12 FKS5

This book was donated to
The King's Institute Library
from the library of
Sam F. Middlebrook
First Executive Director of
The King's Institute.

The International Theological Library.

PLANNED AND FOR YEARS EDITED BY

THE LATE PROFESSOR CHARLES A. BRIGGS, D.D., D.LITT.,

AND

THE LATE PRINCIPAL STEWART D. F. SALMOND, D.D.

HISTORY OF RELIGIONS.

BY GEORGE FOOT MOORE, D.D., LL.D.

VOLUME II.

INTERNATIONAL THEOLOGICAL LIBRARY

HISTORY OF RELIGIONS

BY

GEORGE FOOT MOORE, D.D., LL.D., LITT.D.

PROFESSOR OF THE HISTORY OF RELIGION IN HARVARD UNIVERSITY

II

JUDAISM   CHRISTIANITY
MOHAMMEDANISM

EDINBURGH
T. & T. CLARK, 38 GEORGE STREET
1920

Printed by
MORRISON & GIBB LIMITED

FOR

T. & T. CLARK, EDINBURGH

LONDON : SIMPKIN, MARSHALL, HAMILTON, KENT, AND CO. LIMITED
NEW YORK : CHARLES SCRIBNER'S SONS

TO THE PARTNER IN ALL MY STUDIES

PREFACE

VARIOUS causes have delayed the completion of this volume far beyond what could have been foreseen when its predecessor was issued in 1913. The author may be permitted to hope that the book itself, at least, has profited by the years he has had it in hand, if there is any virtue in *multa dies et multa litura . . . decies castigavit.*

The three religions with which it deals are so intimately related to one another that in a morphological classification they might be regarded as three branches of monotheistic religion in Western Asia and Europe. Christianity originated in a religious movement in Judaism and a Jewish Messianic sect, and though it soon separated from the parent stock, and in the Gentile world became a universal redemptive religion, it was to its inheritance from Judaism that it chiefly owed its religious and moral superiority. Mohammedanism owes its existence to the impression Jewish and, in smaller degree, Christian ideas made upon the mind of the Arabian prophet.

Fundamental in all three is the idea of revealed religion: God has made known to men by revelation in sacred books his soleness, his character, and his will; and this revelation is a law which he has imposed on men not only for ritual and observance but for belief and conduct, thus making faith and morals integral parts of a nomistic religion. All three are in this sense to be described as dogmatic ethical religions. The Bible of the Jews is sacred Scripture to Christians; the Law and the Gospel are acknowledged as divine revelation by Moslems, while in the New Testament and the Koran, Christians and Moslems have their own peculiar Scriptures, completing and in part superseding the former revelations. The Scriptures of all three have the same doc-

vii

trine of creation by divine fiat, according to the first chapter of Genesis; they have the same doctrine of the catastrophic end of the world, when the wrath of God is wreaked in destruction on the heavens and the earth as well as on the guilty race of men. All three are *soteric* religions, proposing themselves as ways of salvation from the doom of all unsaved souls at death and the judgment,[1] and each asserting that it is the *only* way.

Each of them, conceiving itself as the one true religion, attributes to itself finality, and believes itself destined to universality. In them all the ideal of universality assumed political forms. In Judaism, indeed, the dream of ruling over the nations of the earth in the name of the Lord never had a chance to translate itself into historical reality or even into essay. But in Christianity and Islam the idea of empire as the embodiment of religion dominated centuries of history, and ruthless wars of conquest glorified themselves as the victories of the faith. A further consequence of the ideal of exclusive universality in Christendom was the principle that a Christian state should not tolerate within it any other religion than Christianity, nor any other kind of Christianity than the one true kind. Religious liberty logically involves the secularisation of the state.

In modern times the expansion of both Christianity and Islam has been by commerce, missions, and colonisation rather than by conquest, but commerce and missions have often been but steps to protection, occupation, and annexation by Christian states. The belief in ultimate universality must persist as long as each believes itself the one true religion, and so long as it persists the religions must strive in the ways of the time to achieve their universal destiny.

The three religions have never divided the world territorially among them. In the countries conquered by the Moslems were great numbers of Jews and Christians, and under the protection accorded by the Koran to the "Book-people" and the habitually tolerant rule of the caliphs there

---

[1] This is true of Judaism from a time not long before our era.

was much intellectual intercourse and exchange of influence. Contact with Christian theology in Syria opened the eyes of Moslems to some of the theological and ethical problems of their own religion, gave them methods and ideas, and introduced them to the source of both in Greek philosophy. Out of much controversy a theology emerged which came to be generally accepted as orthodox. Before long the Jews constructed a rational and systematic exposition and defence of their own faith on the pattern of the Moslem Kalām. Jewish thinkers followed the Moslems into the field of philosophy, also, and vied with their achievements in it. In Spain, which in the twelfth century was the chief seat of these pursuits, Christians also were drawn into them, and the works of Arabic philosophy and theology translated into Latin soon found their way into France and Italy. The acquaintance with Aristotle and the Arab Aristotelians made an epoch in European thought. The names of Avicenna and Averroes, of Avempace (Ibn Bajja) and Algazel (al-Ghazali), of Avicebron (Ibn Gabirol) and Maimonides, multiply on the pages of the schoolmen by the side of those of the Fathers; the influence of these authors on Christian theology was far-reaching.

In all these intellectual movements Greek philosophy—understood or misunderstood—is at the bottom of the matter. The mysticism of all three religions is essentially Neoplatonic, the scholasticism of all predominatingly Aristotelian. Even a dogmatic controversy like that on the Trinity, which might seem by its subject to be exclusively Christian, has a close counterpart in the hardly less acute and protracted controversies among Moslems and Jews over the reality and nature of the divine attributes; while the doctrine of the Trinity was not infrequently conceived in forms which are hardly distinguishable from Moslem attribute theories, and not unrelated to them.

The resemblances are not superficial or fortuitous. They are, on the contrary, a common element, derived from a common source, shaped by the same philosophic influences, and developed by interchange of ideas. On the other hand, each of these religions has an individuality which is stronger than all their affinities. Especially is this true of Christianity, whose dogma of salvation through the incarnation, death, and resurrection of Christ has no counterpart or analogy in either Judaism or Mohammedanism. This dogma determined both the sacramental cultus of Christianity and its ecclesiastical institutions, and drew both after it into the sphere of dogma.

In the course of their history these religions have undergone many changes, and variations have arisen which depart so widely from the primitive type or the prevailing trend of development that they might almost be described as distinct species, descended from the same remote ancestor and bearing the same generic name. This multifariousness makes the presentation of the religions in the present volume peculiarly difficult. It is not merely that an intelligible account of the variations is hard to give in small compass, but that the narrator is tempted to involve himself in a maze of digressions in which the thread of the history is lost. This can only be avoided by treating them from the point of view of the main movement and subordinating them to it.

The historian of religion has to do more than exhibit the facts impartially and in just proportion, trace the origin and development of ideas and institutions, and define the forces, internal and external, which were operative in this development. He must endeavour to understand and appreciate ways of thinking and feeling remote from his own, and help his readers to a like apprehension. To do this, he must put himself, as far as imagination can go, into the position and attitude of those who formed and entertained these ideas; he must learn to think other men's thoughts after them, as they thought them, and to enter with sympathetic intelligence into their feelings. Accuracy and impartiality without imagination and sympathy can at best give no more than historical materials, not history. How far the present

volume realises this ideal others must judge; it has never
been absent from the author's mind.

Religions like those before us, which have sacred Scriptures and other writings whose authority is recognized as
normative in matters of faith and practice, should be allowed
to present and interpret themselves in conformity with
these authoritative sources, and the same right belongs to
their divisions, and to religious movements and controversies in them.   In this as in the former volume it is primarily the religion of intelligent and religious men that is
described.   Where we are dependent on literary sources, it
is from the writings of such men that the best and most
authentic part of our knowledge is derived.   Such men are
always the minority, but they are the true representatives
of their religion in any age, teachers and examples to their
fellows.   No religion has ever succeeded in bringing all of
its adherents to its standards of right living, or within sight
of its intellectual and spiritual ideals; and in the highest
religions the gulf between the intellectual and moral leaders
and the superstitious and depraved sediment of society is
widest.   But it is not from ignorance and superstition that
anything can be learned about a religion; at that end they
are all alike.

Writers on the history of religions often spend themselves on the beginnings as if they alone signified, and deal
cursorily with everything that came after.   A study of the
origins of a religion can yield nothing but a knowledge of
the origins; the religion itself can be known only in its whole
history.   It is the aim of the present volume, therefore, to
exhibit the development of the religions with which it deals
as completely as the limits of space permit, passing over
no important stage or movement.   In the chapters on
Christianity the author has not purposed either a sketch
of the history of the church or a history of Christian doctrine, but an outline history of the religion itself from the
same point of view from which that of other religions is
written.   It is indeed evident that only this point of view

and a corresponding method of treatment are a sufficient reason for adding another to the innumerable books about Christianity.

To what was said in the Preface to the first volume about the spelling of foreign words, I have only to add that, in Arabic proper names in which the article appears, both assimilation and the liaison with a preceding inflection vowel are neglected.

The index is constructed for the purpose of facilitating the comparison of corresponding phenomena in different religions as well as of following the development of an idea, an institution, or a rite, in any single religion. As illustrations reference may be made to the index under the entries, "Attributes," "Predestination." So far as the matter is similar, the topical entries agree with those in the first volume, so that the comparison may be at will extended to the religions discussed in it; see, for example, "Asceticism," "Eschatology," etc.

Among the many books to which I am indebted, I should make particular acknowledgment of my obligation throughout the chapters on Christianity to Loofs, "Leitfaden der Dogmengeschichte," and in the chapters on the Sequel of Reformation and Modern Tendencies, to the informing and suggestive treatment of the period by Troeltsch in "Die Kultur der Gegenwart." It is hardly necessary for any student of Mohammedanism in our day to confess how much he owes to the learning and insight of Ignaz Goldziher.

Doctor H. A. Wolfson, Instructor in Jewish Literature and Philosophy, was kind enough to look over in proof the chapters on mediæval and modern Judaism, and Doctor George La Piana, of Harvard University, did the same service for the chapters on Christianity. To both of them I am indebted for corrections and suggestions, as I am also to Professor Charles C. Torrey, of Yale University, who read the manuscript on Mohammedanism in an earlier stage of the work, and to Professor William R. Arnold, of Andover Theological Seminary, who read the same chapters in proof. Mr. Albert H. Moore, of Cambridge, who assisted me in the first volume, has had a much larger share in the second, in the preparation and revision of the manuscript and correction of the proofs. The book owes not a little to his constant critical scrutiny.

G. F. M.

CAMBRIDGE, MASS.

CONTENTS

JUDAISM

CHRISTIANITY

MOHAMMEDANISM

HISTORY OF RELIGIONS

CHAPTER I

JUDAISM

THE RELIGION OF ANCIENT ISRAEL

Israelite Tribes in Canaan—The Kingdom—Religion and Migration—
Nomadic and Agricultural Religion—Jehovah and the Baals—
Places and Modes of Worship—Festivals—Priests, Seers, Prophets
—National Religion—Temples and Images.

THE great upheaval of the populations of Asia Minor and
Syria, of which the Hyksos invasion of Egypt was one
result, did not come to rest with the expulsion of the Hyksos.[1] The Syrian wars of the early Eighteenth Dynasty
restored order under Egyptian supremacy in Palestine and
southern Syria, but in the decadence of that dynasty under
Amenophis III and IV, as we learn from the Amarna des-
patches, the country was again invaded by tribes of various
origin and from different quarters, while the Hittite power
in the north was becoming an increasing menace. In the
disorders which followed the death of Amenophis IV the
Syrian possessions of the empire were lost, and we get no
further glimpse of the situation in Palestine until the Syrian
campaigns of Seti I and Rameses II. Under Rameses' successor, Merneptah, European sea-rovers from the coasts
and islands of the Mediterranean made their appearance in
the western delta in alliance with the Libyans, and in the
reign of Rameses III they threatened Egypt both on the
Libyan border and from the side of Syria. In the recoil of
this wave of invasion the Philistines were left behind on the
coast plain from Gaza northward to Dor.

[1] See Vol. I, pp. 178–180.

Among the tribes which in this dislocation of peoples succeeded in gaining a foothold in Palestine were those whom
we know under the collective name Israel. This name
occurs first in an inscription celebrating the devastations
which Merneptah had wrought in Palestine about 1225 B. C.
From their own traditions of the invasion and settlement it
appears that the centre of their strength was in the highlands south of the Great Plain. Kindred or allied tribes
were scattered in Galilee and east of the Jordan, while
another group settled in the south, where its principal member gave its name to the highlands of Judah. It is probable
that these tribes had entered the country at different times
and by different routes. The walled cities were naturally
secure from their attacks unless by a stratagem or a lucky
coup de main, and under the protection of the fortresses the
Great Plain, the seaboard and adjacent foot-hills, and the
wide valleys running inward from the coast long remained
in the possession of the older inhabitants. The Israelites
in different parts of the land were thus separated from one
another, and a line of Canaanite strongholds, of which
Jerusalem, on the main road north and south, was the key,
interposed between Joseph and Judah.

When the period of convulsion following the collapse of
the Egyptian supremacy and the overrunning of the land
by invaders from all quarters was over, the Canaanites
recovered courage and resolved to be masters in their own
country. Meanwhile the increase of the Israelite population in the central highlands constrained them to turn to
agriculture for a living, and they began to cast covetous
eyes on the fields of their neighbours. A struggle for the
possession of the Great Plain ensued, which is celebrated in
the triumphal ode of Deborah (Judges 5). In this poem
the unity of the tribes appears distinctly as a religious bond:
the conflict is the battle of Jehovah with the kings of Canaan, and Israel's victory is the victory of Jehovah.[1] But
though the Israelites in the battle of Megiddo conquered

---

[1] The collective name Israel does not occur in the poem.

their freedom from Canaanite dominion, they did not gain possession of the fortified cities along the plain.

In the eleventh century the Philistines, from their base on the seaboard, subjected the interior. Their main object was, of course, the flourishing Canaanite cities and their rich territories, but the Israelite peasants also were made to pay heavy taxes and submitted to humiliating conditions. This crisis united the tribes in self-defence under the leadership of the Benjamite, Saul, whom after his daring relief of Jabesh Gilead they acclaimed king. The conflict went on. Saul fell in battle with the Philistines, but David succeeded in achieving independence and establishing a Judæan kingdom. After the death of Saul's feeble successor, the other tribes also acknowledged David as king. He captured Jerusalem, which till that time had been a Canaanite city, and made his capital in this strategic position between the north and the south.

His successor attempted to transform the kingdom, in which the tribes preserved their organisation and a large measure of autonomy, into a centralised monarchy whose provinces were administered by governors appointed by the crown, and this, together with the heavy exactions demanded by Solomon's passion for building and the luxury of his court, was more than the Israelites would bear. The king, moreover, was a Judæan, and he was unwise enough to make this conspicuous by special privileges to Judah. At his death the double kingdom of Israel and Judah fell asunder; the Israelite tribes chose a king of their own, while Judah alone with its kindred clans held to the house of David.

At the time of the struggle with the Canaanite city-kings of the Great Plain celebrated in the Song of Deborah, Israelite tribes were seated east of the Jordan from the head of the Dead Sea northward to the Yarmuk (Reuben, Gilead); in the hill country south of the Great Plain (Ephraim, Benjamin, Machir), and in Galilee, from the edge of the Great Plain to the Phœnician hinterland (Issachar, Zebulun, Naphtali, Asher, Dan). All these tribes owned Jehovah as their god;[1] he fought for them, and overwhelmed their foes. This god was not native to Canaan; his seat was a mountain in the south, whence he came on the wings of the storm to deliver his people (Judges 5, 4). One strand of the narrative of their migrations calls his mountain Horeb, another Sinai. At this mountain, after their escape from Egypt under the lead of Moses, the tribes had sworn fealty to Jehovah as their deliverer, and pledged themselves to worship him as they were there taught by Moses. So far all the accounts of the Exodus concur, but on another very important point they differ. According to one, which is by various signs recognised as the tradition of the kingdom of Israel, the tribes had not previously worshipped Jehovah, or, as it is expressed, their fathers had not known him under that name. Judæan sources, on the other hand, make all the patriarchs worshippers of Jehovah, and carry back the origin of this religion almost to the beginning of human history (Gen. 4, 26). This difference may be combined with another: the patriarchal narratives as well as the genealogies connect the Israelites on the one side with Aramæan tribes, from the southern Lebanon eastward across the Euphrates to Harran, and on the other with the nomads of the deserts south of Palestine and in northwestern Arabia. The most natural explanation is the fusion, after the establishment of the kingdom, of northern and southern—Israelite and Judæan—traditions. There are independent reasons for thinking that the tribes to whom the name Israel in the narrower sense belonged were akin to their Aramæan neighbours, and came from the northeast, while the clans which went to make up Judah were of southern extraction. The latter may well have known the holy places of Jehovah from immemorial times, while the Israelites proper only later adopted his worship.

An ancient sanctuary of Jehovah to which great prominence is given in the narratives of the Exodus is Kadesh, a

[1] Hebrew *Yahweh.*

small oasis with abundant springs of water in the desert south of Palestine. In its vicinity the tribes, after leaving Mount Horeb, are said to have encamped for a generation before their entry into Canaan. There are traces, however, of an independent tradition, presumably the oldest of all, according to which, upon their escape from Egypt, they made their way directly to Kadesh, which in this story must have been the chief scene of the work of Moses. Beersheba, farther north, on the borders of Canaan itself, is also a famous holy place of Jehovah, associated especially with the name of Abraham; in the time of the kingdoms it was a favourite place of pilgrimage, particularly for worshippers from Israel. In a similar way Beer-lahai-roi, in the same region, is connected with the names of Isaac and Ishmael. There were thus several spots in the region south of Palestine at which Jehovah was worshipped by the nomads who pastured their flocks thereabout.

In their further migrations the Israelite tribes carried with them a portable sanctuary, a tent, sheltering a chest in which were preserved—so, at least, it was believed in later times—two stone tablets inscribed with the fundamental precepts of their religion. To this tent, which was pitched outside the encampment, Moses resorted to consult the oracle. When the Israelites entered Palestine, the chest was deposited in a shrine at Shiloh, in the heart of the territory of Joseph.

In the religion of Israel in Canaan, as it appears in the earliest sources, it is easy to distinguish certain elements which are an inheritance from the nomadic stage, and others that are as plainly adopted from the settled population of the land, while much was doubtless common to both peoples. Speaking generally, the nomadic elements are original constituents of the religion of Jehovah, and the agricultural rites are engrafted upon it. Of the former the most characteristic is the festival called the *Pesakh*, translated, after a questionable popular etymology, "Passover" (Exod. 12, 13). This festival fell in the spring, on the night of the equinoc-

tial full moon. It was a family feast, though of course
many families might celebrate it at the same place. Each
household provided its own victim, a lamb or kid, which
was roasted, and eaten with a bitter salad. The meal was
consumed "hurriedly," what could not be devoured was
burned, not a scrap must be left over sunrise. In the account of the institution of the ritual in Exod. 12, the blood of
the victim is splashed upon the door-frame of each house to
keep out "the destroyer" who brought death into the homes
of the Egyptians; and although this feature disappears from
later laws—perhaps in consequence of the transfer of the
originally domestic festival to a fixed sanctuary—it can
hardly be doubted that it was one of the most important
parts of the observance. A spring festival, corresponding in
its main features to the Israelite Passover, was kept by the
Saracens of the Sinaitic Peninsula in the fourth century
A. D., and by the Arabs in Mohammed's time; the splash-
ing or smearing of blood on tents and houses, and on cattle
and human beings, for protection against disease and death
is common to-day in all those countries, among both Moslems and Christians.

When the Israelites in their new seats learned from the
Canaanites not merely to grow grain—which even nomads
occasionally do—but to cultivate the vine, olive, and fig,
and to make oil and wine, they learned with the arts of agriculture the religious ceremonies without which their labours
would have been fruitless. Canaanite agriculture, as Hosea
recognised, led directly to the adoption of Canaanite cults:
Israel worshipped the gods of the land, who, as men thought,
gave the corn and wine and oil, the wool and flax.

The Canaanites formed a multitude of petty city-states,
which not even external pressure ever welded into a larger
unity. Each of these had its own god, who was distinguished from the rest only as the god of the particular community; in attributes and functions as well as in the worship
paid them they were essentially alike. The civilisation of
the inland Canaanites was agricultural, and the chief busi-

ness of the local deities was therefore to give to their worshippers bountiful increase of their fields and vineyards.
To these Baals, as the divine "proprietors"[1] of the city and
its fields, their offerings were made for protection and prosperity. Each city and town had its own place of worship,
often upon a hilltop, as the Canaanite name, "high places,"
imports.

Jehovah and the Baals thus occupied in the beginning distinct spheres: Jehovah was the champion of Israel in war,
and it was he who gave the increase of his flocks to the
Israelite peasant as he had to his nomadic ancestors; the
Passover and the sacrifice of firstlings were parts of his
worship, and his name was probably pronounced when an
Israelite cut the throat and spilled the blood of a sheep or a
goat killed for the entertainment of a guest, or to celebrate
by a feast some event in the life of the family or of the community. On the other hand, the Baals were the gods of the
soil, and in their honour the festivals of the husbandman's
year were kept. It is not to be supposed that in thus ac-
knowledging the powers which blessed their labours in the
field and vintage the Israelites thought that they were ignoring their own god or depriving him of his due; agriculture
was not his calling. After the establishment of the kingdom, when the Israelites were in complete possession of the
land which by right of conquest had become Jehovah's land,
so that he was not only the god of Israel but god of Israel's
inheritance, the worship of Jehovah superseded that of the
Baals in their own sanctuaries, preserving the established
ritual custom.

The Israelite places of worship were for the most part the
same high places at which the Canaanites had worshipped
before them, and the furnishing remained essentially the
same. The altar was a pile of rude stones—altars cut in the
living rock or built of cut stone such as the Canaanites
often used are forbidden—the upright stone and the wooden
post (*massebah, asherah*) stood by it. Sometimes there was

[1] This is the meaning of the word *ba'al*.

also a hall for sacrificial feasts, but no temple as a house of the god. At these local altars sacrifices were offered on many occasions of domestic or communal life; there also the annual festivals were held, at which thrice in the year every man was required to "see the face" of Jehovah with an offering in his hand. Worshippers frequented in greater concourse at festival seasons the more famous sanctuaries, such as Bethel, Gilgal, and Beersheba.[1]

In private sacrifices the victim was commonly a sheep or goat; the blood was dashed upon the altar or poured out at its base, the fat of the inwards burned on the altar,[2] the flesh boiled, and eaten by the offerer with his family and guests. Communal sacrifices offered by the elders or heads of the families of a town took the same form. On extraordinary occasions the whole carcass of a victim was burned on the altar. The burning of the fat was attended to by a priest, at least at the greater high places, and he had a toll for his service, which was at first, doubtless, fixed by local custom; later the attempt was made to regulate it by more general rules.

The three festivals to which reference has already been made fell in the spring, in early summer, and in autumn, respectively. The first was the celebration of the beginning of the barley harvest, the characteristic feature of which was the presentation of a first sheaf at the altar and the eating of unleavened cakes of the new crop. This festival in its original local form must have been movable, depending on the ripening of the grain in the region and season; but it was, at an early time, fixed to follow immediately the observance of the Passover at the vernal full moon. The end of the wheat harvest also was marked by a festival, probably once kept when the reaping was actually completed, but in the calendar set seven weeks after the beginning of the barley harvest at the Passover. The greatest of all, often called "*the* feast," by way of eminence, was the har-

---

[1] See Encyclopædia Biblica, " High Place."
[2] The burning of the fat was a Canaanite, not a nomadic, custom.

vest-home in the autumn after the fruits had been gathered and the vintage was over. It was, indeed, primarily a vintage festival, and the booths, from which its familiar name, "tabernacles," is derived, were originally the temporary shelters in the vineyards in which the owners lodged during the season. A uniform date for the celebration, the full moon of the seventh month, was perhaps not established till after the centralisation of worship at Jerusalem had detached it from its natural environment.

In early times the assistance of a priest was not necessary to the offering of sacrifice. The most important function of the priesthood was divination, which they practised by means of a specific apparatus, apparently a form of divination by lot. They had also an expert knowledge of the rules of clean and unclean and of the appropriate purifications and expiations. This knowledge, as well as the art of manipulating the oracle, was transmitted by tradition in certain families, but these families formed no exclusive caste, though at an early time "Levite" priests—whether Levi be the name of a guild or a clan—were regarded as a superior kind. The ancient customs of Israel, which were under the sanction of religion, fell naturally into their province; they gave decisions on questions of customary law as well as of ritual. The priesthoods of such sanctuaries as Shiloh, Dan, Bethel, Gilgal, doubtless had much influence in shaping custom and making it uniform throughout the land, and in harmonising and consolidating tradition.

Besides the priests, with their divination by art, there were men who practised natural divination. They were called "seers," because they had the gift of second-sight, and could tell, like Samuel, what had become of stray asses, or had visionary premonitions of future events, as when the same seer foresaw Saul's meeting with the band of prophets. The visions of Amos (cc. 7–8) are examples of a somewhat different kind. The prophets (nebi'im) whom Saul met coming down from the high place, by whose contagious enthusiasm he was carried away to the surprise and scandal

of his fellow townsmen, were companies of devotees, who
by music and other exercises wrought themselves up to a
pitch of religious excitement in which they acted like men
beside themselves and attributed their doings and sayings
to possession by the spirit of Jehovah. They were zealots
for Jehovah, and doubtless did much to fire patriotism in
the Philistine crisis, as they did in the long Syrian wars.
In the ninth century there were organised societies of such
devotees, living together under a superior, besides many
who do not appear to have been inmates of these establishments. Ahab, on the eve of his fatal campaign against
Ramoth in Gilead, is said to have got together four hundred
of them, who with one voice predicted the success of the
expedition; only one, Micaiah ben Imlah, truly foresaw the
event, and declared that the others were inspired by a lying
spirit sent from Jehovah to lure the king to his doom. In
the stories of Elisha we find him in close association with
the organised prophetic societies, while Elijah stands apart
from them in solitary grandeur, and Micaiah dares to contradict the unanimous herd—precursors in this of the
prophets of the opposition in following centuries whom we
call from the event the true prophets.

The wars of liberation waged with the Philistines, the
establishment of the kingdom, the subjugation of the Canaanite cities, the conquest of neighbouring peoples, with the
exaltation of the national consciousness which accompanied
these struggles and successes, were revivals of the religion
of Israel. In peace men might own their dependence on
the gods of the soil, but in war Jehovah alone was their
reliance, nor did they trust him in vain. With the union
of the tribes in the nation his worship became the national
religion. Solomon built a temple in his capital, and installed
in it the ancient chest ("ark") of Jehovah, which, according
to tradition, had accompanied the tribes in their migrations
from the Mount of God, and after its recovery from the
Philistines had fallen into the hands of Judah. Jerusalem
had no historical association with the worship of Jehovah,

but the king's temple became as such a national sanctuary. When the short-lived union of Israel and Judah under the same king came to an end, the kings of Israel built national temples at Bethel and at Dan, and later in their capitals. At the royal temples, where public sacrifices were offered daily and the festivals were celebrated with much pomp, a more elaborate liturgy was developed; priests of various ranks and offices were multiplied, rich vestments were worn, bands of musicians and singers adorned the service by their art—all after the fashion of their neighbours. On great occasions the kings themselves offered sacrifice in these temples; the priests who ministered in them were appointed by the kings and removed by them at will. Temples did not, however, supplant the old high places in every city and village, nor eclipse the fame of such ancient pilgrim shrines as Beersheba and Gilgal.

Jeroboam is said to have set up in his new temples at Bethel and Dan gilded images of Jehovah in the form of a bull, and thus introduced idolatry into the public cultus. Hosea speaks of the "calf" (*i. e.*, the bull idol) of Samaria, and it is not unlikely that other sanctuaries had similar images. Hezekiah removed from the temple in Jerusalem a copper serpent, believed to have been made by Moses, to which down to his time incense was burned. Idols were, however, not a regular, or perhaps a frequent, part of the furniture of a sanctuary. As among the Phœnicians, the old sacred stones and other aniconic seats of the deity—in Jerusalem the ark—satisfied the need of the visible presence of the god. The multitude of idols of which Hosea and Isaiah speak were household images, probably of protecting demons, or of functional divinities such as the goddess of maternity represented in many clay figurines from Palestinian excavations, rather than of the national god. Domestic idols are mentioned repeatedly in legend and history, as well as by the prophets, under the name "teraphim," but little is known of them beyond the fact that they were not, like the "graven images and molten images," picked up in

Canaan, but were in use among Israelites before the invasion, as well as among their Aramæan kinsmen. The earliest denunciations of idolatry are directed against the "graven images and molten images" of the Canaanites, but the bull images of Jehovah in the northern kingdom were doubtless from the first condemned by conservatives as a heathenish innovation. The story of the "golden calf" at Horeb, conceived from the point of view of the eighth-century prophets, expresses the abhorrence in which Jehovah held this cult.

CHAPTER II

JUDAISM

THE AGE OF THE PROPHETS

Elijah—Jehovah or Baal—The Eighth Century—The New Prophecy:
Amos, Isaiah, Micah, Hosea—The End of the Kingdom of Israel—
Foreign Religions in Judah—The Reforms of Josiah—Deuteron-
omy—Fall of Judah—False Prophets and True—Predictions of
Restoration—Jeremiah and Ezekiel—Individualism in Religion—
Ezekiel's Idea of Holiness—Monotheism—National and Universal
Religion—The Persian Conquests—The History of Jewish Institu-
tions—Myths: the Deluge, the Lost Paradise, Cosmogony—Cultus:
Temple, Priests, Sacrifices—Purifications and Expiations—The Day
of Atonement—Conflicts over Intermarriage—The Samaritans and
their Temple—Theodicy in the Book of Job—Gnomic Poetry.

THE northern kingdom was not only the stronger and
richer, but was in closer contact with civilised neighbours,
the Phœnicians and the Syrians; great lines of trade and
travel passed through its territory, while Judah lay to one
side. It is not strange, therefore, that Israel was in all
things the more progressive of the two states. Its population contained a much larger alien element—Canaanite and
Aramæan—which was more easily absorbed than assimilated,
and it was in disposition as well as in situation more open
to foreign influences in culture and religion. It was inevitable that these tendencies should be opposed by social and
religious conservatism.

A crisis came in the reign of Ahab. The king was married to a Phœnician princess, and built in his residence,
Samaria, a temple for her god, the Baal of Tyre, as Solomon
is said to have built a temple of the Phœnician Astarte for
one of his foreign wives. Some of the prophets of Jehovah
protested—probably not in words alone—and were punished
for their presumption; altars of Jehovah, which had perhaps
been the scene of popular demonstrations, were thrown

13

down by the order of the incensed queen. A three years' drought and famine was interpreted as a manifestation of Jehovah's jealousy. Elijah appears as the head of the zealots, declaring that Jehovah tolerates no rival, no compromise; he will be sole Lord in his own land. The prophet challenges the priests of Baal to an ordeal on Mount Carmel, in which they lose and are massacred by the people; but the instigator of the deed is constrained to flee from the vengeful wrath of Jezebel to Horeb, the ancient Mount of God in the far-off south. It was not the first assertion of the jealousy of Jehovah, but the issue had never before been so dramatically joined: "If Jehovah be God, follow him; but if Baal, then follow him!"

For the sins of Ahab and Jezebel Elijah pronounced the doom of the dynasty; his successor, Elisha, saw that the prediction was fulfilled by inciting a conspiracy among the officers of the army. Jehu extirpated the house of Omri and purged the land of the foreign religion by slaughtering the priests of Baal with the worshipping congregation, and turning the temple into a public latrine.

The first half of the eighth century was a time of great prosperity in both kingdoms. Under Jeroboam II in Israel and Uzziah in Judah successful wars and commercial enterprises enriched the upper classes; they built great houses and enlarged their landed estates, and lived in luxury. The poor, under the same conditions, grew poorer. Bad years threw the small peasant proprietors into debt, and, ruined by usurious interest, they had to cede their ancestral acres to the great landlords, sinking into dependence and often into slavery. The rich and powerful are charged not only with using their right ruthlessly, but with oppression and the perversion of justice. Meanwhile religion was in a flourishing state. The prosperity of the country was proof that the national God was well-pleased with his people, and those whom he had so signally favoured did not grudge him a share of their gains; the sacrifices were more lavish, the ritual more splendid than ever.

There were some, however, who did not take so compla-
cent a view of the times, upright and God-fearing men, who
were moved to indignation by the wrongs of the oppressed
and the decadence of morals, and believed that God must
be as indignant as they were at such doings. This was the
beginning of a new chapter in prophecy. The judicial murder of Naboth had prompted Elijah to predict the ruin of
the house of Omri; the prophets of the eighth century foretell
the fall of the kingdoms of Israel and Judah for the sins of
their people. Looking backward, the historian sees Assyria,
which had been stayed for half a century, about to begin
again its triumphant westward progress, before which the
petty kingdoms of western Syria must succumb. To the
prophets the Assyrian is the rod of God's anger for the destruction of the guilty nations.

Prophecy is one of the most remarkable phenomena in
the religion of Israel. Among some peoples, as in Egypt
and India, the priesthood was most influential in the
progress of religious thought; in Greece it was the poets and
philosophers; in Israel the prophets. A succession of men
of widely diverse genius, station, and circumstance, through
a period of two centuries or more, transformed a national
religion not externally different from that of their neighbours
into a unique ethical monotheism. Some of these prophets
committed their oracles to writing, the words of others were
collected and preserved by their disciples, and thus a new
and distinctive kind of literature arose.

The first prophet of this new type whose utterances are
preserved in the Old Testament is Amos, and he, as if conscious of the difference, disclaims the very name of prophet.
He is a plain herdsman, who, as he tended his flocks in the
wilderness of Judah, heard the call of God to announce the
coming judgment. In the astonished ears of the throng of
worshippers gathered at the royal sanctuary in Bethel on
some high festival he declared that a great catastrophe was
about to befall Israel. The Assyrian armies will overrun
the land from one end to the other; its defences will fall

before them, its palaces will be sacked, its temples desecrated. The city that set a thousand men in the field will
see but a hundred return; the death-wail will resound in
every street and lane, in every field and vineyard. The
pitiful remnant of the people will be carried captive to the
distant east. The prophet chants a dirge over the dead
nation:

"The virgin of Israel is fallen, she shall never rise again;
    She lies prostrate upon her land, there is none to raise her up."

The cause of this irrevocable doom is the violence and
oppression, the fraud and corruption, that may be seen on
every hand. The rich and the great use their power and
wealth to rob their neighbours under the forms of law or
in cynical defiance of law. The poor are their defenceless
prey, whom they sell into slavery for a debt as small as the
price of a pair of shoes.

Their religion is abhorrent to Amos' soul. Men think
by hecatombs to buy the favour of God and bribe him to
condone the outrages which they perpetrate upon their
fellow men! What God requires is not worship, but justice, uprightness, and kindness. "I hate, I spurn your
feasts; I take no pleasure in your great assemblies. Yea, if
you offer me your burnt offerings and oblations, I will not
accept them, and your sacrifices of fat cattle I will not look
at. Away from me with the uproar of your hymns, and the
music of your lyres let me not hear. But let justice flow like
water, and right like an unfailing stream."

The will of God for righteousness, as Amos understands
it, is written in the intelligence and conscience of all right-
thinking men. He calls the very Philistines to see with
horror and indignation the wrongs which are done in Israel.
And since there is for all men but one natural and universal
standard of right, Jehovah avenges transgressions of it not
only in Israel but among other nations. The book of Amos
begins with a series of oracles proclaiming the doom of sev-

eral neighbouring peoples by name, and the ground of the
judgment is in each case their ruthless trampling on the
rights of man—the atrocities of war, the enslaving of the
conquered, the violation of the tomb. The moral conception of God's character is the first step in the path which
led the Jews to monotheism.

When fifteen or twenty years later Isaiah appeared as a
prophet in Jerusalem it was with the same message and in
the same tone. He condemns social conditions in Judah
as sweepingly and scathingly as Amos in Israel, and as unqualifiedly predicts the approaching ruin of the kingdom.
The worship in the temple in Jerusalem is as odious to God
as that which Amos denounced at Bethel.

What do I care for your many sacrifices, says Jehovah. I am sated
with burnt offerings of rams and the fat of stall-fed beasts; the blood of
bulls and lambs and he-goats I have no pleasure in. . . . Your new-
moons and your annual feasts my soul hates; they have become a burden to me that I am weary of bearing. When you spread out your
hands I will shut my eyes not to see you; yea, when you multiply
prayers I will not listen. Your hands are full of blood! Wash you,
make you clean, take your evil doings out of my sight; leave off doing
evil, learn to do well; strive after justice, punish the oppressor, do justice to the orphan, defend the cause of the widow.

We have here a fundamental doctrine of prophecy: the
will of God is wholly moral. Worship for its own sake he
cares nothing about, but he cares everything for justice,
fairness, and goodness among men. The nation in which
these do not prevail he will destroy. Hecatombs and pane-
gyrics cannot bring him to wink at wrong and oppression;
nor will he be softened by distressful prayers in the day of
calamity. Nothing will avail but a thorough amendment
of the relations of individuals and social classes.[1]

With this Isaiah joins a thought of God which had not
previously been uttered with the same intensity and itera-

[1] See Amos 5, 21–24· Isaiah 1, 10–17; Micah 6, 6–8; Jer. 7 (especially
verses 21–23).

2

tion—God's immeasurable might and his lofty majesty.
Everything on earth that lifts itself on high before him
shall be abased; the towering mountains and the impregnable fortresses, the arrogance of men in their pride of
power—all shall be laid low in the dust. The vain self-
exaltation of the creature is an affront to the majesty of
God. The greatness of God must fill man with the consciousness of his own littleness, his power with the sense of
impotence. But while it dissipates vain self-confidence and
reliance on the arm of flesh, it is the ground of a surer confidence. God rules among the nations, he makes them and
breaks them; they execute his will while they think they are
doing their own. Faith in him is the only stronghold: "If
you will not have faith, surely you shall not be established."
These, also, are ideas which enter into the Jewish conception of God and the substance of the Jewish religion.

Isaiah was a prominent figure in Jerusalem for forty years
or more, and gave counsel—not always accepted—to kings.
He witnessed the fulfilment of his own predictions as well as
those of Amos and Hosea in the fall of the kingdom of Israel
in 721, and saw Judah twenty years later brought to the
verge of ruin by Sennacherib. His contemporary, Micah, a
native of a town on the edge of the Judæan lowland, de-
nounces with the utmost vehemence the wrongs which the
country suffered at the hands of the unscrupulous pluto-
crats of the capital, and predicts that Jerusalem shall be
ploughed as a field, and the temple be like a lonely chapel in
the thick of the forest.

The fourth of the great prophets of the eighth century,
Hosea, was, unlike those whom we have hitherto considered,
a native of the northern kingdom. He began to prophesy
in the latter years of Jeroboam II, and in the disorders and
anarchy which followed Jeroboam's death he saw the beginning of that precipitous decline which within a generation
brought Israel to its end. Since there is no allusion in the
book to the invasion by Tiglath-Pileser in 734, it is probable
that the prophet died before that date. Hosea paints his

time in the darkest colours: all classes of the community are alike corrupt—king, nobles, priests, prophets, and people. The cause of this universal moral corruption he finds in religious defection. In Canaan Israel had adopted the religion of Canaan, with all its Baals and its idolatrous and licentious worship. He compares this apostasy from the pure religion of Jehovah to the unfaithfulness of a wife who leaves the husband of her youth to run after other loves. The sin of Israel is, therefore, worse than a transgression of God's righteous will, it is a wrong against his love. By its very nature it makes the continuance of the union impossible; Jehovah will drive Israel out of his house (the land of Canaan). But God's love is not extinguished even by Israel's unfaithfulness. He will, as it were, lead Israel back into the wilderness again, away from all her Canaanitish seducers, that there, alone with him, she may return to the love of her espousals in that golden age of Moses. Then, restored to the favour of God, Israel shall enter upon a better and lasting future.[1]

In Amos the dominant idea of God is his inexorable righteousness; in Hosea it is his inextinguishable love. All that Amos' God demands of men is justice and fairness and goodness to their fellows—a purely ethical definition of religion. The moral demands of religion in Hosea are not a whit less stringent, but he finds the source and spring of all morality in love to God. "Thou shalt love the Lord thy God with all thy heart and thy neighbour as thyself" is the formulation of Hosea's idea of true religion.

The predictions of the fall of the kingdom of Israel which the contemporaries of Amos and Hosea received with incredulity were soon and signally fulfilled. In 734 Tiglath-Pileser conquered the country, annexed Galilee and Gilead to his new province of Damascus, and set a king of his own choice on the throne in Samaria to rule over the remnant of the kingdom. Ten years later a revolt brought the Assyrian armies again upon the field. In 721 Samaria fell before

[1] See Hosea 2, 16 ff.

Sargon, and the kingdom of Israel came to an end. Despite
this warning, Judah vainly attempted to shake off the Assyrian yoke after the death of Sargon. Sennacherib devastated the country, made over a large part of its territory
to his loyal vassals on the seaboard plain, carried away,
according to his own account, two hundred thousand cap-
tives, shut up Hezekiah in Jerusalem "like a bird in a cage,"
and reduced the city to the last extremity. At this juncture he was constrained by an outbreak of pestilence in his
army to raise the siege and return to Assyria, and Judah
thus gained a respite of a century. Hezekiah's successor,
Manasseh, was wise enough to see that further resistance
to the great empire on the Tigris meant annihilation, and
during his long reign kept the peace and paid his tribute
punctually.

The disasters of the preceding half-century had shaken
the confidence of the peoples of Syria in themselves and in
their gods. Had any of the gods of the nations delivered
his land out of the power of the king of Assyria? The
breaking up of nationalities, with the dislocation and com-
mingling of peoples, had for one of its results a mixture of
religions such as on a larger scale followed the conquests of
Alexander. Foreign deities, new rites, strange and extravagant expiations, were eagerly taken up. Judah did not
escape this tendency of the time. Altars were erected in
the courts of the temple and on the roof of the palace in
Jerusalem to the host of heaven; the horses and chariots of
the sun were stabled within the sacred precincts; offerings
were made to the moon and to the signs of the zodiac. The
worship of the queen of heaven (the planet Venus) was
especially cultivated by the masses.

Among the innovations of Manasseh was the sacrifice of
children, particularly the first-born, at a hearth, or fire-pit,
in the Valley of Hinnom, a little way below the temple. The
peculiar form of sacrifice is unquestionably foreign, probably
Phœnician, but the language of the prophets and of the
laws makes it plain that the victims were sacrificed by fire

to Jehovah under the title "the king," [1] and that this was held to be required by such old rules as "Thou shalt make over to Jehovah everything that opens the womb," "The first-born of thy sons shalt thou give unto me." The motive of the story of Abraham and Isaac is to show that the faithful servant of Jehovah would obey without question even the command to sacrifice an only son, but that God has appointed a victim as a substitute. One of the few prophetic utterances that may with probability be ascribed to this period declares that God does not require human sacrifice: "With what offering shall I approach Jehovah, do homage before the God on high? Shall I approach him with burnt offerings of yearling calves? Does Jehovah desire thousands of rams, myriad streams of oil? Shall I give my first-born for my transgression, my offspring for my own sin? He tells thee, O man! What is good and what does Jehovah demand of thee, but to deal justly, and love to do good, and walk reverently with thy God?" [2]

Through the brief reign of Manasseh's son, Amon, and the minority of Josiah, who was but eight years old when he succeeded to the throne, the religious situation was unchanged. A few years after the accession of Josiah the Scythians overran western Asia to the frontiers of Egypt. The appearance of this plague upon the horizon gave occasion to a fresh outburst of prophecy. Zephaniah and Jeremiah pronounce the imminent, irrevocable doom of Judah. The day of the Lord is at hand: "Neither their silver nor their gold will avail to deliver them in the day of Jehovah's fury. By the fire of his jealousy the whole land shall be devoured; for he will make a full end, a dismayful end, of all the inhabitants of the land." To the indictment which the prophets of the eighth century brought against their contemporaries, those of the seventh add the specific sins of

---

[1] "Molech" is not the proper name of a foreign god, but a mispronunciation of the epiclesis ha-melek, "the king." See Encyclopædia Biblica, III, 3183 ff.

[2] Micah 6, 6–8.

Manasseh's generation, the foreign religions and the child
sacrifices. The Scythian flood rolled back. Judah was not
overwhelmed, nor, so far as appears, even inundated by it;
but the terror those uncouth horsemen with their barbarous speech and wild ways inspired was never forgotten; they
became in imagination the very type of the scourges of God,
and from Ezekiel on, in prophecy and apocalypse, the
hordes of Gog and Magog are the harbingers of the end of
the world.

In 621 B. C., in the course of some repairs in the temple,
a book was brought to light purporting to be the ancient
law of God. The reading of this book threw Josiah and his
counsellors into consternation, so different was its prescription from their religion and that of their fathers as far back
as they knew. Convoking the elders of Judah and Jerusalem in the temple, the king entered with them into a compact to conform to the newly discovered law. Thereupon
he proceeded to destroy out of the temple every vestige of
alien cults and to desecrate the spot where children were
sacrificed to the divine king. The second part of the reformation was far more radical. Josiah destroyed all the
sanctuaries of Jehovah himself in his realm, "from Geba[1]
to Beersheba," pulling down the altars, smashing the standing stones, hewing in pieces the sacred posts, defiling the
sites, and carrying the priests off to Jerusalem, where they
were given their living from the revenues of the temple but
not permitted to officiate in sacrifice. Henceforth offerings
should be made and festivals kept only in Jerusalem.

The change he thus attempted to make in the religion
of his subjects was revolutionary. The whole religious life
of the people from time immemorial had centred around
these local altars. On great occasions men might make
pilgrimages to some more famous shrine or to Jerusalem
itself, but the obligatory offerings and the sacrifices which
were connected with every event in the life of the family or
community were brought to their own high places. Provi-

[1] A little way north of Jerusalem.

sion was indeed made in the new law for celebrating the
annual festivals at Jerusalem; but, thus torn up and trans-
planted to a strange and perhaps distant sanctuary, they
necessarily lost their old character altogether.   There is no
record of resistance to the king's edicts, but it is hardly
imaginable that they were carried through without opposition; the desecration of Jehovah's altars and the dishonour
done his priests must have been in the eyes of the common
man an appalling sacrilege and an act of outrageous tyranny.[1]

The book which set all this going is in our hands in Deuteronomy.   This book, though incorporating many older
laws, was composed in the seventh century, probably not
very long before its discovery in the temple, as the programme of a reform such as it actually inspired.   The religions and cults it combats are precisely those which flourished under Manasseh and his successors, and are denounced
by Jeremiah and Ezekiel as the peculiar sins of the age.   In
condemning the worship of foreign gods Deuteronomy follows in the footsteps of the prophets from Elijah on.   Jehovah will endure no rivals in his own land.   The prohibition
of sacrifice to Jehovah himself anywhere but in Jerusalem,
on the contrary, was new.   The worship at the high places
had, indeed, been attacked by earlier prophets; Hosea, especially, looked upon it as Canaanite heathenism, and in this
he was followed by Jeremiah.   But in Deuteronomy there
is more than the objection to the character of the worship
and to its Canaanite origin.   The reformers who framed the
laws against the high places felt an incongruity in the many
altars of the one God: "Hear, O Israel, Jehovah our God is
one Jehovah!"   So long as there was a Jehovah of Beersheba and a Jehovah of Hebron and a Jehovah of Jerusalem,
they were in the apprehension of the worshippers at these
shrines distinct.   Thus, apart from all practical considera-

[1] The attempt of Amenophis IV to make the worship of Aton the sole
religion of Egypt is a striking parallel. See Vol. I, pp. 181 ff. The feeling of the masses about Josiah's reforms and their consequences may be
seen in Jer. 44, 15 ff.

tions, the unity of the sanctuary seemed to be a corollary of the unity of God. The moral standard of Deuteronomy is very high. God demands not alone justice and fair-dealing, but humanity and charity. The spirit of the book appears most conspicuously in such utopian legislation as the provision for a septennial cancellation of debts and the humanitarian rules for the conduct of war.

Deuteronomy is an attempt to embody the ideals of the prophets in principles and institutions by which the whole religious, civil, and social life of the people should be governed. Even in form a large part of the book is prophetic, precept and exhortation rather than statute. With the additions of similar nature and spirit which were made to it in the next generation, it represents more completely than any other single book the outcome of the whole religious development, down to the fall of the kingdom, and more than any other book it influenced the subsequent development.

Only a dozen years after Josiah reorganised religion in his kingdom on the Deuteronomic model, he fell in battle at Megiddo, and his short-lived reforms were borne to the tomb with him. His defeat was the beginning of the end; and as the catastrophe loomed nearer and more terrible, the demoralisation became more general. The picture which Jeremiah and Ezekiel draw of the political, social, and religious decadence is darker than ever. In desperation men turned for refuge to foreign gods; idolatrous mysteries were practised in secret in the chambers of the temple.

Two attempts to throw off the Babylonian yoke ended disastrously. Nebuchadnezzar, who on the first occasion, in 597, treated the conquered city leniently, after crushing the second revolt, in 586, burned the temple and the palaces and breached the fortifications. In the two deportations he carried off to Babylonia the ruling classes, the higher priesthood, the well-to-do citizens, and the skilled artisans, following the Assyrian policy of decapitating rebellious peoples. Many others fled the land, some of them finding refuge in

Egypt. At every turn of events Jeremiah, and latterly Ezekiel in his Babylonian exile, had foretold this outcome, while the great body of the prophets had encouraged the revolts, and up to the last moment proclaimed in the name of the Lord that he would not suffer his holy city to be taken and his temple desecrated by his foes. Their predictions, falling in as they did with the wishes of their hearers, found ready credence and applause, while Jeremiah was thrust into a dungeon and put in peril of his life for his disloyalty to his people and his blasphemy against God. The event proved who was the true prophet, and gave divine authentication to his words; and not to his only but to the whole succession of ethical prophets, in distinction from what we may call the national, or political, prophecy. A new value thus attached to all their words, and their oracles, which had been preserved in the small circle of their disciples, were, we may well believe, sought out and studied more than ever before.

In particular, predictions of a national restoration and a future more glorious than the past, such as are found in Hosea and in Isaiah, were highly prized. Jeremiah and Ezekiel, also, foretold a restoration, though not in their own time. The sins of generations were not to be expiated in a day; but, above all, the prophetic teaching about the character of God and his moral demands of men must sink into the mind and conscience of the people; the restored nation must be a righteous people whose God is the Lord. Judgment itself, while it may constrain to amendment, has no power to work an inner transformation; God himself must be the author of such a change. He will purify the people from all their uncleanness and idolatries: "A new heart also will I give you, and a new spirit will I put within you; I will take away the stony heart out of your flesh, and I will give you a heart of flesh. And I will put my spirit within you, and cause you to walk in my statutes, and ye shall keep my ordinances, and do them" (Ezek. 36, 26 *f.*). When God makes a new covenant with his people: "I will

put my law in their inward parts, and in their hearts will I
write it; and I will be their God, and they shall be my
people: and they shall teach no more every man his neighbour and every man his brother, saying, Know the Lord! for
they shall all know me, from the least of them unto the
greatest of them, saith the Lord" (Jer. 31, 33 $f.$). The
character that is acceptable to God is itself the work of God.

In the dissolution of the nation and the dispersion of the
people in other countries, even the outward observances of
religion became less a matter of the custom of the community and more a matter of individual fidelity to the
religion of the fathers. Whether a man accepted the prophetic conception of religion and gave it its consequence
in his own life could not be a matter of custom at all, but of
personal determination. Jeremiah and Ezekiel, in different
ways, give expression and impulse to the personal aspect of
religion. Jeremiah had stood alone against all the representatives of the national religion—kings, priests, prophets,
and people—and in his own experience had learned that one
man in communion with God possesses the abiding reality
of religion, which would remain what it is though the nation
and all the institutions of religion should perish. The influence of Jeremiah is evident in many of the Psalms of religious experience, which make communion with God the one
all-sufficient good of the soul. Ezekiel emphasises the individual element in religion from the side of the divine retribution. The generation on which the judgment fell salved
their consciences with the proverb: "The fathers ate sour
grapes, and the children's teeth are set on edge." Not so!
the prophet indignantly exclaims; God does not punish a
generation for the sins of its predecessors, nor a man for his
father's transgressions: "The man who sins shall die."
He develops this doctrine with a rigorous logic: The bad
son of a good father will not fare the better in God's judgment for his father's virtues, nor the good son the worse
for his father's vices; every individual is judged by his own
character. The old notion of the solidarity of the nation

and the family are rejected as incompatible with the justice of God.

Correspondingly, repentance, which in the older prophets had been conceived as the return of the people to allegiance and obedience, becomes individual. If a man who has been guilty of the grossest sins against religion and morals turns from his evil ways and does that which is lawful and right, "he shall surely live, he shall not die. None of his transgressions that he hath committed shall be remembered against him, by his righteousness that he hath done he shall live. Have I any pleasure in the death of the wicked? saith the Lord God, and not rather that he should turn from his way and live?"

Ezekiel had the mind of a priest; sin presents itself to him primarily as defilement, and the most heinous of sins is the defilement of holy things, above all, the pollution of the house of God and the profanation of his holy name. He sees Jehovah, mounted on his cherub car, abandon his temple and his land to escape from the midst of such abominations. In the restoration, if Judah is to enjoy the permanent favour of God, every precaution must be taken to make the occurrence of such affronts to his holiness impossible. This is the ruling idea in the plan for the new city and temple and the project of a reformed cultus which Ezekiel outlines in the last chapters of his book. Solemn ceremonies at the beginning of each half-year are prescribed for the purification—or, as it is expressed, the expiation—of the temple by blood from the uncleanness by which it may by inadvertence or error have been defiled. The sacerdotal conception of holiness is throughout pushed to its utmost consequence. A similar point of view is exemplified in the collection of laws in Lev. 17–26, which, from the recurrence of the motive, is often called the Law of Holiness. Here, too, sin is defilement of the people and the land, profanation of holy things or of the name of God. The whole custom of Israel, of which its morals are a part, is subsumed under the ritual category of holiness. The motive for shunning all defilement from beasts and vermin is: "Make yourselves holy, therefore, and be holy; for I am holy," precisely the same motive that is urged for the observance of the fine compend of moral precepts in Lev. 19.

Earlier prophets and reformers, as we have seen, contended against the worship of the Canaanite Baals and of foreign gods from near and far: Jehovah was a jealous god, and demanded of Israel an exclusive devotion. But whatever kind or degree of superiority they attributed to their own god, they did not question that the gods of the nations were the real and powerful deities their worshippers believed them to be. The leaders of thought now went a long step beyond this, to the assertion that Jehovah was the only God. Additions to the book of Deuteronomy made in the sixth century put this doctrine into the mouth of Moses: "Jehovah is God in heaven above and upon the earth beneath; there is no other"; "Jehovah is God; there is none beside him" (Deut. 4, 39; cf. 35). It was, however, the unknown author of Isaiah 40 ff.—the theologian among the prophets, as he has not inaptly been called—who made monotheism the fundamental dogma of Judaism: "Thus saith Jehovah, the king of Israel, and its deliverer, Jehovah of Hosts, I am first, and I am last, and besides me there is no god" (Isaiah 44, 6; cf. 43, 10 f.; 45, 21). He created and he sustains all things;[1] he alone foreknows what he has foreordained. This doctrine of God is for the prophet the corner-stone of faith. The maker and ruler of the universe is the saviour of his people, whose promise of restoration is now about to be fulfilled. Nothing is beyond his power, nothing present or future is beyond his knowledge, nothing can thwart his purpose of salvation.

The coincidence between the fall of Judah, which was in the eyes of all the world the defeat of its god, and the rise of a militant monotheism, averring that Jehovah is the only god, is not such a paradox as to a superficial observa-

---

[1] Creation was attributed to Jehovah much earlier (e. g. in Gen. 2); but creation does not necessarily imply monotheism.

tion it might seem. Long before the catastrophe Jeremiah had foretold the event: for the incorrigible sins of the nation Jehovah would visit them with fire and sword; the temple in which they vainly confided should be desecrated and destroyed. The Babylonians were the executioners of Jehovah's judgment. Nebuchadnezzar was his servant. Not in the might of his arms or his gods did the Babylonian king gain the victory, but by the mandate of Israel's God, who gave over the city and people into his hands. It was Jehovah, not Bel, who triumphed in the fall of Judah. Therein lay the hope of the future. If the Babylonians, like the Assyrians before them, were only the rod in Jehovah's hand to chastise a guilty people, he could break the rod when it had served its purpose—he *would* break it when it exalted itself against him! He who set empires in motion for judgment could use them as well for deliverance. The restoration predicted by the same prophets whose foretelling of doom had been so signally verified was believable only if all the forces of history were controlled by one will, directed by one purpose.

Jewish monotheism is not the outcome of attempts to discover an ultimate principle or a supreme power in the physical universe, nor of metaphysical speculations on the nature of being, but results from the conception of history as a moral order. The prophets of the eighth century, when they declared that the national god punishes the wrong-doing of Israel by the hand of other peoples, were concerned with the application of the doctrine, not with its implications; yet Amos, the first of them, proclaims the like judgment of Jehovah on the neighbouring nations for the like offending. Their successors, with a wider outlook, saw in the great overturnings of their time—the Scythian terror, the ruin of Assyria, the rise and fall of Babylon, the entrance of Media and Persia on the stage of history—the same law at work. Finally the principle is thought through to its monotheistic consequence. The character of Jewish monotheism is determined by its genesis: it is an ethical theism.

Even more distinctive is its teleological character; it finds
in the history of the world not merely the judgment of the
world, but the working out through judgment of the divine
will for a good world which is the end of all God's ways
with man.

This monotheistic development had taken place in a
national religion; the God of Israel had become sole God.
A monotheistic national religion is, however, a contradiction in terms, as thinkers were not long in discovering. If
there is but one God, how is it that the Jews alone know
and worship him, or, rather, how can it be that he has
made himself known to this little people only? The answer
suggested in one of the additions to Deuteronomy, that
Jehovah portioned out the heavenly bodies to the several
nations of the earth to worship, reserving Israel for himself
(Deut. 4, 19), was inadmissible, for it made him the author
of heathenism. A more satisfactory solution was found
by the author of Isaiah 42, 1 *ff.*; 49, 1 *ff.* Jehovah chose
Israel and revealed himself to it, to the end that Israel
should be the prophet of the true religion to enlighten the
Gentiles, that God's salvation may reach to the ends of the
earth. Thus the particularism of the national religion is
reconciled with the universality which is inherent in the
idea of monotheism. The ground is here laid, also, for the
Jewish propaganda of subsequent centuries, and its peculiar
character is determined.

Opposition to idolatry, public or domestic, as a foreign
invention, and particularly as borrowed from the religion
of the Canaanites, is very old; from this point of view it is
condemned by the earlier prophets and prohibited in the
oldest collections of laws. The monotheistic thinkers of
the sixth century reject it on the higher ground that it is
inconsistent with a true and worthy conception of the
nature of God to represent him in the likeness of man or
beast, or to recognise his visible form in sun, moon, or star
(Deut. 4, 15–19). The folly of idolatry is exposed with
trenchant sarcasm by the author of Isaiah 40 *ff.* From the

contemplation of the majesty of the God who "measured
the waters in the hollow of his hand, and meted out heaven
with a span, and comprehended the dust of the earth in a
measure, and weighed the mountains in scales, and the
hills in a balance," to whom all the nations are as nothing, and vanity, he takes us into an idol maker's shop and
shows him making a god, outlining the figure with red chalk
on a block of wood, carving with sculptor's tools the likeness of a man, perhaps overlaying it with silver or gold,
fastening it in place with nails, or securing it with silver
chains. With pieces of the wood he cooks his dinner and
warms his hands, "and of the residue thereof he maketh a
god! . . . he falleth down unto it and worshippeth, and
prayeth unto it, and saith, Deliver me; for thou art my
god!" These utterances found many imitators in later
centuries; satire on idolatry is a *genre* of literature in which
the Jews developed a notable virtuosity, and their talent
for it was not the least of the causes of the universal dislike
entertained for them in a world in which it was good manners to treat your neighbour's religion with outward respect.

In the sudden rise of Persia to ascendancy over Media
and the dazzling victories by which Cyrus wiped out the
kingdom of Lydia and subdued Asia Minor to the shores of
the Ægæan, the Jews saw a presage of deliverance. Babylon's turn would come next! They exulted over its impending, irretrievable ruin. Jehovah is mustering the host for
battle; it is he who stirs up the implacable Medes against
Babylon, "and Babylon, the glory of kingdoms, the beauty
of the Chaldean's pride, shall be as when God overthrew
Sodom and Gomorrah." [1] These vindictive expectations
were not realised; but in 538 the Babylonian Empire fell.
"Jehovah hath broken the staff of the wicked, the sceptre
of the rulers, that smote the peoples in wrath with a continual stroke, that ruled the nations in anger, with a persecution that none restrained." [2] It was in accordance with
Cyrus' general policy towards the subject peoples that the

[1] See Isaiah 13–14.   [2] Isaiah 14, 5 *f.*

Jews should be free to return to Palestine if they chose, and
to rebuild the temple; but it is certain that, though individuals came and went, there was no migration in mass
such as the Chronicler describes in Ezra 2, and a national
restoration entered as little into the plans of the Persians as
of the Babylonians. The conquest of Egypt in 525 only
enclosed Judæa more firmly in the iron ring of Persian
dominion.

The usurpation of the pretender Smerdis, the death of
Cambyses, and the rebellions which broke out at once in all
quarters, not only among the conquered nations but in the
Iranian homeland, and brought the empire to the verge of
dissolution, revived the hope of independence in the heart
of the Jews also. In Jerusalem the prophets Haggai and
Zechariah urged their countrymen on to the rebuilding of
the temple by predictions that God was even now overturning the kingdoms of the nations; they hailed in Zerubbabel,
a descendant of the old royal house, the future king of
Judah, and even, in symbolic act, set the crown upon his
head. The golden age was at hand! Again expectation
was disappointed; Darius Hystaspis put down the revolts
everywhere, and re-established the empire more firmly than
ever.

Of the history of the two centuries that follow little is
known. The Jews were now widely dispersed. From
Babylonia, where they were both numerous and prosperous,
they spread into Persia, Media, and more remote eastern
and northern provinces. In the disasters of the first decades of the sixth century many of the inhabitants of Judæa
had sought refuge in Egypt from the armies of Nebuchadnezzar or migrated thither from the devastated land after
the fall of Jerusalem. Some of them, doubtless, returned
to Palestine when the acute distress was over, others remained. They were found not only in the cities of Lower
Egypt, but far up the Nile; the presence of a Jewish military
colony at Elephantine in the fifth century is established by
recently discovered documents, and the colonists affirm that

their fathers were settled there before the Persian conquest. Doubtless the cities of Syria also had Jewish denizens in larger or smaller numbers, and the trade routes by land and sea led more adventurous members of the race to the emporiums of Asia Minor and the Greek Islands. In all the lands of their dispersion the Jews looked on Jerusalem as the abode of the national God, the religious capital of the race.

The most important literary work of the first half of the Persian period was a history of the origins of the Jewish religious institutions, written with the purpose of showing their antiquity. Thus, the Sabbath was ordained at the creation and hallowed by God's own example; the prohibition of blood was given to Noah at the same time with the permission to eat animal food; circumcision was the seal of the covenant with Abraham; sacrifices were instituted by Moses at Sinai, and so on. It is characteristic of this work that it does not prescribe, in the form of rule, how a thing shall be done, but describes, as precedent and pattern, how it was done in the first instance. Thus the detailed account of the sacrifices at the dedication of the tabernacle constitutes an epitome of the sacrificial ritual. The religious standpoint of the writer is an elevated monotheism; anthropomorphisms are avoided, with everything that might seem unworthy of deity. This history of the sacred institutions was presently combined with the older histories, and in the convenient framework it furnished, the ritual and ceremonial laws were inserted; in this way the Pentateuch took shape. It was not, however, for a long time a finished book; *novellæ* continued to be added to the laws, some actual, some the product of legal theorising; additions to the narrative also were made. This growth apparently did not altogether cease until the Greek time; but before it ceased the development of unwritten tradition had become relatively more important.

The first section (Gen. 1–11) of the great composite work, which beginning with the creation carries the history to the fall of the kingdom of Judah in 586 B. C. (Gen.–

3

2 Kings), comprises almost all that is connectedly preserved of Hebrew mythology: the creation of the world; the lost paradise and the origin of suffering and death; the great flood and the dispersion of nations. Some of these myths received their literary form in the classical period of Hebrew literature, probably in the ninth century B. C., others as late as the Persian time. In the process of stringing them together into a continuous narrative, especially where two versions of the same story were combined in one, some changes were necessarily made, but in general the compilers and editors show much skill in effecting their end with the least possible violence to their sources.

Some of the myths are Palestinian; others are of foreign origin, but adapted to a Palestinian environment and to Jewish religious conceptions; while of others, still, it remains doubtful in which of these classes they should be included. The type of the second class is the deluge, the original of which is the Babylonian myth of the great flood, now forming an episode in the poem of Gilgamesh.[1] In Gen. 7–9 two variant forms of this story are combined, one taken from an early pre-exilic source, the other from the history of the sacred institutions, probably of the fifth century. The agreement with the Babylonian myth is so pervasive and minute as to suggest literary dependence; the discrepancies between the two versions may in part go back to variant Babylonian originals. But while the whole story is borrowed, it is, by comparatively slight yet highly significant changes, brought into harmony with the religion of Israel. In place of the Babylonian hero, the deified Xisouthros, a Palestinian figure is chosen, Noah, the ancestor of three races, who at the beginning of the Israelite kingdom disputed with one another the possession of the land, represented by the names Shem (Israelites), Ham (Canaanites), and Japhet (Philistines?). In the sequel of the flood the three sons of Noah, as sole survivors, become the progenitors of the races of mankind.[2]

[1] See Vol. I, pp. 216 f.   [2] See Gen. 10.

The most characteristic of the Hebrew myths is that of the lost paradise. When the world was still without vegetation because there was no rain, God modelled a man of earth and breathed life into him. For man's abode he planted a garden in Eden ("Delight"), somewhere in the east, in which, among all goodly trees, grew the tree of life, whose fruit would make one who ate it live for ever. In compassion on the man's solitary state God created all kinds of beasts and birds, and let the man give them their names; but no fit mate for him was found among them. So God made a woman out of one of the man's ribs, as the proverb says, "my very bone and flesh." There was one tree of which God forbade them to eat on pain of death, the "tree of knowing good and evil." The serpent, the most astute of the creatures, persuaded the woman that God had deceived them about this tree: its fruit, far from being deadly, would give them godlike knowledge. They ate, and the first-fruit of their dear-bought wisdom was the shame of nakedness, to conceal which they made them aprons of leaves. To the sense of shame fear was added when they heard God walking in the garden in the cool of the day, and they hid themselves among the trees. Brought to account, the man blamed the woman and the woman blamed the serpent. On all three God pronounced sentence: man shall henceforth wring his living from a reluctant earth in the sweat of his brow; woman shall bear children in anguish and peril and be subjected to her husband by desire; the serpent shall crawl on its belly and eat dust. Forthwith, lest they should snatch immortality by robbing the tree of life, the hapless pair were driven out of the garden, and the way of return barred by a guardian demon brandishing a flaming sword.

In this story, as in extended mythical narrations generally, motives of diverse origin appear to be combined. Eden, for example, may have been, as in Ezekiel, the garden of the gods, like the garden of the Hesperides in Greek mythology with its dragon-guarded golden apples in the

far west; the account of creation may be taken from an
independent cosmogony; the description of the site of the
garden at the source of the four rivers seems to be a later
insertion. But from whatever source the setting may be
derived, the myth is concerned, not with cosmogony or
the abode of the gods, but with man and his lot on earth.
The question how man came to be subject to death, which
has always seemed an unnatural thing, or how he failed to
attain immortality, is the subject of many myths, of which
the Babylonian story of Adapa, who through a misunder-
standing did not taste the food of the gods that was offered
him, may serve as an example.[1] With this is joined in
the Hebrew myth the question why man must earn his
living by grievous toil and woman must suffer the pangs
of childbirth—two evils which do not appear to belong to
the nature of things, or, from a higher point of view, to the
plan of God in creation. We do not do full justice to the
answer when we read it, "Man toils and suffers and dies because he disobeyed the commandment of God." The nature of the disobedience reveals an unexpected subtlety.
The forbidden fruit was the knowledge of good and evil, the
knowledge that distinguishes man from the beasts and
makes him like the gods. With fine insight, too, the author
unfolds the psychological consequences of dawning knowledge, and hints at stages of civilisation marked by the
naked savage, the girdle of leaves, and the coats of skins.

To the setting and the incidental motives of this story
analogies more or less close can be found in plenty, but to
the myth as a whole or to its characteristic features no
parallel is known,[2] and there is no intrinsic reason for attributing it to a foreign origin. The conception of God and

[1] See Vol. I, p. 218.
[2] A seal in which two fully clothed figures are seated on opposite sides
of a tree, while behind one of them is what appears to be a snake erect
on its tail, has been interpreted in the light of Gen. 3 as a Babylonian
picture of the temptation, and, solely on the strength of this dubious
circular interpretation, it has been affirmed that the Hebrew myth was
borrowed from the Babylonians.

the religious attitude in general are similar to those of the oldest stratum of Israelite legends (*e. g.*, Gen. 18), with which the style of the narrative also connects it.

The story of Adam and Eve is followed by those of Cain and Abel (Gen. 4, 1–15) and of Cain and his posterity (4, 16–24). The latter has been recognised as a fragment of Kenite legend, while the former is a Judæan ætiological myth, accounting by the not unfamiliar motive of the curse of kindred blood for the reversion of their Kenite neighbours from agriculture to the nomadic life and for the peculiar tribal mark they wore. Neither of these has any connection with the expulsion from paradise, to which they are joined only by a genealogical link. Other fragments of old Hebrew mythology are the descent of the giant races from the commerce of gods with women—a hint which Jewish demonology made the most of—and the confusion of tongues and dispersion of peoples as a consequence of the heaven-storming ambitions of the builders of Babylon, with its lofty temple tower. That Babylon was the scene of the linguistic disaster is proved by the pun, Babel-babble, which is, it must be confessed, rather neater in English than in Hebrew.

The cosmogony (Gen. 1, 1–2, 4) forms the beginning of the post-exilic history of the sacred institutions. The scheme of six days' work in which the series of creative fiats is set does not belong to the original, which more naturally falls into eight or nine acts. The motive of the six-day scheme is transparent—it gives the Sabbath the sanction of God's own observance. In the beginning all was a waste of waters enveloped in darkness. God first created light and divided day from night; then he made the solid vault between the waters of the celestial ocean and the lower waters; he gathered the seas and let the land emerge; he caused the land to produce the various forms of vegetation; he made the heavenly bodies, the birds of the air, and the land animals, wild and tame; last of all he created man, male and female, in the image and likeness of God, to rule over all the crea-

tures in earth and sea and sky, with commission to multiply and fill the earth and subdue it.   As in other pictures of
a vegetarian golden age, fruit and grains are the only food
of man and beast.   The order of creation is a natural progress; the one peculiar feature is the place occupied by the
heavenly bodies, which, as moving and therefore living
creatures, appear at the head of the animal kingdom instead of immediately after the establishment of the firma-
ment.   In this transposition a polemic motive may plausi-
bly be conjectured, a stroke aimed at the sun, moon, and
star worship of the heathen.   As compared with the frank
anthropomorphism of the Garden of Eden, theological reflection is apparent throughout.   In the place of a god who
plants trees and moulds man of earth, or refreshes himself
by a turn in the garden in the cool of the evening, is a god
who speaks, and it is done; he commands, and it stands forth.

The opinion has obtained considerable currency that in
this story of creation a Babylonian myth has been appropriated and recast to accommodate it to Jewish religious
and theological conceptions, as was done by two hands at
different times with the story of the flood.   Thus far, however, no corresponding Babylonian cosmogony has been
recovered.   In the poem on the combat of Marduk and
Tiamat the chapters which probably related Marduk's
creation of plants and animals are so badly mutilated that
a reconstruction is as yet impossible.[1]   In the other remains
of Babylonian cosmogonies the coincidences with Gen. 1
are the mere commonplaces of creation myths, and do not
suffice to establish any connection between the two.[2]

In the prophets and in poetry there are numerous allu-
sions to other myths, among which a victory of Jehovah
over a dragon, or sea-monster (Rahab), occurs with especial
frequency.   The conflict was perhaps originally cosmogonic, a counterpart of the battle of Marduk with the
chaos-monster Tiamat and her helpers (see Job 9, 13); but
if so, this association has receded completely into the back-

[1] See Vol. I, pp. 209–213.   [2] Cf. Vol. I, pp. 382 f.

ground. In some passages the reference is to the cleaving
of the Red Sea (Isaiah 51, 9*f.*; Psalm 74, 12–14; *cf.* Rahab
as an allegorical name for Egypt); in Isaiah 27, 1 the destruction of the dragon and Rahab is still to come, at the
beginning of the last times.

The forms of the Jewish cultus, while exhibiting some
peculiar features, did not in the main differ very widely
from those of other Syrian religions. The temple housed
no image or other material representation of the deity; the
sacred chest which in earlier times stood in the holy of
holies had disappeared even before the destruction of the
temple by Nebuchadnezzar. In later times the cella was
a dark and empty room which no one but the high priest
might enter, and he but once a year, on the Day of Atonement. In the hall in front of the cella stood the table of
the god, on which loaves of bread and flagons of wine[1] were
kept from week's end to week's end; a candelabrum sup-
porting lamps kept always burning; and a stationary bra-
zier, or altar, for incense. The last is not included in the
oldest inventory, which provides only censers carried by
the priests. In the court before the temple was the great
altar for sacrifices, and around the court were rooms for
various uses of the temple service—magazines, stables,
kitchens, and the like.

At the head of the priesthood was a chief priest, whose
importance was much greater than that of his predecessors
in the days of the Judæan monarchy, because there was no
king over him. The local governor, when a native, had
only co-ordinate authority; and when, as commonly, a for-
eigner filled the office, the high priest was not only the
religious head of his people but in many ways their political
representative before the Persian administration. Like
other Syrian high priests, he customarily wore the purple
and the tiara of a ruler instead of sacerdotal vestments.[2]

---

[1] The present text prescribes the flagons but omits the wine.
[2] The high priest assumed the sacerdotal functions of the king, and
with them the royal apparel.

The common priests were numerous; there were among
them several families, without, so far as appears, a corresponding differentiation of function. The inferior ministry of the temple was performed by levites, who, according
to Ezekiel, were descendants of the old priests of the high
places; there were also musicians and singers, guards, door-
keepers, and menial servants. The relations of these classes
evidently changed in many ways in the course of the centuries; fortunately it is not necessary for our purpose to
reconstruct this obscure history.

The public sacrifices, which in older times had been maintained by the king, were now supported chiefly by the people through an annual tax of a third or a half shekel per
capita on the adult males. They consisted of a daily holocaust of a lamb, morning and evening, with a portion of
flour mixed with oil and a libation of wine. On Sabbaths
and new moons, on the civil new year, and at the three
annual festivals, the number of victims was multiplied.
Private offerings were either prescribed or voluntary, and
were of various species which need not be more particularly
described here.[1] The victims were neat cattle, sheep, or
goats; turtle-doves or pigeons were in some cases permissible substitutes for the quadrupeds, an innovation made
necessary by the growth of urban population. The priests
dashed the blood against the altar, and burned the fat with
the appropriate oblation of meal or cakes; for this service
they took their toll in certain portions of the victims.

As in earlier times, the knowledge of the multifarious
rules of clean and unclean, and of the necessary purifications and expiations, was one of the chief functions of the
priesthood. Doubtless under their hands the old rules
were casuistically developed in particulars and brought
under general formulas; but at the bottom this whole side
of religion is a survival from a remote antiquity. Death is
of all things the most dangerous defilement, and at the
same time highly contagious. The dwelling in which a

[1] See Encyclopædia Biblica, "Sacrifice."

death has occurred, and all that is in it, and every person who enters it are unclean for seven days, as is also every one who touches a corpse or a grave. If a man who has been exposed to such infection comes into the sanctuary unpurified he pollutes the holy place and exposes himself to be cut off by the outraged holiness of God. A peculiarly potent disinfectant is demanded; it is not, as among the Persians, cow's urine,[1] but water in which the ashes of a red cow have been stirred. To obtain a store of the purifying ashes a cow was burned whole, with certain woods and herbs; all who assisted in the performance were rendered unclean. With this liquid the habitation with its furniture and utensils, and persons who had been in the house, or who had touched the body, a bone, or a grave, were sprinkled on the third day and again on the seventh; only after this second disinfection might they associate with their fellow men or take part in the worship of God.

Sexual functions, normal or abnormal, are unclean; childbirth requires isolation for seven days and exclusion from the sanctuary and from all contact with holy things for the rest of forty days, if the child be a boy; for double these periods in the case of a girl. At the end of this term a yearling lamb is prescribed as a holocaust, with a dove or pigeon as a sin offering; with this the priest "shall make expiation for the mother, and she shall be clean." Various diseases, also, are unclean, especially the whole class of skin diseases included under the comprehensive name "leprosy." The discrimination between innocent eruptions or inflammations and the leprosy was a difficult matter, and rules for the guidance of the priests in their diagnosis were early formulated. The leper was banished from the abodes of men; he must go about with his garments rent, his hair dishevelled, covering his lips, and warning men of his dangerous presence by crying, "Unclean! Unclean!" In case of recovery peculiar ceremonies of purification were demanded. A bird was killed over an earthen vessel contain-

[1] Vol. I, p. 392.

ing fresh water, in such a manner that its blood mingled
with the water; the priest dipped cedar wood, wool dyed
crimson, and hyssop, together with a living bird, into the
vessel, sprinkled the bloody water upon the leper, and let
the living bird fly away, carrying off the contagion. In the
ritual as it now stands in Lev. 14 other sacrifices are combined with this primitive discharge of the disease, and the
restored leper is anointed with blood and oil in a way rem-
iniscent of the consecration of priests.

Many kinds of animals, birds, and fishes are forbidden
as food. They are unclean, and whoever touches the carcass
of one of them contracts uncleanness; vessels, food, water,
are defiled by contact with them. Similar restrictions
exist abundantly in other religions, savage as well as civilised. A comparison of the Jewish rules with those in the
Hindoo law books, and with the Zoroastrian Vendidad is
peculiarly instructive; there is the same underlying system
of ideas, with many striking agreements in particulars.
The comparison shows also that the Jews were not burdened
beyond other peoples with such interdictions and disinfec-
tions.

The priestly laws are largely concerned with rites of purification, by which men or things which have contracted uncleanness in the religious sense, and are thereby rendered
polluting to men and abominable to God, may be restored
to normal social and religious status. These rites originated in a time when no clear distinction was made between
"uncleanness" (infringement of a taboo), disease, and moral
wrong. As has been said of the Greeks, "evil of all kinds
was a physical infection that could be caught and trans-
planted." In the Jewish laws all these fall under the comprehensive name "sin," which is at bottom a ritual, not a
moral conception. Sin attaches physically to inanimate
objects, such as the stones of a new altar; it is removed by
physical means. The sin offering, in the technical use of
the term, is not an offering for sin, but for inadvertent
transgression of certain ceremonial prohibitions, or is de-

manded after childbirth, leprosy, the completion of a Naz-
arite vow, and the like, none of which involve sin, as we
understand the word. The result of the inclusion of the
moral in the sphere of the religious is that the physical
means efficacious in removing uncleanness are employed to
purify a man from moral defilement or to protect him
against the consequences of his wrong-doing.

Most of the expiations have a specified and limited application, but there was one great annual *piaculum* for the
whole people, the Day of Atonement. In the ritual for this
day two elements may be distinguished. The high priest
first offers "sin offerings" to make expiation for himself and
his house and for the people; with the blood of these victims
he enters the *adytum* of the temple and sprinkles the blood
there, "to make expiation for the holy place, because of the
uncleanness of the children of Israel and because of their
transgressions, even all their sins." In the same manner
the temple and the altar are expiated. The second and
characteristic feature of the ceremony follows. The high
priest lays his hands on the head of a goat, and confesses
over it all the iniquities of the children of Israel and all
their transgressions; the sins of the people in the year past
having thus been laid upon its head, the scapegoat, bearing all their iniquities, is led away into an uninhabited region
and there let go. In later times, at least, to make sure that
the goat with his burden of sin did not wander back to the
abodes of men, he was pushed over a precipice. The man
who led him into the wilderness was unclean for the rest of
the day. Such methods of ridding the community of evils
by loading them upon man or beast and driving the bearer
out or putting him to death are found among many peoples;
it is sufficient here to refer to the *pharmakoi* at the Attic
Thargelia.[1] In the ritual in Leviticus lots are cast over two
goats; the one on which the lot "Jehovah's" falls is sacrificed as a sin offering; the other, designated by lot as "Azazel's," is sent away. The common opinion is that Azazel

[1] Compare also Vol. I, pp. 105–107.

is the name of a demon of the desert, but the Septuagint translators seem to have understood the word favourably, as designating a being who does away evil (ἀποπομπαῖος). There can be little doubt that the name, which is of the ordinary pattern for angels and demons, is a relatively late element in the ritual.

The ritual and ceremonial laws were revised and expanded in the Persian period; it is sometimes possible to recognise successive stages in this process, and to distinguish with some confidence between development in practice and paragraphs that represent sacerdotal theories or desiderata. In its main features, however, the priestly law embodies the ancient custom of Israel from the days of the kingdom or still more remote times. The observance of the rules of clean and unclean, for example, must always have been an important part of religion; infringement of them incurred the mysterious dangers of the violated taboo. Similarly, neglect to render to God the first-fruits and tithes or the firstlings of the flock must always have been regarded as a fraud on God, and likely to provoke retaliation. In this respect there is no reason to think that the attitude of the Jews in the fifth century differed from that of their fathers in the seventh or the tenth.

If these things acquired an enhanced importance in the eyes of the religiously minded part of the people, it was for other reasons than the intrinsic valuation of the observances themselves. In older times they had been the customary law of the national religion, the demands of Jehovah as defined in the tradition and decisions of his priests. Now, following the track of Deuteronomy and the Book of Origins, they were set forth as a body of religious statutes delivered by God to Moses for all time to come. They were, moreover, from the point of view of monotheism, not the institutions of a national religion, but of the one true religion, which was in idea and destiny universal. And, finally, the welfare of the people and the fulfilment of all its hopes of a future were dependent on its being a holy people in the

sense and spirit of Ezekiel and the Law of Holiness, which
included not only religious fidelity and moral integrity, but
ritual purity.

It would be a mistake to imagine, however, that this increased importance of the law in principle, or the elabora-
tion of ritual and rule, choked ethical and spiritual religion.
The literature of these centuries—the Psalms, Job, Proverbs—prove, on the contrary, that the influence of the
prophetic teaching had never before been so wide-spread
or so deep as in this period. Nor does it appear that either
priests or people were excessively scrupulous in legal observances; the picture of the conditions in Jerusalem drawn by
the author of Malachi, or in the memoirs of Nehemiah, are
of quite the contrary implication.

One of the commonest and loudest complaints of those
who had the burden of the purity of religion on their
hearts in this age was the intermarriage of Jews with their
neighbours, to whom the reformers applied indiscriminately
the old name, "people of the land," with the new connotation, "heathen." In early laws (e. g., Exod. 34, 15 f.; Deut.
7, 3) connubium with the populations of Canaan is forbidden on the ground that it inevitably led to contamina-
tion of religion. Intermarriage between different peoples,
or even different ranks or classes of the same people, was
unlawful in many ancient nations, as at Athens and Sparta;
and all peoples who have highly developed rules of clean
and unclean necessarily regard outsiders who do not observe the same rules as unclean, and contact with them as
defiling; the ancient Egyptians, the Zoroastrians, modern
Hindoos, and Shiite Moslems, are pertinent examples. In
Jerusalem, especially among the upper classes, who had
most to gain by untrammelled intercourse with their neighbours and by marriage alliances with them, laxity in these
matters was common; Nehemiah found even a son of the
high-priestly house married to a daughter of Sanballat, the
governor of Samaria. The reformers of the fifth century
were particularly zealous against these mixed marriages,

but it is doubtful whether their efforts had at the time
any large result.

Another point about which they were much concerned
was the observance of the Sabbath. In old times the weekly
Sabbath was the least of the holy days. As one of the distinctive observances which was not dependent on the temple and the sacrificial liturgy but could be kept anywhere,
the Sabbath gained increased importance in the dispersion;
abstention from labour on the seventh day was the conspicuous mark of a godly Jew, a silent profession of his
faith. In Judea this reason for an enhanced reverence for
the day did not exist, but even by older standards the
observance was very lax. According to Neh. 13, 15 *ff.*,
labour in the fields and vineyards was not suspended, and
in the city the Sabbath had become a market-day.

In the Psalms which with reasonable probability may be
ascribed to the Persian period as well as in those of the
succeeding centuries, a note of discord and strife is often
struck. The poets voice the sentiments of those who
called themselves the pious (*ḥasidim*), or the righteous, the
upright—in their own estimate the truly religious part of
the people. They contrast themselves, not without satisfaction, with the wicked, the proud, who act as though
there were no God, and perpetrate all manner of wrongs
on their fellow men. The wicked mocked the godly and
their scruples, plotted against them, persecuted them.
They were, consequently, enemies of God and his saints, and
the pious hated them with a zealous hatred and exulted in
the prospect of their speedy destruction. Even more violent are the denunciations in Isaiah 59; 57, 3–13; 65, 1–7;
66, 3, 17,[1] which charge them with undisguised heathenism,
revivals of ancient cults, and importation of foreign mysteries (*cf.* Ezek. 8). There is no warrant for supposing, as
many do, that these drastic utterances were aimed specifically at the Samaritans; they sound more as if the prophet

---

[1] These utterances are now generally attributed to a Judæan prophet
and to the period under consideration.

had witnessed such abominations in his own neighbourhood; but it must be admitted that the occasion which called them forth is unknown.

The mention of the Samaritans brings us to another difficult question. According to Josephus, the temple on Mount Gerizim was erected by Sanballat, the governor of Samaria, for his son-in-law, Manasseh, a renegade brother of the Jewish high priest Jaddua. These events occurred under the last Persian king and at the beginning of Alexander's rule in Syria. It is commonly assumed that Neh. 13, 28 refers to the same circumstance, and that Josephus has erroneously introduced the story just a hundred years too late. This combination is, however, very dubious, and the intrinsic probability is on the side of the later date.

Whether it occurred in the fifth century or in the fourth, the building of the temple on Gerizim was the occasion of bitter animosity between the partisans of the two sanctuaries. It is a mistake to think that the Jews in the Persian and Greek time looked upon Jerusalem as the only place where acceptable sacrifice could be offered to God. The Deuteronomic Law could reasonably be interpreted as applying to Palestine only, and was, in fact, so understood. The Jewish military colony at Elephantine had a stately temple, erected, according to their own testimony, before the Persian conquest; a regular priesthood ministered in it, and sacrifices of all kinds were offered on its altar. When this temple had been destroyed by a Persian local official at the instigation of the Egyptian priests, the colonists appealed to the high priest of Jerusalem, the Persian governor there, and the sons of Sanballat, governor of Samaria, to use their influence at the satrap's court to get them permission to rebuild. In the time of Antiochus IV the Jews in Lower Egypt built a temple at Leontopolis, which stood till 72 A. D., two years after the fall of Jerusalem; its chief priesthood was of the old line of Jerusalem, and the legitimacy of sacrifices there is acknowledged in a qualified way by the rabbinical authorities of following centuries. In the account

of its foundation we learn incidentally that the Egyptian
Jews in Ptolemaic times had many other temples; nor is
there any reason to imagine that this was peculiar to Egypt.

Shechem, with its sanctuary on Mount Gerizim, was an
old Israelite holy place, and worship had probably been
offered there through all the centuries. But now for the
first time it entered into open rivalry with Jerusalem; its
temple was of the same pattern; its ritual doubtless conformed to the Jerusalem use; its high priest was of unimpeachable legitimacy; in all probability he brought along
with him the Mosaic Law, the Pentateuch. If exclusive
claims were made for Jerusalem, a stronger case could be
made out for Gerizim. The law of the sole sanctuary in
Deut. 12 requires that the Israelites should bring their
sacrifices "to the place which Jehovah, your God, shall choose
out of all your tribes to put his name there." What place
was meant might be learned from Deut. 11, 29 *f.*; 27,
12 *f.*; Josh. 8, 30 *ff.*—it was Gerizim. Jerusalem is not so
much as named in the Law; it had been a Canaanite city till
David's time. How embarrassing this argument was is
shown by the Jewish alterations of the text in all three of
the passages cited. It was not, therefore, the mere existence
of the temple at Shechem by the side of the temple in
Jerusalem, but the pretensions of Gerizim to be the sole
legitimate temple, which made the Jews hate the Samaritans
so implacably.[1]

The greatest literary monument of the Persian or earlier
Greek time is the Book of Job, a dramatic poem on theodicy. The older vague belief that God favours the good
and visits his displeasure on the bad had hardened into a
doctrine of individual retribution, according to which God
in his justice requites to each good or evil exactly according
to desert. Experience contradicts this simple formula; the
good are not always prosperous and the bad do not always
come to grief. Job is a man of exemplary piety and virtue,
who in a moment is stripped of his possessions and his chil-

[1] See John 4, 20.

dren and smitten with a dire disease; but he does not murmur or rebel—"shall we receive good at the hand of God and shall we not receive evil?" His three friends come to comfort him after their fashion. They represent the orthodox view: such unheard-of inflictions must be the penalty of great sin, the greater because hidden. They express this conviction at first in insinuating phrases, but when they cannot bring Job to own that he has deserved his lot, they speak out with the frankness his obstinate self-righteousness seems to warrant. Job will not belie his good conscience: "God forbid! I will not own that you are right! Till I die, I will not repudiate my integrity; I will hold fast my uprightness, and not let it go; all my life my conscience does not reproach me." He swears it by the God who has taken his right from him and embittered his soul. What his miserable comforters call the justice of God is tyrannous injustice. Suddenly God, whom Job has alternately besought and challenged to appear, answers out of the whirlwind, not to defend his government of the world or the justice of his dealings with Job, but to overawe the bold mortal who would presume to fathom the ways of the Almighty; and Job is constrained to acknowledge his error in talking of things beyond his understanding. In the epilogue God justifies Job's words and censures those of the friends.

The poet had no ready-made solution of the problem of theodicy; but he refutes the cruel dogma that all suffering is the proportioned penalty of sin. God's dealings with men may be an inscrutable mystery; they need not be a monstrous injustice unless we insist on regarding them as consistently retributive.

In the fifth century fall also the beginnings of gnomic poetry, which has its highest development in the succeeding period. The aphorisms on the conduct of life which we find in the Proverbs and in Ecclesiasticus are chiefly the words of the "sages," a class of moralists, in part, at least, professional teachers of youth—the Jewish sophists, we

4

might call them, if Plato had not given the word a bad sound. The wisdom which they eulogise as the best thing in the world is not philosophical theory, but the practical maxims by which a sagacious man orders his life. They appeal to prudential motives rather than to the highest ethical principles; but they consistently affirm that morality is the condition of success and happiness, and that religion ("reverence for God") is the foundation of even worldly wisdom. The counsels of the sages are wholesome, even if homely. Warnings against the fascinations of strange women, the serpent that lurks in the wine-cup, indolence, hasty anger, gossip and slander, are common themes. In Sirach we get a vivid picture of the life of the cities stirring with the ferment of Greek civilisation. There is hardly anything specifically Jewish in the moral precepts, nor do the sages give themselves the least concern about ritual and ceremonial; religion is with them not a matter of observances but a serious and reverent temper of mind towards life and the moral order of the world. From reflections on the excellency of wisdom in man some of these thinkers were led to meditate on the wisdom of God, possessed by him before the world, the first of his works, his sportive associate in the creation (Prov. 8; *cf.* Job 28; Ecclus. 24; Wisd. 7). Hellenistic Jewish philosophy, especially Philo, developed these suggestive hints in its own way, making Wisdom an intermediary between its ultramundane God and the world; in Palestinian theology Wisdom is commonly identified with the Law, *i. e.*, with revealed religion (Deut. 4, 6; Ecclus. 24).

CHAPTER III

JUDAISM

SCHOOL AND SYNAGOGUE

Alexander and his Successors—The Asmonæans—Rise of the Pharisees —Doctrine of Retribution after Death, Resurrection, Immortality —Essenes and Other Sects—Philo—The Synagogue—Popular Literature and Apocalypses—Wars with Rome—The Stronghold of Judaism, the Law—Judaism as Revealed Religion—The Idea of God—Angels and Demons—The Golden Age and the Last Judgment—The Talmud.

THE battle of Issos in 333 had made Alexander the master of all western Syria. In the division of his empire Palestine, after some vicissitudes, became part of the kingdom of the Ptolemies in Egypt, and remained in their possession, though not uncontested, until 198 B. C., when it passed into the hands of the Seleucid kings. With the conquests of Alexander began a new and wider dispersion of the Jews; as soldiers, traders, and adventurers they were to be found in all the new centres of politics and commerce which sprang up everywhere in the East. In these cities, where Greek was not only the language of administration but the common language of intercourse among their polyglot inhabitants, the Jews in the course of a generation or two exchanged their Aramaic vernacular for the new cosmopolitan speech. In Alexandria, where they formed from the beginning a considerable part of the population, they found it necessary early in the third century to provide themselves with a Greek version of their sacred Law. In Judea itself the upper classes made haste to acquire at least a veneer of Hellenistic culture, and the unfavourable influences of Hellenism are more apparent there than in the dispersion itself. Particularly under the Seleucids, who in

their perennial financial embarrassment sold the office to
the highest bidder, the high priests strove to commend
themselves still further to their lords by an ostentatious
zeal for Greek manners and customs. One of them purchased the privilege of establishing a gymnasium just below
the temple, and the young priests hurried through the services to resort thither. The Greek hats in the streets and
the naked contests in the gymnasium were an equal scandal
to the godly.

During one of the campaigns of Antiochus IV in Egypt
the high priest Jason, whom he had deposed, took Jerusalem by a *coup de main*, driving out the king's latest creature,
Menelaus. The adventure gave the king a not unwelcome
pretext for confiscating the public and private treasures in
the temple. As this did not put an end to agitation he, in
December, 168, erected an altar to Jupiter on the great
altar in the temple, and shortly after issued a sweeping
edict against the Jewish religion, whose observances he forbade under extreme penalties.

The result was a revolt headed by Judas Maccabæus,
who, favoured by the inefficiency of the Syrian commanders
and by Antiochus' absence in the East, succeeded after
three years in recovering possession of the temple and
restoring it to the worship of the national God, though the
castle in Jerusalem with a strong garrison remained in the
hands of the Syrians for twenty years longer. The religious
persecution ceased, but the struggle continued. The Asmonæans,[1] encouraged by the weakness and disorders of the
kingdom, now aimed at nothing less than the independence
of Judah under their own rule, and this end, after many
turns of fortune, they achieved. Not content with this,
they waged aggressive war against their neighbours on all
sides, and for a brief time the territory over which they
reigned almost equalled in extent the kingdom of Solomon.
Later rulers of this house allied themselves with the old
aristocracy and with the neighbouring dynasties, and their

---

[1] The family of Judas and his brothers.

character and conduct were not more pleasing to their pious countrymen than those of the high priests they had superseded. Family dissensions, artfully fomented by the Idumæan Antipater, Herod's father, opened the way for Roman intervention, and in 63 B. C. Pompey made an end of what was left of the Jewish kingdom after eighty years of independence.

The Maccabæan revolt was supported at the beginning by the earnestly religious part of the people, who called themselves the pious; persecuted for the exercise of their religion, they took up arms against the persecutors. When the persecution was at an end, the worship in the temple restored, and a high priest of the legitimate line—though personally an odious creature—installed by the king, they had no further motive for continuing hostilities; and the more distinctly the Maccabæan struggle assumed a political form, the more completely they drew away from it. Out of this unorganised class, or party, of the godly the Pharisees arose, whose name is first heard in the time of Jonathan (161–143 B. C.). They called themselves by preference "associates," and formed societies, pledging themselves by mutual agreement to a strict observance of the laws, in particular those concerning ceremonial purity and the religious taxes, which were often neglected even by otherwise well-meaning people. The actual members of these societies were probably never very numerous; they included, however, many scholars ("scribes"), and by their teaching and example and their repute for learning and piety they exerted a great influence among the people.

The learning of the scribes was not only in the Scripture but in the traditions, the unwritten Law, which was in part based upon interpretation of Scripture and in part embodied custom that had grown up by the side of the Scripture. The Pharisees employed the principle of tradition not merely in the interest of a strict interpretation and observance of the Law, but to adapt its prescriptions to changing circumstances. It is erroneous to regard them as an ultraconservative or reactionary party. On the contrary, they were less inclined to a hard-and-fast literalness than the priesthood or the sects. With the great body of the people behind them, they constrained the rulers and the priests to accept their interpretation of the Law, and boldly opposed the worldly and corrupt conduct and measures of the later Asmonæans. Under Alexander Jannæus the conflict culminated in open hostilities, in which much blood was shed. His successor, Queen Alexandra, made her peace with them by reaffirming their abrogated ordinances; and from that time forth their power was so firmly established that even Herod avoided coming to an open rupture with them.

It is in this period that the belief in the retribution after death, the immortality of the soul, and the final judgment became current. In older times the Jews had the same notions about the survival of the dead which are found among all races. The tomb was in some way the habitation of the departed, and the strenuous prohibition of the offering of food to the dead in laws of the seventh century bears testimony to the persistence of the belief. By the side of this conception there appears in the same age the idea of a common abode of the dead, a vast cavern beneath the earth, where the shades of all men are gathered. The most vivid descriptions of this dismal place are in Isaiah 14 and Ezek. 32, 18 ff. The resemblance of the Hebrew Sheol to the Homeric Hades and the Babylonian Aralu is obvious, and it is not impossible, though it is by no means certain, that Babylonian imagery may have contributed to these prophetic pictures. The international character of the prophetic Sheol should not be overlooked. In it are found the nations which are the enemies of the Jews, with their rulers.

The lot of the shades is miserable, deprived of life and the joy of living, inhabiting the tomb or the dark recesses of the earth. To be sent to this gloomy realm before one's time is the extreme penalty of offending God. But while death, and particularly premature death, is thus retributive, there was no notion of retribution after death, except, perhaps, in so far as the unburied dead have a worse lot. In the nether world itself there is no separation of good and bad; nor have the great of the earth a prospect of brighter fortune in the company of the gods, as they have in Egypt or in the Elysium of the Greeks. These early notions remained substantially unchanged until the last centuries before the Christian era; the problem of theodicy in Job is so acute because there is no possibility of justification or compensation after death.

There is hope for a tree, if it be cut down, that it will sprout again. . . . But man dies and wastes away; man gives up the ghost, and where is he? As the waters fail from the sea and the river runs dry, so man lies down and rises not again; till the heavens are no more they will not awake nor be roused out of their sleep. —Job 14, 7–12.

From the fifth century on the Jews were in increasingly close contact with three peoples who had much more definite ideas about the hereafter, the Egyptians, the Persians, and the Greeks. Egyptian influence is as little to be discovered in Jewish eschatology as in other sides of religion. The case is very different, however, with the Persians and the Greeks.

Zoroastrianism, the religion of the Persian Empire, taught a judgment of individuals at death, in which each man's destiny was determined by his religion, and by his thoughts, words, and deeds in this life; the souls of the good being admitted to the abode of infinite light and the presence of God, while the wicked were hurled down to hell. When the present age of the world is at an end there will be a day of judgment for all mankind; the bodies of the dead will be raised in a general resurrection, and, reunited with their souls, will stand at the bar of God in the great assize. In the end all evil will be destroyed for ever, and the world will be renewed for the habitation of the righteous.[1]

[1] See Vol. I, pp. 375, 398 ff.

The expectation of a great crisis in history by which the heathen kingdoms which oppressed the Jews should be overthrown and the Jewish state restored in more than its pristine power and glory had been a favourite theme of Jewish thought for centuries, and in apocalyptic prophecies, such as those in Isaiah 24–27, this crisis is depicted with the imagery of a judgment of the world in which the powers of heaven as well as the nations of the earth are involved, and the restoration brings a new heaven and a new earth. The doctrine which extended the sphere of divine retribution for the individual over another life could not but appear, when once the idea was conceived, as a necessary implication of God's justice and a welcome solution of the cruel problems which the incongruity between men's deserts and their fortunes upon this earth created. In the Book of Daniel the notion of a resurrection appears in limited and peculiarly Jewish form. The righteous—specifically, perhaps, the martyrs of righteousness in the Seleucid persecution—who sleep in the dust shall rise from their graves to share in the blessedness of the golden age on earth now about to be ushered in, while the wicked rise to shame and contempt, or, as the words may also be interpreted, are an object of shame and contempt because they do not rise.

The premises of the Jewish eschatology are therefore in the religion itself, but the development of these premises into a definite and articulated scheme must be attributed in the first instance to Persian influence. In fact, the Palestinian eschatology, as we find it in writings from the second century B. C. on, corresponds entirely to the contemporary Persian doctrine, except that place has to be made in it for the Jewish national hope, the golden age on earth. It was the Pharisees and those who followed their leading who took up with conviction and enthusiasm these new ideas. Among other classes they found less ready acceptance. Jesus, son of Sirach, who may be taken as a representative of the sages, ignores them; the author of Ecclesiastes refuses them. The aristocracy of the priesthood, with the conservatism of worldly high churchmen, also rejected them, and their following, the Sadducees, did the same; they stood by the Scripture in its plain meaning, and would none of the ingenious exegesis by which the Pharisees introduced the resurrection into the Law.

Zoroastrianism was not, however, the only side from which new notions about the hereafter came to the Jews in that age. The Orphic sects, from the sixth century B. C., had familiarised the Greeks with the idea of heaven and hell and of a judgment of the dead. Plato presented the same ideas in more refined and moral form, and gave to the belief in the immortality of the rational soul the sanction of his lofty philosophy. The immortality of the soul and the retribution which awaited it at death were, in fact, part of the common belief both of the educated and of the un-learned.[1] In Hellenistic surroundings, as in Alexandria, for example, Jews, even without a scholastic acquaintance with Greek philosophy, naturally picked up these ideas, and found them fit so admirably into the framework of their thought that they seemed to spring naturally out of their own religion. The author of the Wisdom of Solomon is the eloquent apologist of immortality in the common Platonic form, and it seems probable that he accepted also the Platonic corollary, the pre-existence of the soul. From the point of view of Greek dualism, to which the body with its senses is the great hindrance to the realisation of the soul's true destiny, the reincarceration of the soul in its bodily prison-house was the worst thing that could happen to a man after death. Plato, with the Orphics, so thought of the re-embodiment of the soul by transmigration, and those Jews who opened their minds fully to Greek influences for this reason rejected the notion of resurrection. It is instructive to compare 2 Maccabees, in which the resurrection is the sustaining hope of the martyrs, with 4 Maccabees, which uses the martyr stories taken from 2 Maccabees, but effaces every mention of resurrection,

[1] See Vol. I, pp. 443 ff., 504 f.

substituting for it the Greek notion of the immortality of the soul.

It is customary to follow the example of Josephus and speak of the Pharisees as a Jewish sect. The term is hardly exact. They were the representatives of the Puritan tendency, or movement, which through them became dominant in Judaism; they were also the school of tradition, devoted to the development and promotion of the unwritten Law. There were, however, several bodies to which the term sect may with greater propriety be applied, because they separated themselves more or less completely from the mass of their fellow countrymen in religious matters. Of these the Essenes are, through descriptions in Josephus and Philo, the best known. The accounts in these authors do not agree in all particulars, and it is quite possible that the Essene communities did not all follow the same rule. They were a celibate order, living in monasteries, where they had all things in common and supported themselves by labour in the fields. Their life was regulated by a strict rule, the object of which was to unite a superlative degree of ceremonial cleanness with the undisturbed cultivation of a reflective piety. For admission to the order a prolonged novitiate was required, and when the candidates were finally admitted they bound themselves by the most solemn vows to observe the rules of the order and to keep its secrets. They had books of their own, which they carefully guarded from the knowledge of outsiders. Such an institution has, so far as we know, no antecedents in Judaism,[1] and foreign influences are probably to be recognised in some of their peculiar rites and customs. But our knowledge is too indefinite to enable us to say with assurance what these influences were.[2]

Similar in some respects to the Essenes were the Thera-

[1] The prophetic societies of the ninth century present only superficial resemblances.

[2] The assertion that the Essenes were in some way connected with Buddhism—though frequently made as positively as if it were a demonstrated fact—is without any foundation.

peutæ in Egypt, of whom Philo has written at length in his treatise on "The Contemplative Life." They also were withdrawn from the world to devote themselves to piety and meditation on higher things; but while the Essenes were a cœnobite order, the Therapeutæ, like the early Christian ascetics in Egypt, lived in a colony of separate huts and cells, assembling in a meeting-place only for their Sabbath and festival observances.

Recently discovered manuscripts have revealed the existence of a dissenting sect of different character in the region of Damascus. In some time of tribulation in Judea a number of Jews, including priests and levites, migrated to that country. There they subsequently bound themselves by covenant to observe the ordinances and interpretations of the Law they received from a teacher who appeared among them some years after the migration. Their organisation seems to have been modelled on the encampment of the Israelite tribes in the desert, each camp, as they called their communities, being presided over by a supervisor, while above these stood a supervisor of all the camps. In their legal interpretation they were, like all the other sects that we know anything about, more literal and, in general, stricter than the scribes of Pharisaic leanings; this is peculiarly apparent in the rigour of their Sabbath observance and in the dietary laws. They expected the appearance in the future of a Teacher of Righteousness sprung from Aaron and Israel—a peculiar variation of what is commonly called the Messianic hope.

While most of the Jews who were in any way influenced by Greek philosophy were affected by it as by the atmosphere they lived in, there were some who became students of philosophy in a more formal sense. Of these by far the most important, and the only one of whose writings much is preserved, is Philo, of Alexandria, who was born probably ten or twenty years before the Christian era and died some years after 40 A. D. Philo was not only learned in philosophy, but was himself a thinker, if not of the first rank, at

least among the foremost in his own age. He owes most
to Plato, for whom he has the highest reverence, but is also
much influenced not only on the ethical but on the theological side of his philosophy by Stoicism, and has from the
Pythagoreans his fondness for extracting wisdom from numbers. As a Jew, he accepts all the Scriptures as divine revelation; among them the Pentateuch holds the first rank by
virtue of the comprehensiveness and profundity of the
truth which it contains. On the other hand, by reason he
is no less convinced of the truth of Greek philosophy. The
truth of philosophy and revelation is in substance one; it is
taught by the philosophers in abstract, intellectual form,
while in the Bible it is presented concretely for the common
mind. Yet although the substance of truth is the same, it
is clear that the form in which it is presented in philosophy
to the mind of intelligent and thoughtful men is higher than
the symbol or example, the precept or object-lesson, in the
Law. And since the truth in both is God's truth, it must
be God's will that men should not remain on the level of
the Bible, but proceed to the higher ground of philosophy,
from which point of view alone it is possible fully to understand the biblical revelation. His task, therefore, as a
philosophical interpreter of the Scripture was to show how
in its own way it teaches the highest ethical and philosophical truth.

He accomplishes this by the application of the allegorical
method, which had been already developed and employed
with a somewhat similar end by the Stoics, and by this
means has no difficulty in discovering in the seemingly irra-
tional and trivial details of the ceremonial law the most
elevated and inspiring lessons, or in developing out of the
stories in Genesis a series of edifying psychological studies
in character.

Philo's conception of God and of the world reflects the
fundamental dualism of the Platonic philosophy. His
God, when he speaks as a philosopher, is a metaphysical
Absolute of whom nothing can be affirmed but that he is.

He is essentially nameless, and to predicate of him attributes or actions would be to circumscribe him and reduce him to the measure of finitude. The other pole of the universe is an eternal, inert, formless matter. This gulf between a God who by the very idea of godhead does nothing and matter which by its definition cannot do anything is the crux of Philo's metaphysics, as it was for the Neoplatonists who came after him and for the speculative Gnostics. In Philo's solution the influence of both Platonism and of Stoicism is recognisable. Between God and the material world he interposes the *logoi*, which corresponded to the Platonic ideas supposed immanent in God and to the Stoic forces (δυνάμεις), operative ideas immanent in matter. As Plato comprehends all the ideas in the one supreme idea, the Good, so does Philo find the unity of all the *logoi* in the one *Logos*. His premises demand on the one side that the Logos, as reason, should be eternally immanent in God, and, on the other, that as implicated in this material world it should be distinct from God. The vacillations and ambiguities in Philo's treatment of this subject should not be attributed to inability to think clearly, but, as so often in theology, to the necessity of thinking ambiguously.

Philo's dualism has its further consequence in philosophic alienation from the actual world. The soul of man can find its true happiness only in rising above the world and the body, ascending by reason or soaring in contemplation to the world of ideas, or rapt in ecstasy to God. This salvation by philosophy is by its very nature individualistic. Men may further one another in the quest by high communing, but the attainment must be solitary. It is easy to see, therefore, why Philo, with all his attachment to his people, has no interest in the national hope or the restoration of independence; the rule of a Messianic king could not be for him a religious end. The popular notions of retribution after death—the resurrection of the body, a dramatic world assize, a material heaven and hell—he ignores; the Platonic parallels he doubtless took figuratively.

It is an error to take Philo as a representative of Hellenistic Judaism. He is a figure of great interest in himself, but he had, so far as we know, no Jewish disciples, and we find no trace of his influence in the subsequent development of Judaism, or even of acquaintance with his writings, down to the Middle Ages. His importance lies on the one hand in his relation to the later schools of Greek philosophy, in particular to Neoplatonism, and on the other in his influence on the development of Christian theology from the Fourth Gospel and the Epistle to the Hebrews on.

Conceiving Judaism as revealed religion, whose Scriptures and tradition embodied the whole will of God for man's whole life, the task of the religious leaders was to educate the whole people in this religion. To this, besides their conviction of the truth of religion and its vital importance to the individual, they had an impelling motive in the belief that the fulfilment of the national hope, the coming of the golden age when the reign of God should be realised upon earth, depended upon the conformity of the entire people to the revealed will of God. In the centuries preceding the Christian era Judaism created in the synagogue and the school institutions excellently adapted to the accomplishment of this task. In all the lands of their dispersion, wherever Jews were settled even in small numbers, they had their synagogues, in which on the Sabbaths and twice in the week besides, they gathered for prayer and the study of the Scripture. The Pentateuch was divided for this purpose into lessons in such a way that it was read through in the course of three years.[1] In Palestine, and doubtless in Babylonia, the lesson was read from the Hebrew text and accompanied piecemeal by an interpretative translation in the Aramaic vernacular. Among the Greek-speaking Jews the custom of reading the pericope directly from the Greek translation seems to have been early established. The reading from the Law was followed by a second lesson chosen from the historical books and the proph-

---

[1] Later, the custom of reading it through every year prevailed.

ets. How early these prophetic lessons were fixed in a cycle corresponding to the Sabbath lessons from the Law is uncertain; probably not till some time after the Christian era. An exposition, or homily, based upon the lesson of the day, or at least taking it as a point of departure, was also customary. The services in the synagogue have often been compared to the worship of the Protestant Churches. There is, however, one notable difference: the synagogue had no ministry. There was no class of men whose special privilege or duty it was to read the lessons or to comment upon them. Any one who was qualified to do it might take part in the service in either way. Naturally the rabbis or their disciples who were members of the congregation or were present as visitors were preferred as preachers because of their greater fitness for instructive and edifying discourse, but their superior education and authority as teachers gave them no prerogative right.

Schools for elementary instruction were common in Palestine, in which boys learned to read in the Hebrew Bible, and the meaning was explained to them more or less fully by their teachers. In the higher schools the Law was methodically studied, following the rotation of the weekly synagogue lessons, and the unwritten Law was learned in connection with these lessons. The students not only memorised the traditions, but discussed with their teachers their meaning and application, their relation to the written Law and to other traditions. In striking contrast to the contemporary religions, in which theological learning was confined to the priesthood and often jealously guarded by them as an esoteric wisdom, the scribes and rabbis did their best to familiarise all classes of the community to the measure of their capacity, not merely with the form and ceremonial, or with the national legend and history, but with the higher lessons of religion and morals.

In the two or three centuries before the Christian era and the first century after it, a popular religious literature of considerable bulk and varied character was in circulation. There were short stories, such as Esther, Ruth, Judith, 3 Maccabees, Tobit, some originally written in Hebrew or Aramaic, others in Greek. The primæval and patriarchal history was written over in a particular interest, as in Jubilees; the Testaments of the Twelve Patriarchs combine legend with moral lessons and predictions; there are hymns, like the Psalms of Solomon. One of the most abundant species of this literature are the apocalypses, revelations of the last days of the present epoch of history, the judgment, and the golden age to follow; they contain also visions of the unseen world or visits to heaven and hell, and disclose the mysteries of astronomy and meteorology.

The historical apocalypse is the successor of prophecy in one of its aspects. The predictions of judgment assume, in such transitional writings as Isaiah 24–27, Zech. 9–14, and Joel, an increasingly supernatural form. Later authors construct, out of ideas and imagery drawn from many sources, composite pictures of the great crisis and the Messianic times; they set themselves to answer the question how all this shall come about, and when. The Book of Daniel is one of the oldest of these apocalypses, and sets a pattern which its successors imitate and vary. The four great empires, for example, successive representatives of the kingdom of this world in its hostility to God and his people, and the destruction of this power to make way for the kingdom of the saints of the Most High, become a standing scheme. Similarly, the computation of the time when the rule of the heathen shall be overthrown and the golden age begin, operating with a cycle of four hundred and ninety years—seventy times seven, or, as in Enoch, ten times forty-nine—is, from the second century B. C. on, a recurring exercise in apocalyptic arithmetic.

The collection which goes under the name of Enoch contains pieces of various origin and character, comprising eschatology, cosmology, and angelic mythology. Jewish apocalypses underlie the Revelation of John in the New

Testament. After the fall of Jerusalem in 70 A. D., the seers of 2 Esdras[1] and the Apocalypse of Baruch adapt the traditional material and method to the new situation, and discuss with the *angelus interpres* the burning question how the goodness or the justice of God can be reconciled, not merely with the ruin that has fallen on the Jews, but with the damnation of the great mass of mankind. Hellenistic Judaism created its counterpart to the apocalyptic literature in the Sibylline Oracles, the pretended utterances of heathen prophetesses.

Some of these writings are of sectarian origin, and more or less plainly promote sectarian notions and interests; others, without such a distinct tendency, are the work of authors who were in the eyes of the learned uneducated men, and fostered popular superstitions ·and fanaticisms. It is not surprising, therefore, that they found little favour at any time in the eyes of the rabbis, and that in the second century they were condemned in mass; they have been preserved only in Christian hands. There can, however, be no doubt that in certain circles or strata of Jewish society these writings had in their time a great vogue, and represented beliefs widely current among the people, notwithstanding the disapproval of scholars; nay, it is evident that the contents of some of them were transmitted by underground channels for centuries, to come to the surface again in mediæval Jewish literature. But their lasting influence and importance were in Christianity, not in Judaism.

In the crises of Jewish history during these centuries—in the persecution under Antiochus and the Maccabæan rising; on the overthrow of the Asmonæan kingdom and the taking of Jerusalem by Pompey; in the days of the Parthian inroad; when Caligula declared his purpose to set up his image in the temple; during the war of 66–72 A. D.—the chronic expectation of a great overturning flared up in a fever of hope; old apocalypses were revived and recast to fit the situation, and new ones were written. Even in

[1] In the Latin Bible, 4 Esdras.

5

quieter times a comparatively trivial incident, some blunder
of the Roman administration, heedless as it was wont to be
of the prejudices and superstitions of subject peoples, sufficed to set off an explosion. The words of enthusiasts who
read in the events of the times the signs of the end of the
world more than once rallied numbers under the banner of
insurrection. Such outbreaks were ruthlessly suppressed—
it was part of the routine of Roman provincial government;
the throngs that went out into the wilderness to see a
prophet or perchance more than a prophet melted away
and left no record behind; but one of these movements was
destined to be written large in the history of the world
under the name of Christianity.[1]

In 66 A. D. the revolutionary party, in spite of the efforts
of the priests and the scribes to restrain it, precipitated a
conflict with Rome, which resulted in the taking of Jerusalem and the destruction of the temple in 70. Deeply as
the Jews in all lands felt this catastrophe, its actual effect
on the religion was not correspondingly great. Judaism
had long had its real sanctuary in the synagogue and the
schools of the Law; and if the outward institutes of atonement ceased with the sacrifices, it had in repentance and
good works the reality of which sacrifice was only the symbol. In other ways, however, the effect of the fall of Jerusalem was of notable importance. The great council (Sanhedrin), which had had large judicial and administrative
powers, came to an end. The priestly aristocracy, which
had held many seats in the council—if not always the
majority—and the Sadducean party which supported them,
therewith lost their whole influence. From that time on the
Sadducees were a sect in the proper meaning of the word,
and soon sunk out of notice, though not out of existence.
Through these changes the teachers of the Law, almost exclusively of the Pharisaic party, acquired an undivided and
undisputed authority. Their schools, of which that at
Jamnia was for the moment the most celebrated, and the

[1] See below, Chapter V.

rabbinical synods which were convened from time to time, succeeded to the Sanhedrin. Their decisions might have no civilly binding force, but they had a moral authority which made other sanctions needless.

In the following generations the oral Law was gradually formulated in these schools in the shape in which it has come down to us. A systematic codification of this Law was begun by Akiba in the first decades of the second century. In his school, also, a more rigorous interpretation of the written Law prevailed, based on the principle that in the word of God as it is contained in the Scripture no jot or tittle is without significance—a principle which often led to extremely strained exegesis. The Greek translation in use was far too free for those who entertained such views of Scripture, and, moreover, it had now become the Bible of the Gentile Christians, from which they drew their proof texts in controversy with the Jews. Under the influence of Akiba a new and strictly literal Greek translation was therefore made by the proselyte Aquila, and there was more than one revision of the Septuagint intended to bring it into closer accord with the original. The canon of Scripture and the standard Hebrew text were also fixed in this period.

In 132 A. D. the Jews again rose in arms. Different reasons are given for the outbreak. It is possible that a law against emasculation was interpreted as prohibiting circumcision, but the emperor Hadrian's decision to erect a heathen temple on the site of the ruined sanctuary in Jerusalem was cause enough. Unlike the war under Nero, in which the party of action carried the authorities off their feet, the revolt under Hadrian had from the beginning the support of many of the most eminent religious teachers. It found an able leader in Simon bar Cozeba, who was hailed by Rabbi Akiba as the "Star out of Jacob" foretold in the prophecy of Balaam, and is for that reason called Bar Cocheba. The struggle was long and bloody. The Jews defended themselves with desperation, but in 135 the war came to an end with the capture of Bether. As the rabbis had been among the chief fomenters and supporters of the war, to which they had given the character of a religious uprising, it is not strange that the Romans, not purely in retaliation but in self-defence, proscribed the rabbinical schools as hotbeds of insurrection, and put various restrictions upon the exercise of the Jewish religion. Some of the teachers defied the edicts and died as martyrs to the Law. Quiet was gradually restored, and under Antoninus Pius the oppressive edicts, the execution of which had already been relaxed, were rescinded.

In the latter part of the second century there set in among the Jews a reaction against everything foreign. The age of missionary activity which had begun in the century before our era came to an end; even the conversion of proselytes was looked upon askance. Judaism, thrown on the defensive, retreated into the stronghold of the Law, and converted it into an impregnable fortress. When the schools of the Law were restored after the war under Hadrian, Galilee was the seat of the most celebrated. Here, about the turn of the century, the Patriarch Judah gave the Mishna the authoritative form in which it has come down to us, and, backed by the patriarchal authority, it soon superseded the Mishna collections of other schools. Only one of these, the Tosephta, has survived complete, while others are known through the extensive quotations from them in the Talmuds. Collections of religious and moral teachings in the form of homilies or expositions of the Scripture lessons, which form the basis of the older Midrashim, were also begun in this age. By the end of the second century Judaism had assumed the form which, with no substantial change, it maintained until the revival of learning under Moslem influence in the ninth and tenth centuries, and which, indeed, in essentials, it still preserves.

The corner-stone of Judaism is the idea of revealed religion. God has not only made himself known to men, but has declared to them his will for man's whole life. This revelation the Jews possess in their Holy Scriptures and in its complement, the unwritten Law.[1] There is no duty towards God or man which is not either expressly or by plain implication contained in this twofold revelation. The study of God's law is therefore the first duty of every Jew, for upon knowledge of God's will the keeping of it depends. This study is the only rewarding labour; the acquisition of this knowledge is the only abiding gain. But to bring the fulness of blessing, the study must not be pursued to win thereby reward or honour, but for its own sake. He who studies a precept of the Law should think of himself as receiving it immediately from God at Sinai. The Law is the signal proof of God's peculiar love to Israel. It is a universal blessing like the dew and the rain, a tree of life, an elixir of life to him who fulfils it. It delivers him who takes its words to heart from anxiety of war, famine, and folly; it frees him from the oppression of rulers. It illumines the understanding. Its promises sustain Israel through the centuries of hope deferred. Love for the Law and devotion to its study and observance, pride in the Law as the wisest and best in the world, gratitude to God for the gift of the Law—this is the prevailing note in all periods.

The Jewish conception of God is derived from the Bible, and from the purest and most exalted teachings of the Bible, such as are found in Exod. 33 *f.*, Hosea, Deuteronomy, Jeremiah, Isaiah 40–55, and the Psalms. Monotheism was reached, as has been already observed, not from reflections on the unity of nature or of being, but from the side of God's moral rule in history, and it has therefore a more consistently personal character than where the idea of unity has been derived from physical or metaphysical premises. God is supramundane; his abode is in heaven, he is the Lord of heaven, the God of heaven; by metonomy, the name Heaven itself is applied to him, as in the phrase, "the kingdom (reign) of Heaven." But he is not extra-

[1] The oral Law was revealed at Sinai no less than the written Law.

mundane, excluded from his world because he is infinitely
exalted above it. On the contrary, he is everywhere present in the world, filling it as the soul fills the body. The
interest in such assertions is religious, not philosophical;
because God is everywhere he knows everything, and his
providence embraces all his creatures. Similarly, God's
almighty power is emphasised, not because it belongs to
the idea of God to be omnipotent, but because nothing can
defy his justice or thwart his purpose.   He is the sole creator
and sustainer of the world, which he brought into being by
the word of his power according to a wise and unchanging
plan. The world and all that is in it was made for man as
the climax of creation; or, in a profounder conception, it
was made for the Law, that is for religion. Not only the
order of nature but the order of history is all of God's
making. History is interpreted by his moral will or his
revealed purpose.

The holiness of God is his godhead morally conceived,
the sum of moral perfections. Righteousness and loving-
kindness or, as commonly expressed, justice and mercy, are
his two fundamental attributes. His justice is man's assurance that he will not use his almighty power tyrannously.
If God should transgress justice in but one act, the world
would go to pieces. His justice is not that of inexorable
law or of a more inexorable theological attribute, but of a
sovereign whose end is the best interest of the community
and of the individual. God knew beforehand that if he
executed justice according to the strict letter of the law,
none could stand. Consequently, he is long-suffering; he
gives warning, sends chastisements, teaches men the way of
repentance, and forgives the penitent; for forgiveness is his
supreme prerogative, and repentance was created before
the world—the plan of salvation was in existence before
sin. Justice and mercy are not contradictory elements in
his character, but complementary. He is just because he
is good, and good because he is just. But mercy is most
congruous with his nature, while justice is, as the prophet

said, "his strange work." In all this God is an example to men, who are constantly exhorted to imitate his sympathy, his long-suffering, his forgiving spirit.

God is the ruler of the world, the king of kings. He rules in it without a rival. He can do his will in heaven and on earth, and his will is a good world. The most characteristic expression of this conception in Judaism is the "reign of God," or as it is translated in our New Testament, "kingdom of Heaven," the undisputed supremacy of God's will in the world, as Jesus defines it in the prayer, "Thy will be done on earth as it is done in heaven." And as this consummation is the end of God's ways in the world, so it must be man's supreme desire and aspiration. A prayer is no prayer which does not include the reign of God.

As king, God had long been imagined enthroned in heaven, surrounded by ministers who deliver his messages on earth and execute his commands. The latest books of the Old Testament give to some of the angels personal names and particular functions, by which they acquire a more distinct individuality than the nameless messengers, or "agents," of God in the older literature. Jewish angelology goes much further. There are angels who preside over natural phenomena, such as the motions of the stars, the rain and hail; the nations have their angelic regents or champions; there are guardian angels of individuals, and angels who record men's deeds; the destroying angels, with God's commission, bring death and disaster on earth and torment the souls of the wicked in their prison-house. The angels form a hierarchy with numerous ranks, the "angels of the presence" holding the first place. This angelic mythology, it should be observed, has a larger room in apocalypses, such as Enoch, and in the popular literature, than in the rabbinical teaching. The miscegenation of the sons of God with the daughters of men in Gen. 6 grew into myths of fallen angels. The names of these arch-sinners were known, and the evil arts they taught mankind—from them women learned to paint their eyes and wear jewelry, men to make armour and

weapons of war; magic and witchcraft were introduced by
them.

For more reflective minds the operations of God in creation and providence, in history and revelation, were mediated, not by anthropomorphic agents such as angels, but
by qualities of God himself, his Wisdom, his Word, his
Power, to which objective existence was given. Their
activity could only be represented as that of intelligent
agents, and the effort to represent vividly of itself gave
more distinct personality to them. This fell in very well
with contemporary tendencies in Greek philosophy, and
was furthered by the coincidence, as clearly appears both
in Philo and in the Wisdom of Solomon. It is only in
Philo, however, under the exigencies of a transcendent idea
of God, that these personified qualities approximate hypostasis, and become intermediate beings between God and
the world or God and man; and even in Philo this way of
thinking is not consistent.

The old beliefs about demons and their harmful doings
not only persisted, but underwent a development parallel
to that of angelology. It was a cosmopolitan age in superstition as well as in religion. Egypt, Babylonia, and Persia
all contributed to the composite demonology of Western
Asia and to the arts of dealing with demons; exorcism and
demonic magic flourished everywhere. The evil spirits, like
the good, formed a hierarchy of many ranks. At their head
was a "chief of the devils," who was sometimes the ring-
leader of the fallen angels, Azazel or Shemjaza (Shem ḥazai);
in other writings he is Beliar; in others still, the Satan, "the
adversary," of the Old Testament, or Mastema, a name of
the same significance. Demons were, as universally in popular belief, the authors of disease and death; in particular, as we see in the New Testament, mental and nervous
diseases were attributed to possession. But the sovereignty
of God was too firm a corner-stone of Judaism to permit its
religious teachers to cede to the devil a realm of his own;[1]

[1] It is only in the New Testament that he figures as the "god of this
age."

and it is noteworthy that even in the sectarian literature Beliar and his ilk gratify their ill-will to God and men by tempting men to sin and so bringing upon them punishment, rather than by themselves inflicting evils on mankind.

A fact of considerable significance in the history of Judaism is the disuse of the proper name of the God of Israel, Jehovah (Yahweh), in place of which either the appellative God was employed, or a great variety of epithets, such as the Lord of Heaven, the Most High, the Almighty, the Holy One, the Merciful, the Power, the Presence, the Name, the Place (omnipresent). In reading the Scriptures "the Lord" was substituted for the unutterable name, as was done in the Greek version as early as the third century B. C. Several motives doubtless conspired to bring this about. One was the apprehension that the holy name might be uttered irreverently and profanely; another was to prevent its use for magical purposes.[1] But besides these there was a reason of which the Jews may not have been clearly conscious—a proper name for God is needed only to distinguish him from other gods; if there is but one God, he needs no such distinction.

It has been frequently asserted in recent times that the Jewish conception of God in this age was of a being so exalted as to be remote and inaccessible, or, as it is sometimes expressed, a "transcendent" deity; and that the immediateness and reality of religious communion were correspondingly impaired. The whole temper of Jewish piety is a refutation of this singular misjudgment. The loftiest terms of human speech are employed to magnify God—as they are in the Psalms, and in Christian liturgies from the New Testament down—but the greatness of God does not signify his aloofness, his holiness no longer means his inaccessibility. "What great nation is there that has gods as near to it as Jehovah our God is wherever we call upon him?" is spoken from the heart of the Jew in the age of the Mishna as truly as in that of the Deuteronomy. In

---

[1] Here the good motive defeated itself; the "secret name" is the omnipotent spell in magic.

later books of the Old Testament the title "king" is frequently given to God, and, following this usage, he is addressed in the prayers of the synagogue as "our king." In another sense he is the "king of the universe"; and, as in the Old Testament, the sovereignty of God is the cornerstone of redemption.

The characteristic note of Jewish piety in this age is the thought of God as father—not the father of the people only, as in the Old Testament, but of individuals. The name is much more frequent in the liturgy and in the utterances of Palestinian rabbis than in the popular writings, whether Hebrew or Greek. The word expresses love, confidence, and intimacy, and the relation is reflected in the quality of obedience. The attitude of the Jew towards God is contrasted in this respect with that of the Gentile: the former is like a son who serves his father gladly, saying, "If I commit a fault against my father he will not be angry with me, for he loves me"; the Gentile is like a foreign-born slave who serves in fear, saying, "If I commit a fault against my master he will be angry with me." Sinners whose conscience makes them shrink from approaching God are encouraged, "Is it not your father in heaven to whom you come?" In a time of deepest depression after the war under Hadrian, when all other help and hope failed, a rabbi exclaims: "Whom have we to lean upon? One only, our father who is in heaven." The sovereignty of God and his fatherhood are so far from conflicting that one of the most familiar of the synagogue prayers begins, "Our Father, our King."

The disastrous end of the Messianic uprising under Hadrian did not extinguish the faith in a golden age to come; but, with the dear-bought wisdom of experience, the Jews settled down to wait for God's time without trying to precipitate his intervention. The constant features of this expectation, amid many variations in imagery and order, are the coming of a descendant of David to restore the kingdom of Israel; the attempt of the enemies of Israel to prevent

the establishment of this kingdom, and their final overthrow; the gathering of the Jews from all lands to Palestine; an age of peace and prosperity under the wise and
just rule of the Messiah, when virtue and piety shall be
universal.

With this conception of the golden age derived from the
prophets are combined eschatological conceptions appropriated from Zoroastrian sources: the last judgment, when
the dead are raised to stand at the bar of God; the
sentence of the wicked to the fires of hell;[1] the renewal of
the earth to be the abode of the good, who lead in it a trans-
figured existence free from the infirmities of the flesh and
from the power of death. In the details of this eschatology
there is still greater diversity than in the form of the Messianic hope, and the two are often blended or confused.
In the more consistent representations, however, the final
judgment succeeds the golden age; the "days of the Messiah" are a period of shorter or longer duration—forty
years, seventy, four hundred, or, as in the New Testament
Apocalypse, a thousand—intervening between the present
age and the end of the world. Between death and the
resurrection the souls of the righteous are in bliss and
those of the wicked in misery in their respective abodes.

The codification of the oral Law and the promulgation of
the Patriarch's Mishna in the beginning of the third century brought to a conclusion the labours of the Tannaim, or
repeaters of tradition. Their successors found occupation
in the schools for centuries in the discussion of the Mishna,
debating the meaning, ground, and application of its prescriptions, and reconciling apparent discrepancies or contradictions in them. The reports of these discussions
formed a secondary body of legal tradition, which in the
course of centuries grew to vast proportions, and was in
turn codified in the two Talmuds, embodying, respectively,
the work of the Palestinian and of the Babylonian schools,

---

[1] As in Zoroastrianism, these fires are expiatory and purgatorial, not
eternal. Akiba lets the torment last a year.

together with a great variety of other traditional lore. The
Babylonian Talmud was substantially complete by the end
of the fifth century; the Palestinian, perhaps three-quarters
of a century earlier. The decisions registered in the Talmuds, or the outcome of the debate as determined by certain principles, were invested with binding authority. In
the Middle Ages the Babylonian Talmud superseded its
rival even in Palestine, and became the final arbiter for
orthodox Jews everywhere.

In the last centuries of the existence of the temple, under
the influence of the Pharisees, features which had their
origin in the synagogue were engrafted upon the cultus.
Thus, at the daily morning holocaust the officiating priests
interrupted the sacrificial ritual to assemble in a chamber
off the court for prayer, the order including an opening
ascription of praise, the confession (*Shema'*; Deut. 6, 4 *ff.*,
11, 15 *ff.*), the Ten Commandments, and two prayers (for
the people and for the divine acceptance of the offering),
closing with the priestly benediction. The chanting of
psalms in the temple ritual and the use made of them in the
prayers of the synagogue was another point of assimilation.
On the other hand, participation of the people in the worship of the temple was insured by the presence at all the
public sacrifices of representative delegations from different
parts of the land, each of which was in attendance for one
week in the half year. The delegation not only stood by
at the sacrifices, but gathered four times a day for reading
of the Scriptures and prayer, while the community at home
which they represented likewise gathered daily during their
week for a similar service in the synagogue.

After the destruction of the temple such features of the
cultus as admitted the transfer, *e. g.*, the blowing of the
horn (*shofar*) at New Year's, the palm branches and goodly
fruit (*lulab* and *etrog*) at Tabernacles, were introduced into
the synagogue; the priestly benediction (Num. 6, 24–26) was
pronounced in the synagogues, with a difference in the mode,
before the fall of Jerusalem.

While the temple stood, the festivals were observed at home and in the synagogues by those who could not go to Jerusalem to take part in them; after its destruction these services remained the only memorial of the vanished cultus. The proper lessons for these seasons were passages of the Law connected with the festivals. The same principle dominated the subsequent growth of the liturgy; the word, in lesson, prayer, psalms and hymns, must take the place of the ancient ritual of sacrifice, which men could now offer only thus in mind and heart.

The Passover, which had been primitively a family sacrifice, and even in Jerusalem had preserved at least the fiction of the family group, resumed in domestic observance its ancient character. The father, in answer to the questions of a child, narrated the occasion of the institution and explained the peculiar features of the meal, such as the unleavened bread and the bitter salad. The synagogue services of the week had appropriate lessons from the Pentateuch, and similarly for the Feast of Weeks and Tabernacles. The ancient agricultural association of the festivals fell into the background when the Jews were scattered in many climes and were chiefly city-dwellers. The memorial character which is attached to some of them in the Bible itself prevailed for all. Passover commemorates the deliverance from Egypt, the prototype of the greater deliverance yet to come; the Feast of Weeks celebrates the giving of the Law at Sinai, which the chronologers fixed at that season. Tabernacles had always had a peculiarly joyous character, which was emphasised in the later temple liturgy by the festal processions and the new ceremonies of the water libation. It had the same character in later Judaism; the illumination of houses and synagogues was one of the features of the festival. In the Middle Ages the closing (ninth) day was celebrated as the Joy of the Law, marking the end of the annual cycle of readings from the Pentateuch, which then began again at the beginning.

Two festivals, not in the biblical calendar, came in before

the Christian era. Purim celebrated the deliverance of the
Jews from the destruction Haman planned for them as narrated in the Book of Esther, which was the Scripture reading for the day. It had a national rather than a religious
character, and since there was no biblical prescription concerning its observance, the merrymaking freely borrowed
forms from outside, and sometimes ran into excesses which
the graver heads among the rabbis disapproved. In imitation of the example in Esther 9, 19, Purim is a season for
exchanging presents and making charitable gifts. The re-
establishment of sacrifice in the temple after its recovery by
Judas Maccabæus in 165 B. C. is commemorated by the
Feast of Dedication, beginning on the twenty-fifth of Kislev
and lasting eight days (1 Macc. 4, 59). In its general character it resembles Tabernacles, with which it shares the custom of illumination.

The civil year of the Jews began in the autumn, while the
festival cycle began in the spring. New Year's Day, the
first of Tishri, is thus in the ecclesiastical calendar the first
day of the seventh month. According to a widely accepted
view, the first of Tishri was the day on which God began
the creation of the world. The characteristic feature of the
ritual is the blowing of a horn (*shofar*) at certain points in
the liturgy of the day, a ceremony taken over, as we have
seen, from the temple. Next to the Day of Atonement, it
is the most solemn day in the Jewish year. For, probably
under the influence of Babylonian conceptions, it is believed
that on this day all mankind pass for judgment before God,
and in the books of destiny the fate of the righteous and
of the incorrigibly wicked is irrevocably decreed, while for
the mass of men, who do not belong to either of these
classes, an interval of ten days is granted for repentance
before the sealing of the verdict on the Day of Atonement.
The ten Penitential Days have, therefore, a most important
place in the religious thought and life of the Jews.

The Day of Atonement was the great expiation of Judaism, when the sins of the people, solemnly confessed by the

high priest and laid upon the head of the scapegoat, were borne away into the wilderness. The rabbis moralised this ancient rite of riddance by teaching that the expiation availed only for those who sincerely repented of their sins; and after the rite itself ceased with the destruction of the temple, repentance itself remained the sole condition of the divine remission of sins. In the Day of Atonement, therefore, the penitential exercises of the preceding days culminate; confession of sin, sorrow for sin, prayer for the forgiveness of sin, dominate the whole liturgy of the day. The ancient association is preserved by the lesson, Lev. 16, the temple ritual for the Day of Atonement, and by a kind of descriptive paraphrase of that chapter (the Abodah). The liturgy was gradually expanded to such length, by multiplication, especially of poetical effusions, and repetition, that it fills the entire day.

The constant element in the Jewish prayer-book for weekdays and Sabbaths, for use at home and in the synagogue, contains prayers which were in use in the first century of the Christian era or earlier. In the course of centuries the liturgy has grown by accretion, and, with the services for the feasts and fasts, the new moons and special Sabbaths, has come to be voluminous and complicated. It would be more exact to say "the liturgies," for there has never been any uniformity; each country and region has had its own development. Every great religious movement has written itself somewhere into the liturgies. And, on the other hand, probably no liturgy has ever impressed itself on the religious life of a people so deeply as the Jewish.

The situation of the Jews under Roman dominion from the time of Antoninus Pius to that of Constantine varied with the disposition or caprice of the emperors; many burdens and restrictions were imposed on them, but the most stringent were not long enforced, and however irksome they were, the Jewish religion itself was protected by law. The triumph of Christianity made their position worse. Constantine issued edicts forbidding conversions to Judaism

under penalty of death, and imposing the same penalty on
the Jewish party to a marriage between Jew and Christian.
His successors made still more oppressive laws. Great
bishops like Ambrose of Milan and Cyril of Alexandria
goaded the rulers or inflamed the mob against the Jews,
whose case became continually harder both in the East and
in the West. In the Persian Empire they fared better
on the whole; but the more zealous Zoroastrians among the
Sassanian kings persecuted Jews as well as Christians.
Under these adverse conditions it is not strange that learning and culture declined. Yet the Midrashim, or homiletic
catenas, and the corresponding matter in the Talmuds are
evidence that the moral and religious teaching of earlier
times was kept alive. The Palestinian schools died out
about 425 A. D., those in Babylonia were in full decadence
in the sixth century.

CHAPTER IV

JUDAISM

MEDIÆVAL AND MODERN

The Moslem Renaissance—The Karaite Schism—Jewish Theology and Ethics—Saadia—Bahya ibn Pakuda—Ibn Gabirol—Judah ha-Levi —Aristotelianism: Maimonides—Mysticism: the Kabbala, Hasidism—Modern Revival of Learning—Moses Mendelssohn—Reform Movements—Zionism.

THE Moslem conquests in the seventh century embraced the countries in which by far the greater part of the Jews were settled, and delivered them from the persecuting zeal of Christians and Zoroastrians. In the Oriental renaissance under the caliphate the stirrings of the new intellectual life were quickly felt by the Jews. One of its first manifestations was a revolt against the authority of tradition, to which the completed codification of the Talmud had given the character of finality, and the tyranny of its official interpreters, whose opinions and decisions were already beginning to constitute another body of actual law. The leader of this movement was Anan ben David, a member of the family of the exilarchs,[1] himself learned in the Talmud and the micrologic casuistry of the schools, whose intellectual sterility and religious aridity had in his day reached its nadir. It is said that the dangerous habit of having opinions of his own cost him the succession to the exilarchate, to which he had pretensions, and that this personal grievance threw him into open antagonism to the traditionists who had compassed his defeat. Whatever his

[1] The exilarch (Resh Galutha), a hereditary prince of Davidic lineage, was the civil head of Babylonian Jewry, as the Gaon, appointed by him, was its religious and judicial head.

motives may have been, his declaration of independence drew to his side many to whom emancipation from the dominion of the rabbinical authorities was welcome. They formed a sect with an organisation of their own, and made Anan their exilarch.

Over against the authority of the Talmudic tradition Anan asserted the authority of Scripture and the right and duty of private interpretation. "Diligently search the written law," was his watchword. He did not reject traditions as such, but when he found them at variance with Scripture he set them aside, in spite of great names and immemorial prescription, and put the biblical rule, according to his interpretation, in their place. To his successors he seemed to have been unduly conservative, or to have unconsciously brought over too much of the old leaven, and they made more thorough work in purging out the remnants of rabbinism. Compends of the laws and observances made by Anan, though differing in many particulars from those of the great body of the Jews, were superseded by later ones of more radical character.

The sect, which had at first been called after its founder, Ananites, is better known by the name Karaites, which we might translate "Bible Jews." [1] In their rejection of tradition as an authority concurrent with Scripture and their assertion of the right of individual interpretation and judgment, the Karaite movement has a partial resemblance to the Protestant Reformation. "To investigate is a duty; to err in investigation is no sin"; a man should bind himself to no authorities, but examine and investigate for himself; a son need not agree with his father nor a pupil with his teacher if he has reasons for his dissent; if he is mistaken, he has at least the reward of opening men's eyes and enlightening them.

The appeal to Scripture led the Karaites to a kind of study of the Bible that had long been neglected, the en-

[1] From *kara*, "read." We call the sacred books "writings"; Jews and Moslems call them "readings" (Mikra, Koran).

deavour to find out what it really meant, and their opponents were constrained to meet them on the same ground. They had the methods of Moslem interpreters of the Koran as an example. It was the beginning of a new biblical exegesis which later had a notable development in both camps. The literal interpretation of the Pentateuch led the Karaites, as it had led the Samaritans and certain older Jewish sects, to greater strictness in various matters than was the rule among the Rabbanites. Thus, levitical laws, such as defilement by a dead body, were revived, which the Rabbanites held to be no longer in force.

Persecution in Babylonia drove many Karaites to Palestine and Egypt; Jerusalem became their intellectual centre until the Crusades, afterwards Constantinople. Before the end of the ninth century the schism had grown to such dimensions, and its leaders had become so aggressive, that it was a serious menace to orthodox Judaism, and provoked violent polemics; and although this crisis passed, Karaism maintained itself for centuries, and produced a considerable and by no means negligible literature, especially in the interpretation of the Bible. Since the sixteenth century it has greatly declined, and now numbers only a few thousand adherents, chiefly in Turkey and Russia.

The theological controversies among the Moslems raised many questions which were as pertinent in Judaism as in Islam, and they soon became subjects of warm discussion among Jewish thinkers. This came in the days when the Mutazilites were at the height of their influence,[1] and both their rationalistic method and a good deal of their doctrine were appropriated by the Jews. The problem of the divine attributes—how the existence of attributes can consist with the unity of the godhead—first raised by them, continued for centuries to be one of the burning questions of Jewish philosophy. The problem of the freedom of the human will was also part of this inheritance, though, as Judaism had no dogma of predestination, it did not present

[1] See below, pp. 417 ff.

to Jewish thinkers the same theological complication as to
Moslems.

The necessity of an exposition and justification of Jewish belief and teaching led Saadia (d. 942) to write his "Beliefs and Dogmas." The author was born in Egypt in 892,
and was thoroughly versed not only in Jewish but in Arab
learning. In 928 he was called to be the head (Gaon) of
the academy at Sura, in Babylonia, which had fallen into
sad decadence. His uncompromising integrity soon brought
him into conflict with the exilarch, and he was for several
years kept out of his office. During this time he wrote at
Bagdad the book of which mention has just been made.
Saadia made an epoch in almost every branch of Jewish
learning. His translation of the Pentateuch and other
parts of the Bible into Arabic, which was then the vernacular of much the greater part of the Jews, is comparable in
importance to the Septuagint in the Hellenistic age; and
besides this translation, which is in fact and intention an
interpretation, he wrote commentaries in a new style on
several of the books. By his lexicon and grammar, modest
as these first steps were, he has a right to be regarded as
the initiator of Hebrew philology. In the controversy with
the Karaites he was the most redoubtable champion of
orthodox Judaism. The "Beliefs and Dogmas" (more
exactly, "rationally established tenets") is the beginning of
the philosophical treatment of Jewish theology.

The influence of the Moslem liberal theologians is evident
throughout. After an introduction, in which certain preliminary questions are discussed, Saadia proceeds to develop
the cosmological argument for the existence of God, and
from this point of view discusses the nature of God, his
unity, attributes (life, power, wisdom), the commandments
of God (rational and positive), the revelation of God through
prophets and the nature of prophecy, the effects on the soul
of obedience and disobedience, freedom and ability, good
and ill desert, the nature and activities of the soul, soul and
body, the state of the soul after death, the resurrection, the

Messianic age, reward and punishment in the other life; concluding with a chapter on ethics as a kind of appendix.

Saadia shows himself familiar with Greek philosophy, as far as it was accessible to him in Arabic translations, and with Christian as well as Moslem theology. In the first chapter he states and criticises twelve theories of the origin of the world held by different philosophers and religious bodies. Under the head of the unity of God he combats both dualistic theories (Zoroastrian, Manichæan), and the Christian doctrine of the Trinity and the Person of Christ; and in a later chapter controverts the Christian arguments to prove that Jesus was the Messiah, particularly those based on the interpretation of Dan. 9, 24–27. His discussion of the Trinity avoids a polemic against vulgar polytheistic notions of the divine persons, and confines his criticism to the Trinitarian doctrine of the theologians. Like the Moslem controversialists, he finds the root of the error in a misconception of the nature of the divine attributes upon a false analogy drawn from the nature of man, which gave them an existence of their own, beside, rather than in, the essence of God. In the sequel he shows himself remarkably acquainted with the subtleties of Christological speculation, in which he distinguishes four conflicting theories.

In the following centuries Jewish theology and philosophy ran along with the movements of Moslem thought which are to be described in a later chapter. The Neoplatonic elements in the composite Arab philosophy and in the Moslem mystics made themselves felt in Judaism, also, in a greater inwardness of religion and a mystical tone of piety. This is strongly marked in Bahya ibn Pakuda's "Duties of the Inner Man," written in Spain perhaps a century and a half after Saadia, the first methodical treatment in Jewish literature of the religious and moral life—piety and ethics.

Outward, bodily actions, including the external observances of religion, have meaning and worth only as they express what lies beneath them in the mind and heart; it is only with this inner man that the author proposes to deal.

Both piety and ethics have their root in the recognition of
God and gratitude to him; man should therefore seek first
to know God truly and to revere him sincerely. God, as
he is in himself, is indeed beyond man's knowing; he is
the absolute One. What we can know about God is to be
learned from contemplation of nature—from which, indeed,
apart from revelation, we are aware of his existence—and
of ourselves; this, therefore, is the first of the duties of the
inner man. The argument from the created world to the
Creator runs on similar lines to Saadia's, as does also the
proof of God's unity. Different kinds of unity are to be
distinguished; the unity of God is a substantial unity, the
ultimate reality, the unchangeable ground of being. The
attributes of God—existence, unity, eternity—are inseparable from the essence of God; they are, in truth, only nega-
tions of the opposites. Our inability to know God in himself
corresponds to our inability to know our own soul, whose
existence is nevertheless manifest in every thought and
act.

This foundation laid, the author goes on to treat successively of the worship of God (in the heart and under
external forms), trust in God (providence, immortality),
single-mindedness in the service of God, humility, penitence,
self-examination, withdrawal from the world, love to God.
Love of God, which is the end of all moral and religious self-
discipline, is the longing of the soul for the source of its life,
in which alone is its rest and peace. As in the theological
part of the work Bahya is in general accord with Saadia
and the Moslem theologians, so in other parts the influence
of the Encyclopædia of the Pure Brethren of Basra is demonstrable.[1] Nor is his affinity to Ibn Gabirol and al-Ghazali
to be overlooked.

The "Duties of the Inner Man" has been one of the
great forces in moulding the religious life of the Jews. It is
still extensively used as a spiritual guide by all classes, circulating in many editions, and frequently furnished with

[1] See below, pp. 450 ff.

a modern translation for the benefit of women and others whose understanding may not reach to philosophical Hebrew.

Solomon ibn Gabirol (d. ca. 1058) is the most noteworthy exponent of Neoplatonism among Jews or Moslems, though, like the rest, his Neoplatonic ideas run into Aristotelian moulds. God is for him the metaphysical Absolute. This Absolute, or first substance, is at one pole; at the other is the world of matter and form. The gulf is spanned by the divine will, which thus assumes in his system the function of the Logos in Philo's, mediating between the Absolute and finite existence. Unlike Philo, however, Ibn Gabirol makes no attempt to show that this high philosophy is allegorically contained in the Bible; he develops his system in a kind of religious fourth dimension, without reference to Scripture or specifically Jewish beliefs. When the *"Fons Vitæ"* of "Avicebron" became known in Latin translation to the schoolmen, it was not suspected that the author was a Jew; the work was thought to be by some Moslem philosopher. Through it a fresh current of Neoplatonism flowed into scholastic channels; Duns Scotus was especially influenced by it. Among the Jews Aristotle was in the ascendant, and though Ibn Gabirol is one of the most highly esteemed of the synagogue poets, and his great hymn, "Kether Malkuth," [1] is permeated with the spirit of his philosophy, his ideas made little impression on Jewish thought, unless in the mystical circles in which the Kabbala was cultivated.

The modified Arab Aristotelianism of al-Farabi and Avicenna, which made room for emanation theories of Neoplatonic extraction, became in the twelfth century the dominant influence in Jewish religious philosophy. But whatever the alloy of these composite philosophies, their pretension was to be a loftier and purer religion for intellectual men. They had in science and metaphysics the truth of which positive religions were only an adumbration for unphilosophical minds. Knowledge and speculative

[1] "The Crown of Divine Sovereignty."

thinking were the way of intellectual salvation, the attainment of the true end of man's being, to which neither the implicit acceptance of hereditary beliefs nor the scrupulous performance of moral and ceremonial prescriptions conduct man. In interpreting the Bible—or interpreting it away—by the principle that nothing in revelation can contradict reason, they made reason the ultimate and indefeasible authority.

To this presumption of philosophy Judah ha-Levi strenuously demurred. In his dialogue Kuzari (ca. 1140), a pious king of the Khazars, in search of a more satisfactory religion than that of his forefathers, invites a "philosopher"—that is, an Arab Aristotelian—a Christian, and a Moslem, to expound to him their respective doctrines. The king makes pertinent objections to them in turn, and, since both Christianity and Mohammedanism are by their own admission sprung from Judaism, he finally sends for a Jew, who convinces him that Judaism is the best religion; in consequence, he and his people embrace it.[1]

So far from having the decisive word in questions of religion, Judah contends that philosophy has nothing to say about such matters. In mathematics and logic, and in natural science based on observation, its results may be certain or probable; but beyond that, in cosmic physics and in metaphysics, it offers only conflicting and unverifiable hypotheses. The fundamental truths of the Jewish religion—creation out of nothing, particular providence, the immortality and destiny of the soul—are not discovered or demonstrated by reasoning; they rest on the historic fact of a revelation to Israel through prophets. The way to the highest knowledge of God is not speculation, but simple and unquestioning faith.

Judah's antipathy to philosophy is not the jealousy of ignorance. His discussion of the problems of the divine attributes and of the freedom of the will prove, on the contrary, that he was well instructed in philosophy and an

[1] The conversion of the Khazars, a Turkish people, is a historical fact.

acute thinker. Where the disputes of philosophers had
confused men and perplexed their faith, sounder reasoning
must clear up their intellectual difficulties. His attitude
towards the arrogant claims of the philosophers resembles
that of the great Moslem theologian, al-Ghazali, to whom,
indeed, Judah ha-Levi is greatly indebted. Like Ghazali,
also, he finds a ground of religious assurance in religious experience. The Neoplatonic strain in him is strong; it gives
its character to his mysticism, and from its doctrine of
emanation is derived one of the leading ideas of his work,
the influence of the divine Logos on a chosen part of mankind.

The Aristotelian period in Jewish theology begins with
Abraham ibn Daud (d. 1180), who on the basis of the Arab
Aristotelianism of Avicenna develops philosophically the
fundamental religious conceptions, and endeavours to
prove that philosophical theory and Scripture teaching are
in complete harmony, the difference being only that the
Bible presents these truths in popular form for the common
mind.

The greatest name among the Jewish Aristotelians, and
one of the greatest in the whole history of Judaism, is Moses
ben Maimon (Maimonides; d. 1294). Born in Cordova in
1135, he was forced to flee from Spain by the bigotry of the
Almohades,[1] and spent most of his life in Egypt, where he
was court physician to Saladin. His chief theological work
is the "Guide of the Perplexed," addressed to such as have
been led by philosophy to doubt whether revealed religion
can be reconciled with reason. Maimonides undertakes to
show that not only is there no contradiction between the
truths of reason and those of religion, but that the chief
doctrines of religion can be philosophically demonstrated,
and faith thus established on a rational foundation. Indeed, if faith be not merely the assent of the lips but of
the intelligence, this is the only way to it.

Like all philosophic theologians, Maimonides was con-

[1] See below, pp. 470 ff.

cerned above all things to preserve the idea of God in its purity. To this it belongs that God is incorporeal, and in all respects unlike his creatures. But the Bible ascribes to him hands and feet, eyes and ears, besides human—all too human—passions, and among Jews as well as Christians and Moslems not only did the mass of simple people imagine God as what has in modern times been called a "magnified non-natural man," but there were teachers who made it a criterion of orthodoxy to take the words of revelation to the foot of the letter, and denounced the philosophers as confessed unbelievers. The anthropomorphic controversy was a perennial one. Maimonides applies to such expressions in Scripture the same figurative exegesis which from Philo's time on had been employed in all three religions.

He subjects the method of the Moslem theologians (Mutikallimun) and their Jewish imitators to a searching criticism, to show its complete inadequacy. Their argument for the existence of God was invalid against the philosophers who, with Aristotle, denied its major premise, namely, that the world was created; and all their corollaries about the unity and nature of God fell with it. The atomic theory to which the leading Moslem theologians had addicted themselves in their endeavour to make God the sole cause in the universe is false; its authors do not recognise that the universe is an organism governed throughout by law.

Like Ibn Daud, Maimonides would prove the existence of God by the Aristotelian arguments from motion to an unmoved prime mover and from contingent to necessary existence. The prime mover—the ultimate reality—must be incorporeal, absolute and simple unity. Simplicity implies that there can be in it no change. Attributes which appear to assert something of God are admissible only if it is understood that they merely deny that there is any imperfection in him; they cannot define the nature of his perfection, which is beyond apprehension. Even the so-called relative attributes, which express the relations between him and his creatures—attributes, so to say, only from the human point of view—are inadmissible; for God is wholly unlike created things, and analogy of relations is impossible. Against the attributists Maimonides is hardly less zealous than against the anthropomorphists. Those who ascribe to God positive attributes have not a false idea of God; they have none at all. Their God is made after the likeness of man.

Between God and the material universe Maimonides interposes a series of emanations—immaterial intelligences—down through the celestial spheres; the tenth and last of these, the *sekel ha-poel* (actualising intelligence),[1] presides over the sublunary sphere of mundane existence to which man belongs. Into the details of this cosmology, which is based on Avicenna, it is not necessary to go further here.

The *sekel ha-poel* might also be called the creative intelligence in our sphere, since it imposes upon matter, which is pure potentiality, the forms in union with which it becomes actual in the real world. This is true not only of what we call material things but of the human intellect, which in itself is merely potential, a latent, or, in Maimonides' own phrase, a material, intelligence.[2] The realisation of its possibilities through the operation of the "actualising intelligence" makes the latent intelligence of man a real or "acquired" intelligence; we might say, a system of intellectual concepts, or ideas, which disengages itself from the lower faculties of the soul and becomes a substantial, immaterial existence—pure form, and therefore imperishable. In this way Maimonides finds place for the immortality of the soul, or, more accurately, a philosophical substitute for it. The human soul is not by nature immortal; it is only capable of attaining immortality by philosophy, which is a strait gate and a narrow way; and it is difficult to see how, on Maimonides' nominalist premises, its individuality is to be preserved.

In the same way he admits a limited providence. The

---

[1] Aristotle's νοῦς ποιητικός in a new rôle.

[2] "Material" is of course to be understood in the sense of the Aristotelian "matter."

Aristotelians denied God's knowledge of particulars and his concern for them. Maimonides makes the human race an exception in so far as in it God's providence extends to individuals in degrees corresponding to their intellectual and moral attainment; those who have made no such progress are, as their punishment, left subject to the forces and laws of nature.

Prophecy, the highest stage of human attainment, is the work of the "actualising intelligence," operating upon the intellect and imagination of man; on the one side it is an emanation from God, on the other a psychological process. There are different kinds or degrees of prophecy, from dreams up to vision in a state of exaltation, yet of clear consciousness. All the visions and symbolical actions of the prophets are purely subjective. Only in Moses, who is a prophet *sui generis*, was the factor of imagination absent; he stood on the higher plane of pure immaterial intelligence. The discussion of the subject is one of the most interesting and instructive parts of Maimonides' philosophy.

The greatest objection to Aristotelianism was the doctrine of the eternity of the material universe, or of the matter of which it is composed, which seemed to conflict squarely with the biblical account of creation. Maimonides does not think this objection insuperable. In fact, if the eternity of the world were philosophically demonstrated, it would be no more difficult to interpret what Scripture says about creation than to explain its anthropomorphisms. But the Aristotelian argument, based as it was upon astronomical theories which the advance of science had abandoned, was inconclusive. For the philosopher the eternity of the world is an open question; and inasmuch as creation is an admissible hypothesis, there is no reason for rejecting the traditional doctrine and the common understanding of Scripture. The end of God in creation is hidden in his inscrutable wisdom. Man errs when he imagines himself that end. In this sublunary sphere, as an intelligent being, he occupies the highest place; but compared with the vast whole of the universe and with the intelligences that preside over the celestial spheres, he is an insignificant creature.

Maimonides discusses the problem of freedom in relation to universal law and to divine providence, and affirms man's complete freedom. Inherited disposition and the circumstances of his life may make it more difficult for one man to attain to intelligence and virtue than another; but he has in his will the power to overcome these adverse conditions. The notion that a man's character and destiny are determined by his stars is combated on scientific and philosophical grounds. On the much-debated question how the freedom of man can consist with the prescience of God, Maimonides holds that the difficulty arises from the assumption that God's knowledge is comparable to men's. But a knowledge that comprehends all in one intuition is not only wholly unlike ours, but is altogether inconceivable by us. If man were not free, if God interfered in any way with his freedom, there would be an end of all morality, and there would be no place for either law or prophecy.

The "Guide of the Perplexed," written in Arabic, was immediately translated into Hebrew and before long into Latin. It was widely read by Moslems and Christians as well as by Jews. No other work of a mediæval Jewish author had so large and deep an influence.

The "Guide" is not Maimonides' only contribution to theology. The first book of his great codification of Talmudic law, "Mishneh Torah," or as it is more commonly called, "Yad Hazakah," treats systematically the chief doctrines of religion. The "Eight Chapters," prefixed to his commentary on the Mishnic "Sayings of the Fathers," contain an outline of psychology and ethics. In the commentary on the Mishna is also found a concise statement of the fundamental articles of belief, which has become the most widely accepted creed of orthodox Judaism, and as

such has a place in the prayer-books. The articles are in
brief:

I believe with perfect faith that God is; that he is one with a unique
unity; that he is incorporeal; that he is eternal; that to him alone
prayer is to be made; that all the words of the Prophets are true; that
Moses is the chief of the Prophets;[1] that the law given to Moses has
been transmitted without alteration; that this law will never be changed
or superseded; that God knows all the deeds and thoughts of men; that
he rewards the obedient and punishes transgressors; that the Messiah
will come; that there will be a resurrection of the dead.

The philosophical theology of Maimonides was violently
opposed. It was equally obnoxious to the traditionalists,
to the mystics, and to the representatives of the old theology
whose methods he had harshly criticised. Some zealots,
playing with fire, brought his works to the notice of the
Christian inquisition in Provence, and had the satisfaction
of seeing them condemned as heretical and publicly burned
at Montpellier and Paris, as those of Averroes, and even of
al-Ghazali, were burned by Moslem bigots.

The Aristotelianism of Maimonides, as has been remarked
above, is substantially that of Avicenna; with the works of
Averroes (d. 1204) he was not acquainted when he wrote
the "Guide." The most eminent Jewish Averroist was Levi
ben Gerson (d. 1344), who has also the distinction of being
the solitary realist among Jewish philosophers—the rest,
like their Moslem fellows, were nominalists. With Ḥasdai
Crescas (d. 1410) set in a tide of reaction against Aristotelianism of every variety, and the general decadence of Jewish intellectual activity.

In the centuries in which philosophy and theology were
coming more and more under the dominion of Arab Aristotelianism, the esoteric doctrines of the Kabbala ("Tradition") were growing and spreading. The origins of this
hidden wisdom are very remote. The Jewish Gnosticism
which flourished at the beginning of the Christian era, and

[1] This and the two following articles are pointed against the claims
of Moslems and, in part, of Christians.

the theosophy which had its adepts in the same age even in orthodox circles, are reckoned among its spiritual ancestors. It revived, or sprang up anew, in Babylonia in the early centuries of Moslem rule, and one of its products, the "Book of Creation" (*Sepher ha-Yeṣirah*), attributed to Abraham, seemed of sufficient moment for Saadia to write a commentary on it. From Babylonia it seems to have reached Europe in the ninth century, and to have been handed down in initiated circles, taking in time somewhat different forms in different countries. The Neoplatonic elements which were present in the Oriental Kabbala were reinforced in Spain by deeper draughts from the fountainhead, and in the measure in which Aristotelian rationalism gained the upper hand in theology, the Neoplatonic mysticism found refuge in the Kabbala, to which, in return, it gave a more philosophical form.

These various streams flow together in the classical work of the European Kabbala, the Zohar. This book, in form a commentary on the Pentateuch, purporting to embody the esoteric teachings of the great rabbi and saint, Simeon ben Yoḥai (first half of the second century A. D.), is indeed an encyclopædia of kabbalistic doctrines and speculations, and ultimately acquired canonical authority in mystical circles comparable to that of Dionysius the Areopagite among Christian mystics. In the catastrophe that befell the Spanish Jews at the end of the fifteenth century, as has happened over and over again in similar circumstances, men in persecution and exile turned for spiritual refuge to mysticism, and the study of the Kabbala, especially of its theosophic and magical sides, was greatly stimulated, while the scattering of its disciples expelled from Spain spread it in the many lands of their new dispersion. Isaac Luria (d. 1572, at Safed in Palestine) became the founder of the modern school, which flourished in the sixteenth century not only in the East but in Italy. It took root in Poland, where in the seventeenth century it was expected that all rabbis should be learned in the Kabbala as well as in the

Talmud, and in the eighteenth century was disseminated in Germany by Polish teachers. Many Christian scholars, also, from the time of Raymond Lull (d. 1315), particularly in the sixteenth century, busied themselves with this esoteric Judaism, in which some of them found proofs of the truth of Christianity, some a profound symbolical theology, others the secrets of natural philosophy, while its indirect influence may be traced in the Christian mystics.

The metaphysics of the speculative Kabbala are ultimately derived from Neoplatonic sources. God is the Infinite, the Absolute, of which nothing can be affirmatively predicated—neither attributes, will, intention, thought, word, nor deed—and in which change is unthinkable. Between this Absolute and the material world the Kabbalists, like their predecessors, interpose a series of emanations, sometimes conceived in metaphysical, sometimes in more mythological, form (the Sefirot, Adam Kadmon), and a series of worlds. The soul of man is tripartite: the animal soul, the moral nature, and the pure spiritual intelligence, in itself incapable of good or evil. The goal of the last is to return to God. As in the sphere of the will man may be governed by fear of God or by love, so knowledge may be reflective or intuitive; the path of the soul's ascent leads from fear to love, from reflective knowledge to intuitive knowledge; its goal is perfect love and pure contemplation. Other features of the system, such as its solution of the problem of evil and of the fall of man, cannot be touched upon here.

By the side of the philosophy and ethics of the Kabbala stands a practical Kabbala, with a fantastic mythology—cosmogonic, angelic, eschatological—which has come down in part from the Enoch books and cognate pre-Christian literature, in part seems to be of Gnostic origin, with a heterogeneous increment from subsequent generations and various sources. The practical Kabbala is largely occupied with the means of working the supernatural world, warding off the assaults of demons, constraining angels to do man's will, performing all manner of miracles. Among these means, amulets, and particularly the magical power of mythical names, have a great place. The history of religions affords many other examples of the pernicious affinity between mysticism and magic—theosophy and theurgy. For the attainment of the loftier ambitions of the soul the practical Kabbala had recourse to ascetic exercises such as have everywhere been employed in religions which propose a like goal—self-inflicted privations, especially fasting, and suffering of body and mind.

There is no doubt that the study of the Kabbala contributed to promote or confirm popular superstitions, but, on the other hand, by the supremacy that it gave to the inward knowledge of God, and by the high value it set on prayer, it did much to keep alive the spiritual element in Judaism, and to prevent its degenerating into an arid formalism of Talmudic casuistry and of ritual observances. The remarkable religious movement of the eighteenth century, Hasidism, drew no small part of its inspiration from the Kabbala.

The Kabbalists had done their share to revive the expectations of the approaching advent of the Messiah; Luria, among others, believed himself to be the Ephraimite Messiah, the forerunner of the Davidic Messiah. Apocalyptic calculations based on a passage in the Zohar made out that the deliverance of Israel was to come in the year 1648; another computation, which gained wide currency among Christians, also, fixed on 1666. Shabbethai Zebi, the most famous in the long catalogue of Messianic pretenders, gave himself out for the designated deliverer, and found credence not only with great masses of the unlearned in many lands, but with some prominent rabbis. Neither his imprisonment by the sultan nor even his conversion to Mohammedanism, which he accepted to save his life (1666), sufficed to destroy faith in him. Several of his followers made similar claims for themselves, so that there was a succession of Shabbethaian Messiahs in the seventeenth and eighteenth

7

centuries, the last of whom, Jacob Frank, with many of his
dupes, publicly embraced Christianity (1759).

The ease with which these would-be Messiahs found believers, and the pathetic fidelity with which their followers
clung to them even after they were unmasked, are symptoms
of the prevailing unrest and of the dissatisfaction of multitudes of Jews with their spiritual guides, the rabbis, who
were more and more absorbed in the futile casuistry of their
Talmudic studies, and, in the telling phrase of Baal Shem,
"through sheer study of the Law had no time to think
about God." This dissatisfaction found another expression in Hasidism. The founder of this movement, best
known by the name Baal Shem, which the people gave him
as a miracle-worker, was born about 1700 and died in 1760.
He was not a reformer bent on annulling the rabbinical law
or amending it; what he found fault with was not the observance or the study of the Law, but the spirit in which it
was done. His aim was to revive spiritual religion in the
hearts and lives of men.[1]

The ruling idea of Hasidism is the indwelling of God in
nature and man. All things are pervaded by the divine
life; nothing is void of God, for if we could imagine such a
thing it would instantly fall into nothingness. God is in
every human thought; when a man speaks he should remember that the divine speaks through him. He who does not
see the world in the light of God separates the creation
from the Creator, and he who does not fully believe in this
universality of God's presence has never properly acknowledged God's sovereignty, for he excludes God from a part
of the actual world. God did not make the world and then
leave it to itself; creation is a continuous process, a perpetual manifestation of the goodness of God. Revelation
also is continuous, and the organ by which it is apprehended
is faith. It is not prophecies and visions alone that come
from heaven, but every utterance of man, if rightly understood, conveys a word of God.

[1] See on the following, Schechter, "Studies in Judaism," pp. 20 ff.

Since God is in all, there is good, actual or potential, in all. Every man should think humbly of himself and be slow to think ill of another. He should try to recover the erring and sinful by friendliness to them and prayer for them. No man has sunk so low in sin as to be incapable of raising himself to God. Sin is not positive but negative; it is imperfection. With asceticism Baal Shem had no sympathy; pleasures are manifestations of God's love, and, so regarded, are spiritualised and ennobled. Eating and drinking and sleeping, as well as study and worship, are the service of God, which for the truly religious man includes all life. The motive for fulfilling the ordinances of the Law is not to accumulate merit by multiplying observances, but to become one with God. The object of the whole Law is that man should become a law to himself. Of all means of spiritual attainment prayer is the most efficacious. The essence of prayer is not petition, though that has its place, but "cleaving" to God, a sense of oneness in which the consciousness of separate existence is lost, and man finds himself in the eternal being of God. This state is accompanied by an indescribable bliss, which is a necessary element of the true worship of God.

This pantheistic mysticism contains little that is specifically Jewish, though it conserves the outward forms and observances of Judaism. As in similar systems—in India, for example—men who had attained to the heights of this god-consciousness became to their fellows a kind of godmen. What such a man intuitively perceives is divine truth; his utterance of it has the authority of revelation. He lives the divine life among men in its life-giving power— Baal Shem is reported to have given to the words of Hab. 2, 4, the turn, "The righteous can make alive by his faith." "He is a source of blessing and a foundation of grace"; God's grace is bestowed upon those who love him, while those who do not believe in him are apostates from God. Besides all this, divine virtue resides in such holy men; they can work miracles, exorcise evil spirits, lay ghosts,

·and give many other tangible proofs of their supernatural
powers. Such men were called Zaddikim, "righteous men."
They enjoyed a reverence and devotion which would have
turned even heads not prepossessed by a belief in their
superiority to plain humanity. In the last half-century better education and the influence of the movement for enlightenment (Haskalah) have drawn away many of the younger
generation from Hasidism, and its numbers and vitality are
declining.

The persecution of Jews in Spain and Portugal, and of
Jewish converts to Christianity (Maranos), whose Christianity was in most cases a transparent disguise, led in the
sixteenth century to extensive emigration to Turkey, where
they enjoyed the protection of the law, and to those Christian countries in which they found at least comparative
toleration, especially to Italy, France, and the Netherlands.
In Amsterdam there was from the beginning of the seventeenth century a flourishing Jewish community, which
counted among its rabbis some scholars of wide reputation.
The most famous name in the annals of Amsterdam Jewry
is Baruch (Benedict) Spinoza (1632–'77). His philosophy,
in which important elements derived from mediæval Jewish
philosophers, especially Maimonides and Crescas, find a
place in a system which has its starting-point in Descartes,
proves him one of the most profound and original thinkers
of his race. Spinoza belongs, however, to the history of
European philosophy, and his influence on Jewish thought
has been relatively small. Excommunicated by the synagogue, and with no inclination to exchange the bondage of
Jewish orthodoxy for that of the church, he lived out his
short life in solitary freedom, grinding optical glasses and
surveying all things "*sub specie æternitatis*"—from the point
of view of the infinite and eternal.

In central Europe, after the middle of the fourteenth century, Jewish learning gradually decayed, and the revival of
letters and the Protestant reformation did little to improve
the situation. Insulated in their ghettos, even their speech

was untouched by the development of literary High German, and their antiquated German, mingled with Hebrew words, was in the ears of their neighbours a barbarous jargon. The reflux migration from Poland in the seventeenth century and the revival of Talmudic studies by imported Polish rabbis in the eighteenth did not make matters better in this respect. That their intellectual isolation was a greater evil than all the legal disabilities under which the Jews suffered; that from this ghetto of the mind they alone could liberate themselves; and that to accomplish this the barrier of language must first of all be broken down—these were the convictions which inspired Moses Mendelssohn (1729–'86) to advocate and initiate a reform in education which should prepare Jewish youth to appreciate and appropriate German culture. His own German translation of the Pentateuch and other parts of the Bible, undertaken originally for his children, contributed much to the end he had at heart. The Free School in Berlin, founded at his suggestion, was the first institution in Germany for the instruction of Jews not only in the Bible and Talmud but in secular studies and modern languages.

Mendelssohn himself was the friend of Lessing, and moved in the brilliant circle of writers and thinkers who made the Berlin of Frederick the Great illustrious. His philosophical writings were widely read and highly esteemed. Intellectually a child of the "Aufklärung," he was a Jew to the bottom of his heart, and adhered faithfully to the ancient forms of his religion. In one of his latest works, entitled "Jerusalem" (1783), these two sides of his character find instructive expression. Like Leibniz he distinguishes eternal necessary truths from contingent truths, such as phenomena of nature or historical fact. The former are apprehended by reason alone, which God has bestowed on all men; they are not communicated by supernatural revelation, nor, in the nature of things, can miracles afford any confirmation of them. Mendelssohn recognises no other eternal truths than those which are not merely comprehen-

sible by human reason but discoverable and confirmable by
reason.   Judaism is not revealed religion, if by religion be
meant a system of eternal truths, but revealed law; not
what man must think or believe, but what he must do.
Unlike Christianity, therefore, Judaism has no distinctive
dogmas, though Maimonides had been ill advised enough
to formulate articles of faith for it.   Its eternal truths are
the truth of all human religion.   The Law, on the other
hand, was revealed to Israel alone, which God had chosen
to be a priestly nation.   Besides its religious and moral precepts, its ceremonial observances were a kind of symbolic
language inviting men to reflection on the profound lessons
which lay beneath the surface.   This Law, written and oral,
in all its parts is perennially binding: "I do not see how
those who are born in the house of Jacob can at all consci-
entiously emancipate themselves from the Law."

The revolutionary era brought to the Jews in the chief
states of western Europe the more or less complete removal
of their civic disabilities; Jewish students began to frequent
the universities in numbers and to participate in the eager
intellectual life around them.   The spirit of liberty was in
the air, often manifesting itself in revolt against authority
in every sphere.   While the world about them was busy
overhauling everything that had come down from the past,
it is not to be wondered at that reform began to be broached
among the Jews also.   The beginnings were made with
mild changes in the synagogue worship, the introduction of
a sermon and prayers in German, the singing of hymns in
the same language, sometimes with organ and choir, the
curtailment of the inordinately tedious service by dropping
some of the doggerel *piyyutim* ("poetries") with which the
German and Polish liturgy especially was overladen.   These
innovations were vehemently opposed by the conservatives,
to whom they appeared little short of sacrilege.   Insignificant as the specific issue may seem, they instinctively per-
ceived that behind it lay the question whether Judaism was
immutable in ritual as in doctrine, or was to adapt itself to
the changing notions and capricious tastes of the age.

While these controversies about organs and prayer-books were going on, scholars, equipped not only with Jewish learning but with the philological and historical training of European universities, were engaged in critical investigations of Jewish literature, proving that it was the product of a long and complex development, and represented different, and sometimes conflicting, tendencies. The same methods were before long applied to the sacred text itself with a like result. Nowhere was the immutability, nowhere the finality, to be discovered which the opponents of progress made the characteristic of Judaism.

A more radical tendency was represented by the Frankfort Society of the Friends of Reform, who issued their declaration of principles in 1843 in three articles: "*First,* We recognise the possibility of unlimited development in the Mosaic religion. *Second,* The collection of controversies and prescriptions commonly designated by the name Talmud possess for us no authority from either the doctrinal or the practical standpoint. *Third,* A Messiah who is to lead back the Israelites to the land of Palestine is neither expected nor desired by us; we know no fatherland but that to which we belong by birth or citizenship." The more moderate reformers vied with the stanchest conservatives in denouncing this "confession of unbelief," and the antagonism was increased when the Frankfort society resolved that circumcision was not indispensable.

Several conferences of rabbis were held between 1844 and 1846, but the differences were too radical to make it possible to come to a common understanding. The revolution of 1848 diverted interest for a time into other channels; the reaction which followed strengthened religious conservatism among Jews as well as Christians. The reform movement came to a standstill in Germany, where it has only in the last few years begun to make headway again; but it was taken up and carried forward in the United States, whither several of its ablest exponents emigrated in the fourth and fifth decades of the last century. The adherents of reform in this country reject the authority of the Talmud

and the rabbinical codes; they put aside also the expectation of the coming of a Messiah, the return of the Jews to
Palestine, with the re-establishment of Jewish nationality
and sacrificial worship; they do not believe in the resurrection of the body, but in the immortality of the soul.   The
dietary laws, biblical as well as rabbinical, which have their
reason in the ideal of exclusiveness, fall with that ideal.
Sabbath rest is understood as refraining from labour for
gain; all the casuistry about prohibited works and the legal
fictions by which the prohibitions are evaded are swept
away.   While the effort is made to maintain historic continuity in the forms of worship, the ritual and the prayer-
book have been recast in conformity with the principles of
the reform.

The belief that the dispersion of the Jews among the
nations, their "exile," is an expiation of the sins of the
people, and that it is to end with the gathering of the Jews
from the ends of the earth to the Holy Land and the restoration of their nationality, has been a cardinal article of orthodox faith in all the centuries, and though the realisation
of this hope promised by so many would-be Messiahs was
repeatedly disappointed, the faith was unshaken.   In the
Jewish "Aufklärung" of the Mendelssohnian age, indeed,
when, with the political emancipation the Jews became citizens of European states and absorbed with avidity the intellectual and æsthetic culture of their environment, many
cast aside these nationalist aspirations: Judaism was a religion with a mission to mankind which could only be fulfilled by the dispersion of the people.   It was historically
and actually the religion of a race, but none the less the
Jews were nationally and in culture Germans or Frenchmen
or Englishmen, as the case might be.   This was also the
attitude of reformed Judaism.   To the great masses of the
Jews, however, this renunciation of the national hope seemed
to be the pulling out of a corner-stone.

Numerous projects for the restoration of the Jews to Palestine and for securing the autonomy of their settlements

there were put forth in the nineteenth century, some of them by Christians of millenarian prepossessions, but without considerable results. The movement received a great impulse in the last decades of the century from the rise of an aggressive anti-Semitism in European countries. Nationality was conceived not in a political, but in a pseudo-ethnological sense; "national culture" was the expression of the genius of a race. The Jews were a foreign element in the national body politic, socially unassimilable, a peril to the purity of the national culture just in proportion to their intellectual acuteness and their financial power. This antipathy manifested itself in different ways, from otracisms in clubs to wholesale massacres, connived at, if not instigated, by the government; but everywhere it pressed home upon the Jew the fact that he was a member of an alien race. The idea that race is the true basis of nationality, and consequently that each "race" ought to be a nation for itself fell in with the immemorial belief of the Jews and gave fresh energy to it. Zionism and anti-Semitism are, in so far, only two aspects of the same phenomenon.

The appalling condition of the Jews in Russia in consequence of economically ruinous laws and bloody pogroms, and the hardly more tolerable state of their fellows in Roumania, gave a practical turn to the movement. The only hope for these distressed millions was emigration in mass; and it is not strange that the eyes of many of them turned to the land of their fathers. In western Europe, also, the question could not fail to rise in the minds of philanthropists, as well as of idealists; Was not the solution of the perennial Jewish problem an autonomous Jewish state in Palestine under Turkish suzerainty? When in 1896 a Viennese journalist, Theodor Herzl (d. 1904), in his "Jewish State," struck out a plan for the new exodus to the promised land, his words found an instant and enthusiastic response in many quarters. Opposed by liberals as a revival of an old delusion; by hard-headed men of affairs as a visionary scheme; by the ultraconservative, partly out of prejudice against the origin of the movement, partly because in the orthodox programme the advent of the Messiah should precede the return to Palestine, Zionism spread rapidly. A literature of pamphlets and periodicals was created, congresses in which all shades of belief and unbelief met together were held, a programme and measures for carrying it out were adopted, societies for the promotion of the cause were formed in all countries; many who at first stood aloof were swept into the current.

But when it came to realising these exalted ideals insuperable obstacles were encountered. The Sultan was polite, but the expected concessions were not forthcoming; the financiers did not respond as they were expected to. Strident discord, also, early made itself heard in the Zionist counsels; the project of a Jewish colonial state in British East Africa seemed to many nothing short of treason to the enterprise. The revolution of 1908 and the subsequent overturnings in the Turkish Empire seemed to put the realisation of the original plan further beyond the horizon of possibility than ever. The events of the present war, especially the occupation of Palestine by the British army and the prospects held out to the Jews of re-establishment in the land of their fathers, have given a new turn to the affair, the ultimate issue of which cannot at this moment be foreseen.

CHAPTER V

CHRISTIANITY

THE APOSTOLIC AGE

Jesus and his Disciples—The Work in Galilee—Pilgrimage to Jerusalem and Death—The Teaching of Jesus—The Faith of his Disciples—Beginnings of Gentile Christianity—Paul—The Gospel of the Lord Jesus Christ—The Mystery of the Cross—The Law and the Gospel—The Spirit of Christ—The Coming of the Lord—Predestination—Angels and Demons—Influence of Paul—The Epistle to the Hebrews—The Gospel of John—The Incarnate Logos—The Knowledge of God and Eternal Life—Regeneration—The Spiritual Gospel—The Revelation of John—The Millennium and the Last Judgment—The Nazarenes and other Judaic Sects—Early Christian Churches—Heresies—Marcion and the Gnostics—The Consolidation of the Catholic Church.

THE expectation of a great deliverance, in which by the intervention of God the Jews should be liberated from the dominion of the heathen, and of a golden age of righteousness and peace and prosperity to follow the re-establishment of independence, kept alive by the lessons from Scripture which were read and expounded in the synagogues and by revelations bearing the names of ancient worthies, gave birth from time to time to prophets, who announced that the great moment was come, and sometimes drew crowds after them into the desert, where, according to a common belief, the Messiah was to appear. In the year 28 or 29 of our era such a prophet, named John, appeared in Judæa, proclaiming that the reign of God[1] was at hand, the age in which his sovereignty should be universally acknowledged and his righteous will be supreme in the hearts and lives of men. It was a common belief that in that age there would

[1] This is the meaning of the phrase translated in the English versions, "kingdom of Heaven" or "kingdom of God."

107

be no place for sinners; it was to be ushered in by a judgment in which they should perish. John urged his hearers
to prepare for the crisis by repenting of their sins and thus
securing God's forgiveness.[1] Of those who professed repentance, he required a confession of their sins and an ablution
in the waters of the Jordan, which he seems to have treated
as a condition of remission. Hence the name, "John the
Baptiser." The multitudes that flocked to him and his
influence over them roused the suspicion of Herod Antipas,
who deemed it prudent to forestall a possible outbreak by
putting the leader to death.[2] The arrest of John dispersed
his following, but did not destroy their faith in his prediction that a greater than he was about to appear, who would
winnow the chaff from the wheat, gathering the wheat into
his garner and burning the chaff in unquenchable fire.

Among those who resorted to John and were baptised by
him was Jesus, a young man from Nazareth in Lower Galilee. His father, Joseph, was a carpenter, and Jesus had
been brought up to the trade. The names of four brothers
are known, and he had sisters married and living in Nazareth. Of education Jesus had no more than in those days
fell to the lot of youths of his class in a provincial town.
He may have learned to read the sacred books in Hebrew
in a school for boys such as were maintained in many places,
but his knowledge of the Scriptures was doubtless chiefly
gained from the reading and exposition of the lessons in the
synagogue.[3] Of the legal lore that was to be got only at the
feet of the rabbis he had none. His mother tongue was the
Aramaic vernacular of Galilee, a provincial dialect whose
slovenly pronunciation is the butt of rabbinical witticisms.

The religion in which he grew up was the orthodox Judaism of his day, such as has been described in its own place.[4]
The teaching of the synagogue made the people familiar, not
only with the words of the Law and the Prophets, but with

---

[1] See above, pp. 70, 79, on the Jewish doctrine of repentance.
[2] So Josephus reports the matter.
[3] See above, pp. 62 f.   [4] See pp. 68–74.

the traditional interpretation of Scripture and with the doctrines and observances which the scribes founded on Scripture and tradition. The teachers, as a class, were of the Pharisees, who were the recognised religious authorities. Jesus' ideas and beliefs were formed under these influences; the customs to which he was habituated from childhood and the piety that was cultivated in the community about him bore the same stamp.

After the arrest of John, Jesus returned to Galilee and took up, as doubtless others did, the call to repentance, "The appointed time is come; the reign of God draws near." But he did not adopt John's prophetic style of speech or life. The scene of his labours was not the desert, but the populous towns about the northern end of the Lake of Galilee, where he taught in the synagogues or discoursed to the crowds that gathered to hear him on the hillsides or the shore of the lake. He was commonly addressed with the respectful title, "Rabbi," appropriated to religious teachers. There was so little of the ascetic about him that his enemies defamed him as a man overfond of good eating and drinking and on terms of scandalous intimacy with disreputable characters.

Jesus soon gathered about him a group of disciples who kept him closer company and went about with him from place to place. Among them there was an inner circle of intimacy, Simon (Peter), and the brothers, James and John, sons of Zebedee. All of them were men of the common people; several were fishermen, one was a toll-gatherer. There was no scholar among them, and apparently none otherwise of mark except the three just mentioned.

According to the oldest narrative (Mark 1, 21 *f.*), Jesus' first public appearance was in the synagogue in Capernaum, where his words made an impression of authority unlike the ordinary synagogue homilies with their dependence on tradition. From Capernaum, accompanied by some of his first disciples, he made a tour among the neighbouring villages, announcing the coming of the kingdom and teaching in their synagogues. Subsequent journeys took him farther away; the Gospels speak vaguely of all Galilee, but, except Nazareth, no place is named nor is any incident of these tours recorded. Evidently most of his time was spent in Capernaum and its vicinity, with occasional excursions to the other side of the lake, where also, in the tetrarchy of Philip, there was a considerable Jewish population.

The impression his message and teaching made was enhanced by the fame he soon acquired as an exorcist who could expel the most obstinate demons and cure diseases which defied the skill of the physicians. Wherever he went this reputation preceded him; crowds gathered to be healed or to see others restored to health, and listened to his words with the respect inspired by such evidence of power. It was not long, however, before voices were raised in criticism of his disregard for rules of the unwritten Law about which religious men, and especially teachers, were expected to be peculiarly scrupulous. The Pharisees, who were a kind of Jewish Puritans, saw with great concern the lax observance of the Sabbath, the indifference of the common people to the rules of religious cleanness, and their negligence in the payment of taxes for the support of the clergy. Their efforts to reform these abuses gave them an exaggerated importance in their eyes; punctiliousness in such matters became for them the criterion of piety—an error which precisians seldom escape. The study of the twofold Law in the schools had for many a similar result; the minutiæ of the Law and the casuistry of the doctors acquired the factitious value which microscopic points of learning always possess for the academic mind.

Jesus, while recognising the obligation of the Law and the authority of the scribes as its interpreters, made small account of many of their refinements of observance, and thus seemed to encourage the masses in irreligiousness. The most frequent conflict in the Gospels is over the keeping of the Sabbath, about which the lawyers had created a whole code of definitions and prescriptions. The Pharisees, who made a principle of shunning contact with classes presumed to be ignorant or negligent of the strict rules of cleanness, protested against his dining with publicans and sinners, and complained that his disciples did not wash their hands before meals, as the Pharisean rule required. Jesus in his turn condemns the teachers of the Law who set their traditions above the Scriptures, and even nullified by their casuistry the commandments of God.

Such clashes with the Pharisees probably did not impair Jesus' popularity with the common people, who had no love for those "unco' guid," and could well enjoy seeing them taken down; but they were the beginning of an antagonism between him and the religious leaders, who used their great influence against him. They not only combated his loose teaching, but discredited his cures by attributing them to magic—he cast out demons, not by the power of God but by a compact with Beelzebul, the king of the demons. Herod Antipas also manifested a suspicious interest in him; he is said to have been persuaded that Jesus was the decapitated John come to life again, and to have desired to set eyes on him. Perhaps on this account, Jesus left the district where he had hitherto laboured, and betook himself with his more intimate followers to the region northeast of the Lake of Galilee in the tetrarchy of Philip, and thence farther north into the inland territory of the city of Tyre.

In proclaiming that the reign of God was at hand and in his teaching about it Jesus said nothing of the Messiah, with whose coming the beginning of the manifest rule of God in his world was associated in the popular expectation; nor had he either in public or in private done anything to suggest that he thought of himself in that character. He was the sower, who scattered the message of the kingdom broadcast; on most of his hearers it made no lasting impression, but where the seed fell on good ground it bore corresponding fruit. During their wandering in the north, in the neighbourhood of Cæsarea Philippi, Jesus one day asked his disciples what men said about him. Some thought, they

replied, that he was John the Baptist, some that he was
Elijah (the forerunner of the Messiah), others, more indefi-
nitely, one of the old prophets returned to earth. "But
who do you think I am?" "You are the Messiah," answered Peter. It seems to have been the first time that
such an idea had been broached even in the inmost circle
of his companions, and Jesus enjoined them not to utter
this word to any one.

Not long after this they returned to Galilee without
publicity, and then, as the season of the Passover was
approaching, set out with the pilgrim company to go to
Jerusalem for the feast. The expectations with which his
followers drew near the city are exemplified by the attempt
of James and John to get from Jesus a promise that they
should occupy the seats of honour at his right and left, as
the first and second ministers in the kingdom. Jesus himself had a premonition that the great venture would have a
different outcome. He was going to present himself to his
people assembled at the feast. Would they recognise him
as one whom God had sent to inaugurate the reign of righteousness on earth? His experience with the religious leaders in Galilee gave no reason to anticipate a favourable
reception in Jerusalem, where the power of the Pharisees
was much greater. And if he openly announced himself
the Messiah, he could hardly doubt that the chief priests
and their Sadducean supporters would join hands with the
Pharisees and doctors of the Law against him, to say nothing of the Roman governor, always on the watch to quell
incipient demonstrations of religious fanaticism or political
insurgency.

Arrived upon the Mount of Olives, which overlooks Jerusalem from the east, a procession was formed with Jesus in
the middle riding on an ass borrowed in a neighbouring village, the crowds chanting, as they began the descent, a
familiar line of a Psalm: "Hosanna! blessed is he who comes
in the name of the Lord!" with improvised responses:
"Blessed is the approaching kingdom of our father David,"

or the like. The manner of Jesus' entry was symbolic of the coming of the king as it was represented in a well-known prophecy,[1] and was doubtless understood as, so to speak, an acted prediction; but it was not an open Messianic declaration. When his pilgrim escort were asked, "Who is this?" they replied: "Jesus, the prophet from Nazareth in Galilee."

With prophetic zeal for God's house, Jesus purged the temple of the traders and brokers who had stands in the courts. The multitudes, who probably had their own grievances against the licensed monopoly in sacrificial victims and the premium demanded by the money-changers, were with the bold reformer, and the authorities did not venture to interfere, however deeply they resented the invasion of their prerogative. So Jesus came and went, and spoke as he chose to the throngs in the court. The conflict with the religious leaders, however, became more acute every day; they tried to entrap him into compromising utterances—for example, about the tribute to Cæsar—and he in his turn denounced them with increasing vehemence: they would neither enter the kingdom of Heaven themselves nor let others do so; their teaching was a perversion of the Law, and their religious profession a sham. To his disciples in private he spoke of the doom of the city which rejected its day of opportunity, and of the coming of the Son of Man in judgment.

The authorities were not unreasonably apprehensive of what might come of all this. The concourse at the feast was an explosive mass which a spark might set off, and nothing more likely to do it than a prophet or a Messianic pretender. In such an event it would be like Pilate to hold them responsible for not preventing it. They hesitated to lay hands on Jesus, however, lest they should provoke the disturbance they feared, until one of his disciples offered to guide them to him by night in a lonely place outside the city where he would have only a few friends with him.

8
[1] Zech. 9, 9.

Thus Jesus was arrested and conducted to the residence of the high priest. Even when they had him in their own hands the priests did not feel secure, but planned, at the earliest possible hour, to turn over their prisoner to the Roman jurisdiction. Meanwhile a meeting of members of the Council was held to frame the charges they should lay before the governor. Early in the morning he was accordingly brought to Pilate's court, accused of giving himself out for the king of the Jews. On this charge he was executed the same day in the Roman mode, by crucifixion.

Jesus was not in his own thought nor in the apprehension of those who heard him, friend or foe, the founder of a new religion. However different the emphasis of his teaching from that of the school and the synagogue, he had no doctrine about God's nature and character, or about what he requires of men, or on his relation to his people and his purpose for them, or concerning the hereafter of the individual and the world, that would have been unfamiliar to a well-instructed Jew of his time. Nor was he, as some in modern times would make him, a preacher of social reform, taking the part of the poor and downtrodden, denouncing their oppressors, and inveighing against the structure of society that made such injustice possible. The economic reconstruction of society was the last concern of a man who believed that God was on the point of putting into effect his own programme for the new world.

Without any attempt to extract what nowadays is called the "essence of religion," Jesus kept closely to what is essential in religion. About much that seemed to his pious contemporaries of great importance he was little concerned. A simple and natural piety, a pure and upright life, unselfish goodness to all men, taking its example and inspiration from the goodness of the Father in Heaven, who bestows blessings on the evil as well as the good—such is the character God desires to see in men. Here, then, is the emphasis of Jesus' teaching—piety, morality, and charity. He did not come to annul the Law and the Prophets, but to confirm them. Not less than the righteousness of the scribes and Pharisees, but more, is required of those who would enter the kingdom of Heaven. Jesus accepted the institutions and observances of Judaism as a positive element in religion, and conformed to them; but he did not attribute to these externals intrinsic worth in the sight of God nor allow that punctiliousness about them was by itself a sign of superior religiousness. Tithing garden-herbs was well, but not to be so preoccupied with it as to forget that justice, charity, and fidelity are of greater account than mint, anise, and cummin.

The subject of Jesus' teaching was the reign of God. The phrase was associated in Jewish thought especially with the prophecies in Zech. 14, 9 and Obad. verse 21; it was an age in which the Lord should be sovereign in all the world, the one God, universally acknowledged. Though the Jews often connected it with the coming of the Messiah, the idea of the reign of God was in origin and meaning independent of that expectation. God had, indeed, been king from the beginning, but his sovereignty was not recognised by men. When Israel at Sinai uttered the words, "All that the Lord has spoken we will do and listen to," for the first time a people professed its allegiance to God's kingship. And this profession every Jew renewed daily in the recitation of the Shema (Deut. 6, 4–9), submitting himself to the authority of the "kingdom of Heaven." The reign of God was thus a present reality in so far as God's sovereignty was acknowledged, the obligation to obey his law assumed, and his will done. In so far as the Jewish people came short of this, the reign of God was an unfulfilled ideal. But it was their firm faith that the time would come when it should be fully realised, not in this one nation alone, but throughout the world. The reign of God would then be revealed in its glory and power. This was the essentially religious form of the Jewish expectation of the golden age to come.

To these ideas and expectations the teaching of Jesus

attaches itself. The reign of God, manifest and universal, is about to begin. To live in the world as it will be then is the supreme object of desire and striving. Inasmuch as it is the very definition of the reign of God that his will is done on earth as it is done in heaven, only those can have a place in it whose character corresponds to its nature; it is a world in which there are none but good and godly men. Jesus' idea of true religion has already been described. The piety, morality, and charity which constitute it have no esoteric sense or sectarian definition. The conception of piety naturally draws most upon the Psalms as expressions of religious experience; and when Jesus tells his hearers what kind of men the reign of God and its blessings belong to, it is the character of the humble and godly in the Psalms that he depicts. It was the type of piety he exemplified in his own life and tried to cultivate in his followers. A distinctively Jewish feature, as compared with the Psalms, is the thought of God as the Father in Heaven, and the influence of this conception not only on piety but on morality and charity, in all which spheres it has an important place in the teaching of Jesus.

To illustrate the nature and worth of the kingdom of God, Jesus frequently employed parables, or comparisons, a mode of teaching much used in the synagogue. The parables of Jesus display a fertility of invention and a felicity of expression that give them a poetic charm rarely found in the parables of the rabbis.

In what way the reign of God was to be inaugurated, the advent of which he believed to be imminent, is a question with which Jesus does not seem at first to have concerned himself. If we can trust the order of time in the Gospel tradition, it was not till toward the end of his brief career that he spoke to his disciples of the Son of Man who was to come on the clouds of heaven, and of the judgment with which the present period of the world's history should end, as foretold in Daniel and in certain visions of Enoch. The phrase "son of man," which in the mother tongue of

Jesus and his disciples meant simply a human being (indefinite), acquired a specific sense only in this apocalyptic association—the figure "like a man" whom Daniel and Enoch saw in heaven, and whom the latter identified with "the righteous and elect one," the Messiah.

On the arrest of Jesus his disciples fled and made their escape to Galilee. Before long, however, they returned to Jerusalem. They believed that God had brought Jesus to life again and taken him up to heaven, whence he would shortly descend in power and glory. He was himself the Son of Man, of whose imminent coming to judgment he had spoken. Their faith that Jesus was the Messiah was thus re-established, and their expectation took a new form. This faith was connected with visions of their risen Master. According to the tradition Paul received, he appeared first to Peter, then to the Twelve,[1] afterward to others, either singly, as to James (Jesus' brother) and to Paul himself, or to numbers together—once to more than five hundred.

In Jerusalem, where they awaited the descent of the Messiah from heaven, the disciples had their own meetings by night in private houses, but they spent much of their time in the courts and halls of the temple, and used the opportunity which the resort to the holy house gave them to endeavour to convert others to their faith that Jesus was the Messiah. They were the more zealous in these efforts because they believed that only those who, repenting of their sins, acknowledged Jesus as the Messiah would be saved when he came to judgment.

For proof they adduced Scripture texts, especially Psalm 22, in which they found the death of the Messiah foretold in all detail and circumstance just as Jesus died on the cross. In other Psalms they found predictions that the Messiah should be raised from the dead (Psalm 16, 8–11), and be seated at the right hand of God (Psalm 110, 1). That Jesus has been raised from the dead and taken

[1] In the earliest accounts the scene of these first appearances was probably Galilee.

up to heaven they were witnesses, for they had seen him.[1]
In confirmation they pointed to the miraculous cures they
wrought by the name of Jesus. The arguments and exhortations of the Apostles made converts, both among the
residents of Jerusalem and the visitors who came up to the
feasts from many lands. Some priests are said to have
been among them, and later we read of Pharisees who embraced the faith.

The leading men in the little community of believers were
the three who had been the closest companions of Jesus,
Peter and the brothers, James and John, the sons of Zebedee. There were twelve "Apostles"—the number was important because it was the symbol of their mission to the
twelve tribes of Israel—but though as members of this
group they enjoyed a certain precedence, the rest of the
Twelve figure only in the catalogues, not in the history.[2]
James, the brother of Jesus, was not one of the Twelve, but
his relation to Jesus made him an important accession to
the ranks of the disciples, and at a later time he became one
of the pillars of the church in Jerusalem, taking precedence
even of Peter.

At first the disciples seem to have confined their efforts
to Jerusalem, but when the momentary expectation of the
coming of the Messiah subsided, they extended the sphere
of their labours to the surrounding country, while converted
pilgrims returning to their homes carried the gospel to
remoter parts. The spirit and method of the propaganda
are represented in the instructions traditionally ascribed to
Jesus (Matt. 10, 1 ff.). The missioners (Apostles) were to
address themselves to Jews only, avoiding towns inhabited
by heathen or Samaritans. They went from place to place,
depending on the hospitality of the inhabitants for entertainment. If they met an unfriendly reception in any
place they were not to brave persecution, but to flee to
another. Their business was urgent, for before they were

[1] See Acts 2, 32.
[2] The field was thus left free for apocryphal legends.

through with the cities of Israel the Son of Man would come. So Jesus had foretold.

The disciples of Jesus the Nazarene, as they seem to have been commonly called, were orthodox and pious Jews, whose Messianic and eschatological beliefs were their sole peculiarity. They worshipped in the temple and frequented the synagogues with the rest. As their numbers grew they perhaps formed a congregation of their own, as any group of Jews who could muster the quorum for prayer (ten men) was free to do, the synagogue being a purely voluntary association.[1]

Outside of Palestine the disciples of Jesus followed for a time the practice of the Apostles in Jerusalem and addressed themselves with their gospel to Jews only. But in mixed communities, where there were not only proselytes to Judaism but many other "religious persons" who frequented the synagogues and accepted the fundamental ideas of Judaism without becoming proselytes, the knowledge of the gospel filtered by various channels into heathen circles and prepared the way for direct efforts for the conversion of Gentiles.

The preaching to Gentiles was not merely an extension of the missionary field, it was the beginning of a Gentile Christianity. Converts from heathenism necessarily apprehended the gospel in a very different way from the Jewish disciples in Jerusalem. The whole background and setting of the disciples' conception—the life under the Law, Jewish Messianic expectations, and Jewish eschatology—were lacking. On the other hand, they brought their own modes of religious thought, and attached to the words they heard the signification and connotations of their own speech. The greatest difference of all was that the gospel of the Lord Jesus appeared to them, as it could not to Jewish believers, to be a new religion. However close its relation to Judaism might be, in making faith in the Lord Jesus the condi-

[1] Thus we read in Acts (6, 9) of synagogues of the Libertines (Roman freedmen) and others.

tion of salvation for Jew and Gentile alike it set itself over
against Judaism as well as against all the varieties of heathenism, a distinct and exclusive religion.

From what they heard of the life and teaching of Jesus
they would understand that he was the founder of this
religion; but the far more important thing was that he was
the author of the salvation which his religion promised
men. Jesus was to them a purely religious figure, the
Saviour through whom they had the forgiveness of sins
and the assurance of everlasting life. Both their thought
of him and their feeling toward him were thus very different from the personal love and reverence of his disciples,
who had lived with the Master in intimate fellowship, and
among whom the tradition of his doings and sayings was a
sacred memory.

The names and titles applied to Jesus by his disciples
also had a different meaning and different associations in
Greek and to the mind of Gentiles. Messiah, so full of significance to a Jew, literally translated *Christos* ("anointed"),
had no corresponding suggestion in Greek; it was a mere
title, Jesus the Christ, and very soon lost even this distinction and was combined in the proper name, Christ Jesus or
Jesus Christ. The disciples spoke of Jesus in their Aramaic
mother tongue as "our master" (*maran*), the verbal equivalent of which is ὁ κύριος ἡμῶν. In Greek the article was
in most cases sufficient specification, and men said ὁ κύριος
Ἰησοῦς, "the Lord Jesus," or among themselves simply
"the Lord." This became the characteristic title of Jesus
Christ in Gentile Christianity.

If *Christos* had no religious associations in Greek, *Kyrios*
(Lord) had many. It was a standing epithet in the wor-
ship of numerous deities in Egypt, Syria, and Asia Minor.
The Roman emperors assumed the title Kyrios (Dominus)
as the most unequivocal assertion of their divine supremacy.
There were "gods many and lords many," and Gentiles who
heard that men could be saved only through the Lord Jesus
Christ would without question understand Kyrios as a

divine title. This was made doubly certain by the association with salvation. "Saviour" (Σωτήρ) also was a title or epiclesis of many deities, as well as of divine Hellenistic kings and Roman emperors. The religions which professed to have the secret of a blessed immortality all made salvation depend on initiation into the cult of a particular saving divinity, and the Christian churches seemed to Gentiles to be mysteries of this kind.

It was probably in the train of such ideas and associations that the worship of Jesus Christ as a divine Lord and Saviour originated among Gentile Christians. At any rate, it soon became the distinguishing mark of the Christian religion in the Gentile world. To Paul, Christians are those "who invoke the name of our Lord Jesus Christ."

The spread of the gospel among the Gentiles gave rise to a controversy about the relation of such converts to the Jewish Law. The conservative faction in the church in Jerusalem, made up in part of Pharisees and headed by James, the brother of Jesus, who is represented both by Josephus and by the Palestinian Christian tradition as a typical Jewish saint, maintained that Gentiles must be circumcised and bind themselves to observe the whole Law, written and oral; those who would share in the fulfilment of God's promises to the Jews must become proselytes to Judaism. Jesus himself had said: "Until heaven and earth pass away, not the smallest letter or stroke shall pass away from the law till everything in it be done," and "He who relaxes a single one of the very least of these commandments and teaches men so shall be called least in the kingdom of Heaven." They insisted also that Jewish believers should not enter the houses of uncircumcised Gentile converts, much less eat at their table; for all Gentiles and everything belonging to them was unclean. It was the standpoint of rigorous Judaism.

There was, however, among the Jews themselves another and larger way of thinking of God's purpose for the world, derived from the prophecies which predict the universality of the true religion. The reign of God foretold in these prophecies was an age in which the Gentiles also should acknowledge the sovereignty of the one true God and do his righteous will, without being incorporated in the Jewish people. According to the Book of Acts, Peter's experience led him to the conviction that "in every nation he who fears God and works righteousness is acceptable to him." But when it came to the practical consequences in intercourse with uncircumcised believers, he vacillated between the freer attitude which corresponded to this conviction and submission to the authority of James and the pressure of Jewish opinion. Thus two tendencies early appeared in the community in Jerusalem itself.

The Hellenistic Jews were inclined to a less stringent theory than their Palestinian brethren as well as to a freer practice. In a heathen environment they naturally laid the greatest weight on the generic differences between Judaism and the pagan religions around them—monotheism, the rejection of idolatry, the avoidance of heathen vices—and conceived Judaism in these essential articles as the future universal religion. The religious persons who adopted thus much of Judaism, attended the synagogue, kept the Sabbath, and perhaps observed some of the most distinctive of the dietary laws, such as abstinence from pork, certainly believed that they were in the way of salvation, even though uncircumcised, and the Jews undoubtedly encouraged them in this belief. Nor is it probable that social intercourse between Jews and these "God-fearing" Gentiles was confined within the narrow limits that would have been possible under Pharisaic regulation; even the Pharisee was not expected to live according to his pledge outside the land.

These differences about the relation of Gentile converts to the Jewish Law did not necessarily involve a different apprehension of the person and work of the Messiah and the salvation believers should enjoy when he came; the issue was at bottom a conflict between a national exclusive and a universal conception of the mission and destiny of

Judaism in the peculiar Messianic form which the disciples of Jesus believed to be its fulfilment. Meanwhile, however, a Gentile Christianity had grown up whose conception of the Lord Jesus Christ and his salvation was altogether different. To those who embraced this, as has been said, Christianity was not a variety of Judaism, but a new religion, of which Judaism was at most a prophecy and an historical preparation. For them there was therefore no reason why a Gentile who sought his salvation in this religion should become a Jew to do it.

In most places Hellenistic Jewish disciples and Gentile converts seem from the first to have coalesced without difficulty. The Jews brought their Scriptures not only to establish the new faith on the authority of revelation but to instruct their fellow believers in the character of God and the character he required of men. On the other hand, they joined with the Gentile Christians in the worship of Jesus as their Lord and Saviour without being conscious of any defection from the principle of monotheism. Those who had some tincture of Greek philosophy soon found a way, as we shall see, to give Christ an even higher place in their theology. Of the process by which Gentile and Jewish Christianity were fused into a common type which may perhaps best be called Hellenistic Christianity there is naturally no record, but the fact is a secure inference from the whole subsequent development. The elements and proportions varied in different places; we can, in fact, hardly imagine the earliest Christianity in Syria and Asia Minor too diversified.

It is in this composite Hellenistic Christianity, not in the Messianic Judaism of the Apostolic church in Jerusalem, that the antecedents and premises of Paul's teaching are to be sought. He was not its author, as is often assumed, but its ablest and most zealous exponent and its most original and fecund thinker.

Saul of Tarsus, better known by his Roman name, Paul, was born of "Hebrew" (that is, probably, Aramaic-speaking) parents. His father or some more remote ancestor had acquired Roman citizenship, presumably as a freedman. Tarsus, where Paul's youth was passed, was a flourishing Greek city, with considerable reputation for learning and culture; its schools took rank beside those of Athens and Alexandria. As a young man he went to Jerusalem, where he had family connections, and became a student of the Law under the famous Rabbi Gamaliel. A Pharisee, zealous for the religion of his fathers, he saw no good in the new sect with its crucified Messiah and its apocalyptic expectations, and willingly lent himself as an agent of the inquisition which the Sanhedrin set on foot. Suddenly converted to the faith he had persecuted by a vision of Christ in heaven, he took refuge from the indignation of his countrymen in the Arabian kingdom of Aretas. Three years later, after a fortnight's visit to Jerusalem, he returned to northern Syria and Cilicia, where for several years he preached the gospel to the Gentiles. Of this independent activity there is no record, but from the time he followed the summons of Barnabas to Antioch he is the central figure in the Acts; and besides this narrative we have a half-dozen or more of his own letters addressed to different churches, which not only present his teaching and reveal his character, but give a vivid picture of the life of the early Christian communities.

Paul's missionary journeys led him back and forth through Asia Minor, and to Macedonia and Achaia. After several years, while on a visit to Jerusalem, he was set upon by a mob, inflamed by a rumour that he had introduced an uncircumcised heathen into the courts of the temple, and would have been killed had not the Roman commandant rescued him out of their hands by arresting him as the cause of the disturbance. After a long detention at Cæsarea, while his case was still pending before the procurator, he claimed his right as a Roman citizen to have his cause heard by the emperor, and was accordingly sent to Rome. There he lived for two years in military custody but in free intercourse with Jews and Christians. At this point the narrative in Acts breaks off. All that can with reasonable confidence be gathered from other sources is that he was put to death in Rome under Nero.[1]

Such composite Hellenistic Christian communities as have been described above were doubtless established in Syria or Cilicia before Paul found his way thither. It may be assumed that their faith had not yet been the subject of much reflection, and that the problems it contained were scarcely recognised. They inevitably emerged, however, in the discussions with Jews and Gentiles which attended the preaching of the new religion; and it was presumably in the course of his missionary labours in those parts, before his appearance in Antioch, that Paul thought his way to the fundamental doctrines which he calls his gospel. But new conditions and controversies in the wider field of activity to which he was subsequently called kept him thinking on, and the letters we have from the last ten or fifteen years of his life show a steady progress.

Paul was fully conscious that the gospel he preached was his own; he did not receive it, he says, by instruction of men, but through revelation of Jesus Christ. In particular he emphasises his independence of the Judæan Apostles; neither first nor last did he owe them anything. In asserting that he had his gospel by revelation he does not mean that his knowledge of the facts of Jesus' life and death came in that way; he refers more than once to things he had received by tradition. But his gospel is not the facts related by tradition; it is his interpretation of them, and above all his doctrine of the person and work of Christ. Herein his independence of the Judæan leaders needs no demonstration.

To Paul, as to the Gentile Christians, the Lord Jesus Christ was a divine being, the Son of God. He was the creator of the world. Christians have not, like the heathen, many gods and many divine lords, but one God, the Father, from whom ("out of whom," as the source of being) the universe

[1] Nero died June 9, 68 A. D.

proceeds, and one Lord, Jesus Christ, through whom (as
the agent in creation) the universe came into being and is
maintained. The cosmic functions of Christ are set forth
more fully in the Epistle to the Colossians.[1] He is God's
beloved Son, the image of the invisible God, the first-born
of all creation; for *in* him was created the celestial and terrestrial universe, not alone the visible heavens and earth,
but the invisible thrones, lordships, principalities and
powers—ranks of superhuman beings to whom the administration of the universe is committed.

Laying aside the divine form in which he existed before
his appearance on earth, he assumed the form of a servant
by taking the likeness of humanity, and in this semblance
submitted to death on the cross. For this self-abnegation
God exalted him to higher rank, and conferred on him the
name that excels every name,[2] that in the name of Jesus
all beings in heaven and earth and hell should bow in
adoration and confess that Jesus Christ is Lord,[3] to the
glory of God the Father.

Christ is thus a divine being of inferior order, subordinate
to the Father. Such divinity did not conflict with monotheism. The unity of the godhead did not, either for Greeks
or Jews, exclude the existence of beings who, notwithstanding their inferiority to the supreme God, were universally
and properly called gods. And, indeed, the more exalted
the idea of the supreme deity the more need was felt of
some intermediary between him and the world of creation
and providence. The Jewish philosopher, Philo, whose
God is elevated in his nameless and undefinable godhead
above all the concerns of time, interposes between him and
the created universe the divine Logos, whom he calls "Son
of God," "First Born," "Second Deity."[4]

Paul's God is, however, not a transcendent deity after the

[1] The authenticity of Colossians is contested by many critics. The
Christology, however, is only the culmination of ideas which are found
in other letters of Paul.
[2] The name "Lord." [3] Appropriation of Isaiah 45, 23.
[4] See above, p. 61.

pattern of Plato or Philo, but the personal God of the Bible, and Paul's concern is not cosmogony but redemption. To deliver men from sin and death, in whose thraldom all mankind lay, Christ, the Son of God, descended to earth and died upon the cross; the work of deliverance accomplished, and those twin enemies deprived of their power, he ascended to heaven, where he is enthroned at the right hand of God, and whence he will ere long come to take his saints to himself.

Paul's gospel is the gospel of the cross; the death and resurrection of Christ are the foundation of the Christian religion. Without them there is no salvation for Jew or Gentile; in them there is salvation for all mankind. Christ's death is potentially the death of all; in his resurrection humanity triumphs over death and attains eternal life. But only those are actually saved who are so united with him that they were crucified with him and with him are risen from the dead.

This union is effected by faith, which is not merely the intellectual and moral acceptance of the gospel, not simply a trust in God or in Christ, but an undefinable experience in which oneness with Christ is permanently realised. This is the characteristic Pauline conception of faith, the most distinctive feature of his doctrine of salvation. It has no antecedent or analogy in Judaism or among Jewish believers in Jesus, and none in the personal religions (mysteries) or philosophies of the time; it sprang from Paul's individual experience—an experience peculiar both in its outward circumstance and in the temperament of the man. For this reason his mystical idea of faith made little impression on early Christian thought, which held fast to the ordinary and accepted meanings of the word, belief and trust. Of much greater influence, because more in accordance with current ways of thinking, was Paul's teaching about the sacraments. In baptism into the name of Jesus Christ a man goes through Christ's death and resurrection; he is plunged into Christ's death, entombed with him, rises with him to a new and immortal life. In the bread and wine of the Lord's Supper the communicants partake of the body and blood of Christ, not in metaphor or symbol, but in reality. The realism of these conceptions is strikingly illustrated by the practice of vicarious baptism for relatives and friends who had died without the knowledge of Christ, and by the fatal consequences of eating the bread and drinking the cup of the Lord without "discriminating the body" (*sc.* from common bread and wine).

Paul calls his gospel a mystery, and a mystery, in the proper sense of the word, it must have seemed to his hearers. It had its sacred legend of a divine being who met upon earth a tragic fate, and by his triumph over death opened the way of immortality to men.[1] Salvation was by union with him in his passion and his resurrection, and could be achieved only by those who confessed Christ as Lord and became members of his church. The form of initiation, baptism, was common in the mysteries. The sacramental eating of the body and blood of the Lord which made men partakers of the divine nature and so insured them immortality also had analogies there. Enthusiasm was cultivated in the church as in the *thiasoi.* Finally, as in the mysteries, this way of salvation was open to all men, without distinction of race, station, or sex.

It was, indeed, only in the guise of a mystery that Christianity could present itself in that age as a universal personal religion. Its success in the regions where it first spread was due to the fact that it thus offered men the highest good they could conceive—the assurance of immortality—in the form they could best understand—by union with divinity. Not that Christianity borrowed its ideas and rites from the mysteries; Gentile Christians necessarily conceived the gospel and the distinctive observances they received from the missionaries as a mystery.

Christianity differed widely, however, from other mysteries. Its drama of redemption was not a savage myth of lust and violence, but the story of a divine being, a Son of

[1] See Vol. I, pp. 581 *f.*, 589 *f.*

God, who came down to earth and voluntarily laid down his life that he might save men from death, and by his resurrection bestow on them eternal life. Great and characteristic differences were due also to its inheritance from Judaism. From Judaism it took its sacred Scriptures, with the prestige of immemorial antiquity and the authority of divine revelation—no small advantage in an age when men were looking on all hands to revelation for religious, and even for philosophical, certainty. From Judaism it took, also, its idea of the one God, creator and ruler of the universe, thus fitting its scheme of salvation into the larger context of a monotheistic theology in a way unknown in the mysteries.[1] Above all, it laid the emphasis in its idea of God on his moral character and on his insistent demand of a corresponding moral character in man, thus, like Judaism, making morality an integral part of religion. God's relation to men, especially the thought of God as father—not in the sense of author or progenitor, but as the object of filial love and obedience—is also conceived essentially in Jewish fashion. It is the combination of these elements with the mystery of salvation through the Lord Jesus that gives its peculiar character to Christianity.

In the mysteries, as has been shown in another place, death and the dismal existence after death were the lot of mankind because men are men and not gods; it is human nature.[2] For Paul, on the contrary, it is the penalty of sin. Death is universal because sin is universal: Jews under the revealed Law, and Gentiles who have the law of nature written in the human conscience—all have sinned. This universal sin began with the first man, the progenitor of the race. By his disobedience sin entered into the world, and death by sin; through Adam's sin all men became sinners, and all are under the doom of God's broken law. Nor is this all. Sin is not man's nature as it came from the hand

---

[1] In the mysteries generally the supreme god was ignored; the whole interest was in the saviour god.

[2] See Vol. I, pp. 443 f.

9

of God; but by inheritance, example, and habit it has become second nature, and it is as impossible for him to cast it off as if it were his original constitution. The seat of its power is "the flesh," by which Paul does not mean merely the body as material, but body and soul, sense and reason, as they are, corrupted by sin. It renders nugatory all the aspirations after truth and goodness that man finds in his mind (*nous*), and is in permanent antagonism to God and his righteous will, to the gospel and the Spirit; the thoughts and aims of "the flesh" are opposed to God, for they are not and cannot be subject to the law of God. So long as a man is "in the flesh" he cannot please God.

Herein lies the necessity of the death of Christ.[1] Since all have sinned, Christ by his death made atonement for the sins of mankind, and thus rendered it possible for God to "justify" (*i. e.*, to save) the sinner who by faith in Christ avails himself of this salvation. In the mysteries the death of the hero is a meaningless calamity; it is his resurrection only that has religious value. To Paul the death of Christ is an expiation provided by God himself, who sent his Son to redeem the sinful race of men.

Paul is zealous to prove not only that the salvation in Christ avails for every man, but that there is no other way of salvation, and especially that Judaism is none. The Jews believe, he says, that they will be saved by the works of the Law, that is, by conformity to the will of God as revealed in Scripture and tradition; they rely on their own righteousness.[2] But to be found righteous on his own merit a man must have kept the whole Law perfectly, a thing no one ever has done or can do. The Law was given, according to Paul, not that men by obedience might attain to righteousness, but to bring them to a consciousness of their sinfulness, and, by the impossibility of fulfilling its

[1] To the immediate disciples of Jesus his death had no profounder necessity than that the Scriptures must be fulfilled.

[2] The Jewish doctrine of salvation was, in fact, very different (see above, pp. 70 *f.*). Paul implicitly denies that God does, or can, freely forgive the penitent sinner.

demands, to impress upon them the necessity of another righteousness than their own. It was a tutor under whose stern discipline the Jews were put to prepare them for Christ.

The perpetuity of the Law was an axiom in Judaism and to the Jewish believers in Jesus. For Paul the Law was a pedagogic institute, a temporary dispensation. When Christ came and the new dispensation of grace was inaugurated, the Law, belonging to an order of things that had passed away, expired by its own implicit limitation without need of formal abrogation. Consequently, for Christians to be circumcised and put themselves under the obligation of the two-fold Law was nothing short of apostasy.

Paul thus emancipated Christianity from the Law not only in practice but in principle, without impugning the character of the Law, which is "holy and just and good," and without abandoning the ground of revealed religion in the Old Testament. A more radical type of Gentile Christianity, which made its appearance within Paul's lifetime, did both; it rejected the Law as in itself evil, imposed by a deity inferior to the Christian God or hostile to him—ideas which in the next century gained great currency in Gnostic sects.[1]

Paul's opponents accused him, by abolishing the Law, of destroying the very foundations of morality, and some of his converts evidently thought that the logic of no law was lawlessness. He does not meet these inferences, as has often been done in more recent times, by distinguishing between ritual and ceremonial and the moral law. The Law was for him, as for the Jews, an indissoluble unity; as a whole it was given, as a whole it was annulled. But his Christian has no need for an external regulative of conduct in Scripture and tradition, because he has the principle and motive of right living in himself, or, rather, in the spirit of Christ that lives in him. His old sinful nature is dead; it was crucified with Christ—how can he any more live in sin? Such was the theory; experience was a different story, as Paul's letters to the Corinthians testify.

[1] See below, pp. 154 ff.

Religious worship supposes a *præsens numen*, and Christians who worshipped the Lord Jesus necessarily believed that their Lord was present in their gatherings for worship. That he should be thus at once in heaven and on earth did not make them any difficulty; the religions of the time all made the same assumption without ascribing to the gods omnipresence. So, also, among the Jews the Shekina, the invisible presence of God, was wherever ten men (the quorum of the synagogue) were gathered for prayer.

The presence of Christ in the Christian community was manifest in the operations of the Spirit. As in the Old Testament the spirit of God is the author of experiences in which men seem to be possessed and controlled by something above themselves, and endued with supernatural wisdom or power, so in the Christian church the spirit comes upon men, producing enthusiasm or ecstasy; they prophesy, speak with tongues and interpret the unintelligible dialect of the spirit, heal diseases and expel demons, at its prompting and in its power. As in the Old Testament the operations of the spirit are attributed to God, who sends it, so in the church the work of the spirit of Christ is the work of Christ. But besides these occasional and spectacular manifestations of divine possession, the spirit of Christ indwelling in Christians is the permanent source and power of their peculiar religious life. The virtues and graces—"love, gladness, peace, forbearance, kindness, goodness, faithfulness, meekness, continence"—are the work of the spirit; they are in the empirical man as supernatural as the gift of tongues or miraculous powers. The spirit is for Paul a divine atmosphere in which the Christian lives, an element which, like the atmosphere, penetrates and pervades his whole being.

The Jewish ideal of a golden age on earth, which had its origin in the Messianic prophecies, and even in its most universalised form could not be dissociated from the national hope—it always left an invidious precedence, if not pre-eminence, to the Jews—was not the good which Gentiles seeking the salvation of their souls asked of religion. Many Jews, also, living in an atmosphere of Greek thought, entertained the conception of the immortality of the soul which was current in popular religious philosophy and had no affinity to the orthodox Palestinian eschatology. The salvation which such Jews, like their Gentile neighbours, sought was a state of eternal blessedness with God and the souls of the good. A Jewish Hellenist like the author of the Wisdom of Solomon, or a Christian Hellenist like the author of the Epistle to the Hebrews, conceives salvation in the same way; the resurrection of the body has no room in his thought.

Paul was a Pharisee; the resurrection of the body was the distinguishing dogma of his school. He had let go pretty nearly all else of his Jewish orthodoxy, but on this point he was tenacious. The resurrection of Christ and the resurrection of believers were in his mind correlative. In Judaism, as in Zoroastrianism, whence the doctrine came, the resurrection was the redintegration out of its dispersed elements of the identical body that was dissolved at death and the reunion of the soul with it, that the whole man, soul and body, might stand at the bar of God's great judgment and receive the just retribution of the deeds which they had together done in the mortal life. The scene of the blessed hereafter beyond resurrection and judgment was this earth, purified and glorified.

Paul's conception is entirely different. When the Lord comes in the clouds, his saints will be caught up to meet him in the air and go to be for ever with him in heaven. At the same time the dead in Christ will be raised and taken up to heaven. But heaven is no place for flesh and blood, and so those who are living at Christ's coming will be transformed, and the bodies which rise from the tomb will be as unlike those that were committed to it as the plant that springs from the earth is unlike the seed that was buried in it. "It is sown an animal body, it is raised a spiritual body" —that is, probably a body of fiery matter such as angels are made of; it will be like the glorious body of the Lord him-

self.   In another even more significant passage Paul lets go
this slender thread of continuity.   In a familiar (originally
Orphic) metaphor, the body is a tent in which the soul has
its transient habitation; when this tent is struck the soul is
not left naked and homeless; a celestial body awaits it, an
imperishable house of God's own building.   Thus for Paul
"resurrection" is not the restoration and revivication of the
fleshly body, but the assumption to heaven of the soul
invested with a new and heavenly body.[1]

Far the greater part of those to whom the gospel was
preached, whether Jews or Gentiles, rejected it.   The ground
of this rejection Paul sometimes puts in the sinful will of
man, or he ascribes it to a false conceit of wisdom, or to the
influence of superhuman powers of evil—"the god of this
age has blinded the minds of the unbelieving that the illumination of the gospel of the glory of Christ, who is the
image of God, should not enlighten them."   But when he
expresses his deeper reflection on the problem he finds the
solution in predestination.   With his view of the inherent
sinfulness of humanity and its consequent aversion to the
truth, faith was not in the power of man, it must be the
gift of God; and that God had not bestowed on all the will
to believe was plain.   "He has mercy on whom he wills,
and whom he wills he hardens"—so the Scripture taught.
Such reflections were confirmed by his own experience; like
Augustine, his doctrine of election was rooted in his experience of divine grace.   Paul's doctrine of predestination is
not the determinist corollary of an idea of God which asserts for him a causality so absolute as to leave no place for
finite free will; it is his solution of the problem, Why, when
the gospel is so convincing, do not all men believe?[2]

The philosophies as well as the religions of the time, in
proportion as their idea of God was metaphysically or
morally sublimated, made place for a multitude of powers
intermediate between God and the world of nature and

[1] It is perhaps not superfluous to remark that neither the soul nor the
spiritual body is immaterial.   Paul was not a Platonist.
[2] So it was also with Mohammed.   See below, pp. 396 f.

men. Some of them were good, the agents of the divine
will in the administration of the universe; some evil, and
hostile to God and all good. Paul recognises such a hierarchy of evil. They are the principalities, rulers, and
powers which are to be overcome and in the end annihilated
by Christ, but against which, meanwhile, Christians have to
battle. Demons of superhuman might and malignity sur-
round man and strive to compass his undoing; the air—the
whole region beneath the sphere of the moon—is full of
them. At their head is one whom Paul calls "the god of
this age"; in John he is "the ruler of this world."

One class of powers which played a great part in the
thought of the time were the heavenly bodies. Not only a
man's outward fortune and his circumstances but his temperament and moral predisposition were determined by the
stars under which he was born—an astrological fatalism.
These are the στοιχεία τοῦ κόσμου, the elements of the
universe, to which the Galatians seem to desire again to
come into bondage. They are the "rulers of this age,"
who in ignorance of God's secret purpose crucified the
glorious Lord, and thus unwittingly carried out God's plan
of redemption and became the cause of their own undoing.
In Paul's Epistles this dualism is not a part of a reasoned
theory of the universe; it serves him to put in the strongest
light the necessity of the salvation in Christ and the stu-
pendous magnitude of the achievement. For Paul conceives the problem of redemption not merely as the salvation of individuals from sin and death, but as the deliverance of the universe itself from the bondage of corruption, a
problem of cosmic dimensions. In this sense it became the
speculative problem of Gnosticism, which approached it
from the standpoint of a dualism more radical than Paul's,
though it found welcome authority in Paul; his "god of
this age" became in their hands the creator of this evil
world, the god of the Jews and giver of their Law, the author
of everything that was opposed to the higher Christianity
they professed.

Paul was too original, his construction of Christianity

was too individual a combination of disparate elements—
the Apostolic tradition, the primitive Gentile Christian
apprehension of the gospel, the Judaism in which he was
brought up, and the redemptive religions of the time and
region in which he preached the mystery of salvation
through Christ, all passed through the alembic of a singular
personal experience—his presentation of his doctrine in his
Epistles was too occasional and elliptical to be comprehended as a whole by the ordinary mind.   Consequently his
influence in the following generations, considerable as it
was, was the influence of ideas and expressions detached
from their context of thought and sometimes taken in a
sense foreign to his intention, not of the system of ideas
which we construct and call Pauline.   The main current of
Christian thought did not, as is often imagined, take its
rise in Paul, it did not even pass through him; rather it
flowed by him as around a rock in the bed of a stream.

A striking illustration of this is the writing which we
know under the title, "Epistle to the Hebrews."   The unknown author was a Grecian Jew, well versed in the Scriptures of his people and expert in the methods of interpretation which are generally called Alexandrian.   From the
common premises of the Christian propaganda, by the aid
of his allegorical method, he develops a doctrine of the
person and work of Christ and of the way of salvation
through him which, though not entirely independent of
Paul's, displays remarkable originality of conception.

The theme of the Epistle is the incomparable superiority
of Christianity over Judaism: it has a more perfect revelation, a better law, a new covenant, larger promises, a more
efficacious atonement, and all this through Christ.   The
Prophets, Moses, the angels through whose instrumentality
the Law was given, were ministers of God, but Christ is the
Son.   He is an outstreaming of the Father's glory, like the
light that radiates from the sun, of the same nature, yet
distinct; the very image of God's person, as the impression
of a seal is the counterpart of the image engraved on the

gem.[1] By his agency God made the worlds, and by God's mighty power he sustains them. He became man, assuming all the infirmities of humanity except sin, and having made a purification for sins, he took his seat at the right hand of the majesty on high, exalted to a place as much superior to the angels as the name "son" is more honourable than theirs (ἄγγελοι, "messengers"). The conception of the nature of the Son and his relation to the Father is not essentially different from that of Paul in the letters to the Philippians and Colossians or of the Gospel of John, though it is otherwise expressed.

More characteristic is the author's construction of the work of Christ. He is the great high priest, and by once offering himself, the true and perfect sacrifice, and by perpetual intercession in the celestial sanctuary, he makes a priestly atonement, and is the author of eternal salvation. Of these supersensible realities the Aaronic priesthood and the sacrifices of the Jewish Law were but types or shadows, having in themselves no efficacy to expiate sin or to purge the conscience of the sinner. By the blood of Jesus a new way is opened for men into the presence of the holy God; having him to intercede for them, Christians approach with confidence the throne which is now for them a throne of grace. In this freedom of access to God and assurance of his favour is the immeasurable superiority of Christianity.

When this life is over Christians will enter upon an eternal Sabbath, in which they cease from their labours as God did from his when the creation was finished. In the celestial city, with the innumerable concourse of angels, the native citizens of heaven; with God, the judge of all, and Jesus, the mediator of a new covenant; with the spirits of the righteous of the Old Testament who have reached the goal, they too will attain perfection. The resurrection of the body and what goes with a material environment in the

---

[1] Philo uses similar figures of the Logos, but of Philo's transcendent idea of God, and consequently of the metaphysical significance of the Logos in Philo's system, there is no trace in Hebrews.

hereafter has no place in this Hellenised hope of immortality. Like Paul, the author holds fast to the primitive
Christian expectation of the speedy coming of Christ, who is
now seated at the right hand of God, waiting till God shall
make his enemies his footstool (Psalm 110); then he will
appear the second time for the salvation of those who expect him. The day of his advent is visibly drawing near,
and the author insistently exhorts his readers to be ready
for it.

The higher conception of the nature of Christ which is
set forth in the Epistles of Paul and in Hebrews has also
its Gospel, in which the way is opened to a more philosophical apprehension of the person of Christ and his relation to
God through the doctrine of the Logos. The Stoics had
made this term familiar, and Philo had adopted it in a
sense modified both by the Platonic element in his thought
and by the associations of the "word of God" in the Jewish Scriptures, as the most adequate name for the agency
which his ontological idea of the godhead constrained him
to interpose as a "second deity" between the transcendent
God and the world of nature and of men. He makes the
Logos solve the problem of cosmogony; it is fundamental
in his theory of revelation, and has a central place in his
philosophy of the religious life. There is reason to think
that the divine Logos occupied a similar place in the religious thought of some Gentile circles as well as in philosophical speculations.

The author of the Fourth Gospel assumes that the name
and idea of the Logos are familiar to his readers, and therefore rapidly summarises the philosophical doctrine—the
eternal divinity of the Logos, his intimate relation to God,
his work in creation and revelation—to come at once to the
new and distinctively Christian doctrine, the incarnation of
the Logos.

The original Palestinian gospel represented the faith of
the primitive community of disciples in Jerusalem that
Jesus was the Messiah. The Spirit of God came upon him

at his baptism, a heavenly voice saluted him as God's chosen one, his beloved son. In the power given him by God he wrought miracles; he taught with authority the true nature of the reign of God and how men must live to have a part in it. Rejected by the rulers of his people, put to death by the Roman governor as a would-be king of the Jews, God raised him from the dead and took him up to heaven, whence he would ere long come to judgment. The Synoptic Gospels, as we have them, are the Gospels of Greek-speaking churches, and the reflection of their type of Christianity is recognisable in them in various ways; but the figure of Jesus remains in all essentials as the older tradition traced it.

To those a corner-stone of whose faith it was that Christ was a divine being, who became man for men's salvation, and after finishing his work on earth resumed the divine existence he had temporarily laid aside, these Gospels must have seemed inadequate, and toward the end of the century an unknown author in Asia Minor (probably in Ephesus) produced a fourth Gospel, entitled in the manuscripts, "According to John." Having at the outset identified Christ with the divine Logos, as we have seen, this Gospel presents the life and teaching of Jesus as the manifestation of an incarnate deity whose divine glory shone through the veil of flesh, the glory of the Father's only son.

The divine self-consciousness of Jesus declares itself throughout. He not only came hither sent by God, but he issued out of God; not only is he in the Father and the Father in him, but he asserts publicly to the Jews in the temple: "I and the Father are the same thing." Hence, to know him is to know the Father; a man who has seen him has seen the Father; it is God's will that all men honour the Son just as they honour the Father.

Yet the author makes it clear that the divinity of Christ is a divinity, so to speak, of the second order; the Logos as god is distinguished from (the supreme) God; the "only-begotten Son" suggests the familiar contrast to the "unbegotten." [1] By his own account Jesus utters what the Father has given him to say; his miracles are the works which his Father has given him to do; what he does is what he sees the Father do. The miracles of the Fourth Gospel are few in number, and are all signal exhibitions of supernatural power, such as the opening of the eyes of a man born blind or bringing back to life one who had lain three days in the tomb. These works are "signs," evidences of his divine claims.

In accordance with the conception of the life of Jesus as that of an incarnate deity, he exhibits no symptoms of human weakness. The agony in the Garden of Gethsemane has no place in this Gospel. No one takes his life from him, he lays it down of himself; he has power to lay it down and power to take it again. The crucifixion is an exaltation; it is a return to the Father and a resumption of the divine glory he had with him before the world was. The last words from the cross are not the cry, "My God, my God, why hast thou forsaken me?" (Psalm 22, 2), as in Matthew and Mark, but, "It is accomplished!"

Salvation is eternal life, which the Son gives to all whom the Father has given him (the elect). The secret of eternal life, or rather its essence, is to know the only true God and Jesus Christ whom he has sent. This knowledge is not a monotheistic doctrine about God; it is a mystical knowing mediated through the Son; those who possess it, another writer of the school says, are *in* the true God (1 John 5, 20). While in the popular mysteries the initiates sought an eternal life that was only a kind of deified this-life by union, enthusiastic or sacramental, with the saviour-god, more philosophically minded seekers of salvation strove to attain it by the way of γνῶσις, a transcendental knowledge by which man became divine or realised his essential divinity. The *gnōsis* was not an intellectual or rational knowing, it was itself a "mystery"; it had its vision, or rather "sight" (θέα), of God, by which, it was sometimes said, man is

[1] Μονογενής and ἀγέννητος. Philo; the Hermetic Scriptures.

deified in this life. The standing metaphor for *gnōsis* is "light." Indeed, from a figure it becomes a synonym; "light" and "life" in this esoteric dialect are inseparable correlates.

This way of salvation by knowledge, which might not inaptly be called an intellectual mystery, attracted many; it created a considerable religious literature, most of which appears to have been written in the second or third century. The doctrine itself, however, can be traced a good deal further back, outside of Christianity as well as in it. Echoes of its ideas as well as of its characteristic terminology may be recognised in Paul; the author of the Fourth Gospel is more profoundly influenced by them.

The knowledge of God, which is eternal life, can come only from God himself, who reveals himself in his Logos.[1] So John: "No one has ever seen God: an only-begotten (*i. e.*, unique) god (or son),[2] who is in the bosom of the Father, he told about him." This was the mission of Christ on earth. No man has ascended to heaven; the secrets of the heavenly world can be revealed only by him who descended from heaven, the Son of Man who is in heaven. He is the light of the world, and those who follow him will not walk in darkness, but will have the light of life (John 8, 12; *cf.* 1, 4). The consequence of linking eternal life with knowledge is that the function of the Logos-Christ is essentially that of a revealer or a revelation of God. His own people, to whom he first came, did not accept him, but all who did accept him he enabled to become sons of God. Christianity appears here fully self-conscious: it is the only true religion, and has therefore a universal mission. Jesus was sent for the salvation of the world (κόσμος); he preaches to the Samaritans, and is hailed by them as the Saviour of the world. On his last visit to Jerusalem certain Greeks (Gentiles) seek an interview with him;

---

[1] Similarly not only Philo, but the adepts of the *gnōsis* salvation.

[2] Between the rival readings, μονογενὴς θεὸς and ὁ μονογενὴς υἱός, the probability is strongly on the side of the former.

the Jews suspect him of an intention to go abroad and teach the heathen. He himself says: "I have other sheep, which are not of this (Jewish) fold; them also I must lead, and they will hear my voice, and there will be one fold, one shepherd."

"The world" is sometimes, when the author is expressing the universal character of Christianity, all mankind as the object of God's love, the field of Christ's mission; oftener "the world" is the comprehensive term for the opposition to God and all good. This opposition has a superhuman head, the "ruler of this world," like Paul's "god of this age." The mass of mankind belong to the world; Christians are an elect minority. Faith is the belief that Jesus is the only Son of God, by which men are led to turn to him for the knowledge of God which is eternal life. Belief and unbelief do not lie in man's will, but in God's choice.[1]

The idea that the entrance into the new and higher, the immortal life, must be by a spiritual or intellectual rebirth, or rather regeneration, meets us often in the mysteries, and especially in the intellectual mysticisms of the age; ἀναγεννήσθαι, παλιγγενεσία, are familiar terms in them. In John, also, it is the *sine qua non* of salvation. Flesh breeds flesh; spirit alone can engender spirit, and only he who is begotten by the divine spirit can enter the "kingdom of heaven."[2] In the thought of the time spirit was not only the principle of a divine life but of the higher knowledge; so Paul conceives it (*e. g.*, 1 Cor. 2, 14). In John the two are inseparably connected, or rather they are the same thing.

Where salvation consists in knowing God (*gnōsis*), sacraments, as a real means of communicating the divine life or nature, are unnecessary.[3] It is in accord with the ruling ideas of the Gospel according to John, therefore, that the institution of the Lord's Supper is not narrated in it; its place is filled by an esoteric discourse. The sacraments of

[1] All the circles and sects which find salvation in *gnōsis* attribute to themselves a special gift or capacity not shared by the multitude.

[2] "Kingdom of heaven" in this Gospel is not the reign of God on earth, but the realm of God in heaven.

[3] So in the Hermetic circles; so also in some Christian mystics.

the Christian church nevertheless existed; in the author's time they had a central place in its liturgy. The Eucharist seems to have been an especial object of Jewish attacks. As in other cases, John carries back the questions and controversies of his own age and surroundings to the beginning, and lets Jesus himself make answer and defence. The miraculous supply of bread for the needs of the multitude serves to introduce a discussion in the synagogue in Capernaum. Neither that bread nor the manna Moses gave their fathers was the real bread from heaven, but Jesus himself, who came down from heaven; or, more explicitly, his body. Only he who eats his flesh and drinks his blood possesses eternal life. The Jews take him literally and find the assertion absurd; but their cavils only draw from him emphatic reaffirmations in even more paradoxical terms—he will not abate a syllable of the obnoxious expressions. But when he was alone with his disciples, who found the doctrine almost too much for them,[1] he explained that the flesh is of no use at all, the spirit alone gives life. In the discussion in the synagogue the necessity of the sacrament is maintained against objections from without: the flesh and blood of Christ in the Eucharist are a "medicine that makes a man immortal, an antidote for death," as Ignatius wrote to the Ephesians not long after. To the disciples is given what is frequently called a spiritual interpretation of the sacrament: the virtue resides, not in the material elements, but in the words of Jesus, which are spirit and life.

So also with worship. Holy places and sacred times belong to an outgrown order. "God is spirit, and they who worship him must worship him in spirit and in truth." Baptism is but once alluded to (John 3, 5), in a context where it is wholly subordinate to the Spirit. True Christian worship is not a public cultus, but an attitude or relation to God in the mind and heart.

A peculiar development of the idea of the Spirit in this

[1] According to John 6, 66, many disciples fell away from Jesus as a consequence of this discourse.

Gospel is the doctrine of the "paraclete," or counsellor, whom the Father will send after the departure of Jesus, and, so to speak, as his vicar. He will not only recall to the memory of the disciples all that Jesus said, but will be the medium of future communications from him; he will guide them into all the truth. The church thus has in its spirit-counsellor an organ of continuous revelation, of progress in the truth.

A somewhat detailed sketch of the teaching of Paul, of the Epistle to the Hebrews, and of the Gospel according to John has been necessary because these writings contributed more than all others to Christian ideas about the Saviour and salvation. A comparison of Paul with John, and of both with the deposit of primitive Palestinian tradition in the older Gospels and the first chapters of the Acts, shows what widely diverse conceptions existed side by side in the last quarter of the first century; and the variety would be increased if the other writings ultimately included in the New Testament were similarly examined, and the comparison extended to the "heresies" which are combated as erroneous, that is to the peculiar opinions and speculations of small and often local groups of Christians. Such a survey is remote from our present purpose; but one book requires notice by reason both of its peculiar character and of its influence on Christian eschatology, namely the Revelation of John.[1] It begins with a series of seven letters dictated by the Son of Man to the seer in his vision, and containing mingled praise and blame, warning and exhortation, to as many churches in Asia Minor. The rest (chapters 4–22) is an apocalypse in a series of visions such as is familiar in Jewish literature from Daniel and Enoch to 2 (4) Esdras and Baruch. The ideas and imagery are in large part traditional, only regrouped in another way by a new turn of the kaleidoscope and applied to another situation. Most

---

[1] Whether the John who is the recipient of the revelations is meant to be the Apostle, or some other, was disputed in the ancient church, as it is among modern scholars.

of the visions contain so little that is specifically Christian
that it has been seriously questioned whether they were not
appropriated entire from Jewish sources with only a superficial adaptation to Christian use. Whatever degree of
literary originality may be allowed the author, the matter
is Jewish throughout.[1] The resurrection of the saints to
enjoy the thousand-year reign of the Messiah; the war of
Gog and Magog at the end of the millennium, and their destruction; the general resurrection and last judgment; the
new Jerusalem descending from heaven in all its glitter of
gold, even to the river of life and the trees bearing monthly
crops of new fruit and medicinal leaves, are the trite ideas
and imagery of Jewish eschatology in apocalypse and Mid-
rash. Through the authority of the Revelation of John this
materialistic eschatology, with its corporeal resurrection
and its millennial reign, was brought over into the church,
and found acceptance not only among ignorant Christians,
to whose imagination it offered something more tangible than
the ideas of Paul and John, but among men like Justin who
boasted of philosophic education. In the second century
millenarian eschatology was orthodoxy in Asia Minor and
the wide regions which took their theology from that source;
it is the faith of Irenæus. It has survived through all the
vicissitudes of theology, and over and over again has broken
out in epidemics of enthusiasm.

While the gospel was spreading among Greeks and bar-
barians and a distinctive Gentile Christianity was being
developed, the church in Jerusalem preserved the primitive
type of belief and adhered to the Jewish law and custom of
life. It is probable, indeed, that in reaction from the tendencies which were transforming Hellenistic Christianity
into another religion the conservative element in Jerusalem
gained more complete control and became more Jewish than
ever. The church was held in pious esteem, and collections
were made in Gentile churches for the poor brethren in
Judæa; but it had no longer any influence on the movement

---

[1] Sectarian Jewish, it should perhaps be said.

outside of Palestine. James was put to death by the Sanhedrin in 63 A. D., but the act was condemned by the best
citizens and those most scrupulous about the laws, on whose
complaint Agrippa deposed the high priest as the author
of the deed. During the war (66–72 A. D.) the members
of the community in Judæa are said to have taken refuge in
Pella, on the other side of the Jordan. The successor of
James was a cousin of Jesus, named Simeon. He and his
successors down to the war under Hadrian (132–135 A. D.)
are enumerated in the list of bishops of Jerusalem, but it is
hardly likely that the ruined city was their residence.[1]

The calamities which befell the Jews, the internecine strife
of parties, the destruction of Jerusalem and the temple,
doubtless gave a new impetus to the preaching of dire judgment impending, of which all these things were but the
signs foretold in prophecy and apocalypse, and more explicitly by Jesus; and the preaching found readier credence
among men under whose very eyes the world seemed to be
coming to an end. At the beginning of the second century
the disciples of Jesus the Nazarene, as they are called in
Jewish sources, were numerous in Judæa and in Galilee, and
were making such headway with their propaganda that
the leading rabbis of the generation were constrained to
make more rigorous opposition to the spread of the heresy.
The vehemence of their utterances shows that the matter
gave them concern, the more because the heresy had in-
sinuated itself even into their own ranks. It is significant
that it was thought necessary to make a formal pronounce-
ment that the Gospel ($\epsilon\dot{\upsilon}\alpha\gamma\gamma\dot{\epsilon}\lambda\iota o\nu$) is not an inspired and
sacred book. Significant also is the introduction into the
form of public prayer under the direction of the Patriarch
Gamaliel II of a petition, "May the Nazarenes and the
heretics suddenly perish!"—an effective means of preventing the disciples of Jesus from leading the prayers in the

---

[1] The large number of these "bishops"—twelve in a single generation—suggests that the list includes the heads of other communities in
Judæa.

synagogue, or of detecting them, if, as worshippers, they did not join heartily in this curse on themselves. The adoption of such a measure shows that Jewish Christians frequented the synagogues; perhaps it was directed chiefly against those who had secretly embraced the faith.

The Jewish rebellion in the reign of Hadrian took a Messianic character; the leader, Bar Cozeba, was proclaimed as the "Star out of Jacob," the predicted conqueror of Edom (Rome),[1] hence his new name, Bar Cocheba. The Christian Jews could not support him without denying their own Messiah, Jesus, the signs of whose imminent coming they saw in the commotions around them, and they fled again to the regions east of the Jordan. When the war was over, and Hadrian decreed that no Jew, under pain of death, should set foot in the new city, Ælia Capitolina, which he built on the site of the ruined Jerusalem, the Christian Jews fell under the prohibition with all the rest, and the church which was presently established there was a Greek church with Gentile Christian bishops.

The development of catholic theology in the second and third centuries left the Jewish Christians of Palestine behind. From the catholic point of view their antique notions were not a stunted survival of a primitive type of faith, but Judaizing heresies, and it is from the compilers of collections of heresies that the scanty information we have about them chiefly comes. To the middle or end of the fourth century some of them conserved their original beliefs with little change. They bore the name Nazarenes which the Jews gave to all Christians, and were found principally in the Decapolis in the region around Pella, in a district in Basanitis, and in Cœle-Syria about Berœa (Aleppo). By Epiphanius' account, they had the Hebrew Scriptures and lived in all respects according to the Jewish Law, differing from other Jews solely in their belief that Jesus was the Messiah. They had a Gospel in Aramaic, which Epiphanius identified with the original Matthew. Jerome visited the

[1] Num. 24, 17 ff.

Nazarenes of Berœa, which was only a few miles from his hermitage in the desert of Chalcis, and copied their Gospel, which, like Epiphanius, he took for the Aramaic Matthew. The specimens of their interpretation of Scripture which Jerome gives evince hostility to the scribes and Pharisees, beginning with the schools of Hillel and Shammai. They interpreted Isaiah 9, 1, of the liberation of the Galileans from the errors of the scribes and Pharisees by Jesus, and the shaking off of the heavy yoke of Jewish traditions, and verse 2 of the shining out of the gospel of Christ to the bounds of the Gentiles and the way of the great sea by the preaching of Paul, "the last of the Apostles." In their relations to catholic Christians they seem to have occupied the middle ground represented in Acts by Peter and described in the middle of the second century by Justin—the Law of Moses was binding on born Jews, but not on Gentiles.

Other Jewish Christian sects regarded Paul as a renegade and the adversary of the Apostles, and could not say evil enough about him. They had a Gospel related in some way to Matthew, but beginning, like Mark, with the appearance of John the Baptist. They rejected the story of the miraculous birth of Jesus, and believed him the son of Joseph and Mary by ordinary generation. They maintained the position of the adversaries of Paul in Galatia; circumcision and the observance of the whole Law is necessary to salvation. It is from some such party that the original story came which forms the groundwork of the Clementine Recognitions and Homilies, in which the subordination of Peter to James is evidently sectarian. Others, again, with the Catholic Church, confessed Christ born of the Virgin. Some became infected with notions vaguely designated as "gnostic," which were rife in the first centuries of our era among Jews and heathen as well as Christians. Of these general types of Jewish Christianity there were many and constantly changing varieties. They flourished chiefly in the regions east of the Jordan. After the fourth century little is heard of them, but some of them survived to a later time; Mohammed's acquaintance with Christianity came mainly from such sources.

The organisation of the primitive societies of believers was very simple. There were missionaries ("apostles") who were sent out from the principal centres—Jerusalem or Antioch—to preach the gospel or visit other churches, sometimes taking helpers with them. The local societies were called "assemblies," like the Jewish synagogues. The affairs of the society were managed by the seniors (presbyters, elders), whether by the tacit recognition or choice of the community, or appointed by the missionaries. Paul's letter to the Philippians is addressed "to all the saints (ἅγιοι, initiates) in Christ Jesus who are in Philippi, with the overseers and helpers." There were also prophets who spoke as they were inspired; but prophecy was an occasional gift, not an office.

A more advanced stage of organisation is reflected in the instructions for missionaries in the Epistles to Timothy and to Titus, where the qualifications of overseers, and the duties of helpers, both men and women, especially in the administration of the charities of the churches, are defined. We learn that the elders were at the head of the community, and that some of them preached and taught in its gatherings; what the peculiar function of the overseers was, if indeed they are to be distinguished from the elders, we are not informed. The letters of Ignatius, bishop of Antioch, written early in the second century to churches in Asia Minor, show that each church was ruled by a single overseer (bishop),[1] with a plurality of elders (presbyters) and helpers (deacons) under him. A society in which these three orders are not found, Ignatius says, is not called a church. The authority of the bishop is supreme; baptism and the Eucharist are administered by him or by such as he has empowered to do so. This episcopal constitution of the church soon became universal, and all the conditions of the

---

[1] The English "bishop" is Greek *episkopos*, "overseer."

time—the growth of the church, its relations to the civil authority, the conflict with heresy—tended greatly to increase the power of the bishops. The churches in different cities were autonomous, and were not united in any common organisation, but there was much coming and going among them, and frequent intercourse by letters. Christians everywhere felt themselves members of one great religious communion, which Ignatius calls the General ("Catholic") Church, in distinction from the churches of individual cities. The same thing was true of the initiates of the mysteries of Isis or Mithras. Similarly, the Jews spoke of the "Synagogue of Israel," which embraced all adherents of Judaism— we might equally well translate "Israelitish Church."

In the gatherings of the first Christians the greatest freedom prevailed, and scenes of disorderly enthusiasm such as Paul reproved in Corinth may have been not infrequent; but before long, at least in their principal assemblies, instruction and exhortation took a larger place. In the synagogue, in which some of them had been brought up and which many others had frequented, they had before them an institution singularly adapted to these ends, and the reading of portions of the Scriptures (especially the Prophets) and discourse upon them were early taken over into Christian use. Jewish prayers and their biblical models also much influenced the development of the Christian liturgies. Besides the Scriptures, letters of Apostles, especially those of Paul, or communications from other churches, were frequently read.

The distinctive Christian rite of the early church was the mystery, or sacrament,[1] of the Eucharist, the participation in the flesh and blood of the Lord. Primitively this rite concluded a church supper, called *Agape* ("love"); but it was, in some parts of the church sooner, in others later, detached from this connection and transferred to the principal daytime service, of which it formed the solemn culmination.

---

[1] *Sacramentum* is the Latin translation of the Greek μυστήριον.

About the middle of the second century, in a defence of Christianity addressed to the emperor Antoninus Pius, Justin gives a description of Christian worship in Rome, in substance as follows:

In the Sunday assemblies a lesson is read from the Memoirs of the Apostles (Gospels) or the writings of the Prophets; the presiding officer (bishop) follows with a discourse admonishing his hearers to conform their lives to the good teachings they have heard, after which the congregation rises, and all unite in prayers. This part of the service is succeeded by the celebration of the Eucharist: bread, and wine mixed with water, are brought to the bishop, who offers praise and honour to the Father of the Universe through the name of the Son and the Holy Spirit, and gives thanks at length that God has bestowed these gifts on us, the people responding, Amen! The deacons then distribute to each of those present a portion of the bread and of the wine, and carry portions to absent members of the church.

In the sequel an explanation of the sacrament is given as the Christian tradition, which contains substantially the Catholic doctrine of the Eucharist.

In the latter part of the first century and the beginning of the second Christianity spread rapidly and widely. The chief early centres of distribution were Antioch for Syria and Cilicia, Ephesus for Asia Minor, Rome for Italy, and presumably Alexandria for Egypt and the Cyrenaica. Churches were soon planted also at Carthage and at Lyons, from which the gospel was disseminated in Africa and southern Gaul. Somewhat later Edessa became the metropolis of a Syriac-speaking Christianity.

The progress of the new religion presently attracted the attention of the government, all the more because common rumour accused the Christians of abominable orgies in their clandestine assemblies—feasting on human flesh and promiscuous sexual intercourse, Thyestean banquets and Œdipean incests.[1] The charges were believed not only by

[1] Christians spoke of eating the flesh and drinking the blood of the "son of man"; the "brothers" and "sisters" met at night in secret conventicles, and separated with the "kiss of peace."

the masses but in intellectual circles. The magistrates soon found out that Christians not only did not worship the gods, but, what was worse, refused to burn incense before statues of the emperor, take oath by him, or otherwise acknowledge his divinity. This was a species of *læsa majestas*, a capital crime at once political and religious. The procedure was summary; the mode of execution, except in the case of Roman citizens, arbitrary with the magistrates. Exposure to wild beasts in the arena as a spectacle for the populace was a favourite way of disposing of criminals condemned to death, and Christians were frequently sentenced to this fate.

Down to the edict of toleration in 311 Christians were never safe from prosecutions of this kind; but until the middle of the third century those who suffered death for their faith were not many compared with the growing numbers of Christians in the empire. Strenuous repressive measures might be in operation in one province, while in the neighbouring ones the churches were unmolested; a severe persecution in a region was often followed by years of tranquillity; there were periods when the church enjoyed almost unbroken peace throughout the empire. Decius (249–251) was the first to employ the whole administrative machinery of the empire in a general persecution.

In the second century a succession of apologists undertook the defence of Christians against the vulgar calumnies and against the imputation of disloyalty. They protested against the injustice of subjecting them to torture and death for the mere name of Christian, which, though not the form, was the actual working of the procedure commonly employed in their case. They took occasion also to set forth the evidences of Christianity and arguments to prove that it was the only true religion.

In the writings which the church eventually included in its list of Christian Scriptures, divinely inspired and therefore normative for doctrine and life, the readers are often warned against false teachers and their teachings. Such

warnings are especially frequent in the so-called Pastoral
Epistles, in Second Peter, Jude, and the letters to the
churches of Asia in the first chapters of the Revelation of
John; and (outside the New Testament) in the letters of
Ignatius. The teachings thus condemned are sometimes
called "heresies," a word which properly signifies the distinctive principles of philosophical schools, but in ecclesiastical use has from the beginning the connotation of
false and harmful opinions.

The oldest specifically Christian heresy was that Christ
did not in reality suffer and die, but only in seeming. It
was natural for converts from heathenism to think of the
appearance of Christ on earth as the temporary assumption
by a god of a human form, as in so many tales in the mythol-
ogies. To such as had some tincture of philosophy the very
definition of the divine was to be by nature exempt from
suffering and death. Men who regarded matter as inhe-
rently evil could not conceive that Christ was really embodied in human flesh, with all its corruption and defilement. The belief that the humanity of Christ was only a
semblance thus had its origin in the desire to think of him
nothing unworthy of a god;[1] as a doctrine, the docetic theory
of Christ's humanity is linked with the dualism of popular
philosophy.[2]

The Jewish origin of Christianity, the essential identity
of the two religions in their monotheism and their morality,
the appropriation of the Jewish Scriptures by the church,
and the fact that many converts to Christianity in the first
generations came to it by way of the synagogue, explain the
persistent recurrence of Judaising tendencies. If there was
no longer a propaganda such as Paul had to combat in
Galatia, which by accepting circumcision and the obligation
of the whole Law would have transformed Hellenistic Christianity into a sect of Judaism, there was an inclination to
conform to Jewish observances in the keeping of Sabbaths

[1] On a similar phenomenon in Buddhism, see Vol. I, p. 302.
[2] See below, p. 166.

and festivals and of prescriptions about food and drink, such as is censured in the Epistle to the Colossians, along with superstitions like the worship of angels which were as heretical in Judaism as in Christianity. The Judaising against which Ignatius warns the churches of Asia was of a like kind. Christianity (this is the first occurrence of the word) is a way of living different from Judaism: "Let us learn to live according to Christianity"; "for if we continue to live according to Judaism, we confess that we have not received grace."

A more radical opposition appears in the Epistle of Barnabas.[1] According to this author, Christians did not, as was commonly taught, supersede the Jews as the people of God, the true Israel, when the Jews rejected Christ; the Jews never were the people of God. The Mosaic covenant was broken and annulled at the foot of Sinai by the sin of the golden calf before it ever went into effect. God's covenant belongs exclusively to Christians. The Jews, with their literal interpretation and material practice, wholly perverted the spiritual meaning of the Law. God never demanded sacrifices and oblations, but a contrite heart; not the circumcision of the flesh, but of the ears and heart. The narratives of the Old Testament are allegories of Christ; the author claims for Christians the Law (in its spiritual sense), all the prophecies and the promises—in short, he leaves the Bible to the Jews only for a stumbling-block. This attitude is not an exaggeration of the antithesis of Law and gospel in Paul, or of the contrast of type and reality in Hebrews (with which the author has otherwise some affinity), it is the opposite of Paul, as a glance at Romans 11 shows.

Instead of taking possession of the Jewish Scriptures and making of them a preparation for Christianity or a revelation of it, others abandoned it to the Jews altogether, creating a complete contradiction between the Old Testament and the New. This conception of Christianity was com-

[1] The writing which bears this title is not by the companion of Paul.

mon to Marcion and the Gnostics, and led to his being
classed with them, though he does not belong to them.   To
Marcion, Judaism and Christianity, the Law and the gospel,
were so completely opposite in teaching and in spirit that
they cannot have the same author.   The god of the Old
Testament was warlike and a cruel deity.   He laid down
his will in a law, and inexorably inflicted its penalties on
transgressors; in this sense he was a *just* god.   This just
god was the demiurge, artificer of the visible universe, as
is told in Genesis; a god of inferior intelligence and imperfect in character.   Above him was the supreme God, creator
of the invisible or intelligible universe, whose nature is pure
goodness.   This *good* God was unknown—even the demiurge was not aware of his existence—until Christ came
down from heaven to reveal him, and drawing men away
from allegiance to the demiurge, to call them into his own
kingdom.   Indignant at this invasion of his realm, the
demiurge caused him to be crucified.   Christ was not the
Messiah foretold in the Old Testament by the prophets of
the demiurge; the Jewish Messiah is an Antichrist, who
shall one day arise and be overcome.   After this triumph,
the souls of those who are saved through Christ will enter
into the kingdom of God.   The body of man is a work of
the demiurge; the Christian must, therefore, combat and
subdue it, with its appetites and passions.   The ethics of
the system are ascetic; the motive is love to the good God.

Such, according to Marcion, was the teaching of Paul,
the only pure Christianity.   The church, ignoring the warning of its Master, had put the new wine of the gospel into
the old bottles of Judaism, with the inevitable result.   His
mission was to restore genuine Christianity by bringing the
church back to Paul.   Whatever in the Epistles of Paul and
the Pauline Gospel, Luke, was at variance with this doctrine, he deleted as Judaising interpolation, and gave his
followers an expurgated Pauline canon, rejecting the other
Gospels and Epistles altogether.   Failing in his efforts to
reform the church according to his ideas, Marcion organised

a rival church, which lasted till after the empire became Christian, and, to judge from the temper in which the Fathers attack it, must in many places have had numerous adherents.

Others, with a more thoroughgoing dualism, reasoned that the artificer of this world, evil as it is through and through, must himself be altogether bad. Since their doctrine was that an esoteric knowledge (*gnōsis*) is the only salvation from the evils of bodily existence and the world of matter and sense, the commandment not to eat of the tree of knowledge (Gen. 2) was to them plain proof that the god of the Old Testament, the demiurge, was the enemy of mankind. By this prohibition he sought to keep man from his highest good, and when man had tasted the fruit of knowledge, again displayed his malignity by barring the way to the tree of life. The serpent, on the contrary, "the most intelligent of the animals" (Gen. 3, 1), was man's friend, revealing to Eve the envy and falsehood of the demiurge and the true effect of the forbidden fruit: "Your eyes will be opened, and ye will be as gods, knowing good and evil." It was the serpent, they said, who opened to men the knowledge of the heavenly mysteries; the serpent who in the days of Herod appeared in human form (Christ).[1] Some of these Ophites (Serpent Sect) are said to have produced in their sacrament a snake from a box and let it crawl around and over the elements, a rite to which Greek mysteries offer partial parallels. The Law of Moses having been imposed by an evil and inimical deity, it was incumbent on those who knew his true character to go contrary to his commandments. The sinners of the Old Testament, who would not obey the mandates of the demiurge, were the men of light in their time; one sect characteristically chose Cain for their eponymous saint.

The saving knowledge was here a subtle theosophy, there myth and mummery; secret rites and magical charms full of unintelligible and unpronounceable names had a large

---

[1] *Cf.* John 3, 14.

place in it. The number and variety of Gnostic sects or
schools was prodigious; the movement, which began in the
Apostolic Age, was at its height in the latter half of the
second century, and only slowly subsided.   In them all men
sought to attain salvation by an esoteric knowledge (*gnōsis*)
of the mysteries of the godhead, of the universe, and of the
soul, and those who had this knowledge were therefore
called "Gnostics."

The Gnostics not only called themselves Christians, but
professed to be a very superior sort of Christians, if not the
only genuine Christians.   Amid the clamour of these rival
pretensions the question, Where is true Christianity to be
found? was urgent.   Only one answer was possible: True
Christianity was what had been taught and practised in
the church from the beginning.   Peculiar authority naturally belonged to the churches which could assert an unbroken tradition of faith and order from their apostolic
founders.   The succession of bishops conserved and passed
on this tradition, and thus became, so to speak, the living
criterion of orthodoxy, its authoritative exponents.   The
bishops of the leading sees communicated to one another
the doctrine of their churches and co-operated in measures
to combat error.   Before the end of the second century
synods of bishops began to be held, an organ of concerted
action.   Thus the conflict with heresy strengthened the sense
of Catholic unity, and the episcopate, as the bulwark of the
Catholic faith, acquired a greatly enhanced importance.

Another result of the conflict with heresy was the formation of lists of writings attributed to the Apostles, or to their
companions and helpers under apostolic direction, which
the church accepted as Christian Scriptures, excluding the
spurious Gospels, Acts, and Revelations of the Gnostics and
other heretics, many of which also bore apostolic names and
claimed the authority of inspiration.   Here again prescription gave the criterion: books which had long been in use in
all the chief churches were genuine, those which had not
this recognition were rejected as apocryphal; those which

were accepted in some parts of the church, but not in all, were dubious. The oldest list that has been preserved[1] comprises the Four Gospels, Acts of the Apostles, the Epistles of Paul (including Hebrews), James, 1 Peter, 1 John, and the Revelation of John. Unanimity about some of the books in the New Testament was not attained even in the fourth century; but the object of the canon was achieved.

Still another result of the conflict was the employment of brief summaries of the Catholic faith as a test of orthodoxy and a norm for the interpretation of Scripture, which by their allegorical higher exegesis the Gnostics wrested to support their very unscriptural speculations. Such compends of Christian truth had been in use earlier in the admission of converts by baptism; they now became a "standard of the truth" (κανὼν τῆς ἀληθείας). The Roman baptismal confession from which the so-called Apostles' Creed is derived, in its oldest known form ran somewhat as follows:

I believe in God the Father Almighty, and in Jesus Christ his only Son, our Lord, who was born of the Holy Ghost and the Virgin Mary, crucified under Pontius Pilate and buried; the third day he rose from the dead; he ascended to heaven; he sitteth at the right hand of the Father; thence he shall come to judge the living and the dead; and in the Holy Ghost, the Holy Church, the remission of sins, the resurrection of the flesh.

Symbols of similar content in varying phrase were employed in the East also.

Thus in the course of the second century, by its own development and through the conflict with heresy, the church became what Ignatius at the beginning of the century had prophetically called it, the Catholic Church, with an efficient episcopal organisation maintaining an authoritative apostolic tradition, a canon of sacred Scripture, and an explicitly defined rule of faith. In all this progress the church in Rome had a leading part. Before the close of

[1] Muratorian Canon. Roman (not official), about 180 A. D.

the century Irenæus, bishop of Lyons in Gaul, a native of
Asia Minor, who in his youth had listened to the words of
the aged Polycarp, bishop of Smyrna, could write of the
Roman church: "Ad hanc enim ecclesiam, propter potiorem
principalitatem, necesse est omnem convenire ecclesiam,
hoc est, eos qui sunt undique fideles, in qua semper . . .
conservata est ea quæ est ab apostolis traditio." [1]

[1] Every church, that is, all believers everywhere, ought to agree with
this [*i. e.*, the Roman] church, in which the tradition coming down from
the Apostles has always been preserved.

CHAPTER VI

CHRISTIANITY

THEOLOGY AND DOGMA

THE writers who undertook the exposition and defence of Christianity for educated readers—the so-called Apologists—were chiefly converted philosophers of a kind common in those days, half sophist, half rhetorician, who discoursed in public, or to paying hearers who frequented their lecture-rooms, on moral and religious subjects. They found in the new religion the true philosophy; it had the authority of divine revelation, and it gave the assurance of a blessed immortality. Christianity was to them primarily a revelation in the Scriptures and through Christ of the truth about God, of the moral law with its rewards and punishments, and of immortality through knowledge of the truth and obedience to the revealed will of God.

They endeavoured to prove that in its teaching about God Christianity was in accord with the best thought of the age, transcending it by carrying the thinking on under the guidance of revelation to its vaguely adumbrated consequences, and making practical application of its theology to religion and life. The superiority of Christianity to the old religions must be patent, they argued, to all intelligent men; and, lest any should fail to see it, they set out in a glaring light the unreasonableness of polytheism and idolatry and the absurdities and immoralities of the myths—an enterprise in which they had many precursors among the Greeks as well as in Jewish controversial literature.

For the Apologists, as in the popular religious philosophies out of which they came, God was eternal, and in his unchangeable divinity too exalted to be brought directly into action in the changing world of things and men. Like Philo and the Gospel of John, they find the connection between God and the world in the idea of the Logos, which as divine reason was eternally immanent in God, and was emanated from God before creation, that through him the world might be made (Prov. 8, 22 *ff*.). The Logos is the Son of God, generated by his power and will, not as by a division of his essence. All revelation comes from him; it was he who appeared in human form to the patriarchs, he who spoke by the prophets. Nor was the work of the Logos confined to one people; whatever is reasonable and right in the teaching of Greek philosophers and poets is from the same source. The full revelation is made in the incarnate Logos. Combining Pauline (Colossians) and Johannean phraseology, Justin uses the name Christ of the Logos before the incarnation. The Logos, or the Christ-Logos, is thus a deity of the second order, numerically distinct from the Supreme God, but of one mind and will with him, emanated from God, or, in more scriptural phrase of the same meaning, generated by him. In this pluralistic monotheism the Spirit is sometimes distinguished from the Father and the Logos-Son—an anticipation of the problem of the ontological Trinity, not of its solution.

The knowledge of God ($\gamma\nu\tilde{\omega}\sigma\iota\varsigma$) is not in the Apologists an esoteric insight into the mysteries of the divine Being, as with the intellectual Gnostics, but a knowledge of God's unity, character, and will. Faith, that is, the acceptance of the Christian religion and obedience to its new law, is the condition of salvation. Salvation is deliverance from the assaults of demons, of which the world is full, and when this life is over, immortality, or, as it is commonly expressed, "imperishability" (ἀφθαρσία, "incorruption").[1]

In their notions of the hereafter the Apologists, contrary to what might be expected of philosophers with a streak of Platonism, accept the beliefs of unphilosophical Christians, taking the resurrection in material literalness: "We expect to receive our bodies again after they are dead and laid in the ground." Justin, with all whose orthodoxy he regards as unequivocal, looks for a thousand-year reign of Christ on earth with a rebuilt and enlarged Jerusalem as his capital, after which will come the general resurrection and the last judgment, as in the Revelation of John.

Irenæus, Bishop of Lyons (d. ca. 200 A. D.) is in substantial agreement with the Apologists in his conception of the Logos, Son and revealer of the Father, who spoke by the prophets and was incarnate in Christ, and of the Spirit, as well as in his idea of faith (credere ei est facere eius voluntatem), the obligation of the moral law, free will and ability, and in his beliefs about the hereafter. He has, however, a more profound theory of the reason of the incarnation, the germs of which he may have brought from his native Asia Minor—they are found in Ignatius—but the development of which was probably not uninfluenced by contact with the intellectual Gnostics and their doctrine of a fallen world.

God, by his Word (Logos), made Adam after his own likeness. This godlikeness, which included immortality, Adam, by his fall, lost for himself and all his descendants, who inherit his mortal nature; the recovery of the pristine likeness to God is therefore the condition of immortality; its possession is "imperishability." To this end the race must begin over again, with Christ as its head in place of Adam. By the union of divinity and humanity in Christ—a commixtio et communio dei et hominis—he undoes the harm

---

[1] See 1 Cor. 15, 53. The preference for this word over ἀθανασία, "immortality," is due to the fact that in Greek philosophy γίγνεσθαι and φθείρεσθαι are opposites, "come into existence," "cease to exist."

Adam did and restores to mankind the lost divine image. Only man could fairly overcome man's enemy, death; only God could give security of salvation; "unless man were made one with God, he could not share in incorruption." Against the Gnostic doctrine that the humanity of Christ was only a semblance, Irenæus affirms that he took from the Virgin Mary *substantiam carnis;* but with equal emphasis that the deity thus incarnated is "the Son, ever co-existent with the Father, uncreated, of the same essence" (ὁμοούσιος).

The union of deity with a real and true body of flesh and blood makes the body of man capable of immortality. The Gnostics, "despising the creation of God (the body) and rejecting the salvation of the flesh," think that when they die their souls will mount above the sky and go to that imaginary Father of theirs. Irenæus holds, on the contrary, that souls abide in an invisible place appointed by God until the resurrection; then receiving bodies and rising entire, that is, bodily,[1] they will thus come to see God. As for Ignatius the sacramental bread was a medicine that gives immortality, so in Irenæus the flesh which is nourished upon the body and blood of the Lord cannot be destined to destruction. After the invocation, the bread is no longer common bread, but a Eucharist, in which is a heavenly as well as an earthly element; so also our bodies, receiving the Eucharist, are no longer perishable, having the expectation of an eternal resurrection. It is through the sacrament that the salvation of the flesh is achieved.

The doctrine of the Logos seemed to thinkers imbued with the current religious philosophy to furnish a key to the understanding of the Scriptures, and to harmonise the church's worship of Christ as God with its polemic monotheism. There were others, however, to whom this discourse of a second god, the son of the first, begotten by him before the creation of the world—of Father and Son, or of Father, Son, and Spirit, as two, or three, numerically distinct divine beings—had a familiar mythological sound

---

[1] This is the Jewish doctrine. See above, pp. 55 *f.*, 75.

which made the whole Logos theology suspicious; and
this prejudice was doubtless strengthened by the resemblance of the emanation of the Son in this theology to the
theories of the Gnostics. Attempts were therefore made to
interpret the Gospels and the common faith of the church
in a way more conformable to naïve monotheism. Some,
rejecting the Fourth Gospel, held that Jesus was born of the
Virgin, in accordance with the Father's will. He was a
man of exemplary character and deeply religious. At his
baptism the Spirit descended upon him, consecrated him as
the Christ, and endued him with supernatural powers.
Then and thus he became the Son of God in the Messianic
sense, but not of divine nature. If it was permissible to attribute divinity to him, it was only after his resurrection
and ascension, and only in a loose use of the word. This
opinion, which closely resembles that of some of the Jewish
Christian sects described above, was rejected by the church
without further ado.

Others endeavoured to maintain at once the deity of
Christ and the numerical unity of the godhead by the
theory that it was God himself who became incarnate, and
no other. One and the same God was both Father and Son,
now invisible, now visible; now unbegotten, and again born
of the Virgin; now impassible and immortal, now suffering
and dying on the cross. A somewhat more developed
theory taught that the one God assumed in succession
different rôles ($\pi\rho\acute{o}\sigma\omega\pi a$, *personæ*): in the character of Father he was the creator and legislator; in that of Son,
from the incarnation to the ascension, he was the Saviour;
in the present age he is the Spirit in the church. Thus,
these scriptural names stand for modes or phases of God's
operation or self-manifestation, not for a supreme God with
one or two subordinate deities springing in some way out
of him. Those who made the arithmetical unity of God
($\mu o\nu a\rho\chi\acute{\iota}a$)[1] their shibboleth are commonly called "mo-

---

[1] $\mathrm{M}o\nu a\rho\chi\acute{\iota}a$ is the Greek word for "monotheism," or the doctrine of
the divine unity.

narchians" (more correctly, "monotheists," or unitarians);
their adversaries nicknamed them "patripassians," asserting
that by their doctrine of identity they made the Father
suffer on the cross.

There is every reason to suppose that the gospel found its
way to Alexandria at a very early time, probably not much
later than to Antioch; but of the establishment of the church
there and of its history to the close of the first century
nothing whatever is known.   That the Christian community
was by that time numerous, and had gained adherents among
the intellectual class may be inferred from the fact that as
early as the reign of Hadrian two great Gnostic systems
originated in Alexandria.   Basilides undertook to derive
the universe from the metaphysical principle of pure Non-
being instead of absolute Being, without the hypothesis of
emanation, and to construe salvation in an ascending scale
only, without the hypothesis of an antecedent fall of spirits
from the higher realms—a graduated salvation, in which
each attains according to his capacity, while those who
finally remain below are enveloped in "the great ignorance,"
and, knowing nothing above them to aspire to, are content.

Valentinus, like Plotinus, starts with the metaphysical
Absolute, which is beyond the categories of knowing and
being.   From this proceeds by emanation the Nous (Universal Intellect), from it the Logos, from it Anthropos (ideal
generic Humanity).[1]   To each of these is given a (grammati-
cally) feminine counterpart: Mind-Truth, Word-Life, Man-
Church, and by a kind of analysis of the last two pairs of
concepts, secondary emanations proceed from them.   All
this is in what the Platonists of the time called the κόσμος
νοητός, a universe that has only an intellectual (*i. e.*, incorporeal) existence; the Valentinians called it the Plerōma,
the fulness of the godhead.   There was no world of sense,
no matter.   Plotinus arrives at his primordial matter by a
final stage in the self-exteriorisation of the Absolute; Valen-

[1] Compare the system of Plotinus, Vol. I, pp. 533 *f*.   Observe that
in the Valentinian scheme Humanity is in the godhead.

tinus can conceive the very existence of matter only as the result of a fall within the godhead itself.

This is set forth in Platonic fashion in the myth of the fall of Wisdom through its aspiration to know the unknowable. In the remotest of the emanations, Sophia, a desire arose to know the Father and commune with him, which none but Nous can do. This ambition to transcend her bounds and its failure excited in her the emotions of ignorance and grief and fear and perplexity; and when she was delivered from these and they were extruded from the Plerōma, they became the primordial elements of the visible universe—ignorance and grief, fear and perplexity, are the very tissue of nature as well as the warp of human life. Out of them a demiurge fashioned the world; he, or the angels (like Plato's "younger gods"), made man's body and breathed into him a soul. Some men have also received from a higher source a germ of spirit; they are the "spiritual men." [1]

Man is not only mortal, he is sinful; his heart is the habitation of a multitude of demons, which make and keep it unclean. Only the Son can expel them and purify the heart, and only the pure in heart can see God. Christ, the Saviour, was emanated that he might come and recover the spiritual race that is from above—as the fall was in the godhead, the recovery must come from it. It is a poetic imagination that Christ was an emanation of all the æons of the Plerōma, each of whom contributed what was best in it to the making of the most perfect beauty, the Star of the Plerōma (cf. Col. 1, 17; 2, 9). When this Jesus came forth from the bosom of the godhead to earth, he brought a body with him from above, and passed through the Virgin Mary, taking no substance from her womb. The motive of this docetism is plain: he whose mission is to deliver men from the world of matter and sense cannot himself be subject to the infirmities or the defilement of the flesh.

[1] The distinction of material, animal, and spiritual men comes from 1 Cor. 2, 14; 15, 46 ff.

These thinkers undertook to solve the problem of the universe in a monistic sense, starting with Absolute Being or Absolute Non-Being; to account for the material world and all the physical and moral evil in it, without involving God in it or making him responsible for it; to explain how souls, which are by nature divine, came to be in this exile, imprisoned in the body, defiled and corrupted by contact with matter and the desires of the flesh; how they may be liberated, purified, and restored to their native estate; and how the redemption of the universe itself is to be achieved and nature delivered from the bondage of corruption. These were the central problems of contemporary religious philosophy. The specific problem of Christian philosophy was to interpret, from these premises and in this scheme, the nature of the Saviour, and his work in the salvation of individual souls and the redemption of the cosmos. In them, as in the Neoplatonists, a theory of the universe was not the ultimate end of speculation; the relation of the soul to God furnished the basis of an intellectual mysticism the goal of which is the reascent of the soul to God or its union with God.

Expelled from the church, Valentinus and his disciples formed churches of their own, which survived the impartial persecutions of the heathen emperors, but succumbed to the particular persecution of their Christian successors. But putting heretics out of the church did not put the questions they raised out of the world, nor did the refutations of churchmen like Irenæus and Hippolytus answer them. If the church was to gain or hold thinking men, it must offer them a better philosophy than the Gnostics, it must think its faith into a theology. Like the systems of Basilides and Valentinus, like the philosophy of Plotinus, this theology came from Alexandria.

The Christian school in Alexandria, from its foundation, took a prominent place among the schools of that university city. Clement, the second head of the school, was a man of voluminous reading in Greek literature and philosophy, as well as in the Scriptures and Christian authors, both Catholic and Gnostic, and his reputation for learning and eloquence drew to his lecture-rooms throngs of pagan as well as Christian hearers. His peculiar service was to vindicate the right of educated and thoughtful men to an apprehension of Christianity which satisfied their intelligence, and to show that such an apprehension is possible without, like the Gnostics, rejecting the traditional standard of truth. He calls himself a gnostic; the "pseudo-gnostics" are not to be allowed to usurp so honourable a name. His *gnōsis*, however, is not a theosophy, but a knowledge of divine things profounder than that of simple believers, and not accepted on authority but rationally established. The faith of the common Christian is "an epitome of the essentials," the knowledge of the Christian gnostic is "the sure demonstration of the things received by faith." The true gnostic lives on a higher plane than the simple believer, morally as well as intellectually, and Christians should endeavour, by the study of philosophy and the discipline of the religious life, to attain this higher stage. The divine Logos is the source of all intelligence, knowledge, and morality. The education of the human race is the work of the Logos—the Greeks by philosophy, the Jews by the Law, until Christ came. It is the Logos which now turns men from false religions and evil ways, trains them in right living, and is their teacher in the true knowledge.

Clement's successor, Origen, was born in Alexandria of Christian parents, in 185 or 186 A. D., and as a boy had heard Pantænus, the founder of the school, as well as Clement. His father was one of the first victims of the persecution in 202 or 203, and Origen, on whom the support of the family devolved, began his career as a teacher by giving lessons in grammar. After a short time the bishop, Demetrius, appointed him to the head of the catechetical school, over which he presided until 231. Long-standing difficulties with the bishop then came to a head. Origen, deprived of his place in the school and compelled to leave Egypt,

established himself at Cæsarea in Palestine, where the rest
of his life was spent in teaching and writing.   He died in
254 at Tyre.

Origen's productivity was enormous.   Besides his critical
labours on the Greek Old Testament, he made exegetical
commentaries or series of homilies on many books of the
Old Testament and most of the New; he took an active part
in the controversies of the time, and kept up an extensive
correspondence.   His defence of Christianity against the
attack of Celsus is an apology of a new kind.   The treatise
"On the First Principles" (of Christian philosophy) is the
first systematic exposition of Christian theology.   It is this
work with which we are especially concerned here.

At the outset the author gives a succinct statement of
the faith which the church has received by tradition from
the Apostles.   In the conflict of opinions this is the only
norm; nothing is to be accepted as truth which is in any
way at variance with this apostolic tradition.   But the
Apostles delivered thus only the articles which are necessary
for all Christians to believe, and often without explanation
or reason.   To many questions which a thinking mind cannot help asking the rule of faith gives no answer.   Investigation and speculation have, therefore, room and right
beside and beyond, though not against, the ecclesiastical
standards.   Systematic theology thus begins with an apology
for its existence.   Of the four books into which the work is
divided the first treats of God and rational existences; the
second of the world and mundane creatures, and of the
soul and its destiny; the third has for its principal subject
the freedom of the will, and the conflict men have to sustain
with the devil and his hosts; the fourth is on the inspiration
of the Scriptures and their interpretation, concluding with
a recapitulation of the main points discussed in the work.

In the schools of Alexandria Platonism had aways been
the prevailing philosophy.   It had, indeed, appropriated
much from other sources—from Aristotle, from the Stoics,
and from the later Pythagoreans—but it Platonised what-

ever it took, in the faith that all good thoughts were Platonic. The Alexandrian Platonists had a strong antipathy for every kind of materialism. They were not satisfied to rest in the dualism of mind and matter,[1] or, in religious terms, of God and the world, which Plato himself had not overcome; they sought a solution which, from the premises of the immaterialist conception of reality, should be as complete and unitary as the Stoic system from its materialist premises. We find this endeavour in Philo; the speculations of Basilides and Valentinus show further advance in this direction; it was in Origen's time that the goal was reached. He himself, after he had already been for several years the principal of the Christian school, attended the lectures of Ammonius Saccas, the reputed founder of the Neoplatonist school; Plotinus was a younger contemporary; Porphyry in his youth had seen the aged Origen, perhaps at Cæsarea or at Tyre.[2]

As in Valentinus and Plotinus, God is for Origen transcendent in the proper meaning of that much misapplied term. He is the μονάς or ἑνάς, absolute and simple unity. Philo called his Absolute *Nous*, "Intellect"; Origen, with Plotinus, goes beyond this: the One transcends the Plotinian categories of thought and being (ἐπέκεινα νοῦ καὶ οὐσίας). The problem of Origen, as of every similar metaphysical monism, is how from this Absolute, one, simple, unchangeable, the manifold universe of becoming, change, and dissolution can be derived—how the all-exclusive unity can be the origin of all existence; and, above all, how to escape making the Good the source of evil. Plotinus, as has been shown in another place,[3] interposed between God and the material world a descending series of emanations, the first and highest of which was the Nous, or Universal Intellect. Origen, following Philonic and Christian rather than Pla-

---

[1] The Platonic matter is not the gross stuff of which what we call material things are made, nevertheless it is an eternal somewhat besides God. See Vol. I, p. 503 and note 1.

[2] On these philosophers, see Vol. I, pp. 533 *ff.*

[3] See Vol. I, pp. 533 *f.*

tonic terminology, gives this place to the Logos, or Universal Reason. In the Scriptures this intermediary has various other names: Son, First-Born, Only-Begotten, Christ. It is the Wisdom which was the beginning of God's ways, generated before the earth was made (Prov. 8, 22 *ff*.); an efflux of the glory of the Almighty (Wisd. 7, 25 *f*.; *cf*. Heb. 1, 3), and therefore of the same essence with him (ὁμοούσιος); distinct yet not separate, like the sunbeam and the sun. Plotinus uses the same illustration; the figure—but not the meaning—is familiar to those who recite the Nicene creed: φῶς ἐκ φωτός, "Light derived from Light." Another simile, which excludes the imagination of corporeity, is volition proceeding from thought.

For the emanation of the Logos, Origen employs the term "generation," [1] which was established in the use of the church. It is the process by which the Father is father and the Son son, and since this relation is eternal Origen speaks of "eternal generation," *sicut splendor generatur a luce*. "There never was a time when the Son was not"— the words became a watch-cry, or a war-cry, in later controversies.

The Son is generated of the essence (οὐσία) of the Father,[2] an eternally distinct divine *hypostasis*.[3] But though of the same essence with the Father, the Son is not on an equality with the Father. The Father alone is unbegotten, that is, to him belongs the aseity of godhead; he is God himself and of himself. The Son is begotten, a second god, worthy of second honour after the universal God; he is god, but not God. The Father is incomparably good; the Son is not good of himself, but an image of the goodness of God—and so on, consistently. The Logos, or hypostatic divine Wisdom, is inferior to the transcendent God, because it contains in itself the *logoi*, or (immaterial) germinal principles,

---

[1] Plotinus (i. 5, 6 *f*.) uses the same word of the emanation of the Nous.

[2] Οὐσία in a Platonic sense.

[3] The word in Origen's use signifies "rational individual."

of the multiplicity of existences,[1] thus standing between the absolute One and the phenomenal many; he is the first-born of all creation, and *in him* were created all things, visible and invisible (Col. 1, 15–17).

The Spirit is as much below the Son as the Son is inferior to the Father. It is eternally (*i. e.*, timelessly) created by the Son, and of all things (*i. e.*, the rational existences) that were created by the Logos, it is most highly honoured. In revelation it was an instrumentality of the Logos, but its specific operation is in the saints, that is, in the members of the Christian church. It thus occupies the place which Scripture and the unreflective faith of the church assigned it; to Origen's philosophy it is superfluous.

From eternity a multitude of immaterial intelligences, or rational souls, were given existence by the Logos, in all respects equal, endowed with freedom.[2] The Son loved what he had made (*cf.* Wisd. 11, 24), and granted to them to partake of his nature in the measure in which they severally clave to him in love. Some of them were possessed by a more ardent love of the author of their being, others by a slighter affection; and these last had less part in him. Thus, in the exercise of their freedom, the rational souls in different degrees declined from their original, not by positive error but by defect of love.

The consequence of this alienation was that souls were invested with bodies, and a material universe was brought into being for their abode. Those which have declined least from their original have a corporeal vesture of fine ætherial matter; they are principalities, powers, angels. The devil and his angels, the demons of various ranks who swarm in the air, are the souls that have fallen deepest. Between angels and demons are men; they too are rational existences, lapsed from the intelligible world, and incorporated in an

---

[1] The term is Stoic; but the Stoic *logoi* were not immaterial.
[2] In maintaining their equality Origen contradicts the Gnostic theory of the superiority of a favoured class of "spiritual" men; their freedom exempts God from responsibility for the evil that came by their fall.

earthly and mortal body vivified by an animal soul.   Among
human souls, again, some have sunk deeper than others; the
inequalities of birth and fortune, apparently unmerited sufferings—as of one born blind—are thus explained without
admitting chance or fate, or the necessity of attributing the
evils in the world to another power in order to save the justice and goodness of God, as in vulgar Gnosticism.

Freedom of will remains in fallen spirits, and in it the
possibility of rising stage by stage to the highest or sinking
to the lowest.   The goal set before all is to recover their
primal estate.   The human will is free, but its original
equilibrium is lost; in the body the soul is exposed to the
defilement of matter and the temptation of demons who
seek to draw it deeper into ruin.   And not only man, but
the highest angels and the heavenly bodies, with the whole
creation which has been unwillingly made subject to vanity
($\mu\alpha\tau\alpha\iota\acute{o}\tau\eta\varsigma$, Romans 8, 20), are in need of salvation.

To save the world, the Son of God (the Logos) united with
himself a rational soul—the only one of all that had never
erred nor departed from him—and sheathed, as it were, in
this soul, entered an undefiled body.   Origen calls this not
incarnation (*ensarkōsis*, "enfleshment"), but "humanise-
ment" (*enanthrōpēsis*).   Christ is Theanthrōpos, God-Man;
he even uses the word "composite."   But he takes pains
to distinguish in thought what belongs to the divine and
the human respectively.   It was the human body only that
suffered (the divine is impassible); and "the only-begotten
Son of God, the Word of God, and his Wisdom and Righteousness and Truth, is not circumscribed in the confines of
a body" (the divine is not subject to spatial limitations).

Being the image of the invisible God, Christ is a revelation of him, "for by him by whom the Son is known, the
Father also is known."   He is the Way that leads to the
Father; by it those who fell from their first estate may
return.   Christ calls those who are in the flesh, that first he
may make them to be conformed to the incarnate Logos,
and then lead them on to the vision of himself as he was

before his incarnation (the Logos in his divine nature), that so they may say: "Though formerly we knew Christ after the flesh, henceforth we know him so no more."

In his eschatology Origen departs more widely from the common belief of the church. He combated the crassly material imagination of the thousand-year reign of Christ on earth, which was not only entertained by the vulgar, but, in defence against the objections of educated heathen and especially in the conflict with Gnosticism, had become a touchstone of orthodoxy. The Revelation of John, which was the chief source of these conceptions and gave them apostolic authority, Origen interpreted allegorically; it was a cardinal principle of his hermeneutics that whatever sounds material and carnal is to be taken figuratively in a spiritual sense.

Regarding the material body as a prison in which the exiled soul is confined by reason of its fall, the resurrection of the flesh, however purified, contradicted his very idea of salvation. Origen ranged himself on the side of Paul, "Flesh and blood cannot inherit the kingdom of God." The spiritual body with which the soul is hereafter to be invested will be organised by a germinal *logos* which now exists in the body; thus individual identity is preserved, without identity of material constitution. Origen's de-materialisation extends not only to heaven but to hell; its fire is not a material and external fire torturing sensitive bodies, but the inner fires of conscience and remorse, a suffering at once punitive and purificatory.

By progress in knowledge and virtue human souls may attain, through finer and purer embodiments, even to the highest of the archangelic ranks. The goal of all—angels and men and demons—is to reascend to their first estate and be again the pure, bodiless intelligences they were before their lapse, in loving communion and participation with the Logos. Even the devil and his angels will thus return to God, and when this end is reached the material universe will be dissolved into its primal nothingness. This is the "restitution of all things" (ἀποκατάστασις παντῶν) of which the Apostle speaks (Acts 3, 21). Then God will be all in all as at the beginning (1 Cor. 15, 28). But inasmuch as souls are always free, it is possible for them again to fall away, and thus the cycle is renewed. There will be innumerable worlds after this, as there have been before it.[1] The doctrine of the restoration of all things is not the pious hope of a sentimental universalism—from such emotional promptings Origen is wholly free. It is the necessary counterpart of his theory of the nature of souls and of their lapse, and is demanded both by his metaphysics and his theodicy.

In the last book of the "De Principiis" Origen develops a theory of the threefold sense of the divine revelation in Scripture: there is the literal and historical sense, which is all that simple-minded readers see in a passage; the more intelligent find in it a moral lesson; while the truly enlightened man alone discovers, besides these, an allegory of profound spiritual truth. Many things, not only in the Old Testament but in the New, taken literally, are impossible or unreasonable or even immoral. The purpose of revelation in such cases is to constrain the reader, by the unacceptableness of the apparent sense, to search beneath the letter for the hidden meaning. This is the first clear enunciation of the theory of the multiple sense of Scripture which to the end of the Middle Ages was generally accepted.

Origen was attacked from all sides. His theology had ideas enough in it to furnish subjects of controversy for centuries. The simple believers, to whom all philosophising about matters of faith lay under the presumption of unbelief, found more specific heresies in his doctrines. The lapse of souls was palpably Gnostic, and so was the whole conception of salvation. The dematerialised eschatology was one of their great stumbling-blocks. Without a resurrection of the flesh they could imagine no satisfaction in a future life; the delights of everlasting rational thinking and participation

---

[1] The resemblance to Stoic doctrine is obvious.

in the divine Reason were none to them; the final restoration, in which even the devil was to be saved, was peculiarly obnoxious. Besides, it was all against plain Scripture and the immemorial faith of the church. The anthropomorphists, especially strong among the monks, were scandalised by his immaterial deity. Their God was as the Bible described him, with a body and members like theirs. They triumphantly proved his corporeity by Scripture: Does it not say "God is spirit"? and does not everybody know that spirit is material? The antipathy of the common man for Origenism is easy to understand. Deprived of an imaginable God and an imaginable heaven, what would be left of his religion?

The central problem of Christian theology from the beginning had been to reconcile the deity of Christ with monotheism. The Apologists found the solution in the doctrine of the Logos. Origen gave to this doctrine a metaphysical form and foundation. But the unity of the godhead in his system was a metaphysical, not a personal unity; he derived the Logos-Son from the Absolute-Father by a process which, under another name, was the emanation which the Gnostics had brought into disrepute; and the Son remained a deity of inferior rank. In the following generations other theories of the relation of the Son to the Father, based on a different fundamental philosophy, were proposed only to be refused by the church; the Neoplatonic character was permanently impressed on Christian theology by Origen. But Origen's system as a whole was not accepted. In particular, the subordination of the Son to the Father, and the inferiority of the Spirit to both, which was an essential feature of it, the necessary consequence of its metaphysic, was rejected. The eternal equality of the three Persons of the Trinity became, as we shall see, the only orthodoxy. His peculiar theory of the incarnation was forgotten; the apocatastasis was finally branded as heresy. Yet Origen makes an era in the history of Christian theology, and however widely the dogma defined at

Nicæa differs from the Trinity of Origen, it would not have been but for him, and it was ultimately made tolerable to the Eastern church by a return to him.

Down to the middle of the third century the church in different regions and different times had suffered from a number of more or less severe persecutions, which, however, seldom lasted long and did little to check the spread of Christianity. Decius (249–252) was the first to set the whole machinery of the empire in motion to seek out the Christians and constrain them to renounce their faith and conform to the religion of the state. Those who obstinately refused to offer sacrifice or burn incense before an image were tortured and put to death. Many suffered in this way, among them the bishops of several of the great sees. The number of those who fell away was vastly larger; in some places it was almost the whole community. The persecution lasted, with a brief intermission and some changes of method, for about ten years. Then for more than forty years, from the accession of Gallienus (260 A. D.) until the nineteenth year of Diocletian (303 A. D.), the church enjoyed to all intents and purposes complete toleration. It quickly recovered from the ravages of the Decian persecution and grew more rapidly than in any former generation. Christians were found everywhere and in every rank of society—in the army, the government bureaus, in the imperial household, sometimes in high charges. Diocletian's wife and daughter are said to have been Christians.

The last persecution, and by far the worst, was begun by Diocletian in 303, but continued in the East with even greater severity after his retirement. An edict of toleration was signed by three of the four emperors in 311, but it was not until two years later that it brought much relief to the churches in the regions over which Maximin ruled. The Edict of Milan, issued by Constantine and Licinius in 313, put Christianity on a complete equality with the old religions: "Every man has full liberty to worship whatever he chooses." The places of worship and other property of

12

the church which had been seized during the persecution were restored without payment. Not only the religious liberty of individuals but the rights of the church as a corporation were established. In 323 Constantine, himself a Christian,[1] became sole emperor, and with freedom and imperial favour the church entered on a period of great and rapid expansion. Henceforth, except for the short reign of Julian (361–363 A. D.), the emperors were Christians, and before the end of the century the temples were closed and all acts of heathen worship forbidden by law.

The controversies over the deity of Christ continued, only temporarily intermitted in the crises of persecution, and growing in violence with every revival. Parties were formed; bishops excommunicated one another; synods condemned rival opinions as heretical and assumed to define the Catholic faith; ecclesiastical politics played an increasingly prominent part in the struggle. When, on the death of Licinius, Asia Minor, Syria, and Egypt came under the rule of Constantine, he found the church rent by these conflicts, and even the public order disturbed.

The most serious of these dissensions was the Arian controversy. Arius, a presbyter of Alexandria, had in his youth studied under Lucian, the head of the school in Antioch, where the Peripatetic philosophy had greater influence than in Alexandria, and had there imbibed, at least in germ, the views which were later called Arian. In Arius's (ultimately Aristotelian) definition the distinguishing mark of deity is self-existence. It followed that the Son, who owed his existence to the Father, was not God. He rejected the theory of emanation which, whether under that name or another, was involved in the doctrine of the Logos-Son. The Logos was for him a creature, brought into existence by the will of God before the creation of the world, the first of all creatures (Col. 1, 15), existing before time.[2] He, like all

---

[1] He was not baptised till shortly before his death, in 337.

[2] Time began with the creation of the heavenly bodies whose revolutions measure it.

other things, came into existence from non-existence; there
was a time when he was not. So far from being of the same
nature with the Father, the Son is in all respects unlike the
distinctive nature (οὐσία) of the Father.[1] The name God
is applied to him liturgically, we might say; but he is not
God in reality.

For these heresies an Alexandrian synod in 321 deposed
Arius and a dozen or more of his supporters. Arius retorted
the accusation of heresy upon his bishop, Alexander, whom
he charged with Sabellian errors, that is, with making
Father and Son the same being.[2] In Palestine, whither
they betook themselves, Arius and his companions found a
friendly reception. Many bishops in Syria and Asia Minor
sympathised with them. Eusebius, the bishop of the capital (Nicomedia), took up their cause, and tried to array the
episcopate of Asia Minor and Syria to bring pressure to
bear on Alexander for the restoration of Arius. Alexander
was not idle; he circulated a summary of the teachings of
Arius, "the most pernicious of all the heresies that have
ever been, the precursor of Antichrist." Emissaries of the
two parties were everywhere, presenting their side and col-
lecting the signatures of bishops. The entire ecclesiastical
East was in commotion.

Constantine, having failed to compose the strife by good
advice, convoked a council of the whole church to settle
this issue and other dissensions of minor consequence. This
first œcumenical council met at Nicæa, in the near neighbourhood of the imperial residence. There, in the early
summer of 325, about three hundred bishops, or presbyters
delegated by their bishops, assembled. By far the greater
number were from Asia Minor, Syria, and Egypt; the Latin
West had hardly more than a half-dozen, including two
Roman presbyters representing Pope Sylvester. The emperor himself presided at the opening session, and made his
influence felt throughout.

The deposition of Arius was confirmed, and he was ban-

[1] Arius uses οὐσία in a Peripatetic sense.   [2] See above, p. 164 f.

ished to Illyricum. The personal issue being thus disposed
of, the council took in hand the framing of a symbol in
which the Catholic faith, particularly concerning the nature
of Christ, should be so defined as to preclude dispute and
thus secure the unity and peace of the church. How far it
was from achieving this result generations of bitter strife
were to show.

The basis of the Nicene symbol was the creed in use in
the church of Cæsarea in Palestine, which by some changes
in phraseology and the insertion of some new clauses was
fortified on the points in controversy.

The text of this creed is as follows: [1]

We believe in one God, Father Supreme, maker of all things, visible
and invisible. And in one Lord Jesus Christ, the Son of God, begotten
of (ἐκ)[2] the Father, as his only Son, that is, of the essence of the Father,
God of (ἐκ) God, light of light, true God of true God, begotten, not
made, of the same essence (ὁμοούσιος) with the Father, through whom
all things in heaven and in earth came into being; who for us men and
our salvation came down and was made flesh, became man, suffered,
and rose on the third day, ascended to heaven, and is coming to judge
the living and dead. And [we believe] in the Holy Spirit.

To the symbol is added an anathema, specifically condemning the teachings of Arius:

Those who say, "There was a time when he was not, and before he
was begotten he did not exist," or assert that the Son of God is of a
different subsistence (ὑπόστασις) or essence (οὐσία), or created, or subject
to change or variation, the Catholic Church anathematizes.

Some of the expressions in this symbol were objectionable
to many members of the council, especially the use of the
word *homoousios* to define the relation of the Son to the
Father. The word bore the stigma of heresy fastened upon
it a half-century before by a large and representative synod

[1] The so-called Nicene Creed as it is used in modern liturgies is not
the creed adopted at Nicæa or by any other council.

[2] The preposition here and in the following clauses means "out of,"
signifying source or origin.

of the bishops of Syria and Asia Minor which deposed Paul of Samosata, bishop of Antioch, for teaching that the Logos (or Wisdom, or Spirit) in God corresponded to the rational faculty in man, having no distinct personality. "God, together with the Logos, is one person," he said, and he employed the word *homoousios* to express precisely this identity—"the same person." To the great majority of the Orientals, then and afterward, the term seemed to give countenance to a doctrine no less obnoxious to them than that of Arius, a doctrine which maintained the uniper-sonality of God in such a way as to leave no room for per-sonal distinctions in the godhead, and for which the name of Sabellius served as a prejudicial label. The Origenists solved the difficulty for themselves by using οὐσία of the one essence or nature of the godhead and ὑπόστασις for the eternal personal distinctions in it; but the council seemed to obliterate this discrimination by using the two in the anathema as synonyms.

Whatever opposition there was in the council was over-borne. Hosius of Cordova, who had the theological ear of the emperor, insisted on *homoousios*. In Latin οὐσία and ὑπόστασις were expressed indifferently by *substantia;* and *unius substantiæ* seemed the exact expression to contradict Arius's assertion that the Logos was in all respects unlike the *substantia* (οὐσία) of the Father. Constantine let it be known that the word had his approval, and the bishops who objected to it most strongly made haste to subscribe with such grace as they could. They doubtless said to them-selves that, after all, the word was ambiguous enough to cover a multitude of opinions.

The controversy was not long in coming. The protago-nists were on the one side Eusebius of Nicomedia and on the other Athanasius, who as a deacon had attended his bishop, Alexander, to Nicæa, and in 328 succeeded him in the episcopate of Alexandria. Athanasius was so con-spicuous a figure in the half-century after Nicæa as the leader of the party which stood immovable on the *ipsissima verba* of the symbol, above all the *homoousios*, without compromise or accommodation; he wrote so voluminously in its defence, and suffered so much in exile and flight for his intransigeance, that it is not strange that the Nicene dogma is called Athanasian, and that it is popularly supposed that Athanasius had a chief hand in framing the creed—which he assuredly did not.[1]

We may fortunately spare ourselves the history of this unedifying strife. Suffice it, then, to say that before the death of Constantine (337), Eusebius having meantime become his adviser in theology and ecclesiastical affairs, Arius had been recalled from exile; the Arians restored to communion by a council at Tyre, with the approval of the emperor; Athanasius deposed by the same council for abuse of power, and consigned by the emperor to banishment at Trier in Gaul.

The Latin West, with few exceptions, held to the Nicene symbol. They understood that it excluded from the church the heretics who said that Christ was not God, and did not see why the Greeks should make such a pother about the particular words by which this salutary end was accomplished. The influence of Athanasius, who after his second extrusion from his see (339), took refuge in Italy, attached the leading Latin bishops to his person and party. They refused to recognise his deposition, and regarded him as a much-maligned and persecuted man.

In the East, on the contrary, Constantine was no sooner dead than the church laid on the shelf the creed he had imposed on it, by framing new confessions of faith in which the shibboleths of Nicæa are eloquent by their absence, and which could be subscribed by moderate men of all parties.[2]   When

---

[1] It is a much less excusable error that the issue at Nicæa was, as is wittily said, an *iota*—*homoousios* vs. *homoiousios*. Ὅμοιος κατ' οὐσίαν is Athanasius, not Arius; the homoiousian party which arose after Nicæa was no less anti-Arian than the homoousian.

[2] Notable among these is one adopted by a synod at Antioch in 341. It must be remembered that the Nicene Creed had no such sacredness as it eventually acquired. It had the authority of a general council; but no one in that day imagined that the church which had made it had no power to change it or set it aside by another council.

Constantius became sole emperor, in 353, he set himself to bring the Latin episcopate into line with the overwhelming majority of the Orientals. First he forced them to acknowledge the deposition of Athanasius, banishing the few recalcitrants, among them Pope Liberius. The next step was formally to supersede the Nicene symbol. To this end the emperor convoked two councils, or rather an œcumenical council sitting in two sections, that for the Eastern half of the empire meeting at the Isaurian Seleucia (in Cilicia), while the Western bishops met at Ariminium (Rimini), in Italy. Both adopted an identical creed, which contained, indeed, nothing controversially Arian, but on the other hand nothing to which any but the extreme Arians (Anomœans) could not assent. The Son was declared to be "like the Father who begat him, as the Scriptures say"; the phrase "*in all things* like"[1] was carefully avoided. A statement was annexed to the creed to the effect that, inasmuch as there is nothing in the Scriptures about the "essence" ($o\vec{v}\sigma\acute{\iota}a$) of the Father and the Son, nor of the $\vec{v}\pi\acute{o}\sigma\tau a\sigma\iota\varsigma$ of Father, Son, and Holy Spirit, it is the will of the council that these terms be not used any more. The symbol of Seleucia-Rimini was sent around to the bishops who had not been in attendance on the council for their subscription, and almost without exception they signed it. The church thus with virtual unanimity substituted for the creed of Nicæa a symbol from which the essential unity of the Son with the Father and even his essential likeness to the Father was eliminated, and put the very terminology of that creed under the ban. Constantine had tried to restore peace in the Catholic church by a creed that should exclude, as he doubtless was persuaded, a few contentious heretics; Constantius sought to secure unity by a symbol which, avoiding obnoxious phraseology and divisive questions, could be assented to by all but a few irreconcilables at either extreme. Neither plan achieved the desired result.

In November, 361, Constantius died and was succeeded by his cousin Julian, whose heart's desire was the revival

[1] A phrase early used by Athanasius.

of the old religions. In his philosophic detestation of all "Galileans" he ignored their dogmatic varieties. The heretical sects against whom Constantius had legislated enjoyed an interval of repose, and numerous Catholic bishops who were for one reason or another sojourning in foreign parts, among them Athanasius, were allowed to return to their sees, a measure decidedly not conducive to peace where they found another incumbent in possession. The episode did not last long, for after Julian's death in the Persian campaign (June, 363) Christianity came back to power.

The great majority of Latin bishops had given their adhesion to the creed of Rimini, not because they had seen a new light, but because the doctrinal wind had changed at Constantinople. When, therefore, they were left to themselves by Julian's impartial contempt, Athanasius and Pope Liberius had little difficulty in bringing back the Western episcopate, with few exceptions, to the Nicene formula. In the East the movement in the same direction was slower, but it was in the end accomplished. A council of Eastern bishops convened by the Emperor Theodosius at Constantinople in 381, after condemning heresies on the right hand and the left—Arians of both the radical and the moderate type, Semi-Arians, who denied that the Holy Spirit was of the same essence as the Father and the Son, Sabellians, Marcellians, Apollinarians—reaffirmed the Nicene Creed without addition or subtraction, and adopted an explanatory statement on the Trinity, which has not been preserved. The heretics were by imperial edicts dispossessed of their churches, and their assemblies for worship were prohibited. The laws were constantly made more stringent, the enforcement more energetic.

The return to the Nicene Creed pure and simple was made possible by a construction of the doctrine of the Trinity which conserved both the essential oneness of the godhead and the distinctions of Father, Son, and Spirit. The divine nature, or essence ($o\dot{v}\sigma\acute{\iota}a$), is one and the same in all; but Father, Son, and Spirit are three eternally distinct "subsistences" (ὑποστάσεις). The Father is "ungenerated" (self-existent); the Son is "generated" timelessly (in a metaphysical sense) by the Father; the Spirit "proceeds" (John 15, 26) from the Father.

This solution, which was found by theologians of the middle party (homoiousians), comes in the end from Origen. But the transcendent deity of Origen has disappeared, and with it the conception of the Logos-Son as an intermediate being between the Absolute and the universe; with it, too, the inferiority of the Son to the Father and of the Spirit to the Son. The whole tendency was to make the three not only coessential but coequal. The appearance of tritheism in this pluralistic monotheism was not overcome; the unity of the godhead resolves itself into a "source of deity" (Athanasius), or into a mere generic unity; in either case, as such, impersonal. Interpreted in this way, the Nicene Creed excluded all varieties of unipersonalism, Sabellian as well as Arian, and to this it owed its success.

One of the features of this New-Nicene theology was the elevation of the Holy Spirit to equal partnership in the hypostatic Trinity. The creed of Nicæa said only, "We believe in the Holy Spirit," without saying what they believed about it. Athanasius in his later years desired the addition of an explicit statement that the Spirit also was of the same essence (ὁμοούσιον), but found few willing to go so far. Some held, with Origen, that the Spirit was a creature; others found no scriptural warrant for applying the name God to it, nor had it ever been, for itself, an object of worship in the church. At Constantinople, as we have seen, the "adversaries of the Spirit," or Semi-Arians, who would not call the Spirit God, were anathematised in the same breath with the old Arians who denied the name and nature to the Son. Thus the Trinity was completed. The doctrine has been since the fourth century the characteristic of Christian theism, and is still professed, though frequently with extremely unorthodox interpretations, by all Christians who call themselves orthodox.

The outcome of the Arian controversy was the dogma

that the Son, or Logos, who was incarnate in Jesus Christ, was not an inferior kind of deity, but of the same nature as the Father, an eternally distinct person in the unity of the godhead. The incarnation itself now became the central problem, and the strife over the person of Christ was longer and bitterer than over the deity of the Son; the schisms to which it gave rise persist to our day in the so-called national churches of the East.

The mass of plain Christians had doubtless always taken the incarnation mythologically, and found no difficulty in it. Very early the opinion emerged that Christ's body was not a real flesh-and-blood body.[1] The earliest philosophy of it, in the Apologists, was that the Logos, a deity of the second order, intermediary between God and the universe, assumed a human body and dwelt among men to reveal God and the knowledge in which is eternal life. But where it was held that eternal life is not achieved by knowledge of God but by participation in the divine nature, the incarnation necessarily had a different significance: God became man that (through his union with humanity) man might be made god (that is, immortal).[2] This salvation by deification must embrace the whole man; to accomplish it the Son must not merely be God in a human body, but must really assume humanity—must *be* man, body and mind.

The question had been touched on incidentally in more than one phase of the early Arian controversy, but it was brought into the focus of discussion by Apollinarius of Laodicea, in Syria, about 350 A. D. Apollinarius belonged to the strict homoousian party, and stood with his friend Athanasius for the Nicene Creed to the foot of the letter. It was evidently the prevailing conception in his surroundings that in Jesus Christ both the God and the man were complete and distinct. Apollinarius rejects this theory, because the incarnate Christ would then be not one person, but two; not the one Son of God, but two sons, once by

[1] See above, p. 153.
[2] So Irenæus and Athanasius. See above, pp. 162 *f.*

nature and once by adoption; and there would be in the same subject two independent and possibly conflicting wills, a human and a divine. He endeavoured, therefore, to explain the incarnation in such a way as to secure the unity of the person of Christ while maintaining both his divinity and his humanity. The analogy of human personality suggested the solution. As in man, body and soul, or, according to another psychology, body, soul, and intellect (Nous), constitute one person, so in Christ, the body of flesh with its animal soul, and the Logos, which in him fills the place of the human Nous, or rational soul, constitute one person. One *divine* person; for between the Logos and the body is such a union that not only their activity but their *nature* is one. The body of Christ is the body of God; in crucifying his body the Jews crucified God; nay, even "the flesh, as the flesh of God, *is* God." Like Irenæus, Apollinarius draws the sacramental consequence: "His flesh, by virtue of the deity essentially united with it, gives life to men; we are saved by partaking of it (in the Eucharist) as of nutriment."

In this divine-human person the man was evidently incomplete, lacking human intelligence and self-determination. But, opponents urged, if men are saved through the assumption of humanity by the divine Logos, the assumption must be complete or the salvation of man will be correspondingly incomplete. The Catholic faith, so a Roman synod declared, was *perfectum deum perfectum suscepisse hominem*. The doctrine of Apollinarius was condemned; but the issues he had raised were not so easily laid, and before long the whole church was in turmoil over them. Athanasius held views of the person of Christ, which, though less clearly thought out or avowed, were so much like those of Apollinarius that writings of Apollinarius had no difficulty in circulating under Athanasius' name; and throughout the controversy the Alexandrians in general were inclined to assert Christ in the incarnation so wholly God as to curtail or nullify his human nature, while their opponents were no less concerned to maintain unimpaired his complete humanity than his true divinity. The more moderate of the Alexandrians held, against the Apollinarists, that Christ had a human Nous (rational soul), as well as body and (animal) soul, but that this Nous had no independent human activity. The completeness of the human nature was thus preserved in its elements, but not in its functions; the will and the whole rational and moral life of Christ was merely divine. The two natures are only theoretically distinguished; in reality they are fused in an "essential unification"—Apollinarius's own phrase.

The Antiochians denied that there was any such fusion or confusion of humanity and divinity; each was complete in itself and distinct. The man Jesus Christ had a natural human development, human weakness, human needs, and a human will, which, though constantly inclined to good by the Logos, did not for that reason cease to be a free will. He was like all other men, differing in no respect from his fellows except that the Logos was graciously pleased to dwell in him as in a temple, but this gracious indwelling did not change his nature. The unity of the divine and human natures in him was a moral, not a physical, unity. They laboured to overcome the dual personality of which their adversaries accused this doctrine, but with incomplete success.

In 428 Nestorius, a priest of Antioch, became bishop of Constantinople. In a sermon preached shortly afterward he expressed his disapproval of the custom of calling the Virgin Mary "Mother of God" (θεοτόκος): "She did not bear the deity . . . she bore a man, an organ of deity." To plain Christian piety, which worshipped Christ as God, speculations about the number of natures in him seemed nothing short of blasphemy. The monks especially, whose theology was of the muscular kind, demonstrated their reverence for the Mother of God by riots, and the suppression of these disturbances did not increase the bishop's popularity. Cyril, bishop of Alexandria, forthwith entered the lists as the champion of the unity of Christ's nature against those who made two of him. His favourite formula was: "*one* enfleshed nature of the God-Logos"; "*of* (ἐκ) two natures *one*" (*sc.* person). The human nature is impersonal; it is only the garment of the Logos, which has thus embodied itself in humanity but remains in this association the One it was before. Christ was human as having human *nature*, not as a human being.

A general council was convened in Ephesus in the summer of 431. By a stroke of audacity Cyril, who with his partisans was early on the ground, opened the council before the arrival of the Pope's legates or the bishops from Syria and Asia Minor, and proceeded to depose Nestorius. When the Oriental bishops came, they held a session by themselves and deposed Cyril for his violation of conciliar rights. The emperor thought it would be for the peace of the world to be rid of both of them. Nestorius went back to his old monastery near Antioch, whence he was subsequently sent into more distant banishment; but Cyril escaped to Egypt and defied both the sentence of the council and the edict of the emperor. The efforts of the government patched up a temporary truce between the contending parties, but a few years later the strife broke out again, fiercer than ever. A monk named Eutyches, an ultra-Cyrillian, was condemned by a local synod in Constantinople in 448 for denying that the humanity of Christ was of the same nature as ours (ὁμοούσιος ἡμῖν): before the union there were two natures, after it but one (viz., the divine nature). Dioscurus, of Alexandria, seized the opportunity to reopen the hereditary episcopal war on his rival in Constantinople and the Oriental bishops. His influence at court procured the calling of a general council at Ephesus in 449, and his own appointment to preside at it. By this council Eutyches was pronounced orthodox and restored; the bishop of Constantinople, Flavian, and a half-dozen of the leading Oriental bishops were deposed, amid proceedings so scandalous as amply to deserve the name with which Pope Leo stigmatised the council, "latrocinium Ephesinum"; and the "anathemas" of

Cyril, in which he let himself go the whole length both of his logic and his language, were declared to be the orthodox faith.

The death of Theodosius II in 450 was the downfall of the party in the court and the imperial household which had been for Eutyches. The new rulers, Theodosius' sister, Pulcheria, and her husband, the emperor Marcian, leaned the other way. To put an end to the strife they convened another general council at Chalcedon in 451. In numbers it exceeded all its predecessors; more than five hundred and twenty bishops sat in it, all from the eastern half of the empire, except the Pope's legates (one of whom presided) and two African bishops. Dioscurus was brought to account for the doings of his "robber synod" and deposed, the sentence being read by the legate in the name of Pope Leo—"by us and by this council."

The council then, after reaffirming the creed of Nicæa and that of Constantinople (381), adopted a statement intended to exclude on one side the errors which had been labelled with the name of Nestorius and on the other those of Eutyches. The definition of the orthodox doctrine of the person of Christ is in substance that which Pope Leo had sent to the council of 449 (the so-called "Tome of Leo") but for the sake of conciliation as much use as possible was made of the phraseology of Cyril.[1]

The statement affirms that Christ is perfect equally in his divinity and his humanity; he is of the same nature (ὁμοούσιος) with the Father in his divinity, of the same nature with us in his humanity, in all respects like us except for sin. He was begotten of the Father before all ages as regards his divinity, and, as regards his humanity, in these last times born of Mary the Virgin, the Mother of God; the same Christ, Son, Lord, Only-Begotten, in[2] two natures, without confusion, without change, without division, with-

---

[1] Especially as he expressed himself in a letter to Nestorius, penned in a cautious moment and disguising his real opinion.

[2] Leo's ἐν triumphed over Cyril's ἐκ.

out separation; the difference of the two natures being in no wise done away by reason of the union, but rather the peculiarity of each nature being preserved and concurring in one nature and one individual (ὑπόστασις); he not being divided nor separated into two persons, but one and the same Son and Only-Begotten, God-Logos, the Lord Jesus Christ.

The West stood fast by the decree of Chalcedon in the sense of the Tome of Leo. The situation in the East was very different. There a large part of the church regarded this doctrine as a thinly disguised Nestorianism. To them Christ was God without any circumlocution; "two natures," however qualified or extenuated, left him but half God. These Monophysites ("partisans of *one nature*"), as their opponents named them, who were the great majority in Egypt, and everywhere counted in their number most of the monks, took their doctrine from Cyril in those writings in which he spoke out his whole mind, especially from his "anathemas," which had been adopted by the council at Ephesus in 449.

Their watchword was "God was crucified." The emperor Zeno's attempt in 482 to unite the distracted church by a Henoticon, or formula of union, in which the doctrine of Chalcedon was virtually surrendered, failed; but it had an unexpected result—it made a breach with the Western church which lasted for a quarter of a century. The statement of Chalcedon was formally reaffirmed by the emperor Justin in 519. A Cyrillian interpretation was put upon it, to the exclusion of all others, by the Council of Constantinople in 553, and emphasised by the imperial condemnation of the writings of the Oriental opponents or critics of Cyril. The Chalcedonian formula is, therefore, the official orthodoxy of both the Eastern and the Western church, but is officially interpreted in contrary senses. The thoroughgoing Monophysites were not to be won back by such partial concessions; Egypt was almost solidly Monophysite, and the Coptic church, with its dependency, the church of

Abyssinia, the Armenian (Gregorian) church, and the Jacobite Syrians remain unreconciled to this day.

Another effort for union in the seventh century raised a new controversy over the question whether there were in Christ two wills, a divine and a human, or only one, the divine will. After fifty years of contention and vacillation, an œcumenical council at Constantinople in 681 decided for two, the human will obediently following and being subject to the divine; and anathematised, among others, Pope Honorius, for being of the other opinion.

CHAPTER VII

CHRISTIANITY

LATIN THEOLOGY. MONASTICISM

Latin Christianity—Augustine—The Trinity—The Pelagian Controversy—Augustine's Doctrine of Sin and Grace; Incomplete Reception in the Church—Asceticism: Hermits and Monasteries in Egypt—Monachism in other Lands—Benedict of Nursia—Mysticism: Dionysius the Areopagite and Maximus Confessor.

THE Christian church in the West was in the beginning a Greek-speaking church, and down to the end of the second century, in Rome as well as in the provinces, the literature which it produced was in Greek. Proconsular Africa seems to have been the first region where Christianity gained a foothold among a Latin-speaking population. There, in all probability, the earliest Latin translations of the books of the New Testament were made and a Christian literature in Latin had its beginnings. At the end of the second century and in the first decades of the third the African church had in Tertullian a writer who may fairly be said to have created Christian Latinity, and in whom a Western type of Christianity first appears. In the next generation Cyprian, bishop of Carthage (d. 258), was the greatest figure in all the West, a statesman of the church, who did more than any other to define and defend the catholic idea of the church. Before the third century was far advanced the Western church had become a Latin church; but there was close communication with the East. Greek authors were much read in the original or in translations; many of the leading men of the Latin church in the fourth century— men like Ambrose of Milan, Hilary of Poitiers, Lucifer of Cagliari—were learned in Greek theology, and several of them had lived in the East. The Latins were less inclined, in general, to subtleties of theological speculation than the Greeks, but they took their part in the controversies of the fourth and fifth centuries, and both at Nicæa and at Chalcedon the West shaped the dogma of the church.

The man who gave its distinctive character to Western Christianity was Augustine. Born at Tagaste, in Numidia, in 354, of a heathen father and a Christian mother, he was educated for the career of a rhetorician—we should say a professor of Latin literature. While a student at Carthage he was drawn into the company of the Manichæans,[1] and was for ten years or more a catechumen (*auditor*) in their church. His gradual disillusion was succeeded by a period in which Academic scepticism of a Ciceronian type seemed to him the proper attitude of mind in matters of religion. Meanwhile he had removed from Carthage to Rome, whence he was called to Milan to fill a public professorship. There the instruction of the great bishop Ambrose so far overcame his misunderstandings and prejudices about Catholic Christianity that he became a catechumen.

Augustine found his way to an intellectual acceptance of Christianity through translations[2] of Neoplatonic writings which came into his hands in Milan. In this philosophy both dualism and scepticism were overcome; by it, for him, the rationality of Christian doctrine was established. Neoplatonism was for Augustine much more than the bridge by which he passed over to the church; it entered into his religious experience, and its influence on his thinking was pervasive and permanent. In his earlier writings it predominates; in later years he was more biblical and more churchly, but his fundamental philosophy was unchanged. Coincident with the intellectual epoch which Platonism made in Augustine's life was a moral crisis. A recital of

[1] Manichæanism was a composite religion in which Christian (Gnostic) and Zoroastrian elements were combined in varying proportions. Its outstanding feature was a religious dualism. It was for a long time a serious competitor of Christianity, not only in the East, where it arose, but in Africa and Italy.

[2] By Victorinus.

the story of St. Antony and the lives of other ascetics wrought in him a violent revulsion of feeling. He loathed the life of sensual indulgence he had led; and from that time forth "concupiscence" was for him the prime and typical sin. This was the temper of the ascetic piety of the times, pagan as well as Christian; the Platonists no less than Paul taught him that to begin its ascent to God the soul must emancipate itself from the desires of the flesh.

After his baptism in Milan (Easter, 387), Augustine spent a short time in Rome and then returned to Africa. For a while he lived at Tagaste with a few like-minded friends in a kind of voluntary monastic society; but in 391 he was made a priest at Hippo, and in 395 bishop of that see. There he laboured for the rest of his life, and there he died in 430, in the midst of the Vandal invasion.

The Latin church, as a whole, notwithstanding the ter- giversation of Rimini, adhered steadfastly to the creed of Nicæa.[1] Augustine interpreted the accepted dogma from the presuppositions of his Neoplatonic philosophy. God, the *prima essentia, una æterna vera substantia,* is an indi- visible unity. Father, Son, and Spirit *"simul omnes est unus dominus"*; and even in the things which are peculiarly ascribed to them severally he sees the indivisible operation of the Trinity. The distinction of the persons is only rela- tively to one another; that is, in the relation of the Father to the Son and the Son to the Father, and of both to the Spirit, which proceeds from them both. He is well aware that "person" does not properly express such relations. Personality in the proper sense he attributes to the one God, whose *esse* is the same as *personam esse.* He sought to make the Trinity intelligible by psychological analogies, the relations of thinking mind to itself; *memoria, intelli- gentia, voluntas;* or *mens, notitia mentis, dilectio;* we may paraphrase, "intellect, thought (which, as expressed, is word), and volition, or love." And as in our experience

---

[1] The Arians had considerable strength in northern Italy, and Am- brose had trouble with them while Augustine was in Milan.

each of these in operation includes the other two, so it is in God; no one of the Persons ever is or acts alone.

The Greeks, from the Apologists on, had assumed, with the philosophers, the freedom of man's will as the condition of moral responsibility, and had emphasised it in opposition to the current astrological fatalism and to the dualism of the Gnostics. In baptism all former sins were remitted; thereafter it was for the Christian, with the aid of divine grace, to lead a good life in accordance with the will of God. Of his ability to do so they made no question. Athanasius affirmed that many Christians after baptism lived without sin. Salvation was deliverance from mortality by deification, more specifically the deification of the body. The common teaching in the West was similar.

Tertullian, a lawyer with a Roman lawyer's tincture of Stoic philosophy, saw things in a different light. The radical evil is not mortality, but *sin;* and sin is not the voluntary act of an individual endowed with free will, but a corrupt nature which all men have inherited from Adam. This evil of the soul proceeds *ex originis vitio*, and is in a sense natural, "for the corruption of nature is second nature." The idea of a hereditary corruption of the soul made him no difficulty, for he held with the Stoics that the soul is corporeal (we say, "material"), and, with Panætius, that it is propagated by the implanting of a soul-germ in the act of generation.[1] Correspondingly, divine grace is not merely the forgiveness of sins in baptism and the enlightenment of the mind by the knowledge of the truth; "there is a force of divine grace, altogether more potent than nature, which dominates the power of choice." He conceives this force as substantial (spirit); it enters into a man and works in him physically.

Nearer to the time of Augustine, Victorinus and the unknown author who is now commonly quoted by the absurd name "Ambrosiaster,"[2] in their commentaries on

---

[1] Original sin is the continuity of soul-germ-plasm, a Weismannian might say.

[2] Because his writings were formerly attributed to Ambrose of Milan.

the Epistles of Paul had interpreted him in a way similar to Augustine, but without anticipating the far-reaching consequences he drew. Augustine was early led by such passages as Romans 9, 16; 1 Cor. 4, 7; Phil. 2, 13, to the conviction that God is the author of the will to believe, and this corresponded well with his own experience of the way he had been led from error to truth, from doubt to faith. That since Adam's fall and in consequence of it man is unable of himself to do or even to will any good; that his salvation, therefore, depends wholly and solely upon God; and that God's saving purpose cannot be thwarted by man's unwillingness—these convictions, also, find expression in writings from the early years of Augustine's episcopate. The systematic development and co-ordination of these ideas were brought about by the controversy with Pelagius and his followers which began in 411.

Pelagius held that God endowed man at his creation with free will, that is, the power of choosing between good and evil, which is the pre-eminence of the rational soul, the dignity and worth of human nature. This freedom was not lost in Adam's fall; it is in every one of his descendants as it was in him. Further, man has not only a formal freedom, he has the ability to do all that God requires of him; it is inconsistent with the character of God to command what man cannot do. There is no such thing as original sin—sin transmitted from parent to child as *per traducem*[1] —all the way from Adam down. Voluntariness is the essence of sin, which is not a corruption of nature but a misuse of free will. If sin were necessitated in any sense, it would not be man's own sin, and God could not justly hold him accountable for it. The grace of God gives the forgiveness of sins in baptism, and makes men children of God; it enlightens the mind, and inclines the will to good by knowledge of the good—the moral influence of the truth. Predestination, finally, is nothing but God's foreknowledge of those who will believe.

---

[1] That is, as a vine is propagated by layering.

Augustine's doctrine is the antipodes of all this. Adam was created righteous and endowed with free will; if he had willed to abide in this state, God would have given him grace to continue steadfast in his good will, and he and his posterity would have shared the blessedness of the angels who kept their first estate, knowing neither pain nor death. But Adam fell. Abusing his free will, he lost the power to will the good; the consequence of voluntary sin was the *dura necessitas peccatum habendi*. The sin of Adam not only brought on his descendants as by a kind of attainder the sentence of death which God pronounced upon him; the sin itself is entailed upon them. Even infants, who have no actual sin of their own, are born with this *original* sin, that is, the sin which inheres in them from their origin in Adam. The sin of the first man was in reality the sin of all his posterity, for they were all *in* him (Romans 5, 12).[1] The just punishment of that sin is justly inflicted on all men, "who *were* that one man." An infant is punished— though with a *mitissima damnatio*—because it is part of the *massa perditionis*. Every human being comes into the world with this entail of original sin, and being engendered in concupiscence inherits a corrupt nature, in which sensuality is stronger than reason. Every one, as soon as he is old enough to be a moral agent, makes himself guilty of actual sin, and that of necessity; yet this necessity is not his exculpation but his condemnation. When Augustine asserts that free will did not perish from human nature by Adam's sin, he means only that men sin voluntarily, not under outward constraint; for in men subject to the devil the will is impotent to anything but sin; it can will only evil, not good. Such freedom to evil only is but another name for the *dura necessitas peccatum habendi*.

---

[1] For ἐφ' ᾧ πάντες ἥμαρτον, "for that all have sinned," the Latin version has *in quo omnes peccaverunt*, "in whom (*sc.* Adam) all sinned." If the translator had rendered *eo quod*, it is possible that the Western church might have been as little afflicted with original sin as the Greeks or the Orientals.

To this conception of sin, original and actual, Augustine's doctrine of grace and its operation corresponds. Since man can do nothing good, God must do all in man's salvation. Chrysostom represents the Greek standpoint when he says: "It depends on us and on God. First we must choose the good, and then God does his part. He does not anticipate our will, that our freedom may not be impaired; but when we have made the choice, he helps us in many ways." Augustine's man has no such power of choice. The will to believe is a work of God in man; faith is the gift of God. This faith is not merely true belief about Christ, for in that sense demons and wicked men may believe. Christian faith is inseparably joined with hope in Christ and love to him; if a man have not these, he believes that there is a Christ, he does not believe *in* Christ. The faith by which man is justified is faith working by love. Justification is not, in Augustine, a declaratory act, as the reformers of the sixteenth century interpreted Paul, by which the sinner is *pronounced* righteous in virtue of the righteousness of Christ; it really *makes* a man righteous.[1] "This is the grace of God through Jesus Christ, whereby he makes us righteous with his own righteousness, not with ours." The justifying grace of God liberates the will, so that it is free for good instead of evil; it inspires good-will, or love, by which its subject is renewed in the inner man; "by the indwelling of the Spirit there arises pleasure in, and love of, that supreme and unchangeable good which is God"; by shedding abroad love in man's heart it implants good desire in place of evil desire (*concupiscentia mala*).

The saving grace of God, by which alone a man can believe in Christ or even wish to do so, is not bestowed on all, but only on those whom God chooses; and his choice is not motived or conditioned by anything in those who are its object. The very idea of grace excludes desert—the grace of God would not be *gratia*, Augustine says, unless it were

---

[1] *Justificare* is *justum facere*. The Protestants read their Paul in Greek.

gratis. From eternity God elected and predestined to eternal life a determinate number of individuals. These, in their time, he calls according to his purpose; to them he gives faith; in them he inspires love; them he justifies (makes righteous); them he glorifies. God's purpose cannot fail of its end; his grace works *indeclinabiliter et insuperabiliter*. It works *in* the elect the will to believe, works *with* their will for good, and secures them against falling away. The predestinated are sons of God not only before they are reborn, but before they are born, and cannot possibly perish. The rest of mankind God leaves in the sin and guilt and just condemnation in which the whole race lies. This arbitrary and inscrutable predestination of the elect to eternal life and the rest to eternal death does not impugn God's justice, for in *justice* all deserve damnation, and if in his mercy he saves some out of this *massa perditionis et damnationis*, he does no wrong to those whom he leaves to their doom.

A synod at Carthage in 418, attended by bishops from all the African provinces, anathematised Pelagian teachings, and, in contradiction to them, delivered itself on original sin, the necessity of grace, and its operation, in accord with Augustine. That the church had always held, at least implicitly, the doctrine of original sin, the synod proved by infant baptism. Infants were baptised for the remission of sins, and it was the universal belief that infants who died unbaptised could not enter the kingdom of heaven. With this established practice and belief Pelagius' denial of original sin was squarely irreconcilable. The Pope concurred in the condemnation of Pelagius, and the emperor Honorius required all the bishops in the Western empire to subscribe an anti-Pelagian declaration upon pain of deposition and banishment. At the Council of Ephesus (431), where Pope Cælestine joined hands with Cyril of Alexandria, Pelagius was included in the same condemnation with Nestorius, who had espoused his cause; but the doctrines of Augustine never found acceptance in the Greek or Oriental churches, and the controversy which so profoundly agitated Latin Christendom then and thereafter had no echo in Greek.

In the West itself it was one thing to repudiate Pelagius, and quite another to go the whole length with Augustine, when once it was seen how far that was. The total inability of man either to do or to will any good; the irresistibility and inamissibility of divine grace; an election which, without regard to anything in its object, predestines some to salvation and the rest to perdition—these doctrines were quite as radical departures from generally accepted opinion as Pelagius' optimistic estimate of human nature and consequent minimising of the function of divine grace in man's salvation. Unconditional individual election had as its corollary ideas of the church and sacraments widely different from those which the church had always entertained—on which, one might say, it was built. Vincent of Lerinum[1] invoked the principle of prescription against these innovations: "We should take the greatest pains to hold what has been believed everywhere, always, and by all; for this is truly and distinctively catholic." "*Quod ubique, quod semper, quod ab omnibus*"—this famous criterion of Catholic orthodoxy was framed against Augustine, whose total inability, absolute predestination, and irresistible grace met none of these conditions.

The strongest opposition to Augustine's doctrines came from the monks of southern Gaul, where monastic institutions had recently been introduced from the East. For them, as in all Greek theology, free will was an axiom; the premise of all ascetic piety was the potency and merit of man's effort, with the assistance of divine grace, to achieve salvation. Their position was that of the church at large, East and West, before Augustine. Against Pelagius they affirmed that every man sinned in Adam's sin, and that no man is saved by his own works, but by regeneration through the grace of God. But the propitiation in the sacrament of the blood of Christ is offered to all; so that all who will

[1] An island and monastery near the modern Cannes.

to come to faith and baptism can be saved. God predestinated to salvation those of whom he foresaw that they
would be worthy of election, and would depart from this life
with a good end. "Therefore every man is admonished to
believe and to work, so that no man should despair of attaining eternal life, since a reward is prepared for willing devotion." All the distinctive features of Augustine's system
are here conspicuous by their absence.

The Augustinian doctrines, especially of prevenient and
unmerited grace, were embodied in the canons of a local
synod at Orange in 529, to which their confirmation by
Pope Boniface II gave an authority that the synod itself
did not possess. It is a very mitigated Augustinianism,
however, which is expressed in them. Predestination is
mentioned only to deny predestination to evil; of the irresistibility of grace there is no word; and the churchly point
of view appears in the inseparable association of grace with
baptism: "We believe that, grace having been received by
baptism, all baptised persons, by the aid and co-operation of
Christ, are able, if they will labour faithfully, to fulfil all
things which pertain to the salvation of the soul, and are
under obligation so to do."

The form in which the doctrines of grace were transmitted
to the Middle Ages is best represented by Pope Gregory
the Great (590–604): God in his inscrutable purpose chose
some beforehand, and justly left some in their evil ways.
The grace of God—which is not irresistible—is not bestowed
in consideration of any desert in man. Without the grace
of God we can do nothing good; but the good deeds we do
are not God's only but ours; he treats them as our merit,
and rewards it as if it proceeded from us alone. There was
thus a general tendency to abandon irresistible grace, and
to state the doctrine of election in such a way as at least
to mask the implication of predestination to damnation; to
overcome inability by baptismal grace, and to make room
for the merit of good works. Yet unabridged Augustinianism was not without influential representatives of unim-

peached orthodoxy, such as Fulgentius of Ruspe in the sixth century, and was more than once revived in the Middle Ages.

There was an ascetic strain in Christian piety from the beginning. At first the expectation of the imminent coming of Christ to judgment was the prime motive; when this subsided, the conflict of sense and reason, of body and soul, which ran through all the thinking of the time and gave an ascetic turn to religious philosophy and everything that we should call personal religion, took its place. Those who aspired to higher achievements in the Christian life all mortified the flesh more or less in conventional ways. Continence (ἐγκράτεια) was elevated to the first rank among the virtues for the married as well as the unmarried; a meagre diet without flesh or wine, varied by periods of strict fasting, was an approved method of subduing the appetites and passions; the counsel of Jesus to the rich young man, "Sell all that thou hast and give to the poor," was followed by many. This self-discipline did not require separation from society nor the abandonment of ordinary occupations. But in Egypt, in the third and fourth centuries, a new type of asceticism developed, which rapidly spread through the Christian world. At first the ascetics withdrew from the city to some uninhabited spot near by to devote themselves undistracted to religious exercises. Soon the desire for more complete seclusion drew some of them deeper into the desert, where they formed a kind of colony, living singly or two and two in simple huts, and subjecting themselves to such privations as seemed good in their own eyes. Those who excelled in self-mortification were called "athletes," and, as Dom Butler has said, they loved to "make a record" in austerities. One heard that another lived on a pound of bread a day; forthwith he put himself on rations of four or five ounces and a scanty allowance of water. The biographers of the Egyptian monks delight in such anecdotes. Even this mode of life was too sociable for the most ambitious ascetics; they retreated into still more inhospitable solitudes, and built their cells out of sight and sound of one another, meeting only in church on Sabbaths and Sundays. The eremite[1] form of monachism prevailed in Lower and Middle Egypt. Its most famous representative was Antony, who, if he did not establish a rule, gave it direction and became its great example.

About the same time Pachomius originated the cœnobite[2] type. He also had led the life of a hermit in the desert; but towards 320 A. D. he founded in Upper Egypt a monastery on a different model. The monks lived, twenty or more together, under the same roof; they had separate cells, but ate at a common table. The establishment comprised several such houses, each under its own house-master appointed by the abbot. The surrounding wall enclosed also a porter's lodge, a hospice for guests, an infirmary, storehouses, and workshops. The larger monasteries had their own church, where all the monks assembled for the principal services, while the daily offices were said in the several houses. The whole life of the monks was ordered by rule; their worship and their work, their food and their fasts, their garb and behaviour were minutely prescribed. Labour had an important place in it, and various trades were carried on—agriculture and gardening, blacksmithing, dyeing, tanning, shoemaking, and so forth. The monastery was an economic community; what it produced beyond its own needs was sold or exchanged for the common good. The new plan had an immediate success; other monasteries for men were established on its model, and presently similar institutions for women.

The primary aim of asceticism was the subjugation of the flesh, with a pronounced sexual emphasis. These passions were commonly conceived as demonic impulses in man or demonic assaults upon him; hence the battle with the lusts of the flesh became a warfare with the demons who strove thus to compass the undoing of the soul. The biog-

---

[1] Greek ἐρημίτης, "desert-dweller," whence English "hermit."
[2] Greek κοινόβιον, "community life."

raphies of the monks are full of such combats, often in forms so concrete and circumstantial as to suggest genuine hallucination. The positive goal, as in the pagan asceticism of the time, was the mystical experience of the emancipated spirit in communion or union with God. A single passage from a homily of Macarius may suffice for illustration:

When the soul, having attained the perfection of spirit, is completely purged of all passions and united in ineffable communion with the Comforter, the Holy Spirit, then is it also counted worthy to become spirit, most intimately united with the Spirit; then it becomes all light, all eye, all spirit, all joy and bliss and exultation, all love and compassion, all goodness and friendliness.

There was a spiritual as well as a bodily ascesis; we read of withdrawal from the world in the solitude of mental concentration, contemplative prayer, daily inquisition of conscience, reflection on death, walking in the presence of God, and the like.

The monastic movement spread from Egypt to Palestine, and to Syria, where the tendency was to complete isolation and extreme austerity. It soon reached Asia Minor also, where Basil gave it the form which prevailed in the Greek church and has continued to this day. The monks lived together in monasteries under a prescribed rule. Their work was in common, meals in common, prayer in common seven times a day. Their ascetic exercises were directed by the superior, and were moderated by the principle that so to weaken the body by fasting as to unfit it for labour is contrary to Scripture.

Monachism was introduced into Gaul from Egypt in the middle of the fourth century, and Cassian, who had lived among the hermits of the Nitrian desert, set forth in his Institutes their mode of life, with such modifications as the climate of Marseilles demanded. In Italy, whither it was brought about the same time, every variety of monachism was represented—eremite and cœnobite, regular and irregular.

The reformer and organiser of Western monachism was Benedict of Nursia. His famous rule for the monks of Monte Cassino (529 A. D.) may, indeed, justly be regarded as the institution of a new type, whose principle was, no excess in anything. Sufficient simple and nourishing food, comfortable plain clothing suitable to the season, ample time for unbroken sleep, moderation in the length of divine offices, were its distinctive features; reading had its appointed daily hours as well as toil and prayer, and learning was cultivated. The organisation and discipline of the monastery were completely regulated; the rule enjoins the strictest obedience to the superior. Labour and obedience are, indeed, the cardinal principles of the order. Benedict founded also a corresponding order for nuns, with a similar rule; his sister, Scholastica, was its first abbess. The Benedictine rule in time superseded all others[1] and became the universal type of monachism in the Western church, as that of Basil was in the Eastern churches.

The service which the Benedictine monasteries rendered to civilisation in the following centuries is inestimable. They kept the lamp of learning burning through the dark ages. In their libraries was preserved what we possess of the heritage of ancient Rome and of early Christian literature in Latin. The monastery schools educated not only monks and clerics, but youths of secular families. The Christianising and civilising of the Teutonic nations was in great measure their work. Partly through the practical Roman genius of the author of the Benedictine rule, partly in consequence of the tasks which the conditions of the time imposed, Western monachism is distinguished by its practical character from Eastern, with its more exclusively ascetic and contemplative ideals.

Since monachism represented the higher Christian life, priests and bishops were chosen with increasing frequency from among the monks, and this strengthened the feeling that all the clergy should lead an ascetic life after the mo-

[1] Except in the Celtic church.

nastic pattern, so far as the conditions and duties of their
calling permitted.   In particular, clerical celibacy was an
ideal which sought to convert itself into a rule, especially
in the West.   Ambrose, Augustine, and Jerome were zealous
for it; popes and synods enacted it into the law of the church.
Clerics who were married before ordination must live apart
from their wives; marriage after ordination was prohibited.
The perpetual necessity, to the end of the Middle Ages, of
fresh legislation against the marriage or concubinage of the
clergy is evidence of its ineffectiveness.   In the East long-
established custom was made law by the Second Trullan
Council (692), which forbade the *second* marriage of the
clergy and marriage after ordination; married bishops must
not live with their wives, but this rule does not apply to
presbyters.   Most of the bishops, in fact, come out of the
monasteries; priests are almost invariably married, and this
is the case also in the Oriental churches.[1]

The mystical aspiration in Christian asceticism has been
referred to above.[2]   The classic system of Christian mysticism is found in the writings which bear the name of Dionysius the Areopagite (Acts 17, 34), but were in fact composed in one of the last decades of the fifth century.   God
in Dionysius is the Absolute, transcending reason, intellect,
and being ($\lambda\acute{o}\gamma o\varsigma$, $\nu o\hat{u}\varsigma$, $o\dot{u}\sigma\acute{\iota}a$), as in Plotinus and Origen.
In the affirmative way all perfections may be attributed to
him in superlative degree; but if we proceed in the opposite
way to negate of God all the limitations implied in these
ascriptions, we arrive at last at an abstraction of which
nothing can be predicated: the godhead is inexpressible, inconceivable, unnamable.   "God is nothing in anything at
all"; "he is the abstraction of all that is."   This is the common philosophic doctrine, the influence of Proclus, the great
systematiser of Neoplatonism, is evident in other parts of

[1] Those fractions of the Greek and Oriental churches which have
come into the Roman obedience (Uniates) are allowed to follow in this
respect their ancient rule.
[2] See p. 205.

the system.   The "supergodhead, superessentially super-existing, superior to all things" is logically—not in time—prior to the Trinity. Dionysius affirms the identity of the Trinity with the Unity; we should rather say that he makes the Trinity an eternal evolution of the Unity.

His Christology is Monophysite.[1] Jesus stands between the transcendent godhead and the orders of being inferior to him; through him, in different degrees, by a hierarchical series of mediations, they are made partakers of divinity; it is Jesus also who draws them to communion, and finally to union, with God. The orders of beings higher than man, the angelic hierarchy, are nine, in three groups: Thrones, Cherubim, Seraphim; Lordships, Powers, Authorities; Principalities, Archangels, Angels. To this celestial hierarchy the ecclesiastical hierarchy corresponds, through whose agency in the church which he founded Jesus draws men back to God. The three stages in the Christian's progress toward the goal of union with God are purification, illumination, consummation, which in the ministry of the ecclesiastical hierarchy are symbolised by the functions of the deacon, priest, and bishop respectively. The real purification and illumination are intellectual. The consummation is an ecstasy in which, sense and reason being left behind, the soul enters the divine darkness and contemplates the divine Being in complete ἀγνωσία. The agnōsia is "a gloom veritably mystic, within which man closes all perceptions of knowledge and enters into the altogether impalpable and unseen, being wholly of Him who is beyond all and of none, neither himself nor other, and by inactivity of all knowledge he is united in his better part to the altogether unknown, and by knowing nothing, knowing Knowing transcending intellect." Herein the goal is attained, θέωσις, "deification."

---

[1] Accepted on their own pretension as the teaching of a disciple of Paul, these writings, with those of Athanasius (or of Apollinarius under the name of Athanasius) and Cyril, are the great authorities of the Monophysites.

This oneness with God, or identification with the Absolute, is achieved only by love (ἔρως); but in Dionysius love is an intellectual attraction, as in the Greek philosophers, rather than the passion of devotion and self-surrender which the more emotional forms of mysticism mean by love. It is aroused by the contemplation of the divine perfection or of the absoluteness of the divine Being—by what God is in himself, not by what he is to the subject.

The great interpreter of Dionysius was Maximus Confessor (d. 662).[1] In him both the common ascetic-ethical and the emotional elements in mysticism have a larger place. The purification of the soul, which in Dionysius is essentially intellectual, is in Maximus the removal of the moral hindrances to the attainment of perfection, especially the extirpation of the passions. Practical, or ethical, philosophy has thus to cleanse the soul from sin and purge the conscience. The second stage is the contemplation of the divine Being (φυσικὴ θεωρία). Through it the mystical progress is to the "theological philosophy," in which God reveals himself in many-voiced silence and infinite light. The spiritual life has an initial stage (πρόοδος), an ascent of the soul to God (ἀνάβασις), and an assumption (ἀνάληψις) into the mysteries of the divine existence. The soul that loves God is deified. It yields itself wholly to the enfolding divine embrace, is made like God, entering into ineffable communion with him, and losing itself in the ocean of the godhead.

The writings of the Pseudo-Areopagite and of Maximus have been the Bible of mystics in the Eastern church; their influence on Moslem mysticism (Sufis) is demonstrable; it is perhaps to be recognised in the Jewish Kabbala. A copy of the works of Dionysius was sent by the Byzantine emperor, Michael Balbus, in 827, as a present to the Frank

[1] For daring to maintain that there were two wills in Christ (see above, p. 192) when the emperor had decreed that there should be only one, Maximus had his tongue cut out to the root and his right hand chopped off.

14

king, Louis the Pious, to whom the gift was the more precious because he believed that the author, the disciple of Paul, was no other than the legendary first bishop of Paris, the martyr apostle of France. In the next generation, at the instance of Charles the Bald, Dionysius was translated from Greek into Latin by John Scotus Eriugena. It is evident from Eriugena's earlier works that he was acquainted with the Greek Fathers, and much influenced by the teachings of Origen and Gregory of Nyssa, and the doctrines of Dionysius and Maximus Confessor fitted very well in his mind with the Platonising bent he had contracted from them as well as from Augustine, and in some part perhaps more directly from later Greek philosophy.

The esteem in which the works of Dionysius were held in subsequent times is shown by the fact that between Eriugena (ca. 850) and the Renaissance (Ficino, 1492), four other translations were made. Of their influence on theology, not alone among the Greeks—especially in John of Damascus —but in the West, it must suffice here to say that Hugh of St. Victor, Grosseteste, and Albertus Magnus wrote commentaries on them, and that Thomas Aquinas quotes them so often that a bare index of references to passages in Dionysius fills many columns.

CHAPTER VIII

CHRISTIANITY

INSTITUTIONS. WORSHIP

Suppression of Paganism—Uniformity and Schism—Bishops, Metropolitans, and Patriarchs—Primacy of Rome—Liturgies—The Mass—Baptism—Confirmation—Church Festivals and Fasts—Doctrine of the Church in Cyprian—Heretical Baptism—Augustine's Doctrine of the Sacraments—Saints and Martyrs—The Virgin—Angels—Images and Pictures in Churches—The Iconoclastic Struggle—Purgatory—The Church at the End of the Ancient Age.

THE abrogation of the laws against Christianity and the favour Constantine and his successors showed to the church led to a great increase in the numbers of Christians and a corresponding decline of the old religions. Soon the Christian emperors enacted laws against them. Constantius (d. 361) ordered all the temples to be closed, and prohibited sacrifice upon pain of death. It does not appear, however, that any serious effort was made to enforce this law where public opinion did not support it; in the great centres like Rome and Alexandria it was a dead letter. Julian (361–363) did not have to reopen the temples; they had never been closed. The legislation of the emperors who followed Julian went no further than to forbid bloody sacrifices. But in 392 Theodosius prohibited all acts of heathen worship, in the temples, on the highways, or on private grounds, under severe penalties. The offering of sacrifice was explicitly put under the head of high treason (*majestas*), precisely as the Christians' refusal to sacrifice had been treated under the heathen emperors; but the pagans did not display the same zeal for martyrdom. The temples were in some cases converted to municipal uses, others were preserved as architectural monuments. In places where the people held

211

tenaciously to the religion of their fathers, as, for example, at Gaza, the government sometimes winked at the continuance of heathen worship—for tangible reasons. The zeal of the bishops outran the execution of the law by the officials. In 391 Theophilus, bishop of Alexandria, with his army of monks, after riots in which much blood was shed, destroyed the great temple of Serapis. Chrysostom sent out from Antioch raiding-parties of fanatical ascetics, "burning with divine zeal," to demolish the temples in the Lebanon region; Porphyry of Gaza, armed with a special rescript of the emperor Arcadius procured by an imposture worthy of a comedy, razed the famous temple of Marnas. In the West the suppression of paganism was slower and less complete; Christians were relatively less numerous, the hand of the government was less firm, and the Teutonic invasions gave it more urgent occupation.

The Christian emperors were minded to have but one kind of religion in their dominions; they legislated not only against pagans and Manichæans, but against Christian heretics and schismatics of every name. Constantine, as we have seen, ordered that their churches should be turned over to the Catholics and their corporate property confiscated; their meetings for worship, even in private houses, were prohibited. During the controversies in the Catholic church over the nature and person of Christ, first Arius and his followers were exiled, then Athanasius and the uncompromising Nicæans; now it was Nestorius, then Eutyches, and again the Origenists and the Orientals. The heathen emperors had persecuted Christians because they would not conform to the religion of the state in the externals of worship, but left it free to every man to think what he pleased; the Christian emperors demanded conformity of thought, or at least of profession—subscription one day to Nicæa, the next to Rimini; first to Ephesus, then to Chalcedon, as one faction or another inspired the autocrat's theology. The church paid dear for the privilege of being a state church.

The efforts to secure uniformity by more exact definition of dogma, and the use of all the machinery of church and state to force the true faith for the time being, as prescribed in canons of councils and the decrees of emperors, upon dissidents, resulted in new and formidable schisms. The older secessions—Novatians, Donatists, Meletians—had arisen over questions of church order and discipline; those sects were puritan protests against the laxity of the great church. The schisms of the fourth and fifth centuries were doctrinal; they were parties which refused to accept dogmas enunciated by particular councils or to change their faith when the doctrinal weather-cock veered around in Constantinople.

All the conditions of the growth of the church had tended to the concentration of responsibility and authority in the person of the bishops, for which, before the middle of the third century, Cyprian found a *jure divino* theory. To this authority the councils called by the emperors to legislate for the whole church in doctrine and discipline added not a little; the bishops thus assembled were the church, their decision was its collective voice. All bishops were in theory equal; each had in his own sphere the same powers and prerogatives; in synods and councils each cast a single vote. In Egypt only, in conformity with its political administration, the bishop of Alexandria exercised an authority over the other bishops comparable to that which elsewhere the bishop had over his presbyters; he was an ecclesiastical autocrat—his enemies sometimes called him the Pharaoh. The bishops of the great sees such as Alexandria and Antioch exerted a wide influence beyond their diocesan boundaries. Antioch was the leading church not only in Syria but in Cilicia and far into Asia Minor. Ephesus was held in honour by reason of its part in the early history of Christianity, but had declined in actual importance. Before Constantine there was no provincial organisation and no recognised metropolitan authority, though a gravitation in the latter direction is apparent.

In the canons of the Council of Nicæa, however, the grouping of the bishops by provinces and the primacy of the bishop of the chief city of the province, the seat of the civil administration, are assumed, the organisation of the church in the East being thus assimilated to the provincial organisation of the empire as remodelled by Diocletian. The council of 381 went a step farther, in giving to the bishops of Constantinople, Ephesus, and Cæsarea in Cappadocia, with those of Antioch and Alexandria,[1] an authority superior to that of other metropolitans and of provincial councils. Among these, again, it assigned to the bishop of Constantinople a rank second only to the bishop of Rome, that is, in effect, the precedence over the whole episcopate of the Eastern church. Ephesus and Cæsarea soon lost their independent rank to Constantinople, while Jerusalem was erected into a patriarchate with the provinces of Palestine under it. Thus, from the middle of the fifth century there were in the East four patriarchates, Constantinople, Antioch, Alexandria, and Jerusalem. But for the Moslem conquests, which wrested Syria and Egypt from the empire, it is not improbable that the centralising tendencies of the Byzantine empire after Justinian and the weakening of the other patriarchates by the Monophysite schism would have given Constantinople a position in the Eastern church corresponding to that of Rome in the West.

The church of Rome was always the great church of Western Christendom. As the sole church of apostolic foundation, the scene of the labours both of Paul and of Peter, to whom Christ had given the primacy among the Apostles, it was pre-eminently the custodian of apostolic tradition. Its situation also lent it prestige; the church of the capital was naturally looked up to as the capital church of Christendom. The removal of the seat of government did not diminish this prestige, while it left the bishops of Rome all the greater freedom and power. In the inter-

---

[1] Corresponding to the "dioceses" of Justinian's administrative system.

minable strife of the Eastern bishops, the support of the
pope was eagerly sought; they carried their grievances to
Rome and urged its intervention.   The Council of Sardica
(343 or 344)[1] gave to bishops who thought themselves unjustly judged by provincial councils the right to carry their
appeal to the bishop of Rome, who might, if he saw reason,
order a rehearing before a commission named by him, or,
if he remitted the case to the original instance, might be
represented by a legate at the new trial.

The second great centre of Latin Christianity was Carthage, which was in communication with Rome and generally in accord with it.   Disagreements arose, sometimes
sharp collisions of opinion, but there was no rivalry between
the sees, and such perennial strife as raged between Alexandria and Antioch or Alexandria and Constantinople was
unknown in the West.   Nowhere was the precedence of
Rome more cordially acknowledged than at Carthage.   In
the distress which befell the church through the Teutonic
invasions and the establishment of Arian churches in the
kingdoms the conquerors founded in Gaul and Spain, in
Lombardy and Africa, everything that was Catholic in those
lands turned to Rome for guidance and succour.

Many things thus conspired to give to Rome the primacy
in Western Christendom; but primacy was yet far from
supremacy.   At the close of the sixth century there was no
indication that the Latin church would one day become
more strongly centralised than ever the Roman empire had
been.   No one—the popes as little as the rest—seems to
have felt any pressing need of such a thing.[2]

The main features of Christian worship were always the
same, but in time the simple rites described by Justin in the
middle of the second century were elaborated into a stately

[1] The council was convoked as a general council, but the Eastern
bishops withdrew because the Latins would not recognise the deposition of Athanasius; consequently it represented the Western churches
only.

[2] Duchesne, Origines du culte chrétien, 5th edition, p. 44.

cultus. This tendency, inherent in all ritual, was greatly furthered by the influence of the Old Testament when the Christian clergy came to be regarded as succeeding to the place of the priesthood of the former dispensation. The gorgeous raiment of the high priest, the ceremonial vestments of the other priests, the solemn processions, the choirs of Levitical singers intoning psalms, the clouds of incense from swinging censers—all seemed a divine model of religious worship, which warranted the church in rivalling the pomp of the ancient cults.

The Eucharist was the centre of the Christian cultus, and the eucharistic liturgy was the first to be fixed. Doubtless the process is correctly outlined by Duchesne:

> At the beginning the usage was everywhere much the same; not wholly, for a complete identity in details cannot be admitted even for the churches founded by Apostles. It is not at first that men attach to matters of this kind the importance that makes them sacred and fixes them. By degrees customs become rites, and rites are expanded into more or less imposing and complicated ceremonies. At the same time the subject of the prayers and exhortations was fixed; usage indicated to the officiating minister the ideas he was to develop and the order in which he was to treat them. Later, the last step was taken by adopting fixed formulas which left nothing to individual choice and the accidents of improvisation.[1]

Before this last stage was reached local diversities had established themselves and were thereafter perpetuated. In the third century the great centres of Christendom, Rome, Antioch, Alexandria, had their own peculiarities of usage, which followed the expansion of the church into wide regions, again with many local variations. The liturgy now in use in all the orthodox patriarchates of the East, and in the national churches of Greece, Russia, Bulgaria, Servia, is called by the name of St. Chrysostom; it is the liturgy of Constantinople, a development of the Syrian type, while the Alexandrian is perpetuated by the Coptic (Monophysite) church in Egypt and by the Abyssinian church. In the

[1] Origines du culte chrétien, 5th edition, p. 54.

West the Roman liturgy attained its present exclusive use
only at a comparatively late time.   In Gaul, Spain, Britain,
and Ireland, the older liturgies were of the class which is
conventionally named Gallican; Milan long had its own
(Ambrosian) liturgy.

When the whole population became Christian the part of
the ancient service which had regard particularly to converts
not yet admitted to baptism (catechumens),[1] with its long
lessons from Scripture and recitation of Psalms, was much
abridged, especially in the West. The homily had never
had the same importance in Latin Christendom as in the
East; preaching was reserved to the bishop, in person or
by deputy, and was occasional and infrequent. The effect
of all this was to make the public cultus virtually consist
in the Mass.

This tendency was promoted by the conception of the
Mass as a sacrifice, which several factors contributed to
render increasingly prominent: the sacerdotal conception of
the work of Christ developed by the author to the Hebrews
—Christ the priest, Christ the atoning sacrifice, Christ the
intercessor; the sacerdotal idea of the Christian priesthood,
analogous to all the ancient religions and particularly to
the Levitical institutions; the primitive liturgical association of the offering of the congregation with the Eucharist.
What did most, however, to establish the sacrificial conception of the Mass in the theology of the Western church was
that in it atonement was made for sins committed after
baptism, and the forgiveness of the penitent sinner thus
assured.[2]   Pope Gregory I (d. 604) presents the doctrine in

[1] The catechumens were dismissed before the *missa fidelium*, the
celebration of the Eucharist, at which only those in full communion
with the church might be present.

[2] Baptism conveyed the remission of antecedent sins—in the case
of infants, of original sin; but how the forgiveness of sins committed
after baptism could be assured was a question which had exercised
serious minds from early times. The sacrifice of the Mass answered
this question, and in connection with the development of the discipline
and doctrine of penitence constitutes one of the most important features
of Catholic theology.

its classic form: "Christ, by the mystery of his humanity, continually offers sacrifice (*sacrificium immolat*)." "In his sacrament he suffers again for us; for as often as we offer to him the victim (*hostiam*, "the host") of his passion, so often we repeat his passion for our absolution." The Mass is a propitiatory sacrifice by which penitent sinners are reconciled to God, and is efficacious not only for the living but for the dead in purgatory. In the sacrament the essential thing was the *participation by* the faithful in the body and blood of the Lord; in the sacrifice it was the *offering* of the eucharistic victim by the priest *for* the faithful.

The rite of baptism assumed its form in an age when the candidates were chiefly converts from heathenism. It was a solemn initiation into the mysteries of the Christian religion, which usually took place at Easter, after a preparation lasting several weeks. An important part of this preparation was the exorcism of the demons which inhabited every heathen, the opening of the candidates' lips and ears by the application of the priest's spittle ("*effeta*," Mark 7, 13), and the anointing of his breast and back with oil, followed by the renunciation: "Abrenuntias Satanæ?—Abrenuntio. Et omnibus operibus eius?— Abrenuntio. Et omnibus pompis eius?—Abrenuntio." Thereupon the candidates recited the baptismal creed, which had been delivered to them the preceding Sunday. Baptism was by triple immersion; following it, the baptised, clad in new white garments, presented themselves before the bishop, who, after an invocation of the Holy Spirit, made the sign of the cross on the forehead of each with the consecrated anointing oil, saying: "*In nomine Patris et Filii et Spiritus Sancti, pax tibi.*" From the baptistery the neophytes passed into the basilica to their first communion. Such was the Roman rite in the fourth or fifth century; and so, with minor variations and with less imposing accompaniments elsewhere.

Baptism was administered by the bishop or under his direction. The spread of Christianity into districts remote from the cities and the growth of the custom of infant baptism made it difficult to maintain this rule, and it became common for presbyters to baptise. In the West the imposition of hands, however, remained an exclusive function of the bishop as the successor of the Apostles, he visiting the churches in his diocese from time to time to confer it. The episcopal "seal" (*signaculum*), which originally had been the culminating act of the baptismal ritual, was thus detached from baptism, and might be separated from it by a considerable interval of time. The sacrament of confirmation became independent. The effect of the two sacraments was distinguished, after New Testament precedents: the one was the laver of regeneration and the remission of sins; by the other the gift of the Holy Spirit was conferred.

At first, probably, the children of Christian parents were admitted to the church by baptism only when they were of an age to profess for themselves the faith of their parents. The belief that in baptism all former sins were forgiven; the fact that the rite could not be repeated; the uncertainty whether grave sins committed after baptism could be forgiven at all, or more than once, made it seem prudent to defer this obliteration of the record, and many remained catechumens for years, even to their death-bed, that they might pass from the world with a clean slate. The belief that those who died unbaptised could not enter the kingdom of heaven (John 3, 5) had the opposite effect, and led to the baptism of infants. How early this began cannot be determined. The first mention of it is in Irenæus. Origen (d. 254) affirms that infant baptism was an apostolic tradition; his contemporary Cyprian discusses the question whether baptism, like circumcision, should take place on the eighth day or might be administered sooner. A generation earlier Tertullian opposed the custom, but did not assail it as an innovation. The rite was essentially the same as in the case of adults, the parents making the responses for the infant. As in the case of adults, baptism was immediately succeeded by participation in the Eucharist, so that the child was at once fully initiated into the

Christian mysteries. Infant communion, still universal in the Eastern churches, continued in the West until late in the Middle Ages.

Parents frequently neglected to present their children for the imposition of the bishop's hands, and attempts were made to remedy this abuse by imposing ecclesiastical penalties on such as failed to do so within the first three years, and by excluding from communion children who had not been confirmed. A council of the thirteenth century permitted a delay of seven years; and in the sixteenth century the Council of Trent approved the postponement of confirmation till the twelfth year, which is since then the rule of the Roman church. One result of this maturer age was a great revival of catechetical instruction in preparation for the first communion, and consequently an increased knowledge of Catholic doctrine among the laity.

The church had from the beginning held its principal assembly for worship on Sunday, and early made Wednesday and Friday fast-days. In time public worship in the churches were held on these days also, in some with a celebration of the Eucharist, in others (e. g., in Alexandria) without. The great annual festival was the Pascha (Easter), in the spring, at the season of the Jewish Passover, whose name it appropriated. A preparatory period of fasting culminated in the mourning of the day of crucifixion; a silent day followed, during which the Saviour lay in the tomb; on the next was the rejoicing over the resurrection, his triumph over death and hell. With such a theme it was inevitable that the ritual should assume a dramatic character, which is more marked in the Greek than in the Roman liturgy.

The date of this festival was fixed by that of the Jewish Passover, at which season Jesus was crucified. Most of the churches celebrated the resurrection on the Sunday following the fourteenth of the Jewish month Nisan; but in Asia Minor, for a time, they kept it on the fourteenth of the month, whatever day of the week that might be. Differences arose also about the mode of determining on what day of the Julian year the fourteenth of Nisan fell, and the rule adopted by the Council of Nicæa did not wholly end them. At the close of the second century the fast before Easter lasted only a few days. Of the forty-day fasting period (Quadragesima) which we call Lent there is no trace before the fourth century, and the custom of its observance varied greatly in different parts of the church. The usage of the Eastern churches continues to differ from that of the West, which received its present form in Rome in the seventh century.

The festival of the nativity of Christ is of much later origin than that of the resurrection. In the fourth century the Eastern churches had a festival on January 6, which they called the "Manifestations" (τὰ ἐπιφάνια), commemorating the nativity, the adoration of the Magi, and the baptism of Jesus. The observance of December 25 originated at Rome, probably in the fourth century; it was introduced in Antioch about 375 and adopted in Alexandria about 430. The choice of the day (the winter solstice in the Roman calendar) was an appropriation for Christ, "the sun of righteousness," of the Natalis Solis Invicti, the Syrian sun-god, identified with Mithras.[1]

That there is no salvation out of the church was the universal belief of Christians from the first. For Paul the church was the body of Christ, in which his spirit dwelt; he was the head, Christians were the members. To the commoner apprehension the church alone had the saving truth; it alone possessed the sacraments by which men, their past sins washed away, were born anew, and, by partaking of the flesh and blood of the divine Saviour, became themselves divine and immortal.

It has been shown in an earlier connection how the multiplication of heresies, each pretending to be the true way of salvation, was met by the criterion of catholicity and apostolic tradition. In the third century there was acute con-

[1] See Vol. I, pp. 578 f., 597.

troversy over the question whether such as had denied their
faith in time of persecution might be restored to the communion of the church. The rigorists seceded on this issue,
and the churches of Africa were rent by dissension. The
leaders of this schism were men of unimpeachable orthodoxy, and they had the earlier tradition of the church on
their side, which had not admitted any remedy for apostasy. It was this situation which gave occasion to Cyprian's "Unity of the Catholic Church," in which the doctrine
of the church found a classic formulation.

"Extra ecclesiam salus non est." "A man cannot have
God for his father who has not the church for his mother."
The church had often been compared to Noah's ark; only
those who are in it can escape destruction. Cyprian adds
a new simile, particularly apposite to the puritan seceders:
the church is Rahab's house; there is safety within its doors,
but whoever leaves its shelter invites his doom. But the
Novatians professed to be the true church; in refusing to
restore the lapsed they were loyally preserving its purity
and maintaining the ancient strictness of its discipline, to
which the majority was recreant. What was to decide in
these conflicting claims? Cyprian's answer is, the church
is where the regular episcopate is. The church is founded
upon the bishops, and all its activities are directed by them,
as was ordained by divine law. They are the successors of
the Apostles, *vicaria ordinatione*, and to them, through the
Apostles, Christ says: "He that heareth you, heareth me."
The bishop is in the church and the church in the bishop;
if any man is not with the bishop he is not in the church.
In other words, to secede from the regularly constituted
bishop is to put oneself outside the pale of the church and
the hope of salvation. The criterion of the true church is
the legitimacy of the episcopate.   .

There can be but one true church. The unity of the
church is a corollary of the unity of the godhead (John 10,
30; 1 John 5, 10). It is symbolised by the seamless vesture of
Christ, in contrast to the mantle of the prophet Ahijah which

was rent into twelve pieces. The unity of the church, again, rests on the unanimity of the episcopate, the *concors numerositas episcoporum*. The church of Rome is "the leading church, from which the unity of the priesthood springs." "There is one God, and one Christ, and one church, and one throne founded upon Peter by the word of the Lord." The ideal unity of the church has not merely its symbol but its embodiment in the successor of Peter. The throne of the bishop of Rome is the *cathedra Petri*.[1]

The existence of numerous bodies of Christians having a ministry and sacraments similar to those of the Catholic Church early raised a practical problem which in turn opened important questions in the doctrine of the sacraments. If a man who had been baptised in an heretical sect came over to the Catholic Church, was he to be baptised like a convert from heathenism, on the ground that heretical baptism was a counterfeit, or was his baptism to be regarded as valid baptism (which could not be repeated), notwithstanding the heresy of the administrator? The African church, under Cyprian's lead, maintained the former view, which had influential supporters elsewhere also. Pope Stephen held, on the contrary, that whatever errors the heretics might be in, their intention was to administer baptism according to the command of Christ. Those who had been baptised by them were therefore to be received into the Catholic Church by the imposition of the bishop's hands "*in pœnitentiam*."

The Roman view and practice eventually prevailed. In the Donatist Controversy Augustine gave it its doctrine.[2] Baptism by a heretic or schismatic, if formally correct, is Christian baptism, and imparts the *character Dominicus*;

[1] The exposition has a special application to the situation in Rome at the time Cyprian wrote. Novatian had been consecrated bishop by the rigorists, in opposition to Pope Cornelius, the bishop in orderly succession.

[2] The Donatists were a puritan separatist sect which was very strong and aggressive in Africa and Numidia in the fourth century, especially among the native population.

but so long as the subject remains out of the communion of the Catholic Church his baptism remains without effect, it does not avail to the remission of sins. Its potential efficacy, so to speak, becomes actual only when he who has been baptised outside the church comes into it. For love, which is the grace of the New Testament, is to be found and can be conserved only in the church; in the Catholic Church alone can the Spirit be received. The church is the body of Christ; in the unity of the body the members are bound to one another and to their head by love—*unitas servat caritatem*. Augustine's doctrine of grace has here an important influence on his idea of the church. Conversely, one who has been baptised in the church does not lose the sacrament of baptism if he separates from its unity, but he loses the grace of which the church is the sole repository. It is the same with orders, for, like baptism, ordination confers a *character*[1] *indelebilis,* which permanently distinguishes the priest from the layman by the power to administer the sacraments. Once imparted, this power cannot be lost nor taken away. The ministration may be irregular or illegitimate, but the sacraments are not thereby rendered invalid.

As the outcome of these controversies the important principle was established that the efficacy of the sacrament is independent of the person of the minister. Augustine puts this in the strongest way: "Between an Apostle and a drunken man there is a great difference; but between the baptism of Christ which an Apostle gives and that which a drunken man gives there is no difference." The question is not who gives, but what he gives. If the rigorists had had their way, a man could have no assurance that the sacraments he received were the genuine sacraments, efficacious unto salvation.

Augustine's conception of the sacraments corresponds to his doctrine of grace. Sacrament is defined as *sacrum signum,* a sacred symbol, a thing or an act which brings to

---

[1] "Stamp."

mind a *res sacra*, specifically, a gift of divine grace which
is to be received. "What are any material sacraments but,
so to speak, visible words?" Meaning and value is given
to them by the words of Christ which accompany them in
the liturgy: "*Accedit verbum ad elementum, etiam ipsum
tanquam visibile verbum.*" All religions have their sacraments: "In no kind of religion, true or false, can men be
held together, unless they are united by some sort of fellowship in visible symbols, or sacraments." In conformity
with his definition, Augustine applies the term sacrament
to various rites—ordination, marriage (Eph. 5, 4), the salt
given to a catechumen is a sacrament; but baptism and the
Eucharist are the chief sacraments.

The reality, or virtue, of the sacrament is solely the invisible grace of God through the Holy Spirit; without this
inward sanctification it profits a man nothing. When it is
remembered that for Augustine the work of grace is the
inspiration, or infusion, of love (*caritas*), by which the subject is renewed in the inner man, it will be seen how widely
his conception differs from that which attributed to the
sacraments a kind of physical efficacy.[1] Many are in the
church and receive the sacraments who, not being of the
elect, have not the saving grace of God. It does not avail
to have the outward sign, or symbol, of grace, if a man
have not love, the reality. That the doctrine of the sacraments in the West has a more spiritual character than that
of the East is chiefly to be ascribed to Augustine.

The earliest Christian worship was addressed to God the
Father and to the Lord Jesus Christ. In time subordinate
objects of worship were introduced, and a secondary cultus
of the saints. The martyrs had always been venerated;
commemorative services were held at their tombs on the
anniversary of their martyrdom, and feasts[2] only too closely
resembling those of heathen custom, which in fact they
perpetuated. Augustine, who was under no illusion about

[1] Augustine understands Jesus himself to refute this notion in John 6.
[2] Called *agapœ*, and ostensibly a dispensation of charity to the poor.

15

this relation, writes: "Drunkenness and luxurious banquets in the cemeteries are commonly believed by the carnal and ignorant multitude to be not only an honour to the martyrs but a solace to the dead." The Manichæan Faustus taunts the church: "You have turned the sacrifices into love-feasts, and in the place of the idols put the martyrs, whom you worship with similar prayers; you placate the shades of the dead with food and wine." [1]

Originally prayer was made *for* the martyrs, but this seemed derogatory; it was more fitting to pray *to* them, seeking their intercession with God. Chapels were built at their tombs or on the scene of their martyrdom, their relics were enshrined in the churches. To the sacred legend of the martyr were added narratives of signal answers to prayer at his tomb or miracles wrought by the relics. Men resorted to his shrine for supernatural help, and it became the seat of a popular cult. Eminent confessors and champions of the faith were honoured in the same way. Some of the Apostles, notably Peter and Paul at Rome, stood high in the roll of the martyrs; tradition or legend gave the crown of martyrdom to all the rest.

In popular apprehension the saints occupied a place similar to that of the heroes in the later Greek religion; they were patrons and protectors of localities, and objects of a local cult, whose help the people of the neighbourhood sought with offerings, prayers, and vows in various needs. The monotheistic religious philosophies of the time made room for this side of the popular religion by recognising a class of good *daimones*, beneficent superhuman powers, who were properly revered with prayer and offerings. The church had combated this worship, not because it was plural, but because it was heathen; in the cult of the saints it found a Christian substitute. The legal suppression of paganism furthered this development; the saints became the successors of the innumerable local and functional divinities whose worship had always been the chief part of the every-day relig-

[1] Compare what Augustine narrates of his mother, Confessions, vi, 2.

ion of the masses. The chapel of a saint took the place
of the shrine of the dispossessed demon; the new occupant
assumed the functions of his predecessor, the local customs
and superstitions were often transferred to him. Christianity abolished the great gods; under other names it adopted
the little ones.

In correct theological theory, what was sought of the
saints was their intercession with God for the blessings desired by those who invoked them. To the less subtle apprehension of the worshippers at their shrines, the saints themselves answered the prayers and received the offerings of
the faithful.[1] A distinction was also made by the teachers
of the church between the homage paid the saints and the
peculiar worship (λατρεία) which is rendered to God alone;
and, while urging the people to avail themselves of the intercession of the saints, they warned them against confounding
the two kinds of worship.

In the fourth century no pre-eminence over the other
saints was ascribed to the Virgin Mary. Her perpetual
virginity had been much earlier affirmed, and was maintained with especial zeal by the ascetics. Augustine, "for
the honour of the Lord," would hold her exempt from the
sinfulness to which the other saints were subject. The controversies about the person of Christ came to a head in the
question of the Θεοτόκος, and many of the most ardent
champions of the one nature were actuated more by jealousy for the "Mother of God" than by understanding of
the theological issues. The Council of Chalcedon gave to
this title dogmatic significance and authority; the Virgin
was elevated to a rank far above the Apostles and the multitude of saints. In the following period churches dedicated to Mary were erected in great numbers. Festivals
of the Virgin, generally in proximity to Christmas, appear
in various calendars, both Eastern and Western, in the
sixth century. The church in Rome seems not to have
observed such days before the seventh century, when it

[1] On the same phenomenon in Mohammedan lands, see below, p. 484.

adopted from the Greeks four festivals, the Presentation in the Temple (Purification of the Virgin), forty days after the Nativity of Christ; the Annunciation, nine months before Christmas (March 25); the Nativity of the Virgin, September 8; and her death (Dormitio), August 15.

The worship of angels which Paul reprobates in his letter to the Colossians seems to have been especially common in Asia Minor. In the fourth century it was prohibited by a council at the Phrygian Laodicea; but its persistence in that region a century later is attested by Theodoret, who notes particularly chapels dedicated to Michael;[1] those who were addicted to the cult justified it by the argument that, inasmuch as the God of the universe is invisible and inaccessible, it is proper to gain the good-will of God through the angels. The defence gives a true explanation of the increasing prominence of the worship of the Virgin and the saints as well as the angels: the God of the universe, even where he was not exalted, as he was by metaphysical theologians, to a transcendence which excludes all transactions with men, was too great, too remote, too unimaginable, too unhuman, to satisfy the religious need for a power to which the common man can draw near with his every-day cares. To the early Christians Christ had been the mediator and intercessor with the Father, but in proportion as theology dehumanised him and elevated the Son to a deity identical in nature and equal in majesty with the Father, defining him in terms as abstract and incomprehensible, religion experienced the need of other mediators and intercessors, and the theologians themselves commended this way of access to God. The growing pre-eminence of the worship of the Virgin reflects the feeling that of all intercessions the most effectual must be that of the Mother with her son.

One of the commonplaces of the Christian polemic against the old religions was the attack on idolatry, and so long as

---

[1] Michael was regarded by the Jews as the champion of their nation, and it is not improbable that the beginnings of angelolatry in the church came from Jewish sects or superstitions.

the conflict with heathenism lasted it was natural that the church should avoid every semblance that could give the heathen a pretext to retort the accusation. When this stage was passed, the same reason did not exist, and pictures were introduced into the churches, scenes from the sacred history or the legends of the saints, at once decorative and instructive. Representations of Christ were at first of a symbolical character, a lamb at the foot of a cross being the commonest. Beginning as aids to devotion, pictures soon became objects of devotion. The multitude was no more able in the new religion than in the old to realise the presence of the deity without some aid from the senses to the imagination. By the sixth century the worship of the *eikons* was universal in the orthodox East. Some churches boasted the possession of images "not made with hands," as heathen temples had had their idols that fell down from heaven; there were images that bled and images that winked; miraculous cures and deliverances were wrought by the pictures of the saints as well as by their relics, and *ex votos* were hung up before them, as aforetime in the heathen shrines; a rank thicket of legend grew about the wonder-working images. The monks were zealous promoters of both the worship and the mythology; the religion of the ignorant masses was compact of these superstitions.

Several of the emperors, beginning with Leo the Isaurian (717–740), took strenuous measures to abolish this worship, removing the images from the churches and whitewashing the pictures on the walls. A subservient council in Constantinople (754) declared image-worship to be idolatry, contrary to Scripture and the Fathers, and excommunicated its defenders, including John of Damascus, the most eminent theologian of the Greek church. Feminine piety came to the rescue. Under the regency of the empress Irene the second Council of Nicæa (787) condemned the acts of its predecessor as heretical and blasphemous, ordered the images to be restored, and religious veneration to be paid to them, with the use of incense and the burning of candles before them. The laws against them were renewed by Leo the Armenian (813–820); but the empress Theodora caused the acts of the Council of Nicæa to be reaffirmed (842). The conflict, which had lasted more than a hundred years, ended in the complete triumph of the images, and the Festival of Orthodoxy, observed to this day in the Greek Church, was instituted to commemorate it.

Throughout this struggle the Roman Church arrayed itself against the "image-breakers" and anathematised their doctrine. The council of 754 was not recognised in the West; legates of Pope Adrian I were present at Irene's council in 787, where a dogmatic pronouncement in favour of image-worship was made. The Frankish church in those days had a mind and voice of its own. It would neither exclude images from the churches nor approve the veneration of them. When the acts of the Nicene Council of 787 were transmitted by Pope Adrian to Charles the Great, the answer, made in the king's own name, maintained this position, unshaken by the conjoint authority of an œcumenical council and the pope. The new council, he affirmed, was as bad as its predecessor; pictures are properly allowed in churches as representations of events or for the decoration of the walls, but adoration of them should be strictly forbidden. A synod at Paris in 825 accompanied its condemnation of image-worship with an express censure of Pope Adrian for lending his authority to the superstitious practices prevailing in Italy and at Rome, which he ought to have resisted. Through the greater part of the ninth century the worship of images continued to be forbidden in the Frankish kingdoms; but in the end it prevailed there also.

The belief that sins committed after baptism must be expiated by suffering, which is the basis of the penitential discipline of the church, received an extension or complement in the Western church in the doctrine of purgatory.[1] Christians who die with minor sins unatoned for undergo for a longer or shorter time a purification by fire, and only

[1] The Greek and Oriental churches have no corresponding doctrine.

after their release from this place of suffering are admitted to the abode of the blessed. Gregory the Great, who did much to give currency and authority to this belief, taught, as we have seen, that the sacrifice of the Mass avails to atone for the sins of the dead as well as the living, and thus to abridge the time of purgatorial torment or secure release from it, and this is the doctrine of the Western church.

The six or seven centuries with which we have hitherto been engaged are the formative period of the Christian religion. By the end of this period—and for the most part long before—its distinctive doctrines had been authoritatively defined and generally accepted in the terms of the creeds; it had also in the writings of the Fathers a classical theological literature of hardly inferior authority; its organisation, institutions, and forms of worship were fully established; it had developed its own types of asceticism and of mysticism. Certain great questions had not been formally decided—the problems of grace and freedom, in the West, for example; others, like the work of Christ, in distinction from his person, had not been adequately discussed, far less satisfactorily solved. But however much was thus left for future generations to do, the decisions of the great councils, the consensus of the Fathers, the prescription of custom, the body of tradition, were regarded on all hands as the unalterable norm of the Christian religion; such it had always been, and such it should always be. That this was an illusion, both as to the past and the future, may seem to the historian palpable; but it was a conservative force of immeasurable consequence. And this Catholic Christianity, whose origins lie in the Apostolic or sub-Apostolic Age, which appears fully developed before the end of the ancient age and was perpetuated essentially unchanged through the Middle Ages, remains to the present day the religion of by far the greater part of Christendom.

CHAPTER IX

CHRISTIANITY

THE MIDDLE AGES

Moslem Conquests—Final Breach between the Eastern and Western
    Churches—Teutonic Invasions—Conversion of the Germanic
    Peoples—Carolingian Revival of Learning—Eucharistic Con-
    troversies—The Mediæval Penitential Discipline—Indulgences—
    Treasury of Merit—Anselm's *Cur Deus Homo*—Church and State:
    Augustine's *Civitas Dei*—The Frankish and German Emperors—
    The Conflict over Investitures—The Issue of Supremacy: Gregory
    VII, Innocent III, Boniface VIII—Denials of Papal Claims—
    The Great Councils: Pisa, Constance, Basel, Florence—Restora-
    tion of Papal Power.

THE Moslem conquests of the seventh century in the
space of a few years wrested Syria and Egypt from the
empire, while Asia Minor was subjected to ever-renewed
invasions which more than once brought the crescent within
sight of Constantinople. The conquerors did not discrimi-
nate among the theological varieties of their Christian subjects; to the churches which had been under the disabilities
of heresy in the empire the impartial toleration of the
caliphate was a deliverance. The great church, on the other
hand, lost the privileges it had enjoyed as the state church
of the empire and the material advantages that accrued
from this position. All branches of the church were confronted by the urgent practical task of adjusting themselves
to the new situation and of maintaining their hold on the
Christian population, resisting the strong motives to defection which the legal and social inferiority of Christians
and the incidence of taxation presented. It might have
been thought that under these circumstances they would
have been drawn together into some kind of union, but this
was not the case; doctrinal differences had long since been
organised in rival churches which had no communion with

one another, and as the heretical churches had their strong-holds among certain populations—Copts, Armenians, Syrians—language was another and permanent divisive principle.

The intellectual life of the Eastern churches was not extinguished by the advent of Islam. A century after the conquest the Greek church had its first—and last—great systematic theologian in John of Damascus, the son of an official of high rank in the service of the caliph, and himself brought up to the same service. His work became the classic of orthodoxy. But the age was past when Greek theologians took the leading part in the discussion and definition of Christian doctrine. The history of theology in the Greek and Oriental churches is in itself an interesting and too much neglected subject; but it may without injustice be said that since the eighth century those churches have had no appreciable part in the historical development of Christianity as a whole.

Notwithstanding sharp conflicts which more than once temporarily interrupted the communion of the Roman Church with the East, the idea of the unity of the church universal was too firmly established and the actual bond of union too strong to permit non-intercourse to harden into permanent division. But in time the complete separation of the Latin-German West from the Byzantine empire dissolved the political ties; the attempts of the popes to assert their headship of the whole church by intervention in internal affairs of the patriarchate of Constantinople; the conservative orthodoxy of the Greeks, who regarded the more progressive West with suspicion and magnified into heresy all departures from their own formulas and customs, led in 1054 to the final breach, when the Pope's legates laid on the altar of Santa Sophia a bull of excommunication against the Patriarch, to which he at once replied in kind by launching an anathema against the Pope. The Oriental patriarchs naturally sided with their Constantinopolitan colleague against the pretensions of Rome. The severance of the

East and the West was complete, and repeated efforts to reunite them came to naught. Through causes partly theological and ecclesiastical, partly political, the gulf has but widened in the course of the centuries.

The great migrations and their political results brought within the sphere of the Greek church and its missionary activity chiefly Slavic (or Slavonised) peoples, and the national churches of Russia, Servia, and Bulgaria, which are sprung from it, contain the great bulk of its present adherents. The racial characteristics of these peoples and their civilisation have made their impress on their Christianity in manifold ways, while the original Greek element has become relatively inconsiderable.

Of the Oriental churches especial interest attaches to that which is commonly called Nestorian, in which the position of the so-called Oriental party in the controversy over the divine and human natures in Christ was perpetuated. Driven from Edessa, where they had maintained a flourishing school, they sought in Persia the toleration that was denied them in the Christian empire, and established at Nisibis a seminary of biblical and theological learning in which the best traditions of the Antiochian school were perpetuated. In the face of repeated and severe persecutions by Persian kings set on by the Zoroastrian clergy, they displayed much zeal for the conversion of the people; in the following century their missions carried Christianity through central Asia, and by 635 they had reached China. In their efforts to convert the Mongols they found themselves in competition with Buddhist monks, and ere long Islam also entered the field. In our own day a remnant of this once numerous and enterprising church survives on the shores of Lake Urmia and in the neighbouring mountains of Kurdistan, and American (Presbyterian), English (Church of England), Roman Catholic, and Russian Orthodox missionaries have vied with one another to convert this handful of Syrian Christians to some one or other of these varieties of alien Christianity, or from one of them to another.

Christianity in the West down to the end of the fourth century was the religion of the Roman and Romanised population, chiefly in the cities.   Among the barbarous (that is, un-Latinised) Berbers in North Africa, Iberians in Spain, Gauls, Britons, and Germans, it had made few converts; in wide regions it had not gained a foothold at all.   In the more thoroughly Romanised parts of the provinces, and even in large parts of Italy, the country people still clung to the gods of their fathers.   The fifth century opened with the first appearance in Italy of Alaric and his Goths (400 A. D.); in 410 he took and sacked the city of Rome.   Before the end of the century the Western Empire had ceased to exist even in name (476); barbarian kingdoms had been established in Gaul, Spain, Africa, and finally in Italy itself. The invaders were of Teutonic race; the invasions were for the most part the migration of tribes or loose confederations of tribes, thrust out of their earlier seats by a more remote Asiatic migration from the steppes (the Huns), and seeking new lands within the borders of the empire.   The first-comers were often pushed from their settlements by fresh waves of migration behind them, or drawn from them by prospect of richer plunder and wider lands beyond, by the adventurous spirit of their chiefs, or by dissensions among them.   When the movement came to rest the invaders set-tled on the land, and, like the Arabs in Syria and Egypt or in Irak in the seventh century, speedily appropriated the civilisation of the conquered and revivified it by the infu-sion of the energy and ambition of a fresh race.   The sub-sequent history of civilisation and of Christianity in the countries which had been included in the Western Empire derives its distinctive character from the blending of Roman and Teutonic strains.

The first of the Germanic peoples with whom the Roman Empire came into conflict were the Goths, who in the fifth and sixth decades of the third century ravaged the Balkan Peninsula and Asia Minor far and wide.   The emperor De-cius fell in battle against them (251), and though they sustained a signal defeat at Naissus (modern Nish) in 269, the emperor Aurelian in 274 withdrew the Roman garrisons from Dacia, leaving the country north of the Danube in the undisputed possession of the Goths, whose settlements extended eastward along the shores of the Black Sea to the Crimea.

It was probably in the latter region that Christianity first reached them; a bishop of Gothia sat in the Council of Nicæa (325). The apostle to the Goths was Ulfila, who was consecrated bishop for them by Eusebius of Nicomedia in 341. It was in the days of Constantius, when Arianism was orthodoxy, and it was thus to an Arian Christianity that the first Teutonic people was converted. Arians both branches of the Goths remained during the two centuries of their national greatness, in Italy, and in Gaul and Spain. All the other Germanic peoples who were converted previous to the end of the fifth century—Suevi, Vandals, Burgundians, Lombards—were either Arians from the beginning or went over to Arianism under the example of their Gothic kinsmen. Except the Vandals in Africa, the conquerors did not molest the Catholic churches in their new kingdoms. The difference of religions ran on lines of race: Teutonic Christianity was Arian; Catholic Christianity was Latin—that was the outstanding difference. For the rest, priesthood, sacraments, liturgy, were similar; practical religious and moral teaching the same.

The Franks on the lower Rhine, at the end of the fifth century (496), were the first considerable Germanic people to embrace Catholic Christianity and hold to it; and as they speedily became the leading German power they were the chief instrument in catholicising Gaul. They drove the Arian Visigoths out of southwestern Gaul into Spain and annexed the Ostrogothic domain in Narbonne and Provence; the impression of these victories converted the Burgundian king. Thus by the middle of the sixth century all Gaul was nominally Catholic. The Visigothic kingdom in Spain went over to the Catholic Church in 589. Among the

Lombards in Italy Catholic influences made themselves felt within a generation after the conquest, by the middle of the seventh century Catholicism prevailed. The Vandals alone remained steadfast in their Arianism till the overthrow of their power by Justinian (533).

The catholicising of the Teutonic nations was not brought about solely by political influences. The Catholic Church was the principal heir of the ancient Latin culture—language, literature, science, art—and when the newcomers sought to possess themselves of this superior civilisation, the Catholic clergy were their natural teachers. Religious unity in turn greatly furthered the amalgamation which rapidly fused not only the Romanised population and the German invaders into one people, but the pagan Gauls and Iberians, who in this period came into the church in large numbers.

The Germanic invaders of Britain, who in the fifth and sixth centuries had overwhelmed the native British Christianity, were converted in the seventh, partly by missionaries sent from Rome (596), partly, especially in the north, by Celtic monks from Ireland. The Irish church in its isolation preserved many antique usages, and had peculiar institutions of its own which it was not disposed to give up at the demand of the foreign ecclesiastics for conformity to the Roman model; it was a full century before the latter completely prevailed in Great Britain.

The Saxons, whose hostility to the Franks extended to their religion, were converted by Charles the Great in a series of wars from 772 to 803; obstinate paganism, overt or covert, and even the attempt to escape baptism or the failure to fast in Lent, was punished by death. The frontier of Christianity was thus pushed eastward to the Elbe. In the next three centuries the Scandinavian countries, as well as Moravia, Bohemia, and Hungary, were Christianised, while the conversion of Russia was in progress from Constantinople. Finally, between the twelfth and fourteenth centuries, Christianity was established in Pomerania, Baltic Prussia, Lithuania, and in Courland and Livland.

Under the Carolingians there was a notable revival of learning in the Frankish church. Charles the Great drew to his court scholars from other lands, such as Paulus Diaconus and Theodulph of Orleans, and in Alcuin of York (d. 814) he had what would now be called a minister of education. Bishops and abbots were required to maintain cathedral and monastery schools; at the court school many of the young nobility were educated under Alcuin's direction. The fruit of this revival is seen in the fact that in the ninth century the Frankish church was ahead of all the rest in learning and intellectual activity.

The revived interest in theological studies soon reopened old controversies or started new ones. We have seen that the prevailing teaching in the Latin church was a mitigated Augustinianism—so much mitigated that since the sixteenth century it has more commonly been called Semi-Pelagianism. The genuine doctrine of Augustine had, however, been maintained in its vigour and rigour by Fulgentius and others in the sixth century, and had never been subjected to ecclesiastical censure. But when in the middle of the ninth century the monk Gottschalk asserted a twofold predestination, "of the elect to repose, of the reprobate to death," he was condemned for the implication that God constrained man to sin against his will—predestination to evil—and spent the rest of his life in confinement in a monastery. This personal condemnation did not deter other theologians, among them Ratramnus, from maintaining views not substantially different from those of the unfortunate monk, while Hinckmar of Rheims went so far beyond the happy mean in the opposite direction that his propositions were censured by synods in other provinces.

Christians from the earliest times believed that in the sacrament of the Eucharist the communicant really partook of the flesh and blood of the divine Saviour and thus became a partaker of the divine life. But in what way the body and blood of Christ are present in the elements was a question the simple believer did not ask, and about which theologians, from at least the second century, entertained different theories. John of Damascus was the first to formulate a physical-transformation doctrine, which became the orthodoxy of the Greek church. A corresponding stage, but with a different theory, was reached in the West a century later in Paschasius Radbertus' treatise, "De Corpore et Sanguine Domini" (831). In the consecration the substance of the bread and wine is inwardly effectively changed into the flesh and blood of Christ, though to the sight and taste there is no change. Moreover, so Paschasius taught, the flesh and blood of Christ upon the altar are the same identical body which was born of Mary, suffered on the cross, and rose from the tomb. "It was the will of Christ that in a mystery this bread and wine, by the consecration of the Holy Spirit, should be potentially created true flesh and blood, and thereby he should daily be mystically sacrificed for the life of the world."

The most eminent Carolingian theologians, Ratramnus, Rabanus Maurus, Walafried Strabo, standing in the Augustinian tradition, controverted Paschasius, rejecting with especial energy the identification of the body and blood in the Eucharist with the body Christ wore on earth; nor were writers lacking in the succeeding centuries who followed them in the teaching that Christ was in the Eucharist, not corporeally, but spiritually. The whole tendency of the age, however, was to the realistic conception of the sacrament, and when in the middle of the eleventh century Berengar of Tours avowed his agreement with Scotus (Eriugena, to whom he erroneously attributed Ratramnus' refutation of Radbertus), and declared that if this were heresy Ambrose and Augustine and Jerome would have to be adjudged heretics, Lanfranc at once procured his condemnation at Rome without so much as a hearing (1050). At a Roman synod in 1059 he was forced to recant and subscribe a statement in which it was declared: "The bread and wine which are placed upon the altar are, after the consecration, not merely a sacrament (i. e., a sacred symbol), but also the true body and blood of the Lord, and are by the senses, not only sacramentally but in fact, handled by the priest, broken and ground by the teeth of the faithful." After a few years the controversy broke out again, and Gregory VII, at another Roman synod in 1079, exacted of Berengar the confession: "I believe in my heart and confess with my mouth that the bread and wine which are placed upon the altar are, by the mystery of holy prayer and the words of our Redeemer, substantially converted into the true and proper and life-giving flesh and blood of Jesus Christ, our Lord, and after the consecration are the true body of Christ which was born of the Virgin, and, being offered for the salvation of the world, hung upon the cross, and which sits at the right hand of God, and the true blood of Christ which was poured from his side, not merely through the sign and virtue of the sacrament, but in its proper nature and true substance."

The opponents of Berengar accepted the consequences of their position, that even to sinners and unworthy communicants the Eucharist is the true flesh and blood of Christ; but only in *nature*, not in salutary effect. In this controversy the Aristotelian categories of substance and accident were first employed to explain the conversion of the elements; the substance, after the consecration, being the body and blood of the Lord; the accidents, the sensible properties of bread and wine, thus laying the foundation for the scholastic theory of transubstantiation.[1]

One of the most important developments of the Middle Ages was a new form of penitential discipline. In the ancient church certain great, and for the most part openly scandalous, sins excluded the offender from the communion of the church and consequently from sacramental grace. Restoration was possible only by the way of a public penitence solemnly undertaken in the presence of the church, and proceeded only by slow stages; the final reconciliation was also a public act, performed with impressive ceremonies by the

[1] This term became current in the twelfth century.

bishop. For sins which were not included in the ancient category of deadly sins the church knew only the *pœnitentia fidelium*, the contrition of the sinner, his own prayers for forgiveness, and the privations—chiefly fasting and other abstinences—which for the good of his soul he imposed upon himself. Naturally such penitents often unburdened their souls by confessing their faults, and sought the pastoral guidance of priests or bishops; and naturally, too, certain customary modes of penance grew up; but this formed no part of the penitential discipline of the church.

The ancient public discipline was ill adapted to the state of society and conditions in the new Teutonic kingdoms, and, in spite of all efforts to uphold or revive it, fell more and more into desuetude. Meanwhile, the foundations of a new system were laid in the monasteries, where monks who had been guilty of an infraction of the rule of the order or of any of the "principal faults" against which the ascetic life was a lifelong conflict—pride, vainglory, envy, anger, lethargy,[1] avarice, gluttony, incontinence—were required to confess their faults before the assembled brethren in the chapter, to beg forgiveness of any they had wronged, and to seek the prayers of the brethren for divine forgiveness. Fasting, vigils, and multiplied prayers were employed as remedies for these faults, and were often thought of as a satisfaction (that is, as making good the fault) to God.

The extension of this discipline to laymen, requiring private confession to a priest and the assumption of a penance imposed by him, seems to have originated in the Celtic church in Ireland, which had from the beginning a peculiar monastic character—its clergy were monks, and its churches were served from the monasteries—and this adaptation of the methods of monastic discipline to the pastoral regimen for the laity was the more natural because the ancient canonical forms of penance had never taken root in the Irish or British churches. For the guidance of those on whom it fell to impose penance, manuals were drawn up, in

---

[1] *Acedia.*

which the normal penance for various sins of clerics or laymen was defined. Fasting for prescribed periods and of prescribed degrees of severity, and the recitation of a certain number of Psalms, are the commonest forms of penance; in the gravest cases, lifelong seclusion in a monastery, exile from the land for a term of years, or pilgrimage to distant holy places was imposed. The measure of even the milder inflictions is often so inordinate that a very ordinary sinner, by cumulation, might find himself with more years of penance to run than of life. It was in accord with the principle of composition in both the Celtic and Teutonic law that severer privations for a shorter time might be substituted; the penance might also be compounded by the devotion of a man's goods to charity or to the church.

From Ireland and England this system spread to the continent with the missionary monks, and though at first opposed by the Frankish clergy, came more and more into use there. For a time the monks alone received the confessions of such as of their own accord resorted to them, and prescribed penance out of their penitential books; but the secular clergy followed their example, and in 789 Charles the Great ordered all priests who had the cure of souls to confess their parishioners. A synod at Châlons in 813 decreed: "One who comes to confess his sins is to be instructed to make confession concerning the eight principal faults which it is difficult to avoid in this life, whether he has committed them in thought or, worse yet, in deed." The practice of private confession rapidly became general. A law for the whole church, making it obligatory on all the faithful, was first made, however, at the Fourth Lateran Council in 1215: "Every Christian of either sex who has come to years of discretion must privately confess all his sins truthfully to his own priest at least once a year, and endeavour to the best of his ability to fulfil the penance imposed upon him, reverently receiving the sacrament of the Eucharist at least at Easter."

Originally the penitent had to fulfil penance before being

restored to good standing in the church; but the Irish penitentials sometimes provide for his rehabilitation after the lapse of a part of the period, and in the end absolution came to be given upon the penitent's solemn engagement to perform the penance imposed upon him. The form of absolution long continued to be deprecatory, for example: "May Almighty God be thy helper and protector, and grant indulgence for thy sins, past, present, and future." Only about 1200 did the prayer for divine forgiveness give place to the priest's declarative *"Absolvo te,"* and theologians, even later, were not at one about the significance of the priestly absolution. There can be no doubt, however, that those who received absolution, in whatever phrase, took the act as certifying, if not conveying, the remission of sins.

The three essential elements of penitence are *contritio cordis, confessio oris,* and *satisfactio operis.* The older understanding was that the divine remission was conditioned upon all three, and therefore was bestowed only when the penance (*satisfactio*) had been completed. When, however, absolution was pronounced before the performance or even the beginning of the penance, the question arose what significance the *satisfactiones* had. The solution adopted by the schoolmen was that by absolution the sinner is relieved of the eternal punishment justly due to every sin, but not of its temporal penalties in this life or beyond. These must be endured either in providential afflictions borne in a penitent spirit or in the form of penance. The sins of the faithful for which satisfaction has not in one or the other of these ways been made in this life remain to be expiated in the fires of purgatory. In this form and definition penitence is a sacrament through which the remission of sins is assured. Even deadly sins by virtue of it become venial; that is, they do not remedilessly consign the sinner to eternal torment in hell.

Related in principle to the commutations and redemptions of penance to which reference has been made above are indulgences. Bishops, at the dedication of a church, for example, granted those who resorted to the church on that occasion and made their offerings there "indulgence" (that is, remission) of a certain fraction (*e. g.*, half) of the penance they might be under at the time. Subsequently indulgences were granted running for a stated period of time and applicable to the reduction of the penance to which a man might therein become liable. The custom apparently had its abuses, for the Fourth Lateran Council (1215) decreed that bishops should not grant more than a year's indulgence at the consecration of a church, and on other occasions not more than forty days.

Distinct from these episcopal indulgences were the plenary indulgences granted by the popes. The first of this kind were offered by Urban II to the crusaders (1095) in the following form: "Whoever out of pure devotion, and not for the purpose of gaining honour or wealth, shall go to Jerusalem to liberate the church of God, may reckon that journey in lieu of all penance." Papal indulgences were later offered on many occasions, of which the most notable was the Papal Jubilee instituted by Boniface VIII in 1300. To such as, being penitent and confessed, should, on fifteen days in that year (or, if residents of the city of Rome, on thirty days) visit the basilicas of St. Peter and St. Paul, "we grant," so the bull runs, "not only a full and ample, but the very fullest pardon of all their sins." Boniface contemplated a jubilee every hundred years; but Clement VI appointed one in 1350, and the interval was later shortened to thirty-three, and in 1475 to twenty-five years; it was also early extended beyond Rome, and plenary indulgences "in the form of jubilee" have been frequently proclaimed at other times.

The scholastic theologians raised the question: If the church, by the authority given it by its Master, "Whosesoever sins ye remit, they are remitted," released the individual from the satisfaction he was bound to make, how was this debt to God paid? They solved the problem by the theory of the treasury of merits. In this treasury are

accumulated, together with the infinite satisfaction made
by Christ (the *supererogationes Christi, quœ sunt thesaurus
spiritualis ecclesiœ*—Alexander of Hales), the superabundant
satisfactions of the Virgin Mary and the saints; and upon
this treasury the church draws for the payment of the debts
remitted to the faithful by indulgences. Authority was
given to this doctrine by Clement VI in his jubilee bull
(1343). Another question was whether the indulgences
apply only to penances imposed by the church, and therefore expire with this life, or whether they avail also for the
satisfaction that remains to be made in purgatory. Thomas
Aquinas maintained that their efficacy is not limited to this
life; they are valid to release *a reatu pœnœ* in purgatory
also. Down to the middle of the fifteenth century, however,
the contrary opinion was held by some theologians of repute. Moreover, since in mediæval law satisfaction might
be made by one man for another, it followed in theology
that indulgences acquired by the living may be applied to
the benefit of the faithful dead in purgatory. The first
formal grant of indulgences for the dead (*per modum suffragii*) was made in a bull of Sixtus IV in 1476.

The most important contribution of the mediæval church
to the completion of the Christian system of doctrine, the
necessity of the death of Christ as a vicarious satisfaction
for the sins of men, or as it is commonly called the doctrine
of the atonement, is closely connected with the development
of the penitential discipline which we have been following.
The theologians of the early church found the reason of the
incarnation either in the need of a complete revelation of
divinity in the Logos, or in the necessity that divinity should
enter into humanity in order that humanity might participate in divine immortality.[1] But neither of these theories
adequately explained the necessity of the *death* of Christ. A
common explanation, accepted even by Origen, was that
his life was given for mankind as a ransom to the devil, who
overreached himself in the transaction and thereby lost his

---

[1] See above, pp. 160 *f.* and pp. 162 *f.*

right to the death of all men.[1] The same view, along with others, appears in Augustine, and was current down to Anselm's day. Partial anticipations of Anselm's theory may be recognised in Augustine and especially in Gregory the Great, but the more immediate premises were the predominating conception of the death of Christ as a sacrifice to God, associated as it was with the sacrifice of the Mass, and the belief that satisfaction is indispensable to the remission of sins, which, with the related ideas of debt and desert, was firmly established in the mediæval practice and theory of penitence. The argument of Anselm's "Cur deus homo" may be briefly summarised as follows:

Every rational creature owes to God complete conformity to his will. If man does not render this obedience, he robs God of the honour that is his due. This is the nature of sin, and so long as man does not pay to God what he has robbed him of he abides in sin. Nor is it sufficient merely to restore what he withheld; as amends for the dishonour done to God man must return more than he took away. This is the satisfaction which every sinner is bound to make to God. God cannot ignore the offence, for that would subvert the moral order of the world by doing away the difference between the righteous and sinners, and contravene the law of retribution under which by divine ordinance man and his deeds lie.

Sin demands, therefore, either punishment or satisfaction. But if God should punish man as his sin deserves, it would frustrate his purpose in the creation of mankind.[2] Nor can man make adequate satisfaction; first, because he can never do more than it is his duty to do, and, second, because the dishonour done to God by his defection requires amends beyond human measure. The whole world is no equivalent for the smallest disobedience against God, and a satisfaction adequate to man's sin must be greater than all in the universe that is not God.

Such a satisfaction God alone can make, while, as a satisfaction for men's sins, it must be made by a man. He who is to make the satisfaction must therefore be at once perfect God and perfect man. Ac-

[1] This resulted from a combination of New Testament passages in which the death of Christ is spoken of as a ransom (e. g., Mark 10, 45) with 1 Cor. 2, 8.

[2] Which was, according to Anselm, to replace with human beings the number of the angels who fell.

cordingly, by the birth from the Virgin, God took unto himself a sinless man, in a union in which the integrity of neither nature is impaired. This God-man rendered to God the perfect obedience he owed, and freely offered to the Father the life which he had not forfeited—"*tam pretiosam vitam, immo seipsum, tantam scilicet personam tanta voluntate dedit*"—thus giving to God something incomparably greater than aught that is not God, and sufficient to make good all the debts of the human race. Such a gift could not go unrequited; and, needing nothing for himself, Christ made over the recompense to men, that they may share in his merit, that the debt they have incurred by sin may be cancelled, and the grace which on account of their sins they lack may be conferred upon them.

The pivotal points in the theory are that without satisfaction there is no remission of sins, and that, as an offence against God's honour,[1] sin demands such immeasurable amends as could be made only by the death of the God-man, the merits of which are transferred to men. The argument is conducted with notable logical acumen, and the form of dialogue gives the author opportunity to discuss various objections which may be raised against the theory. Most of the schoolmen adopted the Anselmic doctrine. In the form in which it was put by Aquinas it became an article of Catholic orthodoxy, and—what in view of its premises and implications is more remarkable—a central dogma of Protestant orthodoxy as well. In regard to the satisfaction which the sinner himself makes in penance, Aquinas teaches that it suffices, not of itself, but because God accepts it; "and since everything imperfect supposes a perfect by which it is sustained, every satisfaction made by a mere man derives its efficacy from the satisfaction of Christ"—a not unimportant supplement to the theory of penitence.

The only other mediæval theory of the atonement that requires notice, rather as an anticipation of some modern opinions than for its immediate influence, is that of Abelard (d. 1142). Developing the idea of Paul in Romans 5, 8 *f.*— an idea which was of great significance to Augustine—he

---

[1] Offences against *honour* are great in proportion to the dignity of the offended party.

taught that the revelation of the love of God in the death
of Christ inspires in men the love which makes them sons of
God. Abelard finds in this effect not alone a psychological
explanation of justification (in the Catholic sense), but the
rationale of the divine plan of salvation. He speaks indeed
the language of Scripture and of the church—Christ offered
himself as a sacrifice to God; in his death he bore the punishment of men's sins—but he carries this thought no further, and does not, like Anselm, conceive the death of
Christ as a *necessary* satisfaction to God. "Our redemption is that supreme love in us, through the suffering of
Christ, which not only delivers us from the bondage of sin,
but gains for us the true freedom of the sons of God."

So long as the empire was pagan the government seldom
interfered in the domestic affairs of the church; but when
Christianity became the religion of the empire the imperial
autocrat ruled the church as sovereignly as he ruled the
state. The emperors called general councils; appointed the
presiding bishop; openly, or from behind the scenes, determined their action in matters of dogma as well as of administration and discipline, and enforced their decisions. They
issued doctrinal formulas in their own name, and even took
it upon them to pronounce the teaching of great theologians
heretical. They named, transferred, and removed bishops
and patriarchs with at most a *pro forma* respect to canonical
procedure. This supremacy of the state over the church
was taken as a matter of course, and, however great the
dissatisfaction with particular acts, the right of the emperor
over the church, by virtue of his headship in the state, was
not contested.

The West was not so immediately under the eye and control of the autocrat in Constantinople; in the age of the barbarian invasions it was for a long time left to its own
resources. But when the imperial power in Italy was
restored in 536, Justinian resumed the sovereignty in ecclesiastical as in civil affairs. A pope who had been duly
elected by the clergy, people, and soldiers of Rome, in joint

congregation at the Lateran, could not be consecrated without the mandate of the emperor in Constantinople or his representative, the exarch in Ravenna; and this continued the law till the fall of the exarchate in 751.

The ideas of church and state in the Middle Ages were profoundly influenced by Augustine's "De Civitate Dei," a work which embodies his ripest thought and is the crown of his literary achievements, a Christian counterpart to the Republic of Plato. Two states stand over against each other, a heavenly and an earthly. Cain, the builder of the first city, is the founder of the *civitas terrena*, as his brother Seth is of the *cœlestis*. Two diametrically opposite affections created and characterise them: self-love reaching to contempt of God, the earthly; love of God even to contempt of self, the heavenly. The earthly state had its origin in violence. In it selfishness reigns, and the conflict of merely self-regarding aims would make it no better than one great *latrocinium*, did not self-interest itself discover the necessity of keeping order and protecting men against one another. Thus, without change in its nature, the state undertakes to maintain the peace, and achieves an imperfect kind of justice.

The typical representatives of the *civitas terrena* are Babylon and ancient Rome, while the *cœlestis* is represented before Christ by the Jews, and now by the Christian church. The heavenly state is, however, not to be identified with the actual church; it is an ideal commonwealth which numbers among its citizens those who have gone before and those who shall come after, as well as those now on earth. And as in this respect it is wider than the actual church, so in another it is narrower, for it includes only the elect who are predestinated to reign with God. As in the old dispensation there were in the Jewish church many reprobate, so it is now in the Christian church; and these, notwithstanding their external relation to the church and its sacraments, belong to the *civitas terrena*. Inasmuch as there is no certain sign by which the elect are distinguished from the

reprobate, there is thus—to use the language of a later time
—a church invisible within the visible church.

The heathen empire persecuting the church was the embodiment of the kingdom of this world in its opposition to
the kingdom of God. But in Augustine's time, when the rulers were Christians, when Christianity was the religion of the
state, and the laws had in many points been amended and
supplemented to accord with Christian standards, the Roman Empire could no longer be identified outright with the
civitas terrena; all the less because, rationalising the material
chiliastic expectations of the early church, Augustine saw in
the triumph of Christianity in the empire the beginning of
the millennium, the reign of Christ on earth. An analogy
was again suggested to him by the Jewish economy, where
the theocratic state (a *civitas terrena*) was a shadow of the
civitas Dei, in which alone its significance lay, and which it
served. So now, in Christian times, rulers who employ
their power to promote the widest extension of the worship
of God, thus making their power the servant of the divine
majesty, may be citizens of the commonwealth of God.

The Catholic Church and the Christian Empire were not
for Augustine the (ideal) *civitas Dei* and *civitas terrena,* but
they were, so to speak, their historical incorporations, and
it was inevitable that in minds less imbued with Platonic
idealism this distinction should be effaced and the conception simplified by identifying the *civitas Dei* with the church.
Augustine himself, when he writes as a practical church-
man, is not scrupulous to observe his own distinction. The
common idea of the church as an institution in which those
who hold its faith, receive its efficacious sacraments, and
die in its communion are saved, neutralised the Augustinian
doctrine which limited salvation to an unrecognisable congregation of the predestinated within the church, even
among those who accepted it. Thus, Gregory the Great,
while reaffirming Augustine's definitions, asserts that "every
one knows that the holy church is the city of the Lord," and
proceeds to the application, the earthly power (the state)

is bound to serve the church. A corollary of Augustine's theory which had a great influence on the political thinking of the Middle Ages was that, as there was on earth but one embodiment of the celestial commonwealth, the Catholic Church, so there could be but one of the terrestrial, the Roman Empire.

The struggle of the church, first for independence of the civil powers and then for supremacy over them, may be called the leading motive of mediæval history. In the course of this conflict not only was the monarchical centralisation of ecclesiastical power in the hands of the popes brought to consummation, but a doctrine of the supreme authority, by divine right, of the popes over political rulers was formulated, to which the Catholic church has consistently adhered.

The new era which began with the Carolingian kingdom opened with an auspicious harmony between the two powers. The pope gave his sanction beforehand to the deposition of the last of the Merovingian puppet kings, and the elevation of Pippin to succeed him—it was better that the name of king should be borne by him who had the royal power than by him who had none. Pippin was accordingly acclaimed at Soissons, and anointed king by Boniface (751), and subsequently by Pope Stephen II himself. On his part Pippin came to the help of the pope against the Lombards, who had subdued the exarchate,[1] and, having recovered the conquered territory, bestowed it upon the pope, thus laying the foundation of the temporal power of the papacy, which was confirmed and enlarged by Pippin's son and successor, Charles the Great, after the overthrow of the Lombard kingdom in 774.

The coronation of Charles by Pope Leo III in St. Peter's on Christmas Day, 800 A. D., was, in the minds of the participants and of the people who acclaimed him Augustus and Emperor of the Romans, the revival of an independent

---

[1] The parts of Italy which were ruled in the name of the emperors in Constantinople, with Ravenna as the capital.

Roman Empire of the West.   In later times the coronation
of the emperor by the pope was interpreted as a demonstration of the sovereignty of the spiritual power over the
temporal: in the exercise of his divine right the pope had
taken the empire from the Greeks and bestowed it upon
the Frankish king.   Contemporaries did not attach such a
significance or deduce such consequences from the act.
The precedent was nevertheless momentous.   The anointing of kings, after Old Testament example, was a consecration which lent a religious sanction to the succession, or
upon occasion to usurpation; the coronation of an emperor
by the pope came more and more to be regarded as a confirmation of the election by the princes.

The immediate result, however, was that the new rulers
exercised over the election of popes a control like that
which had been exercised by the emperors in Constantinople.   The election by the clergy and people of Rome was
subject to the confirmation of the emperor, represented by
his ambassador (*missus*), who from 824 permanently resided
in the city.   In his own kingdom Charles, like his predecessors, appointed bishops as of royal prerogative, convoked
synods and presided at them, issued in capitularies laws for
the national church, and controlled its discipline by means
of his *missi*.   In the controversy over images the Frankish
church, as has been noted, had a mind of its own, and did
not hesitate to pass censure on Pope Adrian.   The closer
relations of the Carolingians with the Roman Church, which
led among other things to the introduction of the Roman
liturgy in their domains, were not allowed in any way to
infringe on the autonomy of the Frankish church or the
prerogative of the Frankish king.   In Italy itself Charles
assumed the same authority in ecclesiastical affairs as in
his own kingdom; his *missi* exercised oversight even over
papal officials, heard complaints, and entertained appeals.
He himself, before his coronation as emperor, sat in judgment on the charges brought against Pope Leo by his
enemies.

Under the weaker hands of Charles's successors the church strove to emancipate itself from this tutelage, and Nicholas I, one of the great figures in the history of the papacy, vigorously upheld the independence of the church, resisting all interference of the civil powers in ecclesiastical affairs. In the church itself he asserted the supreme authority of the Roman see by virtue of the primacy of Peter; all the rights of bishops and councils are derived from the powers conferred on him by Christ. In the exercise of this authority Nicholas annulled the acts of synods, deposed archbishops, and humbled the most powerful and imperious of Frankish prelates, Hinckmar of Rheims. In pronouncing illegitimate a synod which Hinckmar as metropolitan had convened according to custom, Nicholas laid down the rule, so often cited in later times: "No one has the right to convoke a general council without the consent of the pope."

With the revival of the empire, a century later, the Ottos made and unmade popes at their will;[1] their successors left Italy to itself and the papacy became for a time an appanage of the counts of Tusculum. Henry III delivered the church from the scandal of three popes at once in Rome itself by procuring the deposition or resignation of all three, and caused his own nominee, a German bishop, to be elected to the vacant see (1046). The two following popes were made in the same way. With them began an epoch of reform in the church in the spirit of the movement which had its origin in the monastic reforms at Cluny in the preceding century.

The reformers saw one of the chief causes of the lamentable state of the church in its dependence on the civil power, and one of their first aims was to secure the independence of the papacy by taking the papal elections out of the control either of Roman factions or the German emperor. To accomplish this, the choice of a pope was committed by the

[1] Otto I invaded Italy in defence of the pope, and was crowned emperor in 962. He confirmed the pope in the possession of his temporal power and enlarged the territories subject to him.

Lateran synod in 1059, under Nicholas II, to the cardinals, primarily the cardinal bishops;[1] leaving to the other clergy and the people of Rome only the formality of assent. The appointment to the cardinalate in this period of men of different nations not only made that body more truly representative of the whole church but gave the reforming party a predominant influence in the curia. The synod of 1059 also made stringent decrees against the two inveterate evils, clerical concubinage and the procuring of ordination or promotion in the church for money. Finally, it forbade any cleric to get a church through laymen in any way, whether for a price or gratis.

This decree was meant to strike at the root of lay domination over the church, and the attempt to force this reform inevitably brought the church into conflict with the civil power. Many of the bishoprics and abbeys had large landed possessions, bestowed on them by the piety of rulers and nobles, which under the feudal system the bishops and abbots held as feoffs from their lords, for which they were bound to do homage, pay tallage, furnish a quota of armed retainers, and even to follow their liege to war. In Germany the ecclesiastical vassals were a main support of the king against the more independent dukes and lesser nobility. Ecclesiastical posts were frequently conferred for personal and political reasons on religiously unworthy persons; they were often simply sold—of course under less vulgar names. The bishops in turn sold preferment to benefices and church dignities. Many abbacies were bestowed *in commendam* on laymen, who enjoyed the revenues without concern for the purposes of the foundation, or they were similarly turned

---

[1] Cardinal bishops are the bishops of certain suburban churches in the immediate vicinity of Rome (since the eighth century, seven in number), who assisted the pope in his ritual functions, and constituted a kind of permanent synod. Cardinal priests were the priests serving certain principal ("cardinal") churches in the city of Rome. The class of cardinal deacons grew out of the ancient division of the city into districts for the administration of charity, which in time came to have their centre in a particular church in the district.

over to bishops, whose wealth was thus augmented by the impoverishment of the monasteries. The protection of lay patrons or feudal lords often enabled the clergy to snap their fingers at the authority of their ecclesiastical superiors in their efforts to enforce canonical discipline. Laymen who had built or endowed churches or monasteries on their own lands retained the right of patronage, and followed the example set them from above in disposing of the positions in their gift.

The reformers saw only one way to remedy these evils, namely, to make an end of the system of lay investiture, root and branch. It was accordingly decreed that no cleric should receive the investiture of a bishopric, abbacy, or church from the hand of emperor, king, or any lay person whatsoever. Such investiture is declared to be null and void, and both the secular ruler who confers it and the cleric who receives it incur excommunication *ipso facto*. Vacancies in bishoprics are to be filled by canonical elections, at which the clergy and people choose their pastor under the direction and with the consent of the metropolitan or of an episcopal visitor appointed by the Apostolic See.

This effort to do away with lay investiture and make a reality of canonical election encountered opposition not only in Germany, but in France and England. The entanglement of the church in the feudal system was too complete and of too long standing to permit its cutting itself loose by its own fiat. At one moment, later in the conflict, it was seriously proposed by a pope that the church should surrender all the lands, rights, and privileges it held from the crown, the emperor agreeing on his part to give up the right of investiture. The independence of the church would thus have been purchased at the price of its worldly power and possessions. Such a solution was as impracticable from the one side as from the other, and the plan was quickly dropped. But if the church retained its possessions, bishops and abbots would have to continue to be invested with them in customary feudal fashion, and the sovereigns would continue to determine on whom they would confer the office with the feoff. A compromise, based on a distinction between the political and the ecclesiastical character of the bishop, was arrived at in the Concordat of Worms (1122), in which the free canonical election of bishops, *absque simonia et aliqua violentia*, was promised by the emperor, but they must be held in his presence or that of his representative. The emperor gave up the form of investiture by ring and staff, the insignia of the spiritual office, by which he seemed to confer the episcopate, and invested with the temporalities by touching the newly chosen bishop with his sceptre, the symbol of temporal rule. In Germany the enfeoffment must precede the consecration. The rights of both church and state seemed thus to be safeguarded, but manifestly the emperor was left a very effective way of excluding candidates who did not please him.

In the strife over investitures the larger issue of supremacy inevitably emerged, and Gregory VII developed to its utmost consequence the principle that the church is above the state, and that the pope as the head of the church has by divine right supreme power not only in the church, but *a fortiori* over secular rulers, even the highest. He claimed authority to dethrone sovereigns who did not obey the church and to release their subjects from their allegiance, and enforced his sentence by excommunication, and by the new and tremendous weapon of the interdict, which suspended public worship, the administration of the sacraments, and funereal rites in the territories subject to the recalcitrant prince. In the exercise of this power he declared Henry IV deprived of his royal rights in Germany and Italy, and all Christians released from any oath they had made or might make to him; and, favoured by the political conjuncture in Germany, he compelled Henry to go to Canossa. The picture of the king in penitential garb, presenting himself barefoot in the snow at the gate of the castle on three successive days, seeking admission to the presence of the pope, impresses the imagination not merely by the dramatic fact but by its symbolical significance. But it had its reverse. Henry answered a fresh excommunication by causing synods at Mainz and Brixen to pronounce the deposition of the pope, and a new pope, Clement III, to be chosen. Gregory died at Salerno, where he had taken refuge on Norman territory, a few months after Henry's pope had crowned his master emperor in Rome. His last words were, "I have loved righteousness and hated iniquity, therefore I die in exile."

The ideas of Augustine's "Civitas Dei" are evident in Gregory's conception of the relation of church and state. The origin and nature of earthly government is thus set forth: "Who can be ignorant that kings and dukes started with men who, knowing not God, prompted by the ruler of this world, the devil, by arrogance, robbery, perfidy, murder, and almost all crimes, with blind lust of power and intolerable presumption, assumed to lord it over men their peers." The contemporary factor in Gregory's thinking is the influence of feudal ideas. As in the feudal kingdom all power and authority derived directly or mediately from the king, so in the ecclesiastical hierarchy from the pope. The oath which Gregory required of the metropolitans corresponded to the vassal's oath of fealty to the king; the conferring of the pallium was a form of ecclesiastical investiture; bishops took an oath of submission to their metropolitans. Similarly in the political sphere. Once the principle admitted that the *sacerdotium* has precedence over the *imperium*, and it follows not only that "the priests of Christ are the fathers and masters of kings and princes and of all the faithful," but, according to feudal notions, that whatever rights the empire had were conferred on it by the church. The coronation of kings and emperors was then not merely a religious consecration but a kind of investiture. Gregory draws this consequence: "Those whom the Holy Church, of its own motion, with deliberate intention, calls to reign or empire, not for fleeting glory but for the welfare of many, should be humbly obedient." Gregory's ideal was

17

a feudally organised theocracy, in which the pope, as the vicar of God, was suzerain.

The emperors naturally entertained quite different notions of the way God intended the world to be governed. When, in 1157, Pope Hadrian IV reminded Frederick I, Barbarossa, of the gratitude he owed the Roman Church for conferring on him the imperial crown, and held out to him the prospect of larger "*beneficia*," the emperor bluntly replied: "Inasmuch as our royal and imperial power is derived, through election by the princes, from God alone, who by the suffering of Christ his Son subjected the world to be ruled by the necessary two swords, and since the Apostle Peter taught the world this doctrine, 'Fear God, honour the king,' whoever says that we have received the imperial power *pro beneficio*[1] from the pope contravenes the divine institutions and the teaching of Peter, and is guilty of falsehood."

The climax of papal power was reached under Innocent III (1198–1216). In the church he achieved the concentration of power in the hands of the pope which corresponded to the autocratic idea of the office. It was a corollary of this idea that the function of the bishops was to assist the pope in the administration of the church: "He has called them to help him by taking a part of his care, that thus the burden of his so great charge may be the better borne through subsidiary agencies." The right to name bishops and abbots, to translate bishops, and to depose them is, from these premises, indisputable.

Innocent III also claimed the right to judge of the fitness of the king whom the princes had chosen, and in disputed elections to decide between the claimants, basing his right on the transference of the empire from the Greeks to the Occidentals by Pope Leo III, and on the fact that only the pope could crown an emperor. He exercised this right in behalf of Otto IV against Philip of Swabia; and when Otto failed to keep his impossible promises, crowned Frederick II

[1] Taking the term in its feudal sense, "as a feoff."

in his stead. Nor was it in the affairs of the empire alone
that he thus intervened. Philip Augustus of France, Peter
of Aragon, Alfonso IX of Leon, Sancho of Portugal, Ladis-
laus of Poland, were all forced to submit to his will. The
English king John, who declined to accept an archbishop
of Canterbury named by the pope, was brought to terms by
the threat of a crusade, and consented to hold England and
Ireland as a feoff from the Holy See and pay an annual tribute for them; while in the conflict between John and the
barons Innocent pronounced the Magna Charta null and
void, and forbade the king to observe it or the barons to
enforce it under pain of excommunication. "The Lord left
to Peter not only the whole church but the whole world
to govern"—this was Innocent's doctrine, and he did his
best to live up to it. His next successors followed in his
footsteps, and in their struggle with the empire accomplished
the ruin of the house of Hohenstauffen.

In the second half of the thirteenth century there were
in the course of fifty years no less than fourteen popes; and
even if they had been men of greater mark than they were,
the brevity of their tenure of power of itself would have
prevented them from sustaining the papacy at the height
which it had reached under Innocent III. Boniface VIII
(1294–1303), a man of great ability and towering ambition,
tried to reclaim the supremacy which Innocent had exercised, but the times had changed, and Boniface failed where
his predecessor had succeeded. France, under Philip the
Fair, and England, under Edward I, were altogether different nations to deal with from the loose structure of the
German Empire.

The first issue was the right of the state to tax the property of the church and of clerical persons, a right which
the pope claimed for himself alone. Boniface, under penalty of excommunication, forbade emperors, kings, and
nobles of every rank, to impose under any name a tax or
tribute upon the church or to lay hands on its property,
and prohibited clerics of every rank from agreeing to pay

taxes or making contributions to the state, or keeping any promises they might have made to that effect. Edward I ignored the bull; Philip answered it by forbidding gold and silver to be exported from his kingdom, thus cutting off at a stroke a large part of the papal revenue. A few years later the pope summoned the French prelates to Rome to deliberate on reforms in the French church, and cited the king to appear there in person, haughtily reminding him that a king of France was bound to obey the pope. The states-general supported the king, and forbade the French bishops attending the council. A school of jurists had grown up in France, who from a revived study of the civil law derived a doctrine of the supremacy of the state with which the papal claims were irreconcilable. The church in a nation, they held, was subject to its authority; its property was subject to taxation and must bear its part in the burdens of the state; clerical persons were subject to the jurisdiction of the civil courts in civil and criminal causes. The curialist lawyers and the scholastic theologians stoutly maintained the contrary doctrine.

The conflict produced the explicit and authoritative definition of the supremacy of the church over all civil powers in the bull of Boniface VIII, "Unam Sanctam Ecclesiam Catholicam" (1302). The two swords (Luke 22, 38), the spiritual and the temporal authority, were both committed by Christ to the church, the one to be used *by* it, the other to be wielded *for* it and at its bidding by secular rulers. The spiritual power has to institute the earthly, and to judge it if it goes astray; the supreme spiritual power, the pope, is subject to no human judgment, but to God's only. "He who resists this power thus ordained by God resists the ordinance of God." "This authority, although it is given to a man and exercised by a man, is not a human but a divine power, given by the mouth of God to Peter for himself and his successors in Christ. . . . Wherefore we declare, affirm, define, and pronounce that to be subject to the Roman pontiff is unqualifiedly necessary unto salvation for every human creature." Such guidance must be inerrant; and Thomas Aquinas, who in the preceding generation taught the same doctrine of necessary subjection to the pontiff, joined with it papal infallibility, which was after all only an adaptation of the old tradition that Christ had promised that the Roman church should never err in doctrine.

The bull "Unam Sanctam" formulated unsurpassably the doctrine of papal absolutism. But this extreme assertion of papal prerogative overstrained the bow. The kingdoms of Europe, strong in national spirit and national pride, had no disposition to bow submissively to a foreign dominion. Benedict XI had to recede from the intransigeant attitude Boniface had taken in the conflict with France, and after his brief reign (1303–'04) the French party prevailed in the conclave and elected the archbishop of Bordeaux, who ascended the throne as Clement V (1305–'14). The new pope was crowned at Lyons, and in 1309 permanently fixed his residence in Avignon, an enclave in French territory, where he and his successors were dependent on French support and subservient to French interests.

The whole theory on which the papal claim to temporal as well as spiritual autocracy was based was challenged from more than one side. Dante, in his "De Monarchia," held that the imperial power is derived from the supremacy of the Romans over the whole world, which was given them directly by God and is to exist to the end of the world, assuring the temporal well-being of men, as their spiritual well-being is dependent upon the pope. The conflict between the Emperor Ludwig the Bavarian and Pope John XXII produced the most important contribution to the literature of the controversy, the "Defensor Pacis" of Marsilius of Padua and John of Jandun, which discusses the origin and end of the state and the relations of the secular and sacerdotal powers, and deduces from this exposition a series of conclusions of a much more radical character. Not only is the jurisdiction of the civil ruler over ecclesiastical persons and his control in ecclesiastical affairs set forth with unflinching consequence, but the basis of the pontifical claims in the primacy of Peter is flatly denied. All bishops are of equal authority derived directly from Christ; there is no warrant for the claim that one of them is the superior of others in spiritual or temporal matters. To define what is of faith and to decide doubtful points in the divine law only a general council of the faithful is competent; no partial assembly or individual of whatever rank has such power. Similarly, only a council can make acts which are not prohibited by divine law offences at ecclesiastical law. From the commandments and prohibitions of the New Testament no human being can dispense men. Only the lawmaking power in a Christian state can order the meeting of a general or local council, and only a council so convened is legitimate. In short, the power of the pope to give law to the church in matters of faith and morals or in discipline, with the consequent power of dispensation, and his jurisdiction over the church at large, as well as the supremacy of the sacerdotal over the civil power—one may say, the whole mediæval theory of the papacy—was categorically rejected.

The scholastic theologian Occam,[1] involved in the conflict of the strict Franciscans with the same pope, John XXII, also took refuge with Ludwig the Bavarian, and employed his pen in defence of the emperor's side against the pope. Applying the principle of the sole authority of Scripture, he denied *in toto* the papal claim to rule over rulers: the highest civil power, the empire, and the highest spiritual power, the church, are in their respective spheres independent and of equal authority. On similar grounds he denied the infallibility of the pope in matters of doctrine; the decision of John XXII concerning the poverty of Christ and his disciples was in his eyes flatly against the Scripture and a glaring instance of papal fallibility.

The practical assertion of the principle that the supreme

[1] See below, pp. 275 f.

authority in the church is not vested in the Roman pontiff, but in a general council, was not brought about by controversial writings like the "Defensor Pacis," but by the history of the church itself. The seventy years' captivity, as the Romans called the Avignonese papacy, seemed to be happily ended by the return of Gregory XI to Rome in 1377. Upon his death in the following year an Italian pope, Urban VI, was elected to succeed him, but within four months he had so alienated the cardinals that they declared the election void on the ground that it had been made under duress, and elected Cardinal Robert of Geneva, who took the title Clement VII. Urban maintained himself in Rome; Clement, after an unsuccessful attempt to oust his rival, took up his residence in Avignon. For half a century, the allegiance of the European nations was divided fairly equally between two popes. The situation was not only a clamant scandal to Christendom, but it doubled the burdens and aggravated all the evils of the papal financial system. All efforts to restore the unity of the church by the action of the popes themselves proved futile, and at last the cardinals of the two parties united to call a general council. This council met at Pisa in 1409, and, asserting its right as representing the church universal, deposed both popes on the ground that they were in heresy against the unity of the Catholic Church by the very fact that there were two of them, and elected a new one. Since the deposed popes did not recognise their deposition, the result was that the church had three popes instead of two, and this triad was perpetuated by the election, in 1410, of John XXIII, as successor to the Pisan pope. To put an end to this situation, the emperor Sigismund constrained John to convene a new general council at Constance in 1414.

The Council of Constance affirmed its character and authority with the utmost clearness: "This Holy Council of Constance . . . declares that, being legitimately convened in the Holy Spirit, constituting a general council and representing the Catholic Church, it has its power immediately from Christ, and that every man of whatever station or dignity, even the papal, is bound to obey it in those things which pertain to faith and the extirpation of the aforesaid schism and the reformation of the church in head and members."

The claim of the council to represent the church was not a mere phrase. In it sat not only bishops and mitred abbots, but doctors of theology and of law from the universities, and delegates of civil rulers. Warned by the experience of Pisa, the council endeavoured to bring the popes to resign, holding deposition over them as a last resort. All obstacles being finally removed, a new pope, Martin V (1417–'31), was chosen, under regulations laid down by the council, by an electoral college composed of the cardinals together with thirty other members of the council, six from each of the participating nations. There was again at last one universally acknowledged head of the church. Before and after the election of Martin V there was much discussion of reforms in the administration and discipline of the church, and particularly in the papal fiscal system, but conflicting interests of nations, churchmen, and corporations prevented harmony about the nature and extent of these reforms. Some things were agreed upon and decreed by the council, but it left the rest and most important to be settled by concordats between the pope and the several countries singly.

According to precedent and papal claims a council could only be convoked by the pope, and experience had shown that precisely at the times that a council was most needed the pope was least inclined to call one. To remedy this condition, the Council of Constance decreed that another council should meet at the end of five years from its own adjournment, a second seven years later, and thereafter once every ten years. The pope and cardinals might, if occasion arose, call a council in the interval, but they had no authority to postpone the decennial meeting. Each council, before its adjournment, was to appoint the place of meeting for the next, in concurrence with the pope, or, in default of his action, by its own decision.

Provision seemed thus to be made for a regular succession of councils representing the whole church, and exercising in its name the supreme authority in doctrine and discipline which the popes had claimed for themselves. The Council of Basel (1431-'49) reaffirmed the decrees of Constance concerning the independence and authority of general councils, and replied to an attempt of the pope to dissolve it by denying his power to do so without its consent. Having no schism to claim its first attention, it was free to devote its undivided efforts to projects of reform. The council re-established the ancient rights of episcopal election against papal reservations, which it expressly prohibited, abolished some of the most obnoxious of the papal taxes altogether and greatly limited others. Indeed, it allowed its repugnance to taxation and its hostility toward the reigning pope to carry it so far in this direction as to deprive the curia of a revenue adequate to its legitimate needs, and the longer it sat the greater extremities it seemed inclined to go to.

A favourable opportunity for a diversion was given the pope by the overtures of the Greeks. The Byzantine emperor John VII, Palæologus, hard pressed by the Turks, was willing to do almost anything to gain the support of the West, and the pope conceived that the moment was opportune for the reunion of the Eastern and Western churches. He accordingly directed the council to remove to Ferrara to meet the emperor and a great train of Greek bishops who had come to Italy for the purpose. The majority of the council refused to obey this order, and continued its sessions at Basel. The pope's council was, however, opened at Ferrara, whence it was shortly transferred to Florence. After long discussions on the ancient points of controversy between the East and the West—the *filioque* in the creed,[1] the doctrine of purgatory, the sacrifice of the Mass, unleavened bread in the Eucharist, and the supremacy of the pope—a formal basis of union was given out in the form of a bull of Eugenius IV, "with the approval of the General Council of Florence." The Greeks yielded on all the disputed points, but with an explanation of the *filioque* which they could take in an orthodox sense. When the terms of this plan of union were known in the East, the indignation of the Greeks against their representatives at Florence knew no bounds. The great majority, living under Moslem dominion and therefore free to speak their whole mind, denounced the surrender to the Latins, and many of the bishops who had subscribed retracted. The West did nothing to help the Greeks against the Turks; in 1453 Constantinople fell, and nothing more was heard of the plan of union.

While the negotiations were going on at Florence, the rump of the council at Basel forfeited the remnant of respect and influence that was left it by pronouncing the deposition of Pope Eugenius and electing Felix V, thus creating a new but fortunately short-lived schism. With it the age of the reforming councils came to an end, and the attempt to substitute conciliar parliamentarism for papal monarchy.

In the second half of the fifteenth century a succession of able popes, favoured by European political conditions, restored the power and prestige of the papacy, which had been so sadly shaken by the Avignonese captivity, the great schism, and the arrogation of the councils. Under them, also, Rome succeeded Florence as the centre of the Renaissance culture in art, architecture, and letters. Nicholas V, founder of the Vatican Library, Pius II (1458–'64), Sixtus IV (1471–'84), and at the beginning of the following century,

---

[1] In the Latin creeds the Spirit is said to proceed "from the Father *and the Son*. As the creed said in the Mass purported to be the creed of the Council of Nicæa, the Greeks denounced this addition as the falsification of an œcumenical symbol, and rejected it as a plain contradiction of the Gospel, which spoke only of the Spirit proceeding from the Father.

Julius II (1503–'13), and Leo X (1513–'21) are famous in the history of the Renaissance as well as in that of the papacy. They proved strong enough to reaffirm the supremacy of the pope over the whole church, and over councils, which derived their right from the pope alone. The Fifth Lateran Council under Leo X unqualifiedly asserted this doctrine, and renewed the declaration of the bull "Unam Sanctam" that it is necessary to their salvation that all Christians be subject to the Roman pontiff.[1]

[1] Bull, *Pastor æternus*, 1516.

CHAPTER X

CHRISTIANITY

THE LATER MIDDLE AGES

Rise of Universities—The Schoolmen—Thomas Aquinas—Duns Scotus —Systematisation of Theology; Aristotelianism—Nominalism— Mysticism—Hugh of St. Victor, Bernard of Clairvaux—Eckhart and His Disciples—Monastic Reforms—Military Orders—Franciscans and Dominicans — Sects: Waldensians, Albigenses, Brethren of the Free Spirit—Joachim of Fiori and the Eternal Gospel—Situation in England—Wycliffe and the Lollards—John Hus and the Bohemians—The Italian Renaissance—Humanism in Other Lands.

THE new stirring of intellectual life which began in the eleventh century manifested itself in a greatly quickened interest in theological questions and the introduction of new methods in the treatment of them. In Berengar's discussion of the Eucharist, Lanfranc not only condemned the doctrine, but gave vent to his indignation that Berengar defended his position by reasoning rather than tradition— as if logic had anything to do with such matters! But Lanfranc's pupil, Anselm (d. 1109), was convinced that it was possible by reason alone, without bringing in revelation or the authority of the church, to demonstrate the existence of God, the doctrine of the Trinity, the necessity of the incarnation—in short, all the principal doctrines of Christianity. In Abelard (d. 1142) the dialectic method took a more critical turn. His "Sic et Non," proved that there is no consensus of tradition to which appeal can be made as a final authority. Following a method inaugurated by the canonists, he brought the conflicting *dicta* of the Fathers into categorical opposition, not to overthrow the principle of authority, but to show that where doctors disagree, the contradictions can only be resolved by dialectic and critical methods. Employing the same methods constructively, he was the first Western theologian to endeavour to cover the wide field of systematic theology. What was original in his system found little of favour in his own day or afterward, but his method was generally adopted by his successors.

It was in this age that the first universities began to grow out of the old cathedral schools and supersede them. The transition was so gradual that exact dates are arbitrary. Abelard studied and lectured in the cathedral school in Paris, but not long after his death the community of recognised scholars who held from the chancellor of the cathedral the *licentia docendi* developed into the University of Paris. Oxford followed at no long interval, and in the thirteenth and fourteenth centuries universities were founded in most of the chief cities of western Europe. To the most famous of these, especially to Paris, students resorted by thousands from far and wide.

The loose organisation—or, rather, lack of organisation— of the universities favoured the independence of the teachers and the variety of the teaching. There were no professors appointed by a superior authority; every master who possessed the license to teach might establish himself in a university and lecture to such students as his reputation drew to hear him. Teachings which diverged too widely or too noisily from orthodox opinion were subject to ecclesiastical censure, but short of open conflict with the accepted doctrines of the church there was large liberty, and the teachers made liberal use of it.

In the universities scholastic theology, which is the greatest intellectual achievement of the twelfth and thirteenth centuries, was developed. Abelard is usually taken to mark the beginning of the movement, Thomas Aquinas its culmination; in the fourteenth century its decadence began. The first stage was the application to theological questions of the "modern dialectic," derived chiefly from the logical treatises of Aristotle, of which the early schoolmen possessed only incomplete translations; and the first theoretical question

to breed contention was the nature of universals, a problem
which they found stated in Boethius's translation of Porphyry's Isagoge (Realism and Nominalism).   The doctrines
of the church were now submitted to logical scrutiny.   With
sophistical acumen the teachers raised factitious objections,
drew hair-splitting distinctions, and arrived at paradoxical
conclusions by formally unimpeachable syllogisms, keeping
clear of imputation of heresy the while by enouncing their
novelties as mere conjectures and plausible opinions (*placita*).

These are the *garrulæ ratiocinationes* against which Peter
Lombard inveighs.   In his own "Liber Sententiarum," the
most important work of the first period of scholasticism,
which treats systematically the chief *loci* of mediæval theology, he combines the traditional with the dialectic method.
The propositions are supported, the questions answered, by
testimonia from the Scriptures and the Fathers.   Authorities which seem to contradict his propositions or to conflict
with one another are reconciled by ingenious interpretations
or acute distinctions, by which means he arrives at a harmony between John of Damascus and Augustine on the
Trinity.   To the proof from authority he adds rational
argument, and in resolving difficulties or refuting objections
shows himself an expert dialectician.   On this side the influence of Abelard is manifest.   The orderly disposition of
the Lombard's work, and especially the ample and pertinent
collection of authorities, admirably adapted it to use as a
text-book in theological lectures, and it came into general
use for this purpose; to the end of the scholastic age almost
every celebrated doctor lectured on the "Sentences," and
many commentaries on it were published.

A new epoch in scholastic theology opened when the schoolmen became acquainted through translations, first from the
Arabic, later from the Greek, with the scientific and philosophical writings of Aristotle, and with the works of Moslem and Jewish Aristotelians, especially of Avicenna, Averroes, and Maimonides.[1]   A synod in 1209 and a papal legate

[1] See pp. 89 *ff*. and 453 *ff*.

THE LATER MIDDLE AGES

in 1215 prohibited lectures in the University of Paris on
Aristotle's natural philosophy and metaphysics, permitting
only his logic; but this prohibition was soon disregarded,
and before a generation had passed the domination of Aristotle was firmly established. Philosophy now took its place
beside the mediæval Trivium and Quadrivium of liberal arts
in the enlarged plan of university study under the Faculty
of Arts, through which students passed before taking up
professional studies in the three higher faculties (theology,
law, medicine). The great schoolmen lectured on Aristotle
as on the Scriptures and on the Sentences of Peter Lombard,
and the recognition of philosophy as an independent discipline was favourable to a freer treatment of metaphysical
problems.

The first attempt to construct a complete system of theology in the light of the new learning was the "Summa Uni-
versæ Theologiæ" of the English Franciscan, Alexander of
Hales (d. 1245), and his example was followed by all the
great masters to the end of the period. In his "Summa"
the scholastic method is fully developed, but the material
influence of Aristotle is comparatively small, as it is also in
his pupil Bonaventura (d. 1274). It is much greater in the
Dominicans, Albert of Bollstadt (d. 1280) and Thomas
Aquinas (d. 1274). The former deserved the honorific titles,
"the Great" and "Doctor Universalis" by the comprehensiveness of his erudition, in which he surpassed all the
scholars of his age. On the question of the relation of philosophy to theology he held that philosophical problems
are to be treated as such, and not confused with those of
speculative theology. On the other hand, he was convinced
that, though philosophy may demonstrate the existence and
attributes of God and his relation to the universe, specifically Christian doctrines like the Trinity and the incarnation
are beyond its field; the naïve confidence of the dialectic
theologians of the preceding century in the ability of reason
to discover, or at least to demonstrate, the truths of revelation had been broken by philosophy.

Thomas Aquinas (1225–'74), the son of an Italian count, studied under Albert at Cologne, and followed the master to Paris and back to Cologne, where he began his own career as a teacher. Besides Cologne and Paris, Thomas lectured in Rome, Bologna, and Naples. His "Summa Theologiæ" is the supreme achievement of the scholastic theology; indeed, as a reasoned exposition of the whole body of Catholic doctrine it has never been equalled. No man except Augustine has been a greater power in European theology than Aquinas. And not on theology in the narrower definition alone, but on philosophy, ethics, and political theory, did he leave the permanent impress of his genius.

More even than in particulars, the influence of Aristotle is seen in the structure of Aquinas's system, and above all in the consistent intellectualism of his thinking. Theology, as he conceives it, is a science which brings into an organic and rational whole the knowledge of God which is attainable by reason and that which—above reason but not contrary to reason—is given by revelation. It is not a practical but a theoretical science; knowledge of God is an end, not a means. The precedence which he gives in ethics to the dianoetic virtues over the practical has the authority of Aristotle for it, as well as the tendency and tradition of Catholic piety. This intellectualism is undoubtedly one of the sources of his enduring power.

The Franciscans took a no less active part in the scholastic movement than the Dominicans, but they kept closer to the Augustinian-Platonic tradition. The great light of theological learning in the order was Johannes Duns Scotus (d. 1308), who, educated at Oxford, taught chiefly in Paris and Cologne. He was master of the Aristotelian learning both on its formal and material sides, and of all the schoolmen had the most critical head. His work is in considerable part a running controversy with the writings of Aquinas, much of whose reasoning he deems inconclusive. Duns Scotus sets narrower limits to the competence of reason than Aquinas: not only the superrational doctrines of the Trinity and the incarnation, but the life of God, his reason, his will, foreknowledge and foreordination, the immortality of the human soul, the divine judgment, are not susceptible of demonstration in a strict sense. Theology rests on the authority of Scripture and the church, and the only certainty is that of faith. He is not inclined to allow philosophy a voice in theological questions, assuredly not a decisive voice. In his own philosophy he is more influenced than Aquinas by the Arab Aristotelians, especially by Avicenna, in whom there is a strong vein of Neoplatonism.

Scotus is in line with Augustinian tradition when, contrary to Aquinas, he gives the will precedence over the intellect, puts action above contemplation, and conceives theology as a practical, not a speculative, science. Correspondingly, for Scotus, God is not essentially Pure Thought but Absolute Will. It might be supposed that Scotus would have deduced from this idea of God a strict determinism; on the contrary, the primacy he ascribes to the will in man leads him to affirm its freedom. The (timeless) divine predestination is only in some inscrutable way the background of man's action, whose fate is in his own hands. Thomas Aquinas, on the other hand, combines philosophical determinism with the Augustinian doctrine of predestination in a way which from one point of view seems to go the whole length with Augustine, while from another it was capable of an interpretation more in accord with the common theological compromises.

General chapters of the Dominicans within a decade of Aquinas's death adopted his works as the standard of the order; the Franciscans accorded a similar pre-eminence to Duns Scotus. Theologians who did not belong to either of these orders addicted themselves to one system or the other, and the controversies of Thomists and Scotists long continued to make much noise in the scholastic world.

If we should attempt in a few words to sum up the chief results of the scholastic period, we should remark first the systematisation of the whole body of Catholic theology,

18

and the effort to give it throughout a rational, and as far
as possible a logically demonstrative character. A "Summa"
like that of Aquinas comprehended the fundamental doctrines which had been authoritatively defined by the ancient church through the councils, and by what may be called
the catholic consensus, together with those which belonged
more particularly to the tradition of the Western church,
and had in part been developed and formulated in the Middle
Ages and through the labours of the earlier schoolmen, such
as the doctrines of grace, the atonement, the number, nature, and operation, of the sacraments, the doctrine of the
church and its relation to the state. The system of Catholic
theology was thus formally completed and its method per-
fected, though on many and important points there remained differences upon which no authoritative decision
had yet been reached.

But there is something of even greater consequence than
all this. In the beginning of Christian theology the ancient
conception of the universe in its popular Platonic form with
a measure of Stoic admixture was naïvely assumed by
Christian thinkers, who, like Philo before them, interpreted
the Scriptures in this sense, and thus obtained for their
philosophy the authority of revelation. Origen, the founder
of a more scientific theology, was a Platonist, and in the
development of dogma in the fourth and fifth centuries the
Alexandrian (Platonic) school prevailed; its teachings became orthodoxy, while theologians of Peripatetic leanings
were responsible for many heresies, including Arianism and
Nestorianism. Neoplatonism pervades the thinking of Augustine, the master theologian of the Latin church; Dionysius, the Areopagite, also, whose influence not only on mysticism but on theology was considerable, was a Neoplatonist.
The Western Middle Ages, with no access to the sources,
had their meagre knowledge of Greek philosophy chiefly
through Augustine.

The great schoolmen, on the other hand, adopted the
classical conception of the universe in its systematised Aris-

totelian form—its physics and astronomy, as well as its metaphysics—and with few and partial exceptions accorded to Aristotle in the field of science an authority hardly less decisive than that which in other spheres they attributed to revelation. They undertook to organise all the knowledge of the universe—God, man, and nature—that is attainable by observation and reason, together with that which is given by revelation, Greek philosophy and Christian theology, in one comprehensive, coherent, and rational system of truth. Thus, for the first time, the antique conception of the universe as a whole was incorporated in Christian doctrine. The church accepted the results, and eventually came to endow them with the authority and finality of the Christian religion, thus imposing upon itself in later centuries the task of upholding the science of the ancients against modern science—the Ptolemaic astronomy against the Copernican, for example.

A new turn was given to scholastic theology in the fourteenth century by Occam (d. ca. 1349), a pupil of Duns Scotus at Paris, where he also taught with much success. On the question of universals he took a position contrary to the variations of realism in the great schoolmen before him: universal terms such as "man" are only conventional signs for classes in which the mind groups for itself individuals. In thought, also, "man" is a sign—a natural sign—which owes its universality to its indefiniteness. Our intellectual and logical operations are carried on with such counters. The theory is therefore called "nominalism." Occam's nominalism involved a theory of knowledge, metaphysical and psychological, which led him to deny the possibility of attaining certainty by the rational processes in which his predecessors had such confidence. Not only can the truths of religion not be demonstrated by reason; they cannot even be proved to be rational—rather the contrary. They are to be apprehended solely by faith, on the authority of revelation; and if God in his inscrutable wisdom had ordered that the opposite should be true and right, for ex-

ample, that pure selfishness should be meritorious, it would
have been so, reason notwithstanding. In the history of
thought epistemological scepticism has repeatedly succeeded
a period of bold speculation or confident dogmatism, or has
resulted from the deadlock of dogmatic systems, and it is
not strange that nominalism, or "modernism," as it was
also called, rapidly gained ground at the expense of the realistic schools, especially of the Scotists, from whom it sprang,
and for a century or more overshadowed them.

The twelfth century witnessed not only the rise of scholastic theology but a great revival of mysticism, whose most
conspicuous representatives are Bernard of Clairvaux and
Hugh of St. Victor. Against Abelard and his kind, who, in
the elation of the new dialectic, thought to demonstrate
everything by reason, and thus reduced the mysteries of the
Christian religion to a shallow reasonableness, Bernard and
Hugh maintained that there is a knowing which is beyond
the discursive intelligence, truths that are above reason.
Such truths are to be accepted by faith on the authority of
Scripture and the church; but only by the mystical vision,
or intuition, is it possible for faith to be transformed into
knowledge. The soul rises to the height of immediate
knowledge by three stages, *cogitatio, meditatio, contemplatio*:
the last alone can give an invincible conviction of those
objects of faith which are above reason. The path to this
goal in Hugh is substantially Augustine's. In Richard of
St. Victor the Areopagite influence is stronger. The mysticism of Bernard is distinguished by devotion to Jesus in
his divine humanity, and particularly in the humility of his
earthly life. He is the great exponent of a type of mysticism
in which Christ is the central figure—a mysticism more
specifically Christian and more churchly than the classic
systems.

These theologians combated a one-sided intellectualism;
but it would be a mistake to imagine that scholasticism and
mysticism were contradictory principles or even conflicting
tendencies in mediæval thought. The mystical element in-

herited from Augustine and reinforced by Dionysius appears in varying measure in all the great schoolmen, including Aquinas; and on the other hand, the churchly mysticism of the thirteenth to the fifteenth centuries is all scholastic, and the aberrations, so far as they have any ideas in them, are equally so.

The ideals of the religious life which prevailed among the Franciscans naturally inclined them to the type of mystical piety represented by Bernard of Clairvaux; among the "Spirituals" and their sectarian offshoots the influence of Joachim of Fiori gave currency to pantheistic notions derived from Eriugena, as well as to apocalyptic vagaries; the addiction of the order to its great doctor, Duns Scotus, had its consequences in the sphere of mystical theology also.

Especial interest attaches to a group of German mystics of the fourteenth century belonging to the Dominican order, among whom Eckhart, Tauler, and Suso are the outstanding names. Eckhart (d. 1327), the theologian of the three, was for several years professor of theology in Strassburg and Cologne, and portions of his Latin writings brought to light in recent times show that he was the author of a scholastic theological treatise on a large scale, the introduction to which, exhibiting its plan and illustrating its method, has fortunately been preserved. As a Dominican, Eckhart stands in the Thomist tradition of his order, but in what is peculiar to him the influence of the Moslem philosopher Avicenna is especially marked. His fundamental proposition, "*esse est deus*," leads him to consequences which, not only in the rhetoric of his German sermons but in the Latin of his scholastic writings, have a pantheistic sound, and were gladly appropriated by pantheistic circles and sects. They were impeached by the archbishop of Cologne, and at the end of a process in the midst of which Eckhart died, twenty-eight articles extracted from his works were condemned as heretical or exposed to the suspicion of heresy. In the former category is included the theory of the uncreated and uncreatable somewhat in the soul, the divine spark, which gives its distinctive form to Eckhart's mysticism as well as to his peculiar doctrine of regeneration, a theory which is related to the religious psychology of al-Ghazali, and has a resemblance to certain Gnostic and Kabbalistic teachings. In the depths of the soul, in that uncreated light which as "*scintilla animæ*" is implanted in it, it is rapt in an ecstasy into the silent desert of the divine being, beyond the distinction of the persons into the godhead itself, in which are no distinctions; it enters into the timeless and changeless. The eternal generation of the divine Word realises itself as the regeneration of the soul; Christ is born again in the soul of man which is conformed to his likeness.

Preaching in the vernacular, which had been from the beginning one of the chief businesses of the mendicant orders and especially of the Order of Preachers, the Dominicans, flourished greatly in this period, and Eckhart's sermons contributed more to the spread of his theory and practice of mystical piety than his professorial treatises; they found a grateful soil in religious houses for women and in those lay circles which were seeking to cultivate a purer and deeper religious life. His teachings were disseminated still more widely by the preaching of his followers, the enthusiast and ascetic Suso, and Tauler, whose less speculative genius turned the dubious abstrusities of the Master into the practical channels of religious and moral revival. The Friends of God found in him a teacher after their own heart. Yet in these circles, as in the writings of the Dutch mystic, Jan van Ruysbroeck, and in the anonymous "German Theology," the ideas of Eckhart furnish the groundwork of the mystical theology. The affinities of the "Book of Spiritual Poverty," long erroneously attributed to Tauler, on the other hand, are with the Franciscan type of mysticism, and its way to the goal, union with God, is not the intellectual ascent to God but the complete quiescence of the human will in God's. The "Imitatio Christi" of Thomas a Kempis moves in the common Catholic tradition which had its fountainhead in Augustine, and owes little to the various developments of mysticism in the scholastic period or to fresh infusions of Neoplatonism and Arabian philosophy.

What gives this late mediæval mysticism its great religious importance is that its teachers were not content to reveal to a few singular souls the secret of "the flight from the alone to the alone," or to recall the professed religious to the true end of monastic piety, but preached it as the way of life for the laity as well as the clergy. This popularisation had two results: first, it impressed on men that religion is essentially an inner life having its expression and criterion in Christian conduct, and not merely the acceptance of the doctrines of the church and the use of its efficacious sacraments; the second result, a consequence of the first, was, as in similar movements which throw the emphasis on individual experience, a relative indifference to dogma, the bulk of which had no obvious relation to such experience, and to external authority, all the more that this authority was often wielded by worldly ecclesiastics.

The stirring intellectual activity of the last centuries of the Middle Ages was only one aspect of a quickening of religious life which expressed itself in many ways besides theology—in architecture and painting, for example. One of its first manifestations were reforms in the religious orders aiming to restore not only the discipline but the spirit of the monastic life, and the founding of new orders or congregations, among which may be particularly named the Carthusians, who revived in their monasteries the solitary life; the Cistercians, an offshoot of the Benedictine order, which, largely through the efforts and the fame of Bernard of Clairvaux, soon surpassed in numbers and influence all the rest; and the Premonstratensians, founded by Norbert, who devoted themselves chiefly to preaching and pastoral work among the masses and to missions among the Wends. So many other orders sprang up in the course of the twelfth century that Pope Innocent III felt constrained to forbid the foundation of any more (1215), but the prohibition was not long maintained.

The Crusades gave rise to new orders of a peculiar character, of which the Hospitallers, or Knights of St. John, and the Templars were the most important. Growing out of organisations for the care of sick pilgrims to Jerusalem and the protection of pilgrims on their way to and from the holy places, they became military orders, whose members were knights under the monastic vows of poverty, chastity, and obedience. They received from the popes large privileges and exemptions, and both speedily became powerful, wealthy, and worldly. The Templars were in the thirteenth century the richest order in Europe. Their wealth was their ruin, and led to the dissolution of the order by Pope Clement V and the confiscation of their vast estates in France by Philip the Fair (1312) on charges of heresy, impiety, and gross immorality. A third order, the Teutonic Knights (1199), found its chief sphere of activity in the conquest of the heathen in eastern Prussia and the imposition of Christianity on the conquered.

The religious movements of the thirteenth century produced two new orders of a different type from any that had gone before them, the mendicant friars. The founder of the elder of these was Francis of Assisi. Converted by a serious illness from the ways of an exuberant youth, he resolved in penance for his former sins and in literal obedience to the call of the Lord (Matt. 10; Luke 10), without purse or shoes or staff, to go forth preaching the kingdom of heaven. Others, like-minded, joined him in this mission and way of life. Enterprises for the conversion of Moslems in Syria and Morocco to the Christian faith having proved fruitless, Francis came back to Europe and strove to convert Christians to the Christian life according to the precept and example of their Master. The association and its lay preaching were irregular, and if the work was to go on ecclesiastical sanction was necessary. This was given by Innocent III in 1209, and in 1223 Honorius III approved the rule of the order. The brotherhood was devoted to missions and the preaching of the gospel. Evangelical poverty was the law not only for its individual members but for the community; herein unlike the older orders, in which the corporate wealth of the monasteries was often enormous, and was one of the chief causes of the declension from the monastic ideal which kept them in perennial need of reform and made the very success of a reformed congregation the cause of its decadence. Even before Francis' death (1226) more practical heads in the order found his ideal of pure mendicancy impracticable, and under his successor as general of the order, Elias, the strictness of the rule was relaxed. The result of progressive departures from the ideal of the order was a series of secessions; the stricter sort, in whose eyes amendments of the rule and laxity in observance were a kind of apostasy, separating from the body of the order. The treatment they received from the popes threw some of them into a hostile attitude to the papacy and even to the church, and made them an easy prey to heresy.

Unlike the monks of the older time, who chose by preference solitary places for their establishments, the Franciscans found their field of labour in the cities, where they were soon provided with houses to dwell in and more regular means of support than casual charity. Francis founded also a conventual order for women, who lived in strict seclusion, possessing only the bare walls of the convent with its garden, and wholly dependent on voluntary gifts.

The influence of the Franciscan movement was greatly extended by the institution of the Tertiaries of St. Francis, men and women under the direction of the order, who without giving up their domestic ties and ordinary callings, endeavoured to lead a life after the gospel pattern, avoiding worldly dissipations, practising charity, and cultivating a religious spirit.

The other great mendicant order of the age, the Dominicans, was founded by a Spanish priest of high birth and education, with the immediate purpose of winning back to the faith of the church, by preaching, the heretics who abounded in southern France. They adopted the so-called Rule of St. Augustine, with supplementary regulations of their own, and the order was formally recognised by Honorius III in 1216. At the first general chapter of the order (1220) they added the principle of evangelical poverty, after the example of the Franciscans; but as this was an adventitious part of the rule, not the constitutive idea of the order, adaptation to actual conditions raised no such conflicts as rent the Franciscans. The Dominicans, also, formed a body of Tertiaries, and the order grew very rapidly, chiefly in the cities.

The rise of the mendicant orders is one of the most significant phenomena of the age. They were called into existence by a deep concern for the religious condition of the multitude, and the response their labours found shows that in the masses themselves the need of a revival of the religious life was felt. Both orders made preaching a chief part of their vocation, and found in it the most effective way of reaching the people, who in this respect were much neglected by the secular clergy. The popes gave to both orders general powers to confess penitents, and they soon became the favourite guides of lay consciences, the Dominicans largely in the higher classes, the Franciscans among the common people. The orders had a firmly knit organisation, with a general (Minister Generalis) or master (Magister Ordinis) at the head, provincials, and periodical general chapters. Both were immediately under the jurisdiction of the pope and dependent on him, and in return for his protection and patronage rendered him most efficient service in many ways.

The Dominicans encouraged learning from the beginning. Francis himself regarded learning as belonging to the vanities of this world no less than wealth and station: Jesus and the Apostles were simple and unlettered men, and such those who renewed their work should be. This attitude was, however, not long maintained, and teachers of both orders soon sought to establish themselves in the universities. The

University of Paris resisted this intrusion, but had to yield to a papal mandate. Most of the great schoolmen of the thirteenth century belonged to one or the other, and the rivalry of the orders extended to theological systems. Alexander of Hales, Bonaventura, Roger Bacon, Duns Scotus were Franciscans; Albertus Magnus and Thomas Aquinas were the great lights of the Dominicans.

The same stirring of the religious life, the same dissatisfaction with existing conditions in the church, which gave birth to the mendicant orders manifested itself in movements which found no room in the church and consequently separated from it. One of these sects, the Waldensians, had an origin not dissimilar to that of the Franciscans, but a totally dissimilar fortune. The words of Jesus to the rich young man in the Gospel and the lives of saints who had put them into practice made such an impression upon Peter Valdes, a prosperous citizen of Lyons, that he gave all his goods to the poor, and in obedience to the command of the Master took to the preaching of the gospel, making central in his message the teaching of the Sermon on the Mount and the missionary charge of Jesus to his disciples (Matt. 10). Men and women, chiefly of the lower classes, after his exhortation and example, began to preach, wandering from place to place with no fixed abode, taking food and lodging from those who received their word. Valdes sought papal approbation from Alexander III, but it was denied him (1179). Had he obtained it, as Francis did thirty years later, he might perhaps have been enrolled among the saints instead of the heretics, for there is no intimation that at that time he had departed from the teaching of the church or impugned its authority. But when his irregular evangelism was forbidden, he opposed the commandment of Christ to the prohibition of the pope and continued his work.

His followers multiplied in southern France and Aragon, and spread into Italy, where their centre was Milan. Their societies, which were in the beginning only conventicles within the church for the cultivation of the religious life after their fashion, were presently excluded from the church, and they then created an organisation of their own with a ministry and sacraments. The opposition of the church threw them into antagonism with it, and led them to deny its authority, asserting against it, as the sects always did, the authority of Scripture. Soon also they fell out with some of its doctrines, partly in consequence of their independent reading of the New Testament, of which they had a vernacular version, partly through contact with the heretical Albigenses, among whom they lived and with whom they suffered. Scattered by the crusade against the Albigenses, some of them found a refuge in the valleys of Piedmont, and survived there till the sixteenth century, when they were drawn into the current of the Protestant Reformation and learned to look upon themselves as its forerunners.

Another symptom of the religious unrest was an alarming recrudescence of dualistic heresies from which the West had for centuries been free. Their adversaries stamped them with the historical label, "Manichæans," and in fact many things in the accounts of their doctrines and practices suggest the association. Their own name for themselves was "Cathari" (the Pure), and they were connected in some way with the Bogomiles (Friends of God) who plagued the Greek church in the same age, being especially numerous in the Balkan Peninsula. The Cathari had many ramifications and variations, and were called by many local names, of which Albigenses is the best known.[1] Over against a God of light and the invisible world, they set, as the author of the visible universe, a god of darkness, whom they called the prince, or god, of this world; and upon this basis they erected a system which in its general features strikingly resembles some of the dualistic Gnosticisms of the early Christian centuries. Like the Gnostics and the Manichæans, they drew the practical consequences of their dualism in the rejection of marriage and of animal food. They repu-

[1] In other regions they were called Bulgari.

diated the institutions and sacraments of the Catholic Church, claiming to be themselves the only true church; their own great sacrament was the *consolamentum*, an initiation into the class of Perfecti, in which, by the laying on of hands, the Holy Spirit was communicated, and thereby salvation secured.

In southern France the Albigenses were so large a part of the population that Bernard of Clairvaux writes from his own observation of "churches without people, people without priests, priests without respect, Christians without Christ, the holiness of holy places denied, the sacraments no longer sacred, and holy days without their ceremonies." Protected by many of the nobles, they made light of ecclesiastical fulminations; efforts to convert them by preaching had no success. Finally, in 1209, a crusade was launched against them; the nobles in whose territories they had flourished were dispossessed and the land ravaged by war.

To complete their destruction the ancient episcopal inquisition, which was as old as Carolingian times, was revived. New efficacy was given to its investigations by the obligatory annual confession imposed by the Fourth Lateran Council (1215). Those who came to confession were examined about their own beliefs and practices and those of their neighbours; those who stayed away, by the very fact incurred the suspicion of heresy. Soon a new and more formidable instrument was created in the papal inquisition instituted by Gregory IX (in 1232–'35) and intrusted to the Dominicans, which was promptly set to work in the countries infected with heresy. The procedure of the inquisitorial tribunals was of a kind to inspire terror in innocent as well as guilty; the names of the accusers and the witnesses were kept strictly secret; the examination of the accused, equally in secret, was conducted on the presumption of guilt, and often resolved itself into an effort to entrap the accused; torture was employed to extort confession.[1]   The execution

[1] This procedure was not, as is often imagined, invented by the ecclesiastical tribunals; these were the ordinary methods of the justice of the times.

of the sentence was committed to the secular arm, and laws for the punishment of heretics were enacted by Louis IX of France (1228), the emperor Frederick II (1220 *ff.*), and other princes.

Here and there voices were lifted up against the persecution of heretics or the infliction of death upon them, but without effect. The doctrine of the church is defined and defended by Aquinas: Heresy is a crime which deserves death, for the corruption of the faith is a much graver offence than counterfeiting the coinage, which is everywhere a capital crime. The extirpation of irreclaimable heretics is a measure which the church takes for the safety of others to whom the contagion might spread.

Besides the dualistic heresies of which we have spoken, a pantheistic heresy which seems to have some connection with the teaching of Amalric of Bena (d. 1205)[1] spread widely in the thirteenth and early fourteenth centuries. Its adherents called themselves "Brethren and Sisters of the Free Spirit." The spiritual man, they held, is by nature God. He is therefore impeccable, and whatever he does, it is no sin. Consistently, they denied the peculiar divinity of Christ; every spiritual man is all that Christ was. The perfect man is wholly free, neither bound to keep the commandments in the Bible nor to obey the laws of the church or the orders of prelates. They rejected the belief in purgatory and hell, resurrection and future judgment: when the body dies, the spirit, or soul, returns to him from whom it issued forth, and is so reunited with him that nothing remains but that which was from eternity, God. No one will be damned, no Jew and no Moslem. These ideas to some extent infected the Beghards in the region of the lower Rhine, in whose mystical piety they found a favourable soil, and seem to have found acceptance among a fraction of the Waldensians. The principal seat of the sect was in upper Germany and Switzerland.

[1] Amalric imbibed the ideas that upset him from the Neoplatonic vein in Moslem philosophy.

In a wholly different spirit, Joachim of Fiori (d. 1202), as the result of his studies in the prophets and the Apocalypse of John, taught that a new dispensation was about to begin, the age of the Spirit, succeeding the age of the Son (the New Testament, with the priesthood and sacraments of the church), as that succeeded the age of the Father (the Old Testament, the Jewish economy), an age that should bring full knowledge and spiritual freedom. This consummation was to be brought about through the instrumentality of an unworldly and spiritual monasticism. These ideas were naturally much to the taste of the strict Franciscans. The "eternal gospel" (Rev. 14, 6), the gospel of full spiritual knowledge for the age of the Holy Spirit, was discovered by some of them in the writings of Joachim himself. About the year 1200, they thought, the spirit of life deserted the Old Testament and the New to make way for the "eternal gospel." With their minds thus turned to the interpretation of history, they saw in Frederick II the scourge of the corrupt church, the spiritual Babylon (Rome). To these spiritual Franciscans evangelical poverty in imitation of Christ and the Apostles and conformity to the precept and example of St. Francis was the heart of the gospel, the touchstone of genuine and consecrated Christian life. The efforts of the heads of the order and of successive popes to subdue their obstinacy only confirmed them in the conviction that the church was fallen away from true Christianity and wholly given over to worldliness, and drove them into the position of intransigeant sects, some of which, like the Fraticelli, were separated from the church, and by natural affinity embraced heretical opinions resembling those of the Brethren of the Free Spirit.

The same motives which led great numbers to enroll as Tertiaries of the mendicant orders gave rise to independent movements of a similar character, among which the Beghards and Beguines of the Low Countries and the Rhineland are the best known. The pursuit and profession of a more serious religious life and a more scrupulous morality had its customary effect in these circles. They compared themselves to their own advantage not only with the mass of the laity, but with priests, monks, and friars, who took their religion more comfortably, and they were disposed to contemn the authority of the church as well as the persons of its representatives. Not only the churchly mysticism of Eckhart and Tauler but divers heretical doctrines found adherents among them.

Till the latter part of the fourteenth century England was little affected by the new religious movements of the continent. The king and parliament, supported by a strong national feeling, firmly resisted the encroachments of the papal power—the filling of English benefices by appointees of the pope, the carrying of civil and criminal causes, original or appealed, which belonged before the courts of the realm to a foreign tribunal, and the draining of English gold into the coffers of the Avignonese popes, who were at the beck and nod of the national enemy, France. There was, furthermore, an unmistakable anticlerical temper in both Lords and Commons, to which the wealth and power of the clergy and endowed orders, and the manners and morals of the mendicant friars—a favourite subject of satire and diatribe—contributed. Heresy, however, though it had appeared in England in more than one form, had got no foothold there; the inquisition had not been introduced, and the statute, "*De hæretico comburendo*," was enacted only in 1401.

This law was directed primarily against the Lollards, a sect whose rapid spread in the preceding quarter-century gave cause of apprehension to the ruling classes in the state as well as to the church. The founder of the sect, John Wycliffe, a secular priest and teacher in the University of Oxford, first attracted wider notice by writings in support of the powers of the king against the pope, in which he maintained positions similar to those of Marsilius of Padua and Occam, in conjunction with a development of the theory of *dominium* applied to the origin, nature, and limits of civil and ecclesiastical rule, from which he deduced far-reaching consequences; for example, that it is not only lawful but meritorious for temporal rulers to dispossess ecclesiastical persons or communities of wealth which they habitually misuse. His conception of the fully Christian life under the *lex evangelica* alone was much the same as that of Francis of Assisi; but his theory of *dominium* carries him farther than evangelical poverty. If all men were fully in grace there would be no right of private property, but all would have all things in common; in other words, the ideal society would be communistic. In the world as it is, he recognised that this ideal is impracticable; but it is not strange that the peasants' insurrection of 1381 was charged to the spread of his revolutionary communistic ideas among the masses.

To Wycliffe the striving of the clergy for preferment, wealth, and power was in conflict with the law of Christ; it was evidence that they were not of the number of the predestinated, but were hypocrites, who were in the church only in name, not in reality. Inspired by him, numbers of "poor priests," most of them laymen, went up and down the land preaching to the people in the mother tongue and setting an example of a ministry without worldly possessions or ambitions. In vindication of his doctrine of the *lex evangelica*, Wycliffe maintained in a voluminous scholastic treatise, "On the Truth of Sacred Scripture" (1378), the supreme authority of Scripture, not like the nominalists in contrast to reason, but above the decretals of popes and the teachings of the schoolmen. That the people might know and judge for themselves the issues between himself and the church, and that the unlearned as well as the learned might have the law of Christ, he translated the New Testament from Latin into English, and some of his disciples did the same by the Old Testament.

Beginning with censure of papal abuses (among others, indulgences), Wycliffe advanced to more radical ground: "It appears . . . that the pope and his whole sect, invested

19

with temporal dominion, is a hardened heretic." [1] Christ rendered unto Cæsar what was Cæsar's and sought no worldly power; the pope, who acts quite otherwise, appears to be the vicar, not of Christ, but of Antichrist. He attacked also the doctrine of transubstantiation, affirming that the body and blood of Christ are truly and really present in the Eucharist, but that transubstantiation, identification, or impanation,[2] have no foundation in Scripture. His own doctrine of the Eucharist may be described as a scholastic rendering of Augustine's; his opponents identified it with Berengar's and condemned it accordingly, which was of itself proof to him that the Roman Church can err in matters of faith. Other parts also of the doctrine of the sacraments were questioned or criticised, but without so wide departure from the prevailing teaching.

Wycliffe's defence of the rights and powers of the state gained him influential patrons among the nobility, who protected him against the efforts of the ecclesiastical authorities to bring him to account for his utterances; and though a number of propositions taken from his writings were pronounced heretical and others erroneous, and he was obliged to leave Oxford, he died in the communion of the church (1384). After the accession of Henry IV, of the house of Lancaster (1399), however, the state lent its hand to the church to extirpate the Lollards. Deprived of the countenance they had received from many of the nobility and gentry, they were driven into concealment and before the Reformation of the sixteenth century had ceased to exist as a sect.

The writings of Wycliffe early found their way from Oxford to Prag, and the Hussite movement in Bohemia was largely inspired by his ideas. John Hus, from whom this movement has its name, was a professor of philosophy in the university and a popular preacher in the vernacular, who stood in high esteem not only with king and people but for a time with his ecclesiastical superiors. His severe stric-

[1] The temporal power is heresy in fact.
[2] Two other theories discussed by the schoolmen.

tures on the clergy and the abuses of the church, in which he followed closely in Wycliffe's footsteps, cost him this churchly favour and laid him open to the imputation of Wycliffite heresy. The king and the university took his side; the papal legates sustained the archbishop and the excommunication he had pronounced on Hus. This conflict with the authorities of the church moved him not only to attack the pope (John XXIII) for abusing his spiritual power for temporal ends—the occasion was the proclamation of a crusade against the king of Naples with the customary indulgence—but to write a book, "De Ecclesia," in complete agreement with Wycliffe's work under the same title, of which, indeed, it was substantially a reproduction. On the ground of thirty-nine propositions in this book, chiefly impugning the authority of the hierarchy, he was condemned by the council at Constance and, despite an imperial safe-conduct, burned there in 1415.

Doctrinally, Hus was more conservative than Wycliffe. Like him he opposed the indulgences, and denied that confession to a priest is indispensable to the forgiveness of sins; but he did not follow the English theologian in rejecting the doctrine of transubstantiation. He approved, however, the demand of the reform party in Bohemia, that in the sacrament of the Eucharist the cup should be administered to lay communicants as well as to the clergy.

The death of Hus aroused a storm of wrath in Bohemia, and converted the Hussite movement into a national cause. The attempts of the pope and the emperor to break it united nobles and people in defence, and they maintained for twenty years their political and ecclesiastical independence. The Council of Basel in 1433, by some concessions, notably of communion in both kinds, won back to the church the more moderate party (Utraquists, or Calixtines), who had made this the principal issue; the radical Taborites would not be reconciled. In the civil war that ensued the latter sustained a crushing defeat (1434) which ended their militant career. Thereafter they by degrees merged in the majority, or perpetuated Waldensian and Wycliffite doctrine and practice in the sect of the Bohemian Brethren.

The revival of the study of classical Latin literature and antiquities in the fourteenth century, in which Petrarch's is the shining name, was followed in the fifteenth by the opening to the West of the whole wealth of Greek literature. The Council of Florence (1439) brought learned Greeks to Italy; the fall of Constantinople (1453) drove many others thither, carrying their precious manuscripts with them, and ere long they were teaching the language and interpreting the authors to zealous hearers in all the chief cities of the peninsula. It is difficult for us to imagine the enthusiasm which this rediscovery of antiquity inspired. Hitherto learning had been professional and chiefly clerical; the so-called liberal arts, which had once meant the education of a gentleman, had been desiccated into the Trivium and Quadrivium of the mediæval universities, the Faculty of Arts in which they were taught being merely a preparatory school for the professional faculties of theology, civil and canon law, and medicine. Theology towered above all the rest. The new learning was a field in which clerics had no preeminence and the universities for a while no part. The invention of printing came at the opportune moment; the presses poured out editions, translations, elucidations, which put the newly retrieved treasures of ancient literature in the hands of eager scholars everywhere.

The revival of learning introduced a new, untheological kind of international culture, a culture which drew its inspiration and took the patterns for its imitation from classical antiquity. The civilisation they discovered there was a secular civilisation. It had no church, no hierarchy wielding the two swords of spiritual and political power; its religion had no dogmas prescribing what all men should think on all things divine and human. Greek religion, as they learned it through poetry and art, was a religion of beauty and of freedom. In the poets and the philosophers they found a noble and beautiful ethos, not inferior to the best

Christian teaching; they found high speculation on the universal frame of things, on immaterial reality, on the nature and destiny of man. The name "humanism" implies its antithesis; mankind and its concerns supplanted divinity in the interest of men. All this not only weakened the hold of the church and its doctrines on men's minds, but produced in many an indifference to revealed religion; while in not a few emancipation went to the length of a practical paganism.

The recovery of Plato, few of whose works had previously been known, led to a revival of Platonism, or rather Neoplatonism, of which the Florentine Academy, founded by Cosimo dei Medici, was the great centre; from it proceeded Ficino's translations of Plato and Plotinus, and of the so-called "Hermes Trismegistus." In this renaissance of Platonism many found a soul-satisfying philosophy and a sufficient religion for intellectual men. Aristotle, in some form and extent and interpreted in one fashion or another, had been the final authority in philosophy for the schoolmen; Aquinas had completed the great synthesis which made the Aristotelian conception of the universe an integral part of Christian theology. Now the authority of Plato was arrayed against that of Aristotle, and the foundations of the great scholastic system were shaken.

The humanists, who formed their taste on classical models, had an æsthetic antipathy to the theologians because of their uncouth style and barbarous diction, and they had an equally strong aversion to the scholastic method with its subtle distinctions and its interminable syllogisms. Cicero showed how philosophical questions were discussed by cultivated men in a common-sense way, without any such deafening clatter of dialectical machinery. Many, seeing that in this way much could be finely said on every side without a decisive outcome, inclined to a gentlemanly scepticism of Ciceronian fashion. For a doctrine of the rational guidance of life the humanists turned naturally to Stoicism as they found it in Cicero and Seneca, and it became again, as it had been in the last centuries of the ancient world, the moral philosophy of educated men. Epicureanism, in the vulgar sense, had a large following in practice, but only rarely so outspoken an advocate as Laurentius Valla in his "De Voluptate."

Philological studies soon put men upon investigations of the genuineness of writings attributed to ancient authors, and in this field some of the Renaissance scholars displayed notable critical acumen. Applying the same methods to the "Constitutum Constantini," in which the emperor makes a gift to Pope Sylvester of the city of Rome, with all the provinces and cities of Italy and the western regions, and puts them under the *potestas et ditio* of the pope—the foundation of the temporal power of the papacy—Cusanus and Valla demonstrated that it was a mediæval forgery. Their historical studies taught them to go to the sources, and they discovered that the history of Rome, as they read it in the ancient authors, was a very different thing from the mediæval notions of it. It was inevitable that similar observations should presently be made in the field of Christian antiquity.

In the revival of letters and art the popes of the second half of the fifteenth and the beginning of the sixteenth centuries had an eminent part, and both the refinement of taste and the dissoluteness of morals which are associated with the Renaissance were conspicuously exemplified in the lives of more than one of them. Many of them were before all else Italian princes; political ambitions and the advancement of their families were nearer to their hearts than the higher interests of the church. Savonarola, like one of the old prophets, lifted up his voice in season and out of season against the corruption of the age. His zeal for the liberties of Florence was as obnoxious to Pope Alexander VI (1492–1503) as his efforts to reform the morals and manners of the gay city, and when his hour came the Borgia on the throne of Peter gave order that the monk who had defied the pope and invoked Christendom to depose him "should die, if he were a second John the Baptist."

The tastes of the Renaissance popes in architecture, art, and living were extravagant; the curia followed their example, and the papal finances were correspondingly in chronic disorder. Every means was resorted to to increase the revenues, from tithes for crusades in which the sword was never drawn to tariffs on every step of ecclesiastical advancement and dispensations from all kinds of canonical prohibitions. Complaints against the extortions of the curia were never louder or more universal than at the beginning of the sixteenth century. France and England had long ago found means to protect themselves in considerable part from these exactions; but on Germany, which for want of national unity and national spirit had no such defence, they fell with double weight. The resentment thus created was easily turned into sympathy with Luther in his attacks upon the hierarchy among classes to whom his theological innovations were of no concern.

Beyond the Alps, the Renaissance, which in Italy, amid the monuments and memories of the ancient civilisation, had the ambition to be a resurrection of the culture of pagan Rome, took the soberer form of a revival of learning through the study of the classic literatures, to which was soon added the study of the Bible in the original Hebrew and Greek and of the early Christian authors. The presses poured out not only editions of the classics and of the Fathers, but, far outnumbering them all, of the Bible, in Latin, in Hebrew, in Greek, and in translations into modern languages. Between 1450 and 1520 not less than 156 editions of the Latin Bible appeared; there were seventeen editions of the whole Bible in German (from Latin), besides many more of the church lessons; eleven in Italian, ten in French. The first Greek New Testament, edited by Erasmus, was published in 1516; the first polyglot Bible, the great plan of a Spanish humanist, Cardinal Ximenes, containing the Old Testament in Hebrew, Greek, and Latin in parallel columns, with the Targum on the Pentateuch, and the New Testament in Greek and Latin—six volumes in folio—was issued in 1520.[1]

[1] The printing of the New Testament was finished in 1514.

CHAPTER XI

CHRISTIANITY

THE PROTESTANT REFORMATION

THERE was nothing in the state of the church at the beginning of the sixteenth century that foreboded the great Western schism, the Protestant Reformation. The flood of heresies which in the twelfth and following centuries had spread over Europe had subsided. The crisis of the conciliar age was past, and the power and prestige of the papacy had been restored. The need of reform in the church and of a revival of the religious life was recognised not only by the humanists but in the high places of the church itself. In Spain notable and lasting reforms had been achieved; in Italy the Oratory of Divine Love, which counted among its members some of the most eminent churchmen of the age, including several who became cardinals, set the example of sincere piety and pure life in the midst of the surrounding ecclesiastical worldliness, and exerted a leavening influence in a wide circle. Revival and reform in those countries were alike animated by a thoroughly churchly spirit. There was no similar movement in Germany, though the influence of the mysticism of Eckhart and Tauler had not wholly died out. Theology there was in the depths of its nominalist decadence, and the presumptuous ignorance of the obscurantist monks was a mark for the satire of the humanists, whose pens had been sharpened in the conflict between Reuchlin and the Dominicans of Cologne. Erasmus had written the Praise of Folly, and the Epistolæ Obscurorum Virorum were being read with immense merriment by the friends of the new learning. The exactions of the papal fiscal system gave occasion to frequent recitals of grievances which remained fruitless, but the fidelity of Germany to the church appeared unimpeachable.

The occasion of the outbreak, also, was accidental, and in itself commonplace. Pope Julius II, who had undertaken the rebuilding of the Church of St. Peter in Rome, issued in 1510 a bull offering indulgences *in forma jubilæi*, with various benefits, to those who should contribute to the funds for this work. His successor, Leo X, in 1515, made the Archbishop of Mainz commissioner for these collections in the provinces of Mainz and Magdeburg and the diocese of Halberstadt.[1] The archbishop intrusted the preaching of the indulgences to a Dominican friar named Tetzel, who had had much experience and success in similar business.

According to the instructions issued by the archbishop, four distinct benefits (*gratiæ*) were offered, any of which might be purchased separately. The two which concern us here are, *first*, a plenary remission of all sins, availing also to cancel the pains to be suffered in purgatory, to such as, being contrite and confessed, visited at least seven churches on which the papal arms were set up, reciting in each five

---

[1] In Spain, France, and England, the pope did not venture to offer these indulgences at all; but three commissioners were appointed for Germany, and one for Poland.

Paters and five Aves, and made a contribution rated according to the status, occupation, and income of the giver, from twenty-five gold florins down to one; and, *second*, for souls now in purgatory, a plenary remission of all sins, which the pope bestows and grants *per modum suffragii* (*i. e.*, not by the power of the keys), on condition that the living put into the collection-box a contribution according to their ability.

The doctrine of indulgences, even in the carefully guarded form in which it is stated by the authoritative theologians of the church, is exposed to only too facile misunderstandings by the lay mind, unaccustomed to refined distinctions; and when proclaimed by popular preachers with a strong interest in the size of the contribution, was sure to be misleading, particularly in regard to the remission of sins to souls in purgatory. The elector of Saxony did not permit the sale of indulgences in his territory, but the preachers marketed them just over the border. Their doings and the reports of their sayings provoked a young professor in the University of Wittenberg to dispute their teaching and practice. He accordingly posted on the door of the castle church, the usual place for university notices, ninety-five theses, which he undertook to defend against all comers in a public discussion by word of mouth or in writing. It was a challenge to an open debate, a kind of academic tournament much in fashion in those days.

The theses do not sound very revolutionary. In the main they rest on the ground of the accepted Catholic doctrine. Several of them are directed against the perversions and abuses attributed to the venders of indulgences, which the author assumes that the pope cannot be cognisant of. Others, however, contradict the principles upon which the indulgences were granted. He asserts, for example, that it is not the pope's intention, nor in his power, to remit any penalties except those which are imposed by his own authority or that of the canons; that penalties imposed by the church come to an end with death and are not carried over into purgatory;[1] he denies the doctrine of the treasury of merits on which the pope draws for indulgences. On the other hand, he affirms that the whole life of the faithful should be penitence, inward and outward, and that the words of Christ, "*agite pœnitentiam*," refer to this, not to the sacrament of penance; that a Christian man who feels true compunction for his sins has plenary remission from penalty and guilt even without letters of indulgence; that the pope's remission of guilt is merely declaratory; and that works of mercy are of much higher worth in the eyes of God than the pope's letters of pardon.

What concerned him most in the whole matter was that by the preaching of indulgences men were encouraged to a false security of salvation. He was incensed, also, at the exploiting of the people by the venders of indulgences. "Christians ought to be taught that if the pope knew of the extortions of the mercenary preachers, he would rather see the Church of St. Peter in ashes than that it should be built with the skin, flesh, and bones of his sheep." "Why does not the pope, who is richer to-day than the richest Crassuses, build the single church of St. Peter out of his own money, instead of out of the poor believers?"

The author of these theses was Martin Luther. He was born November 10, 1483, at Eisleben in Thuringia. His father's ambition to make a lawyer of him sent him to the University of Erfurt, where he graduated Master of Arts in 1505. Erfurt, like most of the German universities, was still in the mediæval rut, and was one of the strongholds of the modernist (nominalist) philosophy and theology. With the group of young Erfurt humanists—some of them only too human—Luther seems to have had no contact. Hardly had he taken his degree, when he disappeared into an Augus-

---

[1] The extension of the benefits of indulgences to purgatory was still contested in the fifteenth century; the first formal grant of indulgences for the dead was in a bull of Sixtus IV in 1476. The treasury of merits had papal authority in a bull of Clement VI, in 1343. See above, pp. 244 *f.*

tinian monastery, and after taking the vows began the study
of scholastic theology, which he pursued further in the following years at the newly founded University of Wittenberg. In 1510 he was sent on business of the order to
Rome. What he saw of the capital of the church under
one of the most brilliant of the Renaissance popes was not
of a kind to impress the unsophisticated young monk favourably, and the impression of the moment doubtless became
more deeply unfavourable in his reflective memory as years
passed. Returning to Wittenberg, he finished his studies
and was made Doctor of Theology in 1512. In the following years he lectured upon the Bible—Psalms, Romans,
Galatians, Hebrews—and besides his teaching, had oversight as district vicar of eleven monasteries of his order in
Saxony and Thuringia. Both in the order and in the university he was regarded as a rising man.

The theses provoked both the archbishop, who felt himself censured by them, and the Dominicans, who resented
an attack upon one of their order, and from both sides complaint was promptly made at Rome. In Germany Tetzel
replied in two series of theses, and a more redoubtable con-
troversialist, Eck, professor at Ingolstadt, entered the lists
against Luther. The real issue, as Luther's adversaries
made clear, was the right of the pope to grant such indulgences, and this widened into the question of papal powers
in general. This was well understood at Rome also. Pri-
erias, the pope's Magister Sacri Palatii, wrote a "Dialogue
on the Power of the Pope," in which his supremacy and
infallibility are asserted, and the corollary drawn: "Whoever says that the Roman Church has not the power to do
what in fact it does in the matter of indulgences is a heretic."

In Germany the theses and the sermons and pamphlets
with which Luther followed them up had wide circulation
and found a hearty response among the laity, great and
small, who saw in them, not an attack on the church, but a
defence of the German people against the extortions of the
curia and a telling stroke at the unpopular Dominicans.

They regarded Luther as a champion of the perennial demand for the reform of ecclesiastical abuses, and the matter and manner of the replies to him strengthened this feeling. The humanists, with fresh memories of their own conflict with the Dominican obscurantists of Cologne, were on his side. Luther thus became, almost at once, the leader of a national revolt, unconscious of its own ends. His colleagues in the university stood by him, and the elector, proud of his new foundation and of the young professor who had so suddenly leaped into fame, protected him. A summons to Rome, July, 1518, was changed to an order to appear before the cardinal legate, De Vio (Caietanus), at Augsburg, whose instructions were to insist on Luther's recantation of his errors. The hearing was held in October, 1518, but the recantation was not secured. Luther insisted on arguing the question; Caietanus, one of the most eminent theologians of the age, commentator on Aquinas, was not disposed to enter into discussion with an obscure monk. Luther returned from Augsburg to Wittenberg, leaving behind him an appeal from the pope misinformed to the pope to be better informed, which he presently changed to an appeal from the pope to a future general council. An adroit disputant soon drew from him that even a council was not infallible; infallible was only the Word of God.

The proceedings against him at Rome moved deliberately. In view of the approaching imperial election, the pope had strong reasons not to give offence to the Saxon elector, so that it was not until June, 1520, that the bull, *Exsurge Domine*, was issued, expressly condemning a long series of propositions extracted from the writings of Luther, ordering that his books should be publicly burned, and giving him sixty days from the publication of the bull within which to make his recantation. Meanwhile the movement in Germany had made rapid progress, both in numbers and self-consciousness. Luther himself, seeing farther and growing bolder, published in 1520 three of his most significant writings. In the first of these, addressed "To the Christian

Nobility of the German Nation," he attacks the triple wall by which the church is fortified in its abuses: *first,* the exaltation of the spiritual estate, which sets the clergy above the laity as a class apart; *second,* the claim of an exclusive right to interpret the Scriptures; and, *third,* the pretension that the power to convene a council resides in the pope alone. He calls upon the German nobles to set their hand to reformation by constituting a national church under the primate of Germany. They should prohibit pilgrimages, diminish the number of holy days, abolish the celibacy of the priesthood, reform the universities, and put restrictions upon the power of the trade-guilds—a large programme of ecclesiastical and economic reconstruction. In the "Babylonish Captivity of the Church" he attacks the Catholic doctrine of the sacraments, through which the church has usurped the place of mediator and dispenser of grace, and by which it holds the Christian people in subjection. The third of these writings is on "The Freedom of a Christian Man," in which he sets forth his own fundamental apprehension of religion.

When the bull was published, Luther, so far from showing any disposition to retract, replied with a pamphlet, "Against the Bull of the Antichrist," in which he denounced the papal see as the seat of Antichrist, delivered over to Satan the pope with his bull and all his decretals, and shortly after, amid great enthusiasm of students and townsfolk, publicly burned the papal bull, the tomes of canon law, and various writings of his opponents. Meanwhile the term set in the bull had expired, and the bull of excommunication issued, cutting off Luther and his adherents from the church, and calling on the civil power to put down Luther, with his abettors and protectors.

The elector, unwilling to sacrifice Luther, insisted that he should be heard before the newly elected emperor, Charles V, and the diet of the empire (Reichstag), about to meet at Worms; and notwithstanding the protest of the papal nuncio, the emperor yielded to his urgency. Luther appeared before the diet (April, 1521), but there also declined to retract what he had written and said. On his way back from Worms under safe-conduct he was, by the elector's device, waylaid by an armed band and carried off to the Wartburg, where under an assumed name he remained in safety for several months, employing his enforced seclusion on a translation of the New Testament from Greek into German. A month after his departure the emperor issued the Edict of Worms, putting Luther and all his supporters under the ban of the empire. But three days before the edict was issued the French ambassador had taken his leave from Worms; the war with France began. In this conflict the emperor had need of the united support of Germany, and was constrained to overlook the disregard of the edict. Thenceforth for ten years, France, the popes, and the Turks, singly or in combinations, kept the emperor so fully occupied that he was unable to turn his hand to the extirpation of heresy in Germany. The diets, at his instance, repeatedly resolved that the edict should be enforced as far as possible—which always proved to be not at all—and as often rehearsed the ecclesiastical grievances of Germany and demanded a council to redress them.

The emperor also urged the calling of a council, hoping that by the removal of the just grounds of complaint and by reasonable concessions the Lutherans might be reconciled, or, if they refused to meet these concessions half-way, might forfeit the countenance of moderate men to whom the unity of the church and the peace of the empire was of more concern than the new doctrines. But the popes, partly because of hostility to Charles V, partly out of not unreasonable apprehension that a council on German soil might revive the precedents of Constance and Basel, could not be brought to the point. The result was that the rulers and free cities introduced the Lutheran reforms in doctrine, worship, and church government, and appropriated church property, especially of the monastic establishments, as they saw fit; and the diet of Speier (1526) legitimated this anomalous state of things, "while awaiting the sitting of a council or national assembly."

When, therefore, in June, 1530, the diet convened at

Augsburg under the presidency of the emperor himself, all parties recognised that its task was to find some form of reconciliation by which, if possible, the ultimate resort to force might be avoided. The supporters of Luther had no wish to separate themselves from the church; their aim was reformation, not secession. Accordingly, the princes and cities which had adopted the Lutheran reforms presented a statement of their doctrinal position and an enumeration of the changes they had introduced in worship and discipline, with the reasons for them. This statement, subsequently known as the Augsburg Confession, prepared by Philip Melancthon, was conciliatory in tone, and put the most Catholic face possible on the reformed teaching and practice. "Our churches do not dissent from the Catholic Church in any article of faith, but only remove some few abuses which have come in by the error of the times, contrary to the intent of the canons." The titles of the chapters in the second part show in what points the reformers found their "few recent abuses" to amend: Communion in Both Kinds; Marriage of the Clergy; the Mass; Confession; on Diverse Kinds of Meats (rules about food, fasts, etc.); on Traditions; Monastic Vows; Ecclesiastical Power.

A refutation was prepared and presented by a committee of Catholic theologians, and conferences were held between the two parties, but agreement was impossible. The final action of the diet left the Protestants till April of the next year to turn from the error of their ways. Thereupon the Protestant princes and a dozen of the cities formed a league for self-protection, which was subsequently joined by others; and negotiations were entered into with England, France, Denmark, and other enemies of the emperor. Protestantism thus became a political movement, the Schmalkald League was an *imperium in imperio*, with which new danger from the Turks compelled the emperor to treat. By the truce of Nürnberg (1532) the emperor agreed that the Protestants should be left unmolested until the meeting of a council, or in case such council was not convened within six months, until a special meeting of the diet. Neither the council nor the diet met. More wars with the Turks in the East and on the Mediterranean, a second war with France, and a revolt in the Netherlands, kept Charles too busy to intervene in Germany. Meanwhile, Protestantism gained many additional states and cities.

In 1546, however, the emperor outlawed the elector of Saxony and the landgrave of Hesse, and by his victory at Mühlberg (1547) overpowered all resistance. With the sanction of the diet (Augsburg Interim, 1548) he set about restoring the old order of things in the church, with the reservation of a few minor points which were left to the decision of the Council of Trent. Then all at once his right-hand man among the German princes, Moritz of Saxony, changed sides, and made alliance, at the price of the bishoprics of Metz, Toul, and Verdun, with the king of France, who took the field as the "protector of the liberties of Germany and its captive princes." Charles barely escaped capture by Moritz' army by hasty flight over the Brenner. His work was all undone. The settlement of the religious question was left to the next diet, at which, in 1555, the Peace of Augsburg was concluded.

By its provisions the adherents of the Augsburg Confession were recognised in the empire as a religion having an equal standing with the old. Religious freedom, or even toleration, was not contemplated on either side. The principle was *cuius regio, eius religio*. Every secular ruler might hold either to the old religion or to the Augsburg Confession, and his successor, if so minded, might change his faith; but within his territory no other religion was suffered than that of the prince for the time being. The same right to choose between the two religions belonged to the free cities. Those subjects who were unwilling thus to accept their religion from above had the privilege of expatriating themselves and seeking a new home in a territory of their own religion. Much against the wishes of the Lutherans, an exception was made in the case of the great

20

ecclesiastical princes, the archbishops of Mainz, Trier, and Cologne. If one of them abandoned the old faith, he abdicated with it his principality. Germany was thus divided between territories of the old religion and those of the Augsburg Confession. Reformed churches outside the Augsburg Confession were expressly excluded from this peace.

Almost simultaneously with the Lutheran movement in Germany, a similar movement began in Switzerland under the leadership of Huldreich Zwingli; but, partly through the impress of the leader's personality, and more largely through the peculiar political and social conditions in Switzerland, it took a widely different course. Born within two months after Luther, Zwingli was, like Luther, a man of the people, but his early life and education had been very different. Luther had a scholastic training; Zwingli's was purely humanistic. He had studied in the way of the new learning at Bern and Basel and Vienna; his ideal of a scholar was Erasmus, with whom he early came into friendly personal relations and long continued in correspondence. Theology, whether of the old scholastic or the "modernist" kind, he had never concerned himself with. Immediately upon taking his second degree in arts, he became a parish priest at Glarus and later at Einsiedeln, where he continued his studies in Greek and cultivated his talent as a popular preacher. The reputation which he made in these fields led to his election in 1519 as people's priest, that is to say, preacher and pastor, of the Münster church in Zürich, where he at once began preaching in course on the New Testament, commencing with the Gospel of Matthew. Luther's writings presently became known to him, and although he never acknowledged Luther as his master, and later was at radical variance with him, particularly in the matter of the sacraments, he was furthered in his thinking by Luther.

The conditions in Switzerland were vastly different from those under which Luther laboured in Saxony. The Swiss cantons, autonomous, and really, if not nominally, independent of the empire, united only by a league for mutual protection, subject to no princes, and little disposed to allow the bishops to control their actions, governed themselves by councils of their own election, which even before the Reformation often asserted themselves in ecclesiastical affairs. The path of Zwingli's reform in Zürich, which began in 1522, was therefore plain. Controversy having arisen about the obligation of the Lenten fast, the cantonal government, under Zwingli's influence, decided that the Scripture was the only authority, and that only what has its authority is binding. A series of public disputations was held with conservative opponents on fasting, the celibacy of the clergy, the Mass, the monasteries, and pictures in the churches, and the council decreed that these things, having no warrant in Scripture, should be reformed. A visitation of the churches was ordered and biblical instruction prescribed for the clergy as well as the laity; provision was made for the relief of the poor, which the abolition of the monasteries and charitable foundations had made a public question; civil laws were enacted concerning marriage, for the relief of the burdens that rested on the peasantry, for the creation of schools and the establishment of a university; the property of the monasteries was appropriated for the newly organised parishes and parish schools—so swift was the march of reformation. The movement soon spread to the other cantons, beginning with Bern, the most important city in the southwestern part of German Switzerland. It reached also the cities of southern Germany as far as Strassburg, where reforms were carried through in a similar way by the city councils, and where humanistic preparation inclined the reformers to Swiss rather than the Lutheran ways of thinking, or to a mean between them.

Among the leaders of French humanism, Le Fèvre d'Étaples had taken up with enthusiasm the study of the New Testament, and in 1512 published a commentary on the Epistles of Paul, in which he maintained the final authority of Scripture, brought out Paul's doctrine of justification by faith, denying the merit of works any part in it—salvation

is the free gift of God—had doubts about the obligatory
celibacy of the clergy, suggested that the services of the
church should be in the language of the people, and combated popular superstitions—a position not dissimilar to
that of Erasmus. In 1523 he published a French translation
of the New Testament. With his enlightened humanism,
he combined in his theological conceptions and his personal
piety a mysticism derived from the writings of Dionysius the
Areopagite and Richard of St. Victor. Like Erasmus, Le
Fèvre died in the bosom of the old church; but many of his
disciples, influenced by the writings of Luther and the agitation in Germany, went further than their master. The new
ideas made rapid progress, especially in the circles thus prepared for them; but in France the movement had neither
the protection of princes nor the autonomy of cities to shelter it, and by 1525 a period of persecution began in which
many were put to death, and still more sought refuge in
Germany, especially in Strassburg, and in Switzerland.

By one of these exiles, Farel, the Reformation was introduced into Geneva, and under him and John Calvin, who
joined him in 1536, that city became the centre and main-
stay of the French-speaking reformed churches. Calvin, born
at Noyon in Picardy in 1509, had had what we call a classical
education in Paris, and studied law in Orleans and Bourges.
Like many other young humanists he was in sympathy
with the ideas of Le Fèvre and Erasmus, but it was not
until 1533 that he associated himself with the more advanced party which had broken with the church. In the
following year he left France for Basel. There, in 1536, he
wrote his " Institutio Religionis Christianæ," an exposition of
Christianity in the new light, designed to demonstrate to
the king, to whom a prefatory letter is addressed, that those
who were being persecuted for their faith were not, as was
slanderously reported of them, political agitators or sacri-
legious fanatics, nor were they heretics from the fundamental doctrines of the Christian church.

In the Scandinavian countries (Denmark, Norway, and

Sweden), then united under one sovereign, Lutheranism was introduced by the king as early as 1520, chiefly, it would seem, with the motive of curbing the power of the great ecclesiastics. In 1537 the Danish church was fully reorganised on the Lutheran model, and Norway was under the same laws, though the Reformation there made slower progress among the people. In Sweden, which in the meantime had achieved its national independence, the same stage was reached by 1531.

The humanistic movement had done its part in preparing the way for the Reformation in England as well as upon the Continent. Colet, returning from studies in Paris and Italy, introduced the new methods of interpretation into the study of the New Testament at Oxford as early as 1496. His influence drew Erasmus to England. Linacre and Grocyn taught Greek at Oxford, and had Thomas More among their pupils. Luther's writings, particularly the "Babylonish Captivity" (1520), made no small stir among the students and younger teachers, which not only led Henry VIII to prohibit these books, but prompted him to write a defence of the seven sacraments of the church (1521), for which royal demonstration of orthodoxy the grateful pope rewarded him with the title, "Defender of the Faith." Luther's reply was in his most unmannerly manner, and exasperated the monarch still more against everything Lutheran.

That this "Defender of the Faith" within a dozen years broke with the pope and made the church in England independent of Rome was not due to any access of sympathy with the principles of the reformers about papal authority, much less with their doctrinal innovations, but to the refusal of the curia to annul his marriage with Catherine of Aragon in order that he might marry Anne Boleyn. When the pope threatened him with excommunication, Henry's answer was a series of acts of Parliament, declaring that the bishop of Rome has no more jurisdiction in England than any other foreign bishop; the only supreme head on earth of the Church of England is the king. Bishops are hence-forth to be nominated by the king, the chapter retaining only the empty form of election; they take their oath to the king, all oaths of papal obedience being done away. Denial of the king's supremacy in the church was made high treason, and Bishop John Fisher and Sir Thomas More suffered its penalties. The suppression of the monasteries and confiscation of their large possessions followed. By the distribution of a part of these spoils as royal grants to serviceable supporters, Henry created a powerful vested interest against a return to the Roman obedience. It would have been impossible, even for as strong a monarch as Henry VIII, to carry through and enforce such legislation, had it not been for the national self-sufficiency of the English people and an ancient and deep-rooted hostility to foreign authority and taxation.

Political motives at one moment inclined Henry to enter into friendly relations with the Protestant princes of Germany, and the ten articles which the king himself drew up and convocation adopted in 1536 made some concessions to the Protestant position. An English translation of the Bible was not only licensed, but in 1538 a copy was ordered to be put in a public place in every church. The Lutherans in England were encouraged by these acts to think that if the king went so far he might go farther. They were undeceived by the law of Six Articles (1539), often called the "Bloody Statute," in which the doctrine of transubstantiation was declared to be the faith of the Church of England, and the denial of it was punished by fire and confiscation of goods; communion in both kinds was rejected, and the marriage of the clergy; vows of chastity were declared indissoluble; private masses and auricular confession maintained. Many were put to death under this act; others fled the kingdom, finding refuge in Frankfurt, Strassburg, and Switzerland, where they were fortified in their views by closer contact with the continental reformers. It was of much consequence for the further history of the Reformation in England that the associations thus formed were chiefly with the South Germans and Swiss, so that when the exiles returned under Edward VI it was to cultivate in England a type of doctrine materially different from Luther's.

Henry's death (1547) brought to the throne his only son, Edward VI, a boy of nine years; and under the protectorate of Somerset and later under the guidance of Northumberland, the Reformation was established in England on the continental model, at first with some moderation, later in more radical fashion. The accession of Mary (1553), shortly followed by her marriage with Philip of Spain, brought a reaction in which all the religious innovations of Henry VIII and of Edward VI were swept away; England, purged of schism, returned to the bosom of the church—but the sequestered property was not restored. Five years later her sister Elizabeth, the daughter of Anne Boleyn, succeeded her, and the situation was again reversed.

Elizabeth was her father's daughter: she had been educated under the direction of Cranmer; she resented the stigma of illegitimacy put upon her by the church, and could not forget that under her sister's rule she was constrained against her will to conform to the Catholic cultus. Her first parliament repealed the acts of Mary's reign concerning religion, and revived numerous acts of Henry VIII and Edward VI, re-establishing the supremacy of the crown over the Church of England. In the oath of supremacy it is declared that, "The Queen's Highness is the only supreme governor of this realm . . . as well in all spiritual and ecclesiastical causes as temporal, and that no foreign prince, person, prelate, state, or potentate has, or ought to have, any jurisdiction, power, superiority, or authority, ecclesiastical or spiritual, within this realm." The second—more completely reformed—prayer-book of Edward VI, with some changes, was restored by act of Parliament; his "Forty-two Articles," embodying the reformed doctrine, revised, with some use of the Württemberg Confession of Brenz, were issued as the Thirty-nine Articles of the Church of England.

An act of uniformity prescribed the use of the Book of Common Prayer, and forbade under very severe penalties any deviation from the rites and forms therein contained. The most important changes in the Articles have to do with the headship of the church, in which connection the authority of the sovereign in relation to the word and sacraments is disclaimed, and in the doctrine of the Lord's Supper, where the articles of Edward VI flatly denied the real presence, while the Thirty-nine Articles speak of the presence of Christ "only in a celestial and spiritual manner," and of the reception of Christ in the sacrament through faith— Calvin succeeded Zwingli.[1]

Lutheran doctrine found entrance into Scotland as early as 1528, when Patrick Hamilton was burned for it; but it was not until after the accession of Elizabeth in England that the Reformation made much progress. Then, under the lead of John Knox, it swept everything before it, taking a national form widely different from that of England, and essentially Genevan both in doctrine and polity.

If we look at the religious map of Europe a half-century after Luther's theses, we find that the religion of the Augsburg Confession was established in a considerable number of the states and free cities of Germany, but that its advance in other quarters had been stayed; and in the Catholic states, notably in Bavaria and the Austrian crown lands, where Protestantism had made considerable progress, the repressive measures of the princes and the efforts of the Jesuits promoted a reaction in which it steadily declined. A similar decline took place in the territories of the ecclesiastical princes, the archbishoprics of Mainz and Trier. Switzerland, except the forest cantons, was reformed; the Scandinavian kingdoms were Lutheran; England under Elizabeth was finally separated from the Roman Church; Scotland had just broken away. In France the Huguenots

---

[1] In the liturgy, the form of administration combines the phraseology of the two prayer-books of Edward VI, and is therefore half Catholic, half Genevan.

had multiplied in spite of persecution, and counted among
their leaders some of the strongest men in the nation; the
civil wars, of which differences of religion were the cause
or pretext, had just begun, and were to keep the country
continually embroiled till the end of the century. Philip II
was trying to stamp out the movement in the Netherlands
by arbitrary exercise of power which provoked the great
national uprising against Spanish rule. In Spain and Italy
the movement had been put down by the inquisition before
it gained much headway. Within fifty years the schism
had grown from insignificant beginnings till all western
Europe was divided by it, and no one could foresee how
much farther it might go—certainly he would have been a
sanguine prophet who in 1567 had ventured to announce
that the tide had reached full flood.

The common characteristic of the movement in all lands
was the rejection of the authority of the church whether
speaking through pope or council, and not alone its concrete
authority, but the doctrine of the church on which its claim
to supremacy rested. In contradiction to this doctrine the
reformers set up the dogmatic principle of the final sole
authority of divine revelation in Scripture. The theory, as
we have seen, was by no means new. In Scotus it was
the usual retreat of intellectual scepticism upon revelation.
Occam had taught it in conformity with the irrationalism
of his nominalist premises, and it was perpetuated in his
school, but he had given it application only to the supremacy and infallibility of the pope. Wycliffe had extended it
to other doctrines, notably to transubstantiation; various
heretical sects had founded on Scripture alone their eccentricities of faith and manners; the doctrine had been condemned in the person of John Hus, as Eck triumphantly
reminded Luther.

The final authority of Scripture was, however, not the
real issue, but the authority to interpret Scripture. The
church claimed this as its exclusive right. The reformers
asserted this right for themselves, and, in principle, for every

Christian man—practically, they meant for those who interpreted as they did.

The point at which Luther was led in the controversy over indulgences to array the Scripture against the church was the penitential system; but this opened into the larger question, "What is of necessity to salvation?" The answer he gave was the doctrine of justification by faith; and justification by faith, variously apprehended and interpreted, is the second characteristic dogma of Protestantism. To this conception of the way of salvation Luther had come before 1517, mainly through his interpretation of Paul; but he had not discovered any conflict between it and the teaching of the church, and it was only in opposition to the claim of the church to stand between God and man with the keys of the kingdom of heaven in its hands that the individual immediacy of salvation by faith became the corner-stone of his theology.

That man is justified by faith, not by the works of the law, is written so large in the Epistles of Paul that it could not be overlooked. Predecessors and contemporaries of Augustine speak of justification by faith, or by faith alone, as if the language were familiar in their time; it had never disappeared from Catholic exegesis, and had been revived by the humanists, notably by Le Fèvre.[1] To the apprehension of the common man it may have meant no more than the remission of sins in baptism, but the interpreters of Paul could not so restrict it. For Augustine, as we have seen, justification is a real change in the nature of man, an "*ex impio fieri justum*," by a participation in the divine righteousness (*justitia*). The grace of God, inspiring a faith working through love, in that moment justifies man; but the transformation of his character by which the end of God in him is fully attained is a progressive work—justification is both act and process. This was substantially the teaching of the great schoolmen, especially of Aquinas.

[1] See above, pp. 307 f. Le Fèvre's interpretation was known and commended by Luther before 1517.

To Luther, on the contrary, justification is not a change wrought by divine grace in the nature or character of man, not the overcoming in him of sin and the establishment of righteousness, but solely a change in his relation to divine justice, so that his sin with its guilt (*reatus*, liability to punishment) is not imputed to him; while, as the complement of non-imputation of sin, the righteousness of Christ is imputed by God to man as his righteousness. It is, to speak irreverently, a piece of celestial book-keeping, in which man's debit is carried over to be charged to Christ, while Christ's credit is transferred to man. Melancthon conceived justification more distinctly as a judicial act, and brought into use for it the idea and term "forensic."

To this difference in the conception of justification corresponds a different conception of faith. The Augustinian idea of faith has been sufficiently indicated above.[1] For Luther, faith is the unquestioning acceptance and appropriation of the gospel, that is to say, of the promise of salvation through Christ. His very definition of gospel is "promise," in opposition to law, which is command and demand; and justification follows upon this faith, which God has made its condition *sine qua non*. This definition of faith is not only at variance with the Augustinian tradition in Catholic theology, but it leaves out what is most characteristic in the Pauline idea of faith.

The influence of Luther's scholastic training is especially manifest in his doctrine of salvation. He knew only the nominalist schoolmen, and among them had chiefly studied Gabriel Biel; he had some acquaintance also with the writings of d'Ailly and of Occam. Of Aquinas he never had any considerable knowledge, but he had to the full the nominalist prejudice against him and against the whole Aristotelian scholasticism. It was natural, therefore, that he should reject all realistic conceptions of grace and its operation. He held unquestioningly the theory of the arbitrariness of divine will which Occam and his successors

[1] See above, p. 199.

had inherited from Scotus. The question, How is such a scheme of salvation reconcilable with the moral character of God? was not raised by him; if it had been pressed upon him, he would doubtless have replied with Biel, that whatever God called just was made just by his calling it so; and to say that anything that God ordains or does is unjust, is to impose upon him the limitations of human standards of right and wrong.

If on this side Luther's ideas were cast in the mould of nominalism, in other things they were given form and emphasis by his antipathy to the theology in which he had been educated. Inheriting Scotist teaching concerning the human will, the nominalists conceded to man the ability, under the general influence of God, to predispose himself to salvation. Biel, for example, says, When a man does what in him lies, God necessarily gives him grace, in accordance with an immutable divine ordinance; and to what lies in him belongs the ability to love God above all things. This disposition merits "*de congruo*" the grace which enables him through "*meritum de condigno*" to attain to salvation. Luther believed himself to have in his own experience the proof that man has no such power, so that, in making salvation to such a degree dependent upon man's initiative, theologians were in reality making his salvation impossible. That man could in any sense *merit* divine *grace* seemed to him a contradiction in terms.

No word in the vocabulary of theology was so obnoxious to Luther as "merit." Not only was there no merit of any species in anything that a man did antecedent to justification, but nothing that the justified man did in his whole life possessed merit in any sense or measure, or deserved any reward at God's hands. The only merit is Christ's, imputed to the believer. Obligation (*debitum*) belongs to the same circle of ideas, and is repudiated with desert. For the man justified by faith there is no more obligation; Christ has assumed it all. Obligation, desert, reward, belong to the sphere and economy of law, which as a whole is superseded

and annulled by the gospel. Law and gospel are contradictories. By "law" Luther means not only the preceptive
and statutory parts of the Old Testament, but everything
in the New Testament that demands or commands, or
speaks of God's wrath. "Thou shalt love the Lord with
all thy heart," and, "Thou shalt love thy neighbour as thyself," is "law" as much as "Thou shalt not kill," or, "The
soul that sinneth, it shall die." "Gospel" is all in the Old
Testament or the New which points to Christ as the Saviour
and to salvation through faith alone.

The necessary counterpart of Luther's theory of man's
total inability to any good is predestination. On this point
Luther is more rigidly deterministic than Augustine: "God
foreknows nothing contingently, but foresees and does all
things by his immutable, eternal, and infallible will." He
does not shrink from making God the cause of Adam's fall,
or from saying that, since God moves all things in all actions,
it necessarily follows that he moves and acts in Satan and
in wicked men. These conclusions are not reached from
metaphysical premises, or by abstract reflections on the
sovereignty of God; he is concerned to assert man's mere
passivity in salvation in order to put the certainty of salvation on the one sure foundation, the immutable will of God.
Here, also, the idea of God as absolute will, which he had
from the nominalist Scotist tradition, doubtless helped him
over the moral difficulties of such a conception, which from
other premises might well seem insuperable.

To this doctrine of predestination logically corresponds
the idea of the church as the "*prædestinatorum universitas*,"
which comes from Augustine, and had been explicitly formulated by Wycliffe and Hus. The Christian church is a
spiritual unity, not a bodily or visible one; the church universal is an object of faith. The marks by which its presence in the world is recognised are the preaching of the
gospel and administration of the sacraments. The hierarchy is not the church. All Christians are priests, worthy
to appear before God, to pray for others, and to instruct one

another in religious things. A sacrament, in his definition, exists where an express divine promise is given which calls for faith. This leaves of the seven sacraments of the mediæval church only baptism, the Lord's Supper, and penance (*i. e.*, penitence). Penance stands, however, on a different footing from the others, and before long he excluded it because the promise does not accompany a "sign."

The sacraments were in his view means of grace, but not as vehicles of different kinds of realistically conceived grace. What man receives in and through all the sacraments is the forgiveness of sins; and this grace is conveyed, not in the material of the sacrament, but in the word which accompanies it, so that its efficacy is conditioned upon the recipient's faith that he *has* the forgiveness promised in the gospel. It is obvious that infant baptism fits this theory ill, and Luther made the case as hard for himself as he could by declaring that "baptism helps nobody and is not to be administered to any unless he believes for himself." At one time he thought that "in baptism children do believe for themselves and of their own faith, which God works in them." Later he was content to base the obligation of the rite solely on the command of Christ.

Luther's doctrine of the Eucharist is sharply opposed to the Catholic doctrine by his denial of its sacrificial character. He is at variance with Catholic teaching also when he finds the grace which the sacrament conveys only in the word, and makes its efficacy depend upon the faith of the recipient.[1] On the other hand, he held with compensatory tenacity to the physical presence of the body and blood of Christ in the consecrated elements, taking the words of Christ in the institution, "This *is* my body," with uncompromising literalness. This brought him into conflict with Zwingli, who with the Swiss and many of the South German reformers, interpreted the words figuratively—"This *represents* my body"—and regarded the sacrament as a memorial and symbolical rite. The effort of Philip of Hesse to put an end

[1] In his definition of faith.

to a strife so injurious to the common cause by bringing the protagonists together at Marburg (1529) for discussion was fruitless. Luther made agreement with him on this point a test of Christianity, and treated those who held the contrary opinion as enemies of the gospel. An irremediable schism was the consequence. The theory of transubstantiation, by which Aquinas and other schoolmen explained the mode in which the body and blood of Christ are present in the elements, and to which the Fourth Lateran Council (1215) had given its authority, Luther rejected in favour of another scholastic theory, namely, that the substance of Christ's body is not substituted for that of the bread and wine, but introduced beside it.[1]

In falling back upon the sole authority of divine revelation in Scripture, the reformers were confronted by some difficult questions. The Catholic Church received the Bible as the word of God because the church had always so received it, and the canon of Scripture—the list of books to which this character attached—was determined by the tradition of the church. But when the authority of the church and its tradition was denied, the question arose, How do we know that the Bible is the inspired word of God? Augustine said, "I should not believe the gospel did not the authority of the Catholic Church move me thereto." In place of this objective assurance Luther puts the certification of inner experience: "God must say to thee in thine own heart, 'This is God's word.'" As later reformers expressed it, the *testimonium internum Spiritus Sancti* is the only conclusive proof of the inspiration of Scripture. By such a criterion every Christian might have his individual Bible, which "found" him; and it is plain that if Luther had committed himself to the guidance of this instinct, he would have dropped from his private canon more than one book in

---

[1] This theory is discussed by Peter Lombard, and was later held by Occam and d'Ailly, from the latter of whom Luther adopted it, being moved not only by d'Ailly's argument, but by his own nominalist antipathy to everything Thomistic and Aristotelian.

the New Testament as well as in the Old.   What he actually did with the Old Testament was to fall back upon the Jewish canon as contained in the Hebrew Bible, and to segregate the books of the Christian Bible which are not acknowledged by the Jews, putting them in a collection by themselves under the title Apocrypha.   For this name, and for the judgment which is expressed in it, he had precedent and authority in Jerome; but the segregation was an innovation which established itself in all Protestant versions of the Bible.

He did not similarly revise the traditional canon of the New Testament, but he created by a dogmatic criterion a canon of the gospel within the canon of the books.   "Those Apostles who treat oftenest and highest of how faith alone justifies, are the best Evangelists.   Therefore St. Paul's Epistles are more a Gospel than Matthew, Mark, and Luke. For these do not set down much more than the works and miracles of Christ; but the grace which we receive through Christ no one so boldly extols as St. Paul, especially in his letter to the Romans."   In comparison with the Gospel of John, the Epistles of Paul, and 1 Peter, "which are the kernel and marrow of all books," the Epistle of James, with its insistence that man is *not* justified by faith alone, but by works proving faith, is "a mere letter of straw, for there is nothing evangelical about it."   It is clear that the infallibility of Scripture has here, in fact if not in avowal, followed the infallibility of popes and councils; for the Scripture itself has to submit to be judged by the ultimate criterion of its accord with Luther's doctrine of justification by faith.

The sole final authority of Scripture was not a fundamental proposition from which Luther set out to discover a scriptural doctrine of salvation, much less to develop a new doctrine of the church and the sacraments and all that went with them; the logic of his opponents pushed him farther and faster than his own logic or disposition would have done, and always he was thrown back on the Scripture for authority.   He was more interested in the effect of the new apprehension of salvation on the religious life of individuals than in the outward manifestations of religion, and saw no need for change in the customary forms except where they implied and conveyed false ideas about salvation and led men to put their confidence in aught else than the gospel. To remodel the institutions and liturgy of the church on a consistently biblical pattern was not in his mind. He would do away with private masses, because the sacrificial character was impressed on them with peculiar distinctness, and because they were regarded as good works, by which propitiation was made to God for the sins of living and dead. When he came to revise the Latin Mass (December, 1523), he omitted the canon, and everything which suggested offering, but in other points was inclined to leave large liberty even to weak consciences. Only he was insistent that "the word," in lesson and sermon, should be the chief thing in every gathering of the congregation for worship.

With the sacrificial character of the Mass Luther rejected also the sacerdotal character of the clergy. In the only sense in which there is a priesthood under the Christian dispensation, all Christians are priests. Bishops, presbyters, deacons, in different functions, constitute a Christian ministry—primarily a ministry of the Word—deriving their office and authority not from episcopal ordination in Apostolic succession, but by delegation from the community, every member of which is competent to teach, preach, baptise, and administer the Lord's Supper, though for the sake of order the actual exercise of these functions is committed to certain chosen individuals. There is consequently no such thing as indelibility of orders; the community can depose a minister whom it has itself chosen and ordained.

But though Luther himself applied the biblical test only to things he deemed contrary to the gospel, on the principle that what is not against Scripture is for Scripture and Scripture for it, when he asserted that the word of God is the only norm, and that all Christians have the same right to

21

33

33

33

interpret it, he enounced a principle over which he had no control. Men of a more radical temper were for abolishing everything that could not prove its right to exist by Scripture, and making things over on the model they found in their Bibles. While Luther was in seclusion in the Wartburg, headstrong spirits, under the lead of his colleague, Carlstadt, ran away with the reformation in Wittenberg, the excitement and confusion being augmented by the coming of some prophets from Zwickau, who professed to be inspired, predicting a new Turkish invasion and the approaching end of the world, and declaring the baptism of infants no baptism. It required Luther's return and all his influence to restore the rule of moderation.

The Zwickau prophets were the precursors of the radicals who were opprobriously labelled "Anabaptists," *i. e.*, "rebaptisers," because, holding that infant baptism was no baptism, they baptised adults who joined them. The name covers a wide diversity of opinion and temper. Some of those upon whom it was fastened were biblical literalists who proposed a thoroughgoing reformation of institutions, worship, and life, after the precept and example of the New Testament, with no opportunist concessions to things as they are, such as made Luther and Zwingli stop half-way. Others asserted that the supreme authority is not the Scripture, which is but the dead letter, not the living word of God. The true word of God is internal; from within, in the recesses of his own spirit, a man must hear the eternal word of the Father speak to him. By this inner word of immediate revelation he must be taught, not by Scripture and preaching. To some, again, this doctrine of the indwelling of the divine word became a real incarnation by which man is deified even in this present life. Pantheistic ideas and peculiar views about the Trinity and the Person of Christ, also, early appeared among them. The levelling of all inequalities of class and possession, and the community of goods, were an attractive part of the programmes for an earthly kingdom of heaven, and Anabaptist socialists like Münzer had their hand in the Peasants' Revolt.

This great uprising, which spread like wild-fire through southwestern Germany in 1524–'25, was the outcome of long-standing oppression, which had more than once before provoked local insurrections; but the Twelve Articles in which the grievances and demands of the Swabian peasants were embodied, drawn up probably by a village priest,[1] put in the forefront the demand that each community should have the right to appoint its own pastor and to depose him if he conduct himself improperly; and followed this by the provision they proposed to make for the support of their pastors and of the poor from the tithes, the administration of which was to be in the hands of the community. In the political and social part of the programme appeal is made throughout to the authority of the word of God; if it can be proved to them from Scripture that any of their demands are not in agreement with the word of God, the petitioners will recede from it; if they discover other articles of complaint in Scripture, they will bring them forward. Thus the authors seized upon the watchword of the Reformation in the neighbouring Switzerland as well as in Germany; and they may have expected this argument to be more inconvenient if not more persuasive because so many of the Swabian and Franconian knights were avowed partisans of Luther and reform.

Luther read the nobility and the clergy a lesson on the revolt, which he tells them they alone have brought upon themselves by their resistance to the gospel and their oppression of the peasantry. To the peasants he laid down the law: "Let every soul be in subjection to the higher powers." Rebellion against constituted authority cannot be excused by any wrong the powers that be may have done; it is not for subjects to take judgment into their own hands. He exhorts both sides to submit the matter to arbitrament, and to meet each other in a spirit of mu-

---

[1] This memorial was issued in March, 1525, nine or ten months after the outbreak of the revolt, and was evidently intended as an appeal to the sympathy of the reform party. See particularly the apologetic preamble.

tual concession.   When this exhortation fell on deaf ears,
Luther broke out on the "Murderous and Thieving Rabble
of Peasantry" in his most ferocious manner, crying to the
rulers: "Hither to deliver, hither to the rescue; have pity
on the poor people, stab, smite, throttle, who can."   To this
task the princes and nobles needed no incitement; the
revolt, which had ravaged wide regions with fire and sword,
was quelled with vindictive thoroughness.

The Anabaptists, persecuted with death or banishment
by reformed and Catholic alike, multiplied in secret, especially along the Rhine and in the Netherlands; and, as is
common when the wholesome restraint of publicity is removed, the extravagant elements prevailed more and more
among them, until in 1534-'35, after an abortive attempt at
Strassburg, they undertook to revive theocracy in Münster
as the New Jerusalem, with Old Testament accompaniments
such as polygamy, apostolic community of goods, and a
Leyden tailor for a Davidic king.   The capture of the city
by the troops of Catholic and Lutheran princes put an end
to the militant variety of Anabaptism, with its reign of very
ambiguous saints on earth.   What was left subsided into
the peaceable sect of Mennonites.

Luther's opponents charged the Anabaptists and the
peasants to him: religious, political, and social revolution
was in the logic of his principles, as soon as men got hold
of them who had the consistency to think them through
and the courage to translate the consequence into action.
Luther might try to clear his skirts by writing fiercely
against the peasants, but as Erasmus reminded him, he
could not by these tirades keep many from believing that
by his writings in German against the "greaselings and
shavelings," against monks and bishops, and for gospel liberty against human tyranny, he had given occasion to these
popular tumults.

To Erasmus and his humanist following, who expected
that enlightenment would in time bring about a temperate
reform, Luther's excess of zeal and his vituperative eloquence

had always been distasteful; they now withdrew the measure of countenance they had at the beginning shown him. Erasmus himself, whom many regarded as the real author of the mischief—"Erasmus laid the eggs, Luther hatched them"—now openly came out against him with a treatise on Free Will, aimed at the crude determinism of Luther's hyper-Augustinianism, and drew from him in his reply, "De Servo Arbitrio," a reaffirmation of the incriminated doctrine pushed to a veritable *reductio ad impium*. On the other hand, in his "savage book"—as Erasmus called it—against the peasants, Luther committed religion as completely to the support of power and possession, however ruthlessly used, as ever the mediæval church had done, and dashed the hopes of those who dreamed that the "gospel" had a promise for the life that now is as well as for that which is to come.

But the greatest consequence of the Anabaptist extravagances and the Peasants' War was its reaction on Luther himself. He had begun with enthusiastic confidence that, when the word of God was set free and the gospel of justification by faith proclaimed, it would make men think right and do right. A revival of true religion in the hearts of men would in due time bring all needed reforms. Of the civil power he asked only protection for the gospel. Now, confronted by the varieties of Anabaptist gospels, all claiming, like his own, the authority of the word of God, and by the revolutionary excesses which defended themselves with the same appeal, he was constrained to put his trust in princes to extirpate obnoxious sects and maintain the social order; and the subsequent political history of the Reformation in Germany permanently impressed on Lutheranism a peculiar territorial character. The old order was overthrown and the new imposed by the princes, each as seemed to him good. The religion of the ruler was the religion of his subjects. In place of Luther's original idea of the independence of each Christian community, came a multitude of Lutheran state churches under the autocratic supremacy of the prince for the time being, who not only legislated in church orders on organisation, discipline, and worship, but imposed elaborate confessions of faith on his clergy, all subject to equally arbitrary change by his successor. In the violent doctrinal controversies which rent the Lutheran churches almost before Luther was dead, the parties clamoured and intrigued for the theological ear of rulers as the surest way to make the truth prevail.

Luther despised philosophy and had no intellectual interest in theology. Everything in his mind centred about justification solely by faith, in which alone he found the assurance of salvation he sought. The doctrines which are premises, consequences, or corollaries of this—what are commonly called the doctrines of sin and grace, including the sacraments—he thought out in his own way; the conflict in which he was thereby involved led him to deny the authority of the church and the whole doctrine of the church on which its authority rested, and to assert against it the sole authority of Scripture. What lay outside these controversial issues he did not impugn.

He accepted the three received symbols of Western Christendom, the Apostles' Creed, the Nicene Creed, and the Athanasian Creed, as the doctrine of the church universal; and, though he did not find the phraseology of the theological creeds in the Bible, and recognised, as Augustine did, that "Trinity," with its mathematical implications, is a word the use of which can only be justified by inability to find a better one, he never questioned that the dogmas of the Trinity and the deity of Christ formulated the teaching of Scripture and were fundamental articles of the Christian faith. He took pains to emphasise his agreement with "the true Christian church" on these cardinal points by publishing the three symbols in German translation, with an explanatory comment. The religious faith by which alone man is justified is thus limited not only to the church of the word and the sacraments, but by an orthodox confession. "Whoever wishes to be saved must, before all things, hold the catholic faith, which unless a man preserve whole and inviolate, beyond doubt he will eternally perish"—so runs the beginning of the Athanasian Creed, on which Luther was as sound as the pope himself. That the authority of the creeds lay not in the church but in the Scripture implied that the Bible is a body of revealed doctrine, a conception the evolution of which made the churches of the Reformation dogmatic churches to a degree surpassing Catholicism itself.

The theological teacher of the Lutheran Reformation was Melancthon, who was called to Wittenberg as professor of Greek in 1518. The first edition of his "Loci Communes Rerum Theologicarum" (1521) is little more than a clear and orderly exposition of Luther's ideas; but in the course of time he became more independent, and in the later editions of the Loci as well as in his other writings his views on some important points differed materially though not controversially from Luther's. The principal divergences concerned predestination and the Lord's Supper. Melancthon gave up Luther's deterministic conceptions, with the pure passivity of man and the irresistibility of divine grace. There are three concurrent causes in conversion—the word of God, the Holy Spirit, and the human will assenting to the word of God and not contending against it. In the doctrine of the sacraments Melancthon departed more widely from Luther as time went on. He had comparatively early found himself unable to accept Luther's scholastic theory of the ubiquity of Christ's glorified body—a communication of the divine attribute of omnipresence to his human nature—and inclined more and more to the symbolical interpretation of the words, "This is my body," which Luther always insisted on taking literally.

Both this Calvinistic modification of the doctrine of the sacrament and the synergistic doctrine of salvation became the subject of long and acrimonious controversies among the Lutherans of the next generation, and in these controversies, and in the effort to put an end to them either by the more exact definition of the true teaching of the church or by arriving at consensus of some kind, the corpus of doctrine having a confessional and normative authority in one part or another of the Lutheran churches grew to formidable dimensions; but what was of more consequence than these dogmatic libraries was the fact that sound doctrine now became the dominant idea. It was the possession of the sound doctrine which made the true church—sound doctrine in the Scripture, sound doctrine in the creed and confessions. Under this incubus of confessional controversy and dogma the moral and religious forces which the Reformation had set in motion came to a standstill for a time, and in some places even turned back.

CHAPTER XII

CHRISTIANITY

THE PROTESTANT REFORMATION. II

Calvin—Institutio Christianæ Religionis—Election—The Law of God
—Sacraments—The Church—Lutheran and Reformed Protes-
tantism—The Creeds—Servetus—Antitrinitarian Tendencies—
Socinus—Criticism of the Doctrine of the Atonement.

CALVIN's "Institutio Christianæ Religionis" (1536), as has
been said above, was originally designed as an apology of
the Reformation, which, by a clear presentation of the position of the reformers should convince the king of France
and open-minded Catholics that the reformed doctrines
were neither so heretical nor so dangerous as they were represented. In this first edition of the Institutio Calvin sets
forth substantially the teaching of Luther, with some modifications after Butzer, but in a form which bears the stamp
of his own individuality. The chapters treat, in order, of
the Law, Faith, Prayer, the Sacraments (Baptism and the
Lord's Supper), the False Sacraments, and Christian Liberty, thus including only the reformed doctrine of salvation. In later editions it became a complete system of
theology, with a different and more methodical disposition
of the material, treating, in four books, of the Knowledge
of God, the Creator; the Knowledge of God, the Redeemer,
first revealed to the Fathers under the Law and afterward
to us in the Gospel; the Way in which the Grace of Christ
is Received; and the External Means Leading to Salvation.

In its final form (1559) it is beyond question the greatest
theological work of the Reformation, a pre-eminence due in
part to the logical character of Calvin's mind and the lucidity
of his exposition, in part to his learning and skill as an interpreter of the Scriptures, a field in which he surpassed all
his contemporaries.

Luther defended with the authority of Scripture certain doctrines which were in conflict with those of the church; he made no attempt to construct a system of doctrine on the authority of Scripture alone, or even to develop a doctrine of Scripture. Calvin's Institutio, appropriately to its general plan and divisions, begins with a discussion of the sources of the knowledge men may have of God—the innate *sensus divinitatis* and divine revelation in Scripture. The latter is the *æternæ veritatis regula*, the norm of doctrine and of life; obedience to the will of God revealed in it is the source not only of a perfect and complete faith but of all right knowledge of God. On the Bible are to be based, therefore, the organisation and discipline of the church and the moral standards and sanctions of a Christian community, as well as the whole system of Christian doctrine. To the consistent application of this principle the wide differences between the development of the Reformed and the Lutheran branches of Protestantism are in largest measure due.

Justification by faith is the distinctive article of Protestant doctrine in its Reformed as well as its Lutheran type. Calvin's presentation of this doctrine is more closely and completely Pauline than Luther's. To Luther it was the ground of a subjective assurance of a salvation whose sole condition was the confident appropriation of the promises of the gospel, and he always conceived it in antithesis to the ideas of divine law, obligation, good works, and desert—an antithesis which he forced to a contradiction. Calvin develops an objective doctrine of justification based on an exacter interpretation of Paul. He defines justification as "the acceptance whereby God, having received us into favour (grace), regards us as righteous." It consists of two parts, the remission of sins and the imputation of Christ's righteousness. He holds, with Paul, that no other faith justifies than that which is efficacious by love; but denies that it owes its justifying power to the efficaciousness of love.

The inseparable sequel of justification is sanctification (Romans 8, 30); Christ justifies no one whom he does not go on also to sanctify. The development of a holy character after the divine pattern is the purpose of God in human salvation. It is evident not only that Calvin is here the truer interpreter of Paul, but also that he is much nearer to common Catholic doctrine. He distinguishes between the *act*, in which God accepts the believer as righteous (justification), and the *process*, in which, by the work of the Spirit of God within him, man is made holy (sanctification). Catholic theology covers both act and process with the name Justification. The important thing is that the two, however named, are inseparable.

A central idea in Calvin's thinking is the sovereignty of God, who rules the world, not as abstract and arbitrary will, but as a moral personality, the final cause of all whose ways in creation, history, providence, and redemption is his own glory.[1] From this point of view the predestination of the elect is necessarily apprehended in a different way from that in which Luther viewed it. For Luther, who approached the question from the side of original sin, predestination was essential to the assurance of salvation, not a necessary consequence of God's sovereignty. It is a result of this approach that Luther said little, and evidently thought seldom, of the reverse side of the election of some to faith and salvation, namely, the reprobation of the non-elect. Calvin, on the contrary, faces without flinching this unavoidable consequence, and brings the eternal damnation of the reprobate as well as the salvation of the elect into relation, not only to the positive will of God, but to the one final cause, God's glory. "We give the name predestination to the eternal decree of God by which he decided for himself what should become of every individual man. For we are not all created in the same condition. To some eternal life is foreordained, and to others eternal damnation." Of the former it is said that the end of their election is "that we may be to the praise of divine grace"; of the latter, "that by God's just, but inscrutable judgment, they were raised

[1] This conception he had from Butzer.

up to manifest his glory by their condemnation." Calvin
held this hard doctrine, not because of his own hardness of
heart, but because he found it, letter for letter, in Paul. It
was, as we have seen, the final teaching of Augustine; and
the difference between Calvin and the German Reformers
is only that he, like Zwingli, puts it in plain words. Like
Luther, Calvin also held—as they both believed, in agreement with Augustine—that Adam's fall was not only foreseen but foreordained by God.

Those whom God has predestined to salvation he calls,
not alone by the general external call of the gospel, but by a
special inner calling, which, through the enlightening work
of the Holy Spirit, produces saving faith. Faith is thus not
so inseparably bound to the word and sacraments as it is in
Luther; but Calvin found no warrant in Scripture for Zwingli's large-hearted stretching of the possibilities of absolute
predestination to save, by the mysterious operation of the
Spirit, not only God's elect among Jews and Christians, but
pagan philosophers like Socrates.

Luther had little interest in the organisation of the church;
he rejected the authority of the hierarchy, but did not
attempt to construct from the Scripture a normal type of
church government. He left all that at the outset to the
Spirit of God, and in the end to the civil rulers. Calvin, on
the contrary, believed that he found in the New Testament
a revealed pattern for the church, with a ministry including
pastors; teachers; elders, who were chiefly occupied with the
maintenance of order, morals, and discipline; and deacons,
who were the organs of its charity. He found in the Bible
not only norms of church order and discipline, but a divine
regulative for the life of the community. He had not that
repugnance, both personal and theoretical, to law as law,
which was so strong in Luther. That the law is not a way
of salvation, he held uncompromisingly; but the law in the
Old Testament and in the New was for him the revelation
of God's permanent will for the life of man and the order of
society, upon which human law should be based—the law

of the state and the law of the church, between which there should be entire harmony. When it came to the application of this principle, there was a great deal more to be found in the Old Testament than in the New, so that in the church in Geneva and those which followed its doctrine and example the Old Testament had a very much larger effect than in the sphere of the Lutheran Reformation.

The revelation of God's immutable will for human life in the Scriptures must be essentially one with the law of nature, which is divinely impressed on the intelligence and conscience of all men. Hence the legislation of the Old Testament, adapted to particular times and circumstances, may be interpreted in principle, universalised, and supplemented by the law of nature. Calvin's juristic studies and his early interest in Seneca show here; and this Stoic enlargement of the conception of divine law is characteristic of the Reformed churches, in marked contrast to Lutheran orthodoxy and to the literal legalism of some later sects.

In his doctrine of the sacraments Calvin occupies a middle ground between Zwingli, for whom they are mere symbols, and Luther's semi-Catholic conception. Baptism is the sacrament which confirms and sanctions a covenant into which children are received by God; it is the Christian counterpart of circumcision, the covenant sacrament of the old dispensation. No other immediate efficacy need be attributed to it. When children thus introduced into the covenant come to years of discretion, "the remaining significance of this sacrament will follow at such time as the Lord has foreseen." In the Lord's Supper Calvin rejects Luther's scholastic figment of the ubiquity of the glorified body of Christ and the corporal presence of the body of Christ in the consecrated elements, altogether. In the later editions of the Institutes he formulates his final position as follows: "The matter, or substance, of the sacrament I call Christ, with his death and resurrection. By the effect of the sacrament I understand redemption, righteousness, sanctification, eternal life, and all the other benefits which Christ offers to us. . . . In the mystery of the Supper, by the symbols of bread and wine, Christ is truly exhibited to us, even his body and blood, in which he fulfilled all obedience to gain for us righteousness." This presence is, however, mediated through the Spirit to the spirit, not physically or materially.

Calvin distinguishes clearly, as Zwingli had done before him, between the invisible church, which is the *numerus elec- torum*, and the visible church, which is called church with respect to men. The visible church is present wherever the word of God is sincerely preached and listened to, and where the sacraments are administered in accordance with the institution of Christ; for his promise, "Where two or three are gathered together in my name, there am I in the midst of them," cannot fail. Unlike Luther and Zwingli, Calvin firmly adhered to the principle of the autonomy of the church in its relation to the civil authority. The church of the Genevan ideal is, however, not a voluntary church, an association of religiously minded men and women within the secular community; it is the church of the whole people of the city, all of whom are members of it, under its instruc- tion and discipline. The church and the civil magistracy, each independent in its sphere, should work together har- moniously for the glory of God. In France, in a Catholic state, the Reformed churches constituted themselves, through their local, provincial, and national synods—a kind of re- publican organisation—as a national Reformed Church; and a similar organisation was created in the Netherlands and in Scotland—an adaptation of Calvin's church in a city- state to national dimensions and conditions, and always with the idea of the church of the whole people.

The breach between the German and the Swiss Reformers was never closed; the churches of the Augsburg Confession repudiated fellowship with Zwinglians and Anabaptists in one breath. The Swiss, on the other hand, early drew to- gether in a consensus which accommodated or harmonised Zwinglian and Calvinistic views. The two main branches of the reform movement went their several ways, and remain to this day apart—the Lutheran, or Evangelical, and the Reformed, or Calvinistic. Protestantism in Switzerland, France, the Netherlands, England, and Scotland was of the Reformed kind; the Lutheran Reformation was confined to the Protestant parts of Germany and to the Scandinavian countries, and even in Germany the Reformed gained ground that had once been Lutheran, especially in the Palatinate.

The rapid spread of Protestantism provoked violent measures for its suppression. In Italy and in Spain, where it got only a slight foothold, these measures were completely successful; the Protestants who escaped the Inquisition sought refuge in other lands. In the Netherlands the effort of Philip II to extirpate reform and to override the ancient rights of the provinces with an autocracy of Spanish pattern brought about a general uprising of nobles and cities, and ended in the independence of the United Netherlands and the establishment of a national Protestant church. In France, also, the Protestants took up arms in self-defence, and the struggle assumed a political character which kept the kingdom in a state of intermittent civil war from 1562 to 1589, when the accession of Henry IV, of Navarre, himself brought up a Protestant, gave a more favourable turn to their affairs, and the Edict of Nantes (1598) granted toleration to the Huguenots, recognising them as a body politic within the state. The fall of La Rochelle (1628) put an end to this anomalous condition; and in 1685 the revocation of the Edict of Nantes deprived the Huguenots of protection, and led to emigration on an unprecedented scale, which was an economic disaster for France, since it drove into rival countries thousands of the most skilful workmen in industries which were growing up in competition with France. Protestantism remained a proscribed religion in France until the revolution of 1789.

The rejection of the authority of the Catholic Church, the assertion of the sole authority of the Word of God in Scripture in matters of doctrine, logically demanded a re-

vision of all the questions which the ancient church had
settled by the decisions of the councils as the issue of the
great controversies from the third century on. Luther, who
had comparatively little interest in theology and was not
much troubled by logical consistency, did not draw this
consequence. He accepted, as we have seen, not only the
Nicene but the Athanasian Creed, without demur or criticism. In the Augsburg Confession the exposition of the
Principal Articles of Faith begins with the declaration that
the churches which the statement represents teach that the
decree of the Nicene Council is true, and to be believed
without any doubt; and proceeds to condemn a catalogue
of heretics on the deity and the person of Christ, including
the "Samosatenes, ancient and modern." Calvin was less
enamoured of the ancient symbols: the Athanasian Creed
had never been approved by any legitimate church; the
Nicene Creed was a hymn, suited to be sung, rather than a
confession of faith.[1] Both were the work of the post-apos-
tolic age, and devoid of authority. Yet he found the doctrines of the Trinity and the Person of Christ in the New
Testament, and the heresies of Servetus on these points
seemed to him no less than to the Roman Inquisition to
deserve death.

Servetus' "De Trinitatis Erroribus" (1531) was probably
in Melancthon's mind when in the Augsburg Confession he
gave a special note of condemnation to the "modern Samosatenes." His "Christianismi Restitutio" is a complete system of theology, the aim of which is to restore the primitive
purity of Christian doctrine as it is revealed in Scripture.
Unlike Melancthon's "Loci" and Calvin's "Institutio," the
"Restitutio" did not grow out of the work of a reformer and
the need of a community; it was the work of a solitary
scholar, thought out in secrecy and printed anonymously.
Servetus was the first to bring historical criticism to bear
upon the Nicene dogma. Its Trinity was not only not to be

[1] This way of disposing of the creed has been rediscovered by some
modern Anglicans.

found in the New Testament, but it was not the doctrine of the ante-Nicene church: it was not in the Apostolic Fathers or the Apologists, in Irenæus or Tertullian, above all, not in the great Alexandrians, Clement and Origen, who entertained views widely at variance with it. He therefore regarded the Nicene doctrine, not, like the Reformers, as a correct formulation of the teaching of Scripture and of the church from the beginning, but as a corruption of genuine Christianity, precisely as the Reformers regarded the doctrines of the mediæval church.

In philosophy Servetus had imbibed the spirit of the revived Neoplatonism of the Italian Renaissance, and had great reverence for the writings of Hermes Trismegistos and the Chaldæan Oracles of Zoroaster, as the fountain-head of this sublime philosophy in immemorial antiquity; the same ideas pervade the Old Testament and the New as he interprets them. In his criticism of the orthodox doctrine of the Trinity and in the construction which he opposes to it these prepossessions are evident. His own doctrine is briefly expressed in the thesis which serves as title to the chapter on this subject in the "Restitutio": "De Trinitate Divina, quod ea non sit invisibilium trium rerum illusio, sed veræ substantiæ Dei manifestatio in Verbo et communicatio in Spiritu." Far from reducing Christ to a lower place than he occupied in Catholic doctrine and its repetition by the Reformers, Servetus believed that thus alone was Christ's complete deity affirmed and the truth of the Trinity made consistent with the unity of God. Space forbids an exposition of other parts of his system which are of no less interest; it must suffice to add that he stood opposed to all the Reformers in the assertion of the freedom of the human will.

Servetus had no disciples. When the Genevans burned him, and the Inquisition, out of whose hands he had slipped, burned the whole edition of his book except the few copies that had been privately distributed, they made between them an end of this strictly individual heresy.[1]

[1] The influence of his thinking may be recognized in some individuals, but in no party.

Antitrinitarian tendencies appeared sporadically within the area of the German and Swiss Reformations, commonly in connection with Anabaptist ideas. An Anabaptist council which met secretly in Venice in 1550 and was attended by sixty delegates declared their belief on this point: "Christ is not God, but man, born of Joseph and Mary, but full of divine powers. He died in order to attain God's righteousness, that is, the utmost of his goodness and mercy, and his promise." Unitarian views emerged also in Italy in humanist circles touched by Calvinistic ideas. Driven thence by the activity of the Inquisition, the refugees betook themselves to Geneva and other Swiss cities, where, however, when they made their opinions known, they found no peace. Some of them sought security and a field of activity in Poland and Transylvania, associating themselves with the Calvinistic branch of the Reformation in those countries, and disseminated their ideas with such success that they won over to their view a considerable part of the churches of those regions. A division was the result, and the Unitarians organised their own synods and schools. In their ranks wide differences developed. Some occupied a virtually Arian position, maintaining the pre-existence of Christ and his subordination to the Father; others rejected his pre-existence, but held to his birth from the Virgin, and adored the risen Christ, whence they were known as "Adorantes"; while a third, more radical, party denied the supernatural birth, and condemned the adoration of Christ as the worship of the creature in place of the Creator ("Nonadorantes"). The head of the last-named party in Transylvania, Francis David, was, at the instance of Biandrata, a leader of the "Adorant" Unitarians, sentenced to life-imprisonment, and died in prison.

The overcoming of these dissensions was chiefly the work of Faustus Socinus (Sozzini) of Siena. Socinus' uncle, Lælius Socinus (d. 1562, at Zürich), likewise entertained Unitarian views, without any zeal for propagating them, and had managed to live in reformed cities in Switzerland

and Germany without antagonising the Reformers. Faustus Socinus (born 1539, d. 1604), after living for twelve years in Florence at the Medicean court, spent four years in Switzerland, chiefly in Basel, whence he was called by Biandrata to Transylvania to try to compose the strife among the Unitarians there. In this effort he did not succeed, and after a short time removed to Poland, where the rest of his life was spent. It was chiefly through him that the Arian element, on the one side, and the radical "Nonadorantes," on the other, were won over to the middle way, the few irreconcilables seceding. The Racovian Catechism (1605), chiefly the work of Socinus, represents the doctrine of the main body, the "Polish Brethren," as they called themselves.

The movement made great and rapid progress. At Rakow, its principal centre, a school was established, which in its most flourishing time counted a thousand scholars, and where Protestants and Catholics, Anabaptists and Unitarians, studied side by side. There also was established the printing-press from which their literature was distributed, and there the general synod of the Unitarians in Poland and Transylvania annually brought together the ministers, elders, and deacons of the churches. In the early years of the seventeenth century they had a considerable number of theological teachers and writers of mark, the greater part of them German by birth, and the movement gained a foothold in Germany itself, particularly at the University of Altdorf.[1] After 1632 the Catholic reaction gained the upper hand in Poland, and under John Casimir, Jesuit and Cardinal, who became king in 1648, the destruction of this flourishing church was completed. Only in Transylvania has it survived through great tribulation to our own day. Many Unitarians, driven out of Poland, found refuge in other countries, especially in Prussia and the mark of Brandenburg, and in Holland. In the latter country they associated themselves in part with the Mennonites, in part with the Remonstrants. From Holland, partly by migration, partly

[1] Near Nürnberg.

through literature, Unitarian ideas passed to England, where they attracted sufficient attention to evoke an act of Parliament in 1648, making the denial of the divinity of Christ a capital offence.

It was not an accident that this movement had its origin in Italy. Like the humanistic reformation which Le Fèvre d'Étaples, Colet, and Erasmus conceived and laboured for, it had its roots in the Italian Renaissance and its precursors in Italian thinkers. The renaissance of Christianity by a return to the sources was a natural counterpart of the renaissance of classical antiquity by the same means. The New Testament itself was a piece of the ancient world, and better understood by those who had steeped themselves in the thought of antiquity and interpreted it as other ancient authors are interpreted than by those who read it through the eyes of mediæval schoolmen or of the Fathers. They interpreted Paul, not by Augustine, but in the light of Neoplatonic and Stoic ideas which seemed to them not only to be the acme of ancient philosophy, but to embody eternal verity, and they discovered the same sublime philosophy in Paul's Epistles and the Gospel of John.

Erasmus, in his "Enchiridion Militis Christiani" (1502), set forth in simple and popular form what would to-day be called "the religion of Jesus," as the essence of Christianity, without the modern antithesis to "the Christianity of Paul," but instinctively recognising the fountainhead of Christianity, and making the last step in the ascent to the sources. In his view the teaching of Jesus is a compendium of universal religious and moral truth; Christianity is in substance identical with all the true religion and morality that ever was, to which it adds the authority of Christ and the help of divine grace.

The Italian reformers with whom we are here concerned were the heirs of this spirit; but while Erasmus and such as he laboured for a revival of pure Christianity within the church, their successors, two or three generations later, coming after the schism and in the midst of the reaction, saw hope of a restoration of true Christianity only outside the church, and were restrained from radical conclusions neither by affection for the church and desire to maintain the unity of Christendom, nor, it must be added, by historic sense. There was none among them comparable in learning or intellectual acumen to the great humanists, or to many of the theologians of their day, Catholic or Calvinist; nor were they men of broader minds, but they pushed their biblical rationalism to its consequences, whatever they might be.

The doctrine of the Trinity was criticised by Socinus and his successors, on both biblical and rational grounds. Christ is for Socinus a man of extraordinary kind, miraculously conceived, endued with divine wisdom and power, raised from the dead, and exalted to a place of power beside God, and therefore properly worshipped. His work was primarily that of a prophet; he gave a new and deeper meaning to the law, promised us eternal life, and set us the example of a moral perfection which he sealed with his death. Like the humanists, with their ultimately Greek conception of sin as a voluntary act, Socinus maintained the freedom of the human will, with a theory of divine grace which was promptly branded as Pelagian.

Especially incisive was his criticism of the theory of satisfaction in the Anselmic doctrine of the atonement, as it was held by both Catholics and Protestants. He denies, on Scotist premises, that there is in God any necessity for satisfaction, and declares that the punishment of the innocent in place of the guilty conflicts with the justice of God. Remission of sins and satisfaction for sin are contradictories; the one excludes the other. Vicarious satisfaction in the case of personal punishment is impossible; to allow such substitution would be the height of injustice. Moreover, since the deity is incapable of suffering, the death of Christ, if conceived as substitutionary, could have only the value of a single *human* life, and therefore could not suffice for the whole world; while, if the substitution were intrinsically equivalent, it would necessarily operate unconditionally to the salvation of all, and its efficacy would not be dependent on faith. The whole unbiblical and unreasonable doctrine is immoral in itself, and has an immoral influence on men. Upon the ground of the juridical conception of the satisfaction of Christ, entertained particularly by Protestants, this criticism was in fact so telling that it moved Grotius to a reconstruction of the doctrine of the atonement in which he endeavoured to avoid the Socinian objections.

In this theory the death of Christ is neither humanity's amends in the person of the God-man to God's injured honour (Anselm) nor the execution upon him of the penalty which retributive justice demanded of the whole human race for violated law (Protestant doctrine). The necessity of Christ's death lay not in the satisfaction by an equivalent of offended honour or of inexorable penal justice, but in the maintenance of *public* justice. The moral government of the world cannot be maintained without law and its sanctions, nor would these be effective to secure that conformity which is necessary to public welfare if the ruler uniformly remitted the penalty on the simple condition of repentance, for men would think that he did not take his own law seriously and that they need not. The death of his Son, inflicted by God and voluntarily undertaken by Christ, show in the most impressive way how grave a thing sin is in the eyes of God, and is above all things apt to move men to repentance, faith, and righteous life. Abelard conceived the moral influence of the death of Christ as grateful love; for Grotius it is rather the fear of what a God in whose sight sin is so heinous will do to unrepentant sinners.

The Grotian theory prevailed among the Arminians, and was taken up by influential schools of Calvinism, particularly by Jonathan Edwards and his successors in New England. With many modifications it is at the bottom of most modern "moral influence" theories of the atonement.

CHAPTER XIII

CHRISTIANITY

THE CATHOLIC REFORMATION

The Council of Trent—Reform Decrees—Doctrinal Decrees—Scripture and Tradition—Justification—The Sacraments—Orders of the Ministry—Professio Fidei Tridentinæ—The Roman Catechism—Catholic Dogmatics, Polemics, Historical Studies—Ignatius Loyola and the Society of Jesus—Missions, Catholic and Protestant.

FROM the beginning of the conflict in Germany the call for a council of the church to correct abuses and settle disputed questions of doctrine had never ceased to be heard. The emperor Charles V had urged one pope after another to call such a council, but the reluctance of the popes to convoke a council under the conditions on which the Germans insisted, the bad terms on which they habitually were with Charles, and the political complications of the times prevented, and it was not until December, 1545, that a general council at last was convened in Trent, a city of the Empire on the Italian side of the Alps. Things had by that time gone so far that there was no longer any reasonable hope that the council could achieve the end which had been originally desired, namely, to heal the dissensions by the institution of reforms the necessity for which was acknowledged on all hands, and by a free discussion, and, if possible, a common understanding upon the contested points of doctrine. Whereas in 1537 the more moderate Protestants were in favour of participation in a council, the Protestant members of the Diet at Worms in 1545 refused to have anything to do with it. Consequently the Council of Trent found its task, not in endeavouring to reconcile the differences between Catholics and Protestants, but in a precise definition of Catholic doctrine in opposition to Protestantism and in far-reaching reforms in church order and discipline.

343

Nineteen years elapsed between the first session of the council, on December 13, 1545, and the last, December 4, 1563. Its history falls into three periods. It sat in Trent from December, 1545, to March, 1547, when the pope transferred it to Bologna. Two sessions only were held at Bologna, and then Julius III moved it back to Trent again, where it continued its labours for a year, May, 1551, to April, 1552. During this period representatives of the Protestant princes and free cities, at the instance of the emperor, made their appearance in the council, but with demands which it could not in any case have granted, even if new political complications had not broken off its deliberations. Not until January, 1562, was it able to convene again, and although an invitation was again given to the Protestants to participate, this proposal met no response. In the meantime the religious peace of 1555 had formally recognised the division, and established the rights of the religion of the Augsburg Confession in the Empire; consequently the remaining sessions of the council were devoted exclusively to matters of Catholic interest.

The reform decrees of the council left hardly any side of the church life untouched. At the very beginning they deal with instruction in the Scriptures in the higher and lower schools, and with preaching in the churches, which was enjoined upon the parish clergy under the oversight of the bishops. The reforms are throughout in a conservative spirit. They nowhere depart from long-established and universally recognised principles of Catholic church order and discipline, but upon these principles they correct a multitude of abuses which prevailed in almost every sphere; and although the promulgation of the decrees and the best effort to enforce them could not in a day put an end to evils which were the growth of centuries, and although some of the good plans of the council did not prove practicable, it must be recognised that the Council of Trent inaugurated a new era not only in the administration but in the life of the church.

The doctrinal decrees of the council deal chiefly with

specific issues which had been raised by the Protestant Reformers. So far as the fundamental dogmas of the church are concerned, the council contented itself with solemnly reaffirming the Nicene Creed as it stood in the liturgy. On these dogmas there was indeed no controversy between Catholics and Protestants. Similarly, the general Augustinian construction of the doctrine of grace and the Anselmic doctrine of the atonement were held in common by both parties. In defining the teaching of the church on disputed points, the council had chiefly in view those which had been raised in the Lutheran controversy in Germany.

At the outset it laid down, in opposition to Luther's sole authority of Scripture, the concurrent authority of the Scriptures and the unwritten traditions, "which, being received by the Apostles from the mouth of Christ himself, or handed down by the Apostles themselves at the dictation of the Holy Spirit, have been transmitted to us." These two sources and norms of Christian truth and morals the church "receives and venerates with equal piety and reverence." The canon of the Old and New Testaments is defined in accordance with the tradition and use of the church, including the books not found in the Bible of the Jews, which Luther had segregated under the title Apocrypha, and to which he denied the authority of inspiration. It further prescribed that in all public lectures, discussions, and expositions, the *vetus et vulgata editio*—that is to say, the Latin Bible, as it had for centuries been in use in the church—shall be treated as authentic, and shall be interpreted in the sense "which the holy mother Church, whose it is to judge of the true sense and intention of the Holy Scriptures, has held and holds"; thus asserting the prerogative right of the church to determine the interpretation of Scripture, which Luther and all the reformers denied. The foundation having thus been laid, the council proceeded to the particular doctrines at issue.

The dogmatic decrees deal chiefly with the doctrine of original sin; the nature and operation of justification, and its fruits, good works; and with the sacraments. The decrees were framed with great deliberation and thorough discussion in the commission of theologians which prepared them, and after general discussion in plenary session and adoption by the council, their final form was given them by a committee assigned to that special task.

In the decree on justification (January 13, 1547) the council sets forth the Augustinian doctrine which had been held in substance by the church since the fifth century, as it was defined by Aquinas. "Justification . . . is not merely the remission of sins, but also the sanctification and renewal of the inner man by the voluntary acceptance of grace and of the gifts by which a man from being unrighteous is made righteous (*ex injusto fit justus*) and from an enemy a friend, that he may be in expectation an heir of eternal life." Throughout this long and carefully formulated decree the council meets the Reformers on their own ground; there is no appeal to tradition or the Fathers; every statement is based on Scripture. Indeed, in its endeavour to combine in one harmonious presentation the whole teaching of Scripture concerning this side of man's salvation, the decree is more consistently scriptural than Luther, who seized on one aspect of Paul's teaching, as he interpreted it, to the exclusion of all that did not agree with it.

The subject of the sacraments engaged the council in each of the three periods of its activity. In the first (1547), it laid down the far-reaching principle that all righteousness begins, grows, and if lost is restored, by sacraments; and drew up a body of canons condemning various errors about the sacraments. Among these anathematised errors are the assertions that the seven sacraments, viz., Baptism, Confirmation, the Eucharist, Penance, Extreme Unction, Orders, and Matrimony, were not all instituted by Christ; that they are not necessary to salvation, but that without them, by faith alone, man receives from God the grace of justification; that they do not contain and confer the grace they signify, but are only external signs of the grace received through faith and works of the Christian profession; that they do not confer grace *ex opere operato.*

The decrees on the sacraments proceed from later sessions (1551; 1562–'63). In them the complete mediæval development as it had been consolidated and defined by Aquinas is comprehensively, clearly, and uncompromisingly set forth, and in the accompanying canons the contrary errors are specifically anathematised. Thus, in the Eucharist, after the consecration of the bread and wine, our Lord Jesus Christ, true God and man, is truly, really, and substantially contained under the appearance of those sensible things. By the consecration the whole substance of the bread is converted into the substance of the body of Christ,[1] and the whole substance of the wine into the substance of his blood; this conversion is fitly and properly called "transubstantiation." Yet in each of the elements is the whole Christ, his body and his blood,[2] his soul and his divine nature, by virtue of the hypostatic union. The *cultus latriæ* which belongs to God alone is to be paid to the sacrament: "For we believe that same God to be present in the sacrament, of whom the Eternal Father, bringing him into the world, said, 'Let all the angels of God worship him.'"

In another decree the sacrificial character of the Mass is affirmed and defined. In the divine sacrifice which is performed in the Mass the same Christ is contained and is bloodlessly immolated who upon the cross once offered himself in blood; therefore that sacrifice is truly propitiating; and through it, if we draw near to God with a true heart and right faith, with fear and reverence, contrite and penitent, we obtain mercy and find grace to help in time of need. In accordance with the tradition of the Apostles, it is properly offered not alone for the sins of the living, their penalties, satisfactions, and other needs, but also for the dead in Christ who are not yet completely purified (in purgatory).

---

[1] "Substance" must be understood in the Aristotelian definition, not in any of the modern senses of the word.

[2] Communion in both kinds, on which the Bohemians and the Reformers insisted as essential to the sacrament, is therefore unnecessary.

The necessary counterpart of this doctrine is the sacrament of Orders. The Eucharistic sacrifice of the New Testament requires a new sacrificial priesthood, which was instituted by Christ. To the Apostles and their successors in this priesthood he committed the power of consecrating, offering, and ministering his body and blood, and of remitting or retaining sins. The decree affirms also the necessity of ecclesiastical ordination; the indelible *character* (stamp) impressed in ordination; the divine institution of the hierarchy with its several orders; and particularly, in opposition to the Protestants, of the leading place in the hierarchy held by bishops, successors of the Apostles, superior in rank to presbyters, and "set by the Holy Spirit to rule the Church of God" (Acts 20, 28), to whom belongs the power of administering the sacrament of Confirmation, ordaining the ministry of the church, and doing various other things which are not in the competence of the lower orders of the clergy.

The sacrament of Penance (Penitence) is defined with especial care, in close agreement with Aquinas, and defended against the animadversions of the Reformers.

In the fundamental principle that all grace is imparted through sacraments, the council formulated precisely what had been the unformulated belief of the church from the beginning, and the multiplication of sacraments is rather differentiation than invention. "Out of the church there is no salvation" was self-evident, because the Catholic Church alone had the efficacious sacraments. The hierarchical organisation of the church is as old at least as the early second century; and the bishops, elders, and deacons of the New Testament had always been taken as the Apostolic institution of the three orders of the ministry till the exegesis of some of the humanists made bishops and presbyters the same order, an interpretation in which the Reformed churches followed them. On these points, therefore, the council stood fast in the Catholic tradition and gave it formal dogmatic authority. And it was here, over the church and the sacraments, rather than on points of theology or morals, that the real issue lay.

The decrees of the council were confirmed by Pope Pius IV in the bull "Benedictus Deus" (January 26, 1564), and a congregation of cardinals was appointed to supervise the execution of its reforms. To secure conformity to its doctrinal decrees the "Professio Fidei Tridentinæ" was drawn up, and the pope prescribed that it should be taken by all ecclesiastics having the cure of souls and by the members of all orders, with an oath of obedience to the Roman pontiff as the successor of Peter and the vicar of Christ, and a pledge, with the help of God, to maintain unimpaired to the end of life "this true Catholic faith, outside of which no man can be saved." His successor, Pius V, in conformity with the recommendations of the council, revised the Breviary and the Missal. An authentic edition of the Vulgate was published by Sixtus V (1590), which proved to be very incorrect and was superseded by another, thoroughly revised, under Clement VIII in 1592.

One of the undertakings to which the Council of Trent set its hand, but which in the end it devolved on the pope, was the preparation of a catechism in which the doctrine of the Catholic Church should be set forth for the instruction of the people, with the express purpose of counteracting the influence of the numerous and popular Protestant catechisms. Such a catechism was prepared with great care by a commission under the superintendence of Cardinal Borromeo, and after revision by eminent theologians headed by Cardinal Sirletus, was published in 1566. The "Catechismus Romanus" was designed to be a practical manual for the clergy, particularly for parish priests, upon whom fell the duty of giving instruction in religion, not primarily for the use of the laity, for which end its very dimensions —it makes 500–600 octavo pages—unfit it. Like earlier works of a similar kind, both Catholic and Protestant, it is arranged under the main divisions: The Apostles' Creed, the Sacraments, the Ten Commandments, and the Lord's

Prayer. It is a clear and comprehensive statement of
Catholic teaching in theology and morals, based primarily
upon the Scripture, but fortified by abundant references
to the Fathers. It was highly commended by Pope Pius
V and several of his successors, and while it has never had
exclusive authority or universal use in catechetical instruction,[1] it may be regarded as a standard of orthodoxy in the
chief topics of theology.

The revival of dogmatic theology which had begun in
Spain before the Reformation was greatly stimulated by
the work of the council, in which Spanish theologians took
a leading part. The ablest systematic work which came from
this school is the "De Locis Theologicis" of the Spanish
Dominican Melchior Cano (d. 1560), who naturally follows
in the footsteps of Aquinas, but endeavours to put the scholastic theology on a broader basis. In defence of Tridentine
doctrine and polemic against Protestantism, the learned and
acute writings of the Italian cardinal Bellarmin, easily hold
the first place. As an antidote to the Lutheran "Magdeburg
Centuries," in which church history testified to the antiquity
of Protestantism, Baronius (d. 1607) produced his monu-
mental "Ecclesiastical Annals," a work of enormous erudition and genuine historical spirit. In the vast collections of
works of the Fathers and ecclesiastical writers, and in a
multitude of separate editions, there was in the later sixteenth century and through the seventeenth a veritable ren-
naissance of Christian literature. The apparatus for a
critical study of the original texts and versions of the Bible
was provided in the Complutensian Polyglot (1514–'17) of
Cardinal Ximenes and its more comprehensive successors,
the Antwerp and Paris Polyglots (1569 ff. and 1629 ff.),
both from the hands of Catholic scholars, from whom came
also learned and voluminous commentaries on the whole
Bible and on parts of it.

[1] The Jesuits, indeed, impugned its symbolical character, out of dislike for its too explicitly Thomist attitude on the doctrines of grace,
and even professed to discover heresies in it.

Beside and beneath all this was a greatly quickened religious earnestness, which manifested itself in the founding of new orders and religious congregations, many of them devoted to Christian work—teaching, charitable and spiritual labours among the poor, the care of the sick; and on another side in a revival of Catholic piety which took its habitual ascetic-mystical forms. The mysticism of Santa Teresia and St. John of the Cross, or of St. Francis de Sales, is, however, of a different type from the classical mysticism of the twelfth and thirteenth centuries. It had not the same predominating intellectual character, and sought its goal not in the intellectual vision of God, but in absorbing love and complete quiescence in the will of God.

In this great revival of Catholicism, and in the recovery to the Church of whole regions or countries which had fallen away, no single instrument effected so much as the Society of Jesus, which obtained the approbation of Pope Paul III in 1540. The founder, best known by his Latinised name, Ignatius de Loyola (1491–1556), was a Spanish nobleman brought up to the career of arms, whose heart and mind were turned to religion during a long convalescence from a wound received in the siege of Pampeluna in 1521. The soldier's spirit is impressed on the order in its original name, "Compañía de Jesús," in the military model of its organisation, and in the principle of soldierly obedience which is the essence of its rule. The same spirit is manifest in the long and systematic training to which the members of the order are submitted.

This is the outward side of Loyola's institution; the soul of it is the "Book of Spiritual Exercises," a method of religious experience, in which by meditation on sin, righteousness, and judgment, the abhorrence of sin is aroused by which the soul is purified; in the second stage, meditation on the kingdom of Christ leads to the dedication of life to the service of God; in the following stages this resolve is confirmed, the difficulties of the religious life are presented, and the way to overcome them shown; the end to which this whole discipline is directed is reached when the soul is filled with an ardent love of God. This is not, however, as in quietist mysticism, the ultimate and all-satisfying achievement, but the motive power of a life of intelligent activity in the service of God and his church.

The great influence of the order was gained and exercised in three principal ways: *first*, by preaching, especially in missions, by which they reached the masses; *second*, as confessors and spiritual advisers of rulers; and, *third*, by their schools and colleges, in which great numbers of youth of the higher classes were educated. The Jesuits were the reformers of education in the Catholic countries of Europe; the *Ratio Studiorum* was a great advance both in matter and method over the mediæval curriculum. They cultivated humanistic studies, while guarding against their dangers to faith and morals, and took an active part in the new development of science. In the advancement of Catholic learning, of which mention has been made above, Jesuit scholars vied with members of the older orders.

The discovery of America and the opening of the sea route to the East Indies, in which Spain and Portugal were foremost, and the reopening of the land way to China, coming in this time of quickened religious life, kindled the zeal of Christians for the conversion of the nations of the New World and of the oldest, and a new period of missionary activity began, in which the Jesuits had their full share. Loyola's first plan for his Company had been a mission enterprise, and this purpose was never lost sight of. One of the original little band, Francis Xavier, by his labours in India and Japan earned the title "Apostle of the Indies." He died knocking at the doors of China, but in the next generation Jesuit missionaries gained entrance to the empire and began their remarkable work. Among the aborigines of North and South America, also, Jesuit missionaries were among the foremost names. The Dominicans and Franciscans manifested similar enthusiasm for the Christianising of the world, and large results were achieved by their efforts.

The organisation of the Congregation "De Propaganda Fide" (1622) brought the missionary operations of the Church throughout the world under a central direction in Rome.

Protestants were much later than Catholics in the field of missions, except here and there on the margin of European colonies; it was not till the nineteenth century that they undertook the work on a larger scale through voluntary societies, and in part eventually as church organisations. In the meantime Protestant powers had taken the place of Spain and Portugal as the foremost colonising and commercial nations. In the four centuries that have elapsed since the opening of this third great age of expansion a large part of the world which at the beginning of the sixteenth century lay outside Christendom has been annexed to it by colonisation and by missions, both in the lands of ancient civilisation such as India, China, and Japan, and among races on a lower plane of culture in every quarter of the globe, and millions of converts have been gathered into native churches.

CHAPTER XIV

CHRISTIANITY

THE SEQUEL OF REFORMATION

To present a united front against Protestantism, the Council of Trent had avoided as far as possible explicit pronouncements, and even discussion, on questions which divided schools and orders within the church. The old controversies of Thomists and Scotists, of Dominicans and Franciscans, continued, with an increment of zeal from the universal revival of theological interest. The Jesuits were a new contentious element. They were promptly in conflict with the Dominicans over the ancient issue of divine grace and the human will, and in their antagonism to the Thomist Augustinianism of the older order some Jesuit theologians even went so far as to make grace efficacious *non ex se, sed ex consensu humano præviso*. Antagonism to such Pelagianising assertion of the power of the human will led on the other side to an Augustinian reaction which did not always keep within the bounds of scholastic qualifications, and was the more obnoxious because of its resemblance to Protestant doctrine. The condemnation of the Jansenists was a declaration of the Church against this suspicious revival of a high Augustinianism.

In the Protestant churches the great controversies of the post-Reformation period were in the same field, but in a contrary sense; they had their origin in attempts to modify the Augustinianism of the Reformers and the more extreme positions of the theological epigoni. In the Lutheran churches the synergism of Melancthon and the Philippists was combated by the strict Lutheranism of Flacius and his school. The "Formula of Concord" (1580) decided for the "genuine Lutherans" against the synergists: in conversion man is purely passive; "he is worse than a stock or a stone until God brings him to life from the death of sin." Yet the absolute predestination which is the necessary counterpart of total inability is illogically denied.

In the Reformed churches a reaction against the Calvinistic logic with its double decree of election and reprobation led the so-called Remonstrants in Holland, under the influence of a Leyden theologian, Arminius, to claim toleration in the Dutch churches for modifications of the confessional doctrine in certain important points. For particular election, with its corollary, reprobation, they substituted a universal conditional predestination, a decree of God to save through Christ those of the sinful race of men who, through the grace of the Holy Spirit, believe on him and persevere. They held the universality of the atonement; Christ died for every man, to gain for all the forgiveness of sins, but so that no one actually attains this except the believer. Man of himself is unable, either to think, will, or do, anything truly good; the grace of God is the beginning, continuation, and completion of all good in man, but the operation of divine grace, neither in regeneration nor in the regenerate is irresistible. The controversy had not gone far before the inamissibility of grace was also denied.

The conflict between this party and the strict Calvinists was soon entangled with political issues, the particularist loyalty of the Provinces and the centralising aims of the Stadholder. A national synod was demanded by the orthodox party. To strengthen their position, they enlarged their plan to a representative council of the Reformed churches, and delegates from England, the Palatinate,

Hesse, Bremen, and Switzerland, participated in it. This synod, which met in Dordrecht (November, 1618, to May, 1619), in contradiction to the Remonstrants, formulated the "Five Points of Calvinism" with uncompromising rigour. Its canons contain the most extreme statement of Calvinistic doctrine, halting only before the supralapsarian theory, which made election and reprobation anterior to creation and the fall; and halting there, not out of consideration for the Arminians, but in order to maintain an undivided front against them, since among the churches represented in the council this theory was by no means universally approved. As in the Roman church the repudiation of the revived Augustinianism of the Jansenists was the more energetic because of its resemblance to Protestantism, so in the Reformed church Arminianism was the more zealously combated because it seemed a step toward the "Semi-Pelagianism" of the Roman church, and particularly of the Jesuits. The canons of Dordrecht were formally adopted only in Holland and by the French church, but they were accepted throughout the whole of Reformed Protestantism. It was the first and last general council of the Reformed churches, and was among them not infrequently spoken of as an "œcumenical council." A modern historian would be more inclined to call it the Reformed Trent.

The Arminians, expelled from the national church, and at first exiled from the land, survived as a sect, and, freed from compulsory orthodoxy, presently showed themselves amenable to influences not only from Dutch humanism, represented, for example, by Grotius, but to some extent from the Anabaptists (Mennonites) and from Socinian refugees from Poland.

The Synod of Dort had defined thorough Calvinism in a way to exclude all ambiguity, and therefore to make the inherent difficulties of the system more difficult than ever. Another attempt to get over these difficulties was made by theologians of the flourishing French school at Saumur, who endeavoured to reconcile particular election with the universality of the offer of salvation in many passages of Scripture by the theory of hypothetic universalism, introducing distinctions by which the harshness of Calvinism seemed to be moderated. For example, where the Reformed churches had hitherto unanimously denied to man any ability in himself to exercise saving faith, they taught that men have the *natural* ability to believe, but not the *moral* ability. They maintained, also, the mediate imputation of Adam's sin, through an inherited sinful nature, in conflict especially with the forensic theory of imputation held by the so-called Federal school.

But what aroused even more acrimonious controversy than these mitigations of Calvinism was the proof adduced by Cappel that the Hebrew vowel-points and accents were not part of the original text, but embody the traditional interpretation of the Jewish schools many centuries later. Protestantism, in its controversy with Roman Catholic scholars over the authentic text of Scripture, had been driven by its own logic and that of its opponents to stake everything upon the very letter of inspiration, so that in admitting the right of textual criticism on the original Hebrew and Greek, and not infrequently giving the readings of the Septuagint preference over the Masoretic text, Cappel and his disciples seemed to be undermining the very foundations of Protestantism.

This liberal, or "New School," Calvinism found considerable acceptance in France, Holland, and England, but it encountered, also, the most violent opposition. In particular the Swiss churches drew up against it the "Formula Consensus Helvetica" (1675), in which not only was the inspiration of the Hebrew punctuation made a dogma, but an ultra-scholastic Calvinism was set over against the modifications and distinctions of the new school. On the Lutheran side, the corresponding extreme was reached in the so-called "Consensus Repetitus" of 1664, which, however, never attained symbolic authority.

The most comprehensive of the seventeenth century symbols was the Westminster Confession of Faith, which, together with the Longer and Shorter Catechisms, was framed by a commission established by the English Parliament in 1643, and was adopted by act of Parliament, under the title, "Articles of the Christian Religion," in 1648. It was, therefore, in intention and authority, not an ecclesiastical but a national confession, taking the place of the Thirty-nine Articles, as the Directory for Worship, by the same authority, superseded the Prayer-Book. When at the Restoration, Episcopacy, the Thirty-nine Articles, and the Prayer-Book were re-established in England, the Westminster Confession and Catechisms remained the standards of the Church of Scotland, and through it became the standards of English-speaking Presbyterianism everywhere. It was also adopted, with omissions or changes in the articles on church government, by the English Independents and the Congregational churches in New England, and, with a substitute for the article on infant baptism, by the Calvinistic Baptists, so that no other Protestant confession had an equally wide acceptance and influence. It was also the last, the end of the confessional age.

As a consequence of controversies within and without, the later Protestant symbols are much more definite and detailed than the earlier; the Westminster Confession is a complete system of Calvinistic theology in confessional form. The same influences were at work in the old church from the Council of Trent on; the Roman Catechism is an exposition of Catholic doctrine on an even larger scale. The consequence was, that on both the Protestant and the Catholic sides the intellect and conscience of men were fettered by standards of orthodoxy imposed by authority and enforced not only by ecclesiastical penalties but in most countries by the civil law, to a degree unknown before the Reformation.

The Reformation permanently separated from the Catholic Church a large part of central and western Europe. Beginning as an individual revolt against certain abuses, it gathered momentum as every kind and motive of opposition to the Church flowed into its main channel. It commended itself to the masses by bringing them freedom from ecclesiastical taxation, from the spiritual and temporal dominion of the hierarchy, and from dependence upon the priesthood; it appealed to the Teutonic spirit in its antipathy to Italianisation of the church and the perpetual drain of German revenues into the coffers of the curia. Almost at once it assumed a political character. It was introduced by princes in their territories, with small regard for the preferences of the masses, and in the free cities by the majority of the limited citizen body. It made radical changes in the institutions of the church, and radical, though limited changes, in doctrine. The aberrations and excesses of those who took its principles too largely or too literally soon led to a firmer organisation and more rigid control by the civil authority, which had thus replaced, within its own boundaries, the authority of the Church. This political character led to long and desolating wars—the Thirty Years' War, and the civil wars of religion in France. Doctrinal conflicts between the two great branches of the Reformation, and even more acrimonious controversies within them, gave to theological *differentiæ* an exaggerated importance, and tended more and more to make orthodoxy, according to local and sectarian definitions, not only the mark of the true church but the essence of true religion.

The results of the Reformation in the religious and moral life of communities and individuals fell far short of the ideals of the Reformers and of their first enthusiastic expectation. Neither the freedom of the gospel and its interpretation, from which Luther hoped everything, nor religious instruction and discipline in the churches of the Genevan model, transformed human nature. The reformation of the church was only in very imperfect measure a reformation of Christian life. This was especially true in the countries where the national-political character of the movement was most marked. Dissatisfaction with this failure of the Reformation to realise its own ideals was wide-spread and deep, not so much in the high places of state and church as among the humbler ministry and the people, and resulted in what may be called the second great wave of reformation. This movement had in many ways a striking resemblance to the revivals of lay piety in the Middle Ages, and had an even closer affinity to the sects of the sixteenth century which the Protestant churches, both Lutheran and Reformed, excommunicated and persecuted.

It sought in the Scriptures the rule and model of Christian experience and Christian conduct, as well as of institutions and doctrine. Its theological premises were the radical corruption of human nature—original sin unremedied by sacramental grace—and the universal corruption of the world through sin. "Worldliness" was the great evil; the renunciation of "the world," the very mark of the true Christian. But while in former times those who aspired to the higher religious life took refuge from the world in the desert or within the walls of a monastery, in Protestantism, as so largely in the Catholic Church of the late Middle Ages, men renounced the world, not by withdrawing from it, but by living in it without being of it. They sought a personal experience of religion, which, from their Augustinian starting-point, necessarily had its beginning in conversion, an abrupt intervention of God in the life of the sinner, turning him from the way of death to that of life. Paul, Augustine, Luther, were typical examples of such a miracle of divine grace. The scheme of conversion was often formally laid out: the subject, profoundly conscious of his sin and guilt and his exposure to the just wrath of God, and of his helplessness even to repent and believe, experienced, often suddenly, a sense of deliverance, of forgiveness, of perfect trust, of communion with Christ. In this experience of salvation was the beginning of a new life, conformed to the teaching and example of Christ, for which, also, patterns of religious exercises and regulatives of behaviour were soon framed, the avoidance of worldly recreations and amusements being frequently an unduly prominent part of them. As in the Catholic counterparts of this movement, religious experience frequently attained or aspired to mystical levels; while in the conviction that the evil in the world was nearing its climax, men turned to the Apocalypse to console themselves with the predictions of its imminent dissolution and of the millennial glory thereafter.

In Great Britain this movement bears the name Puritan. It originated in the Church of England, and, as an essentially religious movement, was not immediately concerned with the form of church government. The influence of continental theories and the example of the sister established Church of Scotland, however, gave rise to a party of divine-right Presbyterians, some of whom saw no difficulty in reconciling presbytery with episcopacy—bishops being only a kind of superintendents—while others were for a thorough reconstruction of the constitution of the English church on the presbyterial model. A smaller party, driven into antagonism to the established religion by the severe laws against religious gatherings of every kind outside of the regular services of the church, looked on the state church as hopelessly fallen away to the world; it was to them the Babylon of which the prophet warned, "Come ye out from among them and be ye separate." Some of these took refuge from prosecution in the toleration of Holland, and ere long migrated to New England, whither a few years later they were followed by a more considerable body of Puritans, Presbyterian in their theory of church government and of the relation of church and state. In their new home their churches were the established churches of small communities (towns), with an order and discipline which was an adaptation of the Genevan model to their peculiar conditions.

A similar movement within the established Church of Holland got for its adherents the nickname "Precisians," by its scrupulous regulation of conduct and religious exercises—things in which the great body of the ministry and the people were less disposed to be "precise" than in their scholastic orthodoxy.

Dissatisfaction with the "dead orthodoxy" of the Lutheran churches in Germany gave rise to Pietism, in the early history of which the two great names are those of Spener (d. 1705) and Francke (d. 1727). Neither in Holland nor in Germany were separatist tendencies developed; the pietistic circles or associations were formed within the churches, *ecclesiolæ in ecclesia*, which met in private to cultivate spiritual religion and scrupulous morality. The movement spread rapidly, especially among the middle classes in the towns and cities, and in parts of Germany even reached the neglected peasantry. There, as in Holland, it encountered strong opposition from the clergy, and from the universities, into some of which, however, it eventually found entrance. In the latter part of the eighteenth century, the age of the *Aufklärung*, Pietism declined, and in most regions its societies or circles died out. The religious revival of the nineteenth century in Germany was in the church itself.

Puritan ideals were maintained within the Church of England in what is commonly called an "evangelical" type of piety; and in the eighteenth century, reinforced by the influence of German Pietism, gave rise to the great Methodist revival. The leaders in this movement were the brothers, John and Charles Wesley. The name "methodist" had been fastened upon them and their associates as students at Oxford, because of a regimen of piety which they had adopted for themselves, including weekly communion and meetings in one another's rooms for prayer and spiritual conversation; it was extended to the whole body of their followers, and what had been at first a term of derision was accepted by themselves as a denominational title. The Wesleys addressed their efforts to the masses in the cities and large towns and in the mining districts, who were much neglected by the church, indifferent to religion, and often grossly immoral, drunkenness being a common and rapidly

growing evil among them.   They emphasised in their preaching the lost state of sinners and the necessity of conversion
and the new life, and this preaching found a response in
the consciences of many of the middle classes who had been
quite satisfied with the moderate and moral religion they
found in the churches, but were now impressed by the conviction that these refuges were vain against the wrath of
God upon unrepentant and unconverted sinners, however
reputable. The idea of separation from the Church of
England was not in the thought of the founders of Methodism; what they aimed at was to revive true religion in the
church and to recover to it the great lapsed masses.   The
movement spread with unexampled rapidity and power in
city and country, and ere long was carried across the Atlantic to the English colonies in America, where similar results
attended it.

John Wesley was not only an eloquent and indefatigable
preacher but a born leader and organiser, and fully aware
that it was easier to convert great crowds of people in a
whirlwind of emotion than to keep them converted and
build them up in faith and righteousness. He accordingly
introduced a system in which his converts were gathered in
small groups under the guidance and responsible oversight
of a leader. The ordained clergymen who were drawn into
the movement were far too few for the task as it grew upon
their hands, and laymen were enlisted in the work as itin-
erant gospellers. Superintendents were appointed over the
work in particular districts, who, when the separation from
the Church, made inevitable by all these irregularities, was
accomplished, became the Methodist bishops. To the end
of his life John Wesley kept all the threads of the whole
movement in his own hands, and presided over it like the
general of some great semi-military religious order consecrated to the conversion of the world. A comparison with
Ignatius Loyola inevitably suggests itself—a comparison as
instructive in its differences as in its resemblances.

The characteristic feature of Methodism in its early days

was mass conversion, for the accomplishment of which a highly effective technic was developed; and repeatedly in the succeeding generations these efforts and methods have been revived with results which, if less amazing than those of the first expansion, have nevertheless been of large and lasting consequence.

The excessive emphasis put in the second stage of the Reformation upon conversion as an experience or an act of a subject arrived at years of intelligence and responsibility made the question of infant baptism even more difficult than it was for the Reformers of the sixteenth century. The Anabaptists, who had drawn the logical conclusion in that age, survived in Holland in the sect of the Mennonites, and early in the seventeenth century some English separatists (Brownists) in Amsterdam were led, under Mennonite influence, to baptise one another. The declaration of faith of this first English-speaking Baptist church dates from 1611, and asserts that, inasmuch as baptism is the outward manifestation of dying to sin and walking in newness of life, it is not to be administered to infants; and that churches constituted in any other way or of any other persons than of such adult converts as have been thus baptised are not according to Christ's testament. Noteworthy in this declaration is also the assertion of the principle of religious independence: "No church ought to challenge any prerogative over any other," and "the magistrate (that is to say, the civil government) is not to meddle with religion or matters of conscience, nor compel men to this or that form of religion." These first English Baptists, as might be expected from their Mennonite associations, were Arminian, or, as they were afterwards called, "General Baptists," [1] in distinction from the Calvinistic or "Particular Baptists." [2] The latter, drawn chiefly from the independent Puritan

[1] They taught a "general" predestination to salvation of all who would believe. A later name of the same import is "Free-Will" Baptists.

[2] Holding to a "particular" election of individuals.

churches, became by far the more numerous body both in Great Britain and in America. Neither branch, at first, insisted upon immersion as the only scriptural form of baptism, but both soon came to do so, and to make it a criterion of genuine Christianity.

The most famous name among the English Baptists of the seventeenth century is that of John Bunyan (d. 1688), whose persistence in lay preaching earned him many years of imprisonment. His "Pilgrim's Progress," published in 1678, is one of the most widely read books in English literature. In all the Puritan world probably no book except the Bible was so universally known; and from none can the modern reader get so vivid an impression of what religion meant to a Puritan of the Puritans.

For the Baptists and other Puritan separatists of the seventeenth century, and for the Methodists in the following century, the church was a congregation of adult members who had experienced conversion, and associated themselves to further one another in the Christian life. In theory and intention it was a society of the regenerate; it admitted only such as gave presumptive evidence of regeneration, and cut off such as subsequently disproved the presumption or fell from grace. Terms of communion and exercise of discipline were meant, so far as possible, to make the visible church correspond to the invisible. The old dualism of Christ's church and the world lying in the Evil One was revived in new rigour; and these little and local groups assumed toward the society about them the attitude which the ancient church took toward the heathen world, ignoring the existence of a Christian civilisation and government, and often regarding the established churches of Christendom much as the primitive Christians regarded the pagan religion of the Roman Empire. Each of these bodies, esteeming itself to be a peculiar depositary of truth and righteousness, treated the others as adversaries rather than allies in the common cause.

None of the religious bodies which came into existence in

England in the seventeenth century is more interesting than
the Society of Friends, or, as they were nicknamed, Quakers.
The founder, George Fox (d. 1691), feeling, as did so many
others in his time, that the Christianity around him was
more concerned about formal correctness in doctrine and
church order than about vital piety, began to preach the
necessity of repentance, and of a personal experience of
religion and personal knowledge of the truth—a knowledge
not acquired from the teaching of others, but through enlightenment by the divine Spirit. The subjective, or spiritual,
tendency in Protestantism has its most complete realization
in Quakerism. Since everything depends on spiritual experience and enlightenment, and the ability to instruct and
edify others comes only through the gift of the Spirit on
occasion, they could not acknowledge any class of priests or
ministers who had an official or exclusive right to preach
and teach; that the clergy made a profession and livelihood
of preaching seemed to them a sin against the Spirit. Every
one to whom the Spirit gave a word for his fellows had in
that gift and for that time the call of God to speak; otherwise no one had such a call. They took literally the words
of the Apostle Paul, in Christ "there is neither male nor
female," and therefore saw no reason why the Spirit should
not give a profitable message by the lips of a woman. Paul
had, indeed, also said, "I suffer not a woman to teach," but
Paul lived a long time ago and under other and widely
different social conditions.

In their reaction against formalism, by which the freedom
of the Spirit was restrained and its very life chilled and
deadened, they rejected the set forms of Christian worship
—the reading of lessons from Scripture; obligatory prayers,
whether out of a book or out of the preacher's head; the
singing of hymns by choirs and congregations. They gathered to commune with God in the spirit; to listen to the
word of edification, if such a word was given by the Spirit
to one of the assembly; if not, to commune with God in the
silence of their own spirit. The sacraments—baptism with

water, the communion of bread and wine—they set aside as material symbols which contributed nothing to those who possessed the spiritual reality of membership in Christ and communion with him, and which, as the whole history of the church had shown, were in perpetual danger of being put into the place of the reality.

In other things the early Quakers did not consciously depart from the current Puritan type; but consistently with their view of the inner light, by which the Scripture is interpreted and the truth for the time and occasion brought to the minds and hearts of men, they did not bind themselves, nor impose upon those who joined them any creed or confession of faith. Their organization was after the Presbyterian pattern, but without the Presbyterian insistence on divine right. The mystical element was very strong in the movement from the beginning; Fox himself is one of the great mystics. It is, indeed, the soul of Quakerism. On the ethical side, the outstanding things are the rejection of oaths—even judicial—condemnation of war, the insistence on honesty and truthfulness, on simplicity in living and in speech, and the emphasis on active philanthropy which has made them the leaders in many reforms and charities.

The Puritans were strictly orthodox according to the Reformed pattern—the more stiffly orthodox, in opposition to the Arminianism which was common among the clergy of the Church of England in the seventeenth century; the German Pietists were equally orthodox after the Lutheran pattern, though they set much less value than their opponents on orthodoxy for its own sake, and this relative indifference to confessional theology made Pietism a forerunner of what might otherwise seem to be its antipodes, Rationalism. The greater body of the Baptists, as has been said, were strict Calvinists. Wesley carried over into the main Methodist movement an evangelical Arminianism from the Church of England; but his fellow worker, Whitefield, was a Calvinist, and a smaller body of Calvinistic Methodists grew up beside the larger. Thus, this second wave of reformation brought forth no fundamental modifications of Protestantism, and produced no great new symbol.

A tendency to indefinite subdivision was inherent in all these sects, and after toleration was insured by law in England in 1689, and in the larger freedom of America, this tendency had full play; new sects sprang out of old ones, as in those low types of organism which multiply by fission. Sometimes a secession of the stricter sort was a protest against growing laxity of teaching or practice in the main body; sometimes progressive elements were driven out by an intransigeant confessionalism; sometimes division was the outcome of contention over forms; new methods of revival gave birth to many new denominations. The divisive issues were in the main, intrinsically or historically, insignificant, and the departure from the common types of the Reformed churches, small, compared with differences which existed side by side, if not always amicably, within the established Protestant churches. The most diminutive were often the most contentious and persistent.

The Renaissance and the Reformation lie in the transition from the mediæval to the modern age of European civilisation; they do not belong to the modern age. This is peculiarly true of the Reformation. If we examine either Lutheran or Reformed theology, we find that the Reformers have much more in common with the schoolmen of the Middle Ages than with modern thinkers. The problems which they propose, the way they formulate them, the premises from which they essay the solution, and the methods they employ, are essentially mediæval, not modern.

The Bible was for both Catholics and Protestants, from beginning to end, and in every word, an immediate revelation from God, embodied in an inspired book, and free from every suspicion of error either in the original recording of the revelation or in its transmission. It was interpreted by all as a book of divine oracles. Both Catholics and Protestants inherited and accepted without question the ancient conception and astronomical construction of the universe in the theological form which had been given it by the great schoolmen, particularly by Thomas Aquinas. The earth was the centre of the universe, around which the sun and the moon, the planets and the fixed stars, all in their several spheres, revolved; and these luminaries were created and existed for the sake of the earth and the creatures upon it. At the head of this mundane creation stood man, who was, therefore, the real centre of the created universe. His salvation was God's end in creation; the world was made as a stage for the drama of redemption.

Catholics and Protestants were, or meant to be, equally orthodox on the dogmas defined in the Nicene and Athanasian Creeds, and held, so far as they understood it, the Chalcedonian Christology. Their ideas of God, the Trinity, the Person of Christ, were identical. What is even more important, they agreed that the dogmas formulated in these creeds were revealed truth, an unchangeable deposit of faith.

Both read in the Bible the same religious drama of human history, as it was written in Paul, interpreted by Augustine. The fall of man, original sin, predestination and election, the satisfaction of Christ, the nature and way of justification—in short, the doctrines of sin and grace—were as fundamental in Protestant theology as in Catholic; and the differences, however their importance was magnified on both sides, were of small moment in comparison with their essential agreement. The differences were, indeed, hardly greater than had existed among the schoolmen, from whom they were in considerable part inherited. When Protestant theologians of the second generation began to construct complete systems of doctrine, they not only reverted to the scholastic type and built upon the great mediæval synthesis of Aristotle and revelation as on an impregnable rock, but drew directly and largely on the Neo-Thomist theologians of the Spanish school for material and argument.

Catholics and Protestants were at one in another important point. Both adopted without qualification the medi-

24

æval conception of a homogeneous civilisation under the inspiration and regulation of religion; and however widely they differed about the relation of church and state, none of them dreamed of such a thing as the separation of church and state,[1] or of a secular culture in which philosophy, science, literature, art, are pursued for their own sake. For this reason all the churches of the Reformation, no less than the old church, regarded education as a function of the church, and endeavoured to exercise complete control over it from bottom to top.

The ideal of uniformity in doctrine and discipline was as strongly fixed in the minds of the Reformers as of their opponents, but the sphere of this uniformity was narrowed to the boundaries of a nation, a principality, or a city, or, at the largest, to a confederation of such religious sovereignties; and because the sphere was thus limited, and because everything was new, there was far less room for variety than in the mediæval Catholic church. The idea of liberty of conscience, as we understand it, was not for a moment admitted by any of them.[2] Toleration of sects and heresies by the civil authority was, in the eyes of the Protestant churches quite as much as in the Catholic, a manifest sin. Servetus was burned in Geneva with as good a conscience as he would have been burned by the Inquisition in Lyons, if he had not broken jail. The moderate Unitarian, Biandrata, got the radical Unitarian, David Francis, sentenced to life imprisonment in Transylvania, and in prison the obstinate man who would not worship Christ died. Quakers and Baptists were flogged and banished from the Puritan colony of Massachusetts Bay with as stern a resolve to maintain the purity of the gospel and the unity of the faith as they would have been under the laws of Anglican uniformity. The Catholic, Sir Thomas More, who was beheaded because he would not confess Henry VIII the supreme head of the church in England, was solitary in

[1] The Anabaptists and kindred sects are an exception.
[2] This notion also was confined to the Anabaptists.

imagining, in his Utopia,[1] an ideal commonwealth, in which complete religious freedom existed and no man was subject to pains and penalties for his belief.

The Protestant churches declared the word of God in Scripture to be the only authority in faith and practice, and in theory held that the right of interpretation belongs, not to the church, or its ministers and professors, but to every Christian. The eccentric results this liberty of interpretation produced were alarming, and they soon found themselves under the necessity of bridling the freedom of private judgment by confessions and catechisms which prescribed how the Scripture must be interpreted, and had therefore in fact an authority superior to the Scripture; precisely as the Catholic Church had been compelled to do from the days of the Gnostics on.

[1] Appropriately named "Land of Nowhere."

CHAPTER XV

CHRISTIANITY

MODERN TENDENCIES

THE intellectual movement of the Renaissance was essentially secular. The very names humanists and the humani-
ties are in conscious antithesis to divines and divinity. Few
of the representatives of this movement put themselves
in opposition to the church, but they went their independent way without concerning themselves about the bearing
of their studies and thinking upon the doctrines of the
church. Many of them, as we have seen, hoped for reforms
in the church, not only external but internal, through the
progress of knowledge and enlightenment. This movement
was interrupted by the Reformation. Within a few years
after Luther posted his famous theses the attendance at the
universities had greatly fallen off, and the interest in humanistic studies greatly declined. For a century or more religion was the absorbing subject of thought and controversy,
and religion was more and more completely identified with
doctrine. But although secular intellectual interests were
thus thrust into the background, they were not wholly
superseded. While the Reformation was gaining its first
great successes in Germany and Switzerland, and the world
was ringing with the names of Luther and Zwingli, a Polish
astronomer, Copernicus, was undermining one of the cor-

ner-stones of the mediæval combination of Aristotelian cosmology and ontology with divine revelation on which both Catholic and Protestant theologians rested their conception of the universe. Copernicus' "De Revolutionibus Orbium Cælestium," substantially finished in 1530, came from the press, with a dedication to Pope Paul III, as the author lay on his death-bed in 1543. The observations of Tycho Brahe, interpreted by the mathematical genius of Kepler, corrected the so-called Copernican theory and established it upon a firm basis. It was enthusiastically embraced by Giordano Bruno, who, breaking the shell Copernicus had left about the universe, revelled in the infinity of the universe, an endless multitude of solar systems, which, waxing and waning in the endless course of time, manifest throughout an enduring life.

The Copernican astronomy was condemned in the process of Galileo, who was denounced to the Inquisition in 1615, and compelled to promise for the future neither to defend nor teach that theory. The famous sentence of the Inquisitors ran: "That the sun is in the centre of the universe and motionless is a proposition absurd and false in philosophy, and formally heretical, because it is in express contradiction to Holy Scripture. That the earth is not the centre of the universe, and not motionless, but has also a diurnal motion, is likewise a proposition absurd and false in philosophy, and, theologically considered, at least erroneous in matter of faith." The publication of his "Dialogue Concerning the Two Principal Theories of the Universe," the Ptolemaic and the Copernican (1632), brought him into the hands of the Inquisition again, and he was made to abjure, curse, and detest these errors and heresies.

The full significance of this dislocation of the universe was not at once recognised. But with the new astronomy, the beginning was made in the modern world of an observation and investigation of nature whose object is solely to discover and interpret the phenomena of nature by the exact methods of science, independent of tradition, philosophy, and theology—in other words, of a religiously disinterested science, which sets for itself its own goal and pursues it in its own way.

Of this movement Francis Bacon is a conspicuous exponent, not so much through any notable contributions of his own to science, as by his clear conception and exposition of the nature, end, and methods of science. Knowledge of nature is to be gathered from nature itself by observation and induction, proceeding from the particular to the general, ascending from the fact to the principle or law, not descending from general principles *a priori*, borrowed from metaphysics. The results of such research, being the answer of nature itself to the inquiry of the investigator, are not subject to review in the alien forum of philosophy or theology.

In philosophy the new era began with Descartes,[1] who attempted to establish philosophy on a demonstrative, that is, a mathematical basis. In Descartes, as in Bacon, the important thing, from our point of view, is not his philosophy itself, but the fact that he completely set aside the systems of the ancients and their mediæval successors, and addressed himself to his task with new, primarily mathematical methods; and that in his endeavour to construct an intellectual system of the universe, Descartes was as unconcerned about the consequences to Christian theology as Copernicus with his revolutionary theory of the physical universe. This indifference, indeed, is the characteristic of both natural science and philosophy in this period; they moved, as it were, in another sphere, and let the theologians revolve—or stand still—untroubled in their own.

Descartes laid in mathematics and physics the foundation of a mechanist philosophy of the universe, including not only inorganic nature but organic, and halting only at mind in man. Newton, by his investigations in physics and astronomy, above all by his discovery of the laws of gravitation, made such a construction of the physical universe

[1] 1596–1650.

appear not only conceivable but verifiable. The work of
his successors, culminating in Laplace's Mécanique Céleste
(1799–1825), steadily progressed toward a complete mathematical solution of the mechanical problem of the solar
system.

The thinkers of the seventeenth century framed great
metaphysical systems of the universe—dualistic in Descartes,
monistic in Spinoza, pluralistic-individualistic in Leibniz.
Locke recalled the human understanding to more modest
problems by bidding it recognise its limitations when it
comes to universes; the proper business of philosophy is to
teach man to understand himself by empirical study of the
nature and origin of his ideas and emotions. Hume developed a sensationalist theory of cognition which, excluding
the ideas of substance and causality, leaves metaphysics
nothing to live on. In the levels below high philosophy the
same trends of thought are reflected in English deism and
French naturalism, in English latitudinarianism and German rationalism. Nor were science and philosophy the
only influences. There was a revival of notions of natural
law, natural morals, natural religion, which, ultimately of
Stoic origin, had come out in the age of the Renaissance,
and formed part of the humanist tradition perpetuated by
the side of the Reformation rather than in it. The growth
of democratic ideas in state and church, and the individualism that goes with them, ran easily into the rejection of all
authority for the all-sufficient reason that it was authority.
As in the age of the Greek Sophists, the individual man
made his private reason, or the common sense of his kind,
the measure of all things human and divine. In the latter part of the eighteenth century "free thought," ranging
from deism, through scepticism, to outspoken atheism was
wide-spread, and often noisily triumphant over the superstitions of Christianity; while the ministry and theologians
of the Protestant churches devoted their efforts to making
Christianity reasonable from premises and by methods
dangerously like those of its critics.

The alarm excited by the excesses of the French Revolution brought about a reaction in religion as well as in politics. The critical philosophy of Kant discovered for rational religion room and authority in the Practical Reason which Pure Reason denied it. The idealistic philosophies which succeeded—Fichte, Schelling, Hegel—restored religion to its place in their great metaphysical systems, and presently became the parents of philosophical theologies more orthodox in sound than in sense. In the first half of the nineteenth century religion regained much ground that it seemed permanently to have lost in the eighteenth; and theology in all Protestant countries was in the sign of repristination, with the inevitable consequence of new divisions, among which the Unitarian movement in New England is one of the most significant.

Meanwhile, science was making rapid advances in every field, and the new conception of the universe which, in distinction from metaphysical or theological theories, may properly be called scientific, was obtaining more and more general recognition. Astronomy and physics had already taught men to see in the universe a vast mechanism, impelled by inherent forces under invariable laws. Now, geology and chemistry joined hands with astronomy to create a new cosmology. Botany and zoology, hitherto chiefly descriptive sciences, set themselves to the problem of the origin of species in organic evolution, from the lowest living cell to man; and biological chemistry sought to penetrate the final secret, the origin of life. Thus arose a conflict between science and theology, which had in Genesis a revealed cosmogony irreconcilable with the evolutionary hypothesis, while the creation of Adam in the image of God, his fall, and the entail of sin and death on his posterity, lay at the foundation of its doctrine of redemption.

Nor was it the sciences of nature alone by which the foundations were attacked. Historians applied to the Bible the principles and methods of criticism which they employed on other ancient writings, and to the history of the Jewish and Christian religions the idea of development which belongs to the very definition of history in modern times. Biblical criticism was not a new thing in the nineteenth century, but it was pursued with better-defined method and with more strictly historical motives. The result was a complete revision of the chronology of the Old Testament literature and of the history of the religion of Israel. Not only particular results, but the assumption on which the historian proceeds, namely, that the authenticity, age, and historical value of the writings comprised in the canon of the Jews are to be determined and appraised in the same way as the sources of secular history, conflicts with the fundamental doctrine of sacred Scripture. The same methods were employed on the New Testament, with a corresponding and even more disturbing reconstruction of the beginnings of Christianity. The habit of looking at religious problems historically had a more far-reaching consequence, the introduction of the note of relativity into judgments of truth and right. The idea of development in doctrine is diametrically opposed to the dogmatic conception of an unchangeable deposit of faith, at whatever moment in the past this deposit is supposed to have crystallised in unchangeable formulas.

The historical study of Judaism and Christianity was not the only thing which contributed to this result. In the nineteenth century European scholars attained a much larger and more exact knowledge of the religions and religious philosophies of Oriental peoples, especially through the study of their sacred books—the religions of India, from the age of the Veda; Zoroastrianism, the reform religion of the Iranians; the native religions of China and Japan, and the varieties of Buddhism in those countries. The decipherment of the Egyptian and Babylonian monuments opened a way to the knowledge of the two most ancient religions of western Asia. Great progress was made also in an historical apprehension of the religions of Greece. These investigations revealed large and significant resemblances among the higher religions, and gave birth to a new study, which called itself the Comparative Science of Religion. The material collected by ethnologists in all quarters of the earth among peoples upon the lower levels of civilisation showed a remarkable degree of uniformity in the elementary conceptions and practices of religion, and challenged scholars to the attempt to solve, by historical methods, the problems of the origin and development of religion as a whole.

The consequence of all this was that, in the minds of many, Christianity was deprived of the unique position which it asserted for itself and which hitherto had been conceded to it in Christendom; it might be greatly superior to other religions, but this superiority was only relative—the "absoluteness" of Christianity disappeared.

Through a voluminous popular literature of propaganda and refutation, scientific theories and biblical criticism have been widely disseminated, and are accepted by an increasing number not only of laymen but of ministers in most Protestant denominations. The old confessions from the sixteenth or seventeenth century have seldom been formally set aside or revised, but there is a growing disposition to treat them as venerable historical monuments rather than as adequate expressions of present-day beliefs, and the terms of subscription have often been relaxed till they are hardly more than nominal. This dissolution of Protestant theology has gone much farther in some churches than in others, but none has been able to shut out entirely the mordant atmosphere of contemporary thought.

Speaking generally, the Protestant churches which have retained authoritative confessional standards and require assent to them on the part of their ministers, and which possess a strong ecclesiastical organization, through their control of theological education and of ordination to the ministry, have more successfully resisted these disintegrating tendencies, at least by driving out or keeping out too adventurous spirits. This is especially true of the free churches —the established churches are distinctly laxer. In those denominations, on the other hand, which inherited the tradition of independency, in which the autonomy of the individual church is legally complete, and morally restrained only by the undefined common opinion and sentiment of similar autonomous congregations or their voluntary associations; where each church makes its own terms of communion, and frames its own confession of faith for the assent of its members, or employs only an undogmatic "covenant"; where no convention or "council" has right to frame or power to impose a common creed—the various Congregational bodies in the United States, for example—there is entire ecclesiastical freedom, and in them the abandonment of the theology of the seventeenth century is most general. Yet the Baptists, who are the most radical of independents, have remained among the most conservative of religious bodies.

The task which awaits "advanced" Protestantism is to find a theology, or, some would say, a philosophy of religion, which shall represent modern conceptions of the universe, of the place and part of man in it, of the origin and development of religion in general and of Christianity in particular, and of the specific excellencies of Christianity, as adequately for the present as the scholastic theology did for the thirteenth century or the Protestant confessions of the sixteenth and seventeenth centuries for their time.

The general trend is toward a practical, or "socialized," Christianity, which makes much of the teaching and example of Jesus, of the thought of God as the father of all men, of service to fellow men as the essence of true religion, of the reconstruction of society on the principles of the gospel. It is optimistic about the native possibilities of humanity, has an exalted consciousness of superiority to the past, and conjures with the word "progress," often conceived as a kind of biological evolution of an organism called "society." Original sin and the paralyzed or even enfeebled will are quite antiquated, and with them the Pauline-Augustinian doctrines of grace.

It might be thought that, having come to this common ground, there would be a tendency to a reunion of the multitudinous sects which have forgotten their reason for existence, if for no higher than economic motives. There is, however, no sign of such a result. Most of the Protestant bodies co-operate more freely than formerly and, when they get together, deplore the divisions of Christendom and talk about unity; but, though they are for the most part no longer severed by living doctrinal differences, they are kept apart by the differences of the past embalmed in memories and, above all, embodied in corporate institutions.

The influence of contemporary movements of thought in philosophy, science, and political theory was felt in the Catholic Church also. The rising spirit of nationalism revived the old desire for national autonomy in ecclesiastical as well as in civil affairs. The declaration of the French clergy on ecclesiastical power (1682) renews the assertion of Gallican liberties of the preceding centuries; and a similar broad doctrine was promulgated in Germany in the second half of the eighteenth century by some of the great German archbishops. It was upon the same principles that Joseph II in Austria undertook ·a drastic reform of the church in his dominions; and his example was followed by his brother, Leopold, grand duke of Tuscany, with the support of some of the bishops. The programme of their Synod of Pistoia (1786) was the most radical of the kind. Revolution and the Napoleonic wars gave European rulers other preoccupations; but the readjustments of boundaries and the compensation of dispossessed secular princes at the cost of the lands of the Church, deprived it of a great part of its territorial possessions. The secularization of church property and the suppression of monasteries in almost all European countries, the recognition of freedom of worship and civil equality, and the progressive assumption of all functions of education by the state, seriously impaired the influence of the Church.

Nor were the intellectual and social tendencies of the

time more favourable. The forces which produced the French Revolution were not only anti-clerical, but in large part anti-Christian; and the unbridled individualism which was rife in the philosophies of the time, as well as in the teachings of Rousseau and his followers, made against all religious authority. The eighteenth century as a whole was a period of decadence, which made it, in the judgment of a Catholic historian, the most unchristian of all the centuries. Of the nineteenth century the same historian writes as follows: "The characteristic of political life was its gradual penetration by the principles of democracy proclaimed by the French Revolution, which make the nineteenth century the age of constitutionalism and parliamentary government in its various modifications. In its intellectual life the idealistic philosophy of the beginning of the century did not permanently prevail, nor did any definite conception of the universe to the exclusion of all others; it was dominated by the empirical positivist and rational-naturalistic tendencies of thought which make it the century of the natural and historical sciences. In the field of morals, the striving for the complete autonomy of the individual personality asserted itself far more strongly, and has as a necessary consequence the rejection of the idea of authority, and resistance to the authoritative regulation of the individual's inner life. Finally, social life was marked by the full development of nationalism, which brought the differentiation of the Occidental peoples to a kind of conclusion, and raised to a hitherto unknown pitch the national sentiment, the consciousness that each nation has in it certain special endowments and conditions, and has a right to demand its place in the concert of peoples. There can be no doubt that all these factors were necessarily unfavourable to the religious life."

By these conditions the Catholic Church was forced into a defensive position, which impressed itself on its whole activity. It became more than ever the advocate of the old against the new, of ecclesiastical authority against religious individualism, of dogmatic Christianity against the subjective spirit of the age.

This conflict with the spirit of the age is nowhere more consistently and comprehensively exhibited than in the Syllabus of Errors issued by Pope Pius IX in 1864. The heads under which these eighty errors are catalogued are instructive: Pantheism, Naturalism, Rationalism, Indifferentism, Latitudinarianism, Communism, Secret Societies, Bible Societies, Clerico-Liberal Societies, Errors about the Church and its Rites, About Civil Society and its Relation to the Church (separation of church and state), Errors about Natural and Christian Ethics, About the Temporal Power of the Pope, Errors of Modern Liberalism.

The most important doctrinal deliverance since the Council of Trent was the promulgation by Pius IX in the bull, "Ineffabilis Deus" (1854), of the dogma of the Immaculate Conception of the Virgin Mary, which is thus defined: "The Blessed Virgin Mary, in the very instant in which she was conceived, by the singular grace and privilege of Almighty God, in foresight of the merits of Jesus Christ, the Saviour of the human race, was preserved immune from any stain of original sin." The question whether or not the Virgin Mary shared in original sin had been much debated in the scholastic age. It was a standing matter of controversy between the Franciscans and the Dominicans, which Pope Sixtus IV tried to keep within bounds in 1487 by forbidding the advocates of either doctrine to call the other heretical for opinions upon which the Roman Church had never decided. The Council of Trent, while guarding its decree on original sin from the inference that the Virgin Mary was included in it, contented itself for the rest with reiterating the constitution of Sixtus IV.

The pontificate of Pius IX was signalised, also, by the final decision of another long-controverted question, namely, the supreme authority and infallibility of the pope. The Vatican Council in 1870, besides defining the doctrine of the church upon the topics, God, Revelation, Faith, and Reason, with especial reference to modern errors, framed a dogmatic constitution on the Church of Christ. This constitution deals in four chapters with (1) the institution of apostolic primacy in the person of St. Peter; (2) the perpetuity of this primacy of Peter in the Roman pontiffs; (3) the nature and authority of the primacy of the Roman pontiff (jurisdiction); and, (4) the infallibility of the pope. The definition is as follows: "Therefore, we (*sc.*, the Pope), faithfully adhering to a tradition which has been received from the beginning of the Christian faith, to the glory of God our Saviour, to the exaltation of the Catholic religion and the salvation of Christian peoples, with the approbation of the sacred Council, teach and declare it to be a divinely revealed dogma, that the Roman Pontiff, when he speaks *ex cathedra*, that is, when, in the exercise of his office as pastor and teacher of all Christians, by virtue of his supreme apostolic authority, he defines that a doctrine concerning faith or morals is to be held by the universal church, by the divine aid promised to him in the blessed Peter, is endowed with that infallibility with which the divine Redeemer meant his church to be furnished in defining doctrine concerning faith or morals; and therefore that such decisions of the Roman Pontiff are irreformable of themselves, and not by the consent of the Church."

That the church in its teaching capacity is infallible had always been Catholic doctrine; the question was, whether this infallibility resided in a general council or in the person of the Roman pontiff.[1] The latter position was maintained by Aquinas, and in the post-Reformation controversy by Bellarmin; it had the powerful support of the Society of Jesus. Nevertheless, there was decided opposition to the dogma, both within the council and outside of it, partly by such as were opposed to the dogma itself, partly by others who thought the pronouncement inopportune at that time. Almost all of these opponents promptly made their submission when once the constitution was adopted. Those

[1] See above, pp. 260 *ff.*

who believed that a general council was infallible could not well deny its infallibility in pronouncing the infallibility of the pope. A few, chiefly German, theologians refused to accept the dogma and were excommunicated. The so-called Old Catholic Church, which sprang from this, had, however, nowhere any popular support, and soon ceased even to be talked about.

Leo XIII made it his chief aim to reclaim for the Church the leadership in the modern world; and to accomplish this endeavoured to re-establish a closer relation between the Church and the world of his times, in the conviction that the highest aims of civilisation cannot be achieved without religion and the authority of the Church. His deliverances, consequently, especially on social and political questions, had a more positive and constructive character than those of his predecessor. To the spirit of the age, however, he was as little disposed to make concessions as Pius IX. In the Christian philosophies of the Middle Ages, especially in Aquinas, he found the most complete harmony of divine revelation and human reason, faith and knowledge, and saw in them the proper antidote to the unchristian philosophies of modern times. He therefore enjoined the study of the philosophy of Aquinas in Catholic schools and seminaries, and did much in many ways to further it.

Under Leo XIII and his successors a movement among Catholic scholars to which its adversaries gave the name of Modernism made considerable progress. They believed, like the Pope, that it was the mission of the Church to reclaim its leadership in the modern world; but they believed that it could do so only by finding its place in the modern world, not by turning back to the thirteenth century, with its great synthesis of Aristotle and revelation. Critical and historical studies, in which some of them were eminent, led them to apply the principle of historical development not only to the institutions of the church but to its dogmas, and to assert that, as in the past there had been growth in the church as in a living organism, so there must be progress in the present, continuous progress in the future. Christianity, they maintained, must adapt its modes of thinking to the progress of philosophy and science, and to men's ideas on political and social subjects; it must continually advance in experience and apprehension of religious truth, which in its fulness forever lies beyond men's power of conception and adequate expression. The evolution of dogma was, therefore, not merely a historical theory, it was a programme of progress.

Against these ideas and tendencies the Church has expressly and emphatically pronounced. In the decree "Lamentabili Sane Exitu" (1907) and the encyclical "Pascendi Gregis," of the same year, a long catalogue of Modernist errors is condemned, and precautionary and disciplinary measures are prescribed to check the spread of the movement, particularly in institutions of learning and through publications by Catholic scholars. The church is resolved by all means in its power to prevent the disintegrating effects of modern philosophy, science, history, biblical criticism and exegesis, upon the dogmas of religion, which has been so conspicuously exemplified in contemporary Protestantism.

CHAPTER XVI

MOHAMMEDANISM

MOHAMMED

Mohammed—Religion of the Arabs before Mohammed—The First
Revelations—Hostility of the Meccans—Mohammed at Medina—
Arabia Won for Islam—Mohammed's Mission—The Idea of God
—Predestination—The Koran—The Prophets—The Hereafter—
Worship—Morals in the Koran—The Jews—Nationalising of
Islam.

MOHAMMEDANISM, or to give it its proper name, Islam,[1]
is the most recent of the great religions, and its rise and
early progress lie more fully than any other in the daylight
of history. The revelations of the Prophet during the
twenty years, more or less, of his career were collected in
the Koran within the next years after his death, and of the
authenticity of its contents there has never been any substantial question. Besides the Word of God in the Koran,
the words of Mohammed in his own name, his decisions and
regulations on questions of justice or morals or religious observance, were gathered as precedent; his daily habits were
examples. In the spread of Islam, again, there was no long
period of obscure propaganda, like the first generations of
Christianity; the expansion of the Arab empire carried the
religion of the conquerors with it; it was in the name of
religion that their victorious hosts were set in motion and
that the subject lands were ruled.

Mohammed was born about 570 A. D. Many legends
cluster about his childhood, but all that is known with
reasonable certainty is that he was early left an orphan and
was brought up by an uncle, Abu Talib. As he grew to
manhood he journeyed with the Meccan caravans in their
visits to Syria and to Yemen, and saw something of the

[1] "Submission" (to God).

world from the back of a camel, but the only incident related about these journeys, the meeting with the Christian hermit who recognised the youth's prophetic mission, are pious fictions. Mohammed's first journeys were made in company with his uncle; subsequently he was employed by a widow, Khadijah, whose capital was invested in the caravan trade. He conducted the business so much to her satisfaction that she presently proposed to him a matrimonial partnership. Mohammed was about twenty-five years old; Khadijah was considerably his senior and had already had two husbands, but the marriage seems to have been a happy one, and was blessed with six children, two sons (who died in childhood) and four daughters. Mohammed had great respect for Khadijah, and as long as she lived he took no other wife.

Of the years between his marriage and the beginning of his mission there is no record. We only know that in the period immediately preceding his first revelation, which occurred when he was about forty years of age, he spent much time in solitude upon a mountain near Mecca, engaged in religious exercises in which fasting and vigils seem to have had a large place.[1] From the character of his earliest utterances in the Koran it may be inferred that he had brooded over the idea of divine judgment which he had got from Christian and Jewish sources, until the conviction possessed him that this judgment in all its terrors was impending over his people for their sins, above all for the worship of false gods and idols. Such broodings and forebodings wrought, we can well conceive, with more than common power upon a highly susceptible temperament, and upon nerves overstrung by lonely watching and fasting. The descriptions that are given in Moslem tradition of the way Mohammed was affected in moments of revelation have led some students to believe that he was a victim of epilepsy; others interpret the phenomena as symptoms of a less seri-

[1] Such exercises had no place in the religion of the Arabs, and seem to be in imitation of Christian ascetics.

ous nervous disorder, perhaps of a hysterical character. Some abnormality there undoubtedly was; but, while these experiences may explain Mohammed's faith in his own inspiration, they no more account for the content or effect of his prophesyings than the similar experiences of Saint Paul account for Pauline Christianity.

The religion of Mohammed's countrymen was of a very primitive kind. There were many gods, and two or three goddesses who were held in especially high esteem. These deities had their several holy places, whither men resorted on occasion to seek their aid, fulfil a vow, or consult the oracle. The sacred precincts were marked off by boundary stones. The object of worship, or, to speak more exactly, the object in which the divinity lodged, was most commonly a stone, sometimes a tree or a group of trees. In Mecca there was a small square temple, into one corner of which the sacred stone was built. Idols, like the image of Hubal in this temple, were rare and recent importations.

Apart from local and tribal associations, the gods had little individuality; there was no specialisation of function and no mythology. The goddesses bore feminine names, but they had nothing else of the sex about them.[1] Allah ("the deity," like the Hebrew *ha-elohim*), before Mohammed elevated him to the place of sole God, had, by virtue of the generality of the appellation a certain precedence over gods who were individualised by proper names and local habitations.

The victim in sacrifice was killed with a dedication, "In the name of"—whatever god it might be; the blood was smeared on the holy stone or poured into a pit at the foot. The flesh furnished a feast for the offerer, his family, and guests. There was no sacrificial priesthood; the priests were diviners, and sometimes custodians of the holy places.

At some of the chief sanctuaries there was an annual concourse of strangers from near and far; the religious festival was combined with a great fair, at which the products

---

[1] This is said of Mohammed's time and place; with what they may have been elsewhere and in other times we are not here concerned.

of different parts of the peninsula and foreign wares were exchanged. Mecca was the scene of the most frequented of these festivals in all that part of Arabia. A suspension of tribal wars and blood-feuds during the sacred months, a kind of truce of God, insured the safety of visitors at the festival and on the journey.

In the north of Arabia, the kingdoms of Palmyra and of Hira, vassal buffer-states of the Roman and Persian empires respectively, were Christian; and from them Christianity had spread into the belt of Arab tribes that stretched across the desert between. In Yemen, in the south, then under Persian rule, the population was largely Jewish and Christian. Not so far from Mecca, there were Jewish tribes at Medina and in the oases north of it. The caravan trade with the north and the south brought the Meccans some acquaintance with these religions; Jewish and Christian slaves were no rarity in Mecca. Several of Mohammed's contemporaries in Mecca, Medina, and Taif had discovered the inferiority of Arab paganism, and became in their personal conviction monotheists, with an eclectic appropriation of Christian ideas. They made no effort, however, to win others to their way of thinking, and did not attack the religion of their countrymen. Two of them, in Mecca, were of kin to Mohammed's wife; one was a neighbor, and intimate in his house. Through such channels Mohammed may have got the ideas which worked in his mind with such different effect; he certainly did not get from them the inspiration to his mission.

At the end of one of his retreats on Mount Hira his call came to proclaim the word of God to his generation. Tradition has embellished the fact with a wealth of legendary circumstance; the simplest story is that in a dream the angel of revelation (Gabriel) appeared to him and bade him recite what God revealed to him.[1] According to the most

[1] In other places in the Koran the verb ("*ikra*") means "recite" a sacred text (from memory); it is used also of reading (aloud) a written text, and in the latter sense it is understood by the decorative traditions according to which Gabriel brought down a strip of silk inscribed with the words of revelation.

generally accepted opinion, the words of ·the angel are preserved in the Koran, Sura 96, 1–5.

> "Recite! in the name of thy Lord,
> Who created man of a clot of blood.
> Recite! Thy Lord is most gracious,
> Who taught by means of the pen,[1]
> Taught man what he knew not."

Mohammed, the tradition continues, returned to his
home in great perturbation, not comprehending what had
befallen him; Khadijah comforted him and consulted Waraka
ibn Naufal, who, from his acquaintance with the older
Scriptures, recognised that Mohammed was called to be the
prophet of his people, as Moses had been in his day.

Another very early revelation is the beginning of Sura 74:

> "O thou who liest wrapped up!
> Arise and give warning,
> And magnify thy Lord,
> And purify thy garments,
> And keep aloof from defilement.
> And be not liberal, seeking to gain by it;
> And wait patiently for thy Lord."

These utterances, like the rest of the Koran, are in the
rhymed sing-song in which the heathen soothsayers were
wont to couch their responses. An imitative translation of
an early Sura (93) may give some notion of the form:

> "By the bright day
> And the night without ray,
> Thy Lord forsakes not nor casts thee away.
> The hereafter the present will more than repay;
> Thy Lord will give, nor say thee nay.
> Found he thee not an orphan and became thy stay,
> Found thee wandering and set thee on thy way,
> Found thee poor and did thy wants allay?
> Therefore the orphan do not thou gainsay,
> Nor the beggar drive away;
> But the goodness of thy Lord display."

[1] The reference is to the Scriptures of the Jews and Christians.

For a time Mohammed addressed himself to individuals, chiefly in the circle of his more intimate acquaintance. The first to believe in him were of his own household—his wife Khadijah, his freedman and adoptive son Zaid ibn Harithah,[1] his cousin Ali ibn Abu Talib (who was a lad of ten years at the utmost). Outside the house the first believer was Abu Bekr, one of the most esteemed men in Mecca for his probity and his charity, whose knowledge and experience, sound judgment, and benevolent disposition led men to seek his advice on public and private affairs, and gave his counsel great weight. Abu Bekr made no secret of his faith in Mohammed, and the influence of his words and example induced others to believe. After a time Mohammed was encouraged to speak publicly to his townsmen as he found opportunity; but his converts were not very numerous, and were chiefly young men and "feeble folk," as the narrator phrases it—people of small account in the community. The Meccans at first looked on with a tolerant incredulity; when Mohammed passed a group of them they would point at him and say: "There goes that young man of the family of Abd al-Muttalib who talks about heaven." But when he went farther and reviled the gods they worshipped and dilated on the perdition of their pagan forefathers, their enmity was aroused.

The Meccans had no great religious zeal; they resented Mohammed's attacks not so much for the gods' sake as from loyalty to the institutions of the city. They had, moreover, a strong economic interest in maintaining those institutions, for the importance of Mecca was due in large part to the holy places in its territory, and the multitudes of pilgrims who resorted thither at the festivals brought much gain to the citizens. The remorseless logic with which Mohammed consigned to hell their forefathers who

[1] Zaid had been brought from Syria to Mecca as a slave by a nephew of Khadijah. He came from a region and a tribe (the Kalbites of Dumat al-Jandal) which had long been in contact with Judaism and Christianity.

had died in the days of ignorance incensed men with whom the bond of blood was the most sacred point of honour and obligation. Mohammed later forfeited the protection of his uncle, Abu Lahab, and incurred his mortal enmity, by averring that his father (Mohammed's grandfather) was in the fire with all the rest of the heathen. Opposition only sharpened Mohammed's tone and made his denunciations more vehement.

Mohammed's adversaries urged his uncle, Abu Talib, to silence the troublesome preacher, or to withdraw his protection and let them silence him; but Abu Talib, though he was no believer, stood by his nephew. When the other families of Mecca made a compact to have no dealings with the Hashimites so long as they sheltered Mohammed, the clan allowed themselves to be shut up in their quarter for many months rather than dishonour themselves by surrendering their kinsman. But while Mohammed himself was thus safe from anything worse than insult, those of his followers who had not the protection of a powerful family suffered more seriously, and some of them, finding their situation intolerable, took refuge among the Christians in Abyssinia. Shortly after the interdict was raised Mohammed set out with one companion on a mission to Taif, a flourishing town two days east of Mecca, but met a rude reception, and after a few days was constrained to make his way back to Mecca.

He had better success with some pilgrims from Yathrib,[1] whom the annual festival brought to Mecca. Several of them professed Islam, and by their efforts at home others of their townsmen were converted. In two years' time the movement had made such progress at Medina that Mohammed decided to remove thither. He gave the word to the Meccan Moslems, who in small groups, eluding observation as far as possible, migrated to Medina. Mohammed himself and the faithful Abu Bekr remained till the rest were safely off, and then followed them. Before taking this step,

---

[1] Later known as Medina, that is "the city" (of the Prophet).

Mohammed had, in a family conclave, formally severed the ties of kindred which bound him to his people and put himself under the protection of representatives of the men of Medina. This withdrawal is the Hijra (Hegira), and when, after Mohammed's death, it was made the Moslem era, the chronologers fixed the beginning of the year on a day corresponding to July 15, 622 A. D.

The Arabs of Medina belonged to two tribes, Aus and Khazraj, which had migrated thither no great while before from the south of the peninsula. There were also in Medina and its neighbourhood several tribes of Jews, long settled in those parts, and in everything but their religion thoroughly Arabised, in all probability, also, largely of Arab blood. The refugees from Mecca brought a new element into an already complicated situation. In regulating their relations to the Supporters in Medina, Mohammed established the principle that all the Moslems formed one community, and were bound to protect one another in all things and against all enemies, the bond of the common religion being above all ties of clan and kin, and in case of conflict superseding them. Disputes that arose within the community were to be referred to God and Mohammed, that is, in effect, to the arbitration of the Prophet. The Jewish clans which were clients of the Arab tribes of Medina were to be protected in the exercise of their religion; and of the heathen in the city it was demanded that they should not take the part of the heathen of Mecca against the believers.

In this constitution the foundation of Mohammed's political power was laid. Medina had in recent years suffered much from intestine wars between the Aus and Khazraj, in which the Jews also had been involved, and from their legacy of blood-feuds. The new order put an end to all this, and even those who were least impressed by the religious merits of Islam could not fail to see the great gain it brought in security for life and possessions. Many professed Islam from such motives, without any real heart in it. These "hypocrites" were a constant trial to Mohammed, and at more than one juncture a peril to the cause; numerous revelations express his distrust of them.

Medina lay conveniently near the main route to the north, and Mohammed, after some forays on a smaller scale, laid plans to intercept the annual Meccan caravan returning from Syria. The caravan escaped, but the Meccans felt it necessary for future safety to chastise the presumption. The smart defeat they suffered at Bedr was damaging to their prestige and greatly enhanced that of the Moslems. In the following years the conflict was renewed with varying fortunes, but in the end Mohammed prevailed. Mecca itself was taken by him in the year 8 (early in 630 A. D.), and the idols and other appurtenances of heathen worship were destroyed. In the following year Abu Bekr headed the pilgrimage, and formally proclaimed that Mecca and the holy places belonged to the Moslems, and that henceforth no heathen should be allowed to take part in the ceremonies. Mohammed himself made the pilgrimage in 632 A. D., introduced some changes in the rites, and gave the festival the form it has preserved to the present day.

The authority which Mohammed had acquired at Medina and his successes against the Meccans inclined many of the Bedouins to his side; missionary bands converted some and camel raids convinced others. The catastrophe that befell the Hawazin, who had allied themselves with the citizens of Taif against him after the capture of Mecca, completed the change of heart. In 622, when Mohammed, after prophesying for a dozen years to a stiff-necked generation, shook the dust of Mecca from his feet, the refugees and the supporters together numbered but a few hundred; when he died, ten years later, all Arabia had embraced his religion, and a Moslem army was on foot to carry the truth into Syria.

Mohammed's mission, as he conceived it in the beginning, was to warn his countrymen that the day of judgment was at hand, and to urge them to flee from the wrath to come

by putting away their vain idols and serving the one living
and true God. "There is no god but God (Allah)" is the
corner-stone of religion. God is a jealous God, and tolerates no rivals; to have other gods besides him is the sin of
sins. Not the heathen only are guilty of this sin, but the
Christians, who say "God is the Messiah, the son of Mary,"
or "God is the third of three." [1] The unity of God is the
message of God by all his prophets: "We sent no apostle
before thee to whom we did not reveal that there is no God
but me."

The idea of God is essentially that of the Old Testament,
and doubtless came to him through Jewish channels. The
title, al-Rahman, "the merciful," which in one period of
his ministry Mohammed used as a proper name for God by
preference to all others, is a foreign word, borrowed from
the Jews, and the emphasis on the attribute of mercy, especially on God's forgiving grace, is of the same origin. Stock
and stone worship and idolatry are denounced; God must
not be imaged in any likeness. For the rest, Mohammed
pictured God, as the naïve imagination of Jews and Christians had always done, in the highest heaven, seated upon
a lofty throne, surrounded by angelic ministers, some of
whom continually adore him, while others go to and fro,
revealing his word or doing his will upon earth. The devil
(*Iblis*, Diabolos, or *Shaitan*, Satan), an angel who fell
through pride, is an adversary and tempter, as in Judaism
and Christianity. God is not remote from the affairs of
men: "Dost thou not see that God knows what is in the
heavens and on the earth? There cannot be a secret conference of three, but he makes the fourth with them . . . he
is with them wherever they are, and will declare to them
on the day of resurrection what they did."

God is almighty as well as all-wise, the creator of the
heavens and the earth and of all things in them, and master
of his own creation; "Lord of the worlds," "Lord of man-

[1] The strictures on Christian polytheism are all in Suras revealed
at Medina.

kind." In his controversies with the Meccans Mohammed was naturally led to lay emphasis on God's sovereignty and his omnipotence. His right none can contest, his will naught can resist. Yet he is no despot, wielding his awful power arbitrarily or capriciously, for he is wise and merciful.

Mohammed was so firmly convinced of his mission and of the truth of his message, of the urgency of his warning to flee from the wrath to come, that he could not understand why all men did not believe, and surrender themselves to God's will. They asked for signs, for miracles such as had attested the divine mission of the older prophets; he disclaimed supernatural powers, but what miracles could be so conclusive as the "signs" that were sent down to him, the verses of the Koran itself. Yet the fact remained: only a few believed, even on this convincing proof, while the mass rejected both the claims of the Prophet and his revelations. The only explanation that offered itself was that God had given to some to believe and be saved, and left others to perish in their unbelief, and this of determinate purpose: "God leads astray whomsoever he wills, and guides aright whom he wills."

The idea of predestination in the Koran is not derived from abstract reflections on the implications of God's sovereignty, but is the practical solution of a problem thrust upon Mohammed by his experience. Nor is God's dealing usually represented in the Koran as arbitrary: God leaves to wander to their own ruin, like wayfarers lost in the desert, those who have shown themselves unwilling to be guided by him. Of the Israelites who treated Moses ill, Mohammed says: "When they turned aside from the right way, God turned their hearts aside; God does not guide evil-doers"; of the hypocrites at Medina: "They forget God and he forgets them"; and similarly in many places. Nor does Mohammed, even where he asserts God's agency most unqualifiedly, desist from urging men to believe and submit as if all was in their power. The preaching of predestination is not meant to make the sinner feel his helplessness, but to warn him of his peril if he rejects the message. We shall see how the crude and inconsistent utterances of the Prophet on this subject gave material for great controversies among Moslem theologians. Meanwhile it will not be amiss to remind ourselves that here also Mohammed was walking more closely than he knew in the traces of the Jewish and Christian Scriptures.

There is no stronger evidence of the impression which the two great book religions made upon the "illiterate prophet" [1] than the fact that he could not conceive a divine revelation otherwise than as Scriptures which God "sent down." His own revelations were transcripts of a celestial original, brought to him in parts from time to time as need was by Gabriel. These casual and piecemeal revelations, collected soon after his death, constitute the Koran, the inspired scripture of Islam. The Koran consists of one hundred and fourteen chapters, or Suras, varying in length from a few lines to many pages, and differing no less widely in form and content, from the rhapsodical oracles of which examples have been given above to prosaic legislation on everyday matters.

The compilers, having no historical interest, made no attempt to order the chapters chronologically or by subject; they began with the long chapters revealed at Medina— chiefly legislative, and often composite—and put the short Suras, among which are the earliest revelations, at the end. Partly by the aid of tradition, partly by internal evidence, modern criticism is able to divide the prophet's outgivings into three or four large groups, corresponding to as many stages in his career, and thus to trace with some confidence the development of his ideas and aims. For our present purpose it must suffice to indicate in the proper place the more striking changes which were the result of the new situation in which he found himself at Medina.

God's word to men in olden times was made known

---

[1] Mohammed emphasizes the fact that his doctrine was not learned out of books.

through his messengers, or prophets; and Mohammed, as
he conceived his mission more clearly, took these titles to
himself: he was the messenger of God (*rasūl*), commonly
translated "apostle"), the Prophet (*nabī*) whom God sent
to the Arabs.[1] If the Meccans reject him and his message,
the prophets before him were no better received in their
time. The generation of Noah would not listen to him, and
perished in the flood; the Egyptians spurned Moses, and
were drowned in the Red Sea. The catastrophes that overtook those who refused to hear the prophets were favorite
themes with him; to the examples from biblical history he
added Ad and Thamud, Arab tribes whose ruin, it was
revealed to him, was a judgment for rejecting their prophets,
Hud and Salih. The Old Testament stories came to him
by hearsay, with legendary embellishments, and he retold
them with improvements and some original misunderstandings. What he tells of Jesus comes chiefly from apocryphal
and heretical sources.

Mohammed's notions of the hereafter are plainly derived
from Jewish and Christian sources. The beginning and
very motive of his preaching was the impending judgment
of God. The signs of its approach and the events of the
great day, with its eternal issues, fill a large space in the
Koran and in utterances from every period of the prophet's
career; they are depicted with peculiar vividness in a group
of Suras which reflect the acute stage of Meccan opposition.
The "signs" belong to the common apocalyptic tradition;
portents and convulsions in nature fill men with consternation; the trumpet sounds, the earth gives up its dead, and
the assembled generations appear before the judgment
throne of God; the books are brought forth in which men's
deeds are recorded—all the familiar imagery. The Meccans met these threatenings with a light heart; they mocked
at the resurrection and all the stage-machinery of judgment. Mohammed's definition of an infidel is one who calls

[1] The explicit assumption of these titles begins in the last period at
Mecca, and is common only in the Suras revealed at Medina.

the judgment-day a lie; to such he promises a convincing experience of it.

Hell is a gulf of fire, in which, fettered and chained, sinners broil, unable to die and without escape. "The Fire" is the common and sufficient word for it; the name *jehinnam* is the Hebrew *gehinnom*, the *Gehenna* of Jewish and New Testament eschatology. Paradise is "the Garden"—again the Jewish word. Here Mohammed's imagination was more original. His "garden" was a place of green meadows and shady trees, bearing all pleasant fruits, of springs and flowing rivers—the very heaven for a dweller in the barren, burning valley of Mecca, for the Arab of the desert. There are all things that man can desire in lavish abundance, delicious fruits, streams of milk and honey, wine without a headache in it, silken raiment and rich adornment, rare perfumes. It is frankly a paradise of the senses; fair-eyed maids with complexion like pearls and rubies are one of the attractions of the place.[1] But it is also a place where no false nor foolish word is spoken, and where the saved continually praise God for his goodness. An influential school of Moslem theologians, as we shall see, interpreted these descriptions figuratively, as many Christians interpret the city with streets of gold and gates of pearl, the river of living water, and the trees with twelve kinds of fruit in the Revelation of John.

The rejection of the false gods had as a consequence the abandonment of the whole heathen cultus. In its stead Mohammed instituted a worship of prayer, like the devotions of Jews and Christians. The prayers, which consisted of recitation of verses of the Koran, were individual, though a number of Moslems might come together to offer them at the same time. The hostility of the Meccans made the early Moslems choose secluded places outside the city or the shelter of private houses for their conventicles. At Medina a large house of worship (*mesjed*, "mosque") was

[1] It should be said that the Huris appear only in a small group of Suras.

built where the Moslems might perform their private devotions if they wished, and in which they assembled to pray in unison under the leadership of Mohammed. As the Jews had their Sabbath and the Christians their Lord's Day, so Mohammed appointed the Friday noon hour for public prayer, appearance at which was made a religious duty. In other respects, also, the times and forms of daily private prayer were more exactly regulated. At the gathering in the great mosque Mohammed often addressed the congregation, not only on what we should call religious subjects, but on divers matters of general interest to the community.

With the worship of the heathen gods Mohammed forbade the various forms of divination that were practised at their shrines. Under the same condemnation he put gambling, a vice to which the Arabs were much addicted, and in which they went to excesses that remind us of what Tacitus tells of our Teutonic forefathers. In his later deliverances he prohibited unreservedly the use of wine; wine and gambling are Satan's devices to provoke quarrels among the Moslems and to turn them from the remembrance of God and from prayer.

Infanticide, which was common, especially the burying of supernumerary daughters, Mohammed condemned as murder. He forbade fornication, and prescribed severe and equal penalties for both parties. He set a limit on the number of wives a man might have at one time, and restricted the freedom of divorce; required a considerate treatment of slaves, and made the manumission of believing slaves a meritorious work. It is unreasonable to censure Mohammed for not reconstructing the whole social system of the Arabs in anticipation of modern ideas. For his time and according to his light, including what came to him from Judaism and Christianity, he accomplished notable reforms; unfortunately he gave the finality of revelation to their limitations.

Judged by the same standard, the moral teaching of the Koran is high; it may fairly be compared with Deuteronomy, or such compends of Jewish morals as Lev. 19; as may be seen in the following, from a Meccan Sura (17, 23 *ff*.):

Put beside God no other god, lest thou one day sit condemned and without helper. Thy God had decreed that ye serve no one but him. And that thou treat thy parents well, if one or both of them grow old in thy house, and do not speak rudely to them, nor grumble at them, but use to them honourable speech. And incline to them the wing of humility out of compassion, and say, O Lord, have compassion on them, as they brought me up when I was little. Your Lord knows what is in your hearts if ye be righteous, and verily he is forgiving to the penitent.

And give what is right to thy kinsman and to the poor and to the wanderer; but do not squander thy substance, for the squanderers have always been the devil's brothers, and the devil is ever ungrateful to his Lord. But if ever thou must turn away from them to seek from thy Lord the favour thou hopest for,[1] give them at least a kind word. Let not your arm hang motionless from your shoulder, but do not open your hand quite wide,[2] lest thou shouldest have to sit blamed and impoverished; for thy Lord gives sustenance abundantly to whom he will or sparingly—verily, he knows and sees his servants.

Do not kill your children out of apprehension of poverty; he will provide for them and you. Killing them is a great sin.

Avoid fornication; it is an abomination and a wrong way.

Do not kill one whom God has forbidden you, unless it be for a just cause. As for him who is slain unjustly, we have given his next of kin the right to avenge him; but let him not exceed bounds in killing[3] —verily he is ever helped.

Do not touch the property of the orphan,[4] except to improve it until he arrive at his majority.

Fulfil your agreement. Verily, an agreement is always inquired into (by God).

Give full measure when you measure, and weigh with an honest balance; that is the best and fairest way.

Do not follow what thou dost not know about. What a man listens to and looks at and thinks in his heart—all these will one day be asked about.

And do not walk proudly on the earth, for, verily, thou canst not split the earth nor make thyself as tall as the mountains. All this is an abomination in the sight of thy Lord.

[1] *I. e.*, to seek your own livelihood.
[2] Be neither niggardly nor lavish in benevolence.
[3] In pursuing the blood-feud.
[4] Whose guardian you may be.

Mohammed believed at the outset that the religion he preached to his countrymen was the same that had been preached by the prophets before him; this was, indeed, a necessary consequence of his belief in revelation. Of these prophets Moses and Jesus were the greatest, and the Law of the Jews and the Gospel of the Christians were the most important of the Scriptures that God had "sent down" in former times. What was "sent down" to him was to confirm what was already in their hands. When the Moslems were harassed in Mecca, he sent a company of them to Abyssinia to find a refuge among their Christian fellow-believers. At Medina he expected the Jews to recognise the agreement between his teaching and theirs, and to own him as a prophet in the true succession, perhaps as the Messiah for whom they were waiting. The Moslems, when they prayed, turned their faces toward Jerusalem; the Day of Atonement was made a solemn fast for Moslems, the one great fast in the year. Mohammed did not see why, if he acknowledged Moses and his Torah, the Jews should not acknowledge him and his Koran.

The Jews proved obdurate; their doctrine had no place in it for Arab prophets or messiahs. They took a malicious pleasure in exposing the ignorance of biblical history which Mohammed displayed in his stories about biblical persons, thus impugning his claim to have his stories by revelation. He retorted that his was the true and original version; if it was told otherwise in the books of the Jews it was because they had falsified their Scriptures. The attitude of the Jews was not only vexatious, but had in it a visible element of danger. In conjunction with the "hypocrites," as Mohammed calls the numerous class who outwardly professed Islam but had no real faith in it, they might at more than one crisis have made his position in Medina untenable. In the interludes in the conflict with the Meccans, Mohammed, on one pretext or another, fell upon the Jews, and did not stop till he had driven out all their tribes from Medina, and conquered their strongholds in the oasis of Khaibar.

The breach with the Jews had far-reaching religious consequences. It was now revealed to Mohammed that not toward Jerusalem, but toward Mecca should men turn their faces when they prayed; he abrogated the observance of the Day of Atonement and ordained instead a fast for the whole month of Ramadan; he declared the Jewish dietary laws annulled. Islam was not the same with Judaism and Christianity; it was the restoration of an older and purer faith, the Religion of Abraham. This religion Abraham had planted among the Arabs; with Ishmael, the forefather of the Arabs, he had built the Kaaba at Mecca and dedicated it to the worship of the true God. During his career at Mecca Mohammed had always shown reverence for the Kaaba, notwithstanding that it was a house of idols; now he made it his mission to recover the ancient Arabian sanctuary and restore it to its original consecration. When he ordered the pilgrimage in mass in 628, he doubtless thought of the possibility of seizing the sacred places by a *coup de main;* but the Meccans were beforehand with him, and much to the chagrin of his followers, he had to turn back without accomplishing the pilgrimage. Two years later, as we have seen, he was more successful, and restored the House of God to its true owner. He did more: he incorporated the rites of pilgrimage, a whole piece of unassimilated Arab paganism, into Islam, making them the very culmination of its cultus; taking care, however, to obliterate their address and significance. This nationalising of Islam contributed much to its immediate success among the Arabs; its remoter consequences would have taken more of a prophet than Mohammed to foresee.

While in this way Islam was becoming the national religion of the Arabs, Mohammed was imagining larger things. Having come to think of Islam, not as substantially identical with Judaism and Christianity, but as a later and more perfect revelation superseding them, he seems to have conceived his own mission in corresponding dimensions—a prophet to mankind. He is said to have sent letters to the

Roman emperor Heraclius and to the Persian Chosroes, summoning them to submit to the authority of God and his apostle; and was following his epistle with an army when death overtook him. The history of Islam in the following period was determined by this double character. It was the national religion of the Arabs, and it was their task to bring the rest of mankind under its sway, establishing thus the sovereignty of God in this world. The Arab empire assumed the character of a universal theocratic state; a form, it will be remembered, which the Jewish Messianic hope sometimes took, and an endeavour which has many Christian parallels.

CHAPTER XVII

MOHAMMEDANISM

THE CALIPHATE.   DOCTRINAL CONTROVERSIES

The Caliphs—The Moslem Conquests—Situation of Jews and Chris-
tians—Moslem Law—Custom and Tradition—Development of
Jurisprudence—The Principle of Consensus—The Kharijite
Schism—Early Controversies—The Mutazilites—Their Idea of
God—Doctrine of the Created Koran—Rationalised Eschatology
—Mediating Theology—Al-Ashari—Al-Bakilani.

THE situation in which the death of Mohammed (632
A. D.) left his followers was exceedingly difficult.   During
his lifetime he had kept all authority in his own hands.
Military commanders were appointed for a specific expedition with specific instructions, and when they had accomplished their task, they laid down their command and
returned to the ranks of the believers.   Even when his illness made it necessary to designate a leader for the public
prayers in the mosque, the appointment was made only for
the temporary occasion with no provision for a possible recurrence.   All questions that arose in the community were
settled by him, and if his own authority was not sufficient,
a revelation was thrown into the balance.   He had thus
built up no organisation, no machinery of administration
which might have gone on when the master mind which
had designed and created it was withdrawn.   He had made
no provision for a successor, either by naming one or by
determining the method in which one should be chosen.
As prophet, it was clear to everybody that he could not
have any successor—was he not the last of the prophets?
But the religious-political community which Islam had
become required a head and a central and supreme author-

ity; this was indeed the indispensable condition of its continued existence.

For a moment it seemed as if conflicting interests and ambitions might lead to intestine strife; but better counsels prevailed, and Abu Bekr was recognised on all sides as the vicar of the Apostle of God ("caliph"). Abu Bekr was on every account the right man. His personal character, his intimate relation to Mohammed reaching back to the very beginning of Mohammed's career, his simple-minded faith in the Prophet and loyalty to his word and example, made it sure that the work of Mohammed would be carried on, his unfinished task completed, in his own spirit.

The news of Mohammed's death was the signal for the falling away of all Arabia; Medina, Mecca, and Taif almost alone remained true. Medina itself was for the moment seriously threatened by the tribes from the north and the northeast; it had been almost stripped of its defenders to make up the army despatched under the command of Osama against Syria in accordance with plans which had been formed by Mohammed before his death. Yemen fell away as a matter of course, and Yemama with all the regions beyond. It is an interesting evidence of the impression Mohammed had produced upon the Arabs that the leaders in this attempt to assert Arab liberty almost without exception either gave themselves out for prophets or had prophets at their elbows. The struggle which gave the armies of the caliphate most difficulty was in Yemama, where the prophet Maslama (nicknamed by the Moslems Moseilima), at the head of the tribe Abu Hanifa, was only subdued after great efforts. The turn of Yemen followed, and before the end of 633 all Arabia had been reconverted by the Moslem armies.

The consolidation of Islam in Arabia, the fusion into one body animated by one spirit of men and tribes which had yesterday been engaged in fratricidal war, was accomplished by the aggressive wars which now began against the Roman and Persian Empires. These conquests fell in the caliphate of Omar, who in August, 634, succeeded Abu Bekr and was the real organiser of the empire. This is not the place to recite the history of these conquests; it must suffice to recall a few dates which indicate the successive stages in the expansion of Islam. Damascus fell into the hands of the Moslems in the late summer of 635, and in August of the following year was fought on the banks of the Yarmuk the battle which determined Heraclius to evacuate all Syria. On the other side, the battle of Kadisiya in 637 brought under Moslem dominion those parts of the Persian Empire which had been ancient Babylonia and Assyria. The struggle for the eastern provinces continued for some time longer. A decisive victory was won at Nehawend, in 642, and in a few years all Iran was reduced to subjection. In 640 Egypt fell into the hands of the Moslems without serious opposition. Thus when Omar died by the hand of an assassin, in 644, he was at the head of an empire which extended from Cyrene on the west to the frontiers of India on the east.

Under his successor, Othman (644–'56), the movement of expansion slackened. The Moslem empire had indeed reached what might not improperly be regarded its natural limits. Othman was a weak ruler with an especial weakness for his kinsmen and the old aristocracy of Mecca. Mohammed himself and his immediate successors had, out of motives of policy, shown exceptional favours to these late-comers into the faith, but under Othman they got possession of all the best places, the command of armies, the governorships of the richest provinces. Many of these men, as everybody knew, had little religion in their hearts, though they fully appreciated the political possibilities of Islam. The process of secularisation which was converting the empire of the faith into a monarchy quite after the pattern that prevailed among the unbelievers did not go unobserved nor without protest, and Othman found himself the mark of dangerous opposition from two sides—on the one hand from the old believers, the representatives of the truly religious spirit of Islam, and on the other hand from rival aspirants to the caliphate. These and other discontented elements made common cause against the caliph. In 656 bands from Irak and Egypt assembled at Medina and, when the caliph refused to abdicate at their demand, besieged him in his own house, forced an entrance, and killed him.

Ali, the first cousin and son-in-law of Mohammed, succeeded in getting himself acclaimed caliph, and thereupon a period of civil wars began. Two rival candidates who raised the standard of insurrection in Irak were speedily disposed of; but a more formidable enemy arose in Moawiya, the governor of Syria, who made it his mission to avenge the murdered caliph on the heads of those who had instigated or connived at the crime and profited by it. Ali's supporters were made up of incompatible elements; when he yielded to the dictation of one party he alienated the other;[1] he had, indeed, to put down a formidable revolt in his own army while the decisive struggle with Moawiya was still pending. Moawiya was much stronger in material resources and had a united following. Before the unequal conflict reached its inevitable issue, Ali was murdered (January, 661); in the summer of that year Moawiya entered Cufa and received the oath of allegiance as the "Chief of the Believers." In the course of a few years Moawiya made himself master of the whole Moslem world. He established the seat of government at Damascus, and his successors ruled there for nearly a century, until, in 750, the Omayyad caliphate of Damascus gave place (except in Spain) to the Abbasid caliphate of Bagdad.

The Arab armies did not, as is still sometimes imagined, march up and down the world offering mankind the dilemma, "Islam or the sword!" The Koran enjoins the Moslems to force the heathen (Arabs) to embrace the religion of the one true God; it bids them war with others till they submit to the rule of Islam; but it expressly protects the adherents

[1] See below, p. 414.

of the book-religions, Judaism and Christianity,[1] in the exercise of their religion. The Moslem conquests were not, in fact, inspired by fanaticism, nor marked by sanguinary excesses, as wars go. The capitulation of Jerusalem to Omar in 636 stands out in strong contrast to the ruthless massacre of Jews and Moslems when the crusaders took the city in 1099 A. D. The protected populations had to pay a capitation tax, and taxes on the lands, which were left in their possession, the Moslems being at the beginning regarded as an army of occupation encamped on conquered territory, and not allowed to acquire real property. The early caliphs were not at all zealous for the conversion of tax-paying Christians or Zoroastrians into tax-supported Moslems; and when multitudes began to go over to the religion of their masters, the rulers were seriously embarrassed by a movement which upset their theory and curtailed their finances.

The Moslems were compelled to take over the administrative machinery they found in operation in the conquered countries with its organised staff of secretaries and clerks. Thus, in Syria and Egypt the officials through whom the business of government was carried on were Christians, Greeks and Copts; in Irak, Persians. Some of these officials rose out of the bureaus to positions of confidence and responsibility; the father of John of Damascus, the greatest theologian of the Greek church, held a high station at the Omayyad court, and the son was educated for the same career. More than one of the caliphs entertained himself by listening to discussions between Moslems, Jews, and Christians, on the distinctive features of their respective religions and their relative merits; and the development of Mohammedan theology itself gives ample evidence of intellectual intercourse between Moslem and Christian thinkers. Fanaticism is, indeed, the last sin of which history can accuse the Omayyad caliphs, and if there were among the Abbasids some gloomy bigots, it is well to remember that they persecuted dissident Moslems with more zeal than

[1] Zoroastrianism, also, was included in the category.

other religions. Compared with the Christian emperors in
Constantinople or the Sassanian kings of Persia, it may
fairly be said that Moslem rule was tolerant in principle and
habitually tolerant in practice.

The Koran is anything but a complete body of legislation
for the Moslem theocracy. Some matters of prime importance in religion, such as the forms of worship, are not in it
at all, and the same is true in the secular sphere. Mohammed regulated these matters by his word and example, not
by revelation. Every one in Medina knew them by daily
observation; but when the years of rapid expansion came,
and multitudes of converts in other cities and among the
Bedouin tribes had to be instructed in the ways of Islam,
differences of observance arose, small, perhaps, but none the
less points of dissension. When Arabs from many tribes,
with their inherited peculiarities of custom and law, were
brought together in the armies and the standing camps,
these differences also easily became contentious. In the
conquered lands, amid populations of other races, with
civilisations of their own, many new questions came up for
which there was no provision in the Koran.

It was natural that on many points the custom of the
community in Medina, which had been shaped under the
eyes and by the hand of Mohammed himself, should be
taken as a pattern and guide, and that inquiries should be
made of such as had lived there in the days of the Prophet,
how they did this or that in Medina. Often not only was
the practice reported, but utterances of Mohammed bearing
on the matter were alleged. Much in the Koran itself was
obscure—the reading, the sense, the occasion—and here also
the associates of the Prophet were often the only ones who
could explain, and end dispute. Tradition, thus, almost from
the first moment, became an authority, supplementing revelation and interpreting it.

The volume of tradition swelled with portentous rapidity.
That part of it which reports custom and precedent is called
Sunna; that which preserves sayings of the Prophet is

Hadith, "tradition" in the narrower sense. For the authentication of a tradition it was soon established as a principle that it should be transmitted by an unbroken series of attestors, reaching back to one of the companions of the Prophet. Besides this formal criterion, the trustworthiness of the source was taken into account; some of the companions were discovered to have suspiciously fertile memories, and some of the early reporters were proved to be inventive geniuses. From the first, traditions were fabricated on the right hand and the left. Every party, school, and sect in the Moslem world for centuries adduced traditions in its support; they were arrayed against one another in every controversy. The gathering, sifting, and ordering of traditions became one of the main branches of Islamic science.

For a good while it was held that traditions should be learned by heart and transmitted by word of mouth,[1] but in time the mass became too enormous for even the most capacious memory, and recourse to writing became imperative. The earliest collections of this kind aimed at comprehensiveness rather than strict verification; they took in traditions on every subject—on the Prophet, the Koran, rites and ceremonies, law, theology, morals, and manners—arranged under the names of the contemporaries of Mohammed to whom they were attributed, and prefixing in every instance the complete line of transmission.[2] A more convenient classification, by subjects, was, however, soon introduced, and more serious effort was made to exclude the spurious and note the dubious.

Six such collections came to be generally recognised as authoritative. The highest repute is enjoyed by those of Bukhari (d. 870 A. D.) and Muslim (d. 875), which are supposed to contain only "sound," that is well-authenticated

---

[1] The oral Law of the Jews, the Mishna and Talmud, is an analogous case.

[2] The Musnad of Ibn Hanbal is an example of this type; in print it fills six stout volumes.

traditions. These two collections include historical, doctrinal, and ethical material, as well as legal. Most of the
others confine themselves more strictly to legal traditions,
including under that term the norms of religious observance
as well as matters of civil law.

Moslem law is based upon revelation and tradition—the
Koran and the Sunna. In the development of jurisprudence, the school of Medina and those that followed it went
on the principle that everything should be grounded in tradition, or at least confirmed by it. Others, in dealing with
the new problems that arose out of new circumstances, gave
larger scope to deduction and analogy, and allowed a place
to juristic speculation. The latter school shows in many
ways the influence of the principles and method of Roman
law. Moslem law has also everywhere accommodated itself to local conditions and customs, which under the name
Adat or *Urf* have a considerable place in the actual law, for
example in matters of land tenure. It is an erroneous
notion that Moslem law is—or professes to be—wholly
derived from the Koran, which, as a matter of fact, has no
provisions whatever for many subjects of the first importance in the legislation of a civilised state; or that it is in
fact based exclusively on revelation and tradition, Koran
and Sunna. In a modern Mohammedan state such as the
Turkish Empire, the *Sheria*, or religious law, is clearly distinguished from the civil law (*Kanun*), which has been made
from time to time by the sultans, as the Roman law was
made by the rescripts of the emperors, or is embodied in
codes drawn up by jurists and promulgated by the sultan.

Of the many schools of jurisprudence which flourished in
the early centuries of Islam, four have survived in the orthodox Moslem world to the present time: that of Abu Hanifa
(d. 767), which is generally followed in the countries under
Turkish rule and by the Sunnite Moslems in India; that of
Malik ibn Anas (d. 795), in parts of Egypt, all North Africa,
and formerly in Spain; that of al-Shafii (d. 820), in southern
Arabia and the Indian Archipelago, as well as in parts of

Egypt; that of Ibn Hanbal (d. 855), which formerly prevailed in Mesopotamia and Syria, but under Turkish influence has been gradually superseded there by the Hanifite school. The differences between these schools concern chiefly minor details of ritual, and certain points in the law of succession and inheritance, which has had a large development in Moslem jurisprudence. Although the controversy between these schools was sometimes heated, they are all recognised as orthodox and legitimate. A Moslem removing from one country to another may change the school in which he was brought up for that of his new residence without scruple and without censure. Judges sometimes give decisions according to two schools or more. The adherents of these systems are therefore by no means to be regarded as sects, by which misleading name they are sometimes called in our books.

The same mutual tolerance is manifested in other spheres. A tradition of the Prophet puts in his mouth the saying, "Differences of opinion in my religious community are a sign of the divine goodness." The agreement of the Moslem world to regard the rival schools as alike orthodox makes them so in fact. The principle which underlies this recognition is one of wide application. The agreement of the Moslem world in doctrine or practice not only makes the practice or the doctrine permissible, but puts upon it the stamp of sound orthodoxy. Here again a tradition of the Prophet is produced for authority: "My religious community will never be unanimous in error." This consensus is, in fact, the only authority for many things which are an integral part of Mohammedan religion as we know it. Even for things which are at variance with the fundamental teaching of the Koran itself, such, for example, as the worship of saints, universality is all that is necessary to make them unimpeachable. Consequently, when in the eighteenth century the Wahhabis attacked the worship of saints as pure idolatry, they were regarded by the Moslem world at large as heretics for departing from the consensus of the Moslem community, though they indubitably had the Koran on their side. Islam never developed any formal method of defining its own consensus, such as the Christian church created in its œcumenical councils. So far as there can be said to be any theory on the subject, it is that the agreement of scholars of recognised authority in any age makes their consentient opinion the expression of the consensus of the Moslem world.

The conflict between Ali and Moawiya gave rise to the first schism in Islam. Ali had in his army more than his share of the men who were animated by the religious spirit of the early believers, including many of the Koran reciters. They fought to subdue the world to the faith, not to create an empire after the fashion of the unbelievers. They could not forget that the Meccan aristocrats, Moawiya's father, Abu Sofyan, foremost among them, had been the head and front of the opposition to Islam, and had come over to it only when its triumph was sure. Under Othman these eleventh-hour Moslems had got into power, and were making the most of it to further worldly ambitions. Moawiya represented antecedents and aims that were equally obnoxious to them. But Ali could reckon on their support only so long as he satisfied their exacting notions of how a caliph ought to behave; and when in the course of the struggle he made concessions which compromised his claims, twelve thousand of them marched out of his camp and assumed a threatening attitude. From this secession they got the name Kharijites, as we might say, "Come-outers." In their view Ali had forfeited the allegiance of true Moslems.

The caliphs had hitherto been chosen by a small, self-constituted group of leaders from their own number. The Kharijites maintained that the caliph should be elected by the voice of the whole body of Moslems; the succession was not hereditary in the family of the Prophet, as some of the partisans of Ali claimed, nor was it necessary that the caliph should be of the tribe of the Koreish to which Mohammed belonged; the sole necessity was that he should be the

worthiest man.   The Chief of the Believers must be distinguished by exemplary obedience to the law of God as revealed by his Prophet.   If he failed in this requirement, he
should be deposed and a better chosen in his place.

The question of the legitimate caliph brought with it the
question of the true Moslem.   As the Kharijites saw it, the
great mass of those who bore the name had not the root of
the matter in them.   The profession of Islam, they contended, was not enough to make a man a Moslem, nor the
outward observances of religion; the true Moslem is one
who makes the will of God the rule of his life.   A professed
Moslem who is guilty of grave sin is, notwithstanding the
faith he avows, an unbeliever.   In their sectarian self-consciousness they were the only true Moslems; the rest were
apostates, on whom it was their business to execute the
sentence of God, which was writ plain in the Koran.   The
thorough branch of the Kharijites held that even the infant
children of "unbelievers," that is, of other Moslems, should
be ruthlessly slain; a more moderate sentiment was that
they should be left to grow up, and then given their choice
between adhesion to (Kharijite) Islam or death.   Like all
zealots, they could never agree among themselves, but split
up in endless factions.   The most radical, who were the
very Ishmaelites of Islam, their hand against every man and
every man's hand against them, ended by being extermi-
nated by the armies of the caliphs.   Another branch early
established itself in Oman, where it still survives, and whence
it has spread to the Zanzibar coast.   Others, in the train of
the Moslem conquests, reached northwestern Africa, where
they found a grateful soil among the Berbers, and still
occupy a region about Mzab.   These Ibadites, as they are
called from the name of one of their early leaders in Bagdad, have their own schools of law and theology; they do
not intermarry with other Moslems, and keep more or less
aloof from them, though they have long ceased to wage
holy war on them.

In opposition to the Kharijites, who allowed neither

peace here nor salvation hereafter to such as did not live as good Moslems should, there were many who deemed it presumptuous thus to forestall the judgment of God. A man who professed Islam and conformed to its observances was to be treated as a Moslem; whether he was a true believer they left it to God to decide at the last day. They were called Murjites, "Postponers." By these controversies the questions, What makes a man a Moslem? (What is *islām?*) What is faith (*īmān*)? were bequeathed to the schools.

The first conflicts over freedom and necessity, also, had their origin in practical issues rather than in theoretical reflections on the sovereignty of God and the nature of man. The doctrine that the powers that be are ordained of God was naturally in favour with the powers themselves; and no less agreeable to them was the doctrine that their doings also were decreed by God, so that resistance to them, and even criticism of them, was an impiety. Such determinism could quote the Koran, and tradition adduced sayings of Mohammed more explicitly affirming it. In opposition to this convenient dogma, which made the rulers irresponsible instruments of the inscrutable divine will, man's power over his own actions, and consequently his responsibility for them, was asserted. It is narrated that two disciples of Hasan al-Basri one day came to him with the lamentation: "These kings[1] (the Omayyad caliphs) shed the blood of Moslems and seize their goods, and then say that what they do is decreed by God!" whereat Hasan exclaimed, "By God, the enemies of God lie!" One of these disciples was afterward put to death for the treasonable heresy of affirming that man has power over his own actions. The problem thus raised was the subject of long and heated controversy before the rigorous determinist dogma was finally established.

Other influences contributed to give discussion a wider range and a more academic character. In Syria particu-

[1] "King" was an opprobrious name, as "despot" or "tyrant" to us.

larly, Moslems, in their eager quest for knowledge, made acquaintance of Christian theology with its background of Greek philosophy, and in friendly or controversial discussion were put upon many problems, some of them common to both religions, others peculiar to their own.   Under such stimulus to thinking they commenced to reason about them for themselves and make the beginning of a Moslem theology.   Their enterprise was viewed with undisguised suspicion by the most, especially by the jurists, accustomed to treat the Koran and traditions as final authorities.   As always, the mass of simple believers was on the same side; the very idea of reasoning about matters of faith savoured to them of unbelief.   The incipient theologians were stigmatised as "Debaters," with a depreciatory connotation— men who argued about things that God had put beyond argument by revelation.

It must be admitted that the tendency of the most influential school of thinkers in the second century of the Moslem era was not such as to reassure men who had an antipathy to all philosophising about religion.   For the Mutazilites, as they were called, did what is always suspicious in a religion of authority, they admitted reason as a source of knowledge by the side of sense and revelation; and, having done so, took the next inevitable step and made reason the criterion of truth and right.   In this sense they may be called the rationalists of Islam.[1]   They accepted the Koran as a divine revelation, and held that everything in it, when rightly interpreted, must be in accord with reason, which meant, as the same formula has meant in Christian theology, that everything in Scripture must be so interpreted as to make it accord with reason.

The name they gave themselves, the Party of Equity and Unity, fairly expresses their aims.   They were concerned to purify the idea of God by rejecting all conceptions that seemed to conflict with the unity and uniqueness of the godhead, and everything inconsistent with God's justice and

[1] More exactly, rational supranaturalists.

27

fair-dealing toward his creatures. It is an evidence of the religious character of the movement that the Mutazilites were at the outset much more interested in the ethical part of the programme than in the metaphysical.

We have seen that at an earlier time the freedom of man's will, or, in their own phrase, man's origination of his actions, had been affirmed, in order that evil-doers and oppressors might not put off the responsibility for their wrong-doing upon God. The Mutazilites reasoned also that if man's actions were determined, it would be unjust in God to punish him for them. The premise of their argument was, that God must be just, that is, he must do what the common sense and conscience of men deem just. To the orthodox Moslem that was an enormous presumption. For him, as for Mohammed, God was the absolute monarch of the world he had made, and had a right to do as he pleased with his creatures. To say "*must*" about God was little short of blasphemy; it was to set limits—and the limits of a human judgment—upon his godhead. It was plain, too, that in the affirmation of man's freedom and ability the fundamental doctrine of predestination was nullified.

The Mutazilites went farther in the same path. God having created men—as it must be supposed that he did— with the beneficent purpose of bringing them to blessedness, it was incumbent on him to reveal to them the way of salvation. The sending of the Prophet was what they called "necessary grace"—a phrase that sounds much like a *contradictio in adjecto*. It must be assumed universally that in everything that God does he has the best interest of his creatures in view, and that everything that befalls us, seen from his point of view, which comprehends all, is for the best.[1] There is a great deal in the world that seems to defy so benevolent an interpretation, but, with the compensations of the future life to appeal to, the Mutazilites came off pretty well with their theodicy. Some of them found further relief in an adaptation of theories of transmigration and of

[1] The affinity to Stoic doctrine will be noted.

the fall of souls,[1] doctrines which served them to explain also the sufferings of animals.

If the conservative Moslem, whether simple-minded or juristically sophisticated, was asked why this action was good and that bad, his answer was: "Because God has commanded the one and forbidden the other." The distinction between right and wrong, they maintained, is arbitrarily created by the will of God, and men know what is right and wrong only through revelation. The rationalists, on the contrary, held that man by reason, apart from revelation, recognises some actions as good and right and others as bad and wrong. This difference is independent of God's will; he does not make a thing good by commanding it, but he commands it because it is good. Not only this, but there is a natural knowledge of God—his existence, his character, and his will—which man in the exercise of reason may attain, and is bound to attain; if he does not, he deserves eternal punishment. The heathen are not punished for their ignorance of a revelation that had not come to them, but because they closed their eyes to the light of nature.[2]

The common idea of God was crudely anthropomorphic. Taking the words of the Koran in their natural sense, men imagined God sitting upon a throne in heaven, a being with hands and feet, eyes and ears; a body, therefore, and some doctors of repute did not hesitate to say a body of flesh and blood. To the Mutazilites this material image of God was idolatrous. The language of revelation, they held, is figurative, accommodated to the incapacity of gross minds for philosophical ideas. God is not *somewhere* in space and time, he is infinité and eternal; and anthropomorphic notions, which impose upon him the limitations of a magnified humanity, are a real denial of his godhead. The vision of God in Paradise which the Koran promises is a spiritual

---

[1] Transmigration they might have got from the Indian religions; the combination with the fall of souls, however, is a Greek peculiarity.

[2] Compare Paul's argument in the first chapter of Romans.

vision, not a seeing with the eyes of sense; for God is not a sensible object. To the ordinary Moslem, who could not imagine what a spiritual vision might be, this was a rationalistic denial of the explicit words of revelation; they made the literal seeing of God a touchstone of orthodoxy.

The plain mind and the juristic exegetes took the attributes of God as literally as his members. To God's wisdom, for example, they ascribed a substantive existence; they made of it, in the language of Christian theology, an eternal hypostasis. The Mutazilites rejected this conception as irreconcilable with the unity of the godhead: an eternal divine Wisdom is another god, like the persons of the Christian Trinity. How the attributes of God can be conceived so as not to impair the unity of the godhead was a problem which Mutazilite thinkers solved for themselves in different ways. God, some said, was omniscient, not by an accessory attribute of omniscience, but omniscience was his essence; others taught that omniscience was an aspect of his essence; or a state, or mode, of his essence. The resemblance of some of these theories to certain Christian Trinitarian speculations is obvious, and did not escape Moslem critics. It is probably not a mere coincidence; Moslem theologians were not unacquainted with the discussions of the divine attributes by Christian theologians.

One of the heresies of the Mutazilites which was peculiarly abhorred by the orthodox was about revelation. Mohammed's idea of revelation was derived from Jews and Christians, and, since both had their revelations in Scriptures (the Law and the Gospel), he conceived that a book was the highest form of revelation. From the same source he learned that revelations were delivered to the prophets by angels, particularly by the angel Gabriel. The account he gave of his own revelations conformed to this preconceived type. The "korans" (texts) which God "sent down" to him from time to time by the hand of Gabriel were chapters from a book. God himself was the author of this book, the heavenly original of which was inscribed by the hand of

God (like the Decalogue in Exodus) on a "carefully preserved tablet."[1] The Prophet repeated to his followers what was thus sent down piecemeal; they learned the words by heart or wrote them down; in his later years at Medina he dictated them to a secretary. After his death, as we have seen, the revelations were compiled and put together in a volume to which as a whole the name Koran is given.

It was not long before the Koran, that is to say, the original in heaven, was declared to be eternal. It was Jewish doctrine that the Law existed before the creation of the world, not as an idea in the mind of God, but in a kind of suprasensible reality; but it was created. Christian theology, on the other hand, spoke much of an uncreated and eternal Word of God (Logos), and it is quite possible that the early Moslems who heard these phrases thought that they meant the Christian Scriptures, and, not to be outdone, applied the predicates to their own Koran—*it* was the eternal, uncreated Word of God.

To the Mutazilites this seemed to give the Koran an independent existence, in conflict with the fundamental dogma of the unity of God. The ultraorthodox doctrine of the uncreated Koran was, they asserted, the worst kind of infidelity, polytheism was the only word for it. In excess of zeal for the Word of God, some of their opponents went so far as to declare that the Koran men read or recited was uncreated too. The Mutazilite view was that the original in heaven was created in time. The Korans in men's hands are produced by men; their authority lies in the fact that they reproduce the contents of the original. No controversy of the age was hotter than this. The caliph Mamun in 827–'28 A. D. proclaimed it a heresy to maintain the uncreated Koran; an inquisition was set in operation, and those who persisted in their error were excluded from office, their testimony was not taken in court, and the most obstinate or outspoken were imprisoned. Within a generation the tables were turned, and Mutawakkil (847–'61), per-

[1] That is, protected from alteration.

422

MOHAMMEDANISM

secuted the Mutazilites for the heresy of maintaining that the Koran was created.

The rationalistic attitude of the Mutazilites appears also in their eschatology. Most of them interpreted Mohammed's paradise of the senses figuratively; others hit upon the happy notion that every one will find the kind of a heaven he is capable of appreciating; so long as the thinker might have an intellectual heaven, he was willing that the others should enjoy the Huris. They had greater difficulty with eternal punishment, and various opinions were held about it. Feeling the disproportion between the deeds of a lifetime and an eternity of consequences, some taught that when men had been rewarded or punished in the measure of their desert, heaven and hell would cease to be; others believed in the ultimate annihilation of the wicked; still others held to a kind of conditional immortality—at the resurrection all but true believers will turn to dust. The presence of children in hell was also a disputed point; it was thought by some that those who would have been unbelievers if they had grown up were justly sent thither.

The Mutazilites enlist our sympathy for their endeavour to give prevalence in Islam to a purer and morally worthier idea of God and his dealing with men. But it must be acknowledged that they were trying to put new wine into old bottles, and, as often in like cases, their opponents saw more clearly than they what would happen to the bottles.

The orthodox, "the party of tradition," as they called themselves, the intellectual leaders of which were the jurists, maintained for a long time their logical attitude of opposition to all reasoning about matters of religion; their answer to all arguments was an appeal to authority. In the tenth century of our era, however, conservative thinkers undertook to combat the rationalists with their own weapons and construct systems of theology that should be at once orthodox and reasonable; and though the authoritarians regarded these attempts with great suspicion, it had finally to be allowed that the method was justified by the results.

The most famous name among these founders of an orthodox Moslem theology is al-Ashari, who died at Bagdad in
935 A. D. Al-Ashari was reared in a conservative atmosphere, but as a young man he studied under al-Jubbai,
then the most eminent Mutazilite professor in Bagdad, and
distinguished himself by his controversial ability, which he
demonstrated not only in disputations but in several books
written to expound and maintain Mutazilite positions.
Forty years old, and one of the shining lights of liberal
theology, he suddenly made a public recantation in the
Friday mosque in Bagdad; and thenceforth to the end of his
life devoted all his powers to the demolition of rationalism
and the defence of orthodoxy.

Such sudden conversions are a favourite subject of legend,
the formation of which often begins with the subject himself.[1] The story of al-Ashari's conversion is told with
numerous variations and embellishments; a standing feature
is the appearance of the Prophet to him in a dream, commanding him to write in defence of the revealed truth.[2]
What actually wrought his change of heart is not known.
His former allies, whom he now assailed with a violence not
unusual in converts, accused him of various unworthy motives, but there is no reason to question his sincerity. He
connected himself with the legal school of the Hanbalites,
the narrowest and most bigoted of all, and took pains to
emphasise this association by way of a guarantee of his
unimpeachable orthodoxy.

We have seen that the Mutazilites got over the anthropomorphic expressions of the Koran by taking them figuratively; the hand of God, for instance, is a metaphor for his

[1] Familiar examples are those of Paul and Augustine; another notable
Moslem case is al-Ghazali, on whom see below, pp. 459 f.

[2] The point of the vision is that al-Ashari should not abandon the
dialectic method (kalām), but defend by it the true doctrine. The
story has the marks of an apology addressed to critics who thought that
when he turned his back on the liberals he should at the same time
have renounced their manner of disputation and fallen into the ranks
of the authoritarians whose only argument was, "so it is in revelation
and tradition."

power or his beneficence. The ultraliteralists contended that it was a real hand like a man's. Al-Ashari taught that when the Koran speaks of the hand of God, it is to be taken literally, not metaphorically; but in what manner, it was not for man to speculate. It must be believed without asking how, and without conceiving God in the likeness of man;[1] for the Koran explicitly declares that God does not resemble anything in the universe. The controversy between the rationalists and the traditionalists had been peculiarly keen over the passages in the Koran in which God is represented as sitting on a celestial throne. The literalists held that it must be believed as an article of the orthodox faith that God is literally seated on a literal throne, which is the fixed place where he rests; the Mutazilites took all such language metaphorically. Al-Ashari asserted the inscrutable reality of the throne and of the sitting, while affirming that God was not a body in space. No more after the creation of the throne than before, was his presence limited to one place; nor in his sitting on the throne was he upheld by it, but it was upheld by him.

About the hereafter al-Ashari's position seems to have been that revelation is the only possible source of information; reason knows nothing of the other world or what happens there, and should not pretend to improve on what God has disclosed. The Mutazilites, as we have seen, rationalised the Moslem eschatology, and turned more or less of its picturesque Paradise into figures of speech. Al-Ashari appears here to go the whole way with the traditionalists; the Prophet's pool, where believers arriving in Paradise slake their thirst, is a reality; the balances in which men's deeds are weighed are real; the automatic judgment-bridge is real; the inquisition at the tomb by the angels Munkar and Nakīr is no fable or metaphor.[2] Belief in all

[1] This formula, "Without (thinking) how, and without making him like (anything)," was found to be of great virtue in steering a course between "is" and "is not."
[2] See below, p. 475.

these realities is imperative; they are formally introduced into the creed. With regard to the vision of God in Paradise, the denial of which was in the eyes of the orthodox one of the most scandalous heresies of the Mutazilites, al-Ashari again tries to find the safe middle path: God will in some mysterious way really be seen, but not as the vulgar think, with eyes of flesh and blood; the seeing is a kind of knowing or intellectual apprehension.

When it comes to the idea of God and his attributes, the influence of al-Ashari's education appears in more substantial concessions to reason. The realism of the common mind made the attributes of God, metaphysical and moral indiscriminately, and even the descriptive predicates, a kind of entities, having a substantive existence beside God. To the Mutazilites, as has been shown above, accessory attributes were irreconcilable with the unity of God. Al-Ashari accepts the usual catalogue of the seven divine attributes, including seeing and hearing. He conceives them, not as mere names which men give to different aspects of the divine being and activity, nor as modes of the divine existence, but as real and eternal distinctions inherent in the essence of God, and neither identical with the essence nor existing apart from it. In this way he strives to find the mean between the literalists, who seem to separate the attributes from the being of God, and the rationalists, who seem to leave to the attributes no real existence at all.

In the question which had been so hotly controverted between the Mutazilites and the traditionalists, whether the word of God was created or uncreated, al-Ashari made a distinction which has become the accepted solution in Moslem theology. The word (speech) of God, as an idea in God, is uncreated and eternal; but the words of the Koran as recited or read, and its written letters and words, are produced in time and by men. This theory seemed more rational than even that of the rationalists, who held that the Koran was created by God in time, before its revelation to Mohammed, and it was adopted not only by al-Ashari's immediate successors, but by al-Ghazali. Only the extreme literalists continued to affirm that the paper and the ink and the writing and all that was between the covers of the Holy Book were uncreated.

Al-Ashari held with the orthodox against the Mutazilites that good and evil, belief and unbelief, happen according to the decree and by the almighty power of God. But he goes beyond predestination to a determinism of the most rigid kind. God is for him the only creator, the only being in the universe who has the power to produce or originate. He is the creator of men *and of their acts*.[1] This is true, not only in the physical but in the intellectual sphere. The conclusion which we reach by logical reasoning is not the necessary outcome of the reasoning, but is created in our minds by God. Man has in himself no natural power to act at all; the power to act is in each case momentarily created in him by God. In what we regard as voluntary acts, God creates in man, in addition to the power to act, a power of choice; and in accordance with man's choice, God creates the act itself, so that the potentiality, the choice, and the act are the work of God. All the acts of man are therefore not merely predetermined, they are effectuated by God. An illustration is taken from a man who is writing: God creates first the potentiality of moving the pen; then, the will to move it; third, the bodily motion of the hand; and fourth, the motion of the pen. Man conceives himself to act voluntarily in the exercise of the power of choice and that the act is his own. In reality, the power of choice is created, the choice determined, the act effected, by God; man's participation in it is solely that of appropriation (*kasb*), by which, in his own mind, he makes the choice and the act his.

This theory evidently makes God the immediate and occasional creator of evil as well as of good, and al-Ashari courageously accepts this consequence.[2] His old Mutazilite

[1] Koran 37, 94.
[2] On a similar courage in Luther, see above, p. 317.

teacher, al-Jubbai, held that God was by nature incapable of doing or causing evil; on the contrary, God must will for all his creatures what is for their best interest. Several anecdotes are told to show how al-Ashari, after his conversion, cornered his old teacher with the difficulties of this optimistic theory. According to al-Ashari, God wills the unbelief of the unbeliever, creates it in him, and damns him for it, as truly as he creates the belief of the believer and, of his grace, rewards him for it in Paradise.

Al-Ashari abolishes the category of causality altogether, by making everything that occurs in the inner or outer world the immediate and isolated act of God. Nothing in nature has such a property that, by virtue of this property, it produces an effect. Thus, when a man touches ice, it is not the ice, by virtue of the property of coldness in it, that causes the sensation of cold, but God who produces in man this sensation; and if—so we read in a modern orthodox catechism—God should at any time prefer to do so, he might cause a man to have the sensation of a burning heat when he touched ice. There is no such thing as law in nature, not to say law *of* nature. All we can affirm is that certain antecedents are usually followed by certain consequents because God commonly acts in this way; but there is no other connection between the antecedent and the consequent than our observation of this sequence in the usual way of God. From these premises, miracle is not a violation of natural law or a breach in the law of causality—for there are no such things—but merely an act of God unfamiliar to our experience.

The Mutazilites had held that right and wrong are distinguished by the reason and conscience of mankind, apart from all revelation; that men are under obligation to make this distinction and conduct themselves accordingly; and that if they do not do so they are justly punished. Al-Ashari, with the old orthodox, maintained, on the contrary, that right and wrong are known only through revelation, and that actions are right, not because of anything in their nature or ours, but because God has commanded them, and wrong only because he has forbidden them. On the vexed question of faith and unbelief, al-Ashari holds that every one who turns in prayer towards Mecca is presumptively a Moslem, and is not to be regarded as an unbeliever because he is guilty even of such sins as fornication, theft, and wine-drinking. Only one who commits such sins, *holding them to be permitted*, is an unbeliever. Faith (*īmān*) is a narrower concept than Islam; it includes confession in words and the evidence of works, and is thus capable of increase and decrease. Al-Ashari again sides with the traditional schools against the Mutazilites in maintaining the reality of magic and witchcraft, the belief in demons and their doings, and in the miracles of the saints.

An attempt similar to al-Ashari's to provide Islam with a rational orthodox theology was made by his contemporary, al-Maturidi (d. 944), in distant Samarkand. His writings seem to have almost all been lost. Later writers have transmitted to us lists of the points of difference between the two systems; and a Maturidite creed by al-Nasafi (d. 1142) is still used in schools in parts of the Turkish Empire.[1] The differences are, in part, matters of words rather than substance; and in so far as they are substantial, concern chiefly minor points of controversy. Al-Maturidi denied, for example, that God can impose upon man an obligation to do the impossible, which al-Ashari affirmed. Again, for al-Maturidi "appropriation" has a somewhat different sense from that which al-Ashari gives it. The reader who is curious about other differences may compare for himself the creeds of al-Ashari and al-Nasafi printed in the appendix to Macdonald's "Muslim Theology."

The conservative jurists did not exhibit much gratitude towards al-Ashari for his attempt to make Moslem doctrine rationally tenable, and his followers were not seldom included with the Mutazilites in one comprehensive condem-

---

[1] It was published by Cureton in 1843; a translation in Macdonald, Muslim Theology, pp. 308 *ff*.

nation and commination. Within fifty years after his death, however, his doctrine was widely accepted in Irak, whence it spread into Persia—then under Seljuk rule—and westward into Syria and Egypt; in North Africa and Spain it first gained a firm footing through the influence of Ibn Tumart (d. 1128) at the beginning of the sixth century of the Moslem era.

Among those who came after and developed the system of al-Ashari, the most noteworthy was al-Bakilani. On the divine attributes he adopted the modalistic theory of Abu Hashim: the attributes are modes of the divine being which cannot be conceived apart from it, but import no plurality in the godhead inasmuch as they have in themselves no substantive existence. To him is also attributed the introduction of the atomistic theory, which subsequently became so general that Maimonides ascribes it to all the Moslem dogmaticians. All things are composed of atoms, which are in all respects alike. With the atomic doctrine of matter went necessarily the theory of void space. He held the theory of the atomic subdivision of time, also. Two other propositions are attributed to him by Ibn Khaldun; namely, that an accident cannot inhere in an accident (contrary to Aristotle), and that an accident does not last for two consecutive moments of time. Motion, like space and time, is discontinuous.

The relation of all this to the Asharite doctrine of creation is evident. God brings together the atoms in a body and simultaneously creates its accidents. Since the accidents cannot endure for more than one atom of time, and substance without accidents is inconceivable, it follows that an object which appears to us to be permanent is in reality created anew by God in every instant of time, and if he should for a moment cease to exercise this continuous creative activity, the body would cease to exist. Thus, also, every act of man is not only immediately created by God (al-Ashari), but is momentarily created and recreated by him. What is true of single objects or accidents is true of the universe as a whole; it is created anew by God every instant. There is no such thing as causal connection or natural law, nothing but the arbitrary act of the Creator. Nothing in nature, therefore, is constant; and nothing is impossible. If God willed it so, anything might be the next moment endowed with accidents or properties the exact opposite of those which in our experience it possesses. By this doctrine of the atomic constitution of matter and the momentaneity of accidents, Bakilani believed himself to have provided a theoretical basis and explanation for the doctrine of God's sole and universal creative activity.

CHAPTER XVIII

MOHAMMEDANISM

THE PARTISANS OF ALI

Ali—The Legitimist Party—Infallible Authority of the Imam—His Nature—Doctrine of the Return of the Imam—The Imam-Mahdi—Shiite Sects—Differences between Shiites and Sunnites.

AMONG those who supported the claims of Ali to the caliphate and afterward maintained his cause against Moawiya there were some who were moved by personal considerations. Ali had been one of the early believers at Mecca and one of the staunchest adherents of the Prophet. As a general, he was not the equal of some of the other Moslem leaders, but as a champion in single combat, he had distinguished himself on many fields. A popular saying ran: "There is no sword but Dhu al-Faḳār,[1] and no paladin but Ali." In the first election, which resulted in the choice of Abu Bekr, there were some who, on such grounds, thought that Ali should have been the man. There was also a legitimist party who held that the successor of Mohammed should be of his own family. Ali was Mohammed's cousin, and husband of the Prophet's daughter, Fatima. Thus, both by blood and by marriage, he was nearest of kin to Mohammed. When Ali fell under the dagger of a Kharijite assassin, this party gave its allegiance to Hasan, Ali's son by Fatima, and when Hasan renounced his claim, preferring security and luxury on an ample pension to the doubtful issue of a conflict with Moawiya, they transferred their loyalty to his younger brother, Husein. Husein allowed himself to be drawn from the safety of the Holy Cities to head a hopeless revolt at Kufa, and fell at Kerbela (680), in the eyes of his partisans a martyr in the holy cause. A more serious, though in the end unsuccessful revolt in Irak,

---

[1] The name of Ali's sword.

headed by Mukhtar and supported not only by Arabs but
by many of the native Persian converts to Islam, put forward as the legitimate successor a son of Ali by another
wife, Mohammed ibn al-Hanafiyya.

The principle of legitimacy soon assumed a religious as
well as a political aspect. In the eyes of this party the
successor of Mohammed was not merely the caliph, vicar
of the Apostle of God as the head of the theocratic Moslem
state, who commanded its armies, protected its borders,
administered and enforced its laws, civil and religious; he
was the Imam, the successor of the Prophet as the religious
head of the Moslem world. To this office, they asserted,
Ali was formally appointed by Mohammed; consequently,
the first three caliphs, elected by the companions of the
Prophet, were not only illegitimate in the political sense,
but their rule was from the religious point of view a usurpation by which the true Imam was set aside. The usurpers
and their aiders and abettors thereby put themselves outside the pale of Islam; and to this day it is the mark of
orthodoxy among the great body of the followers of Ali
(Shia) to curse Abu Bekr, Omar, and Othman, in the public
prayers in their mosques.

The legitimate Imam is for them not only the supreme
religious authority, but an infallible authority. God, they
argued, cannot have left the Moslem world to determine
what is true doctrine and sound practice by study and discussion or the vague principle of consensus; he must have
given it an infallible guide, not merely at the beginning,
but in every generation. This infallible guide is the "Imam
of the Age," and to recognise this Imam and submit to him
in all things is the prime religious obligation of every true
Moslem. The Imam is not only infallible in his deliverances on doctrine and practice, he is endowed with sinless
perfection. Mohammed did not claim such perfection for
himself; he speaks of himself as a man like other men, and
urges men to repentance by his own example. But among
his followers the belief that he was without sin early arose.

Some held that he was exempt even from sinful impulses, and the question was debated in the schools whether he was above all sorts of mistakes. Among orthodox Moslems, however, the Prophet's freedom from sin or from error, however far it extended, was ascribed to the singular favour of God, who bestowed it upon him of his grace. The Imam of the Shiites, on the contrary, is sinless as well as infallible *by nature*. One view widely entertained even among the more moderate Shiites was that a particle of substantial divine light was implanted by God in Adam, from whom it was transmitted by a kind of traducianism to elect descendants of his in different ages down to Abdallah and Abu Talib, between whom it was divided, passing to their sons, Mohammed and Ali; from Ali, in whose sons by Fatima the divided lines reunited, it descended generation by generation, to the successive Imams of the Age. It is, indeed, the presence of this particle of divine light in the substance of his soul which makes him the Imam, and gives him the spiritual qualities which raise him above the common ranks of men.

The more extreme sects of the Shiites, the "Ultras," as they are called by the other Shiites as well as by the Sunnites, are not content with this theory of a divine element in the soul of the Imam. For them, Ali and the Imams are incarnations of the godhead; and some of them have gone so far as to hold, not only that one and the same God has from age to age manifested himself in many human forms, but even that the body in which this manifestation has taken place is the same identical body.

Such extravagances, which may be called the radical Gnosticism of Islam, have always been condemned by the main body of the Shiites; but they have embodied themselves in sects, some of which have diverged so widely from Mohammedanism that they are more properly to be regarded as derivative religions.

A doctrine which is held in one form or another by all branches of the Shiites is "the return," which resembles the

28

Jewish expectation of the return of Elijah and the Christian belief in the return of Christ. According to Moslem writers, the first promulgator of the doctrine was a certain Abdallah ibn Saba, a Jewish convert to Islam, which would incline us to look for its starting-point in Jewish ideas; but in its development Christian influence is unmistakable. After the death of Ali, some of his followers asserted that he was not really dead, but had been taken up into the clouds of heaven, whence he would presently return to take vengeance on his enemies and establish the reign of justice on earth. A similar belief attached itself to Mukhtar's Imam, Mohammed ibn al-Hanafiyya, who was said not to have died, but to have withdrawn to a valley called Radwa, in the mountains seven days' journey from Medina, where he waited the hour determined by God for his return. The poets describe this abode of the Concealed Imam in language plainly derived from the Messianic prophecy in Isaiah 11: leopards and lions graze beside cattle and goats, which feed without fear in the same meadow with beasts of prey and slake their thirst at the same drinking-place, precisely as in orthodox Mohammedan belief, at the end of time, when Jesus shall return and bring in the golden age, "Lions and camels, tigers and oxen will graze peacefully together."

The belief that the Imam had not died was not the only form in which the expectation of his return was entertained; some Shiites adopted the theory of the transmigration of souls, in accordance with which it was possible at the same time to admit that the Imam had really died and that he would return. In time, however, the doctrine of the Concealed Imam, who was somewhere alive and waiting the day of his reappearance, prevailed among the principal Shiite sects. The Moslem books on the history of sects abound in such notices as this: Such and such a sect (bearing the name of its Imam) holds that So-and-So (their Imam) "never died, nor ever will die until he has filled the earth with justice as it is now filled with injustice." [1]

[1] It was the caliphs—in the beginning, the Omayyads, later the Abbasids of Bagdad—who filled the earth with injustice.

The Shiite doctrine of the return of the Imam was early combined with the common Moslem belief in the coming of the Mahdi (literally, "the one who is guided," *scil.* by God), which has an important place in orthodox eschatology. According to the common traditions, Mohammed foretold that in the last days a man of his own family, bearing the same name and the same patronymic as himself (Mohammed ibn Abdallah), should arise to establish on earth the reign of righteousness and peace.[1] The Shiites appropriated the prophecy for their Imam; when the Concealed Imam is manifested on the stage of history, he will be the Mahdi.[2]

Some branches of the Shiites did not mean by the "Concealed Imam" one who had disappeared from among men, but only a descendant of Ali whose character and office were not publicly avowed, and who was consequently known as the Imam only by the small circle who were in the secret. Such unproclaimed Imams might succeed one another for generations, until at the right time one of them appeared as the Mahdi. Thus, the founder of the Fatimid dynasty in North Africa and Egypt professed to be the descendant in the seventh generation of Mohammed ibn Jafar, the last of the recognised Imams of one of the chief branches of the Shiites, himself the seventh in succession from Ali through Husein.

The partisans of the line of Ali repeatedly rose in insurrection in the cause of one or another of their Imams, and kept up at all times a secret propaganda which did much to undermine the Omayyads and bring about their fall. The fruits of the legitimist agitation were appropriated by the descendants of Mohammed's uncle, al-Abbas, the caliphs of Bagdad, who made large capital of their descent. Some of them were not averse to taking the rôle of Imam themselves, but the genuine Shiites saw in this only one presumptuous usurpation more. They were as irreconcilable under the

[1] Some anti-Mahdist traditions identify this figure who inaugurates the golden age with Jesus: "There is no Mahdi but Jesus the son of Mary."

[2] The idea of the Imam-Mahdi was at the bottom of the Babi insurrection; see below, pp. 512 *f.*

Abbasids as they had been under their predecessors, and continued their subterranean campaign with results to which there will be occasion to return in another chapter.

Of the innumerable divisions and subdivisions of the Shiites only three need be more particularly considered. The Zeidites are named after Zeid ibn Ali ibn Husein, whom they acknowledge as the Imam instead of Mohammed al-Bakir, the fifth Imam of the other sects. They differ from the rest in denying that Mohammed designated Ali as his successor by a written instrument; the companions who elected Abu Bekr and Omar did not, therefore, deliberately set aside the will of the Prophet, however much they erred in not choosing the best man for the place. Some of them held that Ali voluntarily yielded his right to Abu Bekr and Omar, so that they were legitimate caliphs. Consequently, they do not, like the rest of the Shiites, curse Abu Bekr and Omar as usurpers and infidels. The most tolerant even extended their charity to Othman; but they all agreed in rejecting Moawiya and his successors. A Zeidite dynasty established itself in Tabaristan in 864 A. D., and ruled that province for more than sixty years; in Dailan and Gilan they held on even longer. The Idrisids, who ruled Morocco from 788 to 985, were also Zeidites. More permanent was the sway of the Zeidite Imams in southern Arabia (Yemen), where they gained a footing at the end of the ninth century, and have maintained themselves to the present day. In theology the Zeidites, like the Shiites in general, were much influenced by the Mutazilites, and still preserve the characteristics of their doctrine.

The most important of the branches of the Shiites are the Imamites, or, as they have been commonly called in more recent times, the "Twelvers." The latter name is given them because, in distinction from their chief rivals, the "Seveners," their succession of Imams includes twelve names, beginning with Ali, Hasan, and Husein, and then in the line of Husein to the eleventh, Hasan al-Askari (died A. H. 260). The twelfth, Mohammed ibn Hasan, disappeared from among men, and is the Concealed Imam, the Mahdi who shall come. The Twelvers, who have been called the Shia High Church, have been the state religion of the kingdom of Persia since 1502. The rival sect of the "Seveners" end their series of visible Imams with Ismail ibn Jafar, the sixth in the succession recognised by the Twelvers. From them sprang the Ismailis, of whom there will be more to say hereafter.

The partisans of Ali accuse the other side of mutilating or corrupting the text of the Koran to get rid of the embarrassing passages which established the claims of Ali to the succession. According to them Othman, who supervised the redaction of the existing text of the Koran, suppressed in different places more than five hundred words of revelation, among them the explicit declaration: "Verily, Ali is the guidance." The orthodox naturally retorted on them the accusation of interpolating the text and of falsely interpreting it in favour of Ali, thus dealing with the revelation of God in the Koran as the Jews and Christians had done with their Scriptures.[1]

It is frequently said that the most salient difference between the great body of Moslems and the Shiites is that the former acknowledge and the latter deny the authority of tradition. This error, which is probably due to the fact that the orthodox Moslems call themselves Sunnites ("traditionalists"), entirely mistakes the Shiite position. The authority of tradition has no less weight with them than with the Sunnites, and a considerable part of the traditions found in the orthodox Sunna books are accepted also by the Shiites. The difference between them is that to be authoritative with the Shiites a tradition must be traced back to the "family of the Prophet," among whom Ali himself occupies the place of eminence; while for the Sunnites it is sufficient that an unbroken chain of transmitters ascends to one of the "companions of the Prophet."

In matters of ritual observance the differences between

[1] There is, in fact, no ground for the Shiite charges.

the Shiites and other Moslems are not greater than those which divide the various rites of Sunnite Islam; the main features of these observances were fully established before the schism. In the religious law, also, the differences are comparatively small. One of the most considerable is that the Shiites allow and the Sunnites disallow a form of temporary marriage (*mut'a*) which was customary among the Arabs before Mohammed and which Mohammed himself in the Koran appears to permit. According to the Sunnites, Mohammed later withdrew this permission; while the Shiites maintain that Omar unlawfully prohibited such marriages.

In their theology the Shiites are much more hospitable to Mutazilite doctrines than Sunnite orthodoxy is. The Mutazilites were especially strong in the regions where the Shiites were most numerous, and there was no Shiite al-Ashari. Notwithstanding their more liberal theology, the Shiites are much more intolerant than the orthodox Moslems.[1] One probable reason of this is the fact that many Zoroastrians were converted to Mohammedanism in its Shia form; for Zoroastrianism was a highly intolerant religion. To Zoroastrian influence is probably also to be ascribed the fact that to the Shiites all the rest of mankind, Jews, Christians, and Moslems, are unclean. To the Sunnite Moslem, animals slaughtered by Jews or Christians are clean; to the Shiite unclean. The marriage of a Moslem to a Jewish or Christian woman is permitted by the Sunna, prohibited by the Shiites.

[1] The Mutazilites themselves, when they had the power were, like many other liberals, the reverse of tolerant to the conservatives.

CHAPTER XIX

MOHAMMEDANISM

MYSTICISM AND PHILOSOPHY

Other-worldliness of Primitive Islam—Example of Christian Ascetics
—Early Sufis—Influence of Neoplatonism—The Mystic Way and
Goal—Love to God—Indian Influence—Pantheism—Essays of
the Pure Brotherhood—"Theology of Aristotle"—Moslem Aristotelians: al-Kindi, al-Farabi, Avicenna—Averroes.

Mohammed's call, as it is in one of the oldest Suras of the
Koran, was to give warning that the judgment of God was
impending upon his nation, in which none would escape
destruction save such as, renouncing their vain gods and
their evil ways, made their submission to the one true God
and did his will as revealed through his prophet. The first
believers lived in constant expectation of this great crisis
and in preparation for it. The religious exercises in which
Mohammed had engaged even before his appearance as a
prophet, and which he taught to his earliest followers, were
inspired by the sense of imminent catastrophe; fasting and
prayer were their characteristic features. The small success
of his mission at Mecca and the persecutions which he and
his followers had to endure quickened this kind of piety.
"Other-worldliness" was the ruling idea of the religion.

At Medina the circumstances of the situation to some
extent diverted the mind of Mohammed and his followers
from that world to this. Nevertheless, we should err if we
thought that the character of the religion or the sentiment
of believers underwent a radical change. The possession of
Mecca and the transformation of the Kaaba into the sanctuary of Islam, the conversion of the Arabs in town and
desert, were part of the plan of God for the establishment of

the true religion in the earth; but for pious Moslems who had imbibed the teachings and spirit of Mohammed all this was but a preparation for the last day, not the beginning of a new epoch in the history of the world. The success of these enterprises, however, and above all the wars of conquest waged by the caliphs against the Roman and Persian empires, drew to the banners of Islam multitudes whose aims and satisfactions were altogether of this world. They gained riches and power, and used them to promote the interests of their families and tribes; and if the day of judgment intruded upon their minds at all, they, like men of all times in great and sudden prosperity, postponed the uncomfortable thought to an indefinite future, or turned it into God's vengeance on the unbelievers. The consolidation of the Moslem conquests under the early Omayyads by political necessity took the form of an Arab empire, not of a theocratic socialism.

The Kharijite movement has already shown us that this historically inevitable development was obnoxious to no inconsiderable part of the Moslem community on both political and religious grounds. In that revolt the Koran reciters, who as a class clung tenaciously to the ideas and ways of primitive Islam, took a leading part. In the strife and confusion of the civil wars by which the Moslem world was rent in the second generation, it would be strange if many had not seen the signs of the end of the age, the shadow of judgment cast before.

To this native expectation of an imminent day of doom a foreign influence was added. Even in the days of heathenism, as we know from the old poets, the hermits, spending their lives in perpetual devotion, had made a deep impression on the Arabs who passed their cells as they travelled the caravan routes or rode on forays. Now, in Syria and in Irak, Moslems came in contact with Christian ascetics, living in solitude, macerating their bodies by fasting, keeping long vigils in prayer, in daily preparation for God's judgment. That in reaction from the corruption of religion

and morals which they saw on all hands many religious-
minded Moslems were inclined to an ascetic life after the
monkish pattern is convincingly attested by the great number of fictitious traditions in which the Prophet is made to
disapprove such practices, and the prominence that is given
in traditions about the companions of the Prophet to their
enjoyment of the good things of this life.   An often-quoted
tradition of Mohammed is: "There is no monkery in Islam;
the monkery of Islam is the Holy War."   Protracted fasting is condemned: "The Moslem who keeps up his bodily
strength loves God more than the weakling."   "He who
eats with gratitude to God is as good in his eyes as the faster
who abstains from eating."   Celibacy, which was the universal rule among the Christian ascetics, never had any
place in Mohammed's idea of religion, it is true; but the
traditions which condemn it are the product of other conditions than those which prevailed in Medina in his time.
To a man who had resolved upon a celibate life, Mohammed
is reported to have said: "Some of you have made up your
minds to belong to the brethren of Satan!   Either you propose to be a Christian monk; in that case, join them openly!
Or you belong to our people; then you must follow our custom (sunna).   Our custom is married life."   The use of perfumes and cosmetics was peculiarly distasteful to the ascetic
temper of many pious Moslems.   By way of contrariety,
anecdotes were current about the most admired heroes of
early Islam, telling how those holy persons used to perfume
themselves, dye their hair and beards, and deck themselves
in fine raiment.   One of the chief authorities for the traditions of Medina, Abu Hureira, for example, is said to have
used perfumes so abundantly that the children recognised
him by the smell when he passed the schoolhouse.

A more definite ascetic movement spread from Syria to
Irak early in the time of the Omayyads.   Those who addicted themselves to it were called 'Ubbād (singular, 'Ābid),
that is, men devoted to the service of God.   They fought in
the wars like the rest, but stood aloof from public life, and

some even declined their share in the distribution of spoils.
The influence of Christianity is seen not only in the outward
forms of their asceticism, but in the fact that the earliest
writings which come from these circles abound in undisguised appropriations from the New Testament, frequently
presenting themselves as traditional sayings of Mohammed.
They neither worked for a living nor begged for it, but left
it to God to give them one as he saw fit, and counted it a
peculiar virtue to take no thought for the morrow. He who
trusts God is "the child of the moment"; he neither looks
back to the past nor forward to the future. This quietism
expresses itself in their word, that man should be in the
hand of God as passive as a corpse under the hand of him
who washes it. They cultivated insensibility to hunger and
all bodily privations; if they were ill, they did not seek the
aid of a physician; the praise and blame of men was all
the same to them, and they were indifferent to the treatment they received from men. The ordinary pious Moslem
contented himself with the prescribed prayers at the appointed hours of day and night. These ascetics, on the
contrary, taking their warrant from the injunction of the
Koran, "Call God often to mind, and praise him morning
and evening" (33, 41), developed a kind of litany (*dhikr*),
most commonly made up of the names or titles of God,
which they recited, singly or in company, with endless repetition, as a means of fixing the attention constantly on God
and his attributes.

Thus far the Sufis[1] may be said to represent primitive
Moslem notions and ideals, enriched from the Gospels, and
more or less externally influenced by the forms of Christian monasticism. Among the Christian monks, however,
mysticism had early taken deep root, and doubtless through
them the Sufis got their first mystical ideas and aims. In
time, however, they came to draw more directly upon the
fountainhead of Occidental mysticism, the Neoplatonic phi-

---

[1] The name comes from their coarse woollen garb.

losophy.[1] The influx of Neoplatonism began before the end
of the second century of the Moslem era, and in the third
became the predominant intellectual element in Sufism.
One of the men who had the largest part in the creation of
this new type of Moslem mysticism was Dhu al-Nun Misri,
by race a Copt or a Nubian, whose ideas came to him through
Christian channels.[2]

This philosophy gave a new meaning and end to asceticism.
The soul, it taught, is of divine origin; here on earth and in
the body it is an alien and exile. The goal of the mystic
is liberation from the body and from the world, return to
God, union with God—a union in which the finite personality is swallowed up and lost in the infinite, and in losing
finds its true self. Individuality is the fatal illusion, the
deadly sin. The Sufis allege a tradition of the Prophet:
"Thine existence is a sin with which no other sin can be
compared." Jelal al-Din Rumi in his quatrains sings:
"In the beginning my soul and Thine were but one; my
appearance and Thine; my disappearance and Thine. It
were false to speak of 'mine' and 'Thine.' Between us the
I and the Thou have ceased to be"; and again: "I am not I,
and yet Thou art not I; I am at once I and Thou, Thou art
at once Thou and I. In relation to Thee, O beauty of
Khoten, I am bewildered whether Thou art I or I Thou."

Since the illusion of individuality is produced by the distinctive qualities, or attributes, of the individual, the aim
of the mystic is to rid himself of these: "Purify thyself from
all the attributes of self, that thou may'st behold thy glorious essence!"

This supreme goal is not to be achieved at once by an
audacious bound into the bosom of the Infinite, but only
by progressive stages in the path which has been marked by

[1] See Vol. I, pp. 533 ff.; II, pp. 207 ff. See Index s. v. "Neoplatonism."
[2] The opinion, formerly prevalent and still frequently repeated, that
Sufi pantheism was of Persian origin, a reaction, it was said, of the
Indoeuropean mind against the hard Semitic deism of Mohammedan
theology, is erroneous from every possible point of view.

those who have already attained and been made perfect. The Sufi, therefore, calls himself a wayfarer on the road which leads to "the Truth," [1] that is, the one Reality in the universe. One of the oldest comprehensive treatises on the mystic way names seven "stages" before the sublime achievement; to wit, repentance, abstinence, renunciation, poverty, patience, trust in God, satisfaction. The wayfarer must traverse these stages in succession, making himself perfect in each before he proceeds to the next. They constitute the ascetic and ethical discipline of the Sufi. The first step in the path is repentance, or conversion, which includes not only contrition for past sins against God or men, but the abandonment of them, with full resolve never again to fall into them, and reparation of the wrongs which one has done his fellows.[2] To illustrate the importance of reparation, it is told that when a man who had formerly been the governor of a province wished to become a Sufi, his spiritual director bade him first return to the province and secure the forgiveness of every one to whom he had done an injury—a task upon which he spent four years. Repentance is not merely man's turning to God; it has its origin in God's gracious turning to man. To some one who asked the Sufi poetess, Rabia, whether if he turned in penitence to God, God would turn in mercy to him, she replied: "No; but if he turn toward thee, thou wilt turn toward him."

The penitent seeker next put himself under the guidance of a director, a man of experience and approved piety, whose injunctions he followed in everything. The probationary period was sometimes extended over three years, in the first of which the novice was bidden devote himself to the service of his fellow men; in the second, to the service of God, and in the third, to watchfulness over his own thoughts. He can serve his fellow men only when he esteems all men better than himself; he can serve God only when he worships him without regard to his own advantage in this life

[1] Al-Ḥaḳḳ.
[2] So also in the Jewish doctrine of repentance.

or the other; and he can keep his own heart only when his thoughts are collected and every care dismissed, so that he can commune with God without distraction. Only after this trial was it permitted to assume the patched garment which was the distinctive dress of the dervish.[1]

Distinct from the stages of the path are the states of the mystic. The latter are not progressive attainments of man, but emotions and experiences which God bestows on man when and how he will. The treatise already quoted has ten such "states," namely, meditation, nearness to God, love, fear, hope, longing, intimacy, tranquillity, contemplation, and certainty. "They descend from God into man's heart without his being able to repel them when they come or retain them when they go." When a man has traversed all the stages of the path and experienced whatever states God is pleased to bestow upon him, only then does he enter upon that higher plane of consciousness which the Sufi calls Knowledge and Truth; only then does the seeker become the knower, in whom knower and knowing and known are identical.

This transcendental knowledge cannot be reached by the methods of sense or the speculations of philosophy, nor can it be imparted by teaching. It comes in a flash of intuition, or rather of divine illumination. Those who possess it cannot describe it, for the truth is inexpressible, inconceivable. "Strive to cast off the veil, not to augment booklore; no books will further thy intent. The germ of love to God grows not in books; shut up thy books, turn to God and repent." It is at once self-knowledge and knowledge of God, for these are not two but one; the secret lies in the realisation that the appearance of otherness is nought but illusion.

The ecstasy of this experience is often spoken of as intoxication—an exaltation and expansion in which the consciousness of self is surmounted. Still oftener, as in the mystic poetry of all ages and religions, it is in the love of God that

[1] The garment of rags is the proper garb of the Buddhist monk.

man loses himself and finds the fulfilment of his being.
Love is the principle and motive of Sufi ethics; it is, as
Jelal al-Din says, "the remedy of our pride and self-con-
ceit—the physician of all our infirmities. Only he whose
garment is rent by love becomes entirely unselfish." [1]   He
who loves God supremely sees God in all his creatures, and
expresses this divine love in all his dealings with them.
This motive alone gives meaning and worth to deeds of
charity; so long as man bestows all his goods to feed the
poor that by good works he may earn a reward in this
world or in Paradise, his works are not good.   The true
Sufi would give his life to save the life of another human
being, or even of an animal; he would endure the punishment of hell if so doing he could secure Paradise for its
inmates.[2]

The goal of the Sufi path is not the intellectual intuition
of oneness, but the emotional experience of it, the rapture
of love in the possession of the beloved, or rather in being
possessed by the beloved.   This experience is presented in
imagery borrowed from human love, not by way of inten-
tional allegory, but because it is the only language that is
poetically possible.[3]   God is the perfection of beauty; it is
this supreme beauty which inspires the mystic's love, and
it is his love which enables him to see in God beauty to
which other men are blind, just as "The Madman of Love"
in Arab poetry discerns in his mistress beauties which no
other discovers.

It must be admitted that the bacchanalian and erotic
poetry of Persian and Turkish mysticism not only often
violates the reserve which reverence seems to us to impose,
but frequently transgresses the line between religious emotion at its highest pitch and sensual passion, but that is the
standing peril of the mystical Eros.

Only by love is God known.   Revelation, however true
it may be, cannot give this knowledge, for revelation is a

---

[1] An allusion to the story of Joseph and Zuleikha.

[2] Compare the words of Paul in Romans 9, 3.

[3] Plato naturalised it in philosophy; see Vol. I, p. 501.

necessary accommodation to the incapacity of the common
mind; at best, an attempt to say what cannot be expressed
in words. Equally vain is it to look for knowledge of God
in the definitions and discussions of philosophers and scholastic theologians. Love is also the key to the understanding of God's dealings with men. Why does God deal thus
with me? Reason discovers no answer, revelation gives
none; but he who loves understands, as a child through love
discerns the benevolent motive of a father's severity, if not
his wise design.

Greek and Christian influences are not the only ones
which are recognisable in Sufism. The Moslem conquests in
the eastern provinces of the Persian empire brought them
into regions where Indian asceticism and philosophy had long
been established. The chief agency in the dissemination
of Indian ideas beyond the bounds of the Indian peninsula
was Buddhism; not the primitive Buddhism which is known
to us chiefly through the Pali Canon, but the northern
Buddhism of the Mahayana school.[1] The ontology of the
Mahayana has a strong resemblance to Neoplatonism, but
the characteristic Neoplatonic doctrine of successive emanations from the fulness of Absolute Being had no place in it.
The influence of Buddhism is perhaps most clearly seen
among the Sufis in the idea of Fanā—literally "cessation"
—a term in which may be discerned an attempt to find an
equivalent for Nirvana. The complement of Fanā is Baḳā
—abiding, or continuance, i. e., in God. Al-Kharaz employed these terms to denote the perfection of saintship in
those who have traversed all the stages and found the object
of their search. He defends himself against the imputation
that by Fanā he means the annihilation of essence or personality, or that Baḳā implies a confusion between human
and divine attributes. Fanā is dying to the sight of human
abasement and living in the contemplation of divine omnipotence; the true servant of God is so lost in contemplation
of him that he no longer attributes his actions to himself,
but refers them all to God. Other Sufis, however, less care-

[1] See Vol. I, pp. 303 ff.

ful of the semblance of orthodoxy, conceived Fanā as such an absorption in the Godhead, or identification with it, as meant the end of individual existence. One of them writes: "When the temporal joins itself to the eternal, the former has no more existence. Thou hearest and seest nought but Allah! When thou reachest the conviction that there is no existence except Allah, when thou realisest that thou thyself art He, that thou art identical with Him, then nothing exists but He!"

> "Let me become non-existent, for non-existence
> Calls to me with organ tones, 'To him we return!'"

Al-Hallaj was put to death in 922 A. D. for crying in the ears of the scandalised Moslems of Bagdad, "*Ana al-Hakk*," "I am the Reality"—the sole Reality in the universe, God. According to Hallaj, man is essentially divine. God created man in his own image; he projected from himself that image of his eternal love that he might behold himself as in a mirror. Hence he bade the angels worship Adam (Koran 2, 32), in whom, as in Jesus, he became incarnate. Inasmuch as the humanity (*nasūt*) of God embraces the whole bodily and spiritual nature of man, the divinity (*lahūt*) of God cannot unite with that nature, except by an incarnation or an infusion (*hulūl*) of the divine spirit, such as takes place when the human spirit enters the body.[1] Thus, Hallaj says in one of his poems:

> "Thy spirit is mingled in my spirit, even as wine is mingled with pure water.
> When anything touches thee it touches me. Lo, in every case thou art I! . . ."

And again:

> "I am he whom I love, and he whom I love is I:
> We are two spirits dwelling in one body.
> If thou seest me, thou seest him,
> And if thou seest him, thou seest us both."[2]

[1] Nicholson, *Mystics of Islam*, pp. 150 *f.*
[2] Nicholson, p. 151.

This dangerous extreme led to a reaction among the more moderate Sufis, who, repudiating this self-deification and the antinomian immoralism of the radicals, endeavoured to make their mysticism compatible with orthodoxy. Of this tendency the most notable representative is al-Kusheyri, whose Epistle was published in 1045 A. D. We shall see later how in the person of its greatest theologian, al-Ghazali, Moslem orthodoxy assimilated large and fruitful elements from Sufism.

It is evident that in Sufi pantheism the ground of Islamic monotheism is completely abandoned. In place of the one personal God, creator and ruler of the world, was put the sole reality in the universe, the One, the Truth; while for a religion of submission to the will of the supramundane ruler and obedience to his law, with fear of the divine judgment for its motive and the rewards and punishments of the future life for its sanctions, is put a mystical love in which lover and beloved are one, or a transcendental knowledge of identity in which the illusion of individuality is overcome; for the material fires of hell, the separation of the soul from its origin, its alienation from its true self; for paradise, the eternal reunion. As in all similar systems, the positive elements of religion, its commandments and observances, have no meaning or value to him who has attained the truth; at most, it may be admitted that they have a pædagogic use in that through them man may be led to repent and enter upon the Way. Most of the Sufis outwardly conformed to the religious law and custom to avoid scandal or punishment; but there were individuals and sects who held themselves emancipated not only in spirit, but from the letter of the law. Antinomianism is, indeed, inherent in all mysticism.

The Sufis applied to the Koran an allegorical method of interpretation by which they found beneath the letter a spiritual sense, and the more extreme among them acknowledged no other significance in it.[1] They were called the

---

[1] The Shiite sects practised a similar esoteric exegesis for other ends, professing that Mohammed had given to Ali the key to the hidden sense of the text. Sufis sometimes borrowed this legitimation.

Batiniyya, which we might literally render "Insiders," that is, those who seek—and find—the true inwardness of the teaching or the precept of revelation.

Upon these heights the differences between religions disappear. The love of God, the knowledge of God, may be attained by Jews or Christians as well as by Moslems. Ibn Arabi says: "There was a time when I took it amiss in my companion if his religion was not like mine, but now my heart admits every form. It is a pasture for gazelles, a cloister for monks, a temple for idols, a Kaaba for the pilgrim, the tables of the Law, and the sacred book of the Koran. Love alone is my religion, and whithersoever men's camels turn, it is *my* religion and *my* faith." "The ways of God are as many as the souls of men." The various religions with their creeds and rites, in so far as they divide men, are evil. A poet belonging to one of the emancipated orders of Dervishes sings: "Until mosque and Medresa[1] are laid altogether waste, the work of the Kalender (Dervishes) will not be complete; so long as belief and unbelief are not altogether the same,[2] not a single man will be a true Moslem."

Some of the Sufis drew the practical consequences of the divine all-oneness which put them beyond good and evil, as certain pantheistic Christian sects in the Middle Ages are said to have done; but such extravagances were condemned as severely by the great body of the Sufis as by the rest of mankind.

An interesting effort to propagate a philosophical and mystical conception of reality is found in a collection of essays by members of a society in Basra who call themselves the Ikhwan al-Safa.[3] The fifty essays of this collection are arranged in four main divisions corresponding to the stages of an encyclical education. The first part contains the fundamental sciences (arithmetic, geometry, astronomy,

[1] School.
[2] *I. e.*, so long as any difference is made between Moslem and infidel.
[3] By this name they probably meant "The Sincere."

geography, theory of music, mathematical relations) and logic; the second treats of the natural sciences and of man; the third part is devoted to the doctrine of the Universal Soul (Anima Mundi) and the relations of partial and individual souls to it; the fourth part deals with the theological sciences. The first two parts and the last are in the main Aristotelian; the doctrine of soul is Platonic, but with a considerable admixture of Pythagorean and Aristotelian elements. As in the earlier stages of Arab philosophy generally, the complete harmony of Aristotle and Plato was assumed; Aristotle was read and interpreted through the Neoplatonic commentators.

The Plotinian theory of emanations underlies the whole.[1] First is the One, the Absolute; then the Universal Intelligence; then the Universal Soul; the Primordial Matter; and finally the world of things. Under the influence of Pythagorean number-mysticism, however, these stages are by subdivision increased to nine. The Universal Soul is one, but it has many powers, which permeate all nature, and are distributed in all bodies and elements, from the planets down to the plants; these powers are what are called the souls of these creatures, and, as in Plotinus, constitute a system of souls in the Universal Soul. Man is a microcosm; and the correspondence of his nature to the macrocosm is a favourite theme with the writers. In the material world and in union with the body, the soul is, as it were, in a state of stupor, unmindful of its origin, its nature, and its destiny. When it is awakened from its slumber it seeks to return to its source, the Universal Soul. This attraction is love, the best definition of which is, "Love is a mighty desire for union." Such union is possible only between intellectual subjects. "The Creator is the first beloved, for the universal heaven revolves only in desire toward the Creator." [2] Those who have set before them this goal cleave to the Creator, strive to be like him, and imitate him in work and word, in knowledge and in act.

[1] See Vol. I, pp. 533 f.   [2] Aristotle: κινεῖ ὡς ἐρώμενον. Vol. I, p. 508.

Like the Mutazilite rationalists, these mystics allegorize the materialistic Moslem eschatology. The resurrection is not the re-creation of the body, but the awakening of the soul from its heedless slumber; it is the return from the world of matter and body to the world of spirit or of mind. The great resurrection is the separation of the Universal Soul from the material world and its return to God. Hell is not a place of material torment where an angry God punishes sinners in the fire; the sinful soul has its hell in its own body in this life. The cosmopolitan eclecticism which is natural with such ideas appears in the essays. The authors claim the wisdom of all peoples and all religions. Socrates and Plato, as well as Noah, Abraham, Mohammed, and Ali, are among the prophets; Socrates, and Jesus, and the family of Ali are the holy martyrs of this reasonable faith.

Those who are awakened from the sleep of folly recognise the true values of things. To them every day is a festival, every moment an act of worship; their rest is obedience to God. All times and places are alike to them; there is only one place of worship, only one Kibla,[1] namely, to fulfil the word of God. Their love to God manifests itself in religious toleration, and in kindness toward all creatures; it gives those who possess it, in this life composure of soul, heart-freedom, peace with the whole world, and hereafter the ascent to the eternal light.

The Neoplatonism which underlies this system reached the Moslems through various channels, first, in all probability, through Christian theologians, later through translations from the Greek, directly or through the Syriac. The works of Dionysius the Areopagite[2] were comparatively early known, and their influence can be distinctly traced. One of the most important intermediaries was the so-called "Theology of Aristotle," under which name a work com-

[1] The point toward which the worshipper turns his face in prayer—the Moslems toward Mecca, Jews and Oriental Christians toward Jerusalem.

[2] See above, pp. 207 ff.

piled from the Enneads of Plotinus was accepted without question as a work of Aristotle, and enjoyed the supreme authority which his name carried. It is largely occupied with the doctrine of the soul, as the titles of the several books show: On the Soul, Soul and Mind, Qualities and Names of the Soul, Substance of the Soul, The World of Intelligence, Creator and Creation, the Stars, The Supreme Soul, First Force in Matter, Potentiality and Energy, the Rational Immortal Soul, the Ultimate Origin of Things. Similarly, an abstract in Arabic of the Στοιχείωσις Θεολογική of Proclus (Liber de Causis) was taken for Aristotelian doctrine. Neoplatonising Aristotelians like Alexander of Aphrodisias, and Neoplatonic commentators on Aristotle such as Proclus and Themistius contributed their share to the confusion.

The writings of Aristotle which were earliest known to the Moslems and most highly valued by them were the methodic treatises, especially the logic, and the various writings on natural history. The name philosopher in Arabic has always designated a professed follower of Aristotle, who was to them the philosopher by way of eminence. The first of the Arab philosophers, al-Kindi (d. about 870), lays down what became an axiom with his successors, that the only way to philosophy is through the propædeutic sciences, and he did much to make accessible the logical, mathematical, and astronomical teachings of Aristotle; but at the same time he had some hand in the production of the famous "Theology of Aristotle," and in his own theology was through and through a Neoplatonist.

The great stumbling-blocks in the genuine Aristotle to Moslems, as well as to Jews and Christians, were, *first*, the eternity of the universe, which was the necessary corollary of his conception of God as the First Cause; *second*, the limitation of God's knowledge to universals, which excludes particular providence; and, *third*, his denial of immortality to the individual soul. All these theories are integral parts of Aristotle's system, and they are in flat contradiction to the fundamental doctrines of all three religions, creation, providence, and retribution. The Arab Aristotelians had, however, no doubt of the genuineness of the "Theology," and made the Metaphysics agree with it as well as they could. Al-Farabi (d. 950) and Avicenna (d. 1037) got over the necessary eternity of matter, for example, by inventing the category of the "relatively necessary." Avicenna endeavoured to make a place in his philosophy for prophecy and miracles, divine providence, and immortality, recurring for the last to Platonic arguments. Both of them have an emanationist cosmology for the spheres above the moon, and Avicenna combines with this the Neoplatonic series of emanations. Both were Sufis, and both—Avicenna in larger measure than al-Farabi—had leanings to occultism of various kinds. For subsequent speculation, the most important contributions of these philosophers were in the fields of psychology and epistemology.

Between the philosophers and the theologians there was no peace. The theologians accused the philosophers of infidelity. The philosophers retorted that the theologians did not know what they were talking about; they had the audacity to pronounce on the ultimate problems without either training in science or knowledge of philosophy. Al-Ghazali gave a summary of the systems in his "Tendencies of the Philosophers," as a preparation for the "Demolition of the Philosophers,"[1] in which he undertook to expose the errors of their metaphysics, psychology, and natural science, and to prove their teachings in irreconcilable conflict with revelation. A century later Averroes replied with the "Demolition of the Demolition"—and he made it thorough! The greatest of all mediæval commentators on Aristotle here exposes the superficiality of the critic and the sophisms of the theological dialectic.

The philosophers, most of whom were by their calling physicians and men of science, made no effort to popularise their doctrines; they held, indeed, that no one without scientific education had any business with such questions.

[1] The original title was "The Collapse of the Philosophers."

They enjoyed, therefore, comparative freedom for their speculations, notwithstanding the hostility of the theologians. This state of things came to an end in the East in the first half of the twelfth century, and the writings of the philosophers were more than once publicly burned. In one such conflagration, in 1160, the works of Avicenna and the Essays of the Ikhwan al-Safa were consigned to the flames. When once it was in this business, the Moslem inquisition did not make too fine distinctions, but burned scientific treatises on astronomy in the category of astrology. In the West, however, Arab philosophy had in the twelfth century its short-lived glory. Ibn Bajja, of Fez, known to the schoolmen as Avempace (d. 1138), begins this period, Averroes (Ibn Rushd; d. 1198) ends it.

The Aristotelianism of al-Farabi and Avicenna was of a denatured kind, which Aristotle would hardly have recognised and would certainly not have acknowledged. Averroes made an era in European philosophy by his endeavour to interpret honestly the genuine teachings of the Stagirite, and it does not detract from the magnitude of his achievement that he was not always right in his interpretation. He spurned the subterfuges by which Aristotle was harmonised with the religious dogmas of creation, providence, and immortality. Science and philosophy are one thing; religion is another. Each should confine itself to its own sphere, and not intrude on that of the other. Religion is for all, and is given in a form and language intelligible by the common mind; philosophy is the affair of the few who have the mental power and discipline and the previous scientific training it demands. The philosopher should not, by colporting science in the market-place, undermine the faith of the simple believer; the unphilosophical should not, in the name of faith, put dogmatic restraints on philosophical speculation. The worst enemies of faith, in his eyes, were theologians like al-Ghazali, who undertook to establish the truth of religion by their dialectic reasonments and their pseudo-metaphysics, and demanded that men should believe not only what was revealed but the reasons they gave for it.[1]

This plan for avoiding conflict between philosophy and religion by leaving them no common ground to contend upon has more than once been revived, sometimes in behalf of the freedom of thought, sometimes of the immunity of faith to reason. In some of the schoolmen it became the doctrine of a double truth, according to which a proposition might at the same time be true in philosophy and false in theology or vice versa.

In a history of Moslem philosophy it would be necessary here to go into Averroes' theory of the unity of the intellect, which was to the Christian schoolmen the characteristic heresy of Averroism, and as such was combated by Albertus Magnus and Aquinas. This doctrine, however, by way of which Averroes found something better than the immortality of the individual soul, had no similar echo in Islamic theology; and, indeed, the influence of the last great Moslem philosopher was immeasurably greater in the Christian than in the Moslem world.

[1] See below, p. 474.

CHAPTER XX

MOHAMMEDANISM

ORTHODOX THEOLOGY

Al-Ghazali—His Life and Religious Experience—"Revival of the
Religious Sciences"—The Way of Salvation—The Higher Life—
Theology in the West—Ibn Hazm and the Zahirites—Ibn Tumart
and the Almohads.

IN bringing down the history of Moslem philosophy to
Averroes, its last representative, we have anticipated, and
must now turn back to the man who gave to Mohammedan
theology and ethics the form which in all essentials it has
retained ever since. Al-Ghazali (d. 1111) stands to Moslem
theology in this respect in somewhat the same position that
Thomas Aquinas does to Christian theology. His great
work, "The Revival of the Religious Sciences," may fairly
be compared to the "Summa" of Thomas Aquinas, but his
personal contribution to theology was more considerable
than that of the Christian theologian.

Al-Ghazali was born at Tus, near Meshed,[1] in 1058 A. D.
Early left an orphan, he devoted himself to theological
study, as he himself says, from no higher motive than that
there were scholarships for theological students, and that
teaching offered a career. After studying jurisprudence (of
the school of al-Shafii)[2] he went to Nisabur, then one of
the great centres of learning in the Moslem world, and continued his studies under one of the most celebrated theologians of his time, commonly known by his honorary title,
Imam al-Haramain, an Asharite and at the same time a

---

[1] In Khorasan. For a fuller biography, see D. B. Macdonald, Life
of al-Ghazzali, in Journal of the American Oriental Society, vol. XX
(1899), pp. 71–132.

[2] The Asharites were chiefly of this school.

mystic of the orthodox type, a man of large learning and
deep piety.   Under him al-Ghazali studied logic, the natural
sciences, and philosophy, as well as theology.   After the
death of his master (1085), he left Nisabur, and in 1091 was
appointed by the Seljuk vizier, Nizam al-Mulk, professor in
his newly founded college at Bagdad.   As a teacher he had
a conspicuous success, and his lecture-rooms were crowded
with students; but at the height of his career he suddenly
resigned his chair and left Bagdad.   The reason he gave was
the failure of his health; his ostensible purpose, a pilgrimage
to Mecca.   In an interesting intellectual and spiritual auto-
biography, Munkidh min al-Dalal, the cause of his withdrawal is explained.   The breakdown of his health was the
result of an acute intellectual crisis.   Inquiry into the nature
and grounds of certainty in matters of religion led him into
the depths of scepticism.   Certainty could be assured only by
the evidence of the senses or by the primary ideas of reason,
but further reflection threw even these certainties into doubt.
From this extreme he was delivered, he tells us, not by
reasoning, in which he found no help, but by God, who
cured him of that disease, and brought him back to the conviction that in the ideas of reason there is a basis of certainty.   But recognition that certainty is possible was not
yet attainment of certainty.

Looking about him upon those who professed to have the
certainty of religion, he found four classes: the scholastic
theologians (Mutikallimun), who undertook to confirm the
truth by reason; the esoteric sect (Batiniyya), who had an
infallible guide in their Imam, and held that only by com-
mitting themselves implicitly to him can men be secure; the
philosophers, who relied on logical demonstration; and the
mystics, who thought that truth was revealed to them intuitively in their ecstasies.   Such, then, were the ways in
which he must seek certain knowledge.   To return to a
naïve faith in what he had been taught as a child was impossible—the very condition of that kind of faith is that
a man should not be conscious that it is such.

He set himself, therefore, to examine the methods and results of the theologians and the philosophers. The arguments of the theologians, he discovered, were all very well for those who accepted the Koran and tradition; they could defend orthodoxy against various kinds of heretics, and refute their errors; but against such as denied their premises they were helpless. Some of them indeed ventured farther into the field of philosophy, but, being poorly grounded in the sciences, they only exposed themselves to the ridicule of the philosophers. As for the philosophers[1] themselves, their mathematics, logic, and natural science are all very well, but the metaphysics which affirms the eternity of the world, denies God's knowledge of particulars, and rejects the resurrection of the body and bodily punishments hereafter is mere infidelity; their ethics they have appropriated from the Sufis.[2] Of those who, renouncing reason, took refuge in the infallibility of their Imam, he entertained a very poor opinion; their arguments moved in a circle.[3] There remained, then, only the way of the mystics.

With the general character of this way he was not unacquainted, but he now addressed himself to a more thorough study of their treatises, several of which he mentions by name. The result of this study was a recognition that what he was in search of was not to be got from books. Descriptions of stages and states were not the thing itself. There is as much difference between a definition of renunciation—the condition of a man whose soul is no longer of this world—and the reality of it as between knowing the symptoms and causes of intoxication and being intoxicated.

He had by this time been brought back to firm faith in the three fundamental doctrines of Islam: God, the Prophet, and the Last Day, not, as he is at pains to repeat, by definite

[1] His controversy is chiefly with the Arab Aristotelians.

[2] The agreement, as far as it extends, is in reality due to their common dependence on the same Greek sources.

[3] The sect which al-Ghazali has in mind are the Ismailis (see below, pp. 499 ff., 504); particularly, the branch which Hasan al-Sabbah developed into the Assassins.

arguments, but by circumstances and experiences which cannot be described; and he was sure, also, that the blessedness
of the other life is to be attained by restraining the desires of
the flesh, and by severing the attachment of the heart to this
world and fixing all desire upon God. A severe struggle
ensued. His high position and brilliant future held him
back; fear for the fate of his soul urged him on. His health
broke down under the strain. The physicians declared that
it was a mental ailment for which their art could do nothing.
At last, as has been said, he resigned his place and set out
for Syria. There he remained for almost two years in
retirement, spending his time in prayer and meditation and
in the religious exercises of the Sufis, devoting himself to
"mastering his desires, combating his passions, purifying
his soul, perfecting his character—in a word, preparing his
heart for meditation on God."

At the end of this time he made the pilgrimage to Mecca
and Medina, pausing on his way in Jerusalem and at Hebron.
After that, at the urgency of his children, he returned to
the East, where in semi-retirement he pursued the mystic
way which alone leads direct to God. As he describes this
way, the first thing is to purge the heart of all besides God.
The key to the contemplative life is to immerse the heart
completely in the thought of God; the goal is a total passing away (*fanā*) in God. But this end is only a beginning;
the revelations which come to the mystics, in which, in the
waking state, they perceive the angels and the souls of the
prophets, hear their voices, and gain their guidance, are
succeeded by states which cannot be described or defined.
Men have called this supreme experience a fusion of the soul
with God (*hulūl*), or identification with God (*ittihad*); others
call it union (*wusūl*), but such language is a sin. The experience itself, however, is the firm ground of faith and the
key to the understanding of prophecy. Al-Ghazali thus
learned that religious certainty is to be found only in religious experience; it is experience alone that can put the
existence and character of God, the verity of prophetic reve-

lation, the reality of the future life beyond question and controversy. This conviction explains his hostility—perhaps animosity would be the truer word—to the scholastic theologians and to the jurists.

In 1106, at the command of the sultan, al-Ghazali returned to Nisabur to teach in the college there; it was just eleven years after his departure from Bagdad. He cannot have remained there very long, for before his death (1111) we find him again in his native town, Tus.

The title of Ghazali's great work, *Iḥyā ʿUlūm al-Dīn*, Revivification of the Religious Sciences, implies the conviction, which he elsewhere expresses plainly and emphatically, that theology and ethics in the Moslem world of his days were in a moribund state, and that it was his mission to put new life into them by penetrating them with the spirit of true religion. The sequel proved that he was not mistaken; the "Revivification" gave to orthodox Islam a character and direction which it has never lost.

The work is divided into four parts, each of which is in ten chapters. In the first part, after defining the nature of science and of the religious sciences in particular, the author treats of the fundamental articles of Moslem faith: The knowledge of the being of God, his attributes and his operations; then the particular topics of Moslem eschatology, which men are bound to believe on the authority of revelation; the succession of the four caliphs after Mohammed, with a refutation of the exceptional claims made by the Shiites for Ali; the conditions of the orthodox Imamate. This is followed by a discussion of the controverted questions of the relations of faith (Iman) and Islam, and the increase or decrease of faith. Al-Ghazali next takes up the observances prescribed in Moslem law: the ritual purifications, private and public prayer, alms-giving, fasting, the pilgrimage to Mecca, always describing the proper form of the ceremonial as defined by tradition and the law books, but taking pains to emphasize the proper attitude of mind and heart in the performance of these duties, and the spiritual benefits which man derives from them. Thus, when he treats of the ceremonial purifications, he dwells upon the necessity of purity in the heart, and of the removal from it not merely of the vices which defile the inner man, but of all that is not God. He sets forth the forms of prayer prescribed by tradition, and treats separately of private devotion, the recitation of the names and praises of God, and petitions for moral and spiritual blessings. In this connection he has brought together a number of prayers attributed by tradition to godly men and saints of the older time, Jesus among them.

Throughout, he is concerned to impress upon his readers that prayer is to be offered, alms given, the fast kept—in a word, all the observances of religion performed—in such a way that religious and moral benefit may be derived from them. To recite prayers as a matter of routine and by force of habit, without attention or intention, merely uttering articulate sounds without any regard to the sense, is fruitless; to be of avail, prayer must be made with concentration of attention and understanding of the meaning of the words, a sense of the greatness of God and the nothingness of the creature, and in the fear of God inspired by the consciousness of our own shortcomings, weakness, and inclination to evil, and mindfulness of all that we owe to God. Similarly, the reading of the Koran is an act of devotion as profitable to the soul as it is pleasing to God, if it be performed in the spirit of devotion. The Koran is the word of God written; it is, so to speak, a letter from the Almighty to his creatures; it should be read, therefore, reverently, attentively, reflectively, with meditation on the mysteries of truth which it contains.

Even for the rites of the pilgrimage to Mecca—that undigested piece of Arab heathenism which Mohammed incorporated in Islam—Ghazali succeeded in finding religious meaning and profit. All the other prescribed observances, as he remarks, have some rational end, and are plainly useful to the soul; but the throwing stones into the valley of Mina and going in a circle around the Kaaba have no sense, no spiritual utility, in harmony with the natural inclination of the soul. And precisely therein consists the merit of the observance; man abdicates his reason in obedience to the law of God by performing acts which have no intelligible end. This is the value of the pilgrimage for the simple believer; but for the enlightened these seemingly meaningless acts have a deeper moral and spiritual significance, which is discovered by the way of allegory. Mecca is the symbol of Paradise; the Kaaba, of the abode of God; the circuit about the holy house is a figure of the continual adoration which the angels render to the Lord around his throne; the race back and forth between the hills of Safa and Merwa is an image of the perplexity of the soul before God's bar; the gathering of the pilgrims on Mount Arafat should remind them of the Day of Judgment and the like.[1]

The way of salvation for man is the purification of the heart by the extirpation of vice, and union with God by the acquisition of a virtuous character. Al-Ghazali opens this part of his work with the elementary notions of psychology, "Wonders of the Heart." These notions are essentially Platonic. The faculties, or powers, of the soul are appetite, passion, intelligence,[2] the last also called, in religious language, the heart. The heart of man is like a house with many portals, or like a fortress attacked by archers from every side.[3] It has good thoughts and impulses which are called inspirations, and evil impulses which are called suggestions; the inspirations come from angels, the suggestions from demons. Satan, the great enemy, continually strives to enter the fortress of man's heart and rule in it. His assaults can be averted only by guarding well all the entrances, among which he names anger and lust, envy and

---

[1] The Sufis were fond of these allegories—a more elaborate one from Junaid is quoted by Nicholson, The Mystics of Islam, pp. 91 f.

[2] Ἐπιθυμία, θυμός, νοῦς.

[3] The reader may be reminded of Bunyan's "Holy War," with its fortress of Man-Soul.

avarice, gluttony and the love of luxury, inordinate desire for riches (under which word he includes everything that is not strictly necessary to existence). One of the most dangerous of these avenues of evil is sectarian zeal, which gives rise to rancour and calumny. "When Satan succeeds in making one of these fanatics believe that his school or sect is the only true one, if it agrees with his personal inclination, he will induce the man to justify any idea that occurs to him by saying that it is the teaching of his sect; and so with great satisfaction he will believe that he is labouring for religion, when in reality he is only working for the devil." The temptation of Satan is often so subtle as to leave man in doubt whether it is not a good inspiration. Al-Ghazali illustrates this at some length in an analysis of the temptations of the popular preacher—a passage which has all the more interest, because, as we know, it came out of his own experience. The question at what stage a natural impulse becomes a temptation and the temptation a sin, also leads into a psychological discussion. Against evil impulses and temptations ejaculatory prayers are a defence, but they have this virtue only when they are coupled with man's serious effort to mortify his passions.

There are not only virtuous and vicious actions, but sinful habits, which are diseases of the soul, and virtuous habits —habit being defined as a quality or form of the soul impressed upon it, from which acts proceed without hesitation or the necessity of reflection. The doctrine of the four cardinal virtues is ultimately Platonic; the definition of a virtue as a mean between excess and defect is not only Aristotelian, but follows closely the lines of the Nicomachean ethics; the theologian contributes his part in the shape of proof-texts from the Koran.

Passing, now, to the more specifically ascetic part of the work, it is remarked that it is an error to think that the ascetic endeavour is the complete annihilation of the passions, a thing impossible in itself, since concupiscence, for example, is a power which God has implanted in man for a useful purpose; it is necessary, *necessitate naturæ*. The aim of the good man is to bring the impulses of nature into that harmony which is the just medium between excess and defect. This perfect harmony is in some men, notably in Jesus, John the Baptist, and all the prophets, innate. Most men, however, can only acquire it by effort and discipline in the habitual practice of the virtues, and by imitation of the conduct of virtuous men.

The hindrances to the higher life which must first of all be overcome are riches, honours, sectarian zeal, and sin. Riches and honours must be put aside; sectarian zeal may best be overcome by ignoring the particular tenets of the schools and falling back on the simplicity of the fundamental dogmas of Islam, "There is no god but Allah, and Mohammed is his Apostle." It is not an essential condition of spiritual perfection that a man should belong to any theological or juristic school. The remedy for sin is repentance, which consists in abandoning all unrighteousness, firmly resolving not to fall again into sin, contritely and sincerely mourning over one's past life, restoring what he has taken unjustly from others, and forgiving his enemies.

In this way, man has need of a guide. A spiritual director who is a wise physician of souls knows how to recognise the faults and shortcomings of those under his direction and prescribe for each the suitable remedy. Man is in need, also, of a stronghold, within which he is safe from the assaults of the enemy, the fortress of solitude, silence, fasting, and vigil. The spiritual exercises practised under direction in the monastery and the stages of the mystic's progress are set forth at some length. The author is not unaware of the dangers of these methods, and particularly in the highest stages of meditation, when they are undertaken by men unprepared, or disqualified by nature. In these chapters, as throughout the work, psychological insight and sound sense mark the author's treatment.

This brief summary of the contents of the Ihya, in which many things—for example, an admirable chapter on the edu-

30

cation of children—are passed over altogether, may serve at least to indicate to the reader the character of a work which perhaps more than any other single writing has influenced religious thought and life in the Mohammedan world.

Al-Ghazali never concealed his conviction that one of the chief causes of the wide-spread indifference to religion, not to say scepticism, in his time was the fact that the canonists, with their controversial zeal about the minutiæ of law and observance, and the scholastic theologians, absorbed in their endeavour to construct a rational dogmatics and defend it against other schools, heretical or orthodox, had no vital interest in religion, and were often wofully lacking in piety. His criticisms were sharply resented by the professors of law and theology; he had made himself especially detested by the philosophers; while the representatives of traditional orthodoxy, who would hear nothing besides Koran and Sunna, regarded him with the suspicion which they entertained against all thinkers. Especially in Spain, where at the beginning of the twelfth century learning had almost all run to canon law, his writings were formally condemned and publicly burned. Reformers are proverbially obnoxious to academic scholasticism, whose prestige they threaten. It was not long, however, before al-Ghazali came to be honoured as a pillar of the faith and revered as a saint. Such titles as "the Reviver of Religion," "Proof of Islam," were bestowed upon him. Legends soon attached themselves to his name, and it was said that he was for three days the *Kutb*, that is, "the axis," or invisible head, of the Sufi hierarchy in the world. The superstitious believed that he knew the secret names of God, and by them was able to conjure the Jinns and all the forces of the lower world; he was reputed to have in his possession the book of Jafr, containing mysterious wisdom which Ali had handed down in the line of the Imams, and which al-Ghazali alone, in his old age, was able to interpret.

Down to the eleventh century theology had gained no permanent foothold in the West; the learned in Morocco and Spain were almost exclusively devoted to juristic studies, chiefly in the narrow school of Malik ibn Anas. The Muta-zilite controversies had hardly an echo in that remote end of the Moslem world, and consequently no need was felt of a rational dogmatics such as al-Ashari and al-Maturidi had created in the East. Sceptics, and that of a radical kind, there had indeed been, but with them there could be no compromise or accommodation. The first theologian of note in Spain was Ibn Hazm (d. 1064). He himself had been trained as a jurist of the Shafiite school, and for a short time filled the office of vizier at Cordova, as his father had done before him. After he lost this place he spent his life in study, and in controversial writings which displayed so violent and intolerant a temper that a proverb couples the tongue of Ibn Hazm with the sword of al-Hajjaj.[1] He addicted himself to the Zahirite school of law and exegesis, of which he was the first exponent in the West.

It has been noted above that there were controversies among the orthodox schools of Moslem law over the extent to which inference and analogy might legitimately be employed in jurisprudence. In the third century Da'ud ibn Ali, a Shafiite, pushing to extremes the opposition of his school to speculative methods in jurisprudence, became the founder of a secession which is called Zahirite—we might say the "Obvious-Sense" school. He recognised no authority in law but the express terms of the Koran and tradition taken in their obvious meaning, rejecting extension by analogy of cases, and inferences from the reason or motive of the rule in the Koran or the traditions of the Prophet, refusing to recognise behind the decision in a particular case the implicit enunciation of a general principle. Further, he disallowed the acceptance of a rule of law upon the authority of the founder of a school, and demanded that the student, instead of blindly repeating and following the *ipse dixit* of a fallible master, should make up his own mind

[1] Governor of Irak under Abd al-Malik and Walid, proverbial for his merciless severity in dealing with disloyalty (d. A. D. 714).

about the meaning and application of the language of the Koran and tradition. Ibn Hazm maintained the Zahirite principles with great energy not only in the sphere of jurisprudence, but in the sphere of doctrine. The theologians come off even worse at his hands than the jurists, and al-Ashari receives no more mercy than the Mutazilites; indeed, it is upon al-Ashari in particular that he poured out the vials of his wrath.

This antipathy is due primarily to al-Ashari's employment of a rational dialectic in dogmatics, where he should have confined himself to the letter of the Scripture and tradition and the consensus of the companions of the Prophet. Even where he bases his conclusions upon the Koran, he uses a freedom of interpretation which in Ibn Hazm's view has no other end than that of substituting the results of his own reasoning for the plain sense of revelation. Again, in defining the meaning of words in the Koran, especially of religious terms, al-Ashari, with the majority of Moslem theologians, frequently had recourse to the usage of the old Arabic poets and the language of the Bedouins accumulated by the lexicographers, instead of making the specific usage of the Scripture itself decisive. Thus certain theologians, who defined faith (*īmān*) as signifying merely assent to the truth or professed acceptance of it, alleged in support of this view examples from common speech, in which this is the usual meaning of the word. Ibn Hazm indignantly protests against this. What faith means in the Koran is to be learned from the Koran itself; and even apart from revelation, Mohammed doubtless knew Arabic quite as well as any heathen poet or stray Bedouin. In the Koran, faith includes not only knowledge of God in the heart and confession with the tongue, but works accordant thereto. It is fair to say that this perfectly sound principle of exegesis was not a discovery of Ibn Hazm, but was recognised by many Arabic philologists before as well as after him.

Upon the question of the divine attributes Ibn Hazm emphatically rejected as a product of illegitimate speculation, without any foundation in Koran or tradition, al-Ashari's doctrine of eternal immanent distinctions in the divine being. No less energetically did he reject the view of those who held the theory of eternal attributes distinct from the essence of God. It is at first blush surprising to find this literalist at one with the Mutazilites in denying the existence of the attributes, but the grounds of his denial are quite at the opposite pole from theirs; they are, in fact, the consequence of his literalism. There is not a word in the Koran or the traditions about any attributes of God. God in his word does not talk about an attribute of knowledge; he calls himself a knower, and so with all the rest. The terms from which the theologians derive their doctrine of attributes are, in truth, only names by which God has been pleased to make himself known in his revelation. We are not warranted in going beyond this and ascribing to God an attribute of power, because he calls himself powerful, or life, because he calls himself living. In this fashion Ibn Hazm cuts the ground from under the whole discussion, and dismisses it as not only futile, but presumptuous and almost blasphemous.

Another point in which he assails al-Ashari most violently is the doctrine of the Word of God. The Asharites taught that the word of God is an essential attribute, eternal, uncreated, distinct from God, and different from God's knowledge, and that it is one, sole, and indivisible—"God has only one Word." Ibn Hazm brands this as pure infidelity: "We will ask them, Is the Koran the word of God, or not? If they say, No, they are, according to the unanimous teaching of all Moslems, unbelievers. If they say, Yes, we will ask them further, Is this word of God the Koran which is recited in the mosques, written in manuscripts, and learned by heart? If they say, No, they are again, according to the unanimous teaching of all Moslems, unbelievers. If they say Yes, they contradict their own false doctrine."

It might be imagined that an interpreter who insists so strenuously that the word of God shall be taken in its plain sense would be found in the ranks of the anthropomorphists, who in this matter certainly have the letter of the Koran on their side. Far from it! Anthropomorphism is as repugnant to Ibn Hazm as to the Mutazilites; but he does not, like the rationalists, dispose of the hands and face and other members of God in the Koran as figures of speech; he undertakes by dictionary and grammar to prove that in the passages under dispute the words have a literal meaning altogether different from that in which the reader offhand takes them.

The triumph of the Asharite dogmatics in the West was a result of the conquests of the Almohad dynasty under Abd al-Mumin and his successors. The name of this dynasty is a Spanish corruption of the Arabic, al-Mowahhid, "Unitarian," a party, or sect, which made its creed and its battle-cry the *Tauhīd*, the assertion of the unity of God. The founder of this movement was Ibn Tumart, a Berber of the Masmudah tribe. He had studied in the East under Asharite teachers; and although the legends which bring him into personal connection with al-Ghazali are more than improbable, the influence of al-Ghazali's works is unquestionable. On his return to Morocco he found his first task in a reformation of the life of his countrymen, of which, to tell the truth, there was abundant need. The Mohammedanism of the Berbers was at best superficial; the laws of the Koran against intoxicating drinks were a dead letter; swine roamed the streets of the towns, and their flesh was eaten without scruple. Other customs of theirs were in equally plain violation of Mohammedan law. Among the ruling Almoravids the men habitually kept their faces carefully covered, while the women went unveiled, in disregard of the law which forbade one sex dressing like the other. Nor was he better satisfied with the religious notions of his countrymen. The jurists of the prevalent Malikite school insisted on the literal sense of the anthropomorphic expressions in the Koran and tradition, and the cautionary phrase, "in some inscrutable manner,"[1] with which

[1] "Without thinking how"; see above, p. 424.

they were accustomed to qualify their assertions made little impression on the popular imagination, which was grossly materialistic. Against these "corporealists" Ibn Tumart made war without quarter. They were, in his eyes, infidels, and apostates from Islam. The watchword *Tauhīd* meant for him, as it had done for the Mutazilites, not merely the unity of God, but his incorporeality, and in the creed which he drew up, and to which he required the confession of his followers, this is a fundamental article.[1]

On the question of the attributes Ibn Tumart departs from the position of al-Ashari and al-Ghazali, and agrees with Ibn Hazm, under whose influence on this point he manifestly stands, in denying the existence of eternal distinctions in the essence of the godhead. Like Ibn Hazm—and like al-Ghazali, though for a different reason—he was most hostile to the jurists, with their endless casuistry and superfœtation of "opinions," to the neglect of both the sources of law and its principles. Authority lay only in the Koran, the authentic traditions of the Prophet, and the consensus of the companions of the Prophet.[2]

Before long, however, the reformer took a higher flight. He came to believe himself the Mahdi, sent by God to restore decadent Islam, and to fill the world with righteousness as now it is filled with iniquity, in preparation for the hour of God's judgment.[3] He made a collection of traditions concerning the signs of the last times and the character and work of the Mahdi, including certain alleged sayings of the Prophet which praised the people of the West and foretold the coming of the reformer from among them. It had long been a part of the common tradition that the Mahdi would have the same name and patronymic as the Prophet, Mohammed ibn Abdallah. So small a matter did not stand in Ibn Tumart's way; he simply assumed these

[1] For this creed see Zeitschrift der Deutschen Morgenländischen Gesellschaft, vol. XLI, pp. 72 f.

[2] Not the consensus of the Moslem world, expressed in the agreement of the heads of schools, as in the ordinary interpretation of the principle.

[3] See above, p. 434.

names, and found more easy credence because it was nothing uncommon for a Berber to have an Arabic name as well
as a more familiar one in his native tongue. A genealogy
was also worked out in which his lineage was traced back
to Ali and Fatima.

The Shiite doctrine that the Mahdi was an infallible
Imam, the last in a succession that began with Adam, was
not unfamiliar in Morocco, where a Shiite dynasty had
ruled for nearly two centuries.[1] Ibn Tumart's second confession of faith was an Imamite creed, in which the mission
and authority of the Imam were set forth in a most positive
and circumstantial manner. He did not name himself in
it, but every trait in the description tallied so well with
his person that it had its intended effect when Abd al-
Mumin and ten of his fellow disciples saluted him: "These
signs and characteristics are to be found in thee alone.   Thou
art the Mahdi !"[2]

Before long he had a large following among the Berbers,
with whom he had all the more success because his religious
deliverances, his confessions of faith and exhortations, were
made in their own tongue; he even introduced the innovation of causing the call to prayer to be made from the min-
arets of the mosques in Berber instead of Arabic.   Presently
he summoned the believers to a Holy War against the ruling
dynasty of the Almoravids (al-Murabit),[3] whom, for their
false ideas of a corporeal God and their neglect of the religious law of Islam, he denounced as infidels, and their rulers
as Antichrists. The first encounters went against the
Mowahhids, and Ibn Tumart died (1128) without having
seen the triumph of his cause.

Abd al-Mumin took up the unfinished work, and in the
thirty-three years of his rule conquered Morocco and all
Moslem Spain, putting an end to the Almoravid dynasty,

---

[1] A. D. 788–985.

[2] Compare Peter's confession at Cæsarea Philippi, Mark 8, 27–29.

[3] The name signified originally men who picket their horses on the
frontier, that is to say, "Champions of the Faith."

LIBRARY OF CONGRESS CATALOG CARD ORDER FORM

CUSTOMER NUMBER	BOX A	ALPHA PREFIX	LC CARD NUMBER
444125-101			55-7100

TYPE ONLY IN THESE BOXES

REPORT BOXES						ALPHA PREFIX		LC CARD NUMBER
1	2	3	4	5	6			

(HANDPRINT ONLY. USE NO 2 LEAD PENCIL.)

SEE BELOW FOR EXPLANATIONS.

AUTHOR(S) Gettys, Joseph M

TITLE How to teach the Revelation

PUBLISHER John Knox Press

PLACE

DATE 1955

EDITION

SERIES

FIRST FOURSQUARE CHURCH VAN NU/Y

CUSTOMER NAME

VARIATION IN EDITION ACCEPTED?

Explanation of report boxes (1-6 above).
1. Cards are not currently available for this title. Please reorder at a later date.
2. No cards will be printed for this title. Please do not reorder.
3. No LC card number was found in searching.
4. Charge has been made for searching.
5. Other:
6. LC card number.

LC
(Rev

and subjected, one after another, Algiers, Tunis, and Tripoli, thus bringing all North Africa from the frontier of Egypt to the Atlantic under his sway. Abd al-Mumin had been a student of theology before he became the most famous general of his time, and his first successors, especially Mansur, the third of the line, were eminently learned in the science of tradition. Mansur is said to have made an *auto da fé* of the law-books; cases should be decided by direct appeal to the corpus of tradition, not by the opinions of the jurisconsults. Although the triumph of the Almohads was the triumph of a purer and a more spiritual theology, it does not appear that theological studies flourished much under their rule. Their times are made illustrious in philosophy by the names of Ibn Bajja, Ibn Tofail, Averroes, and of one of the greatest of the mystics, Ibn Arabi; but by no great theologian.

CHAPTER XXI

MOHAMMEDANISM

CREED, WORSHIP, MORALS

Essentials of Moslem Belief—Worship—The Fast of Ramadan—
Pilgrimage to Mecca—Survivals of Paganism—Worship of Saints
—Doctrine of Salvation—Ethics and Morals—The Family—
Slavery—Intoxicating Drinks—Piety—Dervish Orders.

THE obligations of the Moslem were early summed up—
probably during Mohammed's years at Medina—under five
heads: The Profession of Faith, Worship, the Payment of
Poor-Rates, the Fast of Ramadan, and the Pilgrimage to
Mecca. The simple Profession of Faith is: "I bear witness
that there is no god but Allah (the one true God), and that
Mohammed is the Apostle of God." The first article, the
confession of faith in the one God, is, in works on Moslem
theology and books intended for the religious instruction of
laymen, understood to include belief in the teachings of the
Koran and traditions concerning the angels, the prophets
and saints, the Scriptures, and the other life. In all these
topics especial prominence is given to the points which had
been denied or disputed in the period of the great controversies. It is commonly held to be incumbent on every
Moslem to be acquainted with the fundamental articles of
belief as they are contained in the creeds, and with the
grounds on which they are believed. A mere implicit faith,
which accepts these doctrines as a whole upon authority,
without knowing in particular what they are or why they
are held, is not sufficient. This was the position of al-Ashari,
and may be regarded as an integral part of orthodoxy.
Some, like Ibn Arabi and al-Sanusi, went so far as to hold
that blind acceptance of the articles of belief without knowing the rational proof of them is unbelief.

On the existence and attributes of God it is sufficient to
refer to what has already been said of the teaching of al-
Ashari and al-Ghazali.[1] Six attributes are commonly enumerated; namely, life, knowledge, hearing, sight, will, and
speech, which are inherent in the divine essence, eternal, and
unchangeable. The doctrine of predestination, also, and
of the immediate creation of men's actions by God, agrees
with that of the theologians named: "Good and evil[2] occur
by his predestination, by his will, and by his operation."
The angels, in various ranks and with diverse functions, are
always obedient to God's will; they neither eat nor drink,
and are without sex. Among them Gabriel, the angel of
revelation, Azrail, who receives the souls of men at death,
and Israfil, who is to sound the trumpet on the day of resurrection, are particularly named.

From age to age God has had his prophets among men,
the first of whom was Adam and the last Mohammed.
Among the rest, Abraham, Moses, and Jesus hold the highest rank. Prophets have appeared not only among Jews
and Christians, but among many other peoples; indeed,
every nation has had its prophet. To some of these prophets scriptures have been sent down by the hand of Gabriel:
the Pentateuch to Moses, the Psalter to David, the Gospel
to Jesus, and other books to other prophets, each for his
own people. Mohammed was sent as a prophet to all men,
and to the demons.[3] The Koran is the final revelation,
and shall abide until the end of the world.

The rationalists in their time had allegorised away the
whole eschatology of the Koran and tradition; and partly
for this reason, and partly because the spontaneous rationalism of the human mind revived their objections, the several
features of this eschatology are defined as obligatory beliefs:
the inquisition at the tomb, when the angels Munkar and
Nakīr will question the dead about their God, their prophet,
their religion, and their Kibla;[4] the signs of the last days—

---

[1] See above, p. 475.   [2] Moral as well as physical.   [3] Jinns.
[4] The place toward which their face was turned in prayer.

the appearance of Antichrist,[1] the descent from heaven of
the prophet Jesus, who will kill the Antichrist and be converted to Islam; the appearance of the Mahdi, of the family
of the Prophet, who will join Jesus; the outbreak of Gog and
Magog and the Beast of the Earth; the rising of the sun in
the west, and the like—are specified in detail;[2] furthermore,
the weighing in a balance of each man's good and evil deeds;
the bridge stretched over hell, which for the righteous is a
broad highway, while for the wicked it is narrower than the
edge of a sword; the ponds of the prophets, Mohammed's
being the largest of all, at which believers shall quench their
thirst, each with his individual drinking-cup, before entering Paradise; Paradise itself, whose soil is musk and the
bricks of its buildings gold and silver, where the saved
shall have for a wish whatever kind of food and drink they
desire, while unbelieving men and demons will ever abide in
hell, tormented by huge serpents and scorpions, by fire and
boiling water, and when their bodies are burned up and reduced to coals, God will create them a new body to suffer
more torment.

Mohammed is for orthodox Moslems not only the last
and greatest of the prophets, but the most excellent of all
created beings. The tendency which appears early in the
traditions to match and surpass what the Christians claimed
for Jesus exalted Mohammed to inerrancy and sinlessness.
Although Mohammed himself, when challenged by his
scoffing countrymen to prove his assertions by a miracle,
not only refused to gratify the demand of the unbelieving
generation for a sign, but declared that he had no miraculous powers, appealing to the "signs" of the Koran itself,
the words of God given him from heaven, as the only and
conclusive miracle, his followers soon attributed to him
many and amazing miracles as proof of his prophetic office.
Among these miracles in the traditions are the making of

[1] *Al-Dajjāl.*
[2] The details are, in great part, Talmudic or Zoroastrian, or both.
See Vol. I, pp. 398 *f.*; II, p. 75.

CREED, WORSHIP, MORALS 477

the sun stand still, in imitation of Joshua; making water flow, like Moses; and the multiplication of food and drink for his hungry and thirsty followers, like the feeding of the thousands in the Gospels. Moslem doctrine distinguishes the evidential miracles of the prophets, which they work to convince men of their mission, from the miracles of the saints, which God works for them, or through them, out of his special favour to them. The intercession of the Prophet for some believers at the day of resurrection, and the acceptance of this intercession by God is also a belief incumbent upon all Moslems.

The significant name for worship in Islam is "prayer," and it may be said that ritual prayer constitutes the public and private worship of Mohammedans. The canonical hours, which were not fixed until some time after Mohammed's death, are five; namely, at dawn or just before sunrise, at noon, before sunset, just after sunset, and after dark. Prayer should be said in a state of ceremonial purity, and is therefore preceded by ablutions in which the face, the hands and forearms, and the feet and ankles are washed in a manner fixed in general by tradition, but with minor variations in the different rites. In the absence of water, sand or dust may be used, as in Jewish law. The washing of the whole body is required as a purification after numerous ceremonial defilements.[1]

In prayer the worshipper faces toward Mecca, the direction of which is indicated in all the mosques by a niche in the wall. The prayers consist of prescribed ejaculations of praise to God, petitions, and the recital of parts of the Koran, always including the first Sura, which from its frequent repetition is sometimes called by Western writers the Lord's Prayer of Islam:—"Praise to God, the Lord of the Worlds, al-Rahman,[2] the Merciful, the King of the Judgment

[1] Sexual functions and contact with death are the chief of these, as in Judaism and Zoroastrianism.

[2] The name al-Rahman is a Hebrew and Aramaic name of God in common use among the Jews, from whom, directly or indirectly, Mohammed got it. It is not an Arabic word, and Mohammed conjoins

Day! We worship thee, and implore thine aid. Guide us in the straight path, the path of those on whom thou hast bestowed thy grace, not of those on whom thine anger rests, nor those who go astray."

The recitation of the prayers in the mosque or elsewhere is accompanied by a fixed succession of genuflexions and prostrations, which vary slightly in the different rites. The time of prayer is announced by a crier from the tower, or minaret, of the mosque; the prayers may be performed in any place where the Moslem happens to be, though it is preferable to make them in the mosque. On Friday at noon the men of a city are required by law to convene in the principal mosque of the place to recite their prayers in unison, under the direction of a leader (*imām*). The Friday assembly usually includes, besides the congregational prayers, a kind of sermon, for which, however, the congregation is not required to remain. Apart from the obligation of attending the noon prayers, Friday is not in any sense a holy day; unlike the Sabbath of the Jews or the Lord's Day of the Christians, no restriction whatever is put upon either work or play.

The poor-rates, which were originally, as their name *zakāt* indicates, voluntary charity, by which the Moslems whom God had blessed with this world's goods relieved the necessity of their poorer brethren, soon developed into a system of taxation, not only for the benefit of the poor, but for the common purposes of the community, such as the building of mosques. They were then prescribed in amount, and collected by officials; but in modern times the payment of them is in most countries left to the conscience of believers.

As has been said above, Mohammed originally made but one obligatory fast-day in the year, corresponding with the Jewish Day of Atonement, but after the momentous breach with the Jews he put in place of it a fast through the entire

with it an Arabic adjective *raḥīm*, in the meaning tender-hearted, merciful, compassionate. Several other expressions of the prayer are apparently drawn from the phraseology of Jewish prayers.

month of Ramadan, perhaps in imitation of the Lenten fast of the Oriental Christians. During the whole of this month Moslems are required to observe a complete fast from sunrise to sunset, abstaining not only from food and drink, but even from such alleviation of hunger and thirst as is afforded by smoking. It is the custom, therefore, to take a meal before sunrise and a fuller one after sunset. Indifferent Moslems not infrequently spend the night making up for the abstinences of the day; but piety requires that the sentiment of the fasting day should prevail in the night also, which, so far as it is not given to sleep, should be passed in prayer and the recitation of the Koran, or in godly conversation. The Moslem calendar, since Mohammed abolished the rude intercalation of the heathen Arabs, has a year of twelve lunar months (354/5 days), and consequently the months rotate through the solar year three times in a century. When Ramadan falls in summer it is no inconsiderable infliction; yet the fast is pretty strictly observed.

When Mohammed made the pilgrimage to Mecca obligatory on every Moslem he did not foresee the expansion of the Moslem world. He meant the pilgrimage to be an annual observance, taking the place of the pagan Hajj and the fairs in the neighbourhood of Mecca. The obligation is now held to be satisfied if a man makes the pilgrimage once in his life, though it is correspondingly meritorious to make it oftener. Distance and expense, however, render it impossible for the majority to make the pilgrimage at all; and the law books accommodate the duty to the fact by many exemptions.

The rites of the pilgrimage were adopted, combined, and incorporated in Islam, from the ceremonies of pagan Arab festivals. Mohammed changed the forms only so far as was necessary to dissociate them from the worship of the old gods, without attempting to substitute a significant connection with the new religion. These ceremonies are of diverse kinds and are performed at different places in Mecca and outside of it.

The centre of these rites in Mecca is the Kaaba, a cubical structure of roughly thirty to forty feet in its three dimensions. In its southeast corner, built in at a height where it can conveniently be touched by the worshippers, is the famous black stone, a span long, in a silver mounting which holds together the fragments into which it was broken when the Kaaba was burned during the siege of the city by the armies of the Caliph Yezid in the year 683. The Kaaba itself contains a single windowless room, access to which is through a door several feet above the ground. The whole building, roof and sides, has a covering of black brocade, renewed every year, with a broad border on which are embroidered in gold texts from the Koran. A few steps away from the corner in which is the black stone is the well Zemzem, which is believed to be the water that God showed Hagar when Ishmael was dying of thirst in the wilderness.[1] A third holy object in this area is the so-called Makam Ibrahim, by which is now understood the stone that Abraham stood on while he was building the Kaaba.

In the Hajj, as it is usually performed by pilgrims from a distance, two ceremonies of independent origin are combined. Of the first of these the Kaaba is the centre, while the rites of the second group take place outside the city. The first, which may also be performed by itself in fulfilment of a vow or otherwise, is called the Umrah. The ceremonies begin when the worshipper arrives at the boundary of the Haram, or sacred territory, which surrounds Mecca on all sides. To perform the Umrah, therefore, a resident of Mecca or a temporary sojourner in the city must first go outside this limit. At the boundary he lays aside his ordinary dress, and assumes the Ihram, a garb consisting of two pieces, one of which is hung around the loins, the other thrown over the shoulders. In all probability this is merely ancient Arab costume perpetuated, as in many other cases, in a religious ceremony. Thus attired, the pilgrim makes his way to the open space surrounding the Kaaba,

[1] Genesis, 21, 19.

shouting at the top of his lungs the word *Labbaika!* which is explained to mean: "At thy service, O God!" [1] Then, running to the right, he makes the circuit of the Holy House seven times, kissing or touching with his hand the corner where the sacred stone is, and the southwest corner, in which there is another, less holy, sacred stone. His next business is to perform the race between Safa and Merwa, two slight elevations on opposite sides of the valley about five hundred yards apart. This course, also, he traverses seven times; across the bottom of the valley, between two posts set up as markers, he runs with all his might. The exercise begins at Safa, not far from the Kaaba, and ends at the same point. This completes the religious exercises of the Umrah, which may be performed at any time of the year.

In distinction from this, the Hajj ceremonies proper are confined to the pilgrimage month, Dhu al-Hijja. When the pilgrim enters the sacred territory he puts on the pilgrim garb already described, which he wears until the completion of the ceremonies. During this time he must not shave nor cut his hair; he may not take animal life of any kind,[2] and must abstain from commerce with women. On the eighth of the month in the afternoon the pilgrims leave Mecca and go out to Arafat, a hill, or ridge of hills, a short distance outside the sacred territory to the east, on the road from Mecca to Taif, where they encamp for the night. The night should properly be spent in devotion; but for those who are not devotionally inclined improvised coffee-houses furnish opportunities of secular relaxation. During the morning of the ninth the pilgrims wander about as they please; at noon, if so disposed, they may hear a sermon. Later in the afternoon occurs the great event for which they are gathered; it consists simply in standing still, shouting *Labbaika!* and reciting certain texts from the pilgrim manual.[3] The mo-

[1] The meaning of the word and the act are unknown.
[2] Except the sacrificial victims.
[3] In heathen times the obligatory standing and shouting were doubtless the accompaniment of a sacrifice.

31

ment the sun has set, the assembly breaks up, and all start at a rush toward Mecca, to the first halting-place, Mudalifa. The essential part of the performance is to run at top speed. At Mudalifa the night prayers are said, and the pilgrims spend the night in vigil in the open air. Before sunrise, by torchlight, there is another obligatory stand in front of the mosque, and before the sun is really up another rush is started to Mina. The day of Mina is the day of the pilgrim sacrifices. Four distinct ceremonies fall on this day. At the end of the valley there is a pile on which every pilgrim throws seven stones, supposedly stoning the devil. Then a victim, which has been marked for sacrifice ever since entering the sacred territory, is slaughtered. Part of the flesh furnishes a feast for the worshippers, the remainder is dried for subsequent use or given to the poor. When the feast is over the pilgrims shave and lay aside their antique garb. This is evidently the proper ending of the rites; the pilgrim has formally returned from sacred to secular state. In fact, however, there follows a return rush from Mina to Mecca, with a circuit of the Kaaba, and the running between Safa and Merwa—ceremonies properly belonging to the Umrah —after which most of the pilgrims return to Mina and encamp there, sometimes remaining for a day or two, but with no other religious duties than to throw a stone daily on the devil's piles.

The pilgrimage brings to Mecca large numbers of people —estimates vary from 50,000 to 70,000 annually—from all parts of the Moslem world. Formerly almost all made the long journey in caravans, starting from Damascus or from Cairo. Many, especially from India and Persia, but also from Egypt, now travel by steamer to Jidda, the port of Mecca on the Red Sea, about thirty miles from the Holy City. A Turkish railroad has also been built from Damascus to Medina, parallel to the line of the old pilgrim road, and many pilgrims from Syria take this more comfortable, and therefore presumably less meritorious, way of fulfilling their religious duty.

The conversion of the Arabs to Islam was accomplished with great rapidity and corresponding superficiality. It was a long time before the observances of the new religion were thoroughly established among them, not to speak of its ideas. Destruction of the objects of pagan worship, the holy trees and standing stones, was easily accomplished, but this outward abolition of heathenism did not extirpate the beliefs or even the practices which underlay Arab paganism. Among the Bedouins in particular, both in Arabia and in the border-lands, the religion of the *Jahiliyya*—the "Times of Barbarism"—still survives essentially unchanged, with only a thin layer of Mohammedanism superposed upon the depths of native superstition. Sacrifices are still offered at ancient holy places, and offerings to the dead are made at the tombs of kinsmen or of the mythical ancestors of tribes and clans.

Nor is the situation materially different among the peasants of Moslem countries. In Syria, for example, sacred trees are still decorated with rags torn from the garments of the worshippers, miraculous powers are ascribed to the holy waters of sacred wells and springs, the hilltops which were the "high places" of the ancient Canaanites are still places of worship, where Moslems, Jews, and Christians together perpetuate religions which are immemorially older than all of them; and what is true of Syria is true, *mutatis mutandis*, of all other parts of the Moslem world, such as India or North Africa. The religions which Islam supplanted live on in Islam unchanged and unabashed. The most-frequented places of worship in most countries are the shrines of the Welis, the tombs or cenotaphs of holy men and women. In a large part of the Mohammedan world Christian saint-worship preceded Moslem saint-worship, and was adopted by the Mohammedans as the shrines of pagan gods and heroes had been earlier appropriated for Christian saints and martyrs. One not insignificant difference is, however, to be observed: the worship of saints has never found a place in the mosque corresponding to that which it has in Christian churches, even when the mosque is erected in memory and honour of a saint.

The shrines are sometimes the actual burial-places of heroes of the Moslem faith. The tomb of Mohammed in Medina was naturally from the first an object of veneration to the Moslems. The holiest places of the Shiites are the tomb of Husein at Kerbela and that of Ali al-Rida, the eighth Imam, at Meshed, both of them tombs of martyrs. Great doctors of the law, like Ahmed ibn Hanbal, multitudes of Sufi saints, some of them famous in the literature of mysticism, others of only local repute, the founders of Dervish orders and their eminent successors, have contributed their quota to the multitude of shrines. Many, however, are ancient pagan places of worship legitimised in Islam by a legend which makes them the burial-places of a Weli.

In orthodox theory the saints are invoked, in virtue of their merits, to intercede with God for the blessings which the worshippers seek at their shrines. In fact, they are for the vast majority of Moslems local divinities, to whom sacrifice is offered and prayer made, whose aid is sought to heal the sick, to give children to barren women, to prosper men in all their various enterprises. Many of them have only a local celebrity; to others throngs gather from all the region at certain festival seasons; to some pilgrimages are made even from distant parts. Thousands thus resort to Meshed and to Kerbela, and to Tanta in Egypt, where the feast has to this day preserved features of Egyptian religion as it was described by Herodotus.

The voluminous Moslem hagiology is full of the miracles wrought by the saints in their lifetime and miraculous help and deliverance given to worshippers at their tombs. The theologians made a distinction even in name between the miracles of the prophets, which are proofs of their divine mission, and the miracles of the saints,[1] which are wrought by God for the saints as tokens of peculiar favour, but to

---

[1] Miracles of the prophets are $āyāt$, "signs"; those of the saints $karāmāt$, "tokens of favour."

which no evidential value attaches. Since there are no more prophets, the world at large is concerned only with the miracles of the saints.

Relics have never had the religious importance in Islam which they have in Christianity. They are relatively few; venerated for their historical association—real or fictitious —with men of mark in the history of the religion; and this reverence has usually a purely private character. The sword Dhu al-Faḳār, which the Prophet presented to Ali, was one of the treasures of the Abbasid caliphs. In the fourth century the mosque in Hebron boasted of the possession of a genuine shoe of the Prophet, and several other shoes of the Prophet were shown in other places; there are numerous supposed autographs of the Prophet and of the first caliphs. Hairs from Mohammed's beard were particularly prized, and were worn as amulets. In India the veneration of relics and their use as amulets seems to have been particularly developed, in imitation and rivalry of native practice, and there it has even found a place in the public cultus of the mosques.

That, whatever subtle distinctions the theologians might make, the worship of the saints was in reality a relapse into polytheism was plainly seen by the Mutazilites, and in their zeal for the unity of God they therefore condemned it without compromise. In the eyes of the orthodox, however, the condemnation of these rationalists was rather a commendation; and it is significant that the founders of Moslem dogmatic theology from al-Ashari to al-Ghazali, as well as the philosopher Avicenna, took it upon them to defend the miracles of the saints and the benefits to be gained by worship at their shrines and pilgrimages to them. On the other hand, some who are deservedly accounted the most conservative of conservatives were outspoken against both the worship and the miracles. Among these was Ibn Teimiyya, who declared that a pilgrimage to the tomb of Mohammed or the other prophets and saints is a "pilgrimage of rebellion," in defiance of the commandment of God; and it is well-known that the great puritan reaction in Islam in the eighteenth and nineteenth centuries which we know by the name of the Wahhabis, was peculiarly violent against the tombs of the Welis and other intrusions of polytheism into Islam. Against all such efforts to restore the original purity of monotheistic faith and practice, the long-established universal custom prevailed. Ibn Teimiyya had to sit in prison a long time for his heresy on this point; the Wahhabi movement never exerted much influence outside of Arabia, and in Arabia itself is now limited to a small region and has lost its iconoclastic fury.

Mohammedanism has also its living saints, to whom miraculous powers are attributed, and who are objects of superstitious veneration. Eminent ascetics and mystics— Sufis and Dervishes—who have attained in this life to that intimate union with God which for the common apprehension is hardly to be distinguished from deification, have always been thus regarded by many. The Shia Imams, even among the least extravagant sects, have in them a scintilla of divinity which sets them quite apart from common humanity; while the ultra-Shiites see in the Imams incarnations of the godhead, such as in our own time Baha Allah was to his followers. In India the Moslem Pirs, both among the Shiites and the Sunnites, occupy a place and exercise an authority quite like that of the Hindu Gurus, and many would think that a man had a poor chance of salvation who did not put himself completely under the direction of such a spiritual guide. In Morocco and Algiers the marabout (*murābit*) is the Mohammedan successor to the holy men, or living gods, of Berber heathenism; they are accorded little less than divine honours while they live, and their tombs become shrines of pilgrimage after their death.

In the Moslem doctrine of salvation, man is not saved by works, either ritual and ceremonial or moral, but by faith; and faith itself is the work of God by his electing, disposing, and preserving grace, without which no man can believe unto salvation. As we have seen above, there were early and long-continued controversies among Moslem theologians concerning the nature of saving faith: Should faith be understood as creed, the profession of the two great articles, "There is no god but Allah, and Mohammed is the Apostle of God"? Or does it include sincere and firm conviction in the heart of the truth of this profession? And finally, must a genuine and efficacious faith bring forth its proper fruit in a life of obedience to the law of God as revealed in his word and in the teaching and example of the Prophet? Differences in regard to the definition of the term "faith" and its relation to "Islam" still exist; but for the substance of the matter Moslem orthodoxy agrees that true faith should be accompanied by works, though it would hardly say that works are a condition of salvation. It is sinful presumption to judge that a man who professes Islam will at his death be sent to hell because his life is in flagrant violation of the religious law and common morality. Consistently, it is held to be no less presumptuous to predict that the Moslem most conspicuous for knowledge of his religion, most scrupulous in the fulfilment of its obligations, and most eminent in all the virtues of life, will go to Paradise when he dies; for the decree of God is secret, into which no man can penetrate.[1] Exception is made only for ten individuals among the companions of the Prophet, of whom he is reported to have said that they were destined to Paradise, and for the martyrs who seal their faith by dying for it in the "Way of God," to whom the Prophet promised the same good end.

The "Way of God" was, above all, war against unbelievers in defence of the true religion, or to extend its dominion and achieve its supremacy in the world. Later and less militant generations gave the name "martyr" (that is, "witness to the faith") to others than those who laid down their lives in the holy war, for example, to Moslems who lost their lives in some great catastrophe of nature, or to a

---

[1] Compare the decree of the Council of Trent on Justification, c. 12: "*Nisi ex speciali revelatione sciri non potest, quos Deus sibi elegerit.*"

man who is killed while defending his house or property against robbers. The theologians and ascetics gave the notion a still wider extension. The word *jihād*, commonly interpreted "holy war," of itself means only "supreme effort" in the way of God. Traditions were adduced in which Mohammed is reported to have said that a man who recites the Koran to fulfil the will of God is as highly regarded by God as the martyrs; and the arrogance of the jurists at a later time carried some of them so far as the assertion, on the feigned authority of the Prophet, that the ink which flows from the pens of the learned has a higher value in the eyes of God than the blood of the martyrs shed in the holy war. Such extravagances, whatever credence they may have found among some of the learned themselves, made little impression upon popular belief, which has always associated martyrdom with death in war for God's cause.

Not only may no man presume to foretell the salvation of another (with the exceptions just named), but no man can have any assurance of his own salvation. The uncertainty of salvation lies in the logic of predestination; it is orthodox Augustinianism as well as orthodox Mohammedanism.[1] At the intercession of the Prophet some Moslems will at death be admitted immediately to Paradise, but no man can have any certainty that he is one of this number. Thus, a wholesome insecurity serves to counteract the presumption that all who profess the true religion and outwardly observe its ordinances, or do not scandalously neglect them, will enter Paradise. On the other hand, as has already been observed, it has become an orthodox dogma that no one who truly professes Islam will be eternally damned. Even the torments of hell to which the wicked are condemned at the day of resurrection are expiatory; and thus in the end all Moslems will be saved.[2]

[1] Compare again the Council of Trent on Justification, c. 9, against the Lutherans, who incorporated this assurance (*fiducia*) in faith itself. "*Nullus scire valeat certitudine fidei, cui non potest subesse falsum, se gratiam Dei esse consecutum.*" This is also Calvinistic orthodoxy.

[2] This is also Jewish doctrine; see above, p. 75.

The religious ethics of Islam are those of a revealed religion. Its authoritative sources are the same as those of theology and law, namely the word of God in the Koran, the teaching and example of the Prophet, and the consensus of the Moslem community. The disposition to reduce everything to juristic formulation which is so apparent in Moslem dogmatics manifests itself also in ethics, and gives it a formal and nomistic character. This is, however, a tendency that is inevitable in the ethics of a revealed religion which treats morals as a part of the revealed law of God; it may be observed in Judaism and Christianity as well as in Mohammedanism or Zoroastrianism. The sanctions of morals, also, are religious; obedience to God's law is requited by him with a reward which is not of merit but of grace, while disobedience is punished as it deserves. Submission to God's will (Islam) being the first commandment of God, the works of those who disbelieve in his revelation are vain; "they will weigh for nothing on the day of resurrection" (Koran 18, 105); "they are like a mirage in the desert, which the thirsty traveller takes for water, but when he comes thither, finds nothing" (Koran, 24, 39).[1]

Logically it would seem as if there would be no room for either good deeds or evil in a system in which God is the sole and immediate creator of every deed, and that the theory of appropriation, in which the theologians endeavour to account for man's consciousness of choice and the approving and disapproving judgment of conscience upon his choices by making man's actions *subjectively* his own, does not suffice to establish his moral responsibility. Nor is there any question that Moslems have often drawn the practical consequence of a doctrine which makes God's will the cause of all their deeds, and laid the responsibility for their misdeeds upon God's will. The moral teachers of Islam have, how-

[1] This is Christian doctrine also. The Western church, after Augustine, denies that apart from the grace of God in his church there are any good works. Judaism, in which faith has no such determining value, teaches, on the contrary, that God in his justice will requite even the worst of men for his good deeds.

ever, never countenanced this fatalistic attitude, but at
whatever cost of inconsistency with the implications of the
dogma, have inculcated man's obligation to live uprightly,
virtuously, and charitably among his fellows, and endeavoured to inspire the fear of God's just judgment on those
who live otherwise.   In Islam, as in other systems which
have exalted the supremacy of God and extended the scope
of his decree to all the actions of men, the common sense
and conscience of mankind has always been sounder than
the logic of determinism.

While in theory Koran and Sunna are the source of all
Moslem ethics, like the written and oral Law in Judaism and
the Bible for thoroughgoing Protestants, yet in Islam, as in
these religions, many other elements enter into the actual
fabric of morals, other influences into ethical doctrine.
The Arab conquerors in Syria and Egypt were brought at
once into contact with the moral standards and ideals of
Christian populations, in Babylonia and Persia with those
of Zoroastrians.   From an early time, especially in ascetic
and mystical circles, Christian influence is easily recognised.
Many passages from the New Testament, particularly words
of Jesus in the Gospels, were attributed to Mohammed,
and thus became by adoption part of the normative Moslem tradition; while other borrowings were installed in the
practice of Islam with the authority of the catholic consensus.
The elements with which its ethical tradition was thus enriched were appropriated because they were felt to be con-
sonant with the teachings of the Koran itself.   Mohammed
had not failed to emphasise the decisive value of motive and
intention in determining the quality of moral actions, or the
truth that goodness and helpfulness toward our fellow men
in need has a greater religious value than worship and ceremonial observances; and when Moslems became familiar
with the Gospel—which it must be remembered is a divine
revelation and one of the acknowledged sacred Scriptures—
they recognised in its words the spirit of their own religion.
A survey of the collections of Moslem traditions and of the

writings of the Moslem mystics would show how large a part of the teaching of the Gospel had passed by one channel or another into Moslem thought.

Through contact with Christians the Moslems made acquaintance not only with the New Testament but with the ethics of the church, to which Greek philosophy, especially Platonic and Stoic, had largely contributed. Later they drew for themselves on the same source. Moslem ethics is therefore of a composite rather than an eclectic type. The four Platonic virtues furnish the general scheme; the definition of virtue as a mean between two extremes, both of which are vices, is taken from Aristotle, and the Nicomachean Ethics are largely cited; the ideas of the nature and destiny of the soul and the goal of moral endeavour are Neoplatonic. This combination may be seen, with variations, in the Essays of the Ikhwan al-Safa, in al-Ghazali, and in Ibn Miskawaihi's Refinement of Morals.[1] The canonists, so far as they go into ethics, and the rationalistic theologians were inclined to mix less Plato with their Aristotle.

The constitution of a Moslem state leaves no room for a political ethics like the classical systems of the Greeks. Among the Shiites, where the Imam is the divinely ordained head of both church and state, obedience to the Imam is of the very essence of Islam, and in Sunnite orthodoxy, also, obedience to the powers that be, which are ordained of God, is a religious obligation. Even among the radical Kharijites the duty of obedience to rulers was not challenged in principle; but inasmuch as a Moslem ruler whose conduct did not accord with their notions of what a ruler ought to be and do, by that very fact forfeited his right to rule and it became the duty of every true Moslem to join in deposing him, the obligation to obedience was crossed by the religious duty of revolution. It would be admitted on all hands, also, that when, in the great decadence of Islam that foreshadows the last day, the Mahdi appears to restore the

[1] An analysis of the contents of this interesting treatise is given by Boer, Encyclopædia of Religion and Ethics, vol. V, p. 507.

reign of righteousness on earth, it will be the duty of all true Moslems to rally to his standard for the overthrow of the tyrants and Antichrists who reign in that evil time. More than once a self-appointed Mahdi like Ibn Tumart has headed a revolution by which dynasties have been overthrown and new ones established.

The family is probably the sphere in which Moslem morals present the most striking contrast to those of modern Christian countries. The Koran, restricting the unlimited polygamy which had theretofore been lawful among the Arabs, limited the number of wives that a free Moslem might have at one time to four, while a slave is allowed only two. Other prescriptions of the Koran, establishing the equal rights of wives, increase the economic hindrances to polygamy, and it has probably always been true that by far the largest part of Moslem men have had but one wife at a time. Divorce, however, is easy, and advantage is largely taken of this facility, the only restraint upon which is that the husband loses the *mahr*—originally the price paid to the woman's family, but actually a settlement which the husband makes upon his bride at marriage—together with the usufruct of his wife's dowry. Consequently, what might be called consecutive polygamy has always been very frequent. In addition to his lawfully wedded wives, a Moslem may have as many female slaves as his station and means allow, and his connection with these slaves is as lawful as that with his free wives. If such a slave bears a son who is acknowledged by her master, she becomes a "mother of a child"; thereafter her master cannot sell her, and at his death she becomes free without further formality. A son thus acknowledged is free and shares in his father's inheritance with the sons of the wedded wives. While the Moslem law thus allows to a man as many women as he can support in his family, it makes adultery, fornication, and prostitution not only heinous sins, but under certain circumstances crimes most severely punished by the law.

Women form an inferior class in Moslem law and in Moslem society. In inheritance, for example, the portion of a woman is one-half that of a male kinsman in the same degree, and in cases where the testimony of two witnesses is required by law, they may be either two men or a man and two women. But popular notions in the West about the status of Moslem women are in many ways erroneous; for instance, that Mohammed taught or Mohammedans believe that women have no souls, or that there are no women in Paradise. On the contrary, believing women have in the Koran the same promise of Paradise as men, and husbands are promised the company there of such of their wives as they may desire. In the Koran no distinction is made between the religious obligations which are incumbent upon women and those prescribed for men. Women do not, as a matter of fact, much frequent the mosques; they are much more often to be found at the shrines of the Welis or in the cemeteries. The pilgrimage to Mecca can be performed by women only under conditions of company and guardianship which make it impossible for most women. The obligatory alms fall out because few women possess property in their own right.

A tradition which goes back to an early time in the history of Islam makes the study of the religious sciences obligatory on every Moslem, man or woman; and the annals of Moslem learning are adorned with the names of not a few women who distinguished themselves in these fields. In the science of tradition, for example, two women taught the traditions which they had heard from Malik ibn Anas at Medina; and the most highly reputed name in the transmission of the famous corpus of Bokhari is also a woman, Karima bint Ahmed, of Merw. The latter part of the sixth and the first half of the seventh centuries of the Moslem era abound in names of women eminent for learning in this and other branches of Moslem science, whose signatures on their diplomas were sought by some of the best-known scholars of the age. As such an authorisation[1] was given only to

---

[1] *Ijāza.*

students who had personally heard the instruction of the teacher, it follows that these learned ladies had, at least in some cases, given public lectures, with men as their hearers. A modern example of the same kind among the Shiites, who in this respect are quite as strict as the Sunnites, is that of Kurrat al-Ain, as famous for her beauty as for her learning and her eloquence, who gave regular lectures in Sheikhi dogmatics at Kerbela and at Bagdad, before she became one of the apostles and martyrs of the Babi reform.

In the roll of Moslem saints the names of many women stand. Among them the women of the family of Ali take the most prominent place, not only among the Shiites but even in Sunnite Egypt, by survival and reminiscence of the Fatimid times. The tomb of the Sitta Nafisa is one of the most sacred spots in Egypt, and the miracles which were wrought by the saint in her lifetime and after her death are the subject of a whole cycle of legend. The Sitta Nafisa was the great-granddaughter of Hasan and daughter-in-law of the Imam Jafar al-Sadik, and is celebrated for her piety and charity as well as for her learning in the Koran and its interpretation. The greatest number of sainted women is contributed by the Sufis, whose religious mysticism had a peculiar attraction for women. In the Sufi literature more than one woman shines; Rabia is most eminent in the double character of saint and poet. In the flourishing days of Moslem monasticism there were many convents for women, and some still remain in its general decline.

If at the present day, as in former centuries, most Moslem women are very ignorant in religion beyond that limited sphere of the law which falls in their domestic cognisance, it is not because they have intentionally been kept in ignorance, but because there is no one to teach them except their fathers and brothers, or their husbands, most of whom do not themselves know a great deal more and are not much concerned to teach the little they know.

Slavery in most Moslem countries has been, and is, almost exclusively domestic slavery, and the slaves—who usually

become Moslems—are treated as members of the household
and feel themselves to be such; so that the institution is of
a much milder form than slavery in the Roman Empire or
in Christian countries like America in modern times. It
has always been a meritorious act to set slaves free, and this
is often done by the owner in his lifetime, or in the anticipation of death. Many slaves are allowed by their owners to
carry on trade or business on their own account, and are
thus enabled to purchase their freedom.

Gambling, which was evidently a favourite pastime of
the heathen Arabs, is strictly forbidden in the Koran, and
the lawyers have construed the prohibition as extending to
forms of chance to which even the most rigorous of Christian moralists would hardly stretch the definition; for example, to life insurance and fire insurance; this, in connection
with the similar casuistic extension of the laws against usury,
which are made to forbid everything that lies under the
remotest suspicion of speculation in future values, constitutes
a serious hindrance to the economic development of Moslem
countries. The lawyers, however, like their kind in all the
world, have been fertile in legal fictions by which the excessive stringency of their own casuistry is more or less
circuitously evaded.

The Koran contains different and not altogether consistent prescriptions in regard to drinking, and even the final
prohibition of drinking wine left room for abundant controversy in the legal schools. Was the prohibition to be
construed strictly as applying only to *wine*, that is, the fermented juice of the grape? Or should it be assumed that
the lawgiver's intention was to prevent drunkenness, and the
prohibition consequently be extended to all other kinds of
fermented drinks containing alcohol, and to all narcotics,
Indian hemp, opium, and tobacco? The straightest sect
of Islamic pharisees, the Wahhabis, put the "drinking of
tobacco" under the same ban with intoxicating liquors;
while at least one unimpeachably orthodox creed declares
the drinking of *nabidh*, an intoxicating drink made from the

fermentation of dates or other fruit, not to be prohibited. Contrary to prevalent opinion—most prevalent opinions about Islam are wrong—the prohibitory laws of the Moslem religion have proved, on the whole, as ineffective as modern Christian experiments in the same direction. There is probably not a literature in the world so reeking of wine as that of the golden age of the highly religious Abbasid caliphate in Bagdad, and this odour clings to the literature of later times, such as the stories of the Arabian Nights, for example, the scene of many of which is laid in Bagdad. It is true nowadays, and doubtless always has been true, that many pious Moslems, with puritan strictness in morals, abhor the use of intoxicants of every kind as a great sin; and it is also true that in Mohammedan cities the drink-shops, like the bagnios, have always been kept by Christians or Jews; but that, as is sometimes said, a single verse in the Koran has made the Moslem world a world of total abstainers has not a shadow of warrant in the facts.

In the cultivation of personal religion in Islam the first place belongs to the public and private prayers, which are always said with decorum and apparent devoutness. When the appointed hour of prayer arrives and the call of the crier is heard, the Moslem, wherever he may be, performs his ablutions, spreads his prayer-carpet, and goes through the number of rounds of prayer prescribed by his rite and such supererogatory ones as he may prescribe to himself. He has not the least of the feeling common to many Christians that private devotions are a thing for the privacy of the closet. The set forms of prayer which constitute the Moslem liturgy are accompanied by short personal prayers, for which there are special manuals. Thus, before beginning the ablutions: "I am about to cleanse myself of my bodily impurities to prepare myself for prayer, a sacred act which will bring me near to the Most High. In the name of the great and exalted God, Praise be to God who has graciously made us Moslems! Islam is truth; unbelief is falsehood." Every subsequent stage of ablution is accompanied

by a brief ejaculatory prayer, appropriate to the particular
act, as, for example, when it comes to the ears: "O my God!
make me of the number of those who hear thy word and faithfully follow it." "O my God! let me hear, one day, the invitation to enter Paradise with the upright." At the end of
the ablutions is recited a confession of sin and a prayer for
forgiveness.

The public worship of Islam, however sincere and devout
it may be, has in it no mystical element. This side of religion, which has had so large a development in Islam, not
only among the Sufis, but through their influence among
the masses of the people, is cultivated particularly by the
various Dervish orders. In the early centuries those who
addicted themselves to the spiritual life put themselves
under the direction of a teacher or guide, by whom they
were inducted into the mystical way; they lived with him,
followed his instruction, and imitated his example. Al-
Ghazali put himself under such a director at Damascus,
and in his later years presided over a group of disciples
at Tus, who lived together in a common habitation, a kind
of monastery. In these older associations there was no
continuity; the death of the master dissolved them. In the
century after al-Ghazali, however, they developed into
orders bearing the name of the founder, and perpetuating
his teaching and methods. One of the oldest of these Dervish orders, and still one of the largest and most influential,
is that founded by Abd al-Kadir al-Jilani (d. 1166). It
has many branches, and is widely distributed through the
Moslem world. The Dervish orders claim for themselves
all the Sufi saints, and carry back their origin to the beginnings of Islam, most of them claiming Ali as the original
founder, though a minority trace their spiritual pedigree to
Abu Bekr.

Each of these has a rule ascribed to the founder, and a
ritual of its own, differing in particulars, though not in general character, from that of the others. They have monasteries in which the professed members of the order live to-

32

gether under the direction of their Sheikh, and where they perform together their common religious exercises. Some of the members are celibates, but, with rare exceptions, celibacy is not a part of the rule. The exercises consist primarily of the recitation of *Dhikrs*, repetitions of names and praises of God, in the particular form in use in the order, accompanied by movements of the head or of the whole body. The end and effect of these performances is to induce an exaltation which may go to the length of autohypnosis. The so-called Whirling Dervishes (Maulawi), who derive from Jelal al-Din Rumi, and the Howling Dervishes (Refaii), are familiar to all readers of books of travel in the Ottoman Empire. Each order has a distinctive dress or badge by which its members are recognised. Many of the monasteries were originally pious foundations, but their endowments have in modern times greatly diminished. Most of the inmates live by their own labour, or upon the charity of religious persons; many of them are beggars and go about with a begging basket, as it were the sign of their trade. In some orders, on the contrary, begging is forbidden.

Besides the professed members of the Dervish fraternities, many laymen are associated with them in a relation which has been not inaptly compared to that of the Tertiaries of the Franciscan order. They live in the world and pursue their ordinary occupations, but assemble weekly, or sometimes daily, usually in the evening, at the house of the order, to take part in such religious exercises as have already been described, under the direction of the Dervish Sheikh. By these means they strive to attain a personal experience of religion, a sense of the nearness and the power of God, which they do not feel in the same way in the staid and decorous worship of the mosque; or, beyond that, a state of enthusiasm or ecstasy. In the monasteries the practice of secluded meditation at certain seasons is still perpetuated by a few of the inmates who have progressed farthest in the way.

CHAPTER XXII

MOHAMMEDANISM

EXTRAVAGANT SECTS AND DERIVATIVE RELIGIONS

The Ismailis—Doctrine of the Sect—Karmatians—Assassins—Druses
—Sheikhis—Babis and Bahais—The Ahmediyya.

IN a former chapter the general characteristics of Shia
Mohammedanism have been described, and its main divisions enumerated. Some of these are far removed from
common Moslem orthodoxy, but may, notwithstanding these
departures, properly be covered by the name of Islam. There
are, however, offshoots of the Shia which have deviated so
widely from the type that they are not to be classed as heretical Moslem sects, but as distinct religions, which have grown
out of Mohammedanism, or in whose comprehensive syncretism the most important elements—or those which they
themselves think it expedient to put in the foreground—are
derived from Shiite Mohammedanism. Some of these call
themselves Moslem, and even proclaim themselves the only
true Moslems, while others wear the name only as a disguise,
which they throw off when they venture to speak freely.

The common stock from which most of these religions
have sprung may best be designated by the name Ismaili.
Their line of historical Imams contains seven names: Ali,
Hasan, Husein, Ali ibn Husein, Mohammed ibn Ali, Jafar
ibn Mohammed, and Ismail ibn Jafar.[1] Ismail died in his
father's lifetime, leaving as his successor in the Imamate, a
son, Mohammed, who disappeared in India; according to
others, Ismail did not die. In the former view it is Moham-

---

[1] The "Twelvers" count as their seventh Imam, Musa, a younger
son of Jafar, holding that Ismail had been excluded by his father from
the succession because he was addicted to drunkenness.

med, the son of Ismail, who is to reappear as the Mahdi; the latter hold that it is Ismail himself.

The founder of the Ismaili *sect* and the author of its peculiar system was a certain Abdallah ibn Maimun, a man of Persian descent, who lived about the middle of the third century of the Hegira in Khuzistan. His aim seems to have been, by means of a secret order, to undermine Islam, and to substitute an altogether different religion. His system, the basis of which is Neoplatonism, is thus described by De Goeje:[1]

From God, the mysterious Being who is wholly incomprehensible to mankind and cannot be defined by any attributes, emanated by his will the Universal Reason, which produced the Universal Soul, the creator of Primal Matter, Space, and Time. These are the five constituents of the universe, and consequently of man, the microcosm. But as every emanation has a tendency to return to its source, man's object in life is perfect union with the Universal Reason. This, however, would be wholly unattainable by him without heavenly help. Therefore the Universal Reason and the Universal Soul have manifested themselves to the world in human shape, the one as prophet-legislator, the other as his assistant and supporter. So appeared successively Adam and Seth, Noah and Shem, Abraham and Ishmael, Moses and Aaron, Jesus and Peter, Muhammad and Ali. After the disappearance of the prophet-legislator, the assistant continues his work, and is the Imam, or leader, the sole interpreter of the true meaning of the divine word. He is followed by six other Imams, after the death of the last of whom a new incarnation takes place. . . . Muhammad, the son of Ismail, is the seventh incarnation. His assistant is Abdallah ibn Maimun, who, with his successors, has to preach and promulgate his law, till, with the reappearance of the last of these as the Mahdi, the end and scope of human life will be reached. All these legislations, though each in succession is better than its predecessor, so that the last is the most perfect, are in reality one, only adapted to the understanding of the men of each period. Moreover, it is always the same Being that incarnates itself in different forms, even as the soul of each Imam passes into the body of his successor.

Thus there have been, since the world began, six prophets, incarnations of the Universal Intelligence, and in the inter-

[1] Encyclopædia of Religion and Ethics, vol. III, p. 222.

val between each two successive prophets a series of seven Imams, incarnations of the Universal Soul. The last incarnation of the Universal Intelligence was near at hand, as was proved by apocalyptic arithmetic, operating with the theory of chronological periods in the history of the world. Abdallah professed to be in communication with the Concealed Imam and to communicate his teaching and commands to his followers. He organised an extensive propaganda by means of missionaries (Dā'īs), whom he sent out to disseminate his doctrine among men of all religions; and, in fact, by their efforts many converts were made, not only among Moslems, but among Christians, Jews, and Zoroastrians, all of whom, it must be remembered, expected the coming of a Messiah. The converts were made to swear with the most solemn oaths that they would never reveal aught of the Ismaili doctrine. There were several stages in the disclosure of the doctrine, or degrees in the mystery, and the missionaries were often not acquainted with the complete system. The method they employed was to raise questions and instil in men's minds doubts about the religion they professed. Then the Ismaili doctrine of the succession of prophets and their assistants was communicated, and the inquirers were taught that each of the prophets had given a religious law adapted to his age. The positive religious law had, however, in itself no religious value; it might be an allegory of higher things to the man who brought to it a knowledge of the higher things derived from elsewhere, and it was only this esoteric sense of the scriptures of the various religions which had any worth. Those who after long testing and preparation were initiated into the higher degrees were taught that the philosophers are superior to all the prophets, Plato and Aristotle to the Koran and the Gospel; for philosophy is the universal form of truth, and all the philosophers express one and the same truth. From this point of view all positive religions are equally good, or equally bad—at any rate, equally negligible. What relation there is between all this and the

Essays of the Ikhwan al-Safa,[1] whose authors are also suspected of having been a secret society with political ends, it is impossible to determine.

Abdallah's ambition was, not merely to be the founder and head of a new religion which should supplant all others, nor even to rule with unlimited authority a religious community organized as a great secret society; he aimed to undermine not only the Moslem religion, but the Moslem states, by the employment of the same means by which the Shia missionaries had undermined the Omayyad caliphate and—not by any intention of theirs—brought the Abbasids into power.

The chief apostle of the Ismaili faith in Irak was a certain Hamdan, nicknamed Karmat, after whom his followers were called Karmatians. The seat of government—for from the beginning they were a political as well as a religious community—was established in the vicinity of the ancient Babylon in the year 890. In this region they soon made so many converts that the Moslem governor in Cufa found it profitable to tolerate them, imposing upon them for his own benefit a tax of a dinar a head. The government in Bagdad began to see danger in the movement, and its founder, Abdallah ibn Maimun, finding that the authorities were on his track, fled to northern Syria, which remained the headquarters of the sect until 900. Meantime the doctrine had been preached with great success in Yemen, and within a generation the Karmatians conquered nearly the whole province, so that Mecca itself was in great alarm. In Bahrain, also, a Karmatian state was founded, between 893 and 903, and successfully resisted all the efforts of the caliphate to bring it into subjection. A large army sent against it in 927 was totally defeated, and even Bagdad was seriously threatened. The following year Karmatian armies from Bahrain took Mecca at the time of the pilgrimage, with great slaughter both of the inhabitants and of the pilgrims, and carried off to their capital at Lahsa the sacred black

[1] See above, pp. 450 ff.

stone from the Kaaba, the veneration of which they pronounced mere idolatry. The stone remained in their possession for more than twenty years, and was only restored
by them at the instance of the Fatimid caliph Obeid Allah.
For many years they made the road to Mecca so dangerous
or imposed so heavy a toll upon the pilgrims whom they
allowed to pass under their conduct, that the pilgrimage
from Irak nearly ceased.

In 900 Obeid Allah, a grandson of Abdallah the founder
of the sect, fled from Syria by way of Egypt to the far west
of north Africa, where ten years later he makes his appearance at Kairwan, the capital, in the character of the Mahdi.
He found the ground prepared for him, for from the time
of the Idrisid dynasty in Morocco (788 to 985) the Berbers
had been familiar with Shiite doctrines and claims. The
new Mahdi gave himself out for a descendant of Ali and
Fatima through the seven Imams of the Ismaili scheme and
a succession of Concealed Imams following Ismail. He
established his capital, called al-Mahdiyya, near Tunis; and
sixty years later his descendants, as the Fatimid caliphs,
added Egypt, and subsequently Syria, to their empire, ruling,
thus, from the borders of Morocco to Aleppo. In pretending
to be descendants in direct line from Ali, the Fatimid caliphs
gave their rule the semblance of Shiite legitimacy, and thus
assumed the character of the only rightful Moslem rulers,
in opposition to the Abbasid usurpers.

In Egypt and Syria their subjects were chiefly orthodox
Sunnites, and while the Fatimids made no concealment of
their adherence to the Shia, on which indeed their claims
were founded, and caused the call to prayer in all the
mosques to be made with the Shiite formula, they in general observed a politic regard for the prejudices of the
masses. Their relation to the Ismaili movement, both on
its political and its religious side, on the other hand, was
carefully kept in the background. Yet in the palaces of the
caliphs at Cairo secret assemblies were held, where among
the initiates doctrines were taught and discussed subversive

of the very foundations of Islam; from these circles the movement proceeded which gave rise to the religion of the Druses.

Another offshoot of the Ismailis, which made for itself a name of mystery and of terror, is that which Europeans know by the name of the Assassins.[1] By Moslem writers they are sometimes called Hasanites, after the name of their founder; the name they themselves used, at least in the beginning of their career, seems to have been Talimites, that is, those who make the following of an infallible religious teacher their distinctive tenet. The main structure of their doctrine is the same as that of other Ismailis, but seems in some particulars to have been more highly elaborated. Their esoteric teaching, as might be expected in a secret society of the kind, is only imperfectly known. The founder of the Assassins was Hasan Sabbah, who after studying the Ismaili doctrines, apparently in Egypt, returned to Persia as a missionary. The operations of this kind of missionaries were, however, not appreciated by the police, since they were not unjustly regarded as equally dangerous to religion and to the state. Hasan accordingly conceived the brilliant idea of securing a safe basis for these operations by seizing (1090 A. D.) the stronghold of Alamut, an isolated rock on the edge of the Elburz Mountains near Kasvin, which he fortified in such a way as to make it almost impregnable. The rock was about three hundred yards long and very narrow, rising precipitously about two hundred feet above the plain. Around the fortress the land was cultivated with such diligence that, we are told, it was like the garden of Paradise. Hasan wrote a number of controversial treatises which were of sufficient importance to evoke formal refutations from al-Ghazali, and Alamut was a seat of learning as well as the stronghold of the Assassins. When Hulagu and his Mongols stormed and destroyed the place

---

[1] Arabic *hashshāsh*, one who intoxicates himself with *hashīsh* (Cannabis indica.)

in 1256, they found in it a large library, which they committed to the flames.

Not long after they established themselves at Alamut we find them at Aleppo also; and their numbers continued to increase, until in the latter part of the twelfth century they had ten or a dozen strongholds in Syria. Here the crusaders came in contact with them, and through the crusade historians we hear a good deal about them and their chief, the "Old Man of the Mountain."

The name Assassins in the European sense is properly applicable only to one, the lowest, class of the members of the order, who among themselves were called Fidā'īs, "The Devoted." They were not inducted into the deeper mysteries of the order, but were carefully trained in the use of arms and the arts of disguise, sometimes also in foreign languages, and were bound to absolute obedience to the command of the Grand Master. They were taught to be patient and bide their time until the right opportunity for the execution of their mission should come. They did not often survive their victims, for they were fond of doing their work in the most dramatic way, striking down a Moslem ruler or minister in the mosque on a Friday, or a Christian prince on a Sunday in church, thus inviting the martyrdom which insured them a high place in Paradise. The emissaries who in 1192 killed Conrad of Montferrat, Signor of Tyre and titular king of Jerusalem, had spent six months in the crusaders' camp disguised as Christian monks. Christian rulers as well as Moslem are said to have hired the services of these experts to put their enemies out of the way.

Their Syrian fortresses were all occupied by the Egyptian Sultan Baibars in 1273; but they afterward regained some of them, and as late as 1326 held as many as five. Though their political power has long been broken and they have given up their murderous practices, this branch of the Ismailis still survives in the region of the Lebanon, where their numbers were estimated a few years ago by a Moslem official at 20,000; but there are believed to be in the cities

many more who conceal their sectarian beliefs under the
general protection of Islam, nor are they by any means ex-
tinct in Persia, where, however, among the more fanatical
Shiites, they are under still greater necessity of concealing
their true character. In western India, where they are
called Khojas, there are said to be 50,000 or 70,000 of them.
Their head, who bears the title Agha Khan, a lineal descendant of the last Grand Master of the Assassins in Alamut,
through whom he traces his pedigree in the line of the Fatimid caliphs from Ismail, the seventh Imam, resides in Bom-
bay, and not only enjoys the veneration of the sect, but derives large revenues from their annual tribute. The Agha
Khan of our day is very much a man of the world, with a
modern education, who has visited Europe and the United
States, and even Japan. Of the peculiar doctrines of the
Ismaili and their elaborate organisation and initiation by
degrees little if anything has survived.

Another religion, further removed from orthodox or even
heretical Mohammedanism than the Assassins, is that of the
Druses, who to the number of perhaps 150,000 still occupy
considerable parts of the southern Lebanon and an extensive
district in the Hauran. The characteristic feature of their
creed is that the Supreme God was incarnated, or manifested in the flesh, in the person of Hakim Abu Ali Mansur,
the sixth of the Fatimid caliphs and the third to reign in
Egypt, who died or, according to their own doctrine, disappeared, in 1020. Hakim's career impressed his contemporaries as more like that of an incarnate devil than an incarnate god. He persecuted not only Moslems who refused
to acknowledge the exclusive claims of Ali to the caliphate,
but Jews and Christians. The record of his deeds leaves no
room to doubt that he was insane, and in many ways re-
minds us of the emperor Caligula. During his reign an
Ismaili missionary named al-Darazi, a Persian or Turk by
race, came to Egypt, where he was received by Hakim with
favour. Before long al-Darazi began publicly to teach that
Hakim was God, the Creator of the Universe, and exhorted

the people to embrace this doctrine. In a book which he wrote he said that the soul of Adam had passed into Ali, and from Ali into the ancestors of Hakim, and finally embodied itself in that prince. This was too much for the masses; he was attacked by the mob and narrowly escaped with his life. Hakim did not dare openly to take his part, but got him safely away to Syria, where he carried on an active propaganda in the region west of Damascus and in the southern Lebanon. The name Druses, apparently derived from that of this Darazi, was given them by outsiders; they called themselves only Mowahhidin, that is, "Unitarians."

Another Ismaili missionary, Hamza ibn Ali, succeeded him in Egypt, proclaiming that Hakim was God, and he, Hamza, the prime minister of God. Hakim now took courage to play the rôle assigned to him. He ceased to attend the Friday prayers in the mosque, and for several years interrupted the pilgrimage to Mecca under pretence that the Arabs made it too dangerous, and failed to send the covering for the Kaaba, which was annually renewed. Having thus openly broken with Islam, he suddenly became tolerant toward the adherents of other religions.

In 1020, as has been said, Hakim disappeared, probably the victim of a secret murder, which a Moslem account attributes to his sister. Those who believed in him held that he was not dead, but had withdrawn in the manner of the Concealed Imams, and would in due time return. His disappearance left Hamza the earthly representative of the divine power, and he pretended to be in direct communion with Hakim. In this way he made himself the real head of the movement, and presently succeeded in supplanting al-Darazi among the Syrian converts of the latter, so that in the Druse tradition al-Darazi has become the great adversary of the faith of which he was in fact the founder. The sacred scriptures of the Druses are ascribed to Hamza, who was himself a manifestation of the Universal Intelligence, as Hakim was the incarnation of the supreme godhead. The doctrine of the Druses is better known than that of other

similar sects, because during the Druse wars in the nineteenth century their sacred books, which they preserve with
the utmost secrecy, fell into the hands of Moslems and
Christians.

With the common features of the Ismaili system and its
successive emanations from the Absolute Unity of the godhead, are combined new elements which have an obvious affinity with Christian Gnosticism and perhaps with Manichæ-
ism. Thus, notwithstanding the fundamental importance of
the doctrine of the divine unity, a dualistic principle is introduced into the very first stage of emanation: the Antagonist, Pure Darkness, proceeds from the Universal Intelligence, which is Pure Light, as a consequence or punishment
of the sin of the latter in looking with complacency upon
his own glorious light. The Universal Soul, the second
emanation, in like manner brings forth an opposite principle called the Foundation, or Companion, and so on through
succeeding stages of emanation. Human souls, when they
come into being, contain both light and darkness—good and
evil are both found in them from the beginning.

The Druses are divided into two classes, in their own terminology, the Intelligent and the Ignorant. Only the former
are initiated into the profounder teaching of the religion,
and constitute an esoteric circle like the higher degrees
among the Gnostics, or among the Pure Brethren and in the
Ismaili sects generally. For them the Koran and all the
observances of Islam are abrogated; though they may profess or practise them, when necessary, as a disguise. The
uninitiated, on the other hand, if living among Moslems,
habitually conform to the custom of the country. The Intelligent are just as willing to confess themselves in substantial agreement with Christians—not, of course, the Syrian
Christians whom they have around them, but Christians of
European, and particularly of the Protestant, type. Under
the solvent power of their esoteric philosophy all positive
religions are only forms or names of the one true and universal religion, which they possess in its purest and highest

form. In this respect their attitude is the same as that of the modern Bahais.

The Druses are unique, so far as I know, among the religions of the world in constituting a closed religious community, neither seeking converts nor admitting those who seek to join them. Their gospel was preached for twenty-six years, and those who accepted it became Druses. At the end of that time the door was shut, and cannot be opened again. At first the return of Hakim was expected soon, but as time went by, the Druses, like the early Shiites or the early Christians, postponed their expectation, and settled down to live in the world that now is. They have, like other religions in similar circumstances, books in which the signs of the end of the age and the approaching return of Hakim are set down, and the final triumph of the true religion described. When Hakim comes, he will abide forever as visible Manifestation, having his capital in Egypt. The Moslems, Christians, and Jews will be subjected to the rule of the Druses, who will fill all places of rank and power in the theocratic empire.

The latest offshoot of the "Ultra" Shiite heresies are the Babis and Bahais. While most of the eccentric religions with which we have been engaged sprang from the branch which recognises seven Imams, the Babis originated among the sect of the Twelve Imams, but they are themselves the proof, if any were needed, that in these circles, also, the more radical Ismaili doctrines of the incarnation or, to speak more exactly in their own terms, the "manifestation" of the godhead had taken deep root. Indeed, the Bektashis, and the Ali-Ilahis or Kyzylbashes, who belong to the branch of the Twelve Imams, are not behind any variety of the Ismailis in the multiplicity of emanations of the godhead, or of godheads themselves, in their Points and Manifestations.[1] Among the Nusairi these sublimities are united in an interesting syncretism with the survivals of a pagan nature-worship. Fadl Allah, the founder of the Shia

[1] To the Ali-Ilahis Ali is the Supreme God in person.

sect of the Hurufis, from whom, at least indirectly, the Bab
and his followers contracted their propensity to find cabal-
istic significance in numbers, also gave himself out for a
Manifestation of the godhead (1398), his doctrine for "the
most perfect revelation of truth," and was put to death by
Timur for his blasphemy.   The Babi-Bahai "Manifestations" had therefore many predecessors, and the fundamental philosophy in all is the same.

The next antecedents of the Babis are to be found in a
sect founded by the Sheikh Ahmed al-Ahsai (d. 1826), who
called themselves Sheikhis, "Followers of the Sheikh." The
essential features of his doctrine were that God in himself,
as the Absolute, cannot be known "even by the heart"—a
rejection of Sufism as well as of scholasticism. All the divine
attributes are found in the Imams, and the actions ascribed
to God are produced by them; they are—this is the essence
of the heresy—the four Causes of Creation.[1] Ahmed says
of the Imams: "I believe in your return; each of you the perfect cause of all that is not God." The Imams, or Imam,
for they are in reality one in all their manifestations, are
thus intermediary between the Absolute God and the world
of sense.   Abstractly, this intermediary may be called the
Truth; it is the first emanation of the Absolute, and corresponds to the Universal Intelligence of the Ismailis, the Intelligence, or Will, of the Druses.

More distinctive and of greater consequence for the future
was the doctrine that there must be among the Shiites, the
true Moslems, in every generation one perfect man, serving
as a channel of grace between the absent Imam and his
church. The Sheikh Ahmed and his successor, Kazim of
Resht, were such perfect Shias in their generation. Another
name for this intermediary between men and the Concealed
Imam in whom are all the divine attributes, is the Door
(Bab), a term and idea which are current also among the
Ismailis, Druses, and Nusairis. The orthodox doctrine in the
sect of the Twelve was that after the disappearance of the

[1] Efficient, Material, Formal, and Final.

twelfth Imam, in the year 873/4, communication was maintained with him through an intermediary called the Bab. There were in this period of the "minor occultation" successively four Babs After the death of the last of these the door was closed and communication with the Imam ceased (940/1). It was believed, however, that the door would be opened again in the generation preceding the return of the Imam. When, therefore, Sheikh Ahmed and Kazim of Resht professed to be in communication with the Imam they virtually claimed the function of the Bab, and this title was given to them by their followers, even if it was not assumed by themselves.

Among those who came under the influence of the Sheikhi movement was a young man named Ali Mohammed (born about 1820), the son of a tradesman in Shiraz. At Kerbela, whither he had gone to visit the tomb of the martyr Husein, he heard Kazim of Resht, who was lecturing there, and made the acquaintance of a number of Kazim's disciples. Ali Mohammed had no more education than is common in his class, and it may fairly be assumed that Kazim's lectures on the Sheikhi doctrine were beyond his depth, but at least he picked up at Kerbela the ideas which determined his own career. These ideas, especially the expectation of the advent of the Imam, wrought strongly upon a temperament predisposed to religious exaltation, and a couple of years later (1844) at Shiraz in a mosque near his home he announced himself as the Bab; in him was reopened the door which, according to the common Twelver doctrine, had been closed for centuries; he was the precursor of the Imam Mahdi.[1] In this quality he vehemently assailed the corruption of the Mollahs, the clergy of the state church—always a fruitful theme for reformers and grateful to the ears of the masses.

Shortly after, he went on the pilgrimage to Mecca, and there also he is said to have made some sort of demonstra-

[1] The year 1844 A. D. corresponds to the Moslem year 1260, exactly a thousand years from the accession of the twelfth Imam (260 A. H.).

tion, which does not, however, seem to have had any consequence. Returning to Persia, he sent out missionaries
(Dā'īs) to disseminate the faith. The proclamation which
was made in his name by one of his followers in a mosque
in Shiraz shows that, from believing himself to be the door
of communication with the Concealed Imam, he had come
to claim to be the Imam Mahdi himself; and he accordingly demanded that the Shah of Persia should recognise
him as such, and acknowledge that he held his royal authority from the Imam, that is to say, from the young
tradesman of Shiraz, Ali Mohammed! Nor was this the
climax of his claim. A Shiite tradition, of which the Druses
and Nusairi had already availed themselves, was that Ali
had declared that the essence of the revelation in the Koran
is concentrated in the Bismillah ("In the name of God")
at the beginning; the whole of the Bismillah is in the letter
Ba, and the whole of the Ba in the diacritical point under
it. Ali Mohammed presently declared himself this "Point
of Revelation," "the Primal Point," that is to say, the sum
and substance of divine revelation. But the "Point" was,
in the extravagant doctrine, not merely the quintessence of
revelation, it was the first emanation of God, which in each
prophetic cycle manifested itself again in the revealer or
embodied revelation of that epoch. In all these persons,
from Adam on, it is the same identical Point, as the sun
which rises new every day is always the very same sun.
Each Manifestation is more perfect than its predecessor;
and this progressive revelation will continue cycle by cycle,
a new Manifestation coming when men are prepared for it.

The Sheikhi sect had been split by the claim of Ali Mohammed to be the Bab, the successor of Kazim of Resht.
There was another claimant, a certain Mohammed Karim
Khan, whom Ali Mohammed usually spoke of as the "Quintessence of Hell-Fire," or the "Infernal Tree of Zakkum."
Many of Kazim's disciples, and they, it would seem, the
élite of his following, acknowledged Ali Mohammed, among
them a notable group at Kasvin, to which the poetess Kur-

rat al-Ain belonged. To them he was, not the mere Imam
Mahdi of the vulgar expectation, the militant Messiah who
was to lead the hosts of Islam to the conquest of the
world, the righteous ruler who was "to fill the earth with
justice, as now it is filled with oppression," but the manifestation of the Universal Will, or Intelligence, the primal
emanation of the Absolute, with whom began a new era
in the history of religion. His revelation, the Beyan, superseded and thus abrogated the Koran and all the ordinances
of Islam.

The disclosure of this more exalted doctrine at a great
gathering of the Babis at Bedesht was a crisis which for a
moment threatened a fatal schism. The danger was overcome, chiefly by the diplomacy of Kurrat el-Ain—a diplomacy as audacious in execution as it was ingenious in conception. The masses, however, while giving their adherence
to the higher conception of Ali Mohammed's nature and
mission, were not diverted from the execution of the Mahdi
programme as they conceived it, and before long were in
arms in different parts of the country against the Shah's
government. The insurgents were suppressed with difficulty after fighting which lasted for many months, and the
vanquished were treated with great severity. While the
revolts were still in progress, the government decided to
strike at the root of the evil by putting to death the pretender to supreme authority in state and church. The Bab,
who had been imprisoned even before the conference at
Bedesht, was executed at Tabriz, July 9, 1850.

The revelation for the new dispensation is called the
Beyan. In it the transcendent God declares to the recipient of the revelation (the Bab): "Verily I have created
thee, and I have established two degrees for thee. The
first of these two degrees is that which belongs peculiarly
to me, and in this degree no one can see anything in thee
except myself. Therefore it is that thou sayest on my
authority, 'I am God; there is no God beside me, the Lord
of the universe'; in the second degree thou dost glorify me,

33

praise me, confess my unity, adore me, thou art of those
who bow down before me." That is to say, in his divinity
he is the only God, the Lord of the universe; in his (apparent) humanity he is a worshipper of God. So much for the
theology of Babism. The practical part of the Beyan is the
constitution and law for a Babi commonwealth. It contains regulations for religious worship—prayers, pilgrimage
to the birthplace of the Bab, for marriage and succession,
and the like. In relation to unbelievers, the fundamental
law is that believers when they have the power are to take
possession of all the property of those who have not "entered into the Beyan," and directions are given for the distribution of the spoil of conquered cities. In Persia proper
no other religion is to be tolerated; no unbeliever to set
foot in it, unless he be licensed for the sake of trade. All
Moslem shrines are to be demolished. In their place,
shrines shall be erected for the eighteen "Letters of Life,"
the apostles of Babism, richly decorated from the plunder
of the older holy places.

A good deal of the Beyan sounds to us like a Utopia, but,
however Utopian its provisions, it was in intention the
divinely revealed law for the state which the Bab's followers
were fighting to establish on the ruins of the kingdom of
Persia.

The Bab had before his death designated as his successor
a youth named Yahya of Nur, who is called in the religion
Subh-i-Ezel, Dawn of Eternity, and commissioned him to
complete the Beyan, which the Bab himself left unfinished.[1]
Subh-i-Ezel was recognized by the majority of Bab's followers, though dissensions were caused by the claims of
others to be the promised Manifestation. An attempt on
the life of the Shah in 1852 led to the execution of twenty-
eight of the leading spirits among the Babi, including
Kurrat al-Ain and several others of the "Letters of Life,"
the apostolic circle of eighteen. Subh-i-Ezel had an elder
half-brother, Husein, who assumed the name Baha Allah,

[1] It does not appear that this was ever done.

Splendour of God. He also was a disciple of the Bab, and after the attempted assassination of the Shah was imprisoned, but, being released, after some months followed his brother to Bagdad. There Subh-i-Ezel lived in seclusion, only his brothers and some of his most intimate followers being admitted to his presence; while the conduct of affairs outside "the veil" was in the hands of his abler and more experienced brother, Baha Allah. The most important of the writings of the sect in this Bagdad period is the Ikan, or "Book of Certainty," an exposition of Babi doctrine and demonstration of the mission of the Bab, composed by Baha Allah in 1861/2.

Bagdad was a convenient base for Babi propaganda and agitation in Persia, and in 1864, upon representations by the Persian government to the Porte, the two brothers, with a considerable number of their disciples, were transported, first to Constantinople, and a few months later to Adrianople. In the latter city, in the year 1866/7, Baha Allah formally announced himself as "Him whom God shall manifest," for whom the Bab had bidden his disciples look. This declaration caused a schism in the Babi community. Most of them attached themselves to the cause of the new Manifestation, but a conservative minority adhered to Subh-i-Ezel. The Turkish authorities found it necessary to separate the factions. Subh-i-Ezel, with his family and a few followers, was sent to Famagosta, in Cyprus, while Baha Allah and his party were deported to Acre on the Syrian coast. In Persia also the Babi church was split over the two brothers, but in the end almost all recognised Baha Allah.

"He whom God shall manifest," so the Bab had foretold, would bring a new and fuller revelation, abrogating and superseding the Beyan as that superseded the Koran. Such a law for the new dispensation Baha Allah gave in the Kitab Akdas, the "Most Holy Book," which was from time to time supplemented by numerous *responsa* and epistles. Like the Beyan, the Kitab Akdas resembles the Koran, the

only sacred scriptures with which the authors or their
disciples were familiar, and both in its ideas and in its
phraseology the reader is constantly reminded of the older
revelation, for whose ordinances in matter of civil law and
religious observance it substitutes others of the same general nature.

The Most Holy Book begins with the fundamental dogma
of the religion. "The first thing that God has prescribed
for the servants of God is that they should recognise the
sunrise-point of his revelation, and the eastern horizon of
his word, which is 'the place' of his essence in the world of
the word and the creation." The terms in which this utterance of God is couched, however cryptic they may sound
to Western readers, were plain and unambiguous to Persians
familiar with the doctrines of the esoteric Shia sects. "The
place" is here, as in the scriptures of the Druses, the human
being, or rather, the human form, in whom the godhead
itself is embodied and manifested in this world.

The counterpart of the recognition of this divinity in
human form is unquestioning and unqualified acceptance of
his teaching and obedience to his commands. "Whoever
lays hold of him lays hold of all good, and he who rejects is
lost, even though he bring all good works. If ye accept
this most exalted 'place' and most lofty 'horizon,' every
one must obey what is commanded by the 'Desired.' These
two things go together; man cannot take one of them without the other."[1]

Baha Allah in fact made for himself as extravagant
claims as were made by or for any of his predecessors in
that vein. According to Abd al-Baha, the ground of Baha
Allah's vast superiority to all who gave revelations before
him is that they were only manifestations of the Supreme
Intelligence, or Will, or—when he talks to Occidentals—of
the Holy Spirit, while in him is manifested, not an emanation from the divine essence but that Essence itself. The

[1] The two things are to acknowledge Baha Allah as God and to do
whatever he commands.

Druse Hakim also is the Supreme God in the flesh; but he preserves something of the mystery of the godhead by disappearing, leaving Hamza, the manifestation of the Universal Intelligence, to reveal his religion to men.

Like the Beyan, the Kitab Akdas is a legislation for a church-state, including its constitution, laws, ceremonial, and liturgy. The legislation, upon the whole, exhibits a larger mind and more knowledge of the world than the Bab's. Into the details of this legislation it is impossible to enter here. It ranges from the regulation of the canonical hours of prayer and the number of series of prayers to be said at each, the worshipper's face being turned in "my most holy direction," that is toward the abode of Baha Allah, to the frequency with which the finger-nails should be cut and the superiority of a douche bath over a plunge. These institutions are unchangeable for a millennium. "Whoever before the completion of a full thousand years shall claim authority (amr),[1] he is a liar and a fraud. . . . Whoever interprets this verse allegorically, or explains it otherwise than it is revealed in its plain sense, is cut off from the spirit of God and his mercy which was before all worlds."

In one important respect the attitude of Baha Allah differs entirely from that of the Bab. The latter was the Imam Mahdi, whose mission it was, in accordance with the common expectation, to dethrone the rulers of this world and establish the reign of righteousness; accordingly, when the Shah refused his submission to this supreme authority, the followers of the Bab drew the sword for the holy war. Baha Allah, on the contrary, took pains at the beginning to make clear that the establishment of the true religion by force was no part of his programme. He held—herein adopting the position of the Fatimid (Ismaili) caliphs in Egypt—that religion should win men's hearts by persuasion, not constrain their allegiance by the sword.

As the founder of a universal religion, he endeavoured to

[1] To produce a new revelation.

demonstrate his claims, not only from the Koran and the previous Shia systems, but from the Jewish and Christian Scriptures, and from Acre he addressed his apologetic and propaganda to the Christians of Europe and America, and with considerable success. This Occidentalised Bahaism has, however, a very remote resemblance to the genuine teaching of the "Most Holy Book" and the complementary scriptures which must be regarded as the authentic sources for the knowledge of the religion.[1]

Upon the death of Baha Allah, in 1892, his sons—of whom he left four, besides three daughters[2]—quarrelled about the headship of the community. Abbas, who called himself Abd al-Baha, had been ornamented by his father with the title "Mightiest Branch," while his brother Mohammed Ali was the "Greatest Branch." Abbas was accused by his brothers of claiming that authority which it was declared in the Most Holy Book no one should claim for a thousand years. In another of his writings Baha Allah had affirmed: "The manifestations are ended with this greatest Manifestation (sc. himself), and whoever claims such a thing is a forger and a liar."[3]

What foundation, if any, there is for these charges we have no occasion to inquire. The main thing is that the quarrel of the brothers became a schism in the religion which has persisted to the present. The party of Abd al-Baha, however, prevailed, and its rival has sunk into relative insignificance.

The authority which Abd al-Baha claims for himself, and which is asserted for him by his sect, is based upon the right to interpret the revelation made by Baha Allah. For practi-

[1] The Most Holy Book is an effectually sealed book to the Occidental adherents of the religion, who cannot extract illumination or edification from the Arabic original.

[2] He had two wives and a concubine, all of whom survived him.

[3] From the frequency and emphasis of such utterances it is clear that Baha Allah apprehended that some one of his followers, and very likely of his sons, would try to supplant him as he had supplanted the Bab.

cal purposes it serves as well to be the sole and infallible
interpreter of a revelation as to give a new one. Upon the
death of Abd al-Baha the headship in the religion and the
power of interpretation will pass to a Council called the Bet
al-Adl, House of Justice, which will preside over all the
interests of the religion, and in its decisions and interpretations will be divinely and infallibly guided.

The numbers of the Bahais are very variously estimated.
The great mass of them are in Persia, but the religion has
adherents in other Moslem countries also, and it has made
a few thousand converts in Europe and America. In Persia, Bahai writers claim from a third to a half of the population of the country, which would give them three millions
or upwards, while some American Christian missionaries
would reduce these figures to one or two hundred thousand.
One reason for this surprising difference in the figures is the
difficulty of determining how much of a Bahai a man must
be in order to be counted. The principle that religious
beliefs should be concealed or disguised when it is dangerous
or inconvenient to avow them is so ingrained in the Shiites
of all stripes that religious statistics are impossible.

A still more recent syncretistic incarnation religion of this
type, with other heretical Moslem premises but similar universal pretensions, was started in India in 1889, by Mirza
Ghulam Ahmed, of Kadhian, in the Panjab. A Moslem
tradition runs, "In the beginning of every century (of the
Moslem Era) God will raise up one who shall reform the
faith," and as early as 1880 Ahmed had announced himself
as the reformer who was due at the beginning of the fourteenth century of the Hegira. In 1889 he came out with
much grander claims. He was the Mahdi whom the Moslem world expected—a denatured, peaceable Mahdi, it must
be added; he was the Christ whose second coming Christians awaited; while to the Hindus he presented himself as
the latest Avatar. As one of his supporters writes, "These
three claims point to the universality of the Ahmediyya
mission.

The gist of the founder's doctrine of himself may be briefly
stated in his own words: "As I have been given the name
of Messiah by God, with reference to the creatures' rights,
and am an incarnation of Jesus Christ, on account of having
been sent in his spirit and character and cast in the same
mould, similarly I have received the name of Muhammad
Ahmad by virtue of my function as a reformer of the transgression of Creator's authority to spread the unity of God,
and therefore I have been sent in the spirit and character
and cast in the mould of the holy Prophet Muhammad,
may peace and blessings of God be upon him. Thus I am
at once *Isa Messih* and *Muhammad Mahdi*. Messiah is a
title given to Jesus Christ, and it means one who is anointed
and blessed by God, his vicegerent in earth and a truthful
and righteous person. The title of Mahdi was given to the
holy Prophet Muhammad, and it means one who is naturally
guided and the heir to all truths, and in whom the attribute
'guide' of the Almighty is fully represented. The grace
of God and mercy have made me the heir to both these
titles in this age, and manifested them conjointly in my person. This is the true interpretation of my claim to the title
of *Isa Messih* and *Muhammad Mahdi*. The way in which
this manifestation has taken place is known in Islamic terminology as *baruz*.[1] I am therefore a *baruz* of Jesus as well
as of Muhammad, peace be with them, and my person is
spiritually a combination of the persons of these two eminent
prophets."[2]

In contradiction to both Christian and Moslem belief that
Jesus, after his crucifixion, rose from the tomb and was taken
up to heaven, whence in the last days he will return, Ahmed
felt it necessary to his own pretensions to prove that Jesus
did not die, but, his wounds having been healed by a magical
ointment, made his escape to Galilee, and thence found his

---

[1] "*Baruz* means the spiritual appearance of one in the person of another, the two bearing a striking resemblance to each other in their
qualities and characters, and being as like one another as two peas."

[2] See Revue du Monde Musulman, vol. I, pp. 534 *ff.*

way to the East, where his tomb was opportunely discovered at Srinagar, in Cashmere.

Apart from the claims for the founder's own person, the movement appears on its own presentation as an endeavour to revive a religious spirit among Indian Moslems, and to reform some of their ways. It appeals for authority to the Koran, the Old and New Testaments, and to "trustworthy" Moslem traditions. Under the stimulus of the educational work of Christian missionaries, considerable stress is laid upon similar efforts by Moslems. Ahmed died in 1908; but the progress of the movement continued, and it has been recently estimated that its adherents now number perhaps 50,000. It, also, has established its missionary outposts in the West, and publishes in English the "Review of Religions" in India, and the "Islamic Review" in England. An edition of the Koran in sumptuous form, with an English translation, and a commentary embodying the sectarian interpretation, has been begun.

LITERATURE

The sole aim of the following list is to direct the reader who may desire to inform himself more fully about one of the religions treated in this volume, or some aspect of it, to books which he may with advantage consult for that purpose. Books of a highly technical character are not included, nor, on the other hand, purely popular works. Especial mention is made of the books in any of these fields in which fuller bibliographies may be found. So far as possible, reference is made to books accessible in English; but the most important books in other languages are also named. Investigations of special topics in monographs or periodicals are not entered in the list.

GENERAL

Works of Reference.—*Encyclopædia of Religion and Ethics*. Edited by JAMES HASTINGS. Vol. I. 1908. This comprehensive work has now reached the tenth volume ("Picts—Sacraments," 1919), and its completion may be expected within a comparatively short time. It contains many articles on the religions to which the present volume is devoted—articles historical, theological, philosophical, and biographical —besides the discussion of many features of these religions in large, comprehensive articles upon religious, moral, and social phenomena. Most of these contributions are from scholars of recognised competence and some of high rank in their special field. The selected bibliographies appended to the articles will serve to guide the inquirer to the most important literature on the subject. The general periodicals on the history of religions, such as the *Revue de l'histoire des religions*, frequently contain articles of value on subjects which fall within the scope of this volume, but they have not the same relative importance as in the field of the former volume. In the *Lehrbuch der Religionsgeschichte*, edited by P. D. CHANTEPIE DE LA SAUSSAYE (3d ed., 1905), the religion of the Israelites is treated by J. J. P. Valeton, Jr., of Utrecht, but comes to an end with the beginning of the Christian era. The chapters on Islam are written by the very competent hand of M. Th. Houtsma, of the same university, but within cramping limits of space. Judaism since the first century of the Christian era is ignored, and Christianity is excluded, as is the case in several other of the larger comprehensive works on the history of religions, probably because it was thought that it had a sufficiently large literature of its own. Of recent works designed for general readers, especial mention may be made of HOPKINS, E. W., *The History of Religions*, 1918, which treats of the so-called primitive religions and those of the barbaric civilisations, as well as those of peoples upon a higher plane of culture, including Christianity.

Inasmuch as the Old Testament is sacred Scripture to Christians as well as to Jews, the Bible dictionaries covering the Old Testament and the New are of use as works of reference to the student both of Judaism and of Christianity. Two such works may be particularly recommended here: *Encyclopædia Biblica.* Edited by T. K. CHEYNE and J. SUTHERLAND BLACK. 4 vols. 1899–1903. *Dictionary of the Bible.* Edited by JAMES HASTINGS. 4 vols. 1898–1902; with an Extra Volume, containing supplementary articles, 1904. The former, notwithstanding some provocative eccentricities, is a superior piece of apparatus; the latter better represents the middle way in criticism, which is supposed to be safe. Both are for the most part the product of the best English and American scholarship. Some of the more comprehensive encyclopædias, particularly the Real-Encyklopädie für protestantische Theologie und Kirche and the Catholic Encyclopedia, include in their scope the field of the Bible dictionaries, and the Jewish Encyclopedia does the same for the Old Testament.

JUDAISM

Works of Reference.—*The Jewish Encyclopedia.* 12 vols. 1901–6. Indispensable for biography, philosophy, theology, ritual, etc.

History.—The only work covering the whole history on a large scale is GRAETZ, HEINRICH, *Geschichte der Juden von den ältesten Zeiten bis auf die Gegenwart.* 11 vols. 1853–74. English translation, omitting the notes and appendices of the original: *History of the Jews.* 5 vols. 1891–2. American edition, revised and continued, 1891–8, with a sixth (index) volume.—For the Old Testament period, or to the beginning of the Christian era, EWALD, HEINRICH, *Geschichte des Volkes Israel.* 3d ed. 1864–6 (4 vols. to the beginning of the Christian era). The most important work on the subject from the critical presumptions of the middle of the nineteenth century. English translation, edited by Russell Martineau: *The History of Israel.* 8 vols. 1869–86. STADE, BERNHARD, *Geschichte des Volkes Israel.* 2 vols. 1887–9. The first considerable work upon the basis of the newer criticism. WELLHAUSEN, JULIUS, *Israelitische und jüdische Geschichte.* 7th ed. 1914. The most illuminating and suggestive treatment of the subject. McCURDY, J. F., *History, Prophecy, and the Monuments; or Israel and the Nations.* 3 vols. 1895–1901. SMITH, H. P., *Old Testament History.* 1903.—From 200 B. C. to 200 A. D. SCHÜRER, EMIL, *Geschichte des jüdischen Volkes im Zeitalter Jesu Christi.* 3 vols. 3d and 4th eds. 1898–1901. With full and almost exhaustive bibliographies of every part of the subject. English translation (from the 2d German edition): *A History of the Jewish People in the Time of Jesus Christ.* 3 vols. 1885–91. In part parallel to Schürer, but extending into the subsequent period, JUSTER, JEAN, *Les Juifs dans l'empire Romain; leur condition juridique, économique et sociale.* 2 vols. 1914 (an index volume is to follow). A work of enormous learning and the highest value.—For the history of the Jews after the war under Hadrian, besides the history of Graetz (above), the articles in the *Jewish Encyclopedia,* under the various countries in which Jews were settled,

e. g., "Babylonia," etc., and the selected bibliographies appended to
them, offer the best approach to the subject. **Literature.**—For the
current opinion about the age and authorship of the books of the Old
Testament and other critical questions the student may profitably
consult: DRIVER, S. R., *Introduction to the Literature of the Old Testament.* 6th ed. 1897. A smaller book which may serve for a first
approach to the subject is MOORE, G. F., *The Literature of the Old
Testament.* 1913. For the historical literature see the article under
that title in Encyclopædia Biblica. More detailed information will
be found in the articles on the several books of the Old Testament in
Encyclopædia Biblica, Dictionary of the Bible, and elsewhere.—On
the Apocrypha, Apocalypses, etc.: KAUTZSCH, EMIL (and others), *Die
Apokryphen und Pseudepigraphen des Alten Testaments.* 2 vols. 1900.
Translations, with introduction and notes. CHARLES, R. H. (and
others), *The Apocrypha and Pseudepigrapha of the Old Testament in
English, with introduction and critical and explanatory notes.* 2 vols.
1913. For those who read German, Kautzsch is preferable.—Rabbinical and later Jewish literature: WINTER, J., und WÜNSCHE, AUG.,
Geschichte der jüdisch-hellenistischen und talmudischen Litteratur. 3 vols.
1894–6. Includes all branches and periods of the literature in mono-
graphic treatment by many scholars, with illustrative extracts in translation.—Religious and moral teaching of the Jewish school and synagogue: BACHER, WILHELM, *Die Agada der Tannaiten.* 2 vols. 1884–90
(Vol. I, 2d ed., 1903). Palestinian masters down to about 200 A. D. in
chronological order, with their moral and religious teachings and interpretations of Scripture, etc., topically arranged. Of the greatest
value for the age of the New Testament. By the same author, a corresponding work, *Die Agada der palästinensischen Amoräer.* 3 vols.
1892–9. To the beginning of the fifth century. **Religion.**—SMITH,
W. ROBERTSON, *The Religion of the Semites.* 2d ed. 1894. Reference may also be made to CURTISS, SAMUEL IVES, *Primitive Semitic
Religion To-Day.* 1902. On survivals of prehistoric heathenism in
the popular religion of Syria and Palestine.—Inasmuch as religion is
the chief interest in the history of Israel, the subject is treated more
or less fully in all the histories the titles of which have been given
above. On the history of the religion specifically, SMEND, RUDOLF,
Alttestamentliche Religionsgeschichte. 2d ed. 1899. KAUTZSCH, EMIL,
"Religion of Israel," in *Dictionary of the Bible* (Hastings), Extra Volume,
pp. 642–734. SMITH, H. P., *The Religion of Israel; an historical study.*
1914. PETERS, JOHN P., *The Religion of the Hebrews.* 1914. With a
classified bibliography. SCHULTZ, HERMANN, *Alttestamentliche Theologie.* 4th ed. 1889. English translation (from the 4th German edition): *Old Testament Theology.* 2 vols. 1892.—Particular subjects:
MOORE, G. F., "Sacrifice," *Encyclopædia Biblica,* Vol. IV, cols. 4183–
4233. With bibliography. MITCHELL, H. G., *The Ethics of the Old
Testament.* 1912. HUGHES, H. M., *The Ethics of Jewish Apocryphal
Literature.* 1909. CHARLES, R. H., *A Critical History of the Doctrine
of a Future Life in Israel, in Judaism, and in Christianity.* 1913.
Jewish School and Synagogue.—SCHÜRER (above), with extensive
literature. WEBER, FERDINAND, *Die Lehren des Talmud.* (1880, under

another title) 1886. To be used with caution, and hardly without
independent knowledge; the author has imposed upon the subject a
system wholly foreign, and even antagonistic to it, and adduces testi-
monies indiscriminately from any place or time. BOUSSET, WILHELM,
Die Religion des Judentums im neutestamentlichen Zeitalter. 2d ed.
1906. (Literature, pp. 54–59.) This presentation depends far too
largely upon apocryphal and apocalyptic writings which Judaism itself
has never regarded as authoritative, and Judaism is in the author's
mind too clearly a foil for Christianity. An excellent treatment of
certain important subjects, to be particularly commended to Christian students, is SCHECHTER, SOLOMON, *Some Aspects of Rabbinic
Theology.* 1909. VOLZ, PAUL, *Jüdische Eschatologie von Daniel bis
Akiba.* 1903. The most thorough monograph on the subject. Valuable
studies on special topics are: ELBOGEN, J., *Die Religionsanschauungen
der Pharisäer.* 1904. KLAUSNER, JOSEPH, *Die messianischen Vor-
stellungen des jüdischen Volkes im Zeitalter der Tannaiten.* 1904.—On
Jewish worship in the Synagogue: DEMBITZ, L. N., *Jewish Services in
Synagogue and Home.* 1898. OESTERLEY, W. O. E., and Box, G. H.,
Religion and Worship of the Synagogue. 2d ed. 1911. A recent work
in this field, of the highest value but of a more technical character is
ELBOGEN, ISMAR, *Der jüdische Gottesdienst in seiner geschichtlichen
Entwickelung.* 1913. **Middle Ages.**—On the Karaites and the Jewish philosophies and philosophised theologies of the Middle Ages, it
must suffice here to refer to Winter und Wünsche, *Litteratur* u. s. w.,
(above), and to the relevant articles in the Jewish Encyclopedia, where
the literature may be found with all necessary fulness; see also GOLD-
ZIHER, IGNAZ, "Die islamische und die jüdische Philosophie" (below,
under Mohammedanism). Particular mention may be made, however,
of KAUFMANN, DAVID, *Geschichte der Attributenlehre in der jüdischen
Religionsphilosophie des Mittelalters von Saadja bis Maimûni.* 1877.
MAIMONIDES, *Guide for the Perplexed.* Translated by M. Friedländer.
2d ed. 1904. A translation of select parts of BAHYA IBN PAKUDA,
Duties of the Heart, by E. Collins, 1911.—**Kabbala.**—GINZBERG, LOUIS,
"Cabala," *Jewish Encyclopedia,* Vol. III, pp. 456–479. History and
doctrines; ample literature. BLOCH, in Winter und Wünsche, *Littera-
tur,* Vol. III, pp. 220–286. **Theology.**—KOHLER, KAUFMAN, *Jew-
ish Theology Systematically and Historically Considered.* 1918. ABEL-
SON, J., *The Immanence of God in Rabbinical Literature.* 1912. See
also, ABELSON, J., *Jewish Mysticism.* 1913. MARGOLIS, MAX, *The
Theological Aspect of Reform Judaism,* in Year Book of the Central
Conference of American Rabbis, 1903, pp. 185–338, and separately,
1904. **Zionism.**—See *Jewish Encyclopedia,* Vol. XII, pp. 666–686.
GOTTHEIL, RICHARD J. H., *Zionism.* 1914.

CHRISTIANITY

For a lucid and accurate, though extremely condensed, presentation
of the external and internal history of Christianity, the reader is
referred to WILLISTON WALKER, *History of the Christian Church,* 1918,
to which, under the modest title, "Bibliographical Suggestions," is

appended a select bibliography, classified and annotated. The following list has a much more limited scope.

Works of Reference.—*Real-Encyklopädie für protestantische Theologie und Kirche.* 3d ed. 24 vols. 1896–1913. *The New Schaff-Herzog Encyclopedia of Religious Knowledge.* 12 vols. 1908–12. Largely indebted to the preceding, but not a translation of it. *The Catholic Encyclopedia.* 15 vols. 1907–14. A work of excellent learning, and especially to be commended to Protestant students. *A Dictionary of Christian Biography, Literature, Sects, and Doctrines.* Edited by SMITH, W., and WACE, H. 4 vols. 1877–87. Covering the first eight centuries. **History.**—GIBBON, EDWARD, *The History of the Decline and Fall of the Roman Empire.* Edited by J. B. BURY. 7 vols. 1896–1900. *The Cambridge Medieval History.* Edited by GWATKIN, H. M., and WHITNEY, J. P. 2 vols. I. The Christian Roman Empire and the Foundation of the Teutonic Kingdoms. 1911. II. The Rise of the Saracens and the Foundation of the Western Empire. 1913. *The Cambridge Modern History.* Edited by WARD, A. W., PROTHERO, G. W., and LEATHES, S. 13 vols. 1902–12. I. The Renaissance. II. The Reformation. III. The Wars of Religion. IV. The Thirty Years' War. The Cambridge Histories are a series of monographs by many scholars, with ample bibliographies accompanying each section. EMERTON, EPHRAIM, *The Beginnings of Modern Europe* (1250–1450). 1917. An instructive and extremely interesting book on a critical period. **Literature.**—MOFFATT, JAMES, *The Historical New Testament.* A new translation, with prolegomena, historical tables, critical notes, and an appendix. 2d ed. 1901. MOFFATT, JAMES, *Introduction to the Literature of the New Testament.* 1911. JÜLICHER, ADOLF. *Einleitung in das Neue Testament.* 5th and 6th ed. 1906; reprinted 1913. English translation: *Introduction to the New Testament.* 1904. KRÜGER, GUSTAV. *Geschichte der altchristlichen Litteratur in den ersten drei Jahrhunderten.* 1st and 2d ed. 1895. English translation: *History of Early Christian Literature in the First Three Centuries.* 1897. Of larger works on the same subject especial mention may be made of BARDENHEWER, OTTO, *Geschichte der altkirchlichen Litteratur.* 3 vols. (Vols. I and II, 2d ed., 1913–14; Vol. III, 1912.) To the end of the fourth century. **History.**—HERGENRÖTHER, Cardinal JOSEPH, *Handbuch der allgemeinen Kirchengeschichte.* 4th ed. By J. P. KIRSCH. 3 vols. 1902–7. A work of great learning; very full registration of the literature. MOELLER, WILHELM, *Lehrbuch der Kirchengeschichte.* 3 vols. (Vol. III bearbeitet von Gustav Kawerau.) 2d and 3d eds. 1897–1907. English translation: *History of the Christian Church.* 1892–1900. I. The Ancient Church (A. D. 1–600). II. Middle Ages. III. Reformation and Counter-Reformation. DUCHESNE, LOUIS, *Histoire ancienne de l'église.* 3d and 4th eds. 3 vols. 1906–10. English translation: *The Early History of the Christian Church, from its Foundation to the End of the Fifth Century.* 2 vols. 1909, 1912. HOLTZMANN, HEINRICH, *Lehrbuch der Neutestamentlichen Theologie.* 2 vols. 1897. WEIZSÄCKER, CARL VON, *Das apostolische Zeitalter der Christlichen Kirche.* 2d ed. 1892. English translation: *The Apostolic Age of the Christian Church.* 2 vols. 1897. MCGIFFERT, A. C.,

History of Christianity in the Apostolic Age. 1910. EUSEBIUS, *Ecclesiastical History,* translated and annotated by A. C. McGIFFERT. HARNACK, ADOLF VON, *Die Mission und Ausbreitung des Christentums in den ersten drei Jahrhunderten.* 3d ed. 2 vols. 1915. English translation: *The Mission and Expansion of Christianity in the First Three Centuries.* 2 vols. 1908. DOBSCHÜTZ, ERNST VON, *Die urchristlichen Gemeinden; sittengeschichtliche Bilder.* 1902. English translation: *Christian Life in the Primitive Church.* 1904. HARNACK, ADOLF VON, *Entstehung und Entwickelung der Kirchenverfassung und des Kirchenrechts in den zwei ersten Jahrhunderten.* 1910. English translation: *The Constitution and Law of the Church in the First Two Centuries.* 1910. **Doctrine.**—Sources for the history of Christian doctrine. *The Ante-Nicene Fathers;* translations of the writings of the Fathers down to A. D. 325. 9 vols. 1885–96. Bibliography and General Index (to 1st 8 vols.). 1887. *Nicene and Post-Nicene Fathers.* Series I, 14 vols. 1886–94. Series II, 12 vols. 1890–5. On the history of doctrine the most useful work for the student is, LOOFS, FRIEDRICH, *Leitfaden zum Studium der Dogmengeschichte.* 4th ed. 1906. With copious extracts from the Fathers and other sources. A convenient work of similar kind accessible in translation is, SEEBERG, REINHOLD, *Lehrbuch der Dogmengeschichte.* 2d and 3d eds. 3 vols. 1908–13. English translation: *Text-Book of the History of Doctrines.* 2 vols. 1905. On a much larger scale and of more individual character is, HARNACK, ADOLF VON, *Lehrbuch der Dogmengeschichte.* 4th ed. 3 vols. 1909–10. English translation (from 3d German edition): *History of Dogma.* 7 vols. 1894–9. SCHAFF, PHILIP, *The Creeds of Christendom.* 4th ed. 3 vols. 1905. A collection of the creeds and confessions, ancient and modern, with translations and notes, and an historical introduction. For the history of early Christian worship the most useful book is DUCHESNE, LOUIS, *Origines du culte chrétien.* 5th ed. 1909. **Middle Ages. Papacy.**—MIRBT, CARL, *Quellen zur Geschichte des Papsttums.* 3d ed. 1911. CREIGHTON, MANDELL, *History of the Papacy, from the Great Schism to the Sack of Rome.* 6 vols. 1899. PASTOR, LUDWIG, *Geschichte der Päpste seit dem Ausgang des Mittelalters.* 3 vols. 1886–95. A supplement to this is, PASTOR, *Ungedruckte Akten zur Geschichte der Päpste.* 1904–6. English translation: *History of the Popes from the Close of the Middle Ages.* 2d ed. 11 vols. 1899–1912. HEFELE, CARL JOSEPH VON, *Conciliengeschichte.* 2d ed. 1873 *seqq.* English translation: *History of the Councils of the Church.* 1871–96. **Scholastic Philosophy and Theology.**—WULF, MAURICE DE, *Histoire de la philosophie médiévale; précédée d'un aperçu sur la philosophie ancienne.* 1900. English translation: *History of Medieval Philosophy.* 1909. STÖCKL, *Geschichte der Philosophie des Mittelalters.* I, 1864; II, 1865; III, 1866. HAURÉAU, BARTHÉLEMY, *Histoire de la philosophie scolastique.* 3 vols. 1872–80. TAYLOR, H. O., *The Mediæval Mind.* 2 vols. 1914. MACLEAR, G. F., *A History of Christian Missions during the Middle Ages.* 1863. FORTESCUE, A., *The Ceremonies of the Roman Rite Described.* 1918. Technical. TREVELYAN, G. M., *England in the Age of Wycliffe.* 1899. LECHLER, G. V., *Johann von Wiclif und die Vorgeschichte der Reformation.* 2 vols. 1873. SCHAFF, D. S.,

John Huss, His Life, Teachings, and Death, after Five Hundred Years. 1915. **Renaissance.**—See the *Cambridge Modern History.* Vol. I. **Protestant Reformation.**—LINDSAY, T. M., *A History of the Reformation.* 2 vols. 1906–7. MCGIFFERT, A. C., *Martin Luther; the Man and His Work.* 1911. SMITH, PRESERVED, *Martin Luther.* 1911. KÖST-LIN, J., *Martin Luther, sein Leben und seine Schriften.* 2 vols. 2d ed. 1883. By one of the leading German Luther students. GRISAR, HARTMANN, *Luther.* 3 vols. 1911–12. A learned Catholic historian, who makes use of a good deal of material recently brought to light. Authorised English translation: *Martin Luther.* 6 vols. 1915–17. WALKER, WILLISTON, *John Calvin.* 1906. For other biographies, histories of particular churches or sects, etc., reference must be made to the bibliography in Walker (see above). The best general survey of the history of Christianity since the Reformation is *Geschichte der Christlichen Religion* (Die Kultur der Gegenwart, I, 4). 2d ed. 1909: EHRHARD, ALBERT, " *Katholisches Christentum und Kirche West-europas in der Neuzeit* " (pp. 298–430); TROELTSCH, ERNST, " *Protestan-tisches Christentum und Kirche in der Neuzeit* " (pp. 431–755). The former is by an eminent Catholic historian, the latter by one of the leading Protestant theologians of Germany. Both are furnished with excellent classified bibliographies.

MOHAMMEDANISM

Works of Reference.—HUGHES, THOMAS P., *Dictionary of Islam.* 1885. Convenient, but with serious limitations. The great *Encyclo-pædia of Islam* is only in its beginnings. A large annotated bibliography is appended to *The Presentation of Christianity to Moslems.* 1917. **Literature.**—NÖLDEKE, THEODOR, *Geschichte des Qorāns.* 1860. 2d ed. Bearbeitet von Friedrich Schwally. Part I. 1909. The most important critical work. SALE, GEORGE, *The Koran.* 1734; very often reprinted. A paraphrastic translation, embodying the interpretation of Moslem commentators; with notes, and a Preliminary Discourse on the life of Mohammed, Moslem doctrine and practice (now in part antiquated). RODWELL, J. M., *El-Ḳor'ân; or The Ḳorân:* translated from the Arabic, the Suras arranged in chronological order. 1871. 2d revised and amended edition. 1876. The attempt to arrange the chapters in chronological order is conjectural and inconvenient. PALMER, EDWARD H., *The Qur'ân.* 2 vols. 1880. Sacred Books of the East, Vols. VI and IX. Not equal to Palmer's reputation, either in the translation or the introduction. The only translation which gives any notion of what the Koran is like in form is RÜCKERT, FRIED-RICH, *Der Koran im Auszuge übersetzt.* Edited by August Müller. 1888. WHERRY, E. M., *Comprehensive Commentary on the Quran.* 4 vols. 1882–6. **History.**—MÜLLER, AUGUST, *Der Islam im Mor-gen- und Abendland.* 2 vols. 1885–7. The best comprehensive history. *Encyclopædia Britannica.* 9th ed. 1875–88. "Mohammedan-ism," "Mohammed" (Wellhausen), "Early Caliphate" (Stanislas Guyard), "The Koran" (Theodor Nöldeke). In the 11th edition the excellent article on the "Caliphate" by de Goeje, and the brief articles,

34

"Mohammedan Institutions," "Mohammedan Law," by D. B. Macdonald may be commended. **Religion.**—The Arabs before Mohammed. WELLHAUSEN, JULIUS, *Reste arabischen Heidentumes.* 2d ed. 1887. JAUSSEN, ANTONIN, *Coutûmes des Arabes au pays de Moab.* 1908. Survivals of immemorial Arab heathenism; a work of very great value. **Mohammed.**—MARGOLIOUTH, D. S. *Mohammed and the Rise of Islam.* 2d ed. 1905. The author brings to his task a large knowledge of the Arabic literature, and gives in the light of it a fresh presentation of the subject—also one coloured by various prejudices. GRIMME, HUBERT, *Mohammed.* 2 vols. 1892, 1895. I. Life of Mohammed. II. Introduction to the Koran; Theological System of the Koran. ALI, SYED AMEER, *The Spirit of Islam, or the Life and Teachings of Mohammed.* 1896. An attractive presentation by a modern liberal Moslem. **Islam.**—GOLDZIHER, IGNAZ, *Vorlesungen über den Islam.* 1910. From Mohammed to the latest sectarian developments (Babis, Ahmediyyas, etc.). By the most eminent of living Islamic scholars; with copious notes and references to the literature, Oriental and Occidental. GOLDZIHER, IGNAZ, *Muhammedanische Studien.* 2 vols. 1889, 1890. KLEIN, F. A., *The Religion of Islam.* 1906. MACDONALD, DUNCAN B., *The Development of Muslim Theology, Jurisprudence, and Constitutional Theory.* 1903. With classified bibliography. A good introduction to the subjects. BOER, T. J., DE, *Geschichte der Philosophie im Islam.* 1901. English translation: *The History of Philosophy in Islam.* 1903. See also de Boer's article, "Philosophy, Muslim" in *Encyclopædia of Religion and Ethics*, Vol. IX, pp. 877–883. (Literature, p. 883.) GOLDZIHER, IGNAZ, "Die islamische und die jüdische Philosophie," in *Allgemeine Geschichte der Philosophie* (Die Kultur der Gegenwart, I, 5). 1909. pp. 45–76. A sketch by the hand of a master. HORTEN, M., *Die philosophischen Probleme der spekulativen Theologie im Islam.* 1910. HORTEN, M., *Die philosophischen Systeme der spekulativen Theologen im Islam.* 1912. ARNOLD, T. W., *The Preaching of Islam.* 2d ed. 1913. MACDONALD, DUNCAN B., *The Religious Attitude and Life in Islam.* 1909. BLISS, FREDERICK J., *The Religions of Modern Syria and Palestine.* 1912. On Mysticism (Sufism), see GOLDZIHER, IGNAZ, *Vorlesungen*, u. s. w., lecture 4, and NICHOLSON, R. A., *The Mystics of Islam.* 1914. With a bibliography, including the principal translations of Sufi authors. **Babis and Bahais.**—BROWN, EDWARD G., "Bab, Babis," in *Encyclopædia of Religion and Ethics*, Vol. II, pp. 298–308. With a full bibliography, down to 1910. **Ahmediyya.**—A history of the movement and description of its character and aims by an adherent is printed (in English) in the *Revue du Monde Musulman.* Vol. I (February, 1907), pp. 535–576.

INDEX

ABBAS, al-, uncle of Mohammed, 435.
    Abd al-Baha, 518.
Abbasid caliphate, 408, 435.
Abd al-Baha, 516, 518 *f.*
Abd al-Kadir al-Jilani, 497.
Abd al-Mumin, 472 *f.*
Abdallah ibn Maimun, 500 *ff.*
Abelard, 268 *f.*
    theory of atonement, 247 *f.*
Ability, natural and moral, 357.
Abraham, Religion of (Islam), 403.
Absolute, Neoplatonic, 165.
    Bahya ibn Pakuda, 86, Kabbala,
        96.
    Valentinus, 165 *ff.*, Origen, 170.
    Dionysius the Areopagite, 207 *f.*
    Maximus Confessor, 209.
    Ikhwan al-Safa, 451 *f.*
    Ismaili, 500.
    Sheikhi, Babi, 510, 512.
Absolution, form of, 243.
Abu Bekr, first caliph, 391, 392, 406.
Abu Hanifa, jurist, 412.
Abu Talib, uncle of Mohammed, 392.
Abyssinian Church, 191 *f.*
Accidents, momentaneity, 429.
Adam, sin of, in Paul, 129.
    Irenæus, 162, Tertullian, 196.
    Augustine, 197, 198.
    Pelagius, 197.
    Massilians, 201.
    See also Original sin.
Adam and Eve, 35 *f.*
Adam Kadmon, 96.
Adat, Moslem customary law, 412.
Adorantes, Unitarian party, 338 *f.*
Adrian I, Pope (772–95), 230.
Æons, 166.
Africa, Proconsular, Christianity in,
    193.
    Mohammedanism in, 407, 436,
        466 *ff.*, 503, 506 *f.*
Agape, 150, 225.
Agha Khan, 506.
Ἀγνωσία, 208.
Ahab, king of Israel, 13.
Ahmediyya, 519 *ff.*
Ailly, Pierre d', 315, 319, *n.* 1.
Akiba, Rabbi, 67.
Alamut, fortress of Assassins, 504 *f.*
Alaric, 235.
Albertus Magnus (Albert of Boll-
    stadt), 271.
Albigenses, 284 *f.*
Alexander Jannæus, 54.

Alexander of Hales, 271.
Alexandria, Jews in, 51.
    church in, 165.
    Christian school, 167 *f.*
    philosophy and theology in, 169
        ff., 178 *f.*, 181 *f.*, 187 *ff.*
    rivalry with Antioch and Con-
        stantinople, 188 *f.*
Ali, fourth caliph, 408, 431.
    party of (Shia), 432.
    incarnation of godhead, 433, 509.
Ali Mohammed (the Bab), 511 *ff.*
Ali-Ilahis, 509.
Allah, "the deity," 388.
Allegory, in Philo, 60.
    Barnabas, 154.
    Origen, 175.
    Sufis and Shiites, 449 *f.*
    Ismaili, 501.
Almohads, 470 *ff.*
Almoravids, 470, 472.
Altdorf, university, Unitarianism in,
    339.
Amalric of Bena, 286.
America, Protestantism in, 358, 361,
    363, 368, 376, 378 *ff.*
Amos, his message, 15–17.
Anabaptists, 322, 324.
    See also Baptists.
Anan ben David, 81 *f.*
Angels, in Judaism, 71.
    Christian worship of, 154, 228.
    nature of, Origen, 172.
    Moslem doctrine, 475.
Anima Mundi, 451, 453, 500 *f.*
Anomœans, radical Arians, 183.
Anselm, 268.
    theory of atonement, 246 *f.*, 345,
        369.
Anthropomorphism, in Judaism, 90.
    Christian monks, 176.
    Moslem, 419, 423 *f.*, 470–472.
    Mutazilite rejection of, 419 *f.*
    mediating theory, al-Ashari, 424.
    combated by Ibn Hazm, 470.
    by Ibn Tumart, 471 *f.*
Anthropos, in Valentinian Plerōma,
    165.
Antichrist, Moslem, 476, 492; *cf.* 472,
    in Christian polemics, 290, 302.
Antinomianism, Marcion, 155.
    Gnostics, 156.
    Sect of the Free Spirit, 286.
    Anabaptist, 322.
    Sufi, 449 *f.*

INDEX

533

Avicenna (Ibn Sina), 87, 89, 91, 94,
270, 273, 277.
Aristotelianism of, 454 *f.*
Avignon, popes at, 261, 263, 288.
Azazel, 43 *f.*, 72.
Azrail, angel, 475.

BAAL of Tyre, temple in Samaria, 13 *f.*
Baal Shem, founder of Hasidism, 98 *f.*
Baals, gods of Canaanites, 6.
Israelite worship of, 7, 19.
Bab, " Door " (of communication with
God or the Imam), Ismaili, Druse,
Nusairi, 510.
Imamite doctrine, 510 *f.*
Bab, Ali Mohammed, the, 511 *ff.*, 517.
higher claims, 512 *f.*
godhead, 513 *f.*
successor, 514.
Babel, Tower of, 37.
Babis, offshoot of Ultra Shiites, 509,
512 *ff.*
schism, 515.
See also Baha Allah, Bahais.
Babylon, fall of, 31.
Bacon, Francis, 374.
Baha Allah, 514–518.
Bahais, offshoot of Babis, 509.
Baha Allah supplants the Bab,
515.
revelation, Kitab Akdas, 515 *f.*
fundamental dogmas, 516 *f.*
schism among, 518 *f.*
numbers, 519.
Bahaism, as universal religion, 517 *f.*
Bahya ibn Pakuda, 85 *ff.*
Baka, abiding (in God), 447.
Bakilani, al-, 429.
Balance, in judgment of dead, 424,
476.
Baltic Prussia, conversion of, 237.
Baptism, in mysteries, 128.
Christian, in Paul, 127.
in Gospel of John, 143.
ritual, 218 *f.*
remission of sins, 196, 200, 219.
regeneration, 219.
postponement of, 219.
infant, Catholic Church, 219.
remission of original sin, 200.
Luther on, 318.
Calvin, 333.
Anabaptists, 321, 364.
heretical, 223 *f.*
See also Baptists.
Baptists, Mennonites, 364.
English, origin and branches, 364,
367.
theory of the church, 365.
See also Anabaptists.
Barbarossa, on church and state, 258.
Bar Cocheba, 67, 147.
Barnabas, Epistle, 154,

Baronius, Ecclesiastical Annals, 350.
Baruch, Apocalypse of, 65.
Basel, Council of, 265 *f.*, 291.
Basilides, 165.
Basra, " Pure Brethren," see Ikhwan
al-Safa.
Batiniyya, 450, 458.
Beast of the Earth, in Moslem escha-
tology, 476.
Beelzebul, 111.
Beghards, 286, 287.
Beguines, 287.
Bektashis, 509.
Beliar, demon, 72.
Bellarmin, Cardinal, 350.
Benedict of Nursia, 206.
Benedictine rule and monasteries,
206.
Benedictus Deus, Bull, 349.
Berbers, Mohammedanism of, 470.
accept Ibn Tumart as Mahdi,
472.
Berengar of Tours, on Eucharist,
239 *f.*
Bern, Reformation in, 307.
Bernard of Clairvaux, 276.
Bercea (Aleppo), Nazarenes at, 147 *f.*
Bet al-Adl, Bahai council 519.
Beyan, Scriptures of Babis, 513 *f.*
legislation in, 514.
Biandrata, 338.
Bible, first Latin version of New Tes-
tament, 193.
editions and translations at re-
vival of learning, 295.
Luther's translation of New Tes-
tament (1522), 303.
infallible divine oracles, 368.
See also Scriptures.
Biel, Gabriel, 316.
Bishops, in New Testament and Igna-
tius, 149.
organs of Apostolic tradition,
157.
synods of, 157.
parity, 213, 262, authority, 213.
Cyprian on the episcopate, 222.
canonical election, 255.
Luther's theory of the ministry,
321.
in Church of England, 310.
powers of, Tridentine decree, 348.
Methodist, 363.
Bishops of Rome, see Popes.
Bismillah, 512.
Black stone, at Mecca, 480, 481, 502 *f.*
Bogomiles, 284.
Bohemia, conversion of, 237.
Hussite reformation and wars,
290 *f.*
Bohemian Brethren, 291 *f.*
Bonaventura, 271.
Boniface II, Pope (530–532), 202,

Boniface VIII, Pope, 259–261.
    conflict with Philip the Fair, 259.
    Bull, Unam Sanctam, 260 *f*.
Brandenburg, Unitarians in, 339.
Brethren and Sisters of the Free
    Spirit, 286.
Bridge, judgment, 424, 476.
Britain, conversion of, 237.
    See also England, Scotland.
Brownists, 364.
Bruno, Giordano, 373.
Buddhist influence in Sufism, 447.
Bulgaria, national church, 216.
Bull, Unam Sanctam (1302), 260, 261,
    267.
    Exsurge Domine (1520), 301.
    Benedictus Deus (1564), 349.
    Ineffabilis Deus (1854), 382.
Bunyan, John, 365.

CABALA (Kabbala), 94–97, 209.
Cæsarea Philippi, Peter's confession,
    111 *f*.; *cf*. 472, *n*. 2.
Cain, 37, 249.
Calendar, Christian, Easter, 220 *f*.
    Moslem, 479.
Caliph, functions of, Sunnite theory,
    432.
    Shiite Imam, *ibid*.
Caliphate, primitive, 405 *ff*.
    administration, 409.
    Kharijite theory, 414 *ff*.
Caliphs, the Four, 405–408.
    Omayyad, 408.
    Abbasid, 408, 435.
    Fatimid (Ismaili), 503.
Calixtines, 291.
Calvin, life, 308.
    Institutio Christianæ Religionis,
    308.
    theology, 329–334.
Calvinism, symbols of, Swiss, 334.
    Canons of Dort, 356.
    Westminster Confession and Cat-
    echisms, 357 *f*.
    Formula Consensus Helvetica,
    357.
    See also Reformed Churches.
    "Five Points," 356.
    "New School," 357.
Canaanites, religion, 2 *f*., 6, 7 *f*.
Cano, Melchior, De Locis Theologicis,
    350.
Canon of Scripture, ancient Chris-
    tian, 158.
    Protestant revision, 319 *f*.
    Council of Trent, 345.
Cappel, Louis, 357.
Cardinals, 254.
Carlstadt (Andreas Bodenstein), 322.
Carmatians, 502 *f*.
Carthage, church in, 193, 215.
    Synod at (418), 200.

Carthusians, 279.
Casimir, John, king of Poland, 339.
Catechetical instruction, 220.
Catechism,
    Racovian, 339.
    Westminster, 358.
Catechismus Romanus, 349 *f*., 358.
Cathari, 284.
Catholic Church, modern conditions
    and tendencies, 380–385.
    See also Church.
Catholic Reformation, 343 *ff*.
Causality, category of, al-Ashari, 427.
Celibacy, clerical, 207, 254, 308, 310.
    Luther's rejection of, 302, 304.
    condemned in Moslem tradition,
    441.
    among Dervishes, 498.
Certainty, religious, ways to, 458.
    through religious experience only,
    460.
Chalcedon, Council of, 190 *f*., 227.
    doctrine of Person of Christ,
    190 *f*.
Charles the Great, 251 *f*.
    revival of learning under, 238.
    on image-worship, 230, 252.
Charles V, Emperor (1519–58), 302 *f*.,
    305, 343.
Chiliasm, see Millennium.
Christ, the name, 120.
    faith of Jewish disciples, 117 *f*.,
    138 *f*., Nazarenes, 147 *f*.
    a divine being, 121, 123.
    worship of, 121, 123, 132.
    Paul, 125 *f*., Hebrews, 136 *f*.,
    John, 139 *ff*.
    docetic heresy, 153.
    Marcion, 155, Gnostics, 156.
    Apologists, 161, Irenæus, 162 *f*.
    Monarchians, 163–165.
    Valentinus, 166, Origen, 171 *f*.,
    176.
    Paul of Samosata, 180 *f*.
    Arian and Nestorian controver-
    sies, 180–191.
    Council of Chalcedon, 190 *f*.
    Reformers, 326, 336.
    Amalricians, 286.
    Servetus, 336 *f*.
    Anabaptists, 338.
    Socinus, Socinians, 338–340, 341.
    See also Trinity.
    death of, meaning and neces-
    sity; disciples of Jesus, 130,
    n. 1.
        Paul, 126 *f*., 130, Hebrews,
        137.
        ransom to the devil, 245.
        Anselm's theory, 245 *ff*.,
        Abelard, 247 *f*.
        See also Atonement.
    Spirit of, Paul, 132.

Dhu al-Nun Misri, 443.
Diaspora, see Dispersion.
Diets of the Empire (Reichstag):
Worms (1521), 302 f.
Speier (1526), 303.
Augsburg (1530), 303 f., (1555), 305.
Diocletian, Emperor, persecutions, 177.
Dionysius the Areopagite, 207–210.
influence, in the church, 209 f., 276, 308.
in Moslem mysticism, 209, 452.
Dioscurus, bishop of Alexandria, 189.
Director, Spiritual, Dervishes, 497.
Sufi, 444, 465.
Disciples of Jesus, first, 109.
their faith, 117 f., 119, 138 f.
Discipline, ecclesiastical, 240 ff.
Reformed churches, 332 f.
Protestant sects, 365.
See also Monasticism.
Dispersion of the Jews, 32 f., 52.
Divination, Israelite, 9.
forbidden in Koran, 400.
Docetism, 153.
Valentinus, 166.
Dogma, ancient church, 180, 184 f., 190 f.
Mediæval development, 273–275.
Tridentine, 344–349, Vatican, 382 f.
Protestant position, 336, 368–371.
Moslem, 474–477.
See also al-Ashari, al-Ghazali.
Dogmas, in Judaism, Maimonides' Creed, 94.
Mendelssohn on, 102.
Reformed Judaism, 103 f.
Dominicans, 281–283, 271 f., 273, 300, 350, 352, 354.
Donation of Constantine, 264.
Donatists, 213, 223.
Dordrecht (Dort), Synod of, 355 f.
Druses, 506–509, 510, 517.
Dualism, Paul, 135, John, 142.
Marcion, 155, Gnostics, 156.
Manichæans, 194.
Cathari, Albigenses, 284.
Duns Scotus, John, philosophy and theology, 272 f., 283, 315 f., 317.
influence of Ibn Gabirol, 87.
See also Scotists.

Easter, 220 f.
Eastern churches, national, 191 f., 234.
See also Greek Church.
Eck, antagonist of Luther, 300.
Eckhart, 277 f.
Ecstasy, Dionysius the Areopagite, 208, 209.
Eckhart, 277 f.

Sufi, 445.
al-Ghazali, 460 f.
See also Mysticism.
Eden, Garden of, 35 ff.
Edict of Milan, 177.
of Worms, 303.
of Nantes, 335.
Education, Jewish schools, 63.
Christian, Carolingian revival, 238.
Renaissance, secular, 292.
Jesuit reforms, 352.
function of the church, 370.
assumption by the state, 380.
Moslem, 493 f.
Egypt, Christianity in, 165 ff., 201 ff.
Mohammedanism in, 407, 409, 503 f.
Elders (presbyters), 149.
in Calvinistic churches, 332.
Election, doctrine of, Paul, 134.
John, 140.
Augustine, 200, 201, Gregory I, 202.
Gottschalk, 238.
Reformers, 331 f.
Jansenists, 354.
Arminians, 355.
School of Saumur, 356 f.
Synod of Dordrecht (Dort), 356.
Elements, of the universe, 166.
astrological, 135.
Elijah, prophet, 13 f., 15.
Elisha, prophet, 14.
Elizabeth, Queen, 311.
Emanation, Neoplatonic, 165, 170, 451.
Valentinus, 165 f., Origen, 170 f.
al-Farabi, 87, 454, Avicenna, 87, 91, 454.
Maimonides, 91.
Ikhwan al-Safa, 451.
Kabbala, 96.
Ismaili, 500 f., Druse, 508.
Sheikhi, 510.
Babi, 512 f., Bahai, 516 f.
Emperors, Christian, supremacy over church, 248 f.
Carolingian, 251 ff.
the Ottos, 253.
See also Church and State.
Emunot we-Deot, Saadia, 84 f.
England, in Middle Ages, 255, 259, 288.
Wycliffe and the Lollards, 288–291.
Reformation in, 309 ff., 335.
Puritanism, 361, 365, 367.
Methodism, 362–364.
Baptists, 364 f.
Friends, 365–367.
Church of, 309 f., 311 f., 358, 367.

INDEX

539

Florence, Council of (1439), 265.
Medicean Academy, 293.
Fons Vitæ, of Ibn Gabirol, 87.
Foreknowledge of God, 197.
    See also Predestination.
Formula Consensus Helvetica, 357.
Formula of Concord, 355.
Fox, George, 366, 367.
France, Christianity in, 236 f.
    resistance to papal claims, 259 f.,
    261.
    Reformation in, 307 f., 312 f.,
    334 f.
    New School Calvinism, 356 f.
    Gallicanism, 380.
Francis de Sales, Saint, 351.
Francis of Assisi, Saint, 280.
Franciscans, 277, 280 ff.
    spiritual, 287.
    schoolmen, 283.
Francke, August Hermann, 362.
Frank, Jacob, 98.
Frederick I, Barbarossa, 258.
Free Spirit, Sect of the, 286.
Freedom of the will, in Judaism, 83,
93.
        Greek Fathers, 196, 199.
        Pelagius, 197.
        Scotus, 273.
        Erasmus, 325.
        Servetus, 337.
        Arminians, 355.
        Moslem controversy, 416.
        Mutazilites, 418.
        See also Determinism, Predesti-
        nation.
Friday prayers, Moslem, 400, 478.
Friends, Society of, 366 f.
Friends of God, 278.
    Bogomiles, 284.
Fulgentius, 203.

Gabriel, angel, 475.
Galileo, condemnation of, 373.
Gambling, forbidden in the Koran,
400.
    in Moslem law, 495.
Gaza, pagan worship at, 212.
Generation, eternal, Origen, 171.
Geneva, Reformation in, 308.
Gentile Christianity, 119 ff., 125,
132 f.
    See also Christianity.
Gerizim, Samaritan temple, 48.
"German Theology," 278.
Germany, Christianising of, 235–237.
    religious conditions, sixteenth
    century, 297.
    Reformation, 297–306, 313–328.
    Anabaptists, 322, 324.
    Peasant's Revolt, 323 f.
    Reformed Church in, 335.
    Pietism, 362.

Ghazali, al-, life and religious expe-
    riences, 457 ff.
    Ihya Ulum al-Din, 461 ff.
    mysticism, 460 f., 465.
    theology and ethics, 461 ff.
    hostility to the philosophers,
    454, 459.
    reputation and influence, 466,
    470 f.
Ghulam Ahmed, founder of Ah-
    mediyya, 519–521.
Giant races, origin of, 37.
    Druses, 507 f.
Gnosis, in John, 140 f.
    Apologists, 161.
    Gnostics, 156 f.
    Clement of Alexandria, 168.
    See also 208 f., 276.
Gnosticism, its speculative problem,
135, 167.
    in the Kabbala, 96.
    in Islam, 433, 500 f.
    Druses, 507 f.
Gnostics, 156 f., 163.
    Basilides, 165.
    Valentinus, 165 f.
God, character of in the prophets,
16–19.
    monotheism, Jewish, 28 ff., 122.
    idea of, in Philo, 60 f., 72.
    rabbinical, 69 ff.
    names and epithets, 73.
        Father in Heaven, 74, 116.
    word of, 72.
    See also Attributes.
    Christian ideas, 123, 125 f., 129,
    139, 140 f.
    theology of the early church,
    161–186.
    Augustine, 195 f.
    Dionysius the Areopagite, 207 f.
    schoolmen, 270–276.
    Luther, 315 f., Calvin, 331.
    See also Trinity.
    Mohammed's conception, 394–
    396.
    Mutazilite views, 417–420.
    al-Ashari, 424, 425–427, al-
    Bakilani, 429 f.
    al-Ghazali, 460 f.
    Sufis, 442 f., 447 ff.
    Ikhwan al-Safa, 450 ff.
    Moslem philosophy, 452–456.
    orthodox Islam, 474 f.
    See also Attributes.
    Ismaili doctrine, 500.
    Incarnation, or Manifestation,
    506 f., 509, 513 f., 516 f.
    Word of, see Word, Logos.
Gods, Canaanite, 6 f.
    Arab, 388.
Gog and Magog, 145, 476.
Golden Age, Messianic, 74 f.

THE INTERNATIONAL THEOLOGICAL LIBRARY

Designed to cover the whole field of Christian
Theology, it forms an invaluable Series of
Text-Books for Theological Students. . .

'A Series which has won a distinct place in
Theological Literature by precision of work-
manship, and quite remarkable completeness
of treatment.' *Literary World.*

Twenty-five Volumes of the Series are published, viz.:—

AN INTRODUCTION TO THE LITERA-
TURE OF THE OLD TESTAMENT.

CHRISTIAN ETHICS.

APOLOGETICS.

HISTORY OF CHRISTIAN DOCTRINE.

A HISTORY OF CHRISTIANITY IN THE
APOSTOLIC AGE.

CHRISTIAN INSTITUTIONS.

THE CHRISTIAN PASTOR.

THE THEOLOGY OF THE NEW TESTA-
MENT.

THE ANCIENT CATHOLIC CHURCH.

OLD TESTAMENT HISTORY.

THE THEOLOGY OF THE OLD TESTA-
MENT.

CHRISTIAN DOCTRINE OF SALVATION.

THE REFORMATION.
Vol. I.—IN GERMANY.
Vol. II.—IN LANDS BEYOND GERMANY.

CANON AND TEXT OF THE NEW
TESTAMENT.

THE GREEK AND EASTERN CHURCHES.

CHRISTIAN DOCTRINE OF GOD.

AN INTRODUCTION TO THE LITERA-
TURE OF THE NEW TESTAMENT.

THE PERSON OF JESUS CHRIST.

HISTORY OF RELIGIONS.
Vol. I.—CHINA, JAPAN, EGYPT, BABY-
LONIA, ASSYRIA, INDIA, PERSIA,
GREECE, ROME.
Vol. II.—JUDAISM, CHRISTIANITY,
MOHAMMEDANISM.

THEOLOGICAL SYMBOLICS.

PHILOSOPHY OF RELIGION.

HISTORY OF CHRISTIAN MISSIONS.

THE LATIN CHURCH IN THE MIDDLE
AGES.

Detailed on following pages.

All Prospectuses of the Series issued prior to January 1920,
are now cancelled.

' "The International Theological Library," to which
we have already learned to look for the best and
most recent in the historical, literary, and linguistic
study of the Bible.' *Biblical World.*

Edinburgh: **T. & T. CLARK,** 38 George Street.

January 1920.

Second Edition. In Two Vols., post 8vo (1180 pp.), price 12s. net each,

A HISTORY OF THE REFORMATION

By THOMAS M. LINDSAY, D.D., LL.D.,

LATE PRINCIPAL OF THE UNITED FREE CHURCH COLLEGE, GLASGOW.

Vol. I.—The Reformation in Germany, from its Beginning to the Religious Peace of Augsburg.
Vol. II.—The Reformation in Lands beyond Germany. With Map of the Reformation and Counter-Reformation (1520–1580).

'At last the English public possesses an adequate History of the Reformation. The work is planned with great comprehensiveness, and executed with singular balance of thought and impartiality. It represents immense labour, with learning of most unusual breadth and depth.'—*Times.*

In post 8vo (540 pp.), price 14s. net,

OLD TESTAMENT HISTORY

By HENRY PRESERVED SMITH, D.D.,

PROFESSOR OF BIBLICAL LITERATURE AND HISTORY OF RELIGIONS, MEADVILLE, PA., U.S.A.

'The history of the little nation out of which was to arise the Sun of Righteousness is clothed with an added charm of actuality as it is presented in these sane and balanced pages.'—*Academy.*

In post 8vo (692 pp.), price 14s. net,

A HISTORY OF CHRISTIANITY IN THE APOSTOLIC AGE

By ARTHUR CUSHMAN McGIFFERT, PH.D., D.D.,

PROFESSOR OF CHURCH HISTORY IN UNION THEOLOGICAL SEMINARY, NEW YORK.

'Not only the fullest, but the most impartial, many-sided, and stimulating book on the subject in the English language.'—*Critical Review.*

In post 8vo (598 pp.), price 14s. net,

CHRISTIAN INSTITUTIONS

By ALEXANDER V. G. ALLEN, D.D.,

PROFESSOR OF ECCLESIASTICAL HISTORY IN THE EPISCOPAL THEOLOGICAL SCHOOL IN CAMBRIDGE, MASS.

'Unquestionably Professor Allen's most solid performance : and that, in view of what he has already accomplished, is saying a great deal.'—*Christian World.*

Third Edition. In post 8vo (538 pp.), price 12s. net,

APOLOGETICS

OR

CHRISTIANITY DEFENSIVELY STATED

By ALEXANDER BALMAIN BRUCE, D.D.,

SOMETIME PROFESSOR OF APOLOGETICS AND NEW TESTAMENT EXEGESIS,
FREE CHURCH COLLEGE, GLASGOW.

'In this noble work of Dr. Bruce, the reader feels on every page that he is in contact with a mind and spirit in which all the conditions for a genuine apologetic are fulfilled. The great powers of the writer—philosophical, critical, and, let us add with emphasis, evangelical—have never been more signally displayed. . . . At the end of Dr. Bruce's book the reader is uplifted with a great and steady confidence in the truth of the gospel ; the evangel has been pleading its cause with him, and he has felt its power.'—*British Weekly.*

Second Edition. In post 8vo (600 pp.), price 14s. net,

HISTORY OF
CHRISTIAN DOCTRINE

BY

GEORGE PARK FISHER, D.D., LL.D.,

SOMETIME PROFESSOR OF ECCLESIASTICAL HISTORY IN YALE UNIVERSITY.

'It is to me quite a marvel how a book of this kind can be written so accurately to scale. It could only be done by one who had a very complete command of all the periods.'—Professor W. SANDAY, D.D., LL.D., Oxford.

Third Edition. In post 8vo (508 pp.), price 12s. net,

CHRISTIAN ETHICS

BY

NEWMAN SMYTH, D.D.,

AUTHOR OF 'OLD FAITHS IN NEW LIGHT,' ETC. ETC.

'There is not a dead, dull, conventional line in the volume. It is the work of a wise, well-informed, independent, and thoroughly competent writer. It removes a reproach from our indigenous theology, fills a glaring blank in our literature, and is sure to become *the* text-book in Christian Ethics.'—*Bookman.*

In post 8vo (558 pp.), price 14s. net,

THE CHRISTIAN DOCTRINE
OF SALVATION

By GEORGE B. STEVENS, D.D.,

SOMETIME PROFESSOR OF SYSTEMATIC THEOLOGY, YALE UNIVERSITY.

'It is a great book upon a great subject. If preachers want to fit themselves for a winter's work of strong, healthy, persuasive preaching, this book will fit them.'—*Expository Times.*

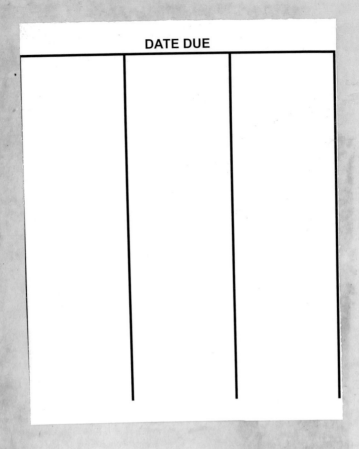

DATE DUE